LEARNING TO LOVE THE BOMB

ALSO BY SEAN M. MALONEY

Campaigns for International Security: Canada's Defence Policy at the Turn of the Century
(with Douglas L. Bland)

Canada and UN Peacekeeping: Cold War by Other Means, 1945–1970

Chances for Peace: Canadian Soldiers in the Balkans, 1992–1995, An Oral History
(with John Llambias)

Enduring the Freedom: A Rogue Historian in Afghanistan

Operation KINETIC: The Canadians in Kosovo, 1999–2000

Securing Command of the Sea: NATO Naval Planning, 1948–1954

War Without Battles: Canada's NATO Brigade in Germany, 1951–1993

LEARNING TO LOVE THE BOMB

Canada's Nuclear Weapons During the Cold War

SEAN M. MALONEY

POTOMAC BOOKS, INC.

WASHINGTON, D.C.

Library of Congress Cataloging-in-Publication Data
Maloney, Sean M., 1967–
  Learning to love the bomb : Canada's nuclear weapons during the Cold War / Sean M. Maloney.
    p. cm.
  Includes bibliographical references and index.
  ISBN-13: 978-1-57488-616-0 (alk. paper)
  1. Nuclear weapons—Canada. 2. Canada—Military policy. 3. Cold War. I. Title.
  UA600.M36 2007
  355.02'17097109045—dc22

                              2006034892

Printed in the United States of America on acid-free paper that meets the American National Standards Institute Z39-48 Standard.

Potomac Books, Inc.
22841 Quicksilver Drive
Dulles, Virginia 20166

First Edition

10 9 8 7 6 5 4 3 2 1

**This book is dedicated to the Members
of The Organization.**

"Nowadays you have to think like a hero, merely to
behave like a decent human being!"

—JOHN LE CARRÉ, *THE RUSSIA HOUSE*

Contents

Illustrations

Abbreviations

1 RDU: 1 Radiological Detection Unit
ABAI: Agreed British-American Intelligence
ABC: American-British-Canadian
ABM: antiballistic missile
ACAI: Agreed Canadian-American Intelligence
ACE: Allied Command Europe (NATO)
ADC: Air Defense Command (RCAF or USAF)
ADCANUS: Air Defense Canada-US (proposed command)
ADM: atomic demolition munition
AEC: Atomic Energy Commission (US)
AEW: airborne early warning
AFB: Air Force Base (US)
AFCENT: Allied Forces Central Europe (NATO)
AFSWC: Armed Forces Special Weapons Center (US)
AIR-2A: See MB-1
AIRCENT: Allied Air Forces Central Region (NATO)
AMC: Air Material Command (RCAF)
AMF(A): ACE Mobile Force (Air) (NATO)
AMF(L): ACE Mobile Force (Land) (NATO)
ANF: Allied Nuclear Force (NATO)
ANZUS: Australian-New Zealand-United States
AOC: Air Officer Commanding (RCAF)
APCC: Army Policy Coordinating Committee
ARPA: Advanced Research Projects Agency
ASP: Atomic Strike Plan (NATO)
ASROC: antisubmarine rocket
ASW: antisubmarine warfare
ATAF: Allied Tactical Air Force (NATO)
ATC: Air Transport Command (RCAF)
AVM: Air Vice-Marshal (RCAF)
AVRO: A. V. Roe (Canada)
AWRE: Atomic Weapons Research Establishment (UK)
BAOR: British Army of the Rhine

BCS: British chiefs of staff
BMD: ballistic missile defense
BMEWS: Ballistic Missile Early Warning System
BOMARC: Boeing Michigan Aeronautical Research Center
BUIC: Back Up Interceptor Control
CADIN: Canadian Air Defence Integration
CADOP: Continental Air Defense Objectives Plan
CAG: Canadian Administrative Group
CANCOMLANT: Canadian Commander, Atlantic (NATO)
CANUKUS: Canada-United Kingdom-United States
CAORE: Canadian Army Operations Research Establishment
CAS: Chief of the Air Staff
CASS: Canadian Army Signal Station
CBC: Canadian Broadcasting Corporation
CBNRC: Communications Branch of the National Research Council
CDC: Cabinet Defence Committee
CDS: Chief of the Defence Staff
CENTAG: Central Army Group
CEP: Circular Error Probable
CF-100: Avro Canuck interceptor aircraft
CF-104: Lockheed Starfighter strike/attack aircraft
CF-105: Avro Arrow interceptor aircraft
CFHQ: Canadian Forces Headquarters
CFS: Canadian Forces Station
CGS: Chief of the General Staff
CIA: Central Intelligence Agency (US)
CIB: Canadian Infantry Brigade
CinC: Commander in Chief
CJSM-W: Canadian Joint Staff Mission Washington
CNO: Chief of Naval Operations (US)
CNS: Chief of the Naval Staff
COG: Continuity of Government
COSC: Chiefs of Staff Committee
CONAD: Continental Air Defense Command (US)
CPX: Command Post Exercise
CSMAS: Counter Surprise Military Alert System
CUSBSP: Canada-US Basic Security Plan
CUSMSG: Canada-US Military Study Group
CUSRPG: Canada-US Regional Planning Group (NATO)
CUSSAT: Canada-US Scientific Advisory Team
CVL: aircraft carrier, light (ASW)
DC: Direction Centers (SAGE)
DCF: Defense of Canada Force
DDE: antisubmarine destroyer

DDH: helicopter-carrying destroyer
DEFCON: Defense Condition (US)
DEW line: Distant Early Warning line
DND: Department of National Defence
DOD: Department of Defense (US)
DRB: Defence Research Board
ECM: electronic countermeasures
EDP: Emergency Defence Plan
EMO: Emergency Measures Organization
EMP: electro-magnetic pulse
ESM: Environmental Sensing Mechanism
ETC: emergency telephone conference
FIS: Fighter Interceptor Squadron
FLN: Front de liberation Nationale
FLQ: Front de liberation du Quebec
FOAC: Flag Officer Atlantic Coast (RCN)
GE: General Electric
GCI: Ground Controlled Approach air navigation system
GIUK gap: Greenland-Iceland-United Kingdom gap
GPF: General Purpose Frigate
GSP: Global Strategy Paper, 1952 (UK)
GSP: General Strike Plan (NATO)
HMCS: Her Majesty's Canadian Ship (vessel or shore establishment)
HRP: Human Reliability Program
IANF: Inter-Allied Nuclear Force (NATO)
ICBM: intercontinental ballistic missile
ICI: Initial Capability Inspection
IM: interceptor missile
IMSOC: Interceptor Missile Squadron Operations Center
IRBM: intermediate-range ballistic missile
JABCS: Joint Atomic Biological and Chemical School
JCS: US Joint Chiefs of Staff
JCSAN: Joint Chiefs of Staff Alerting Network
JIB: Joint Intelligence Board
JIC: Joint Intelligence Committee (Canada or US)
JPC: Joint Planning Committee
JPS: Joint Planning Staff (U.K.)
JSPC: Joint Strategic Plans Committee (US)
JSTPS: Joint Strategic Targeting Planning Staff (US)
JSWC: Joint Special Weapons Committee
JSWPC: Joint Special Weapons Policy Committee
kt: kiloton
LABS: Low Altitude Bombing System
LADD: Low Angle Drogue Delivery

LOFAR: low frequency analysis and recording
LPH: Landing Platform Helicopter
LRMPA: Long Range Maritime Patrol Aircraft
MAC: Maritime Air Command (RCAF)
MAD: magnetic anomaly detection
MB-1: Douglas Genie nuclear air-to-air rocket system
MC: Military Committee (NATO)
MCC: Canada-US Military Cooperation Committee
MAP: Mutual Assistance Plan
MBF: Medium Bomber Force (UK)
MCL: Mid-Canada Line
MDAP: Mutual Defense Assistance Plan
MET: Military Effects Test
MIDAS: missile defense alarm system
MIRV: Multiple Independently-Targeted Reentry Vehicle
MIT: Massachusetts Institute of Technology
MLF: Multilateral Force (NATO)
MOU: memorandum of understanding
MPA: Maritime Patrol Aircraft
MRBM: medium-range ballistic missile
MRV: Multiple Reentry Vehicle
MSF: Mobile Striking Force (Canada)
MT: megaton
MTDP: Medium Term Defense Plan (NATO)
NAC: North Atlantic Council
NADOP: North American Defense Objectives Plan
NAG: New Approach Group (SACEUR)
NAORPG: North Atlantic Ocean Regional Planning Group (NATO)
NAS: Naval Air Station (US)
NATO: North Atlantic Treaty Organization
NDB: nuclear depth bomb
NBCD: nuclear, biological, and chemical defenses
NIE: National Intelligence Estimate (US)
NNR: Northern NORAD Region
NORAD: North American Air Defense Command (Canada-US)
NORTHAG: Northern Army Group (NATO)
NRC: National Research Council
NSC: National Security Council (US)
NSTL: National Strategic Target List (US)
NWEF: Naval Weapons Evaluation Facility (US)
OAS: Organization of American States
ORI: Operational Readiness Inspection
OTU: Operational Training Unit
PAL: permissive action link

PARL: Prince Albert Radar Laboratory
POEADQ or "the Panel": The Panel on Economic Aspects of Defence Questions
PJBD: Permanent Joint Board on Defense (Canada-US)
PMO: Prime Minister's office
QOR of C: Queen's Own Rifles of Canada
QRA: Quick Reaction Alert
RCAF: Royal Canadian Air Force
RCMP: Royal Canadian Mounted Police
RCN: Royal Canadian Navy
RMC: Royal Military College
RPG: Regional Planning Group
SAC: USAF Strategic Air Command
SACLANT: Supreme Allied Commander, Atlantic (NATO)
SAGE: Semi-Automated Ground Environment
SACEUR: Supreme Allied Commander, Europe (NATO)
SAM: surface-to-air missile
SAS: Special Ammunition Storage
SCARS: Supreme Commander Alert Reporting System
SCOD: Special Committee on Defence
SCODE: Special Committee on Defence Expenditures
SEATO: Southeast Asia Treaty Organization
SECDEF: Secretary of Defense (US)
SHAPE: Supreme Headquarters of the Allied Powers, Europe (NATO)
SHOC: Supreme Headquarters Operations Centre
SIGINT: Signals Intelligence
SIOP: Singly Integrated Operational Plan (US)
SLBM: submarine-launched ballistic missile
SLOC: sea lines of communication
SMLM: Soviet Military Liaison Mission
SOSUS: Sound Surveillance System
SONWEC: Senior Officers Nuclear Weapons Employment Course (US)
SSBN: nuclear powered ballistic missile–carrying submarine
SSG: Special Studies Group
SSM: surface-to-surface missile
STRIKEFLETLANT: Striking Fleet Atlantic (NATO)
STRIKEFORSOUTH: Striking Forces, Southern Europe (NATO)
SUBROC: submarine rocket
TOA: Transfer of Authority
TOR: Terms of Reference
TREE: Transient Radiation Electrical Effects
UAR: United Arab Republic
UN: United Nations
UNEF: United Nations Emergency Force
UNTSO: United Nations Truce Supervisory Operation

USAF: United States Air Force
USAREUR: US Army in Europe
VCAS: Vice Chief of the Air Staff
WERPG: Western European Regional Planning Group (NATO)
WUDO: Western Union Defense Organization
ZEEP: Zero Energy Experimental Pile (Canada's first nuclear reactor)

Preface

On a warm night in June 1964, a C-124 Globemaster transport belonging to the United States Air Force (USAF) landed at Royal Canadian Air Force (RCAF) Station Zweibrücken in West Germany. The four-engined machine taxied to a cluster of concrete bunkers surrounded with coils of barbed wire and protected by sentries armed with submachine guns and vicious guard dogs. USAF security guards armed with assault rifles leaped from the belly of the aircraft into the glare of arc lights while Canadian and American armorers used special lift trucks to remove the C-124's deadly cargo. All the activity was conducted with a professional sense of urgency.

Soon six low-slung aluminum silver CF-104 Starfighter jets—emblazoned with Canada's Red Ensign on the tail, "RCAF" on the fuselage, and maple leaf roundels on the wings—would stand ready at Zweibrücken next to those forbidding concrete and sod bunkers, ready to take off at a moment's notice. Aircraft no. 12839 would have a thirteen-foot-long bomb attached to its underbelly while stern sentries kept a vigilant watch. This mechanism, sometimes called "a bucket full of sunshine" by those who worked around it, would be one of four types of nuclear bombs made available to the RCAF in Europe. In its smallest configuration, the "gadget" could explode with a yield similar to the bombs dropped on Hiroshima or Nagasaki. In another configuration, it could yield one megaton, or sixty-seven times the power of the weapons used against Japan.

In short order, eight Canadian Starfighter squadrons in West Germany, or almost a quarter of the aerial nuclear-strike force controlled by NATO's Supreme Allied Commander Europe (SACEUR) in his central region, would have access to firepower greater that that used by all Canadian forces during the First and Second World Wars. Every bridge, rail junction, missile site, airfield, and command bunker behind the Iron Curtain would be a smoking, radiating ruin if the command came from SACEUR to execute the Nuclear Strike Plan.

On the other side of the world, in the forested environs of Lamacaza, Quebec, RCAF officers checked the special communications circuits between the twenty-eight BOMARC missiles and the advanced Semi-Automated Ground Environment (SAGE) computer direction system. The ram-jet-propelled BOMARC, loaded horizontally in its "coffin" launcher, looked like something from a Buck Rogers science fiction serial. This cruise missile was a deadly hunter of bombers, bombers that, if they got through, would in minutes kill or injure through radiation exposure some seven million Canadians. If the isolated radar crews on duty conducting the long polar watch in the Canadian north gave the alarm, BOMARCs would be ripple-launched in a swirl of smoke. Controllers huddled over green scopes deep underground in a bunker in North Bay, Ontario, would direct the missiles to their targets. A BOMARC's electronic brain would come alive, orbit the target area, home in, and vaporize enemy bombers with a flash of energy half the size of the Hiroshima explosion.

If necessary, Canadian army rocketeers from 1 Surface-to-Surface Missile Battery in West Germany would attach nuclear warheads to their Honest John rockets and fire them over the border into East Germany at the Communist forces lined up to storm this bastion of the North Atlantic Treaty Organization (NATO). Over northern Ontario, squadrons of CF-101 VooDoo interceptors would vaporize intruding aircraft or fry the Soviet crews and bombs with radiation generated by MB-1 Genie rockets. Royal Canadian Navy (RCN) Tracker and RCAF Argus patrol aircraft would drop sonar buoys into the cold, dark depths of the North Atlantic to find Soviet missile submarines, which they would in turn crush and send to a watery grave with nuclear depth charges similar in yield to the Nagasaki bomb, before those submarines could launch missiles against Halifax, Montreal, and New England. B-52 bombers of the USAF's Strategic Air Command (SAC) would attach themselves to their KC-135 tankers in an aerial ballet over bases in Alberta and Manitoba before proceeding to targets in the heartland of the Communist menace, the Union of Soviet Socialist Republics.

So much for the myth of Canada as the inoffensive, irrelevant, and neutral peacemaker. Why did Canada pursue a nuclear strategy and acquire such means to implement it?

This book was undertaken for two reasons. First, Canadian access to nuclear weapons is an integral part of Cold War history and little has been done to detail these important aspects of that long conflict. The second reason relates to a closed conference convened in the fall of 1992 at Queen's University that had as its objective attempting to understand Canadian nuclear weapons acquisition. The lack of accurate historical data precluded in-depth analysis by most participants and thus the conclusions to be drawn at that time were extremely tentative ones. In the broad scope of books dealing with nuclear weapons and alliance politics, there is no comprehensive study dealing specifically with Canadian nuclear weapons policy, policy that was fundamental to explaining the ebb and flow of post-1945 Canadian national security policy and protecting Canadian interests. This should strike people as an odd state of affairs given Canada's crucial position within the West's deterrence system. Canada deployed a wide variety of nuclear delivery systems (including defensive tactical weapons as well as offensive theatre weapons in the megaton-yield range), in the defense of North America and the protection of Strategic Air Command, in the defense of the Atlantic sea-lanes, and in the defense of Western Europe. She also provided storage, dispersal, communications, and early warning facilities in support of the Western deterrent against Soviet expansionism. However, this critical position has been almost completely overlooked by almost all non-Canadian, and even by most Canadian, historians.

The main argument of this book is that Canadian national security policy and the place of nuclear weapons in it was designed not only to influence Canada's enemies and thus deter them from attacking and destroying her, it was also designed to influence Canada's allies and further other Canadian interests. Though an extension of an existing Canadian strategic tradition, the new state of affairs produced effects that forced Canadian policy makers to transcend past Canadian foreign policy methods and objectives and take a position of increased importance on the world stage. By 1972, however, Canadian civilian national security policy makers were unwilling to adapt to the rapidly changing strategic and technical aspects of national security policy. Canada's uniformed national security policy makers were able to do so, but the gulf between the two groups grew wider and deeper over time, which resulted in dismantling Canada's substantial nuclear capability and a reduction in the level of influence within NATO.

Unforeseen and unplanned benefits of Canada's contribution to alliance deterrent structures included prestige, honor, and self-esteem. This outcome leads us to the penultimate question of influence and the relationship between the development of armed forces and national policy objectives. There is a huge body of literature dealing with the relationship between the opposing superpowers during the Cold War; there is, however, a paucity of literature dealing with the relationships between the larger and smaller members of the NATO alliance. In Canadian terms, the eternal historical question is, how does a smaller power formulate and obtain her objectives while in alliance with great and super powers? This question linked Canada's strategic tradition with the development of a Canadian national security strategy that included nuclear weapons.

Canada's nuclear involvement was an extension of Canadian strategic tradition. In his work *China's Nuclear Weapons Strategy: Tradition Within Evolution*, Chong-Pin Lin defines strategic tradition as "a set of persistent strategic traits characteristic of a nation."[1] Canadian strategic tradition rests on three pillars. The first pillar is *alliance warfare*. Canada has rarely operated alone and will fight a war or Cold War only as part of an alliance or coalition. Second, Canada retains a *forward security* principle that is primarily based upon Canada's relative geographic isolation from the rest of the world. By fighting or deterring war overseas, Canadian strategic policy makers have believed that they could keep war at arms length from North America.[2] The third pillar is *relative military autonomy*. It is politically dangerous and militarily anathema to relinquish national command and control over Canadian military forces engaged in alliance or coalition warfare. Because of the relatively small numbers of her troops deployed, Canada was unable to avoid releasing such control prior to the Cold War. The most disastrous historical examples of the misuse of Canadian forces include placing Canadian forces at the disposal of the British for the Hong Kong operation in 1941, the Dieppe Raid in 1942, and aspects of Canada's participation in the strategic bomber offensive. During the Second World

War Canadian commanders continuously struggled to retain national control over Canadian forces. They did so, more often than not, in the face of Canadian political indifference.[3]

This study does not argue the process that created Canada's strategic tradition. Rather, it seeks to explain how the three pillars had a dramatic influence on Canadian nuclear weapons policy. Canadian operational commanders, instead of Canadian policy makers, have had to find innovative means of protecting Canada's lifeblood and treasure from misuse. In the Cold War period, Canada's military leaders protected the third pillar by building *operational influence* into the command and control organizations that were in charge of the Canadian military alliance commitments. In most cases this meant placing Canadian staff officers into sensitive positions within the planning and operations sections of integrated alliance headquarters, which in turn commanded Canadian forces assigned to them.

Linked to operational influence is the concept of *saliency*. Maintaining operational influence led to linking the Canadian military contribution to higher aims. For political reasons, Canadian military contributions also had to have a disproportionately high profile because of their smaller relative size within the alliance. This requirement prompted a quest for operational roles, missions, and capability that would provide Canada with saliency. Given that Canada had a strategic tradition that saw expression through alliance structures, what exactly did Canada hope to achieve by acquiring nuclear delivery capability?

A secondary argument in this work relates to the long-standing problems of creating a force structure (formations and command/control arrangements) to respond to continually changing alliance and national strategic concepts. There are those who believe that the Canadian response to the Cold War was "a strategy of commitments," with all of the inflexibility and irrelevance to Canada's needs that this phrase implies. The belief that Canada merely served other countries' interests (particularly those of the United States) at the expense of her own has become the mantra of many Canadian analysts who seek to distance Canadian history from Canadian involvement with nuclear weapons. This book argues that the Canadian force structure, as it developed in the 1950s and 1960s, was far more flexible and responsive to Canadian national requirements than previously believed and that Canada did incorporate Canadian national interests into her own approach to national security and nuclear weapons policy during the period in question.

This study is an exposition of the process by which Canada acquired her extraordinary nuclear capability. Initially Canadian policy makers had to recognize the nature and magnitude of the Cold War military threat to Canadian interests. This was an ongoing process and is discussed in chapters 1 and 2, the early years of the Louis St. Laurent government. Second, Canadian policy makers had to establish an agreed-upon strategy; this development is also discussed in chapter 2 and chapter 3. A military force structure was then needed to implement the strategy. Building it was a laborious and intricate process. Critical nuclear weapons effects information had to be made available so that the necessary training and doctrine could be prepared (chapter 4). Equipment acquisition and planning were intertwined with training and doctrine. In Canada's case, this had to take place in her two separate potential theatres of operations: Europe and North America. Each theatre had different requirements for differing forces, equipment, and diplomatic support. Chapters 5 through 7 deal with these disparate but critical aspects of national security policy.

Finally, the forces had to have access to nuclear weapons themselves to participate fully in a strategy that gave primacy to their use in peacetime (deterrent function) and wartime (war-fighting function). The divergent force structure aspects converged by 1960, but diplomatic problems—brought to bear by the new John G. Diefenbaker government's relationship to USAF Strategic Air Command operations (chapter 8), domestic politics in Canada, and the dramatic deterioration in the world situation as well as a deterioration in Canadian-American relations (chapters 9, 10)— prevented the military force structure from fully taking its place in the deterrent system. Chapter 11 deals with Canadian actions taken during the Cuban Missile Crisis, both overt and covert. Eventually the deadlock was broken and nuclearization could occur with its putative deterrent and diplomatic benefits (chapter 12), but only after the Diefenbaker government was defeated. Chapter 13 examines the technical aspects of what the Lester B. Pearson government wrought in the nuclear force structure realm.

The Limits of the Study

It is a truism to state that no study can cover everything, and *Learning to Love the Bomb* is no exception.

The economic framework in the study is admittedly skeletal. We do not have a single-volume history or analysis of Canadian defense economic policy formulation during the period in question. I have elected to sketch the outline only in round figures and indulge in detail only when it was possible given the existing data.

As the reader will see, this study takes pains to examine the technical and operational aspects of Canadian commitments in relation to strategy formulation. This approach may discourage readers not *au fait* with military affairs. It is my contention, however, that this information is of critical importance to the creation of Canadian national security policy and that the lack of understanding of it in certain policy-maker quarters has drastically affected policy in a negative way. This is not merely an *ex post facto* argument relating only to the 1951–1972 period. This problem is endemic to today's policy-making process in Canada since the latter is so much based on myths, half-truths, outright distortion, and incorrect historical interpretations. Indeed Canadian historiography on national security policy is deficient *because* these matters have not been fully understood by historians as well as policy makers. No matter what decisions are made in Ottawa's smoke-filled rooms, Canadian soldiers, sailors, and airmen still have to carry them out. Their ability to do so is therefore integral to the execution of policy.

Acknowledgments

There are so many people to thank given the scope of this project. First, I would like to thank the members of my doctoral dissertation committee for their guidance and editorial remarks, particularly those of my primary advisor, Dr. David Alan Rosenberg, whose own important work on nuclear weapons issues and strategy contributed to my interest in the field long before we met. David's enthusiasm, dedication, methodology, and specifically his acceptance of new and challenging ideas from a non-American (and younger) scholar are all traits that should be held up as an ideal model of professor-student relationships. I should also like to thank Dr. Russell Weigley and Dr. Richard Immerman from Temple University for their continuous and overwhelming encouragement during the course of this project as well as their unstinting enthusiastic support and endorsement of *Learning to Love the Bomb* and its controversial conclusions, despite the fact that these conclusions flew in the face of conventional wisdom of American historiography and methodology. I would particularly like to thank my friend and colleague Dr. Michael A. Hennessy from the Royal Military College of Canada who also provided sage advice on numerous occasions and with whom it was a pleasure to work in formulating the "emergent nationalist" approach to Canada's involvement in the Cold War at the University of New Brunswick in those dark days of the late 1980s and early 1990s.

This book would not have been possible without the enthusiasm and support of two other people that I have had the privilege of knowing for many years: Fritz Heinzen and Rick Russell. In the struggle to convince the publishing and academic communities in the United States that there is some benefit to learning about the history of America's closest ally and the special relationship which exists between our two countries, Fritz and Rick deserve substantial recognition.

In the pantheon of those studying Canadian-American relations, I must also include and thank Dr. Joel J. Sokolsky from the Royal Military College of Canada. In the fall of 1992, we jointly presented a rather controversial paper on Canadian nuclear issues to a skeptical audience at a conference at Queen's University: this present work bears out in great detail what we set out to do ten years ago.

No historical project can hope to succeed without the backing of knowledgeable and competent archivists and the counsel of other historians. The research for *Learning to Love the Bomb* was undertaken over a number of years, so there are a large number of people to thank.

At the Directorate of History and Heritage (formerly known as DHIST): I would especially like to single out Isabelle Campbell, Donna Porter, and Andrea Schlecht for their attention to detail and ceaseless pursuit of obscure material on my behalf; and Dr. Serge Bernier, Suzanne Bourgeois, Dr. Shawn Cafferkey, Mjr. Bob Caldwell, Charmion Chaplain, Dr. Carl Christie, Dr. Alec Douglas, Dr. Steve Harris, Dr. Bill McAndrew, Cpl. Monica Morneau, Dr. Roger Sarty, Terry Shaw, and especially Michael Whitby.

Department of National Defence: Lieutenant Comander Richard Gimblett, Lieutenant Comander Doug Mclean, and Dr. Scot Robertson for their counsel. Thanks also to Dr. Peter Archambault, a longtime friend and colleague who also worked on the new approach to Canada and the Cold War (while studying at University of New Brunswick with Mike Hennessy and me) and then the University of Calgary.

National Archives of Canada: Tim Dube, Dan German, George Lafleur, Paul Marsden, Anne Martin, Dr. Ian McClymont, Edwich Munn, Michael Way, Glenn Wright, and all the Access to Information personnel who suffered through my endless requests. Never forget!

US Navy Contemporary History Division and the Operational Archives: Gina Akers, Dr. Jeff Barlow, Bernard Calvacante, Kathy Lloyd, and Dr. Ed Marolda.

US National Archives: John Taylor and Eddie Reese (who unfortunately has since passed away).

The Brookings Institution: Bruce Blair.

I would especially like to thank Bill Burr and all the staff at the National Security Archives; Oberstleutnant Winfried Heinemann and Oberst Norbert Wiggershaus of the Militargeschichliches Forshungsamt; Bruce Siemons and Warner Stark from HQ US Army Europe. I would also like to thank Dr. Reg Roy for his time and the staff of the University of Victoria Library for assisting me with the Pearkes Papers at long range; Joan Champ at the Diefenbaker Centre, David Haight at the Dwight D. Eisenhower Library, and Regina Greenwell at the Lyndon B. Johnson Library.

Many people also agreed to be interviewed or to correspond with me. I would like to thank David Anderson, USAF; Colonel William J. Anderson, CF/RCAF; Lloyd Burnham; Captain William Dickson, CF; Air Marshal C. Dunlap, RCAF; Keith P. Farrell; Major General J. C. Gardner, Canadian Army; General Sir John Hackett, British Army; the Honorable Paul Hellyer; Colonel Tom Henry, CF/RCAF; Lieutenant General A. Chester Hull, CF/RCAF; Vadm. Yogi Kaufman, USN; Major General Reg Lane, CF/RCAF; Col. Fred Lockwood, USAF; Brigadier General Don Macnamara CF/RCAF; Captain Don Nicks, CF; Colonel Jack Orr, CF/RCAF; Group Captain Joe Schultz, RCAF; Lieutenant Colonel Randy Stowell, Canadian Army; Brigadier General Herb Sutherland, CF/RCAF; Major General A. J. Tedlie, Canadian Army; and Lieutenant General Henri Tellier, CF. There were a number of serving and former CF members who assisted me but wish to remain anonymous at this time.

It would not do to ignore the vital administrative support provided by Joanne Follmer of the Temple University history department and the support of my colleagues and friends from those days: Randy and John Balano for their hospitality in

New Jersey; Julie Berebitski, who I will never be able to thank enough and only she knows why; Deryk Byess, for his Teutonic sense of order, and for playing the "Panzerlied" while driving his red MG through West Philly; "Red" Chris DeRosa and his pronounced skepticism as well as his ability to live with and then marry Katie; Alexandria Frederich, at the very least for being Austrian and charming, but mostly for her sense of humor and witty intelligence and ability to tolerate another maniacal friend, Tom Sisk, who throws one hell of a Mardi Gras party; Peter and Marty Kindsvatter and ninety-nine bottles of Molson XXX on the wall, plus some Jack D. sipping whisky: Marty drove, we didn't; John McNay for rational calmness under ideological fire, usually mine; and Chris Preble for being able to pull off the suburbanite thing despite his true anarchic inclinations. Others helped out a great deal by providing lodging and other valuable support while I was undertaking research: Kevin, Joan, Jennifer, and Danny Scott; Robert, Shirley, and Julie Scott; Al, Judy, Mike, Andy, Kevin, and Stephanie Maloney; Deborah Stapleford; Loretta Scott; Matt and Lisa Larson; Glen Barney; and Robert and Pam Silliman.

This book was financially supported by the following institutions, all of which I would like to thank for their foresight and courage to fund a project dealing objectively with nuclear weapons when the politically correct tide of the 1990s ran against supporting such things: the Department of National Defence; the Social Sciences and Humanities Research Council of Canada; the Canadian Embassy to the United States; and the Temple University history department. I would also like to acknowledge Dr. Douglas Bland and the Defence Managemant Programme at the Queen's University School for Policy Studies for their financial assistance.

This book was financially supported by Dr. Douglas Bland who is the *Chair of Defence Management Studies* (CDMS) at Queen's University at Kingston, Canada, a research centre engaged in the development of theories, concepts, and skills required to manage and make decisions within the Canadian defence establishment. The immediate objectives of the Chair is to provide continued leadership to research projects on defence management; organize research conferences and workshops on defence management; publish the results of this research; provide governments with a non-governmental source of information on defence administration; develop graduate-level defence management courses and teaching within the MPA program; and build and strengthen links between the *CDMS;* the Canadian defence establishment, defence industries, universities in Canada and abroad, and public and private individuals and institutions interested in defence management generally. Information on all aspects of the program and its publications are at www.queensu.ca/sps/defence.

1

CANADA AND THE COLD WAR TO 1951

The next greatest misfortune to losing a battle
is to gain such a victory as this.
—WELLINGTON

Introduction

This chapter outlines the origins of Canada's national security policy during the Cold War. Practically all policy and operational themes diverge after this early period and later converge during the nuclear weapons crisis of 1960–63. The period 1945 to 1951 was critical in several ways. First, it saw the emergence of the policy process that dominated Canadian decision making for the next fifteen years. Second, it saw creation of Canada's primary long-term alliance commitments, NATO and the North American Air Defense Command (NORAD), and of the forces necessary to satisfy them, which would also remain in place for a decade and a half. Third, Canada made its first major policy decisions on nuclear weapons, namely, the lack of a decision on an independent nuclear weapons program and the decision to allow the USAF's Strategic Air Command to operate from Goose Bay, Labrador. Finally, the two men who had the greatest influence on Canadian nuclear weapons policy rose to prominence: Lieutenant General Charles Foulkes, Chief of the General Staff (CGS) and the first Chairman of the Chiefs of Staff Committee (COSC); and Lester B. "Mike" Pearson, initially Undersecretary of State at the Department of External Affairs and later Secretary of State from 1948 to 1957.

Chapter 1 looks first at the immediate postwar years, with Prime Minister W. L. Mackenzie Kings's continentalism contrasting with St. Laurent's and Pearson's internationalist approaches. We then consider foreign policy under Pearson, from 1948, and the elaboration of the US-Canadian defense relationships, the American-British-Canadian (ABC) nexus, and the articulation of a defense policy structured to deal with these new realities. The third section of this chapter shows how, despite these efforts, Canada still had a merely reactive defense structure that the crisis in Berlin and, above all, Korea, severely challenged. Lack of a nuclear policy led to Canada's permitting SAC to operate in Goose Bay without nuclear weapons—the subject of the fourth section. Finally, the appointment of Charles Foulkes to chair the COSC permitted a stabilization in defense policy making.

Internationalism Versus Continentalism:
St. Laurent and Pearson Versus King

Events in 1946 conspired against Prime Minister W. L. Mackenzie King's vision of a return to the pre-war status quo of an isolationist Canada. The American's use of the atomic bomb against Japan in August 1945, though spectacular, took a back seat to the revelations of widespread Soviet espionage in Canada and the United States in shaping Canadian policy. Soviet cipher clerk Igor Gouzenko defected to Canada in 1945 and brought with him a vast amount of verifiable evidence that shocked officials in Canada, the United States, and Britain. King's attitude shifted ever so slightly, however he was unwilling to reverse demobilization.[1]

A number of observers have argued that the King government decided deliberately not to produce nuclear weapons and that it did so based on morality. These commentators have linked this alleged decision to Lester Pearson's attempts to foster early United Nations (UN) efforts at arms control in 1945–6. It appears, however, that at the time the matter of independent production of nuclear weapons in Canada was never seriously raised outside the External Affairs bureaucracy. The best disincentive to production was economic. Why should Canada spend massive amounts on an independent program if it could profit from sales of uranium to the United States while deriving protection from the Americans, who would spend money for nuclear weapons and the associated delivery systems? Yet Canada's atomic energy research program actually accelerated in 1945–6.[2]

Even with the US Congress's passage in 1946 of the McMahon Act, which prohibited sharing of information on nuclear weapons, Canada was still closely monitoring British efforts to build a weapon and could conceivably derive protection in any case. Canadian policy makers in the late 1940s saw no need for an independent nuclear weapons program, although, as we see below, it could have prevented some of the events of 1960–1963. Although the written record is unclear, it appears as though the King government was hedging its bets in case Canada did need to develop a nuclear weapons program. Later in 1956, however, the Cabinet would discuss the need for an independent program (see chapter 3).

Canada joined the United Nations in 1945. Many prominent officials at External Affairs hoped that the UN would become the primary guarantor of world peace and security. King finally appointed Louis St. Laurent to replace him and ended the tradition of the Prime Minister also serving as Secretary of State for External Affairs. St. Laurent had an extremely able second in command, Lester B. Pearson.

The word most often used to describe Mike Pearson is "affable." Fellow Cabinet member, Judy LaMarsh, described Pearson in this fashion:

> To know Mike Pearson a little was to love him—a little. To know him better was to be disappointed and disillusioned—the better, more disillusioned. . . . Pearson is easy to approach, humorous, self-deprecating, lovable. He has simple tastes, and dislikes formality and ostentation and bombast. Sometimes petulant and irritable, forgetful, child-like and not to be depended upon, his favourite word is "flexible." He will back off from any

fight and seek a compromise. It isn't that he lacks courage, he just prefers to talk rather than fight.[3]

In addition to his outwardly pleasant demeanor, Pearson's trademarks were his bow tie and his slight lisp. Born in 1897 in Newtonbrook, Ontario, and the son of a Methodist minister, he had a background which originally emphasized that "British loyalty, Canadian nationalism, and Methodist faith were stems of the same plant." The future Prime Minister was a baseball enthusiast who also played hockey and football. During the First World War, Pearson served in a medical unit in Egypt and Salonika. He transferred to the Royal Flying Corps, where an instructor thought that "Lester" was "too sissified" and promptly dubbed him "Mike." During flight training Mike was diagnosed with "neurasthenia," which appears to have been some variant of what we would today call operational stress.[4]

His illusions about Empire somewhat muted after viewing war's effects in the hospital unit, Pearson attended Oxford in the 1920s. He went on to teach history at the University of Toronto, where he met O. D. Skelton. Along with Norman Robertson and others, Pearson was recruited into the new Department of External Affairs. His first assignment was to the Canadian delegation at the London Naval Conference of 1930. He returned to London in 1935 and served at the Canadian High Commission there in the early years of the Second World War. In 1945 he became ambassador to the United States.[5]

Together St. Laurent and Pearson fashioned an agenda to ensure that Canada would remain "thoroughly and lastingly in the web of international organizations" and would thus contribute its fair share internationally to peace and security."[6] Unfortunately, the UN's ability to function in this capacity was, St. Laurent and Pearson believed, limited by four-power control and by dangerous Soviet actions in Greece and Iran. Inability to harness the atomic genie greatly concerned both men. By 1946, both were disillusioned with the UN and sought other security mechanisms in which Canada could participate.

Although King was extremely hesitant about getting Canada involved overseas, he did want contingency plans particularly because strategic bomber aircraft could now carry more destructive payloads over longer distances. King, prompted by his defense minister, Brooke Claxton (in office 1946–54), altered the defense policy process to reflect this new thinking, and several new organizations emerged.

These changes included the creation in late 1945 of a permanent Cabinet Defence Committee (CDC) and the Chiefs of Staff Committee. Previously the service chiefs had reported directly to their respective ministers (there were three), who in turn reported to the War Cabinet. Now, they were to meet together to sort out interservice problems and then refer them to the Minister of National Defence, who in turn represented them in Cabinet.

The CDC which consisted of the ministers of National Defence, External Affairs, and Finance, the chiefs of the Air Staff, General Staff, and the Naval Staff, and in many cases the Prime Minister, handled defense matters. The new arrangements streamlined the defense policy process and reduced the administrative burden from four bureaucracies to one.[7]

On the international front, King decided that the Canadian-US relationship was useful for the development of postwar defense, given the greater possibility that North America itself might be attacked. In the already-established, bilateral Permanent Joint Board on Defence (PJBD), Canada participated as an equal partner, not as a subordinate. During the war, the PJBD had functioned as a semiformal advisory body with no direct authority; it acted as a channel for an exchange of views so that the two countries could make recommendations on joint defense issues that were reasonable to both parties. In the words of Brooke Claxton, "It had no public functions, no dinners, no press relations and no leaks."[8] It consisted of a Canadian Section from External Affairs and a US Section from the State Department. The country hosting a meeting chaired the sessions. Military coordination during the war was handled directly through the Canadian Joint Staff Mission in Washington and the US Joint Chiefs of Staff (JCS).[9]

This arrangement changed in 1946. The PJBD retained its advisory role in foreign policy and defense production, but military connections changed dramatically with the formation in May 1946 of the Military Cooperation Committee or PJBD/MCC. The MCC was the direct link between the COSC and the JCS. By this time, the COSC had formed its own Joint Planning Committee (JPC)—which was the equivalent of the US JCS Joint Strategic Plans Committee (JSPC)—and a Joint Intelligence Committee (JIC). Canadian and American members met regularly in sessions of the MCC subcommittee, which were dedicated to completing a joint intelligence appreciation of the threat to North America and a Canada-US Basic Security Plan (CUSBSP) to react to the threat. The crucial session on intelligence included members of both nation's JICs. Theoretically subordinate to the PJBD, the MCC, in fact, took on a life of its own.[10]

Events of 1948 would, however, force a chasm between Canada's strategy and its force structure.

Pearson in Charge: North America and NATO

King stepped down as Prime Minister and "Uncle Louis" St. Laurent succeeded him in 1948. St. Laurent, a Roman Catholic from Quebec, harbored little nostalgia for the pre-war imperial relationship. Not that he was anti-British; he just held a larger view of Canada's place in the world. His faithful subordinate in External Affairs, Pearson, sought a seat in Parliament and succeeded him in the minister's position at External Affairs.

St. Laurent's leadership style could be described as "hands off" and decentralized. The problems in national unity brought on by the 1944 conscription crisis dictated that a closer watch be kept on the domestic political scene. St. Laurent was the perfect man for this role. He had able ministers in Pearson (External Affairs), Brooke Claxton (National Defence), and C. D. Howe (Defence Production); St. Laurent coordinated defense efforts at the CDC level.[11]

St. Laurent's hands-off attitude, as well as Pearson's tendency to make decisions on his own, without developing a consensus with his staff and colleagues, allowed Pearson to implement the agenda that the two men had developed. Pearson firmly believed that sovereignty was not enough; Canada had international responsibilities as well as international interests. With Britain in decline as a major power and the imperial bond weakened by the war, Canada was in a position to do one of three things: remain in the imperial sphere (the Commonwealth of Nations); shift into a significantly closer economic relationship with the United States; or develop some modicum of independence in world affairs.[12]

Pearson selected the third, believing that the old imperial relationship was harmful, not only domestically but economically, and that there was "the need to ensure our survival as a separate state against powerful, if friendly, social and economic pressures from our American neighbour."[13]

In this light and based on wartime experience, Pearson formulated several Canadian foreign policy objectives: national unity, political liberty, the rule of law in international affairs, the values of Christian civilization, and the acceptance of international responsibilities in keeping with Canada's conception of her role in world affairs.[14] Postwar Canada, Pearson reasoned, was now in a new position of strength and influence in world affairs; retreating into isolationism would, in effect, throw away all the gains made in the war.

Translating this agenda into action was not unmanageable in such forums as the UN and the Commonwealth. However, the agenda fell down in the area of military policy. Pearson did not allow for the problems of coordinating a new foreign policy with a new military policy to support it, nor did Claxton attempt any such coordination. As we will see, contradictions developed.

The Czech crisis of 1948 brought into much sharper focus the Soviet military threat to Canada and its allies. Work on the Basic Security Plan under the auspices of the PJBD/MCC accelerated; the two countries forged a stronger intelligence relationship and a closer tripartite relationship among the military leadership of Canada, the United States, and Great Britain emerged.

The PJBD/MCC had by 1948 progressed beyond coordinating planning for Canada-US continental defense. Certainly the Basic Security Plan was an accomplishment. The real importance of the PJBD/MCC for Canadian strategic policy was the insight that it provided into American strategic thinking and the strategic intelligence it gave Canadian planners.[15] The CUSBSP was not a static plan; it was regularly updated as new intelligence flowed in and new weapons systems were deployed. Intelligence came from both Canadian and US sources. Canada's lack of a strategic intelligence assessment body during the war had not limited its ability to collect intelligence but these mechanisms had languished until they were refurbished in 1948. The PJBD/MCC intelligence subcommittee used both nations' intelligence flow to produce the Agreed Canadian-American Intelligence (ACAI) estimate, which was then used to generate changes to the CUSBSP. To produce an effective plan, the US joint chiefs had to tell the Canadian chiefs where the Basic Security Plan fit within the larger context of American global strategy.[16] On the other side of the coin, however:

> In the assessment of the threat, Canada is dependent upon the United States for virtually all principal intelligence estimates. The Canadian contribution is limited to the analysis and assessment of the information and to

collaboration in a joint estimate of the threat. The joint estimate has always been a compromise and not always been accurate. As a result, it has been necessary for Canada to make considerable change and expensive adjustment to its contributions to continental defense.[17]

Canada's lack of an intelligence coordinating body was noted and steps were taken to rectify it in 1948. As Claxton noted in his memoirs: "The flow of intelligence from friendly countries as well as from our missions and representative abroad was so large that it required a considerable organization of well informed people to see that the information went to the right people."[18] Three special organizations were set up to handle this:

- The Defence Research Board (DRB), consisting of the three service chiefs, the president of the National Research Council, the Deputy Minister of National Defence, and at least six of Canada's more prominent scientists, functioned under the Canadian Chiefs of Staff Committee as though it were an equal but separate armed service.
- Second, DRB, led by Dr. O. M. Solandt also possessed the Joint Intelligence Board (JIB). Unlike the chiefs' JIC, JIB's purpose was to coordinate scientific intelligence and provide a link between the armed services and the scientific elements in Canada supporting the defense effort.
- Third was the Communications Branch of the National Research Council (CBNRC). The NRC was essentially a RAND Corporation, a National Security Agency, and an Atomic Energy Commission combined; it was an advisory body to the Prime Minister. The CBNRC, along with the signals organizations from the armed services, collected signals intelligence.
- External Affairs also had a small economic intelligence unit and a member from External Affairs sat in on DRB meetings.[19]

The increased tension with the Soviet Union in 1948 also produced the American-British-Canadian relationship. Unlike other security arrangements, it was a conglomeration of connections established in the immediate postwar period among the three countries. It had no overall framework. Instead, the ABC relationship consisted of several standardization committees, intelligence sharing arrangements, plus attempts to coordinate global strategic planning. The standardization committees, which derived from war-time experience, sought to standardize communications, codes and ciphers, ammunition calibers, and, perhaps most importantly, screw threads. They soon grew to encompass other areas of military cooperation.

The most famous tripartite project had been the creation of the atomic bomb during the war. Even though restrictive American legislation prevented the development of an ABC nuclear relationship in the 1940s, this did not apply to other weapons of mass destruction. All three parties had separate (and thus expensive) chemical and biological weapons programs. If each party had something to contribute to the other members, there was no reason why standardization should not encompass chemical and biological weapons.[20] It took little effort for Solandt to convince Claxton that this would be a beneficial relationship: "The chiefs and Dr.

Solandt persuaded me that this was a big league and that in order to obtain the advantages of membership, including the exchange of information, it was necessary that Canada should make a proper contribution. In other words, we should have some secrets to trade."[21] This discussion was instrumental in the developing Canadian quest for nuclear weapons information necessary for the construction of an armed forces capable of fighting a nuclear war.

Cold War tension also drew together the ABC countries' planning staffs, specifically the Canadian JPC, the American JSPC, and the British Joint Planning Staff (JPS). There was opposition from King in the waning days of his government, probably because he was concerned about Canada's apparent inability to influence how her forces would be used in a future war. Nevertheless, combined planning flourished. Guidance for the planning staffs, as established among General Charles Foulkes (CGS), Field Marshal Bernard Law Montgomery (Chief of the Imperial General Staff), and General Omar Bradley (US Army Chief of Staff and later Chairman of the JCS), focused on the possibility of war with Soviet Union. The three staffs were to exchange intelligence and formulate plans for the conduct of such a war.[22]

Meeting initially on a purely informal basis and without consulting the foreign policy organizations, the planning staffs sought to coordinate and reconcile national conceptions of how a global war would be fought. Matters like command and control, areas of responsibility, and logistics planning were discussed on a number of occasions. Each planning staff sent a monthly list of current projects to their counterparts for informational purposes. Eventually, joint strategic concepts were formulated even though the specifics of an American strategic bombing campaign against the Soviet Union were watered down or omitted. The penultimate ABC strategic concept, completed in the summer and fall of 1948 and which formed the basis for NATO's first strategic concept MC 14, was called DOUBLESTAR by the Americans, SPEEDWAY by the British, and BULLMOOSE by the Canadians. Canadian military commitments did not change at this point from those established under the CUSBSP.[23]

Canadian political oversight over combined strategic planning became more tightly controlled. Claxton noted in retrospect that planners, in their enthusiasm, overstepped the real capabilities of the nation:

> The great danger of planning activities of this kind is that the planners live and work without regard for the facts of national life. Unless they are very closely supervised they are apt to draw up plans that are utterly unrealistic and impossible of fulfillment . . . the final decision must be made under our system by the government or minister acting within a framework of governmental policy. . . . General Foulkes and I found that the planners were getting out of hand.[24]

In 1949, Canadian joint planners almost committed Canada to sending two divisions to the Middle East in the event of war. There was no supporting mobilization or logistical plan, let alone any discussion of the strategic policy implications for the Canadian war effort.[25]

While these connections were being formed without reference to Pearson's strategic policy framework, Pearson himself was not keeping the military services informed. Moves towards the creation of a collective security organization in Europe were well known to External Affairs, who were kept informed by the British Foreign Office. Consultations between St. Laurent and Clement Attlee, the British Prime Minister, had also raised the possibility of an "Atlantic Security System" to include Canada and the United States. The establishment of the Western Union Defense Organization (WUDO) in March 1948 prompted Pearson to explore the Atlantic idea further. The steps by which NATO was formed are too complex to be included here; suffice it to say, Pearson did not want the Canadian military organizations involved in the WUDO discussions initially. Eventually WUDO formally invited Charles Foulkes to London to participate in defense discussions in September 1948.[26]

Pearson's agenda, in keeping with his previously established foreign policy aims, was to maintain world peace and security and to have Canada play a role in doing so. He did not like bilateral or trilateral organizations with larger allies. Such organizations, he believed, limited Canadian influence. How could Canada achieve its aims while maintaining her independence? Four-power bickering had destroyed the UN's ability to perform the mission. An Atlantic Pact, including the non-Communist countries in Europe, Canada, and the United States was the answer.[27]

Pearson, however, saw an Atlantic Pact as something greater than a military alliance. This was another aspect to the counterbalance idea. Clearly, the smaller nations could not compete with the Americans and British in terms of military forces; to use a paraphrase, "he who has the weapons makes the rules." Incorporating non-military aspects into the Atlantic Pact would strengthen connections among the smaller nations and force a more conciliatory line in coalition relations. This plan also served a Canadian purpose, that of national unity. Now Quebec could no longer use the old "it's an imperial war and we won't play" excuse to not contribute to any military effort if it was required.[28] What Pearson did not understand was the link between deployed Canadian military forces and the credibility necessary ability to counterbalance the American preponderance of influence within an alliance. Membership was not enough.

The First Berlin Crisis of 1948–1949 was a catalyst for the creation of the North Atlantic Treaty Organization, of which Canada became a charter member. In its wake Canada did, however, exert a great deal of influence over the NATO's early civil and military structures. The concept of NATO as more than a military alliance was the subject of great debate; the United States and Britain initially were skeptical since it might dilute their overwhelming influence. Nonmilitary aspects of NATO were, however, included as article 2 of the North Atlantic Treaty. This was somewhat of a victory for Pearson, but the overriding concern for the military security of Western Europe took priority over such matters.[29]

Disconnection

King's strategic policy and Pearson's strategic outlook differed. King's postwar continentalism had a limited objective (the security of continental Canada) and a limited military force to support it (the Basic Security Plan commitments). Pearson created a new international foreign policy but a congruent military policy, and force structures were not developed to support it. This disconnection posed problems for Canada when she was asked to contribute military forces for NATO and the Korean War. There was no understanding within External Affairs of the need for detailed integration of military structure and foreign policy goals, nor did the military leadership push for the development of such a structure. At this point (1947–9), the three services reported to the Minister of National Defence and could not present a unified front. Claxton was in the process of reorganizing the department, dealing with several mutinies in the Royal Canadian Navy, and fending off criticism in the press that focused on the dilapidated state of the armed forces, a state for which he was partially responsible.[30]

The Cabinet Defence Committee still was the main forum whereby External Affairs representatives met with Claxton and the service chiefs. The main preoccupation in 1949 revolved around the political and military organization of NATO and where Canada was to fit into it. There was little discussion of developing Canadian military forces for NATO. Discussion focused on continental defense.[31]

World events, however, stimulated further reactive changes. The explosion of the first Soviet atomic bomb late in 1949 and the invasion of South Korea in 1950 shook Canadian policy makers out of their complacency. A crisis mentality developed in Ottawa. The first item on the CDC agenda for the next three years was "Imminence of War." CDC members commissioned and presented detailed intelligence analyses on Communist global strategy. The media also added to the crisis atmosphere. After the Chinese intervention, *Maclean's* (the national newsmagazine) displayed on its cover a globe with clock arms indicating five minutes to midnight. The lack of a force structure suited for collective security almost torpedoed Pearson's plan for Canada's place in the world.[32]

The government's approach to Korea was ad hoc. Canada's foreign policy connections and economic interests were with Europe, not Asia. St. Laurent announced that Canada would participate in defensive measures under a UN-designated commander. Only after the United States announced a huge defense build-up did St. Laurent authorize and announce the dispatch of three destroyers and two transport squadrons to support the UN effort. These forces were allocated to the defense of North America under the CUSBSP; Canada would later renege somewhat on this commitment.[33]

While the destroyers HMCS *Cayuga, Athabaskan,* and *Sioux* steamed for Korea and RCAF North Star aircraft carried American soldiers to Japan, the American press castigated Canada for sending a token force. There was literally nothing else to send, however. The force structure authorized by Mackenzie King was geared toward continental defense and no provision had been made for expansion. In an attempt to stave off American pressure, the Canadian ambassador to the United States met with members from the US State Department.[34]

Behind the scenes, General Foulkes was in contact with his American and British counterparts. Eventually, through British channels, the concept of a Commonwealth Division consisting of Canadian, British, Australian, and New Zealand troops was passed on to the Cabinet via the Canadian Chiefs of Staff Committee.

Since there had been no formal request made of Canada by the UN to send ground forces, the idea was placed in suspended animation.[35]

Prodding by Canadian public opinion expressed through the press, the joint UK-Australian-New Zealand announcement of a Commonwealth Division, and an official US request for a Canadian brigade group finally forced Ottawa to send a land force to Korea. Pearson had to admit "the furnishing to the United Nations on short notice of expeditionary forces capable of quick deployment to distant areas had not entered our planning."[36]

The Mobile Striking Force (MSF) could not be deployed, since this ran counter to the Basic Security Plan commitments, which had already been depleted. There was no peacetime mobilization plan; everything was geared to supporting a long war with adequate build-up time. As a result, one battalion from the MSF was sent to Korea while 25 Canadian Infantry Brigade was raised. 25 CIB's activation was a fiasco. Though it fought with distinction in Korea, the chaotic recruiting plan netted several amputees, a number of criminals, and even a man blind in one eye. It took some time to weed out and build up 25th CIB, much longer than had been anticipated. The process, from recruiting to deployment, took from July 1950 to April 1951.[37]

If the Korean commitment was an example of reactive force structuring, the commitment of Canadian forces to NATO's Central Region was based on a bureaucratic mistake. The original NATO military organization was established by December 1949. It was the product of a compromise between US and British positions and a Canadian proposal fielded by Foulkes. Essentially, the North Atlantic area was divided into a number of geographical Regional Planning Groups (RPGs). NATO nations participated in the creation of a force structure and emergency defense plan for each region. The Military Committee (a body consisting of the chiefs of staff from each NATO country and an integrated staff) and an Anglo-American-French body called the Standing Group coordinated these plans. Under the guidance of the CDC, Canada committed military forces to the Canada-US Regional Planning Group (CUSRPG) and the North Atlantic Ocean Regional Planning Group (NAORPG); Canada also was an "observer" on the Western European Regional Planning Group (WERPG).[38]

Canada allocated a number of ships to protect the sea lines of communication to Europe and started a modest reserve ship refurbishing program to supplement the ships dedicated to continental defense. The CUSRPG was, in reality, only a front organization for the PJBD/MCC. Its emergency defense plan was a highly diluted version of the MCC's Basic Security Plan. This action was done ostensibly for security reasons; in all probability, Canadian and US planners had a "special relationship" and jealously guarded their "turf."[39]

Canadian observers at the Western European RPG soon were doing more than observing. This organization solicited forces from its constituent members for planning purposes so that an Emergency War Plan would be available more or less immediately if the Soviets used Korea as a feint and attacked NATO. Canadian observers were instructed by the CDC that one brigade group and nine squadrons of fighter aircraft (of an unspecified type) could be used in Emergency War Plan deliberations.[40]

Sometime after the Chinese intervention in the Korean War in November 1950, the NATO RPGs submitted their emergency war plans to the NATO Military and Defence committees. When combined, these emergency war plans were the basis for NATO's Medium Term Defense Plan (MTDP). By some bureaucratic glitch, the Medium Term Plan was approved as a definite force structure plan by NATO without consulting the governments involved. There was no conspiracy underlying the glitch; NATO bureaucracy was still immature at this point, and stresses of a possible war generated problems within its middle levels. Canada was now more or less locked into a European commitment. St. Laurent and the CDC had several options: they could protest the issue and withdraw from the commitment, Canada could make good on the commitment, or it could modify the commitment. Since any public display of disunity within NATO at this crucial juncture could have been exploited by the Soviets, St. Laurent chose to honor the commitment.[41]

Further talks between Canadian representatives and General Dwight D. Eisenhower, now NATO's Supreme Allied Commander, Europe, raised the Canadian contribution to two divisions at some unspecified point in the future. Foulkes and the COSC reasoned that a full division could be formed when the Korean War was over and a second division could be raised from the reserves and sent to Europe thirty days after the start of a war in Europe. For the time being, Foulkes committed one brigade group to Europe in 1951 as a display of Canadian solidarity with SACEUR's Integrated Force. Once the Korean commitment was complete, the other two brigades for the division would be stationed in Canada and transported to Europe in the event of war.[42]

The COSC knew well the problems that were faced in raising the Korean force. In order to avoid a similar situation it, with input from the CDC, chose to raise two brigade groups from the reserve forces instead of recruiting a special force off the street as it had for 25 Brigade. Composite units were formed from militia units starting in May 1951, training commenced in June, and the formation, called 27 Canadian Infantry Brigade (27th CIB) deployed to Europe in November 1951. Unfortunately, the training standards were not progressing well and it took the better part of 1952 to bring 27th CIB up to fighting standard.[43]

Despite the ad hoc nature of their formation, the dispatch of 25 Brigade, 27 Brigade, and 1 Air Division were approved by Parliament. Though the government could have sent these formations overseas unilaterally, members of the CDC knew that Opposition and public support was necessary.[44]

The situation with 1 Air Division involved overly eager RCAF officials and an ambitious Cabinet minister in Ottawa. The Canadian MTDP commitment for Europe included nine squadrons of aircraft. SACEUR had, however, invited the chiefs of NATO members' air staffs to develop NATO air requirements. The resulting document was called the Paris Plan. Without consulting the CDC or the COSC, the Chief of the Air Staff, Air Marshal Wilfred "Wilf" Curtis, postulated that Canada should be able to provide twelve fighter squadrons and twelve light bomber squadrons.[45] When word of the situation got back to Ottawa, Claxton feared the worst. Upon investigating the situation, he concluded that:

Nothing but the unbridled enthusiasm of our airmen could have produced such a result. I was exceedingly annoyed . . . this whole episode I am sure was an attempt by the Chief of the Air Staff to do an end run around the NATO military command so as to bring about pressure for a substantial increase in the overall aircraft strength.[46]

In the end, Canada committed twelve fighter squadrons to NATO.

There were other political factors in play, however. It appears as if the original WERPG figure of nine squadrons for planning purposes emanated from the RCAF. Clarence Decatur Howe (Minister of Trade and Commerce, formerly Minister of Munitions and Supply, and generally known as the "Minister of Everything") supported the establishment of three aircraft companies in Canada: A. V. Roe (AVRO Canada), Orenda, and Canadair. The RCAF required modern jet aircraft, and Howe wanted a Canadian-owned and -operated aircraft industry. During the war Canada did not have control over allied aircraft built in Canada, even if they were destined for RCAF units overseas. In many cases, British and American munitions control boards interfered with Canadian production. Now the RCAF was free to set the requirements for two aircraft types, a long-range all-weather interceptor and a day fighter. The commitment of air defense squadrons to the CUSBSP allowed design and production to commence on the interceptor (the AVRO CF-100 aircraft); as there was no need for a day fighter, that project was put on hold.[47]

By 1949 the RCAF realized that it could produce a requirement for the day fighter, thus the NATO MTDP requirement. Howe was more than happy to provide the aircraft, but Ottawa decided not to produce an indigenous fighter for this role. Howe approached North American Aviation in the United States and signed an agreement to produce the F-86 Sabre aircraft. As there was a shortage of GE (General Electric) engines in the United States, Orenda Engines set about producing a Canadian design that exceeded the capabilities of existing jet engines.[48] This aircraft, dubbed the F-86 Sword, was the backbone of the Canadian air commitment to NATO after 1951.

In addition to producing aircraft for the RCAF NATO commitment, Howe had his sights on bigger targets. With the exception of the United Kingdom, no country in Europe in the early 1950s was capable of mass-producing jet fighter aircraft. There was no reason why Canada should not take economic advantage of the NATO requirements for vast numbers of jet fighters. In all, 430 Sabres were exported to the United Kingdom; 300 to West Germany; and Italy, Greece, Turkey, and even Yugoslavia received Canadian Sabres under Canadian and US Mutual Defense Aid Programs.[49]

Goose Bay and SAC Support Agreements

An important product of the increased anxiety caused by the Korean War was the promulgation of the first two significant nuclear weapons agreements between the US and Canada. SAC wanted to use Goose Bay as an emergency bomber base in the event of war and thus wanted to pre-deploy nuclear bombs for its B-36 aircraft there. The most secret form of arrangement available, a Meeting of Consultation, was conducted in 1950. It involved the deputy ministers of External Affairs,

National Defence, and the ambassadors of both countries, as well as the Chairman of the US JCS. No written records were kept. By October 1950, Canada authorized SAC to build a nuclear storage site at Goose Bay, but nuclear weapons were not to be permanently stored in it without Ottawa's approval. The approval was never given, though SAC used the site from December 1950 until June 1971 to store its nuclear weapons and components in transit from North America to overseas bases, clearly a liberal interpretation of the agreement.[50] There were two reasons for Canada to accede to the American request. Foulkes thought that allowing SAC to use the base would increase the efficiency of SAC if it came to war. Pearson, in contrast, looked for a means to get the United States to consult with Canada prior to the use of nuclear weapons and saw SAC use of Goose Bay as an insurance policy.[51]

There was a second Meeting of Consultation in January 1951. SAC wanted permission to fly bombers carrying nuclear weapons through Canadian airspace with only routine flight clearances. The crash of a B-36 and loss of its nuclear weapon over Canada in 1950 probably gave policy makers pause, but by June 1951 the two nations agreed that SAC overflights would be allowed on a case-by-case basis.[52]

These meetings were important in that they laid the groundwork and established the mutual trust necessary for the more extensive air defense discussions and information exchange arrangements that would come in the 1950s. It also gave the first indication of the divergence of opinion within the Canadian policy-making community regarding how nuclear weapons should be used as tools of influence.

Stabilization

Canadian strategic policy up to 1951 was geared to the short term and reactive by nature. The only exception was the already-established continental defense system, which did not require radical alteration. The haphazard response in other areas resulted from not considering what military forces were necessary to back up the new foreign policy. As External Affairs minister, Pearson carried on after 1950 as he had before, opening up new areas and expanding Canada's global connections. Claxton and Foulkes reorganized the defense policy process and struggled to bring the varied commitments under rational control.

The realization that Canada had to focus its strategic process resulted in what was called the Expansion of the Defence Programme. This amounted to reassessing Canadian strategy and determining Canada was going to pay for it. Late in December 1950, the COSC advised the CDC that

> our planning and action should have the twofold aim of (a) preparing Canada against the conditions of a total war; and, (b) continuing to assist and support the provision of deterrent forces in the hope that time will be available to make them effective.[53]

For example, Canada's peak defense expenditures during the Second World War occurred in 1944–45 and totaled almost $3 billion. By 1948–1949, Canada was spending $2.6 billion (Canadian). The 1950–51 expansion brought it up to $7.8 billion. By 1951, Canada had land forces deployed overseas, an air commitment in Europe that was twice the size of the continental defense commitment, naval forces off Korea and in the Atlantic, an aircrew training plan for its allies, and, to boot, was giving away weapons and equipment. The need to maintain, support, train, build, and improve military forces, as well as to produce military hardware, required a modified defense organization.[54] (See figure 1.1.)

The most important change in 1951 was the establishment of a new position: the Chairman of the COSC. Previously, the three service chiefs reported to the Minister of National Defence and were responsible for running their own shops and having direct ties with other allied services. The COSC was, prior to 1951, a forum to coordinate joint efforts and solve interservice problems. The chiefs now had one leader, and the Minister of National Defence could get advice from one man.

That man was Charles Foulkes. Born in England in 1903, Foulkes moved to Canada in his teens and received his education in London, Ontario, at Western University. Foulkes became a Machine Gun Corps Militia officer in 1923 and joined the

Figure 1.1
CANADIAN STRATEGIC POLICY ORGANIZATION, 1951–1963

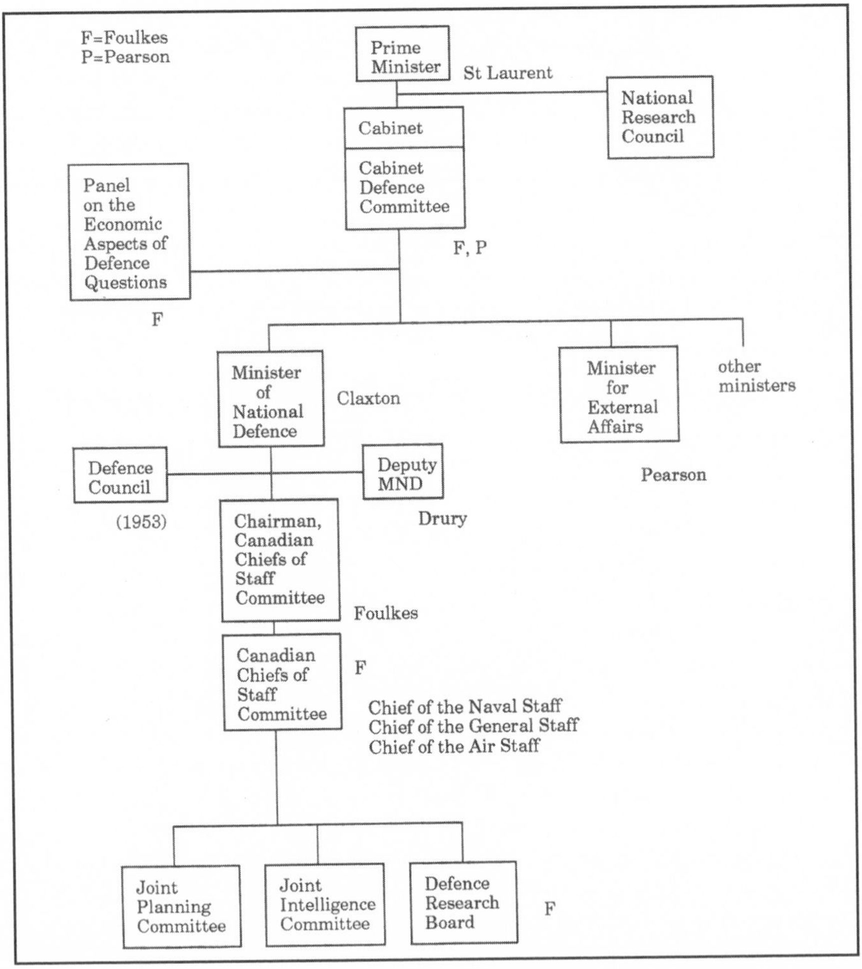

regular force as an infantry officer in 1926. Eventually, after a series of appointments, Foulkes attended the Staff College at Camberley, England. In the war he commanded the Regina Rifles and later Third Canadian Infantry Brigade. By January 1944, he had command of Second Canadian Infantry Division and led the division from Normandy to Antwerp and into the Netherlands. In November 1944 he moved to Italy to command First Canadian Corps and then took the corps to northwest Europe in January 1945 to participate in the final push of the war. He accepted the surrender of the German forces in the Netherlands at the hotel in Wageningen on May 4, 1945. He then took over as Chief of the General Staff. At forty-two years old in 1945, he was one of the youngest men ever to lead the Canadian army.[55]

Foulkes was not well liked by a number of officers who served with him. One subordinate, Major General Harry Foster, thought him a "know-it-all" with a mouth that was "as mean and narrow as his hard shelled Baptist mind." In a mess dispute while junior officers, Foulkes wanted to settle matters with Foster in the boxing ring (Foster declined). Foulkes was not a graduate of the Royal Military College (RMC) and had militia roots. This background clashed with the more status-conscious officers in the Canadian army (Foster was an RMC graduate) throughout Foulkes's career. These men thought Foulkes was an ambitious "climber," merely punching tickets. Despite these views, there are no apparent indications that Foulkes's command of Second Division and First Corps in northwest Europe was anything less than competant.[56]

Assessing Foulkes's performance as CGS in the immediate postwar period is problematic. King's government was hell-bent on rapid demobilization, and even Claxton could not arrest the decline. Foulkes chafed under unrealistic mobilization and planning conditions imposed by King, but there was little he could do about it. The 25 Brigade fiasco and the problems encountered in raising 27 Brigade were most likely catalytic events for Foulkes, who was determined that Canada could not afford to be caught unprepared again. Foulkes was intimately involved in the creation of the NATO command structure: it was his plan for the regional planning groups that was implemented in 1949.[57]

Foulkes's personal connections were extremely important to the creation and implementation of Canadian strategic policy. Foulkes enjoyed the confidence of Claxton, Howe, and A. D. P. Heeney (later ambassador to the United States and then ambassador to NATO).[58] The Director of Central Intelligence in the 1950s, General Walter Bedell Smith, for example, was a close wartime friend. Foulkes's relationship with the Chairman of the US JCS, General Omar N. Bradley, was also built on a wartime foundation, as was his relationship with Field Marshal Montgomery. US Army General (and later SACEUR) Alfred M. Gruenther and Foulkes also had a positive relationship dating back to the war. Historian J. L. Granatstein notes that Gruenther's briefing notes state Foulkes was "pleasant but unimpressive, restrained and thin-skinned. He is not a forceful leader nor is he endowed with any great amount of brains. He appears to think highly of US military leaders and enjoys associating with them. In dealing with him a little flattery and personal attention on a 'first name' basis would be helpful." The correspondence between the two men, as well as Foulkes's central, forceful, and positive role in molding postwar Canadian defense policy, is at odds with this appraisal.[59]

The creation of Foulkes's new position reflected sound organizational principles but the most important of these related to NATO. Canada needed direct and permanent representation on NATO's Military Committee, which developed and implemented strategy for the NATO area. Pearson had blocked Canadian participation in NATO's Standing Group, a group essentially formed to ensure American, British, and French control over NATO military strategy. Pearson believed participation in the group ran against his view of NATO (and Canada's position within it) as more than a military alliance. It would demonstrate to the smaller NATO nations that Canada was not on their side, which would disrupt Pearson's idea that Europe and NATO were counterweights to the US and Britain. Still, Canada had forces deployed in the NATO area and should have some say over how they would be employed, and Foulkes lobbied for Canadian representation. With Claxton on board, the changes were formally introduced in Cabinet and Parliament on February 1, 1951, and the new position of Chairman of the Chiefs of Staff Committee became a reality.[60]

The creation of the chairman position had several effects. The service chiefs now had to go through Foulkes to talk to Claxton, which caused some resentment with Chief of the General Staff Guy Simonds who:

> objected, on occasion, to the way Foulkes involved C. M. "Bud" Drury, the civilian deputy minister of national defense, in military decision-making. He found that Foulkes and Drury often made decisions after reaching an arrangement behind closed doors with one or more chiefs of staff or with the minister. Obviously compromises were necessary when an examination of the detailed papers supporting each service's case did not yield a decision in open committee. Simonds had almost an obsession, though, that the resulting "political" decision was second best militarily . . . [The process] gave the chairman too much influence.[61]

Foulkes was now at almost the same level of influence as the minister, and influenced him through Drury, who had been a Foulkes subordinate during the war. The government formed the Defence Council in 1953, ostensibly to assuage the service chiefs by allowing them access to the minister. Theoretically, the Defence Council consisted of the Chairman of the COSC, the service chiefs, the deputy minister, and the DRB chairman. In reality, it was not a significant factor in the creation of strategic policy.[62]

Foulkes also had direct access to NATO's Military Committee, which allowed him to observe and influence NATO military strategy at its highest level, rather than just observing American and British global strategy through the ABC connections. Foulkes's bilateral connections with the Americans were already strong, but he also favored the absorption of the ABC relationship into NATO in as many areas as possible for practical reasons. Clearly, "If known [the ABC relationship], would be resented by the other countries . . . the U.S. view was that, for security reasons, this planning could not be done inside NATO at present."[63]

The other major alteration in the defense policy process was the formation of a body called the Panel on the Economic Aspects of Defence Questions (POEADQ).

Although the Panel had originally met in February 1950, the commitments that developed thereafter increased its necessity. Succinctly, the Panel's purpose was to

> provid[e] machinery for interdepartment consultation on those aspects of defense which are of concern to other Departments in the economic, financial and supply fields, particularly those arising in connection with the North Atlantic Treaty. The Committee [sic] reports to the individual ministers or to the Cabinet Defence Committee on such of the above matters as are appropriate.[64]

The Panel consisted of the Secretary to the Cabinet, the Deputy Minister of National Defence, the Deputy Minister of Finance, the Undersecretary of State for External Affairs, the Deputy Minister for Trade and Commerce, the Chairman of the Chiefs of Staff Committee, the Chairman of the Defence Research Board, and the Deputy Governor of the Bank of Canada. Note that deputy ministers were professional civil servants from their respective ministries and not elected officials.[65]

An analysis of the Panel minutes indicates two things. By the late 1950s, particularly after the 1957 election, the Panel actually functioned as a shadow Cabinet Defence Committee in the sense that the various ministries gathered together before each CDC meeting in order to coordinate position papers within the Panel. The Panel members who were present at the CDC included the Chairman of the COSC and the Secretary of the Cabinet; the deputy ministers were normally in charge of producing position papers for their politicized ministers and could thus control the information being transmitted to them for use in the CDC meetings. Secondly, those who controlled governmental financing were on the Panel itself and thus privy to what direction defense matters were going. Their presence also gave them time to react to defense finance needs without waiting for a Cabinet decision on some items.[66] In effect then, the Panel did not actually replace the CDC, but was in a position to control much of the information that the CDC saw, and the presence of Foulkes on both bodies gave ideas created in the Panel some continuity in CDC decisions.[67]

In this way, Foulkes developed greater influence in formation of national security policy than Claxton or even Pearson. Claxton served only on the CDC; Pearson was on the CDC, controlled External Affairs, and represented Canada on the North Atlantic Council (NAC), a body that exerted little control over the NATO Military Committee. Foulkes, on the other hand, was a member of the CDC, chaired the Chiefs of Staff Committee (which handled defense planning with the Permanent Joint Board/MCC through the Joint Planning Staff and the Joint Planning Committee), was a member of the POEADQ, was part of the Defence Research Board, and, most importantly, was a member of NATO's Military Committee. In sum, Foulkes was into all levels of the national security policy-making process and in a position to add continuity to whatever policy he could convince other "players" to agree to.

Canadian military commitments overseas stabilized, as did the continental commitments developed by the PJBD/MCC. Two separate defense systems (analogous to theatres of war) developed: the continental system under the PJBD/MCC, and the Atlantic system under NATO. Each possessed intelligence collection and dissemination organizations, force planning and command organizations, and strategic concepts. The continental system was a bilateral Canada-US relationship. Strategic intelligence flowed back and forth across the border, which in turn directly affected force requirements and planning. It was a closed system until 1952–1953. The Canadian joint committees interfaced directly with their American counterparts and had a strategic concept in the Basic Security Plan. The Atlantic system was also a closed system. Integrated NATO headquarters generated intelligence and force requirements with Canadian military input. Command and planning were also handled by integrated NATO headquarters, again with Canadian military input. NATO's strategic concept, MC 14, was derived from the now-defunct ABC strategic planning relationship. Only matters affecting the financing of the forces within the systems were elevated to the national political decision-making level.

These cycles were broken only when political and/or technological developments raised substantial threats to the status quo. Two new factors altered this all too brief status quo: development of thermonuclear weapons and means to deliver them intercontinentally. Once the Soviets had this capability, the MC 14 concept in the Atlantic system would be obsolete. The pattern of war established under this concept involved a Second World War–style conflict fought in a largely conventional mode with a limited number of kiloton-yield weapons. The CUSBSP would also become obsolete. It emphasized airborne/air-transported and naval threats to North America; some kiloton-yield weapons might be used by the enemy if they could acquire forward bases for their TU-4 bombers or V-2-type missiles. When CUSBSP was conceived there was no real intercontinental SAC deterrent force; now there was one and its bases in North America had to be protected. How Canadian strategic policy makers took these factors into account is the subject of chapter 2.

Conclusion

The selection of Louis St. Laurent as Prime Minister and the elevation of Lester B. Pearson to Secretary of State for External Affairs resulted in a new strategic policy framework for Canada. Though the relationship with the United States was a subset, this new framework was multilateral and sought to involve Canada seriously in several international relationships. These relationships included the UN, NATO, and the Commonwealth. There was, however, no change in the military force structure or recognition that mobilization planning based on the Second World War experience was obsolete.

The 1950–1951 period exposed weaknesses in the development of Canadian strategic policy and military forces to support it. Pearsonian policy remained in effect and Canada had to make good on its paper commitments with blood, steel, and aluminum. The resultant reactive force structure formed would be subjected to unforeseen pressures and agendas, which sometimes differed from those projected in the strategic policy framework. The Atlantic system and UN operations temporarily superseded continental defense as priorities within the overall framework. The stabilization process would continue into 1952 and provide the basis for long-lasting change in Canadian strategic policy that included the formulation of a NATO and then a Canadian strategic concept, as well as the eventual nuclearization of the Canadian force structure.

2

FEAR IS NOT AN OPTION: A NEW STRATEGY, 1952–1955

"You must realize that, in this business,
fear is not an option."
—TRUE LIES

This chapter examines four stages in the development of Canadian strategy: NATO's enunciation of strategic concept MC 14/1 in 1952; early American and Canadian joint responses to MC 14/1 in terms of coordinating continental air defense; Canada's reaction to the US "New Look" policy of October 1953, which incorporated defensive use of nuclear weapons; NATO's MC 48 (November 1954), its linking of NATO's European and North American strategy, and its role in consolidating Canadian strategic planning and force structure.

The Chiefs in the Early 1950s

First let us look at the four members of the Chiefs of Staff Committee who oversaw the acceptance and initial implementation of Canada's strategic policy from 1952 to 1956. We met General Foulkes in the previous chapter. Chief of the Naval Staff (CNS), Vice-Admiral E. R. "Rollo" Mainguy, had commanded the destroyer HMCS *Ottawa* during the Second World War and was credited with the first enemy submarine sunk by the RCN. A dynamic naval officer, Mainguy then commanded the cruiser HMCS *Uganda* in the Pacific campaign. After several mutinies in 1949, Brooke Claxton appointed Mainguy to handle the groundbreaking inquiry. The "Mainguy Report" was a critical step in facilitating the RCN's attitudinal shift from a Royal Navy to a Canadian Navy. He was a logical successor to the somewhat befuddled Vice-Admiral H. T. W. Grant given the political climate of the times.[1]

Like Foulkes, Chief of the General Staff Lieutenant-General Guy Granville Simonds was born in England. Unlike Foulkes, Simonds was raised in England by his father, who was an artillery officer. Simonds was accepted into Royal Military College in 1921. Apparently, he asserted to his fellow cadets early on that he would eventually become the CGS. Joining the Royal Canadian Horse Artillery in 1925, Simonds continuously aced officer professional exams and even carried on a lively public correspondence relating to divisional organization with the future General E. L. M. Burns in *Canadian Defence Quarterly* during the 1930s. During the Second

World War, Simonds rapidly rose to command a Canadian corps in Italy and became Montgomery's protégé. Simonds trod on many toes and ruthlessly fired those subordinates who he believed were incompetent. During the Normandy Campaign, Simonds pioneered the mass use of fully tracked armored personnel carriers. After the war, many thought that Simonds was a "shoe in" for CGS, but the position was given to Foulkes, who it was believed was more "effeciant, organized, and cold, a man who lived for compromise and conciliation." It is possible that the powers that be believed that Simonds was too British and too closely linked to Montgomery for a postwar Canada that was trying to shed imperial ties. In any case, Foulkes and Simonds were generally antagonistic toward each other.[2]

Chief of the Air Staff was the portly Air Marshal W. A. "Wilf" Curtis. Born in southern Ontario in 1893, Curtis served as an infantry officer from 1914 to 1916 and then transferred to the Royal Naval Air Service, where he flew on the western front for the rest of the war. He joined the embryonic Canadian Air Force (pre-Royal) in the 1920s and served in a wide variety of staff and training positions. By 1941, Curtis was the Deputy Air Officer Commander in chief of the RCAF's overseas headquarters. He led the fight for Canadianization. The RCAF staff overseas was adamant that RCAF squadrons be under Canadian, not RAF, control. There were too many Canadians in the RAF, and the RCAF units, particularly those serving with Bomber Command, had little autonomy. Curtis was not impressed with British interference in RCAF affairs. Much of his time was spent protecting Canadian interests. When posted to Canada in 1944, he also blocked attempts to place Canadian aircrews and squadrons under RAF control in the Pacific campaign. Curtis was promoted to the Chiefs of Staff Committee in 1947. It was Curtis who, along with C. D. Howe, pushed for the production of the first Canadian jet interceptor aircraft, the AVRO CF-100 Canuck, in the late 1940s.[3]

Curtis retired late in 1953. The man overseeing the RCAF's implementation of MC 48 was Air Marshal C. R. "Roy" Slemon. Slemon was a member of the first RCAF pilot's course in 1923 (six people, of whom Slemon was the only one to remain in the RCAF by 1924—the others were killed in accidents). During the Second World War, Slemon was the senior air staff officer at No. 6 Group (RCAF), Canada's contribution to Bomber Command (he flew missions as well as conducting staff duties).[4] Taking over in 1953, he guided the RCAF into the nuclear age before becoming deputy commander in chief of the North American Air Defense Command (NORAD) in 1957.

These were the men to whom fell the burden of dealing with rapid technological change in the thermonuclear age. In general terms, Foulkes handled the large political questions and the relationship between requirements and policy. Mainguy, Simonds, and Curtis were experts in their fields and were adept at relating technological requirements to operational ones.

Canada, NATO, and MC 14/1: 1952

The NATO Ministerial Meeting in Lisbon during April 1952 concluded that maintaining a large conventional force structure in Europe was not economically feasible and that the existing structure was incapable of deterring the Soviet Union without nuclear weapons to supplement it. Acceptance of these facts initiated a reassessment of how NATO would fight a war. This reassessment would take another two years and be altered continuously given the rapid pace of technological change and threat estimates.[5]

In his capacity as NATO Military Committee (MC) chairman, Foulkes raised the issue of developing an implementation plan for nuclear weapons during the annual review process after Lisbon. The political side of NATO was slow to react, but the MC expressed enthusiasm. Supreme Headquarters of the Allied Powers, Europe (SHAPE), Foulkes believed, should take the lead in this planning since it directly affected planning at all levels. General Alfred Gruenther, after discussions with Foulkes, was interested in conducting such a study, but lack of information on specific nuclear weapons would delay it.[6]

British perspectives on NATO strategy produced the influential Global Strategy Paper (GSP) in 1952. This document formulated the basis for NATO's 1954 strategic concept by envisioning the form that future war would take. It was driven both by the need to determine where nuclear weapons fit in Allied strategy as well as by reductions in the British defense budget. The document postulated a war in which the first phase would be one of immediate and widespread nuclear weapons use, lasting perhaps a few weeks, followed by a period of conventional military operations. The paper cautioned against planning for a short war, though it emphasized that more peacetime resources should be allocated for the first phase so as to ensure the survival of the nation if deterrence failed.[7]

Earl of Tunis Alexander, governor general of Canada from 1946 to 1952 and now Britain's Minister of Defence, authorized Marshal of the RAF, Sir John Slessor (the GSP's architect) to release it to Foulkes and to Bradley, with the intent to coordinate alliance military thinking. Foulkes and Bradley met in September 1952 to discuss these matters. A tripartite military concept was out of the question but British thinking had prompted Bradley to ask SACEUR (General Matthew Ridgway) to produce a plan incorporating nuclear weapons into NATO defense plans for Europe. The problem was releasing information on nuclear weapons, something prohibited by the American Atomic Energy Act. Foulkes got Bradley to release enough information so that preliminary planning could start. Characteristics and composition of the weapons were not part of this information. Bradley was not sure what the GSP's likely long-term impact would be on US planning, but promised to keep Foulkes informed of any future changes in American thinking.[8]

The Cabinet Defence Committee was briefed on the GSP in October 1952. Canadian analysis of the paper concluded that not enough nuclear weapons information would be available to NATO by the December 1952 meeting to dramatically alter the Alliance's strategic concept, and that the GSP would not affect Canada's force structure until 1954. Secondly, Canadian strategic planners agreed with the two-phase war concept and predicted that NATO nations would pour their resources into forces dedicated to deterring war and then fighting it in the first phase, rather than providing forces for both phases.[9]

Lester Pearson was concerned that the British would reduce their conventional forces in Europe to pay for their strategic nuclear force. He "hoped that a fuller exchange of information between the United Kingdom and the United States and a reasonable division of effort in atomic warfare, including coordination of target priorities, would be achieved in order to lighten the pressure on the UK defence budget." He also thought "it was unfair of the United States to ask European countries to make plans on the basis of information in the possession only of the United States." This situation had to change. Claxton thought that the Soviets would match American strategic nuclear efforts. With larger nuclear weapons coming into existence "it would be profitable to an enemy if only one bomber got through to a North American city." Early warning and air defense should be improved.[10] Foulkes thought that strategic air warfare could not affect the immediate course of the defensive battle in Euorpe at once, but would do so over time.

Cabinet took note, but the recording secretary stated "a recent statement of United Kingdom views on global strategy, which gave greater emphasis to the place of atomic weapons, was resulting in a re-examination of plans for the defense of Europe. It would not in any event affect present Canadian defence planning."[11]

For the time being, it did not appear to. NATO Military Committee's document MC 14/1, tabled in December 1952, updated strategic guidance for the major NATO commands (SHAPE and SACLANT— the Supreme Allied Commander, Atlantic) and the Canada-US Regional Planning Group. NATO's aim was to "convince the USSR that war does not pay, and to insure a successful defence of the NATO area should war occur."[12] The method was to stabilize the Soviet offensive in Western Europe and conduct a counter-offensive. North America "possesses the principal Allied production and offensive capacity and is geographically well placed to provide several of the bases required to control vital sea lines of communication. . . . In addition it provides the main base for the strategic air offensive."[13] As for North America:

> In terms of priority of effort, the Canada-US Region was to ensure that it would devote to defensive purposes only that portion of their total forces which is necessary to provide a reasonable degree of protection for the essential elements of North American war-making capacity. . . . the first call on the forces considered necessary to provide the minimal acceptable degree of protection of North America must be allotted to the defence of its productive capacity, communications, bases, mobilization and training facilities. . . . in 1956 the Soviet Union may have a formidable atomic potential against North America, and an adequate defence for this area thus becomes essential in order to permit NATO to accomplish its military objectives.[14]

Canadian planners did not like the original wording, which omitted the possibility the Soviets might attack Canada. They were also not happy with the imprecise discussion on the impact of nuclear weapons use by both friend and foe and thus pushed to have some discussion included. Nevertheless, NATO approved MC 14/1 in December 1952.[15] Changes were in the offing, however: the United States exploded a hydrogen device in October 1952 (the MIKE test), though the test's implications were not disseminated in time for the December NATO meeting as there were no formal nuclear information channels within NATO at the time.

The Continental Air Defense Focus: 1952–1953

NATO's continuing strategy debate proceeded concurrently with significant developments in the Canada-US relationship, particularly those concerning the air defense of North America. Despite the hazy thinking in MC 14/1 about this issue, the two nations made great strides on their own and, even more importantly, worked closely in coordinating, planning, scientific development, and implementation. They did so not under the umbrella of a NATO strategic concept (as later decisions would be) but through personal contacts.

A Soviet air threat to North America was not a new theme. Early coordination was achieved through the PJBD and MCC, resulting in the Basic Security Plan air warning and intercept appendix in 1947. Construction on the American PERMANENT radar system started in 1951, as did a limited number of USAF radar stations (the PINETREE line), which were located in central and eastern Canada, covering the approaches to the industrialized northeast United States. The main threat was the Soviet TU-4 BULL, a B-29 copy, equipped with biological, chemical, atomic, or conventional weapons.[16]

The fear-laden atmosphere in the United States stimulated interest in civil defense. A special study, Project EAST RIVER, concluded that an air defense system was essential to prevent catastrophic damage to the United States as a socio-economic entity. Three to four hours warning was needed. Such a system would have to be based in Canada. Consequently, a Summer Study Group was assembled at the Massachusetts Institute of Technology's (MIT's) Lincoln Laboratory (Project LINCOLN) to discuss what an air defense system might look like. Project LINCOLN was significant in that two Canadian scientists, Dr. John S. Foster of McGill University and Dr. George Lindsey of the DRB, were provided unlimited access.[17]

The study group believed that the Soviets would, by 1954–58, have a stockpile of fission bombs with a yield greater than the nominal 20-kiloton bomb that most planners assumed already existed. The Soviets would eventually develop thermonuclear bombs. Better Soviet aircraft similar to the B-47 would be available, with Intercontinental Ballistic Missiles (ICBMs) coming on-line by 1965. Submarine-launched missiles were a distinct probability, but the group was interested in air defense, not antisubmarine warfare at this point. If there was no warning, twenty large atomic bombs delivered against North America would expose forty-five million people to radiation and kill at least half of them.[18]

The group concluded that air defense was feasible and that improvements were urgent. The system should consist of two Arctic radar chains (later reduced to one); another radar line in central Canada; a tracking and control system; and interceptors.[19] Defensive forces should consist of Canberra-type bombers equipped with air-to-air missiles, perhaps equipped with nuclear warheads:

> Atomic bombs were considered as air-to-air weapons. Against a formation
> of bombers they appear to be an economical weapon. If the launching plane

is to escape the results of the explosion, and the time of flight is to be short enough to prevent the enemy from escaping evasive action, then some simple form of rocket propulsion will be required. The lethal radius is estimated to be 4000 ft. head-on or tail-on, but 8000 ft. side-on.[20]

In addition to manned fighters there should be a local area defense weapon, perhaps either or both of the BOMARC and Nike systems then being tested.[21]

The study group had access to information regarding US technological developments. In 1949, the USAF Air Defense System Engineering Committee undertook a project to improve interception control with computers. It modified a British information system, the Comprehensive Display System, to include a "Whirlwind" computer connected by telephone and high frequency radio to a series of radars. This technology evolved into the Lincoln Transition System, called the Semi-Automated Ground Environment or SAGE in 1954. SAGE was the predecessor of today's Internet.[22]

In 1950, the USAF had approved the development of an interceptor missile, the IM-99, also called the BOMARC (BO=Boeing, MARC=Michigan Aeronautical Research Center). BOMARC was modified in 1953 so that it could interact with SAGE. The first version, BOMARC A, had a proposed range of 125 miles and a proposed high-explosive warhead. The Nike Ajax, a US Army project, was a supersonic point defense missile with a 25-mile range. Over three thousand of these were deployed in the United States in 1953 and 1954. Like the initial BOMARC model, the Nike Ajax was also to be equipped with a conventional warhead. Detailed information on BOMARC made its way to the RCAF as early as 1952.[23] BOMARC's nuclear capabilities had by this time been reassessed, with USAF Air Defense Command (ADC) announcing internally on 31 January 1952 that there was a requirement for a BOMARC nuclear warhead.[24]

The nuclear air-to-air weapon discussed at MIT was the Douglas MB-1. Dubbed the "Genie," the MB-1 was suggested in 1951 for use as an anti-bomber weapon. Formal requirement for its development was tabled in January 1952, but it would not be deployed for another five years.[25] The study group, including the Canadian participants, clearly understood what technologies were currently available and would be available for a future air defense effort.

The DRB's George Lindsey assessed the report in terms of implications for Canada. The Distant Early Warning Line (DEW Line) would cost a lot if Canada built it. If the Americans constructed it, it would involve a major infringement on Canada's sovereignty. The same applied for interceptor aircraft and their bases. Dr. Lindsey noted that

there is a sinister implication for Canadian target cities. If the prediction of heavy attacks proves accurate, and these attacks are met by strong forces deployed in depth to inflict successive stages of attrition as the attack penetrates farther into the system, then the targets which will be better protected are those deep in the interior of the defended area. . . . If the enemy believes this to be the case he is likely to concentrate his attention on the outer surfaces of the system. . . . For this reason it would behoove the inhabitants of the outer fringe to develop the layers of defence outside of their target areas.[26]

After a divisive budgetary battle between air defense proponents and SAC, the Americans' National Security Council approved NSC 139 on 31 December 1952. NSC 139 stated that a distant early warning capability should be developed and ready by 1955.[27] Formal Canadian-American discussions could now begin.

Canadian policy makers, particularly Mike Pearson, were disturbed about sovereignty. Canada was anxious to participate, but there were conditions. They wanted advance knowledge of American thinking regarding air defense matters, particularly American force requirements, and also wanted some form of joint planning along with joint command arrangements for any air defense system involving both nations. These conditions, they believed, would alleviate problems like those "caused on occasion by the USAF's tendency to utilize informal channels of communication owing to a lack of appreciation of the impact on Canada."[28]

Canada was already developing air defense projects that included the McGill Fence (later called the Mid-Canada Line or MCL) and a new interceptor aircraft. The MCL differed from manned radar stations. It consisted of a series of ground stations that projected a signal upwards in an arc. It was directional in the sense that it could determine whether aircraft were headed north or south. In effect, the Mid-Canada line was a trip-wire laid out along the 55th Parallel.[29]

As for interceptor aircraft, Canada designed, produced, and built her own all-weather jet interceptor, the CF-100 "Canuck." Though this aircraft had a proven capability by 1953, many technological advances had been made since its introduction, particularly in aerodynamics and weapons systems. A replacement was needed. Canadian intelligence appreciations indicated that the Soviets would have 750 four-propeller and 50 jet-propelled bombers capable of reaching North America by 1954, with more available by 1958. The RCAF assembled a team in January 1952 to generate requirements for a CF-100 replacement. Essentially, it wanted a twin-engined two-seat aircraft equipped with guided missiles that could fly at Mach 1.5 and have a six-hundred-mile range. Cabinet approved construction of two prototype aircraft in December 1953.[30]

Undertaken by Avro Aircraft of Canada, the CF-105 Arrow program evolved to the point where the speed requirements increased to over Mach 2. In addition the aircraft needed the ability to launch the latest guided air-to-air missiles. The initial weapons system planned for the Arrow involved only conventional missiles, but between 1954 and 1957 designers and air defense planners moved towards equipping the aircraft with nuclear air defense weapons like Genie. In effect, the Arrow would be Canada's first domestically designed and built nuclear delivery system.[31]

Canada, therefore, had more to offer than geography. Combined with clear indications to American policy makers that any air defense effort would be a collaborative one, this understanding produced a new relationship: the Canada-US Military Study Group. It consisted of representatives from the RCAF's Air Defence Command and the American Air Defense Command, with scientific support provided by the Canada-US Scientific Advisory Team, which had members from DRB in Canada and the various American air defense technology bodies. It was responsible for acting as a "medium of exchange" for scientific information.[32]

The new study group oversaw the implementation of Project CORRODE, throughout 1953. CORRODE replaced LINCOLN and the study groups as the primary scientific body dealing with air defense. Project CORRODE included a Canada-US project to determine the feasibility of establishing a high Arctic radar chain. CORRODE also established a series of experimental stations to test men, radar, and communications systems in the extreme Arctic climate and to learn more about electromagnetic anomalies there which might affect early warning.[33]

The concept of operations discussed in Project LINCOLN took shape. In effect, the early warning system was one of four things necessary for the defense of North America. The first was early warning derived from signals intelligence and other sources within the Soviet Union. The second was the effectiveness of SAC; that is, how much damage SAC bombers could produce against the Soviet bomber force before it took off. The third component was the early warning system. Fourth was the ability to disrupt an attack over North America, both at the area and point defense levels. Six hours warning was necessary from the initial penetration of the early warning system by the bombers to the time they had to be disrupted.[34]

The CORRODE test sites were built and tested in the Arctic throughout 1953, while Canadian work continued on the McGill Fence project. In April 1953, the SAGE development team got the go ahead. SAGE would coordinate and control the air battle. NSC 159/4 had recommended the development of air defense projects including SAGE, the MCL, and additional peripheral radars (gap fillers, airborne early warning [AEW] aircraft, and "Texas Towers" at sea).[35]

These projects were accelerated in August 1953 after the Soviets tested their first thermonuclear weapon. American press hysteria was communicated to the Cabinet in Canada while the members deliberated air defense matters. The CUSMSG recommended that MCL construction begin, as it would provide at least two hours warning and it could be in place before the DEW line, which would take longer to build. Cabinet approval was given for MCL construction in November 1953.[36]

Canadian Reaction to the "New Look": 1953–1954

The Eisenhower administration announced its "New Look" policy (NSC 162/2) in October 1953. The New Look policy was no surprise to Canadians. Foulkes developed a close relationship with General Omar Bradley's replacement, Admiral Arthur W. Radford, the new chairman of the JCS. While he was chairman, Radford met with Foulkes more times than any other allied military leader. The two men on many occasions smoothed the way between both nations' foreign policy representatives, particularly on continental defense.[37]

One example occurred in October 1953. Radford was under pressure to accelerate the American continental defense effort, and the perceived slow pace of the Canadian policy process frustrated his attempts to show American policy makers (and the media) that there was, in fact, progress. Foulkes arranged a meeting that included the Director of Central Intelligence, General Bedell Smith; Admiral Radford;

Canadian ambassador to the United States, A. D. P. Heeney; and George Ignatieff from External Affairs. The aim was to clear the air. Some restrictions on nuclear and intelligence information were informally lifted for the purposes of the meeting. In a frank discussion, both parties examined the progress of the Soviet thermonuclear program, delivery systems, intent, and potential methods of limiting damage to North America if attacked. The American's hoped

> to achieve in a rapid and orderly manner and to maintain, in collaboration with Canada, a readiness and capability which will give us a reasonable assurance of:
> (a) contributing to deterring Soviet aggression
> (b) preventing devastating attack that might threaten our national survival
> (c) minimizing the effect of any Soviet attack so as to permit our successful prosecution of the war
> (d) guarding against Soviet inspired subversive activities
> (e) preventing the threat of atomic destruction from discouraging freedom of action or weakening national morale.[38]

Canadian participation, the group agreed, was essential if the deterrent system was to be effective.

The second example was a paper informally passed to Foulkes in December 1953 by an American officer on the NATO Standing Group. Passed on to the Canadian chiefs, this paper laid out American thinking on the place of nuclear weapons in NATO strategy. The Lisbon goals could not be met. Therefore, battlefield nuclear weapons would augment conventional forces. Tactical nuclear weapons "have been given high priority," but they would be useless without knowing what the "empirical effects" were. Though the data remained subject to restrictive American laws, SHAPE and SACLANT would initiate a training program for NATO members as soon as feasible. In the Standing Group's view, "atomic and other new weapons will not . . . obviate the need for standard battle-tested weapons."[39]

The paper emphasized the need for an efficient communications and alerting system. This was "a grave problem, largely political in nature." Most significantly "even short delays in granting Commanders the authority to initiate retaliatory operations might lead to a serious disintegration of our military position." There was no immediate answer to this problem. As for nuclear forces, a mix of aircraft-delivered bombs, missiles, and artillery was necessary given operational factors on the field. Missiles were adequate against fixed targets, but aircraft were needed for targets of opportunity. Nuclear-armed air defense missiles were vital once the Soviets developed a nuclear strike force.[40]

With the October 1953 meeting and December 1953 paper as background, the New Look policy caused some concern in Ottawa. Canadian officials were split as to what impact the New Look would have on Canada's participation in both NATO and the continental defense system. The most important tenets of NSC 162/2 were communicated to the media and thus via the Canadian Embassy to Ottawa. These included the central role of nuclear weapons in counterbalancing Soviet power, the renewed emphasis on strategic striking power, the use of nuclear weapons to support conventional NATO forces in Europe and elsewhere, and the fact that nuclear weapons information must be shared with the Allies so that their forces would be more effective.[41]

However, the message received in Ottawa was garbled during "media transmission," and the confusion was compounded by US Secretary of State John Foster Dulles's explication of the new policy. An Alliance debate (conducted primarily through the media) broke out over where and under what circumstances the United States would use "prompt retaliation" with nuclear weapons at places of its choosing.[42] The Americans were alarmed at the debate. Radford knew that some NATO nations sought Canadian views on such matters, and he was anxious to get Canadian support. Radford secretly informed Foulkes that the phrase "prompt retaliation" was inserted "mainly for propaganda purposes and would not be applied without consultation with allies."[43]

Canadian diplomatic personnel were not overly concerned. A. D. P. Heeney correctly concluded in January 1954 that the most likely effect of the New Look on Canadian defense policy would probably involve "increased attention to continental defence in co-operation with Canada to protect the main base of the striking power of the free world."[44]

An early Joint Planning Committee study indicated that the New Look would affect the Canadian defense program materially, to include extending the early warning system out to sea and dramatically increasing air defense forces. The Canadian joint planners thought that it might prompt Canada to acquire BOMARC or Nike, build more interceptor aircraft, and base American fighters in Canada. Ultimately it would lead to the complete integration of both nations' air defense commands. In terms of Canadian commitments in Europe, the joint planners noted that there was some concern that the American forces might reduce or withdraw from Europe because they were currently deploying nuclear weapons there. The fact that the conventional forces had not been drawn down indicated that they would probably stay. Consequently, withdrawing Canadian forces from Europe would be precipitous. The Canadian joint planners also noted that American nuclear weapons policy was "obscure" and that it was "difficult to determine at this time what the possible implications to Canada" were.[45]

On the other hand, Canada's ambassador to NATO, Dana Wilgress, thought that:

> the protection of this retaliatory power will assume progressively greater importance and, in the end, it will become inseparable from the power itself. . . . A few years hence, the main front may shift from Europe and centre in the armament competition between the offensive-defensive capacity of the Soviet Bloc and the American Continent. The race will not only involve better weapons but also a redeployment of those weapons. Unless we can reduce our commitments outside the American Continent, our defence bill in future years may therefore be higher.[46]

The joint planners were tasked to report in more detail on the possible impact of the New Look, once more information became available from American sources. The JPC paper, "United States Defense Policy and the Possible Implications for Canadian Defense Policy," provided a Canadian interpretation of what the New Look meant. The JPC concluded that the New Look was motivated by economic and domestic political factors and, more importantly, the projected availability of "tactical and strategic atomic and thermonuclear weapons" that "constituted the real strength of the power to deter aggression." In addition, "The realization that the Soviet Union had developed thermonuclear weapons and the capacity to strike any target in North America, gave the Eisenhower Administration the basis on which to divert more resources to the strengthening of American air power and of continental air defence." The JPC also concluded that atomic and thermonuclear weapons might not necessarily be used, "but they are now considered a part of the United States' conventional military strength."[47]

With regard to the Canadian defense program, the JPC noted that the defense of the Atlantic area remained a high American priority. The emphasis on the continental system, however, revolved around protecting the main deterrent force, SAC, as much as protecting Canada and the United States as socioeconomic entities. In effect, "The Canadian government may be faced with requirements for additional radar systems, interceptor forces, anti-aircraft and guided missile installations, further integration of air defences into one command and generally closer measures of cooperation in planning and defence commands . . . demands on Canadian resources—financial, physical and manpower—are likely to be substantially heavier."[48]

Mike Pearson was concerned that Canadian policy makers might use the New Look to withdraw from the European NATO commitment, perhaps citing cost. Pearson's counterbalance concept would be irrevocably altered if this new "continentalism" took root. The aim was to influence the Americans through the NATO medium. Fully committing Canada to continental defense would dramatically reduce her ability to influence the other NATO allies in the diplomatic forums. Canadian and American withdrawal from Europe would even be interpreted by the allies (and certainly the Soviets) as a weakening of the Alliance itself. Canada, therefore, must use her diplomatic capital in Washington and Paris to ensure that spats caused by the New Look announcement remained just that and did not erupt into divisive debate. In a memorandum to the Prime Minister, Pearson concluded that

> Canadian defence policy has been, firmly and rightly, founded on NATO, and we should do everything we can to keep this foundation strong. On the other hand, it is not going to be easy, politically, to maintain at full and unimpaired strength our forces overseas, if our neighbours begin to reduce their commitments through "new decisions" and new strategic concepts. It may be that the American Administration will not be the only ones who will, before long, have to make an "agonizing reappraisal" of foreign policy.[49]

This debate was reflected in the COSC. Simonds did not believe that the Soviets would use the bulk of their nuclear stockpile against North American targets. He thought that the primary Soviet aim was to secure Western Europe and, in particular, the United Kingdom. What if the Soviets did not use nuclear weapons in a conflict at all and relied on their conventional strength in Europe? It would put the moral onus on the West regarding nuclear use. Air Chief Marshal Roy Slemon disagreed. He thought that SAC bases in North America would be the primary targets. What good would securing Europe be without taking out the main threat against the Soviet homeland? Foulkes had to intercede. Canada had to be able to contribute to meeting both threats in a flexible manner. The new Soviet jet bomber, the M-4 BISON, was an indicator of Soviet intentions, Foulkes stated, but the indications were also strong that the Soviets believed they could cut Europe off in the Atlantic and attain victory.[50] Canada, therefore, needed to contribute forward defense forces in Europe, forces at sea, and air defense forces in Canada.

Foulkes was influenced by developments in Europe. General Al Gruenther had established a New Approach Group (NAG) at SHAPE earlier in 1954. The group's purpose was to develop a strategic policy without US JCS or NATO Standing Group interference. In addition to the bureaucratic inefficiency inherent to the Standing Group, other NATO members were not happy about having a committee consisting of American, British, and French military leaders vetting the deliberations of the Military Committee.[51] As Deputy Minister Bud Drury put it in a note to Foulkes: "I see that the basic plans of NATO are subject to review and comment by the . . . [Chiefs of Staff] of [the] U.S., U.K., and France and that it is the function of the . . . [Standing Group] to reconcile such views before they are passed on to lesser breeds."[52]

Specifically, the NAG was to "(1) determine the effect of the introduction of new weapons on the size of the forces that would be needed by 1957; (2) to see what effect new weapons would have on the composition of national forces (land, sea, and air); and (3) to try to determine what effect the new weapons would have on the balance as between regular and reserve forces."[53] The NAG operated on several assumptions. First, war would be short and the decisive phase would come early. This in turn was dependent on the effective delivery of nuclear weapons, instead of a conventional reinforcement buildup over the long term. The emphasis, then, was on forces in being which might consist of a conventional-tactical nuclear shield to hold the line in Europe for up to thirty days. Nuclear weapons would be used from the outset. The NAG submitted its reports in July 1954 to the Standing Group.[54]

In effect, the NAG reports went directly to the Standing Group without going through the Military Committee. Foulkes found out and was not impressed. He pushed for and got a meeting with the Standing Group on 7 June 1954. Foulkes was adamant: Any implementation of NAG recommendations was

> a subject of vital NATO military policy which must be decided on equal terms by all of the fourteen Chiefs of Staff and we cannot agree with the Standing Group countries making up their minds, the other eleven countries being expected to accept the stand taken by the three national governments. This position is unacceptable to the Canadian Chiefs of Staff and the Canadian Government.[55]

This was unacceptable for several reasons, but most importantly for Foulkes:

As this may involve financial and other policy matters of the Canadian Government, the Government will require the Canadian Chiefs of Staff to be in accord with the recommendations, and decisions on policy must be arrived at as equal partners any time they involve Canadian participation.[56]

The American member, General Whiteley, attempted to convince Foulkes that the other NATO members could not participate because of the high security relating to nuclear weapons planning and capabilities. Foulkes told him, "this argument did not hold water at all." SACEUR already knew what the limits were and had not exceeded them in the production of the NAG studies. Foulkes knew the limits also because of his relationship with Gruenther. Foulkes then pointedly told Whiteley, "it is common knowledge that the worst security in NATO is in a country which is represented on the Standing Group" and he "could not accept the fact that anything which could be seen by France could not be seen by Canada."[57]

Whiteley then tried to convince Foulkes that political (as opposed to military) security was another reason the Military Committee should be avoided. In Whiteley's view, "there was a possibility that this paper would reveal that we would not be able to defend Denmark and part of Holland." Foulkes again "pointed out that this was no secret." Foulkes was "not at all convinced that the Standing Group" could solve *any* security problem, military or political.[58]

Foulkes won, and the Standing Group agreed to incorporate the Military Committee into the process.[59] It is possible that if this had not occurred, the very central and important NATO strategy MC 48 might not have existed as a Military Committee–vetted concept.

Shortly afterwards, Gruenther came to Ottawa to brief the Cabinet Defence Committee in June 1954. Foulkes arranged this meeting.[60] Gruenther discussed the activities of the SHAPE New Approach Group, and noted that SHAPE assumed that atomic bombs would be available and used. Gruenther believed that the decision to use them would be at the highest political level, while the SHAPE staff decided how they would be employed: targeting would focus on enemy airfields. SACEUR concluded by asking that Canada not withdraw fighters from the RCAF's 1 Air Division in Europe for continental air defense in North America; this would open a serious gap in SACEUR's air defenses. Nor should Canada withdraw its divisional commitment to the Central Region, asserting that the Canadian contribution to the forces under his command were "magnificent" and "would be very hard to replace."[61] Canada, he said, "had an influence far out of proportion to its 15 million people and could do much to remove the ill feeling that existed between friendly countries. Canadians . . . were not viewed as having any specific axe to grind. . . . much could be done to improve relations between France and the United States."[62]

SACLANT, Admiral Jerauld Wright, also had his turn to address the CDC and the panel. Too many policy makers, in his view, neglected the fact that the Atlantic Ocean was a major factor in the defense of NATO and, as far as he was concerned, continental defense was inseparable from the defense of Europe. After making reference to the magnitude of an emerging missile-launching submarine threat in the North Atlantic, Wright emphasized that Canada contributed significantly to

Anti-Submarine Warfare (ASW) forces and this was welcomed by SACLANT. Wright told the Cabinet that "atomic and thermonuclear weapons would play just as big a role in naval as in other forms of warfare and were just as useful against naval targets . . . include[ing] Soviet submarine bases and airfields from which maritime operations could be launched. . . . SACLANT had made plans to use these weapons and established liaison arrangements with those agencies capable of delivering them."[63] Wright wanted to believe that these weapons would "do the job," but personally "he was quite sure that more conventional forms of armament would [also] be required."[64] Intelligence on the Soviet submarine fleet indicated there were about 400 submarines, of which 80 were long-range, 130 for intermediate distances, and the rest dedicated to coastal operations. Wright also briefed the Cabinet on the American nuclear submarine program. In sum, Canada retained its vantage point on Atlantic issues and was, later on, able to factor this information into the Canadian defense program.

There was one major change in July 1954. Brooke Claxton stepped down as Minister of National Defence. He was replaced by Ralph Campney. Campney was from Picton, Ontario, and was a Queen's University graduate. Like many of his colleagues, he served in the First World War in a hospital unit, then with an infantry battalion in France, and finally with the Royal Flying Corps. A lawyer with strong liberal connections (he had been King's secretary in the 1930s), Campney was assistant to Brooke Claxton in 1951 before taking over the defense portfolio in July 1954.[65] The relationship between Foulkes and Ralph Campney was a cooperative but unremarkable one. Campney "seemed content to adopt a low profile and preferred to react to recommendations of the Chiefs of Staff in implementing defence policy rather than the initiation of new measures and policy."[66]

As 1954 progressed, Canadian planners were receiving better information regarding Soviet intentions and capabilities. Why exactly this was the case is difficult to determine. One possibility is that the informal personal channels between the Canadian and American scientists and policy makers were producing a more fruitful exchange. Perhaps Canadian technical methods improved, or perhaps the Canadian intelligence community improved its organizational structure to move information more efficiently. Whatever the reason, the Defence Research Board and the newly inaugurated Joint Special Weapons Policy Committee (JSWPC) were tasked to report to the Joint Planning Committee on the projected enemy intentions and capabilities.[67] After a semiannual review of intelligence in the fall of 1954, the joint planners concluded that the Soviets were displaying very flexible tactics in dealing with the West, though there was no relaxation of control over Eastern European nations. The Soviet economy had improved, as had its military capabilities. A significant indicator was the fact that "the international Communist movement continues to attempt to undermine governmental authorities wherever opportunities arise throughout the world."[68]

Canadian understanding of the Soviet Union's capability to threaten North America was refined. The estimate stated that the Soviets would possess 34 boosted uranium or plutonium weapons in the 1000-kt yield range and 125 60-kt weapons by mid-1955. That said, the JPC also concluded "a true ballistic-type missile of the requisite range [that is, to North America] will be in service use before 1960–63. An intercontinental missile of the aircraft type might, however, be available by 1957–60."[69]

Weapons effects information was coming in from open sources. Worldwide public outcry in 1954 over the American CASTLE BRAVO test and the "Lucky Dragon" episode in the Pacific raised public consciousness about radioactive fallout and scientists scrambled to understand the phenomenon.[70] The JPC was then asked to report on what effect megaton-yield nuclear weapons would have for the Canadian defense program. This report was a significant step in the formulation of Canadian nuclear weapons policy.

The potential effects of MT-yield nuclear weapons staggered the JPC. In their view:

the use of megaton nuclear weapons could be so devastating to mankind that the primary aim must be, in both the political and military field, to prevent their use. . . . It is considered that the use of any form of tactical nuclear weapon would lead to the eventual use of megaton weapons and, therefore, the possibility of a war involving tactical nuclear weapons only, is unrealistic.[71]

Furthermore:

a very few enemy aircraft penetrating to the vital areas of Canada and the United States could create such havoc that it might become virtually impossible for either country to continue the war. Therefore, an adequate defence against this threat is of vital importance to North America. . . . an attack by submarine is a less likely form of attack than by air but it cannot be discounted. Submarine attack could be by two means—
(a) By use of guided missiles or rockets
(b) By submarine mining (including the off-shore detonation of megaton weapons) [consequently] the detection and destruction of enemy submarines assumes greater importance.[72]

Thus:

Because present defence do not give adequate protection, nor provide sufficient deterrence to such an attack. The only military measure which will prevent the initiation of the use of nuclear weapons in war is the threat of retaliation. The retaliatory forces, therefore, become not only a deterrent, but North America's first line of defence. Now, more than ever, the defence of these forces [must] be given the highest priority in the overall defence programme.[73]

The joint planners argued that the complete air defense of North America was not possible in 1954, but until there was some form of interception, early warning was still useful and vital. ICBMs would be available in the 1960–65 time frame and money should be put into developing countermeasures against them. The entire civil defense system would require reassessment, as would the role of reserve forces.

Canadian forces serving in Europe were not ignored in this appraisal:

SACEUR's concept of defence in Europe is based on the unrestricted use of nuclear weapons. Without these, the forces now in Europe would be inadequate and the Soviets, using its preponderance of manpower, could quickly overrun Western Europe. It becomes apparent, therefore, that under such circumstances SACEUR forces in Western Europe would have to be strengthened.[74]

The JPC paper thus reflected a compromise between the two positions. Though the air and sea defense of North America was a priority, land and air forces would remain part of the NATO shield in Europe.

In a follow on discussion, the DRB recommended to the chiefs that "steps should be taken to obtain some types of US weapons for use by the Canadian Forces."[75] The lack of a medium to acquire information on weapons blocked any further discussion of the issue in 1954, as Foulkes told Solandt: "You should not forward to the Chiefs of Staff any recommendations regarding atomic weapons for Canadian use until a more appropriate time than the present."[76]

Canada started to forge a closer relationship with SAC in late 1954. The first part of the relationship was to confirm that the MCL and DEW lines, once operational, had the primary role of alerting intercept aircraft to protect SAC bases in North America. The air staff assumed that enemy bombers had SAC bases as their primary target. The secondary task was to alert the civil defense organizations in both countries. Until the MCL and DEW systems were up and running, SAC had to rely on the existing PINETREE line, which had spotty coverage and could not guarantee two to three hours warning.[77]

More and more SAC training was conducted in Canadian airspace. The RCAF greatly appreciated the long-range SAC flights attempting to penetrate Air Defence Command's cover around St. Hubert (some of the SAC flights lasted twenty hours). This allowed CF-100 all-weather interceptor crews to participate in extremely realistic training exercises. SAC was, according to the RCAF, "the greatest deterrent force in existence on the side of the Western democracies and it would be undesirable to impose restrictions which would limit its effectiveness." However, there was some confusion on the part of the civilian policy makers. Did the training flights, in fact, carry nuclear weapons? The RCAF thought not, though the issue was not addressed in this specific memorandum of understanding. The bombers probably carried practice nuclear shapes, but not components or bombs minus the "physics package."[78]

External Affairs raised the issue of future USAF (and thus SAC) basing. A media leak in the United States noted that the USAF would soon request more fighter and bomber bases in Canada.[79] In addition to the special nuclear storage arrangement established in 1950, the US Joint Chiefs also established (with Canadian agreement) a unified command for American units handling the northeastern approaches to North America. These interceptor units would come under Canadian operational control in the event of war, something not done in other NATO countries.[80] The first unit to arrive was the 59th Fighter Interceptor Squadron (FIS) with its F-94B Starfire interceptors. It was based at Goose Bay, with a detachment in Thule, Greenland. The 61st FIS was located at Ernest Harmon AFB (Stephenville, Newfoundland) in 1953. It also had F-94B Starfires. Both units were in the process of converting to F-89D Scorpions and considerations were being made regarding dispersal airfields.[81] SAC was interested in basing bombers and tankers out of Torbay, Newfoundland; Churchill, Manitoba; and Edmonton, Alberta.

The RCAF's enthusiasm to support SAC touched off another row in the Joint Planning Committee. There were not enough air defense resources in 1954 to cover every potential target in Canada. The RCAF sought to create a target protection priority list to govern the deployment of RCAF and army air defense resources.[82] Montreal, Toronto, and Ottawa all were priority one targets, while Goose Bay, Halifax, and Vancouver were priority two. RCAF Air Defence Command, with USAF, concurred (no one was sure who initiated the discussions) that the air defense of North America should be considered a single air defense problem. Thus, first priority for the air defense forces should be given to SAC refueling and main operating bases.[83]

Other JPC members were appalled. This plan meant that Goose Bay, a USAF SAC base, was to be given a higher defense priority than the capital of Canada and all of her largest cities. The members concluded "the RCAF recommendation, under brief, is designed to establish the highest priority for Goose Bay in order to substantiate a further recommendation concerning air defence forces at this base." In other words, the RCAF wanted to use the plan to garner more air defense resources, perhaps at the expense of the other services. The JPC members pointed out that a USAF squadron already defended the base.[84]

In the end, the joint planners headed this one off at the pass. They believed that it was ADC's responsibility to defend Canadian targets and "the population or the Government would not accept anything else." In other words, if the Americans wanted it, they could request it directly and it would be considered at the government level. Policy was not to be made by the RCAF Air Defence Command on such a matter.[85]

The accelerated air defense requirements produced equally accelerated analyses of what weapons systems would fulfill those requirements. The RCAF had been sparring with the army throughout 1954 over who would acquire which anti-bomber missile system and who would control it.

The RCAF report "Guided Missiles as a Part of the Air Defence Weapons System," briefed to the chiefs of staff in November 1954, was a clear indication of RCAF thinking and set the ground for future missile developments.[86]

The RCAF's air defense plan was based on the prevention of war through the West's ability to conduct an effective counterattack against the Soviet Union with thermonuclear weapons. An effective and overwhelming threat to this capability would produce instability in the deterrent. The Soviets would not be in a position to produce this effective threat until 1957. There was, therefore, still time to develop effective countermeasures against the future threat.[87] (See figure 2.1.)

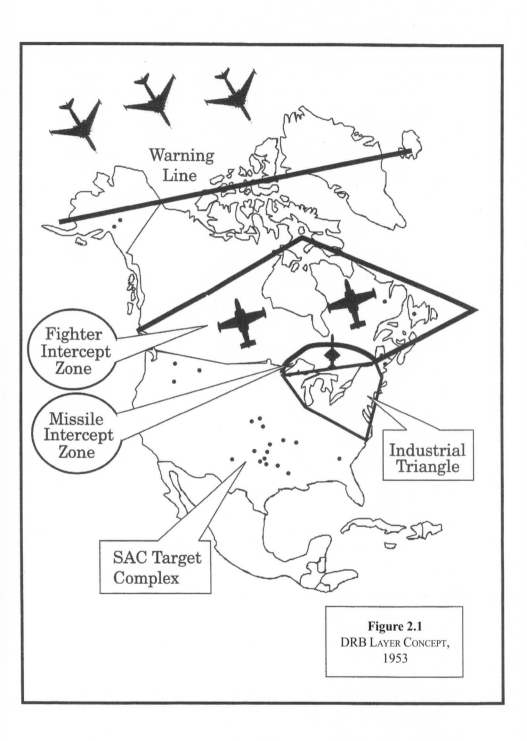

Figure 2.1
DRB LAYER CONCEPT,
1953

The RCAF identified SAC bases as the priority targets that required defense. To compromise with the problems noted by the JPC, RCAF planners noted that the thirty-four SAC bases and the vital industrialized areas of North America formed the same target system and could be defended. Other isolated areas would require special handling. Goose Bay was one of these and the planners did not think it was defensible at all. Early warning was still critical, particularly for SAC: Two or three hours were necessary so that the bombers could disperse. This warning should come from strategic warning sources (that is, signals intelligence) as well as the DEW line and MCL.[88]

The RCAF gave short shrift to the Army's quest to acquire the conventionally armed Nike point defense system. Megaton-yield weapons, argued the DRB, negated point defense systems if these were sited too close to the targets themselves:

> Even if the vehicle carrying the bomb is destroyed in the vicinity of the target and the bomb still explodes, very little real defence has been achieved. We understand that, unless the bomb itself is struck by a fragment, the bomb's barometric fuze will almost certainly be set to detonate in the event that the carrier is shot down. Thus the area in which the carriers are destroyed becomes a matter of very great concern. . . . Short range weapons sited near the target will no longer protect it.[89]

The RCAF saw the air defense system progressing in time in three phases. In Phase I (1955–58), the main threat was the TU-4 BULL and the Type 39 (probably the TU-16 BADGER), and submarine-launched cruise missiles. The enemy aircraft would be operating from bases in the Murmansk and Chukotski areas. Canada would have CF-100 and CF-86 interceptors: The CF-100s would, in theory, be armed with Sparrow II air-to-air missiles. They could stop a small-scale raid but would be unable to dramatically attrit an attacking force if it consisted of Type 39 aircraft.[90]

Phase II (1958–61) was assessed as a "very dangerous" period. The threat would consist of the Type 37 heavy bomber (probably the Mya-4 BISON) and Snark-like intercontinental cruise missiles. The RCAF anticipated that the air defense forces would be equipped with CF-100s with Sparrows and CF-105 Arrows equipped with an undetermined air-to-air missile type. The manned aircraft would be supplemented with a surface-to-air missile similar to the BOMARC A. The aim was to have a 94% kill rate against a mass raid. This would require either six hundred BOMARC As or nine hundred Nike missiles. More would be required to defend all of North America, as this was only enough to minimally defend the industrialized northeast United States, southern Quebec, and southern Ontario. Radar cover south of the MCL and DEW lines would have to be increased so that intercept operations could be conducted. BOMARC would be used against high-speed cruise missiles (air or sea-launched).

Phase III (1961+) posited a similar threat estimate and response. The exception was that the enemy would supplement his forces with a supersonic cruise missile similar to the planned American Navaho system.[91]

The RCAF rated the planned surface-to-air missile systems. Not surprisingly, BOMARC B, an improved version, was the most effective, followed by BOMARC

A, Talos, Nike B, Nike, and finally a British system called RED SHOES. One BOMARC B was the equivalent of twenty-six Nike, four BOMARC As, or twelve Nike Bs. Was the RCAF data reliable enough to base a multibillion dollar decision on? The Chiefs of Staff Committee chose to consider the question at an undetermined point in the future.[92]

The Cabinet Defence Committee met in November 1954 to discuss the defense program in light of the past year's events. It was at this point the matter of a North American emphasis versus a European emphasis came to a head. Ralph Campney was adamant that there was a distinct relationship between the two:

> There was a conflict between the requirements for the continental defence of North America and the defence of Europe. The United States had made a greater contribution to the defence of Europe than Canada. For a large scale U.S. contribution to continue, it would be necessary to have the support of the U.S. public and that required defences of North America considered adequate by the U.S. public. Canada was not willing to let the U.S. government establish defences here . . . without regard to Canadian sovereign interests and we had to avoid giving the Canadian public the impression that the U.S. had vested rights in the northern half of the continent . . . [in order to meet these two requirements] Canada had to contribute to the development of the overall warning system. This might mean that the Canadian contribution to European defence would not be as great as might otherwise have been the case but it would mean that if the United States were satisfied that it was properly protected, it would continue to carry a large share of the burden of defending Europe.[93]

In addition to contributing to the air defense of North America, Canadian forces serving in Europe (the brigade group and 1 Air Division), were still needed and required upgrading. In this way, Canada remained committed to both areas, and the link between them was slowly forged.

A New Strategy: Canada and MC 48

The thermonuclear weapons problem produced tension in deciding where Canada should place her primary military effort, given scarce resources. How much Canadian defense effort should be given to protecting SAC, and how much to protecting NATO in Europe and in the Atlantic?

The link between the Canadian continental and European systems was the new NATO strategic concept MC 48, formally adopted in November 1954. The recognition that MC 48 was this link, however, was not made in an explicit fashion in the same way that NSC 162/2 became identified as the New Look. Rather, Canada's acceptance of MC 48 defined her national strategy and became a *deus ex machina* of sorts. Almost all defense projects prior to 1964 were defined in terms of their relationship to MC 48 and its successor concept, MC 14/2. (MC 14/2 will be examined in more detail in later chapters). Consequently, a detailed description of MC 48 and Canadian reaction to it is warranted in this section.

As noted earlier, MC 48 was the product of an exhaustive NATO strategy process. Gruenther's New Approach Group studies were sent to the Standing Group in July 1954. The Standing Group report on the NAG studies, SG 241/3, was revised in October 1954, when it was sent to the Military Committee under the designation IPT 178/15. It was then released as "Decision on MC 48: A Report by the Military Committee on the Most Effective Pattern of NATO Military Strength for the Next Few Years" on 22 November 1954.[94]

What, then, was MC 48? The document states that NATO's aim is defensive in nature. This defense will be provided by presenting a major deterrent to aggression, presenting a credible forward defense of Europe, and demonstrating a "high measure of confidence."[95] Thus, NATO must convince the Soviet Union that Europe cannot be overrun quickly and, in the event that they try, "they will be subjected immediately to devastating counter-attack employing atomic weapons." Notably, NATO ruled out preventative war, placing the onus of aggression on the Soviet Union or by miscalculation. The only hope the Soviets would have of winning a war would be to destroy NATO's ability to "counterattack immediately and decisively with atomic weapons." Even if the Soviets attacked conventionally, NATO would use nuclear weapons in response. Consequently, a future war would have two phases similar to those envisioned in the British Global Strategy Paper of 1952. There would be "an intensive initial phase of operations—approximately thirty days or less—in which each side would strive to deliver a large proportion" of its nuclear weapons "as rapidly and effectively as possible in an effort to neutralize the opponent's atomic delivery capability." While this atomic assault was in progress, naval, land, and air forces would be initiating operations "to achieve strategic advantage and to be prepared to conduct continued operations."[96]

In the second phase, assuming that one side had not surrendered, "there would be a subsequent period of readjustment and follow up, the exact nature of which would largely depend on the outcome of the initial phase." NATO's ability to defeat the enemy was dependent on its "ability to survive and gain superiority in the initial phase." As a result, "our peacetime force pattern must be designed primarily to achieve success during this initial phase and emphasis must be placed upon development of the forces which can participate more effectively in these operations."[97]

To accomplish its aims, NATO had to develop a better intelligence system and to "ensure to the maximum extent possible the security of [the] vitally important strategic air forces and atomic striking forces in Europe," which included the development of an alert and communications system, passive air defense measures, and dispersion. NATO forces also had to be able to "initiate immediate defensive and retaliatory operations including the use of atomic weapons." NATO forces in Europe were to prevent the overrunning of Western Europe from the outset and preserve the integrity of the NATO area. The state of anti-air forces in Allied Command Europe (ACE) was poor, and therefore "the counter-air offensive is the most important factor in air defence. The only presently feasible way of stopping an enemy from delivering atomic weapons against selected targets in Europe is to destroy his means of delivery at source."[98]

Soviet forces would conduct a surprise attack against NATO nuclear delivery means, followed by "widespread attacks by the Soviet army and tactical air forces against Europe." Attacks would also be made against NATO naval forces, bases, and merchant shipping in order to isolate Europe. The control of sea communications was important in MC 48. Traditional naval tasks did not change dramatically since "NATO naval commanders are to control and exploit the seas for NATO purposes and to deny their use to the enemy." NATO naval forces in being had to be able to conduct "powerful offensive preparations" against enemy targets, and they were to form part of the deterrent in peacetime.[99]

How did MC 48 differ from previous concepts? Unlike MC 14 and MC 14/1, there was no area planning guidance included. This absence bedeviled those who wanted a clear statement asserting that protecting the deterrent was more important than forward defense in Europe. Both were coequal in MC 48. Though MC 14/1 assumed limited nuclear use (that is, limited by the numbers of weapons available to NATO), MC 48 called for a buildup of nuclear forces to supplement the conventional forces in Europe and for those forces already in Europe to develop means of passive defense in the face of nuclear weapons. The aim was to deter Soviet action by having the means to repel attacks against the NATO area and having the means to strike at the Soviet Union directly. Notably, the naval mission did not change dramatically.

Foulkes, who relinquished his position as chairman of the NATO Military Committee in 1953, was still Canada's representative to that body while he was chairman of the Canadian Chiefs of Staff Committee. He was thus able to monitor MC 48's progress throughout 1954. He was able to get a copy of IPT 178/15, which he passed on to the COSC late in October 1954. The chiefs' remarks were far-sighted.

Air Marshal Slemon was concerned because there was "a tendency to assess the damage potential of the new weapons as being simply larger than the old weapons. The effects of fall out have not been considered." He was also concerned that "the papers seem to be written primarily for European eyes. The fact that a successful atomic attack on North America could be disastrous to NATO as a whole is not brought out."[100]

Chief of the General Staff Guy Simonds prophetically noted that:

SACEUR's plans for the defence of Western Europe are built around the use by both sides of nuclear weapons. The Soviet knows this and the Chief of the General Staff is of the opinion that the Soviets may, therefore, use only conventional weapons, thus placing the West in the position of having to initiate the nuclear war. As the relative size of Soviet and NATO stocks of nuclear weapons and delivery capabilities begin to balance, there may be great reluctance on the part of the West to initiate the use of nuclear weapons. This would result in a conventional war in which the Soviets would have a huge advantage . . . and as a result it may become necessary for NATO nations to create larger forces in being. . . . insufficient weight is given in these papers to force requirements which may be necessary to avoid *defeat in the ensuring phases*.[101]

Admiral Mainguy noted that the enemy submarine force would have to be a priority target in the initial phase of the war, or it could wreak havoc in attempts to reinforce Europe in the second phase.

These comments were not passed on in a formal way to the Standing Group: To Simonds's chagrin, Foulkes did not even make use of them for the Military Committee meeting in November. Foulkes believed that there was too much talk about the second phase and forces for it:

> It appears to me that the greatest danger to NATO is that we might get defeated in the first stage and if we get defeated in the initial stage, we won't have to worry about the subsequent stage . . . one of the greatest difficulties we are going to face with this paper in taking it to our political masters is to convince them of the necessary measures that have to be taken to ensure that we can win, or not lose, this initial phase because the steps which we have to take to ensure that we will not succumb to the initial phase are questions which are very difficult for democracies to take.[102]

These questions involved the transition from peace to war, the relationship of launching forces in response to alerts, and the problems of getting the politicians to agree to immediate nuclear weapons use:

> The only way in which the Soviet Union has an opportunity of defeating NATO is by a sudden blow. The initiative will always rest with the Soviet Union it will not rest with us. Therefore, it is going to be frightfully difficult for us to plan to meet this initial onslaught unless we get sufficient priority in putting this forward to our political masters. . . . [a war of attrition] doesn't worry me so much because [we] can win. . . . [the Soviets] are in a position, or may be in a year or two, to strike a sudden disastrous blow and if we aren't ready we haven't taken the measures which have been recommended that we should take, we may not survive the first phase and I would appeal to you that when explaining this to our masters this is the point which is going to be most difficult, the point of getting them to agree to be in a position to withstand this first terrible blow.[103]

While Foulkes addressed the Military Committee, a heated discussion on MC 48 broke out at a North Atlantic Council luncheon. Almost all present were concerned about the implications of immediate nuclear weapons use by NATO. Did the council's acceptance of MC 48 imply that approval had been given for NATO military authorities to plan on the basis "that atomic and thermo-nuclear weapons may be used in the future war?" The American representative noted that planning should continue and that the NAC could withhold authority to actually use the weapons. This assurance calmed the representatives down temporarily. Pearson was informed of this exchange immediately.[104]

Foulkes forwarded a record of the Military Committee meeting and a copy of MC 48 to Ralph Campney at the end of November; these documents were also passed to Secretary of State for External Affairs Mike Pearson. Campney also sent along Foulkes's covering letter in which he noted that there were some changes from the original. NATO ministers "would no longer be asked to approve the use of mass destruction weapons, but rather to approve the authorization for NATO military authorities to plan [for their use at the onset of hostilities]."[105]

At least three participants in the Military Committee discussion over MC 48 expressed concern. These were Admiral Jerauld Wright (SACLANT), Admiral Sir Rhoderick McGrigor (Royal Navy), and General B. R. M. Hasselman (Netherlands). Their problems with MC 48 amounted to what they saw as a lack of detailed explanation about the transition from the initial phase of the war (nuclear phase) to the subsequent (non-nuclear) phase. They believed that naval operations were not handled well within the MC 48 framework, since there would be continuity of action at sea which transcended the two phases. Naval forces were required for both phases and there was some concern that the proponents of strategic airpower would use MC 48's emphasis on the first phase to attack the utility of navies in future wars. Foulkes reiterated his previous views on the need to be ready for the first phase and, most importantly, to appear ready, since the Soviets held the initiative. Admiral Radford, the US Joint Chiefs chairman fully agreed, as did Air Marshal Dawson (RAF) who represented SACEUR at the meeting.[106]

The Military Committee also discussed the problems of the wartime coordination of NATO-dedicated national forces and those national forces that were not earmarked for NATO. A discussion paper had recently been put forward dealing with air defense in the NATO area but it made no reference to North America. Foulkes expressed surprise at this omission and pointedly noted that MC 48 recognized the relationship between air defense and protecting the strategic deterrent forces (SAC) that directly benefited NATO. Foulkes noted "the Canada-US Regional Planning Group was part of NATO and he felt sometimes this was forgotten. . . . The purpose was not to defend North America for North Americans but to ensure the effective defence of the retaliatory capability of North America which would provide the greatest deterrent to war."[107] The committee agreed to recognize this contribution. Confusion over how "NATO" the North American air defense system actually was would reassert itself in the future during the NORAD debate in the late 1950s.

The British government had reservations about MC 48. Pearson transmitted these concerns to Foulkes along with a note stating, "You may wish to show this to Mr. Campney." In essence, the British thought "it would therefore be possible for SACEUR to begin a thermo-nuclear war in certain eventualities without reference to governments. We are sure that public opinion in the west would not, in general, be willing to accept this situation."[108]

The British were sponsoring a NATO resolution that would allow SACEUR to respond with nuclear weapons if attacked, but would also require him to refer nuclear weapons use in all other situations to the vaguely defined "governments" for permission. This was a British maneuver to leverage the preponderance of influence in NATO out of American hands. In other words, the British were creating their own counterweight, but were not going about it in a subtle fashion. Note that the British had over the years lost out to the Americans on several instances over issues, particularly over who controlled NATO naval operations in the Atlantic and Mediterranean. Foulkes underlined "governments" and wrote "President" next to it, indicating he knew that this was an unrealistic proposition at this time given American laws and their proclivity to maintain a nuclear monopoly. This problem would also arise again and again throughout NATO's history.[109]

The British position then leaked to the *Times of London* prior to the December NATO meetings. Despite General Gruenther's masterful briefing to the NAC, the perceived problem of nuclear weapons release continued to dog MC 48's acceptance by that body.[110]

This situation was extremely serious in all respects. NATO military authorities had taken almost eighteen months to reach a consensus on a strategic concept which was a precondition to building forces to carry out NATO's prime function: deterring the Soviet Union. This concept was predicated on immediate nuclear weapons use both to deter the enemy from attacking in the first place and then using nuclear weapons to offset the massive Soviet manpower and material advantage during a war. Western governments did not have the money to maintain huge conventional forces in being and remain stable and prosperous democracies. Pearson and Foulkes had to work together to find a solution that was acceptable in the NAC, or NATO would be incapable of presenting an effective deterrent.

Foulkes produced a history of the issue for Pearson's use in Paris. The original MC 48 redraft discussed in October 1954 included the problematic statement: "In the event of war involving NATO, it is militarily essential that the NATO forces should be able to use atomic and thermonuclear weapons in their defence from the outset." Foulkes had, at the time, indicated to the Military Committee that there would be "some political difficulty here in getting authority to use [nuclear weapons]." In discussions with the American representatives, the Military Committee agreed that political guidance issued alongside MC 14/1 in 1952 constituted such authority: SACEUR was permitted "to arrest and counter as soon as practicable the enemy offensive against the North Atlantic Treaty powers by all means necessary." The final draft of MC 48 altered the original wording, replacing "*should be able to use*" with "*plan for the use of*."[111]

NATO had no alert system yet, though the need for one had been raised in the Military Committee earlier in 1954. In his planning, Gruenther thought he had to have the NAC's authority to call an alert before he could deploy his forces, that is, a one-stage alert system, yes or no. He now wanted to have predelegated authority to call an alert if there was no time to contact the NAC and his forces were in danger of being overrun. This was a separate issue from MC 48 but was now intertwined with it. Foulkes was alarmed and thought "There are grave dangers in a discussion on the restriction on the use of atomic weapons" in the NAC. In his view, "Any idea of restricting the use of these weapons would seriously reduce the value of the atomic weapon as a deterrent and would create an advantage for the Soviet Union if they attempted to take Western Europe without using atomic weapons in the hope that we would not retaliate with mass destruction weapons." Finally, Foulkes noted: "Any discussion of this nature would be bound to leak into the press and provide the greatest possible propaganda value to the Soviet Union."[112]

Pearson then approached John Foster Dulles, US Secretary of State, who told Pearson he had to talk to Eisenhower since the President had his own views on the situation. Eisenhower was "most reluctant to see this matter the subject of formal action by the . . . [NAC]." The President thought that MC 48 was a planning paper and not authorization for nuclear use, since, if the time came, "circumstances rather than any formal procedure would dictate the manners in which the authority to SACEUR was given." The Americans wanted some form of informal understanding, something that would not needlessly constrain. They had the perception that most of the other NATO members did not care one way or another: It was only Canada and France that expressed reservations. Dulles then informed Pearson that he had also "toyed with the idea of including in a resolution some provision enabling SACEUR to use atomic weapons automatically if the other side used them first." Eisenhower had shot this one down, however.[113]

Pearson was frustrated. Wishing the problem away was not acceptable in the NAC arena. It was Foulkes's turn. Campney, Pearson, and Foulkes met to coordinate the effort to stave off the issue before it was brought before the NAC. Foulkes contacted Radford and was able to persuade him to back having the MC 48 draft modified before presentation. This modification amounted to adding more ambiguous language ("should," "may") into the troublesome section as opposed to eliminating the section outright.[114]

The debate over ambiguous words continued for another twenty-four hours as Foulkes, Radford, and Gruenther tried to get Air Marshal Dickson (the British representative) on side. In discussions with Dickson, Radford noted that he had "strict instructions" from the President that he was in no way to indicate that the United States had any intention of giving any commander the authority "to start a war or authority in advance to use thermonuclear weapons." Foulkes noted "in the course of our discussion it was quite obvious that this subject was really academic as the President could authorize the use of thermonuclear weapons by [SAC] even though NATO nations might decide that they would not allow their use in Western Europe; this would present a most ridiculous situation and could contribute to the loss of Europe."[115] Eventually, French General Jean Valluey was brought in, and all finally agreed that MC 48 would be presented to the NAC as "the first of a series of planning papers and not an authority for the use of mass destruction weapons."[116]

Pearson understood the need to keep the issue out of the NAC. He proposed a meeting with Dulles and Anthony Eden, the British Foreign Minister, before the NAC meeting to ensure that the British would not move on it. Pearson's objective was to get the NAC to accept MC 48 as it stood, with the ambiguous language, so that the force structure plan could be implemented. Authority to release nuclear weapons could be the subject of future meetings.[117] The informal meeting between Dulles, Eden, and Pearson was held in London on December 13, 1954. Pearson remained concerned because "the report could still be misunderstood by the public who would think that it had committed wholesale to the use of hydrogen weapons."[118] Fortunately, he noted, the final MC 48 draft was ambiguous enough, and it would "take several years to carry out the plans during which we could study further the political question."[119]

The Military Committee meeting of December 14, 1954 produced no discussion of the nuclear weapons release authorization issue. The policy makers did not want to deal with it publicly, and with good reason. A damaging leak to the *New York Times* by an "informed source" claimed that France was leading other European powers in opposing the use of *all* nuclear weapons in the NATO area without reference to the North Atlantic Council. In the end, the British relented, and the issue was not given great exposure in the NAC in 1954.[120]

Canadian participation in the MC 48 process demonstrated that Canada could influence aspects of the NATO strategy process. It was neither the first nor was it the last time Canadian national security policy makers would do so to protect Canadian interests.

In January, Dr. Omond Solandt of the DRB approached Foulkes and complained that the lack of a realistic long-term Canadian defense policy was inhibiting his staff's ability to provide long-term defense research policies. Could the chiefs produce a paper outlining the nature of a future war and what the Canadian armed forces' roles would be in it? Foulkes told Solandt:

> as the whole of the Canadian defence effort was devoted to NATO . . . the nature of a future war and the roles of the Canadian forces were worked out within NATO (Military Committee Strategic Guidance Report MC 48 and Supreme Commanders Capability Plans) in which Canada contributed in the development of Appreciations and Studies through our JIC and JPC, which were discussed and agreed [to] at the Chiefs of Staff Committee. He also reminded [Dr. Solandt] of the unfortunate delay in being able to have meaningful discussions with the US . . . until the US was able to release to Canada their relevant atomic information.[121]

Foulkes then passed a copy of MC 48 to the Defence Research Board along with a cover letter reiterating Canadian defense commitments in Europe, the North Atlantic, and North America.[122]

Pearson commissioned an External Affairs study on MC 48's implications. The draft, "The Strategic Concept of the Nuclear Deterrent," was an insightful assessment: It in fact presaged the future flow of and future problems with Canadian defense policy in a number of areas.[123]

The authors noted that MC 48 formally inaugurated nuclear deterrence as NATO strategy. It was implicit in previous concepts, but was explicit now. This "raised the stakes involved in the East-West conflict" and it had three implications for NATO: First, it restricted Soviet freedom of action. Second, a consequence of this was that the Soviets would resort to other methods to achieve their objectives, probably methods that "will not provoke nuclear retaliation." Third, it restricted the West's response in that the West could not miscalculate, or it would be obligated to use nuclear weapons to retain credibility.[124]

What did this concept mean for Canada? The drafters thought that continental defense planning was now indistinguishable from NATO planning, since the nuclear deterrent and its defense framework served NATO ends. Therefore, a new NATO command, a North American Air Defense Command, should replace the CUSRPG and perhaps other bilateral Canadian-American arrangements. With regard to the continental versus European focus, the report stated:

> To judge the extent of Canadian participation which is necessary or desirable, it is necessary to strike a balance between the demands of Western European defence and North American defence on Canadian resources. Both are vulnerable to Soviet nuclear retaliation, but both come under the umbrella of United States nuclear deterrent power . . . since it must be assumed that one of the aims of the Soviet Union is to isolate North America from its Western European partners and thus disrupt NATO, the military threat cannot be divorced from the important political consideration of maintaining the unity of the Alliance which is itself an important element of the deterrent.[125]

Canada would be asked to provide increased support to SAC, and that support should be freely given, but her forces in Europe should also be maintained.

The authors were skeptical about the distinction between tactical and strategic nuclear weapons and were also concerned that the "United States and United Kingdom governments will be restrained by moral and spiritual conviction brought to bear by their public opinion from initiating nuclear or any other kind of war, except in retaliation."[126]

MC 48 was ambiguous when it came to wars outside the NATO area and in dealing with sublimited conflict within the area. Consequently, the External Affairs authors thought Canada could play a significant role:

> If . . . the risks of all-out or nuclear war are not justified, and yet important interests of the free world are involved, it is essential that the Western Powers should be prepared to deal with limited wars with limited means and within limited objectives, Canada itself would not participate in such limited or local wars unless by a decision of the United Nations which it had accepted. . . . Allied strategy must therefore combine political and economic rather than military measures to deter the indirect threats which may be posed by the Communists in an effort to outflank the nuclear deterrent.[127]

Thus, Canada was an integral part of a multinational and global deterrent system. There was no serious thought given to extracting herself from her substantial commitments. Still, some Canadian leaders were concerned about the possible overreliance on nuclear weapons. Cabinet Secretary Robert Bryce expressed his views to Foulkes prior to a Chiefs of Staff Committee meeting in February 1955. Bryce did not like NATO's emphasis on immediate nuclear use, but agreed that nuclear weapons use was probable in a general war with the Soviet Union. He thought:

> there was still a probability that they would not be used due to the increasing realization of the truly catastrophic damage that would result. . . . As

this realization grew and spread it was possible that the United States and United Kingdom might come to the conclusion that it would be better to suffer defeat . . . [in Europe] and the Middle East than suffer the consequence of a nuclear exchange. . . . Public opinion . . . might so develop that the USSR might feel that there was a good chance that atomic weapons would not be utilized . . . they might come to believe it sufficiently to take a chance on invading Western Europe and the Middle East. It would appear important, therefore, for the Western World to be prepared for war without nuclear weapons.[128]

It may appear odd that the Secretary to the Cabinet was involved in defense policy making. Known by some as the Universal Joint, Bryce was a senior civil service Mandarin who, in his position, coordinated Cabinet meetings, the agenda, and the distribution of papers (he had worked at senior government levels since 1935). Therefore, if the COSC wanted to present a paper to the Cabinet, they had to go through Bryce. Foulkes, of course, would not allow Bryce to modify papers, but Bryce was a senior advisor and it was good to have his understanding to facilitate policy coordination with Finance.[129]

Foulkes agreed with Bryce, but the facts were these: The West had the bulk of the world's nuclear capability. It was too expensive to maintain conventional forces. Eisenhower had given instructions for American forces to plan on the unrestricted use of nuclear weapons. NATO agreed that nuclear weapons would be used from the outset. Canada had to plan on this basis now, not continue to deliberate the issue. Things would change in the future, yes, but the situation they had to deal with had to be dealt with today.[130]

Looking to the future, the chief's External Affairs observer, R. A. Mackay, mused: "If a state of equality in holdings of atomic weapons and the means of delivering them was arrived at between the USSR and the United States, a stalemate might ensue and the possibility of war be averted."[131]

The COSC took note of this view.

MC 48 was accepted as the basis for Canada's strategic outlook and force structure to support it after 1954.[132] Minister of National Defence Campney instructed Chairman of the Chiefs of Staff Committee General Foulkes in March 1955:

At the Council meeting in December 1954, MC 48 (Final) was approved and represents Canadian Government policy. This policy provides that priority must be given to the provision of forces in being capable of effectively contributing to success in the initial phase. Other forces are required to contribute to subsequent operations, but in view of the importance of the initial phase and taking into account the limited resources which it is anticipated will be available, the build up of these forces must be given a lower priority. Budgetary considerations and the plans of other countries in relation to the build up of forces described as having a lower priority will make it difficult for Canada to proceed with the implementation of plans for forces other than those capable of effectively contributing to success in the initial phase.[133]

MC 48 therefore became Canada's strategy. Deputy Minister Bud Drury noted, however,

> There will, of course, be very considerable resistance to a recognition of the realities of the situation and the taking of decisions to act in accordance with this reality. Because of this resistance and the desirability of overcoming it in an orderly and mannerly way, the changed situation is likely to be reached as an evolutionary process rather than suddenly and in a clear-cut fashion.[134]

Acceptance of MC 48 as the national strategic concept was confirmed later in 1955 by Canadian policy makers in two ways: First, by noting them in the public defense estimates for the 1955–56 period, and second, by Canadian acceptance of MC 48/1.

The 1955 annual report on Canada's defense program noted: "We are convinced that the best way to avoid a war of annihilation is to make plain to any potential aggressor that collectively we have the strength to defend ourselves and that we value our freedoms sufficiently to fight them." Noting that the main problem now was finding the correct balance between conventional and nuclear forces, the report stated "Canada will continue to make such adjustments in her defence programme." These adjustments included "new weapons, new tactics, and strategic concepts," as well as a new sense of vigilance. In a special section entitled "Nuclear Bombs and the Future," the report stated that Canada was directly threatened and that fallout was a serious problem for military personnel and civilians alike. Any future war would be a war for national survival. As such, the priority for defense expenditures would be on air defense efforts in North America. Canada would, however, continue to maintain her NATO commitments at the same levels.[135]

The announced policy was also accompanied by a modest increase in the defense budget for 1955, followed by a larger one the year after. For comparative purposes Canada spent CAN$1,882,418,467 in 1952–53, followed by CAN$1,805,914,922 in 1953–54. Though this figure dropped to CAN$1,665,968,960 in 1954–55, it rose to CAN$1,775,000,000 in 1955–56. It would peak in 1956–57 at CAN$1,806,934,000,000 before steadily dropping during the Diefenbaker government's reign.[136]

The amplification of MC 48, a report called MC 48/1, or "The Most Effective Pattern of NATO Military Strength for the Next Few Years-Report No. 2," was tabled and agreed to by NATO members by December 1955. Though SACEUR and SACLANT both championed MC 48's emphasis on the use of nuclear weapons as critical to the deterrent and the survival of NATO should war beak out, the accession of Germany to NATO in 1955 posed a new problem. Germany could now no longer be sacrificed to protect the rest of NATO. True forward defense was now a political necessity, in addition to nuclear deterrence. NATO forces, in addition to fighting Phase I with nuclear weapons, also had to have the ability to preserve the NATO area as far forward as possible on land, at sea, and in the air. Deliberately sacrificing NATO territory was out of the question. Conventional and nuclear forces assigned to NATO had to be available and ready in peacetime and deployed as far forward as possible, particularly in Europe. An alert system to preserve them was required, since there would be increasingly less time because of technological and geographical factors. This, in turn, lead to a requirement for an early warning system and better air defense forces in the NATO area. The need for mobilization was less than before but was still encouraged for Phase II.[137]

Campney agreed and stated: "The best way to prevent war was to ensure that NATO was sufficiently strong to deter any possible aggressor." Since the mainspring of this effort was SAC and RAF Bomber Command, "It was therefore essential to have an effective early warning system to enable bombers to get off the ground." In his view, "Canada-US regional air defence plans were not for the purpose of making North America safe for North Americans but to protect the Strategic Air Command, which was of vital importance to NATO."[138]

The only hint of a problem regarding Canada and MC 48/1 came from the Americans, who were concerned that, in connection with Britain's desire to reduce her forces in Germany for budgetary reasons, Canada might also want to withdraw her European forces and base her argument on the belief that North American air defense was the only way Canada could contribute to NATO.[139] American fears were unfounded. Canada, of course, had no plans to or even indicated that it might withdraw the brigade group and 1 Air Division from Europe. Canadian policy makers were more concerned about how to allocate money to support both continental defense and European defense commitments, and they favored a strategic reassessment as soon as possible to ensure NATO was on the right track (this assessment, conducted throughout 1956, would result in a new NATO Strategic Concept in 1957 called MC 14/2).[140]

Conclusion

The first strategic question raised during the 1952–1955 period was: Where should the main emphasis on Canadian national security policy be placed: in protecting North America or defending Europe? With Canada already committed to NATO in Europe, and with Mike Pearson actively using Canadian participation in NATO to counterbalance the preponderance of American influence within the Alliance and in North America, the answer was to do both. This fit within the framework of Canadian strategic tradition: forward security and alliance warfare. Without a massive increase in resources, however, Canadian continental defense planners then wanted an answer to the next question: Should the continental defense effort protect the American deterrent forces (SAC) or the population and industrial centers? The answer was to place primary emphasis on protecting SAC, since it was the mainspring of the entire NATO defense effort. Though originally created to handle the European situation, the NATO strategic concept, MC 48, was the culminating point of this debate process in 1954. It solved the "North America versus Europe" and "SAC versus population" problems, and subsequently served as the basis for Canadian national strategy.

MC 48 was not imposed on Canada by her allies: The need for such a strategic concept was imposed by the massive Soviet conventional and emerging nuclear capability that directly threatened Canada and her allies. Canada was not a helpless bystander; she was consulted and had input into the formulation of alliance strategy. The British passed their groundbreaking Global Strategy Paper to Canada before implementing it themselves. The early NATO strategic concept MC 14/1 was modified to conform to Canadian wishes. Foulkes ensured that the NATO Military Committee, not just the Standing Group, examined the New Approach Group reports. Canadian policy makers were kept informed about the details of American strategic policy changes during the New Look period, which in turn allowed Canada to adjust her strategic policy in advance to ensure that Canadian national interests were protected. Finally, a potentially dangerous and divisive debate over NATO nuclear weapons release policy was averted through Canadian efforts. It should be noted, however, that the temporary conciliation on this matter generated by the efforts of Pearson, Foulkes, and others produced long-standing debates within NATO for years to come.

All of this served multiple purposes. First, it confirmed that the third pillar of Canadian strategic tradition, relative military autonomy, was important in the nuclear age. Throughout the entire process that produced MC 48, Charles Foulkes ensured that Canadian interests (which included prestige as well as command and control aspects) were protected. Canadian policy makers would not be pushed into doing something they chose not to do. In the end, it provided Pearson the forum to perform his counterweight activities.

3

THE GOALIE'S BIG STICK: CANADIAN STRATEGY AND THE NEW LOOK, 1955–1957

Invincibility lies in the defense; the possibility of
victory in the attack.

–SUN TZU, THE ART OF WAR

"Mr. President, we are rapidly approaching a
moment of truth both for ourselves as human
beings and for the life of our nation. Now, truth is
not always a pleasant thing. But it is necessary now
to make a choice, to choose between two admittedly regrettable, but nevertheless distinguishable
postwar environments: one where you got twenty
million people killed, and the other where you got
a hundred and fifty million people killed. Mr.
President, I'm not saying we wouldn't get our hair
mussed! But I do say no more than ten to twenty
million killed, tops. Uh, depending on the breaks."

–DR. STRANGELOVE OR: HOW I LEARNED
TO STOP WORRYING AND LOVE THE BOMB

Introduction

As we saw in chapter 2, the MC 48 strategic concept rationalized the separate NATO commitments into a Canadian strategy. Canada now had to have the forces to implement the strategy. Canadian policy makers identified, however, that effective military participation was critical to avoid American dominance in North American affairs and thus to protect Canadian sovereignty. Three themes emerged from this realization. First, Canada needed to update and expand her forces. Second, Canada was now deeply involved in continental air defense. Finally, Canada was deeply involved with providing support to USAF Strategic Air Command operations, operations that were critical to the survival of that deterrent force. These three areas evolved significantly during the St. Laurent years. At first, the St. Laurent defense program was interrupted by changes to the strategic environment, which in turn affected Canadian strategy. The second interruption was more serious: the St. Laurent

51

government fell in 1957 and the Progressive Conservatives, led by John Diefenbaker, took over. Incomplete evolution in all of these interconnected areas was the basis of future serious problems in Canadian nuclear policy encountered by the Diefenbaker government after 1957 and leading up to the Cuban Missile Crisis.

SAC Support Arrangements

While the air defense program got off the ground, the secret arrangements relating to Goose Bay nuclear weapons storage were modified. The American purpose was to confirm that they had, in fact, "secure[d] [Canadian] agreement to those necessary measures short of actual strikes which would improve our position in the event of hostilities."[1] The 1952 arrangement was that SAC training flights equipped with non-nuclear components could overfly Canada and non-nuclear components could be stored at Goose Bay on a notification basis; that is, SAC called up RCAF HQ and effected liaison with the appropriate authority there. Code-named WISER and better known as the "XYZ" procedures, there were three methods of clearing SAC overflights:

X: Routine flights carrying non-nuclear components, general flight programs, and individual flight clearances on a service-to-service basis.

Y: Routine flights carrying nuclear components but with no immediate strike contemplated in the immediate future, general clearance of program on government-to-government basis with individual clearance between chiefs of air staffs.

Z: Flights carrying nuclear components and engaged on strikes or deployment for strikes, clearance on a government-to-government basis (State—External Affairs).[2]

SAC aircraft were authorized by the Canadian government to land at Canadian bases in an emergency.[3]

At this point, the United States had not developed sealed-pit nuclear weapons. The nuclear component in the casing or "physics package" was removable. The Mk. 4, Mk. 5 and Mk. 6 weapons, which formed the bulk of SAC's inventory until 1955, were non-sealed-pit weapons.[4] If whole nuclear weapons had to be flown over Canada or positioned temporarily at Goose Bay, this had to be done on a government-to-government basis, usually through the Canadian Embassy in Washington, DC. If SAC were to use Goose Bay for actual nuclear strike operations, it would also have to be done on a government-to-government basis. Similar arrangement were made with the British for SAC operations in the United Kingdom; but the French, for example, were not informed that actual weapons were stored at SAC bases in French Morocco.[5]

In 1955, things changed. SAC implemented operational aerial refueling in 1951, and with the deployment of B-47 bombers and KC-97 tankers in significant numbers between 1953 and 1955, wanted to increase their reach. SAC wanted to rotate a KC-97 squadron of twenty aircraft through Goose Bay every ninety days and four additional KC-97 squadrons every thirty days. They also wanted to rotate a B-47 wing of forty-five aircraft for ninety-day periods. The stated purpose "was to provide these units with familiarization and simulated combat operational training."[6] The request went to the Cabinet Defence Committee for discussion. Some argued that this was just the first foot in the door for SAC, which would then want additional concessions that would in turn "imperil more and more Canadian sovereignty over its own territory."[7] These same Cabinet members were concerned that SAC would want permanent nuclear storage rights next. Other members pointed out that aerial refueling might mean that nuclear weapons would not have to be stored in Canada. In any case, it would be "embarrassing and difficult" to refuse the proposal since "as part of the Canada-U.S. region we [have] an obligation to our NATO partners to support SAC operations. . . . unless Canada changed her attitude and policy and ceased to encourage the support and the making ready of retaliatory forces, it was almost impossible to refuse the request."[8]

Cabinet gave its assent and SAC started to operate KC-97 tankers and B-47 bombers at Goose Bay, Labrador, and KC-97 tankers at Ernest Harmon AFB in Newfoundland on a rotational basis. These activities were part of a larger worldwide SAC measure that included similar operations at Thule AFB, Greenland, and bases in the UK and French Morocco.[9]

SAC looked to expand its operations further north.[10] In March 1956, the RCAF inquired about future SAC plans. SAC intimated that it would like to survey several airfields and bases in Canada with an eye toward supporting the SAC tanker force either in an emergency or in peacetime. New planning generated this requirement that directed SAC to "increase the weight of its attacks and increase the range of its forces."[11] Two benefits accrued to the SAC bomber force. First, northern expansion would dramatically increase the ranges that the B-47s could operate, in this case several thousand miles. Second, in the present operational environment, the B-47s had to wait for the KC-97s to reach the limit of the B-47 range before refueling. The B-47s and KC-97s were co-located at the same bases in the continental United States. The KC-97s were propeller-driven and therefore slower than the B-47 jets. Therefore, the B-47s had to be held on the ground for some time until the KC-97s were in position. This situation increased the vulnerability of the B-47 force to enemy action. By placing tanker bases in northern Canada, fewer tankers were needed so that B-47s could get to their targets in the Soviet Union and the time delay would disappear. Even the planned B-52/KC-135 combination would need similar refueling plans and this would even increase the speed of a future attack if it had to be directed against the Soviet Union rapidly.[12]

By June 1956 SAC asked permission to survey eleven northern Canadian base sites.[13] The planned magnitude of future SAC operations in Canada, in addition to other American defense projects in Canada, would pose political problems if it were handled on a completely informal basis between the RCAF and the USAF. Consequently, Minister of National Defence Ralph Campney was notified. He wanted a full briefing by SAC, which promptly sent a team to Ottawa to explain why the expansion was needed.[14]

SAC had 28 wings of 45 B-47s, each with 17 wings that were based in the United States. The other 11 were on constant rotation overseas to French Morocco, the UK, Iceland, Greenland, Libya, Turkey, the Philippines, Japan, Okinawa, Hawaii, Alaska, Bermuda, and Spain. Rotation forces also were located in Canada at Goose Bay and Harmon AFB in Newfoundland. In a war situation it would take the first wave of 243 B-47s 13 hours and 20 minutes to reach what SAC called the "R-Line" or the Soviet radar cover. The KC-97s had to fly out three and a half hours *ahead* of the B-47s because they were propeller-driven and therefore slower. The bombers had to wait, which made them vulnerable (there would also be a second wave of 200 more bombers).[15]

With a northern Canadian refueling base complex, a strike of 1000 bombers (B-47s and B-52s) could be accomplished in six hours, which was less than a third of the time (18 hours) without the refueling bases. With the planned basing situation in the United States, the B-47s would proceed over northeast Canada, while the B-52s would fly over central Canada. With the tankers deployed up north, there would be no wait. The SAC briefers also noted that ICBMs and possibly nuclear-powered bombers would be in service by 1965–67: Aerial refueling requirements would thus diminish.[16]

Once surveyed, each site would be improved to meet SAC requirements. For example, each site needed a secure communications system, accommodation, underground fuel storage (to reduce vulnerability), a 9000-foot runway, and parking space for 40 KC-97s or 30 KC-135s. SAC did not want defensive arrangements for the sites in peacetime, to avoid undue attention.[17]

The Cabinet Defence Committee discussed the matter. Campney learned that there were other factors involved in the SAC concept of operations. There was considerable political pressure being brought to bear on the United States to remove SAC facilities from Iceland, North Africa, and Okinawa. The northern basing plan could go a long way toward lessening such pressure. It not only affected alliance relations, but was important in the propaganda war with the Soviets:

> In a large measure war had been avoided because the Russians now thought that if they attacked there would be prompt retaliation by U.S. bombing forces. U.S. authorities were concerned with the possibility of interference with the maximum effectiveness of the deterrent. If SAC were forced to withdraw from some of its existing bases closer to the USSR, the U.S. authorities would want it known publicly that compensating arrangements were being made to maintain the effectiveness of the deterrent. It seemed necessary to make a choice between maintaining [this effectiveness] and a serious domestic political problem arising from a large increase in U.S. facilities and personnel in Canada. There would be serious consequences if Canada contributed to a lessening of the free world's strength.[18]

Canada would benefit militarily and economically by having new improved air bases up north. There was residual concern in the Cabinet about "salami tactics" and nuclear weapons storage, but permission was given to Foulkes to liaise with General Nathan Twining on the matter.[19]

Meeting with Twining, Foulkes learned of political problems at other SAC operating locations. Saudi Arabia and the Philippines were having second thoughts about hosting SAC. There were even rumblings in the United Kingdom. SAC wanted to get into Spain, but there were difficulties. Twining really needed Canada's help on this one. Foulkes told him, "We want to keep this matter very secret," and instructed that the survey teams should come up on non-SAC aircraft. There were to be *no* leaks. There were serious domestic political factors at stake in Canada. Foulkes was concerned about Congress, which leaked all the time, to Canada's embarrassment, but Twining told him he had no control over that process.[20]

The SAC team examined sixteen potential sites (see figure 3.1) and then discussed the matter with the RCAF. Three of these sites were ruled out because of geographical factors (Ft. Chimo, Winisk, and Saglek Bay). The USAF liked Namao (Edmonton, Alberta) and Cold Lake, Alberta, both major RCAF bases. The RCAF would not relinquish Cold Lake, while Namao was close to a major city that was a potential target. In terms of priority, SAC liked Cold Lake, Namao, Churchill (Manitoba), and Frobisher Bay (NWT). Second priority included Great Whale River, Knob Lake, Coral Harbour, the Pas, and Fort McMurray.

External Affairs, however, delayed the deliberations. Its planners believed that the tanker base issue should be integrated into a larger agreement that dealt with SAGE installations in Canada, an expansion of the radar system, and "the integration of atomic capabilities into the air defence system."[21] It also wanted Canadian civilians (thus jobs and, more critically, a reduced American presence) to maintain the facilities in peacetime. This attitude continued while the Suez Crisis erupted in November 1956. SAC increased its rotation flights of KC-97s and B-47s through Goose Bay, culminating in Operations POWER HOUSE and ROAD BLOCK, which put several hundred aircraft over the Arctic regions later that month.[22] SAC was concerned enough about the crisis to get in touch with the Chiefs and concede that Canadian service or civilian personnel could maintain the bases in order to speed up the process. Little could be done on 29 November 1956 as the tension produced by the Suez Crisis lessened with the introduction of UN peacekeeping forces, and the matter was put off to the new year.[23]

SAC indicated that financial considerations would reduce the number of bases needed to four. It still wanted Frobisher Bay, Churchill, Cold Lake, and Namao, with surveys of the other five for an emergency basis. The Cabinet approved this in February 1957.[24] And there the matter lay until after the June 1957 election.

SAC overflights were routine events from the inception of the XYZ procedures in 1952 well into 1957. An example of a routine flight was the passage of five B-47s equipped with nuclear weapons en route from a base in the United States to the UK, with aerial refueling over Sault Ste. Marie, Ontario, in October 1956. SAC called State, which then called the Canadian Embassy. The Canadian Embassy checked with Ottawa and approved the flight within forty-eight hours. SAC then coordinated its flight plans with the RCAF and the planes left on 5 October.[25]

The same lines of communication were used for Operation ROADBLOCK, held on 29–30 November 1956 at the height of the Suez Crisis. Seventy-two B-47s, of which 36 were carrying nuclear and non-nuclear components, overflew Canada

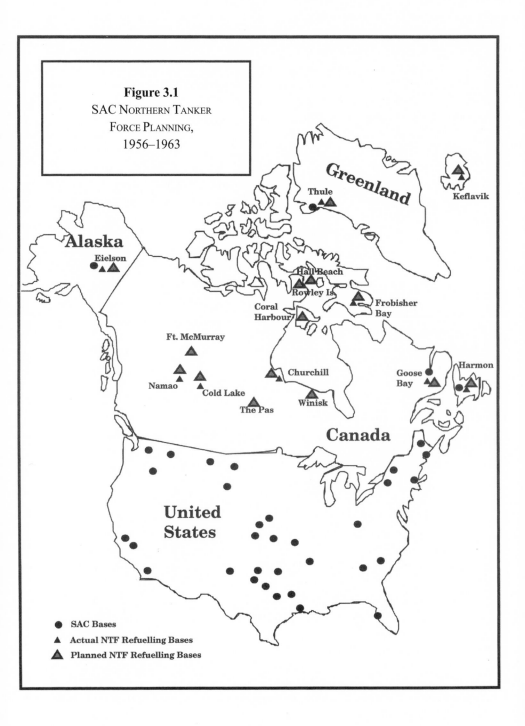

Figure 3.1
SAC NORTHERN TANKER
FORCE PLANNING,
1956–1963

Greenland

Thule
Keflavik

Alaska

Eielson

Hall Beach
Rowley Is.
Coral
Harbour
Frobisher
Bay

Ft. McMurray

Namao
Cold Lake
Churchill
Goose
Bay
Harmon

The Pas
Winisk

Canada

United
States

● SAC Bases
▲ Actual NTF Refuelling Bases
▲ Planned NTF Refuelling Bases

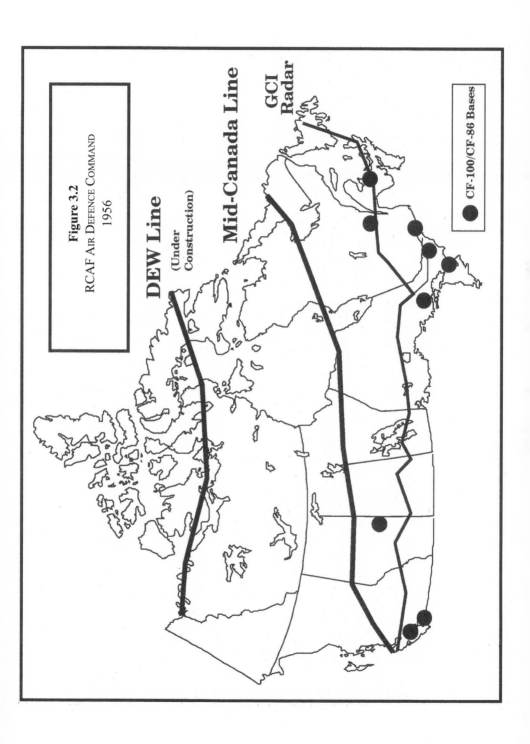

Figure 3.2
RCAF AIR DEFENCE COMMAND
1956

DEW Line
(Under Construction)

Mid-Canada Line

GCI Radar

● CF-100/CF-86 Bases

and returned on 3–5 December carrying the same cargo. Another operation, PINEGROVE, was coordinated for 13–16 January 1957. It consisted of 180 B-47s, with 72 carrying nuclear and non-nuclear components. These were two of the largest SAC deployments to date and may have been intended to "signal" the Soviets during the crisis. This aspect of the operations was not lost on the diplomats coordinating the efforts and there would be long-lasting ramifications in the future for Canada-US relations.[26]

The RCAF and Continental Air Defense
To defend this atomic armada, the RCAF continued to study the best plan for a continental air defense system. The struggle was manifest in several ways: the CF-105 Arrow program and its associated problems as to armament selection; the BOMARC-versus-Nike guided missile debate; the nature of the continental air defense system and how it would be commanded. How the RCAF dealt with these problems between 1955 and 1957 had intricate long-term and far-reaching effects on Canadian nuclear weapons policy.

In terms of continental air defense forces, the RCAF deployed nineteen squadrons of fighters as part of Air Defence Command in Canada between 1954 and 1958. Generally, there were eight to ten CF-86 Sabre day fighter squadrons and nine CF-100 Canuck all-weather fighter squadrons spread out across the country.[27] All of these aircraft were conventionally equipped, though some thought was given to providing nuclear air-to-air capability. All aircraft were tied into Ground Control Intercept centers displaying data provided by the various radar systems (see figure 3.2). RCAF ADC consistently deployed 342 interceptors, while the USAF deployed between 1139 in 1954 to a peak of 1490 in 1957. Thus, RCAF ADC provided between 19% and 23% of fighter interceptors assigned to continental air defense missions.[28] The bulk of USAF ADC flew F-86Ds until 1956 and converted to the F-89 Scorpion in 1957. The F-89 and CF-100 had similar operational characteristics with the exception of the F-89J, which carried the MB-1 Genie nuclear weapon.

RCAF Air Defence Command HQ, located at St. Hubert, Quebec, did not report to a formal integrated command prior to the advent of NORAD in 1957–58. There were extensive cooperative arrangements with USAF's Air Defense Command, but RCAF air defense squadrons did not come under American operational command. In fact, the two USAF fighter squadrons based in Newfoundland and Labrador came under Canadian operational control in wartime.[29]

In terms of quality, USAF pilots were continually impressed with RCAF Air Defence Command's performance, which added to Canadian saliency in the air defense system:

> In a dogfight, the Mk. 5's were formidable opponents . . . We used to fly up to Chatham and play games with the Canadian 86's up there. They had a bigger Orenda engine, and they'd turn us every way but loose. That was ridiculous. . . . We could never touch those hot 86's. They'd leave us. Canadians thrived on action. The more dangerous a situation, the funnier they thought it was . . . [the] CF-100's could outperform the F-94C's. They weren't

really much faster than us, but they had that big wing and could really get up there. They were much more formidable.[30]

In January 1955, right after MC 48's acceptance by NATO and Canada, Air Marshal Slemon queried two of his primary commands, Air Defence Command and 1 Air Division, as to how the new strategic concept affected them. The ADC view was that the main threat consisted of jet bombers carrying hydrogen bombs capable of launching a "sudden high-performance attack with a comparably small force, with a good possibility of eliminating the North American forces or retaliation and razing at least some of the major centers of government, populations, and industry in one blow."[31] The aircraft and its accompanying nuclear weapon had to be destroyed completely far away from populated areas. Canada needed guided missiles, a computer control system, the means to totally destroy enemy aircraft, and some form of integration with American air defense forces to increase the chances of destroying intruders.[32] The RCAF proposed three regional air defense forces, each consisting of surveillance, command, and interception forces. Two should be American, one should be Canadian, with the aim to "make possible Canadian control of all weapons that could be employed over Canadian territory."[33] More importantly,

> the arrangement of the entire structure provides a means whereby Canada could still exercise an extraordinary degree of influence over US air defence planning in matters which directly affect Canada. Altogether, these considerations should serve very considerably indeed to offset the danger of compromise of Canadian sovereignty which independent US air defence planning, programming, funding and implementation has already gone so far towards creating.[34]

If Canada did not negotiate an integrated air defense arrangement, the United States would be forced to plan for its air defense as though Canada did not exist. By being part of an integrated air defense system, American systems could be located to cover targets vital to Canada as well as the United States. Canada would not have to expend financial resources necessary to produce her own system and Canadian sovereignty could be protected. This thinking led to the creation of the North American Air Defense Command, or NORAD.

The Avro Arrow issue seized the RCAF's attention throughout 1955. The RCAF encountered opposition from General Simonds in the Chiefs of Staff Committee. Simonds argued that, in the future, ICBMs would make bombers, and thus the CF-105 interceptors, obsolete. Canada should, in his view, buy an existing American or British aircraft and put its money into building an antiballistic missile system, which could also be used to shoot down bombers. Foulkes sided with the RCAF. The immediate threat was from the M-4 BISON bomber, and nobody knew when it would be replaced, if at all, by an ICBM. Slemon agreed and noted that no allied aircraft met Canadian operating requirements (climatic, distance, and weapons). BOMARC would not be available for at least five years. In fact, Slemon said, "if the development of BOMARC or some similar missile overtook the CF-105 program it may be considered wise to stop or modify further work at that time but in the interim the one should not stop because of the possibilities seen in the other."[35] Simonds failed in his effort to cancel the Arrow and the Chiefs recommended the program to the Cabinet Defence Committee.

Cabinet level policy makers were concerned about the cost of an indigenous aircraft design. Some prescient members were worried that "if for a variety of reasons [the CF-105] had to be abandoned, embarrassment and criticism would be severe."[36] Would the project be cheaper if RCAF squadrons in Europe were equipped with the Arrow as well? Would other nations buy it? Some members argued that "the only way to provide an effective deterrent to aggression was to improve, modernize and develop the warmaking capacity of the free nations. . . . [there] was no alternative but to proceed with the maintenance of suitable deterrent strength."[37] What, some members queried, if the Soviets produced ICBMs? Would that not make manned aircraft obsolete?

> Because of developments in progress, the effectiveness of the deterrent was always only temporary. The Russians and the U.S. were equipping their forces with subsonic and supersonic bombers. . . . If the Russians succeeded in getting [an ICBM] into large scale production before the U.S, there would be a major shift in the balance of power since there was nothing available that could deal with it. The date of this was so uncertain, however, that the West could not afford to gamble on having no deterrent at all in the intervening period.[38]

With regard to the Arrow's mission, it was a

> defensive aircraft. However, atomic weapons were being reduced in size and it might well be that the aircraft could carry one of these and have a valuable offensive capability, albeit at a relatively short range. On the other hand, there had been no suggestions that Canada provide offensive aircraft and, in any event, under present U.S. law atomic weapons from U.S. sources could be handled only by U.S. citizens.[39]

Although a "non-formalized requirement to retain the capability of using weapons with atomic warheads" existed, "it is expected that the aircraft will accommodate air-to-air atomic weapons but firm information on this point is not yet available."[40] "Atomic Arrows" were put on hold for the time being. However, the Cabinet approved the production of the first forty Arrows.[41]

The mounting costs of the program prompted the Cabinet to review the situation in September 1955. Could allied aircraft like the American F-102 or the F-101 take on the role instead? Cabinet also heard that the USAF had plans to "modify its F-101 long-range escort fighter to the all-weather role."[42] Cabinet wanted the Chiefs to present a thorough brief on all aspects of continental air defense, not just the manned interceptor component, so that an informed decision could be made with regards to the future of the Arrow. They wanted to know "How, for example, did

Canadian air defence weapons fit in with U.S weapons systems? What was the relationship of our system to the command structure? Would it be desirable to have a combined command? What effect would the development of ground-to-air missiles have on the CF-105 programme?"[43]

The Chiefs agreed. They too wanted to deal with new and potentially alarming problems like American plans to deploy

> a line of weapons firing guided missiles along the border. . . . [This] would enable missiles fired from the U.S. to engage targets over a narrow strip of Canada. To a certain extent, any influence that could be exerted in the right direction on these plans depended on the contribution Canada was willing to make to the defence of North America.[44]

This concern played to Cabinet members' fears, particularly Pearson, who was worried about Canadian sovereignty. If Canada wanted influence, she had to put up or shut up.

By November 1955, Slemon had a special working group produce the appropriate briefing, which was "field tested" on the Chiefs first.[45] Restating that the protection of and warning for Strategic Air Command was paramount and that protection of industry and administration was a secondary role, Slemon caught his audience's attention by stating "that the war-making capacity of this continent could not tolerate more than 50 successfully delivered thermonuclear bombs. If the enemy were able to launch an attack involving as many as one thousand bombers, it would mean that more than 950 of these would have to [be] destroyed en route, in the perimeter regions beyond the built-up areas."[46]

SAC's dispersion to the US mid-west in the mid-1950s dramatically increased the defended area beyond the previously envisioned northeastern industrial/governmental "triangle." These factors dictated several things. The air defense system had to find a way to increase the probability that the incoming bombers would be utterly destroyed on an individual basis. More interceptor bases, contiguous internal radar coverage (as opposed to early warning from the DEW Line and other sources), better interceptors, and "the provision of an . . . Air Defense Command Organization" were all needed, again a reference to what would become NORAD in 1957.[47]

Slemon endorsed the layered defense envisioned by the Defence Research Board. There should be two lines of interceptor bases (both missile and manned aircraft). The first should be between the DEW Line and the second line (North Bay, Ottawa, St. Hubert), which would be protecting the northeastern triangle. Canada should get SAGE and coordinate with USAF SAGE sites. The air defense problem, Slemon noted, was not just a Canada–north US–south problem. American air defense forces in Alaska and on the eastern seaboard extension of the DEW Line contributed to the defense of North America as much as Canadian air defense forces in the center and to the north. It required an integrated effort.[48]

Slemon proposed five courses of action to the Cabinet:

> (a) Acquire the CF-105, give the CF-100 an air-to-air missile, introduce SAGE, and buy BOMARC.

(b) Same as (a) with only a few CF-105s

(c) Buy American F-102B, improve the CF-100 with missiles, and buy BOMARC.

(d) Same as (c) with no CF-100 improvement.

(e) Same as (a) with more CF-105s and no CF-100 modification.[49]

The preferred "staff solution," of course, was (a).

Guided missiles, multiple radar systems, SAGE, and interceptors were all needed to counter the variety of threats envisioned by the air defense planners. The air defense system was vulnerable to electronic countermeasures. If only one type of system were employed, the chances of the enemy's countering it were higher. Even though multiple systems drove up costs, it was deemed by both Canadian and American air defense planners to be necessary. The F-102B was not a suitable replacement for the Arrow, since it did not meet RCAF standards for aircraft performance (it had one engine instead of two, which would pose problems for aircraft survival in the northern reaches of Canada), weapons system flexibility (differing and changing missile types), or data processing.[50]

The briefers were instructed to delete the word "cheaper" when comparing the F-102B and the CF-105, and the decision was made not to be too specific when briefing the Cabinet about the exact nature of the threat, weapons capabilities, or employment dates/availability of aircraft, as this would be "unwise."[51] For example, the detailed threat estimate was deleted from the presentation.

The RCAF believed that the Soviets had "tested all plutonium, composite, and all uranium fission processes. They have used processes in their tests which indicate a capability for original research and processes which may not necessarily be based on purloined or demonstrated US development."[52] The Soviet stockpile in 1956 was estimated to consist of 44 1-megaton weapons, 150 60-kiloton weapons and 450 5-kiloton weapons. By 1958 the stockpile would increase to 93 1-megaton, 265 60-kiloton, and 785 5-kiloton weapons. All were assumed to be boosted uranium or plutonium weapons. If the Soviets accelerated their thermonuclear program, there would be more megaton-yield weapons, probably in the 10-megaton range.[53]

In terms of delivery capability, ICBMs would eventually be deployed, but the bomber threat was formidable. The Soviets were estimated to have between 1100 and 1300 bomber aircraft (TU-95 BEARs, M-4 BISONs, and TU-16 BADGERs) capable of reaching North America.[54] By 1960, however, the Soviets might introduce 200 additional supersonic jet bombers based on the American B-58 Hustler design currently under development for SAC. BISONs and BEARs would eventually have a cruise missile system, according to the intelligence estimate. Other threats included submarine-launched cruise missiles, with supersonic missiles, thought to be available by 1965.[55] When briefed, the Cabinet deferred the issue until the United States could be sounded out about "sharing in or taking over the whole of the [air defense] programme."[56]

Dr. Solandt, Chairman of the DRB, retired in March 1956. The reasons are unclear. The media reported that Solandt thought that his work was done, however they speculated that he wanted more money (he moved to a higher paying position at

Canadian National Railroads).[57] The media did not know about increased friction between DRB and the RCAF over who made air defense policy. Air Vice Marshal Max Hendrick noted, there was:

> A tendency on the part of DRB in the newer fields of ICBM etc. to collect all information and consider themselves the sole source thereof for Canadians. Also a tendency to consider themselves the authority to decide on our new weapons system and what they shall be. . . . [The services] should have direct access also to the same sources of information and not depend upon getting this information second-hand from Canadian scientists who themselves have got it from the Americans.[58]

After his retirement, Solandt went to the media with his views. He thought that ICBMs would be built, and that it would take a long time to develop effective defenses against them. ICBMs, in his view, made the entire air defense system obsolete. The CF-105 Arrow, he said, would be Canada's last aircraft, and nuclear-tipped air defense missiles would take over its role. In the press briefing, a reporter asked Solandt if a "functioning continental air defence system require[d] the stockpiling of nuclear defensive weapons on Canadian soil."[59] Solandt confirmed that it would, which then prompted more questions about whether a nuclear Sparrow missile would be mounted on the Arrow, questions that Solandt fended off with non-answers.[60]

Solandt was probably removed after RCAF pressure had been brought to bear. His assertion that ICBMs would render the antibomber system obsolete was in direct contradiction to RCAF thinking and threat estimates. Casting doubts on the Arrow program, the jewel in the RCAF's crown, was nothing short of heretical.

A related air defense problem was the selection of armament for the CF-105 and the CF-100s. As early as 1953, the RCAF had considered the GAR-1 Falcon, an infrared, high-explosive, air-to-air missile for the CF-100. The Falcon was, at the time, a projected system and did not as yet exist operationally. DRB initiated its own conventional air-to-air missile program, code-named VELVET GLOVE. While it was under development, DRB discovered that it would be effective only against TU-4 BULL-type targets and would be unable to deal with faster jet bombers. Consequently, the RCAF chose to pursue acquisition of the AIM-7 Sparrow II, which was on the US Navy's drawing boards at the time. Sparrow II was an active radar homing missile that was originally configured to carry a high-explosive warhead. In 1955, the RCAF considered using Sparrow II to increase the CF-100's capability.[61]

In September 1955 Slemon's staff reminded him that the Americans were pursuing nuclear air-to-air weapons development and that this topic kept coming up in bilateral discussions. RCAF participants in these discussions had no guidance, since the RCAF did not as yet have an explicit policy on them. RCAF planners were concerned that there was not enough information on the weapons to incorporate them into future interceptor designs or the Arrow.[62]

The signing of the 1955 Canada-US nuclear information sharing agreement permitted Slemon to ask the USAF for the appropriate information on nuclear air-to-air missiles. The request was phrased as a "weapons compatibility study" for the

CF-105 Arrow and CF-100 Canuck aircraft. The USAF was enthusiastic and sent a team to Avro to study the two aircraft and make recommendations. The Air Staff was "impressed by the sincere willingness of the USAF to cooperate in the exchange of atomic information."[63]

The Arrow armament development team was now able to compare the conventional GAR-1 Falcon and AIM-7 Sparrow missiles with the nuclear MB-1 Genie (see figure 3.3). It would take eight Falcons in multiple attacks to achieve an 82% chance of killing a BISON and four Sparrows to get a 75% chance, but two Genies had an 80% chance with one pass. The Falcons and Sparrows would not totally destroy the target aircraft, and thus the bomb on board might go off. The Genies would either "cook" the bomb so it would be useless, or physically destroy it along with its carrier aircraft.[64]

The path leading to accepting the MB-1 was not clear, however. The analysis team did not possess information on the nuclear versions of Falcon and Sparrow, though they probably had some inkling that they were in the works. Development of the W 42 warhead for Falcon and Sparrow did not, in fact, start until 1956. In addition, a complicated legal process to acquire the right to build conventional Sparrows in Canada was underway. Sparrow II, in any case, encountered severe developmental problems of all kinds and the RCAF looked towards the Sparrow III, a conventional radar-guided, as opposed to a radar-homing, missile (Sparrow II).[65]

The RCAF was now prompted to examine acquisition of the nuclear MB-1 Genie for its interceptor aircraft. In October 1956, the Chiefs were apprised by the Americans that the MB-1 Genie/F-89J Scorpion combination would be deployed in November (it is unclear what impact the Suez Crisis had on this decision, but it was probably a major factor given the severity of the Soviet nuclear threat against NATO members). The Americans were concerned about the political impact of MB-1 overflights in Canada and requested guidance from their Canadian counterparts. Foulkes did not think the Chiefs had enough information on the MB-1 system to go to the Cabinet and explain the situation. Slemon informed Foulkes that:

> any agreement which might be entered into with the United States should include complete exchange of information on atomic defensive missiles. While there had been continued improvement in the exchange of operational information concerning such missiles, technical information which would allow an appreciation of the risks involved in the use of such weapons was still not available."[66]

An urgent request was sent to USAF for an MB-1 briefing: the team was sent immediately.[67] The rapid American response to this request was brought on by the fact that the first F-89J Scorpion squadrons were going on alert with their MB-1s in November 1956: The first squadron was located at Presque Isle Maine, practically on the Canadian border.[68] Major General Richard Coiner, USAF, briefed the Chiefs later that month.

Before he went to the Cabinet, Foulkes stated that three matters had to be sorted out. Agreements had to be made regarding the use of the weapon from Ameri-

Figure 3.3
PLANNED CF-105 ARMAMENT COMPARISON, 1955

Missile Type	Warhead	Number	p/k BISON-type	p/k B-58-type
GAR-1 Falcon	High Explosive	8	82%	38%
AIM-7 Sparrow II	High Explosive	4	75%	46%
MB-1 Genie	Nuclear	2	80%	40%

Source: NAC RG 24 vol. 2071 file2-3-2 pt.5, 4 Nov 55, "Report by the Working Group to the AD Hoc Interdepartmental Committee for the Reappraisal of the CF-105 Development Programme.

can aircraft in Canadian airspace, as well as criteria for landing and taking off of MB-1-armed USAF aircraft from Canadian bases. The Chief of the Air Staff had to be convinced that the weapons were safe. Finally, there had to be some public affairs arrangements made for public consumption if the matter came to light in the press.[69]

If permission were given to operate MB-1-equipped aircraft over Canada, the Chiefs and USAF agreed that the same conditions would apply as in the United States. If an already-identified hostile aircraft was inbound, conventionally equipped interceptors would make confirmation first before an MB-1 would be used. Coiner invited an RCAF team to inspect the weapon itself, along with its safety precautions. If a weapon were inadvertently dropped or fired over Canada, the RCAF had authority to handle the cleanup, along with American teams if necessary. If the weapons were deployed to Canada, Canada would be consulted first, not merely informed.[70]

Ralph Campney briefed the Cabinet in December 1956, after the RCAF/DRB team inspected the MB-1's safety precautions. Cabinet saw no real problem with the Chiefs of Staff Committee–USAF arrangements, except for the publicity part. The members were extremely concerned about political fall-out if they had to explain "why Canada had to rely on the U.S. to defend us with this type of weapon when they were not prepared to let us have any of them." If, however, "the U.S. law were changed, the U.S. might offer to sell similar weapons to Canada and RCAF aircraft would be equipped with them. Indeed, Canadians would probably be surprised if the request were refused."[71] One member noted that there would be a "difficult problem of who would decide when these would be used."[72] In the end, the Cabinet decided to develop a permanent Canada-US agreement in the future.

The USAF was authorized to conduct MB-1-armed interceptor overflights for the next six months if they adhered to the informal Chiefs of Staff Committee–USAF agreement.[73] The Americans made the announcement in February 1957, after consulting with External Affairs. The news evoked only mild curiosity in the House of Commons and then only from one member of Parliament who wanted to ensure that the MB-1 was not actually tested over Canada.[74]

The information acquired by the RCAF and the DRB altered the course of thinking with regard to CF-105 Arrow and CF-100 Canuck armament. The Sparrow was slow to appear and the Falcon was unsuitable. Now there was the MB-1, already operational in the United States. If American legislation was altered, the RCAF could acquire MB-1 for its interceptors.[75] The Arrow's cavernous weapons bay, which could carry eight Falcons or four Sparrows, would require little modification to carry two or more MB-1s. The problem would be the fire control system. Could it be modified to handle the MB-1? Would the new government of John Diefenbaker push the Americans to allow Canada to buy the MB-1? The outcome was not certain in the waning days of 1956, during a national election campaign in which the Liberal government of Louis St. Laurent was on the ropes and did not know it yet.

The RCAF also pursued nuclear guided missile acquisition concurrently with the Arrow program. This was inspired by the 1954 RCAF/DRB–guided missile air defense study. The Canadian Army logically tried to develop a requirement for the Nike system, which they of course would man. This approach was modeled on the US Army's experience with the Nike-versus-BOMARC debate with the USAF in 1952. The US Army was able to produce a functioning antiaircraft missile before the USAF and thus was able to stay in the game.[76] The Canadian Army had limited success. It was able to convince the Chiefs to establish, with the RCAF, a Combined Air Defense Study with the express purpose of examining the guided missile situation. The working committee handling this project concluded that perhaps there should be a BOMARC area defense line and a Nike B (nuclear-tipped Nike) point defense line in Canada. Other missile alternatives like Talos, Nike 3, and the L253, however, should be studied as well.[77] Naturally, the RCAF was not too enthusiastic about this plan and reiterated the point that defense missiles were useless if the enemy employed thermonuclear weapons.

The problem was complicated by a 1955 US Army request to station Nike sites on Canadian soil in Ontario to cover the Detroit-Windsor and Niagara-Welland areas. This request posed political problems similar to those encountered with the MB-1 overflight situation.[78] How could the government explain to the public the need for more American continental defense forces equipped with nuclear weapons to be stationed in Canada? Who would command them? The Chiefs were able to nip this problem off at the bud. In discussions with the Americans, Foulkes argued that Canada could not afford to buy Nike. It would "raise grave political issues as to why [such a defense] was not put into effect for every major Canadian population centre." A US Army Nike unit positioned in southern Ontario would lead to further requests elsewhere for Nike coverage. The Chiefs believed that acquisition of an area defense system and placing it further north under Canadian command would solve the problem.[79]

Figure 3.4
SURFACE-TO-AIR MISSILE COMPARISON, 1955

Missile	Warhead	p/k BISON	p/k B-58-type
Talos	High Explosive	80%	50%
Talos	Nuclear	80%	80%
BOMARC	High Explosive	50%	35%
BOMARC	Nuclear	80%	80%

Source: NAC RG 24 vol. 2071 file2-3-2 pt.5, 4 Nov 55, "Report by the Working Group to the AD Hoc Interdepartmental Committee for the Reappraisal of the CF-105 Development Programme.

The Army and the RCAF eventually reached a rapprochement, but only after Simonds retired and General Howard Graham took his place. Point defense was too costly for Canada to get involved with: It would tie-up already scarce dollars that should be spent on higher priority systems, like the Arrow and BOMARC.[80]

The RCAF was now free to explore area defense systems. There were four choices: nuclear and conventionally-armed BOMARCs or Talos (the RCAF did not understand yet that there would be no conventionally-armed BOMARCs: a variety of conventional warheads were tested between 1956 and 1959, but "one by one for reasons of economy or impracticality...were cancelled."[81]) Talos was a liquid-fueled ramjet missile under development by the US Navy. In its nuclear version, Talos had a W 30 warhead with a .5 kt yield.[82] Unlike the BOMARC B with its projected range of 250 miles, Talos could reach out only to 100 miles. Where the BOMARC had a ceiling of 80,000 feet, Talos could reach 70,000 feet (see figure 3.4 for the probability of kill against BISON and B-58-type targets).[83] Even though the Army proposed a Talos line stretching from Montreal to Sault St. Marie to back up an RCAF BOMARC deployment,[84] the path was clear: BOMARC with a nuclear warhead was the area defense weapon of choice for the RCAF, in conjunction with the Arrow, which would handle the more distant targets.

An Independent Canadian Nuclear Weapons Program?

The Canadian government had eschewed nuclear weapons production in 1945, and there is no hint that a purely Canadian production program was ever seriously contemplated before 1955.[85] However, Army planners within the Directorate of

Weapons Development and the Director, Artillery, along with General Simonds, argued in September 1956 that:

> to carry out its assigned roles in a nuclear war effectively, the Canadian Army must either be armed with nuclear weapons or contain elements of Services from other countries which are so armed. Nuclear warfare is now reaching the point where a nuclear capability is required within small field formations such as a division or brigade group. This means that formations of the size envisaged for the Canadian Army require organic nuclear weapons systems.[86]

Some thought had apparently been given to this issue in 1954, but Foulkes told the planners to back off until better information was available. With the new information sharing agreements, the Army planners figured they could make their move now. The planners took into consideration exercise data and were concerned that the delay in releasing weapons from allied corps or higher headquarters would endanger a smaller Canadian formation subordinate to them, particularly since it would not be Canadian. If weapons were dispersed to lower levels by an ally, or if Canada made tactical weapons herself, the Canadian Army would not have to worry about this problem.

The Army planners believed that the Army required artillery-delivered (tube or rocket) weapons in the .5 to 1 kt and 1 to 10 kt classes. Furthermore, the planners wanted a "prepositioned nuclear weapon" with a variable yield between 1 and 50 kt (similar to, but much larger than, the contemporary American Medium Atomic Demolition Munition, and possibly with a jumping capability to produce an airburst). The Army also wanted two types of nuclear air defense missiles: a high altitude anti-aircraft weapon, and an "Anti-Missile Missile System," yields unspecified.[87]

The Defence Research Board had undertaken studies, led by Alex Longair, on Canadian warhead production, studies that the Army drew on. DRB noted, "The Canadian atomic energy program, which so far has been an entirely civil one, has about reached the stage where the possible requirements of the Department of National Defence should be taken into consideration." The Atomic Energy of Canada Limited NRU reactor, under construction in 1955, was projected by DRB to produce weapons-grade plutonium at a rate of 60–75 kg per year (4 kg of plutonium will produce a 20-kt fission bomb or provide a trigger for a thermonuclear explosion).[88] Though the plutonium from NRU was committed to be sold to the US weapons program, Canada was permitted to hold back any or all of it for her use by agreement. Canada would also need to build a gaseous diffusion plant to produce Uranium 235, but this posed no problem since Canada had abundant and cheap electrical power. All necessary technologies were within Canada's grasp. DRB noted that both U-235 and plutonium methods were desirable to retain flexibility, and that U-235 was cheaper to produce than plutonium by a factor of 3 to 5. DRB wanted such a capability in any event, because it was concerned that "consideration should be given to the possibility of production in Canada the essential portions of the weapons rather than relying on their provision (perhaps questionable) by USA in time of emergency." Thus, "from a purely technical point of view, excluding financial considerations, it is possible for Canada to develop nuclear type warheads or projectiles."[89]

The Army/DRB study did not make it to the Chiefs of Staff Committee or any higher level for lengthy consideration. The reasons are unknown, but a cryptic conclusion in the DRB study by Alex Longair suggests "There is probably no reason why Canada should make its own weapons [paragraph deleted]."[90] It is probable that the DRB figured that it would be cheaper to get them from the Americans.

Canada and the Development of MC 14/2 (revised), 1956–1957

Other NATO nations were having problems with adapting to the MC 48 strategic concept. The popular conception of nuclear weapons in Europe revolved around the idea that nuclear weapons reduced defense expenditures by decreasing the need for large, expensive conventional forces. Consequently, pundits argued, these forces could be reduced and money saved. The reality of the situation was that nuclear weapons replaced the *projected* large conventional forces above and beyond those already in existence, not those forces *already* deployed in Europe. Implementation of the MC 48 concept would in fact increase costs in certain areas like airfield infrastructure. NATO policy makers asked that some form of priority be placed on the buildup.[91]

A further problem arose over how nuclear support would be provided by the United States if the other NATO members restructured their forces to fight in a nuclear environment. Foulkes noted

> At present . . . the support of the forces in Europe by atomic tactical weapons, both missiles and bombs, must be handled by U.S. detachments attached to European formations. This oblique support is not convincing enough to persuade the Europeans that they can count on this kind of support to replace the conventional weapons which now exist. This . . . creates some uneasiness as there is no assurance that it will be a continuing support if the United States decides to reduce its efforts in Europe. Therefore it will be necessary for the United States to amend its laws and give a much wider interpretation . . . so that the European partners can be assured of continuous tactical support and eventually have this support in their own hands. Considerable feeling still exists in Europe that the United States treats the European forces as second-rate forces.[92]

At the same time, the British were in financial trouble and sought to reduce defense expenditures by reducing their forces in West Germany. Pearson noted in a February 1957 Cabinet meeting that there was a "good deal of confusion in U.K. thinking," and that British individuals conveyed the impression that "the U.K remained an independent world power but this was no longer economically or physically possible."[93] This belief, however, did not prevent the British from pushing their perspective in NATO circles.

The other European NATO members and the Americans were horrified, since existing conventional forces stationed in Europe were already below the minimum needed to defend the NATO area. The British, at the same time, pushed for a reappraisal of NATO strategy so that the role of conventional forces could be "clarified," that is, modified.[94]

Canadian policy makers were concerned, as they understood the need to keep forces in Germany for forward defense and they feared a serious disruption in the Alliance which could be exploited by the Soviets.[95] The British favored an ad hoc committee approach for strategic reappraisal, which they would try to influence directly. Almost all Canadian policy makers opposed this method, particularly Foulkes. He thought reappraisal should go to the Standing Group, while others, including the new Deputy Minister, Frank Miller (who replaced Bud Drury and would later become Chief of the Defence Staff) thought that SHAPE should handle it.[96] Any alternative to an ad hoc committee approach was desirable to stave off the British proposal.[97]

Over the course of 1956, the so-called "trip wire thesis" emerged internally within NATO. Under a "trip wire" strategy, the conventional/tactical nuclear forces in Europe were not expected to defend the NATO area. If Soviet forces attacked, it would trigger SAC and RAF Bomber Command to attack the Soviet Union immediately. Thus, the logic went, conventional/tactical nuclear forces could be reduced dramatically in Europe, since they would merely be serving as sacrificial offerings. Thus everybody would save a lot of money.[98] Not surprisingly, the British were the primary proponents of a "trip wire" strategy, closely followed by elements within USAF's Strategic Air Command.

Trip wire proponents gave no serious thought, however, to why the Soviets would suddenly attack Europe in the first place. No thought was given to conflicts peripheral to the NATO area and their possible effect on a NATO–Warsaw Pact confrontation. West Germany would be completely sacrificed if such a concept were adopted. What if the enemy was not deterred? Even President Eisenhower was having second thoughts on NATO's planned heavy reliance on nuclear weapons.[99]

Mike Pearson took note of these developments. By July 1956 Canada formally pushed for a reappraisal of NATO strategy to prevent the trip wire strategy from being adopted. The NATO permanent representatives would supervise the Military Committee, who would produce a strategic concept for the 1956 Ministerial Meeting to be held in December.[100]

In a meeting with US Joint Chiefs Chairman, Admiral Arthur Radford, Foulkes tried to steer Radford to support this position. Foulkes informed him that, against the British Chiefs of Staff's advice, "the British [Foreign Office] assess the danger of a world war as practically negligible, therefore, they come to conclusion that NATO ground forces can be reduced to the 'trip wire' formula."[101]

Both SACLANT (Wright) and SACEUR (Gruenther) presented their view to the NATO Military Committee. They wanted to include regional planning guidance similar to that included in MC 14, but which had not been included in MC 48. This would assist the nations contributing forces in their quest to apply their resources more efficiently. Wright pointed out that NATO needed clarification on pre-Phase I operations and their relationship to MC 48, a concern expressed by Pearson and his staff back in 1955 when they assessed the impact of MC 48 on strategic planning. Wright wanted to develop a limited war concept as an adjunct to MC 48 or as an integral part of any new concept.[102]

All of these factors coalesced in a process that produced MC 14/2, a document which was hotly debated in the Military Committee throughout the fall of 1956. The draft for the Military Committee was, in George Ignatieff's view, "a rewrite of several Military Committee papers, it is inconsistent in many places."[103] Initial Canadian comparisons between MC 48 and MC 14/2 revealed that the draft under consideration in the Military Committee actively promoted "NATO responsibility to deal with aggression in adjacent non-NATO areas."[104] Canadian diplomatic and military analysts looking at countering the trip wire thesis were concerned that

> There is no indication that this question of Soviet aggression in non-NATO areas has been dealt with by the [North Atlantic] Council, and it appears that the Standing Group and the International Planning Team[105] have attempted to deal with this subject without securing political guidance from the Council.[106]

Admiral Jerauld Wright had succeeded in getting the Military Committee to recognize that NATO might become embroiled in a conventional war outside the NATO area that might spill over (with or without Soviet involvement) into the NATO area, prompting a conventional response. For procedural reasons, Canadian analysts wanted this problem recognized and formalized by the NAC so that it would have legitimacy if the British tried to eliminate it from consideration using more subtle diplomatic methods.

Canadian diplomats, on the other hand, were concerned that recognition of peripheral threats might prompt NATO nations to embark on an action outside or on the periphery of the NATO area and draw the rest of NATO into a larger action that might precipitate war. (Note that Jules Leger, the Canadian representative to NATO, made this point on 5 October 1956, less than a month before the Anglo-French Suez adventure, a peripheral situation which could have drawn NATO into nuclear war.[107]) They were concerned, as they had been in 1955, "as to the interpretation which might be placed on minor actions, such as border incidents, initiated by the Soviet Bloc, and whether such incidents would be countered by atomic retaliation,"[108] a point with which Foulkes agreed.

In October 1956, Foulkes addressed the NATO Military Committee and presented the Canadian views relating to MC 14/2. In the Canadian Chief's view, "so far NATO strategy has succeeded and we believe that a considerable amount of caution should be used in any attempt to water down" the existing strategy. The Soviet leadership "agrees that NATO is the biggest stumbling block to Russian expansionism in Europe. No matter what other people say about NATO we have succeeded in our primary task." In essence, Foulkes noted, the strategic concept should not move away from two primary points. First, the primary purpose of NATO was to defend the defined NATO area. Second, "that we will retaliate with all the means at our disposal should the NATO area be attacked by any means." Canada was "mindful that there are brushfires on the periphery of NATO which cannot be ignored, but we want to ensure that in dealing with such situations nothing is done to in any way weaken the determination to defend the NATO area."[109] The Canadian Chiefs recognized that the priority was the NATO area and it was to be defended by a mixed nuclear-conventional force that gave primacy to nuclear weapons use. Peripheral operations were of secondary consideration, but were not to be completely ignored if they directly affected the NATO area.

MC 14/2 was accepted by the Military Committee on 14 October 1956. It was essentially similar to MC 48 but included a more detailed examination of peripheral matters and the possibility that the Soviets might initiate conventional measures short of general war against NATO. It also included forward defense (conventional and nuclear) of the NATO area as first priority, followed by strategic nuclear use as second priority.[110]

The British reacted violently to MC 14/2. They argued, as the Canadian analysts predicted, that adding the conventional/peripheral elements had not been sanctioned by higher authority and that this approval should be obtained before any such alteration was incorporated into the new strategic concept. The Military Committee agreed and sent an information copy to the NAC and the original to the drafters for revision.[111]

What did this mean in the larger sense? The British did not want to spend money on conventional forces and wanted to rely on strategic nuclear use as the only deterrent. If NATO recognized that peripheral or small-scale conventional conflict were possible forms of conflict that the Soviets might use against NATO, then money would have to be spent on conventional, tactical, and strategic nuclear forces if the British wanted to participate in, and have influence over, NATO strategy and operations. If Britain chose to limit itself to one or two of the three activities, it would limit its influence. It did not have enough money to do all three, so the British attempted to force NATO to limit its activities so that the level of British participation would remain high and thus the British could maintain influence.[112]

The other perspective, championed by Canada, recognized that strategic nuclear forces had limitations in their ability to deter all forms of Soviet activity, but that strategic nuclear deterrence was the primary factor that limited Soviet activity against NATO directly. The enemy would, as Canadian analysts argued earlier in 1955, try to operate on NATO's periphery and NATO had to have some means to counter such actions short of strategic nuclear use. In addition, West Germany and the factors relating to its proximity to the main threat produced the forward defense imperative. West Germany was the key to European defense. Consequently, all being fair and just, Norway, Turkey, and Greece deserved the same consideration, which in turn produced the need for conventional and tactical nuclear support to preserve the NATO area. A mixture of conventional, tactical nuclear, and strategic nuclear forces was required on land, in the sea, and in the air. NATO members noted that the monopoly on nuclear weapons access produced "second class" NATO members. Thus, the appropriate universal solution was to give all NATO members access to nuclear weapons, which in turn ran into American legal blocks. Some compromise had to be found.

This entire problem was further aggravated by the Soviet intervention in Hungary and by the Suez Crisis. The Franco-British operation (which stripped a considerable number of conventional British and French NATO-assigned army, navy, and air forces) was designed to retain control over the vital waterway that was on the periphery of the NATO area. A case was made that Abdel Gamal Nasser was influenced by the Soviet Union, and Egyptian nationalization of the canal served Soviet ends. When the Soviets threatened conventional intervention and then nuclear use against Paris and London, the American nuclear umbrella was not automatically extended over the British and the French. Canada used the United Nations to solve NATO's problem by introducing an ad hoc peacekeeping force to reduce tension and monitor Anglo-French withdrawal. Canada was therefore able to demonstrate that conventional forces did, in fact, have a role to play in peripheral operations involving NATO.[113]

While this operation was underway, the NAC met to discuss MC 14/2. An NAC working group dealing with MC 14/2 argued that NATO had to have a "fully effective nuclear retaliatory force as the major deterrent to Soviet aggression." NATO land, sea, and air forces had to have the ability to:

(a) Keep confidence in the military effectiveness of NATO to prevent external intimidation. To this end the continued stationing of British, Canadian, and American forces in Europe is essential.
(b) Deal with local infiltrations and incursions.
(c) Enable Soviet or satellite aggressive intentions to be identified as such.
(d) Deal with limited attacks.
(e) Defend NATO territory against a major Soviet aggression in accordance with the concept of forward strategy and to sustain operations until the strategic counter offensive has achieved its objectives.
(f) Protect and maintain sea communications.

Significantly,

[NATO] forces required for an effective shield must, of course, have the capability to deal with limited armed attacks without recourse to nuclear weapons. Should the situation so require they must also be prepared and capable of responding quickly with nuclear weapons to any type of aggression.[114]

The working group report was analyzed by members of Canada's Panel on the Economic Aspects of Defence Policy. The External Affairs members on the Panel were confused. Did the working group want forces that could enact a conventional pause prior to nuclear weapons use if a limited situation went out of control? Foulkes thought not. After consultations with his European counterparts, he discovered that:

the concern among European members of NATO about the use of nuclear weapons was largely due to their worry that a revolt in East Germany, for instance, might create such a demand for action in the Federal Republic that fighting across the border might take place. The Europeans feared that if nuclear weapons were used in such an eventuality, World War III would be precipitated.[115]

Conventional forces were still needed to contain such a situation so that it did not escalate into nuclear use. After more heated debate, the NAC sent MC 14/2 back for revision, and the process continued into 1957 after the fallout of the Suez Crisis subsided.[116]

In addition to the final version of MC 14/2, another important document was tabled: MC 48/2 or "Measures to Implement the Strategic Concept." MC 14/2 laid out the strategic concept, while MC 48/2 laid out the pattern of forces necessary to implement the concept. Both were approved by the NAC in May 1957. What were the main tenets of MC 14/2 (revised), and how did it differ from the 1954 MC 48 concept and the 1956 version of MC 14/2?

According to the MC 14/2 (revised) concept, war might result from "miscalculation on the part of the Soviets, a misconstruction of Western intentions, or as the result of military operations of a limited nature which the Soviets did not originally expect would lead to a general war."[117] NATO's priority was to develop a defense system that would deter war and, if war occurred, be able to achieve NATO objectives. Nuclear weapons would be used once general war was initiated. If the Soviets started it as a result of a calculated decision, they would use nuclear weapons against NATO nuclear delivery systems first, then other military targets. If war arose from some form of miscalculation or limited conventional operations, the Soviets might use massive conventional forces first, perhaps without immediate nuclear use. In both scenarios, Soviet forces would attempt to isolate Europe from North America and attempt to overrun Europe. To ensure that this did not happen, NATO had to use tactical and strategic nuclear weapons first and use its forces to preserve the NATO area.[118]

In a section entitled "Alternative Threat to NATO Security," MC 14/2 (revised) stated that the Soviets might deliberately

> initiate operations with limited objectives, such as infiltrations, incursions or hostile local actions in the NATO Area, covertly or overtly supported by themselves, trusting that the Allies in their collective desire to prevent general conflict would either limit their reactions accordingly or not react at all. NATO must also be prepared to deal immediately with such situations without necessarily having recourse to nuclear weapons. NATO must also be prepared to respond quickly with nuclear weapons. . . . [I]f the Soviets were involved in a local hostile action and sought to broaden the scope of such an incident or prolong it, the situation would call for the utilization of all weapons and forces at NATO's disposal, since in no case is there a NATO concept of limited war with the Soviets.[119]

With regard to threats outside the NATO area:

it is necessary to take into account of the dangers which may arise for NATO because of the developments outside that area. In this light, planning for the most efficient organization and the equipment of NATO forces must take into account of the possible need for certain NATO countries to use some of their NATO forces . . . such as may arise because of the various and changing forms of the Soviet-inspired threat on a world front. This need, however, should, in conformity with their NATO commitments, be harmonized with the primary importance of protecting the NATO area.[120]

MC 14/2 (revised) reiterated the Phase I/Phase II concept which was the foundation of MC 48. The exact division between the two, in MC 14/2 (revised), was unclear since "anti-submarine operations are likely to continue for an indeterminate period."[121] As with MC 48, MC 14/2 (revised) reminded its readers that priority must be given to forces that would contribute effectively to Phase I, though "forces of certain NATO nations may need to retain the flexibility required to permit action to meet limited military situation short of general war outside the NATO area."[122]

MC 14/2 (revised) included regional planning guidance as MC 14/1 had, but MC 48 had not. The areas affecting Canada included Western Europe, the Atlantic Ocean, and North America.

In Western Europe, SACEUR was to be prepared to "carry out a nuclear strategic counter-offensive and to sustain operations to maintain the integrity of Western Europe until the ability and will of the enemy to pursue general war has been destroyed." SACEUR had to be able to respond to any level of attack with appropriate force. All air, land, and sea units in the region were to have an integrated nuclear capability, as well as air defense. SACEUR was to focus his efforts on destroying the Soviet "nuclear capability, forces, resources, and communications," while defending ports and industrial areas from attack.[123]

With regard to North America, MC 14/2 (revised) reiterated the basic assumptions used by Canada and the United States in their air defense planning,[124] that is, the aim was to protect SAC first and the industrial mobilization base second. The means used to attack North America would include nuclear weapons launched from aircraft and submarines. The Canada-US region was to provide an effective base for and effective protection of, the strategic nuclear counter-offensive capability, maintain an effective early warning and air defense system, and protect as much of the industrial mobilization base as possible.[125]

As for the Atlantic Ocean, NATO was to use it to project nuclear weapons against the Soviet Union in support of NATO forces; to maintain the vital sea lines of communication (SLOC) to resupply and reinforce Europe in Phase II; and to "reduce to the minimum the number of his units which can penetrate to the broader reaches of the Atlantic and threaten" those lines of communication.[126]

The companion to MC 14/2 (revised), MC 48/2, presented force requirements amplifying those established in MC 48/1.[127] Extrapolating from the logic of MC 48/1, if NATO were to fight a sustained (thirty-day) nuclear war, it would need intelligence and warning systems, a high degree of readiness, an alert system, a decentralized civil and military command system with delegated authority, and better civil defense measures so that the population base could exist to fight Phase II, all in addition to Shield (tactical nuclear and conventional forces) and Sword forces (strategic nuclear forces). Nuclear weapons had to be ready for immediate use, and forces with their logistic and support elements were to be dispersed.[128]

Both documents were accepted by the North Atlantic Council by 9 May 1957. The British still were against accepting alternative forms of conflict, since they believed that "[NATO] must never allow the Soviets to think that there is a NATO concept of limited war. . . . to do so would invite the Soviets to start such limited wars." In the NAC meeting, they attempted to amend MC 14/2 (revised) yet again. The Canadian representative, Dana Wilgress, headed off the British effort, stating that the NATO planners' intent was to have the ability to respond to any level of aggression that the Soviets chose to initiate. If the force structure was not designed to handle such alternative courses of action, NATO would be constrained in its response to Soviet aggression. The rest of the NAC members backed Wilgress, pressured the British representative into accepting his view, and the new strategy was adopted.[129]

The first two parts of the strategic reassessment battle were over. NATO had to implement a force structure to support the strategy. The process which produced this would, in Wilgress's words, "translate for the first time the general strategic concepts into numerical force requirements."[130] This process would produce a force plan, known as MC 70, that would integrate nuclear weapons into NATO's force structure.

Canada's force structure, as it had developed since the 1954 MC 48 concept, resonated with MC 14/2 (revised). The requisite flexibility required to deal with alternative threats existed; that is, Canada's forces could (and did in 1956) handle conventional, peripheral threats. Prior to the advent of the Diefenbaker government in 1957, the only thing stopping Canada from acquiring the nuclear capability required by MC 14/2 (revised) and MC 48/2 was the legal inability of the United States to provide the weapons. The new Canadian government's unwillingness to fully accept MC 14/2 (revised) further complicated the problems. This situation was further aggravated by problems brought on by the evolution of the air defense system in North America prior to the 1957 election and the problems of implementing changes to it afterward.

4

INFORMATION IS POWER: CANADA AND NUCLEAR WEAPONS TESTING

6: What do you want?
2: Information . . .
6: You won't get it!
2: By hook or by crook, we will . . .
–The Prisoner

Introduction

In the early 1950s, Admiral Arthur Radford, the Chairman of the US Joint Chiefs of Staff, was anxious that Canada have access to American nuclear weapons information so that the continental defense program could proceed smoothly. His predecessor, General Omar Bradley, felt the same way. Successive SACEURs, Generals Ridgway and Gruenther, wanted nuclear information released to NATO so that realistic planning could occur. The main block was a piece of American legislation, the Atomic Energy Act of 1946, also known as the McMahon Act for Brian McMahon, the Connecticut senator who sponsored and drafted it. This law basically stated that any information regarding nuclear weapons could not be transferred to a foreign government. Generated by the hysteria surrounding the discovery of the atom bomb spy ring, the McMahon Act inhibited nuclear planning until 1954, when it was replaced with new legislation generated by the New Look.

If a national force structure was to adapt to a nuclear battlefield, the forces had to understand the nature of weapons' effects on terrain, weather, equipment, communications, and, most importantly, people. The side possessing such information not only would have a force structure attuned to the new environment; it would also possess an advantage over its enemy.

Nuclear weapons were not merely a larger explosive device. The electromagnetic and radiation effects could function as directional "death rays" if employed properly. Underwater bursts might be employed to use the sea and its surrounding environment against a target as much as blast or heat. If Canadian forces were to function as an integral part of allied defense arrangements, they had to be able to fight in a nuclear environment, and this meant knowing what the weapons were capable of. Canadian planners employed a wide variety of formal and informal information gathering activities in this effort.

Chance and Happenstance: Nuclear Cooperation to 1953

The wartime atomic bomb program was a tripartite project from its inception. Canada had a representative on the six-man (including three American and two British) Combined Policy Committee established in 1943 after the Quebec conference. Canada also provided heavy water from a facility at Trail, British Columbia, and uranium from the Eldorado mines in the Northwest Territories. A joint British-Canadian laboratory was established at Montreal: It was tasked with developing a heavy water–moderated nuclear reactor, in contrast to the American facilities at Oak Ridge and Hanford, which used graphite as a moderator.[1]

For a variety of reasons related to Anglo-American nuclear policy disputes, the Montreal lab partially disassociated itself from the American nuclear weapons program. In 1944, construction began on the Zero Energy Experimental Pile (ZEEP) at Chalk River, Ontario. ZEEP was the first successful nuclear reactor outside of the United States. The British had pressed for the construction of an Anglo-Canadian plutonium production facility for their nuclear weapons program during the war. Even though the King government declared that Canada would not build her own nuclear weapons in 1945, work was also started on the NRX reactor at Chalk River. Building on the work conducted at Montreal and the ZEEP, NRX came on-line in 1947. NRX would serve as the basis for future energy-producing reactors. In sum, Canada was in the forefront of nuclear energy research in the late 1940s.[2]

There were two important Canadian scientists whose work contributed directly to the production of the information required to modify the Canadian force structure. The first was Dr. Omand McKillop Solandt. During the Second World War, Solandt represented Canada on a tripartite operations research team in England. The intimate contacts that he developed with his British counterparts prompted Defence Minister Brooke Claxton (who was in turn influenced by Foulkes) to name Solandt as Canada's representative to various tripartite scientific endeavors in 1946. Eventually, the Defence Research Board was formed in 1947. Solandt, at age 37, became its chairman.[3]

Solandt made his contribution to Canadian strategic policy in many ways. In 1945 he was selected to participate as part of the British delegation to the Strategic Bombing Survey; specifically, that portion of the survey dealing with nuclear weapons use against Japan. Led by Professor W. N. Thomas, representatives of the Civil Defence Department of the Home Office (British) along with Solandt and an Indian representative, left for Japan in October 1945.[4] Solandt was instructed by the British Chiefs of Staff "not [to] make any inquiries, constructional or operational aspects of atomic bombing that are outside the scope of the USSBS terms of reference."[5] The group was restricted to gathering information on the immediate effects of the bomb (heat and blast) including "special effects" ("radio-active or electrical" and contamination). They were particularly interested in the effects of weather and terrain, but the most important aspect was the effect on personnel.[6]

The joint survey team was allowed access to the "Rikken Group" report, a Japanese study conducted immediately after the bombings. This group focused almost exclusively on weapons effects on people and was incorporated into the joint study. Solandt also conducted his own investigations. This information, communicated back to Canada, formed the basis of the first Canadian military doctrinal pamphlet dealing with nuclear weapons and warfare, *Medical Aspects of Atomic Warfare*, published in 1948. Other information derived from the Japan survey was integral in producing the civil defense pamphlet, "The Effects of an Atomic Bomb Explosion on Structures and Personnel," which came out in 1951.[7]

Solandt, in his capacity as the DRB Chairman, commissioned a detailed study examining the effects of nuclear weapons and their relationship to Canadian cities. Part of this study contributed to "The Effects of an Atomic Bomb Explosion on Structures and Personnel"; but the staff was hampered by the fact that "the Atomic Energy Act prohibits the divulging of any information on the military aspects of atomic energy to a foreign power. . . . [I]t was not until March 17 [1950] that the Branch received the authority to discuss the subject with the writer and the resulting discussion was only in the most general terms."[8] The study members were able to get access to the United States Strategic Bombing Survey (USSBS) studies on Hiroshima and Nagasaki. They were also able to get access to two British studies dealing with the "Physical Aspects of Atomic Bombs—Damage to Ships by Under Water Explosion of Atomic Bombs."[9]

The second Canadian whose work helped modify the Canadian force structure was Louis Slotin. Slotin was a 35-year-old scientist working in Los Alamos as a researcher on the Manhattan Project. Working with a multinational team of scientists, Slotin tested the cores of each "gadget" to ensure that the proper reaction would take place between the components. In a procedure known as "tickling the Dragon's tail," Slotin mounted the two reactive halves of a gun-type weapon on a framework and progressively moved them toward each other so that the reaction could be measured. Slotin usually used a screwdriver to ensure that the halves did not come too close and cause a reaction. Unfortunately, when Slotin and his team were testing the cores destined for the CROSSROADS tests at Bikini in 1946, the "Dragon" turned on him and he had to separate the spheres physically with his hands. His body blocked most of the radiation emitted by the brief blue burst, and he took a lethal dose. Instructing the other members to stand still, he measured their distance to the device so that accurate radiation effects measurements could be taken to determine their exposure dosage. Slotin died in agony several days later, but not until the effects on his body could be studied in detail by the Los Alamos researchers. This information eventually found its way into weapons effects data used during training in the 1950s.[10]

Canada undertook its own program to collect the by-products of the first Soviet nuclear test in 1949. Without allied prompting, Solandt initiated a collection system:

> We had not made any advance preparation for airborne sampling but had all the facilities to mount a very competent programme extremely quickly. The chemical warfare lab in Ottawa had the equipment and skills to design suitable filters for continuous airborne sampling. . . . The RCAF were ready and willing to fly on a moment's notice and Canadian scientists were at the forefront of mass spectrography. . . . What Canada totally lacked was the knowledge to translate the results . . . into useful information. DRB very

quickly has a series of flights underway from the West Indies to the Arctic. . . . [Canada passed them to the Americans and the British] the AEC and the US intelligence discovered that our results were far better then theirs. They subsequently came to depend heavily on our filters . . . [T]here is no question that we received an ample return of information from them.[11]

The Royal Canadian Navy was the first Canadian service to use nuclear weapons effects information for a practical purpose. The RCN announced the construction of seven new antisubmarine vessels in 1948, the DE 205-class (better known as the *St. Laurent*-class). The design team included Constructor Captain Rowland Baker of the Royal Navy, on loan to Canada for the project, who had access to British thinking on nuclear warfare at sea and its impact on ship construction.[12]

The *St. Laurent* design team had access to the Operation CROSSROADS data relating to the effects of tests ABLE and BAKER on the diverse "ghost fleet" which was sunk during the tests. RCN Captain Horatio Nelson Lay, Director of Operations, led a small Canadian observation team to Bikini in 1946 (including future RCAF Chief of the Air Staff, Air Marshal Larry Dunlap) and concluded that the main impact of a nuclear weapon was a vast shockwave out to two thousand yards, followed by large amounts of radioactive contaminate. If ships were properly dispersed and had the means of clearing off radioactive water, they could operate in a nuclear environment.[13]

The *St. Laurents* (and the follow on classes) all incorporated passive nuclear, biological, and chemical defenses (NBCD) into their designs. The hull structures were designed to dissipate shock, and each subassembly unit in the hull consisted of an "egg box" system of longitudinal and transverse members made from "T" bars. This construction made for a strong but flexible hull able to take the air and underwater shock of a nuclear explosion, albeit at range. There were a minimum of fittings to the weather decks, since these would cause spray and hinder the clearance of radioactive waste. The ships possessed a distinctive curved "turtledeck" bow, which was originally designed to improve the sea keeping qualities of the ship. It actually provided an efficient means to keep contamination off the weather decks. All deck edges were rounded and the anchor wells faired over.[14]

The ships also possessed a wash-down system, which sprayed contamination off the upper surfaces of the ship. The *St. Laurents* also were the first ships in NATO to utilize the Citadel concept. The DE 205s and their follow on ships were capable of airtight operation. Once certain rapid close-down hatches were activated, the central part of the ship used the beefed-up air conditioning system to filter out contaminants using carbon filters. The Citadel concept, however, could not be extended to the machinery spaces since these required great volumes of air to operate. The first *St. Laurent* was launched in 1950.[15]

Another benchmark in the Canadian effort occurred during the war in Korea. The Canadian Army deployed 25 Canadian Infantry Brigade to Korea as part of the UN effort there. For some reason, Headquarters 25 CIB forwarded copies of eight US Army training directives to the Chief of the General Staff in Ottawa in November 1953. These directives, probably given to the British divisional headquarters by a higher American headquarters, related to the tactical employment of nuclear weapons and methods by which forces in the field could protect themselves from weapons effects. The receipt of this information did not appear to distress the Army Staff to any great degree.[16]

25 CIB incorporated NBCD techniques into its training program. It requested and received guidance from the CGS on nuclear training and equipment scales. The Army Staff, with some rapidity, also forwarded the results of an Army study (Exercise FORWARD ON, August 1953) in mid-November 1953. This study, "The Protection of Men and Equipment Against Atomic Weapons," used the nominal 20 kt bomb paradigm for weapons effects developed in the United States as a training aid. FORWARD ON stated that a formation could expect 100% casualties in twenty-four hours if all of its forces were in the open within two thousand yards of ground zero. Most importantly, FORWARD ON noted that nuclear weapons would have a debilitating effect on communications because high-frequency traffic would be impaired for two hours and, however, VHF traffic would be usable.[17]

The second part of the study, delivered to 25 CIB in early 1953, was called "The Tactical Use of Atomic Weapons." It stated that there were three weapons effects: heat, blast, and radiation. These effects would be limited by the weather and terrain. The weapon would be delivered by aircraft or missile against an enemy airfield, logistical complex, or in the close support of ground forces.[18] Ground forces had to be strong enough to prevent defeat by enemy conventional forces. And they had to disperse to prevent an enemy attack against a concentrated target. A mobile reserve was required to repel an enemy counterattack trying to exploit gaps made by the atomic attack.[19]

It is exactly this type of information that was denied to NATO planners up to 1954. Why would 25 CIB in Korea and the Army Staff have access to it? The obvious conclusion is that the UN forces in Korea were preparing for possible nuclear weapons use and wanted their personnel trained for such an eventuality. In fact, nuclear weapons annexes were incorporated in American plans for Korea from 1952 onward. These were based on a US Army study, HUDSON HARBOR, which contemplated the use of nuclear weapons to develop gaps in the Communist front so that UN forces could exploit them. By 1953, the Eisenhower administration threatened nuclear use if North Korea did not subscribe to an armistice. Thus, the measures taken by 25 CIB were prudent given the situation.[20]

In addition to the DRB, there were two important Canadian organizations involved in gathering nuclear weapons information. The first was the Joint Special Weapons Committee (JSWC), which reported to Chiefs of Staff Committee. The second was No. 1 Radiation Detection Unit, Royal Canadian Engineers (1 RDU).

The JSWC was formed around 1948 and had triservice plus DRB representation. Its purpose was to coordinate research and disseminate information to the armed forces on nuclear, biological, and chemical weapons matters. The bulk of the JSWC's work prior to 1952 focused on biological and chemical weapons, two areas in which Canada held the lead in the West in developing state of the art weapons and defensive measures.[21] The JSWC shifted its priorities to nuclear effects by 1952. It developed an emphasis on producing and testing personal protective measures (NBCD suits, respirators) and unit radiation detection devices (known as RADIAC devices) for the three services.[22]

By 1954, the JSWC expanded its mandate to function as the clearinghouse for data collected by both formal and informal methods. The committee also handled the security arrangements and standards provided by the US and the UK. This, in addition to the increased cooperation produced by the information sharing agreements, dictated a change in the organization and mandate of the JSWC. It was renamed the Joint Special Weapons Policy Committee (JSWPC). The JSWPC was responsible for: service participation in nuclear tests; offensive and defensive special weapons use policy; special weapons equipment requirements; security classification guides for information; coordination of requests for classified atomic information, for example, US Restricted Data and UK Atomic Information; and interservice military characteristics for equipment.[23]

The Chiefs of Staff Committee also created the ZED List, which was a special list of Canadians who had access to atomic information. Those personnel who were "Zedded" were carefully screened. Documents themselves were "Zedded" and given a Zed List control number.

1 RDU was a triservice unit consisting of five officers and twenty-one men (later increased to more than sixty), divided into a Radiation Calibration Laboratory and a Ground Detection Troop of six mobile Monitor Teams. Formed in March 1950, 1 RDU was to assess radiological hazards for field commanders; function as a nucleus reconnaissance and field radiological lab; and calibrate RADIAC equipment. In peacetime, the unit was to test and evaluate equipment under nuclear test conditions.[24] It also assisted in the clean up of nuclear disasters in Canada. 1 RDU was involved with Exercise CHARITY I at the Chalk River reactor in December 1952. The unit conducted a radiation survey after the NRX reactor was "scrammed" and one million gallons of radioactive water were dumped by the cooling system into the basement of the building. The reactor calandria and core were severely damaged and had to be removed and buried.[25]

With the exception of Operation CROSSROADS in 1946, Canada did not directly participate in American nuclear tests until Operation TEAPOT in 1955. Admiral Radford recommended to the Secretary of Defense in December 1953 that "Canada be permitted to conduct a radiological defense field exercise" during the next scheduled test series in Nevada. This request was turned down with the excuse that the McMahon Act prohibited such participation.[26]

There was some Anglo-Canadian collaboration. The British were casting about for an atomic weapons proving ground between 1949 and 1950 and thought that the port of Churchill, Manitoba, on Hudson's Bay should be surveyed. The British Atomic Weapons Research Establishment (AWRE) estimated that the site had to be able to accommodate twelve nuclear detonations over a number of years, with each test severely contaminating a 500-yard circle that could not be reused in later tests. The Canadian government was not keen on this, and AWRE surveyors went to Australia instead.[27]

The site picked for the first British nuclear weapons test (Operation HURRICANE) was the Monte Bello islands northwest of Australia. Dr. William Penney, a

British scientist who had worked at Los Alamos, was in charge of the test program and was a friend of Solandt's. Solandt was invited along as a "Health Monitor" on HURRICANE in October 1952 (possibly because the HURRICANE device contained some Canadian plutonium).[28] This test, rudimentary in nature, was an ocean surface burst that yielded about 25 kt. It was designed as a confirmatory test of British capability. It is unclear exactly what information Solandt brought back to Canada with him after this test, but whatever material he had was provided to the COSC and DRB.[29] It is equally unclear whether Solandt was an impromptu observer at the two Operation TOTEM shots held in October 1953 at Emu Field in Australia. The TOTEM shots, designed to test the composition of material needed for the RAF's BLUE DANUBE nuclear bomb, included test effects trials on Centurion tanks (vehicles also used by the Canadian Army) and other army equipment exposed to the weapons. Operation HOT BOX featured a Canberra bomber flying through the radioactive clouds produced by the explosions so that the aircraft and crew could be tested on return. Canada was eventually supplied with the HOT BOX data, including the flight report.[30]

Solandt and Foulkes pushed the British for closer cooperation. In a letter to the British Chiefs of Staff (BCS), they thanked them for the limited technical information given to Canada from the Monte Bello test, but noted that "valuable as these reports will be, however, there will be specific Canadian problems which have not been investigated. In addition, reports cannot substitute for actual participation by Canadians in a test."[31]

The Canadian shopping list was comprehensive. Foulkes canvassed all three services as to their information requirements and passed them on to the BCS. The Army was interested in weapons effects on all manner of equipment, obstacles, and personal movements. The RCN was interested in the impact of air, surface, and subsurface bursts on ships and harbors, while the RCAF wanted to know about how radiation affected aircrew while they were flying and the impact of blast on airflow. The RCAF was especially interested in the adaptability of nuclear warheads for air-to-air missiles, antisubmarine weapons, and close support weapons. All wanted to know about the best procedures for decontamination

Within the Chiefs of Staff Committee, Foulkes expressed concern that the information gathering program not be based on a purely "defensive attitude" because:

> it was important that because of thermonuclear weapons we not be panicked into thinking only in terms of defence. Atomic and thermonuclear weapons must continue to be considered merely as a type of weapon. Regardless of enemy capabilities in the thermonuclear field, we must still plan to carry out our assigned tasks.[32]

Personal and Informal Relationships

One important method in information gathering employed by Canada was the extensive use of personal contacts among Canadian, American, and British people involved in defense science, planning, and policy. It is, however, an extremely difficult area to document. In many cases, there is no written record. The fact that two men were friends, met frequently, and corresponded does not always prove that there was some form of detailed information passage, particularly when it came to nuclear weapons, their construction, effects, and employment. On the other hand, some close friendships did develop. For example, James Forrestal, the American Secretary of Defense, actively corresponded with his Canadian counterpart Brooke Claxton, even to the point of Forrestal sending the 1949 American defense budget to Claxton while it was under debate.[33]

In intelligence matters, both Foulkes and A. D. P. Heeney, Canadian ambassador to the United States, had a close relationship with Allen Dulles, the Director of Central Intelligence. Foulkes even referred to Dulles as "our man in the CIA [Central Intelligence Agency]," while Heeney wrote to Dulles and noted, "You are aware of how much we have appreciated the frankness and confidence with which you and your officers in the CIA have treated us in Canada and the extent and cooperation and assistance we have received from you for a long time."[34] In fact, the CIA regularly provided Canadian policy makers in External Affairs with American National Intelligence Estimates (NIEs). Raw intelligence material was passed on throughout the 1950s and 1960s: American liaison officers noted:

> The Canadians were less interested in our evaluations than they were in the raw material on which these evaluations were based. This does not reflect a particularly flattering assessment of us but we were willing to go along with them if there was any possibility of our convincing them of our views.[35]

The diplomatic circuit provided information on a wide variety of topics, but hard information on nuclear topics outside of general policy was rarely transmitted.

Other forums for informal relationships included the PJBD, the MCC, the Canada-US Military Study Group (CUSMSG), and the Canada-US Scientific Advisory Team (CUSSAT), as well as affairs like the Lincoln Summer Study Group. Relationships that developed at this level tended to be long lasting. For example, Admiral George Anderson, who eventually was American Chief of Naval Operations (CNO) from 1961 to 1963 (and who would play a role in requesting Canadian forces during the Cuban Missile Crisis in 1962), served on the PJBD between 1946 and 1948, was a member of the MCC at various times between 1948 and 1960, and was a SHAPE staff officer between 1950 and 1953. Through this medium he met General Andrew McNaughton, the Canadian member of the PJBD who handled the early air defense planning (and was later the go-between on many Canadian-American projects).[36]

On the NATO side, Anderson knew General Lauris Norstad well from the SHAPE period. Norstad eventually became SACEUR. Foulkes had arranged with Gruenther (and Norstad, who worked for Gruenther at the time) to have Air Vice-Marshal Frank Miller become the SHAPE Air Deputy in 1954.[37] Miller worked with Norstad during this period and Miller eventually became Chairman of the Chiefs of Staff Committee in 1960. Norstad also was involved with placing Canadian Air Marshal Hugh Campbell as Deputy Chief of Staff Operations at SHAPE in 1957, followed by Air Vice-Marshal Larry Dunlap. Both of these appointments were at Foulkes's behest.[38] Campbell was the first commander of 1 Air Division RCAF under Eisenhower when Eisenhower was SACEUR.[39] Anderson's predecessor in the CNO position, Arleigh Burke, had known Canadian Vice-Admiral Harry De Wolfe, the Chief of the Naval Service between 1956 and 1960 (and head of the Canadian Joint Staff Mission to Washington (CJSM-W) before that), from the Second World War. De Wolfe was probably the first non-American naval officer to sail on an American nuclear submarine. Burke invited De Wolfe and a small Canadian team (which included Omand Solandt's replacement, Dr. Adam Hartley Zimmerman of the DRB and Brigadier Jean Victor Allard, the Vice Chief of the General Staff and later Chief of the Defence Staff) to travel on board the nuclear-propelled USS *Seawolf* in 1957 after the Atomic Energy Act was amended.[40]

Another extremely important informal information exchange mechanism that Canada possessed was the hunting and fishing lodge located at Eagle Lake in Labrador. Eagle Lake started out as a ramshackle fishing camp consisting of a number of tents located near a fish-laden lake within floatplane distance of Goose Bay. The facilities became considerably more elaborate as time went on. Eagle Lake became the primary point of informal contact between the USAF and the RCAF at the highest levels. No notes (and no secretaries) were taken to Eagle Lake, and, as such, there is no written record of the deliberations that went on there. Yet Generals Curtis E. LeMay, Lauris Norstad, Earle Partridge (Commander in Chief of US Continental Air Defense Command, or CONAD) and others were frequent visitors. RCAF officers did not just catch fish at Eagle Lake.[41]

There was what appears to have been an accidental exchange of nuclear information. In 1952 the Joint Intelligence Board was involved in the previously mentioned DRB vulnerability study. While the study was underway, the director requested a copy of an American study, "Capabilities of Atomic Weapons." After the vulnerability study was completed, the document arrived in Ottawa. The JIB was confused. The McMahon Act clearly applied to this paper. Was this release an accident, or did it indicate a new American attitude towards releasing it to Canada, perhaps on the "QT?" The Joint Special Weapons Committee did not really want to know and disseminated the document within the Department of National Defence (DND) and the armed forces. It is probable that the information in "Capabilities of Atomic Weapons" contributed to the FORWARD ON study and thus was part of the material sent to 25 CIB in Korea in 1953.[42]

As noted earlier, there is little doubt that Dr. Solandt, as Chairman of the DRB, used his extensive contacts in the United Kingdom and the United States to acquire nuclear weapons information. There is little documentary evidence of what exactly he did acquire, however:

> nearly all the [nuclear] information was very highly classified and some of it came to us quite informally and partly because many of the interchanges were so informal that they were never recorded. . . . I kept no personal diaries except in a very few special cases and deliberately did not record many discussions in which I was voluntarily given access to highly classified information that was theoretically unavailable to Canadians.[43]

Finally, DRB possessed another resource: Dr. Alex Longair. Joining DRB in 1952–1953, Longair was a British scientist who was a liaison officer to the British Joint Staff Mission, Washington. Solandt brought him on board because "he had a real gift for acquiring information and as a result DRB soon was very connected through a combination of the contacts that I had made and the much more extensive network that Alex had built up."[44] These contacts would prove their worth later in the 1950s, when Canada participated in American and British nuclear weapons trials.

Share and Share Alike?: The Information Sharing Agreements

The development of a formal Canadian-American information agreement in 1954 was an outgrowth of American overtures to meet the need for NATO members to adapt their forces. Generals Eisenhower and Ridgway, in their capacities as SACEUR, had in the past requested information on American nuclear capability dedicated to NATO so that the nuclear targeting staff in SHAPE, the Special Air Staff, could do its job. Some information, specifically the numbers and types of delivery systems, was communicated, but the actual characteristics of the weapons themselves were not. Notably, the Special Air Staff's targeting section, Group Able, included all Americans, so information could be released to them and then they would coordinate with the United Kingdom.[45]

Ridgway pushed for releasing more information to the NATO staffs and also wanted to establish courses so that NATO staff people could be trained in weapons effects, defensive measures, and weapon employment. Even though more information was released to SHAPE in 1953, it was not enough. The McMahon Act was far too restrictive, and there were limits to how far American commanders would go in using informal means.[46] SACLANT, Admiral Lynde McCormick, had gone as far as he thought he could. He recommended "at this time [1954] only certain selected United Kingdom and Canadian officers (attached to my staff, the principle SACLANT subordinate commanders and their planning staffs) be given access to info."[47] McCormick wanted a whole grab bag of information released, including the size, weight, and shape of those weapons already in the American stockpile; approximate yield options; fusing options and penetrating capabilities; nuclear safety procedures; damage parameters; and delivery capabilities, techniques, and accuracy.[48]

This information was remarkably similar to what SACEUR wanted for his staff,[49] and one wonders about the nature and extent of coordination between the two NATO commanders. In any event, this information would provide the form of the NATO-US information sharing agreement and the bilateral Canadian-American agreement in 1955.

Eisenhower was eventually able to convince American legislators to alter the terms of the McMahon Act. In 1954, Congress produced the Atomic Energy Act of 1954, with a special paragraph, 144b. This allowed for the establishment of multilateral (NATO) and bilateral (United States to specific nation) information sharing agreements to proceed on a case-by-case basis, as deemed necessary by the President of the United States.

The first formal agreement under the auspices of 144b, naturally, was the "Agreement Between the Parties to the North Atlantic Treaty for Co-operation

Regarding Atomic Information." Drafts were passed on to Pearson and Foulkes in December 1954 in time for the NATO Ministerial Meeting held at that time. Both concurred that this was a very positive step and that Canada would support it. The only dissenters were the Netherlands and Norway and then only because of their need to consult on matters of constitutionality with their governments. The Canadian Cabinet gave approval for External Affairs to sign the agreement in February 1955.[50]

The actual agreement adopted by NATO in December 1954 stated that the United States would provide information to NATO military and civilian leaders for the purposes of the development of defense plans; defensive training; enemy capabilities; and delivery system development.[51]

The agreement included a special annex, which basically reproduced the same list of information that SACLANT and SACEUR wanted so that they could conduct realistic planning. This annex also allowed for information exchange on the extent of interchangeability of nuclear weapons components, which weapons went on which delivery vehicles, and an estimation as to how the SAC air offensive would affect NATO planning.[52] It did not allow for the passage of nuclear weapons design or fabrication information. Both SACLANT and SACEUR established Atomic Warfare Indoctrination courses for their NATO staff officers so that they could put this information to use. SACEUR organized the NATO School at Oberammergau, West Germany, while SACLANT created a course for this purpose in Norfolk, Virginia. Canadian staff officers enrolled in courses at both locations.[53]

The bilateral Canadian-American agreement on the use of atomic energy for mutual defense purposes was put together between March and July 1955, more or less simultaneously with a similar Anglo-American bilateral agreement, both under the auspices of the 144b portion of the Atomic Energy Act.[54] Initial work on the agreement actually preceded the NATO agreement,[55] but the Americans wanted the NATO agreement to come first, probably so that other NATO allies would not be offended by preferential treatment of Canada by the United States. The original draft was prepared by the Canadian Department of National Defence and sent to the JCS for modification and comment. The JCS strongly supported it and even added an expanded annex.[56]

The American legislative bodies had to first be convinced that the agreements were actually needed so that they would not interfere with the signing of them.[57] The appropriate committees had been briefed on and accepted without debate the necessity of the NATO agreement. Could the NATO agreement not convey the information required to Canada and the United Kingdom?

The bilateral agreement with Canada was, in some respects, different from the NATO agreement. The defense relationship between Canada and the United States was unlike that with Europe as a whole, according to Deputy Assistant Secretary of State C. Burke Elbrick:

> You will recall that the United Kingdom and Canada are partners in the original development of nuclear weapons during the crucial period of the second world war [sic]. Indispensable supplies of uranium ore came from

Canada, while the United Kingdom contributed vital information and techniques. . . . As you are aware we have a network of indispensable arrangements with Canada by means which we hope to have warning of enemy attack hours earlier than if we were forced to depend on [our own facilities]. . . . In fact the military planners realize more and more that the defense of the United States and Canada is one inseparable problem and must be approached as a virtual unity.[58]

Vice-Admiral Arthur C. Davis, the Deputy Assistant Secretary of Defense (International Security Affairs), elaborated on the specific differences:

each agreement consists of three parts, an unclassified cover agreement, an annex classified as Secret which lists the types of atomic information to be exchanged subject to the limitations imposed by law, and a second annex, classified Confidential, containing the security arrangements [for the information itself]. . . . Both texts are identical. . . . [W]e visualize that these agreements will entail much more of a true *exchange* of information than was possible with NATO, they have been expanded to reflect a much greater degree of reciprocity. . . . It will also permit Canada and the United Kingdom with U.S. concurrence to discuss, with NATO, information made available to NATO by the United States. It will not permit Canada or the United Kingdom to exchange with each other information made available by the United States unless this is authorized by the United States and the same information has been made available to both countries.[59]

The primary document, "Agreement Between the Government of the United States of America and the Government of Canada for Cooperation Regarding Atomic Information for Mutual Defense Purposes," thus was structured for exchange, not just dissemination. The information to be released followed that of the NATO information requirements established by SACEUR and SACLANT.[60] The annex detailing what specific information was to be transferred remains classified today. It probably was similar to McCormick's 1954 list and probably did not include weapon design and fabrication information because of the 144b portion of the 1954 Atomic Energy Act, which forbade such disclosure. The annex originally contained exchange of information on military nuclear reactors as an item, since the United States planned to install nuclear reactors in the Arctic to power the DEW Line. This item was removed, as it was covered under a parallel civilian use agreement regarding reactor research. Further, this project was never fully implemented.[61] The Cabinet Defence Committee approved signature of the agreement and it was signed on 5 August 1955.[62]

In the Land Where the Giant Mushrooms Grow: Canada and Nuclear Weapons Tests

Under the terms of the new agreements, Canada asked for and received American test data from the SNAPPER, BUSTER, and JANGLE test series held in Nevada in 1951 and 1952. The BUSTER series consisted of five air-dropped weapons of varying yields up to 31 kt. JANGLE featured Shot UNCLE, a cratering demonstration with a 1.2 kt weapon, while SNAPPER dealt with more air-dropped weapons yielding 1 to 19 kt. The JSWPC was particularly interested in the effects of the weapons on animals, gamma radiation, thermal flash damage, and, in the case of JANGLE, nuclear cratering.[63]

Foulkes and Radford arranged for two groups of Canadians to travel to Nevada for Operation TEAPOT in 1955.[64] The first was an observer group that the JSWPC suggested should consist of "those senior personnel whose influence on Canadian developments is likely to be greatest."[65] Some of the Canadian observers were Commodore Ken Dyer, Commodore Herbert Rayner (later Chief of the Naval Staff), both of the RCN; Major General John Rockingham (formerly of 25 CIB in Korea and later 1st Canadian Infantry Division commander), Brigadier Geoffrey Walsh (formerly of 27 CIB in Germany and later CGS) both from the Army; and Air Commodore F. S. Carpenter of the RCAF.[66] The second group was 1 RDU, which, after training at Fort McClellan, Alabama, would deploy to Nevada for Exercise SAPLING, the Canadian code-name for 1 RDU operations during the TEAPOT series. General James M. Gavin, US Army Deputy Chief of Staff for Research and Development, informed the Canadian Joint Staff Mission Washington. 1 RDU was to observe Shot ZUCCHINI from trenches and then conduct a ground survey. The observer group would watch a Military Effects Test (MET) shot.[67]

Shot MET was a 500-foot tower detonation with an estimated yield of 22 kt. The observation party consisted of twelve British and twelve Canadian officers. They inadvertently observed Shot HA, which Canadian observers estimated was airburst at 40,000 feet (the actual height was 36,620 feet).[68] While waiting for Shot MET, the party also saw Shot POST (2 kt), which was set off to prove technical data. MET was fired on 15 April 1955 and yielded 22 kt. The observer party, with protective clothing, was allowed to look at the test equipment three hours after the detonation. Sampling drones had to be shot down for safety reasons while this was occurring. The party saw the effects of the weapon on a runway (the asphalt ignited); vehicles (badly damaged and thrown about); and trenches (which survived, as did vehicles behind berms). Walsh noted that "there is no doubt that with the proper use of ground and protective measures, the effects of such weapons can be considerably reduced. The impression gained was that the weapon will always be more effective against base installations and civil population than an army in the field."[69]

1 RDU, accompanied by LCol R. A. Klaehn, who would be instrumental in developing Canadian Army nuclear doctrine, participated in Shot APPLE TWO instead of ZUCCHINI. 1 RDU moved to trenches 3200 yards from ground zero on 5 May 1955. In this exercise, an American armored task force, Task Force RAZOR equipped with fifty-five M-48 tanks, moved to within 890 meters of ground zero eight minutes after detonation. The aim was to determine how well armored units could operate after a nuclear explosion: Could they exploit a gap created by a nuclear blast? APPLE TWO yielded 29 kt. 1 RDU assisted in predicting the contamination pattern and conducting the ground radiation survey after the blast with their specially equipped jeeps.[70]

Foulkes was also dealing with the British, gambling that if the Americans would not assent to Canadian participation in TEAPOT, the British might allow Canadians to come along in their next test. But the Americans did allow Canadians to go to Nevada, while the British program encountered delays in 1955, and their next test series was put off till 1956. Alex Longair acquired information regarding the forthcoming BUFFALO test series from British sources. With the latter indicating that the information was not to be transmitted to the Americans, Longair's material was forwarded to the JSWPC, which then directed that plans be drawn up for Canadian participation while others lobbied the British to allow Canadians to go to Australia. Foulkes received the "go" in April 1955: The bulk of 1 RDU, ten DRB scientists, nine staff officers, and two administrative staff for a total of fifty people were permitted to attend.[71]

There appears to have been no Canadian participation in Operation MOSAIC. This British test series was held in May–June 1956, four months before BUFFALO. MOSAIC consisted of two shots, G-1 (15 kt) and G-2 (98 kt),[72] both fired off at Monte Bello. These shots were instrumental in the development of the British hydrogen bomb program and perhaps the British were somewhat disinclined to allow "foreign" observers. Notably, Operation HOTSHOT FOXTROT occurred during G-1 and G-2. HMS *Diana*, a destroyer, sailed through a contaminated area to test passive shipboard NBCD measures. Britain did, however, pass on information regarding aircraft decontamination procedures.[73]

In a similar vein, Canada was not invited to Operation RED WING, an American test series conducted at Enewetak and Bikini between May and July 1956. RED WING was the fourth American hydrogen bomb test series, which included GREEN-HOUSE (1951), IVY (1952), and CASTLE (1954). RED WING tested advanced thermonuclear weapons designs that clearly were not for foreign eyes to see. There were seventeen shots, many of which had a megaton-range yield. Notably, Shot CHEROKEE was the first airdrop of an American thermonuclear weapon.[74] British observers and airborne sampling aircraft were allowed to participate in CASTLE, but there is no indication that specifics were directly passed on to Canada.[75]

In preparing the Canadian BUFFALO teams, the British Atomic Weapons Research Establishment forwarded many controlled documents to the JSWPC and DRB. Though the exact nature of the documents remains classified, JSWPC personnel were surprised at the depth of the information and implied that the British were being generous with Canada beyond the bounds of the information exchange agreements.[76] Foulkes, with AWRE scientist Sir William Penney's help, was even able to get a Canadian engineer officer appointed to the AWRE itself. Captain H. E. Rankin of 1 RDU functioned as the Canadian liaison officer to AWRE and was tasked with "keeping the Canadian agencies ... fully informed on UK plans, proposals, requirements, and decisions concerning, or of interest to [Canada]."[77] There was even an attempt by Canada to get Canadian scientists permanently employed at AWRE, but this was an absolute no-go.[78] The RCAF even wanted to bring an entire CF-100 interceptor, an Orenda jet engine, and a CF-100 prototype nose with a new fire control system. Unfortunately, the landing strip at the test site itself could not take the CF-100, so portions were crated and brought in piecemeal along with comparable British aircraft.[79]

The British wanted Canadian participation in BUFFALO kept secret and Canadian planners concurred. Eventually, the British downgraded the security classification of the extent of Commonwealth participation but would confirm that other nations were participating only if directly asked. Even the United States was not to be informed initially, but this changed when Penney did so in November 1955: "He did not invite the US to the trials. He did not mention Canadian participation [to the Americans]. He said that he hoped he would, for a change, have some information for the US as a result of these trials."[80] Inexplicably, AWRE sent three sealed envelopes to three Canadian DRB scientists, Drs. J. A. Carruthers, R. H. Johnston, and G. Luchak. These envelopes contained the estimated yields and types of weapons that were to be tested in the BUFFALO series. Longair apparently facilitated this, but for unknown reasons.[81]

The degree of trust is notable and in direct contrast to American behavior in the TEAPOT series. Circumstantial evidence suggests that Canadian scientists and military personnel were provided with actual weapons design data for the BUFFALO test weapons. Unlike previous British tests, BUFFALO dealt with working weapons as opposed to test devices. The elaborate security precautions were transmitted to Canada so that any documentation that Canada possessed or received would be handled properly. For example, the British top secret/guard level included the "specific nature and purpose of each weapon trial"; "design details of the weapons"; and "nuclear efficiency" (the physical process produced by the firing of the weapon). Secret/guard documents related to experimental weapons yields, the types and methods of radiation detection and trial recording equipment, and the height of the detonation towers.[82]

The BUFFALO force had 1350 men total, including a 250-man Commonwealth Indoctrination Force that was structured to act as a training cadre for Commonwealth armies.[83] The Canadian BUFFALO contingent consisted of eleven officers and a staff sergeant; 1 RDU (twenty Army, five RCAF); and twelve DRB scientists. These personnel were integrated into the British AWRE units at Maralinga. For example, there was a Target Response Group consisting of Ordnance, Explosive, Structures, Aircraft, Electronics, and Materials teams. There was a Decontamination Group, a Radiological Measurements Group, a Measurements Group (Gamma Survey), and a Health Physics Group. Arrangements were made to pass the final reports of these groups from AWRE to the DRB in Canada once the test series was concluded.[84]

The BUFFALO series consisted of four shots conducted between 22 September and 22 October 1956 at the Maralinga Atomic Weapons Test Range in southern Australia (Maralinga, in the Australian aboriginal language, means "field of thunder"). Shot ONE TREE was a tower detonation to test the 16 kt RED BEARD tactical nuclear bomb, which would later be employed on Canberra, Scimitar, and Buccaneer strike aircraft. MARCOO, fired during a rainstorm, was a ground burst BLUE DANUBE aerial bomb with a small 1.5 kt core, while KITE was the first airdrop of a BLUE DANUBE bomb by a Valiant strategic bomber. This was another low-yield version, topping out at 3 kt. The final test, BREAKAWAY, used a RED BEARD variant exploded from a 100-foot tower at midnight. Its yield was between

10 and 16 kt.[85] In effect, BUFFALO provided its observers with a cross section of British operational nuclear weapons capabilities.

1 RDU was not happy about how its personnel were used in preparing for the shots. There was no time for the highly trained men to consolidate what they learned while on the ground at Maralinga and many wound up doing menial labor in preparation for ONE TREE and MARCOO. It was during the final event, BREAKAWAY, that 1 RDU shined. The unit conducted a detailed ground radiological survey wearing protective gear and driving jeeps during the day and at night, possibly the first time this was ever done. The unit experienced a number of phenomena including partial communications blackouts. All 1 RDU vehicles were heavily contaminated, and personnel developed new methods to decontaminate them in the field. The 1 RDU after-action report noted that "the fall-out areas decayed very quickly and in about three or four days personnel could work in all areas except in the near vicinity of ground zero, in normal clothes, gloves, and rubber boots, carrying a respirator to be worn if winds created a dust hazard."[86] A second important exercise involving 1 RDU simulated a brigade advance with two Australian battalions up and 1 RDU conducting the radiological survey in front with reconnaissance troops. This exercise was conducted in an already contaminated area. 1 RDU was able to test all versions of the experimental Canadian RADIAC monitoring equipment, which would eventually be provided to almost all units, bases, ships, and aircraft in the Canadian armed forces. Many deficiencies in this equipment were noticed and corrected.[87]

RCAF personnel accompanied the British and Australian air survey teams and also assisted in aircraft decontamination procedures. An S-55 helicopter and a Varsity transport aircraft equipped with air sampling sensors flew weaving paths through the egg-shaped fallout pattern created by each of the four shots to determine the extent and flow of the radioactive material.[88]

There is no doubt that BUFFALO provided Canada with a unique opportunity to learn about nuclear warfare. On the whole, though, the British test program was hurried and austere, and the base was ramshackle in the extreme. In the final measure, the Commanding Officer of the Canadian contingent recommended "1 RDU should not return to Maralinga if similar opportunities exist for training and indoctrination at Las Vegas."[89]

While Canadian defense policy dictated that the Canadian armed forces learn as much about nuclear weapons as possible, the Department of External Affairs was deeply involved in fruitless international nuclear disarmament negotiations throughout the 1950s.[90] Normally this did not directly intrude on defense policy, but there was the possibility that a proposed atmospheric test ban treaty could prevent Canada from getting the information she needed to provide her part of the deterrent system. External Affairs was concerned and sought defense guidance on what Canada's requirements were so that negotiations would not interfere with information acquisition. The DRB informed External Affairs that Canadian military requirements for nuclear weapons included the need to "destroy a winged aircraft, manned or unmanned" with a relatively low yield weapon either to knock down the target or "render inoperative" the incoming nuclear weapon with radiation. ICBM interception would require a high-yield weapon: "It should not be assumed that these would be small weapons, it depends on what the weapon is required for." DRB was against any test or weapons ban that placed limits on yields.[91]

External Affairs also queried Foulkes on this issue. On October 1956 he replied:

> Inasmuch as the defense of the NATO Area is dependent on the use of atomic weapons, Canada should support the continuance of the minimum tests necessary to ensure that the use of these weapons will be effective. . . . the annual world limit for atomic test explosions would be acceptable provided any such limit meets the defence requirement of NATO without endangering public health throughout the world.[92]

The testing continued.

Canadians were extensively involved in the American test series Operation PLUMBBOB held at the Nevada testing grounds between May and October 1957 and in the British series Operation ANTLER at Maralinga in September and October.

In the case of PLUMBBOB, the COSC approved a triservice request for participation in an American test series in December 1956. Utilizing the bilateral agreement as a basis for the request, CJSM-W approached the US Armed Forces Special Weapons Project directly. Canada wanted to send 1 RDU to conduct ground surveys, RCAF and RCN teams to learn aircraft decontamination, and an infantry platoon to work with an American ground unit conducting operations. This would be the largest Canadian contingent involved in nuclear testing: 483 men. The AFSWP (Armed Forces Special Warfare Program) passed the request to General Gavin, who, along with the Department of Defense, approved it in March 1957.[93] The Department of Defense was enthusiastic, noting that Canadian participation "is desirable to the maximum extent possible."[94]

The AFSWP also invited Canada to send senior military observers to a planned Principal Military Effects Shot. Canada concurred. All three services sent general officers or commodores involved in the technical, doctrinal, and operational aspects of military planning and equipment acquisition. Some notable observers were Commodore A. H. G. Storrs (the Assistant Chief of the Naval Staff [Warfare]); Commodore H. L. Quinn (Chief of Staff, Atlantic Command); Major General George Kitching (Vice CGS); Brigadier C. B. Ware (Director of Military Training); Brigadier D. C. Cameron (Commander, 4 Canadian Infantry Brigade); Brigadier J. V. Allard (future Chief of the Defence Staff); Air Vice-Marshal Max Hendrick (Air Member for Technical Services and future commander of Air Defence Command); and Air Commodore G. G. Truscott (Chief of Armament Engineering and involved with making RCAF aircraft nuclear-capable).[95] All influenced Canadian armed forces nuclearization.

The USAF approached the RCAF and asked if the RCAF would like to observe the first live test of the MB-1 Genie. The RCAF, naturally, sent a special "Air-to-Air Shot VIP Group" specifically for Shot JOHN. Secretary of State Dulles even asked if External Affairs would like to send an observer as part of an international group separate from the military groups. Albert Edgar Ritchie, Canadian ambassador to the United States, was nominated.[96]

Canadian participation in PLUMBBOB was a tapestry of activity, with Army, RCAF, and RCN personnel involved with no less than ten separate shots out of the twenty-four total in the series. The Canadian Administrative Group (CAG) personnel apparently observed the odd shot beyond the ten, since they were on the ground all the time and had the opportunity to do so. There were, in effect, eleven different Canadian groups at PLUMBBOB: the CAG, 1 RDU, the VIP Group, the Air-to-Air Group, two RCAF and one RCN Working Parties, three triservice groups of observers (code-named BOBCAT I to III and consisting of Major to Lieutenant-Colonel equivalent grade officers, including many battalion and regimental commanders who eventually would command brigades in Europe or, in the case of J. A. Dextraze, become the Chief of Defence Staff), and 7 Platoon, 1st Battalion, Queen's Own Rifles of Canada (QOR of C), led by Lieutenant R. Bridgeman.[97]

PLUMBBOB had multiple objectives, some of which Canadian planners were not aware of from the outset. The American operations order, not released to the Canadian contingent, stated that the PLUMBBOB series was "designed to conduct experiments advancing technical understanding of nuclear and thermonuclear weapons, to test prototypes and develop further information on their military and civil effects."[98]

Most tests involving Canadian observers or the infantry platoon were either weapons effects tests like PRISCILLA or troop trials like SMOKY. HOOD, however, was billed as a "clean" bomb test to other international observer groups, that is, a weapon theoretically capable of producing less radioactive fallout than earlier designs. The Canadian VIP Group and the BOBCAT I observer group were completely unaware at the time that they witnessed the only thermonuclear detonation to occur inside the continental United States, and since Canadians had not been allowed to observe at CASTLE or RED WING, they could well have been the first Canadians ever to witness a thermonuclear shot.[99] Shot HOOD yielded 74 kt and was the largest atmospheric weapon test exploded in Nevada. HOOD was a prototype enhanced radiation device, or a "neutron bomb" as Canadian documents refer to it as early as 1961.[100] It released an "abnormal" amount of initial radiation, eventually inflicting long-term damage on some of the soldiers stationed at the three-mile mark (or closer) from ground zero.[101]

Albert Ritchie, the only Canadian diplomat present at PLUMBBOB, made some pertinent observations that are worth recounting here in detail. Ritchie observed Shot SMOKY, which, he was informed, would yield between 40 and 45 kt (it was actually 44 kt). In his secret after-action report to External Affairs (a report which was widely distributed within that organization), he provided a human account of what occurred:

As the count entered the last minute the excitement was high. It did not seem to matter much whether the observer was a military man, a foreign service officer or scientist. At least some of the suspense among the watching scientists when the first bomb was being tested at Alamagordo in 1945 was undoubtedly being experienced by those present on this occasion. As the count reached "...3...2...1..." and nothing but blackness could be

94

seen through the goggles which everyone was then wearing, not quite knowing what to expect or whether in fact anything would really happen . . .

And then at ". . . ZERO . . ." or ". . . NOW . . ." (I cannot recall for
certain which word was used), there was the most spectacular and brilliant
burst of flame imaginable which even the goggles could hardly dim. The
effect was greatly increased by the fact that simultaneously the whole hillside behind ground zero (which apparently was at a distance of a mile or
two on the other side of the bomb site . . .) caught fire. In those first few
seconds, one saw a massive ball of many coloured fire against the background of a flaming hillside. It would not be possible to say exactly what
colours were in the fireball, but the most striking was a bright mauve or
violet which seemed to be prominent around the outer edge of the ball at
one stage. All of this was the more impressive and the more eerie since it
was not accompanied by any sound at all. . . .

When about four seconds had passed, the colonel shouted that goggles
could be removed. I looked towards the ground before taking mine off, as
I wanted to get my eyes accustomed to the light before facing the brilliant
spectacle across the desert. Even at that distance I found that the sand
around my feet was glowing with a golden hue apparently more brightly
than in the middle of the day. Although by then the fireball had been trans-
formed into the beginnings of the usual mushroom-shaped cloud, the desert
was still covered by a bright light although the dawn had scarcely begun
to appear in the sky. The sagebrush and cactus on the distant mountainside
continued to burn.

It was weird to watch the illuminated smoke or vapour curling around
and literally sucking up the dust and debris from the earth. The mushroom
cloud when it was eventually formed reached high into the sky and one
could see an ice cap forming at the top. According to our Colonel the height
of the cloud when it reached mushroom form was about eight or nine miles
. . . shortly after the rockets had passed through the cloud it was possible to
see one or two aircraft skirting the top of the cloud and penetrating it slightly.

All of these things must have happened in the space of a minute or a
minute and a half since it is my recollection that they preceded the arrival at
our location of the shock and sound waves from the explosion . . . the
progress of the shock wave across the desert could be clearly seen. When it
reached us it seemed to take the form of a loud and deep noise accompanied by the sort of gust of wind that one experiences when standing behind
an aircraft as the propellers are started.[102]

Ritchie also speculated as to American motives for inviting an international
observer group: he thought that the real aim was to make an impression. The international observer group consisted of representatives from NATO, the Southeast Asia
Treaty Organization, the Central Treaty Organization, and the Inter-American Defense Board, people who "may have been so impressed by the spectacle that they
may have become all the more keen for their governments to acquire or develop

such an excellent device."[103] Perhaps the observers were supposed to come away with a positive impression that "smaller nuclear weapons are relatively harmless and controllable and therefore might be safely employed in certain situations."[104] This, Ritchie thought, was unlikely after SMOKY. With regards to Canadian participation vis-à-vis the international observers, Ritchie also noted that:

> There were some private comments on the fact that Canada seemed to have been especially favoured by being allowed to have troops participate in the project, and one or two observers thought it a little strange that their countries had not been offered the same facilities. More might have been heard of this alleged favouritism if there had not been a Canadian in the general group in the same position as other NATO observers. The apparently special position of Canada would then have been considerably more conspicuous.[105]

7 Platoon's experience is important since it was the only time that a Canadian combat unit was involved in the test series in the 1950s. 7 Platoon was incorporated into Task Force WARRIOR, which was the 1st Battle Group of the 12th Infantry Regiment, 4th Division stationed at Ft. Lewis, Washington. The 12th Infantry had been reorganized into one of the five battle groups in a Pentomic Division, part of the US Army reorganization for tactical nuclear warfare in 1956–57. With a Pathfinder team from the 82nd Airborne Division, two transport helicopter squadrons, the 1st Battle Group and 7 Platoon conducted airmobile and ground operations during shots STOLES, SHASTA, and SMOKY. Two Canadian exchange officers were with the helicopter units. During SMOKY, the Pathfinder unit was inserted about one hundred yards from ground zero, fifteen minutes after the detonation, followed by the airmobile force one hour later.[106]

The RCAF sent twenty high-ranking observers to Shot JOHN, the live MB-1 Genie test. Many were instrumental in RCAF nuclearization, like Air Marshal Roy Slemon (Chief of the Air Staff and later, Deputy CinCNORAD); AVM C. R. Dunlap (Vice Chief and later Chief of the Air Staff); Air Commodore Claire Annis; AVM L. E. Wray (Air Defence Command); and Air Commodore D. A. Bradshaw (a future commander of 1 Air Division).[107] The F-89 Scorpion piloted by Captain Eric Hutchison, USAF, fired the 2 kt rocket and conducted a back-flip escape maneuver seconds before the weapon exploded in mid-air. Two more F-89s penetrated the cloud after the weapon was detonated so that the effects on the crew and aircraft could be measured. Six volunteer CONAD officers then raised a sign scrawled "Ground Zero-Population 5" several thousand feet below on the ground.[108] One Canadian observer who looked directly at the blast saw spots for several days afterwards every time he closed his eyes.

Many PLUMBBOB tests were not open to foreign observers. These included the weapons safety tests Projects 57 and 58, COULOMB A and B, PASCAL A and B, and SATURN. The lack of Canadian scientific representation at the PLUMBBOB series compared to, say, the BUFFALO tests, indicates that Canadian access to weapons design information was minimal. PLUMBBOB was a "military show" from a

Canadian point of view. It certainly gave a wide variety of Canadian officers first-hand experience.

There is a possibility that at least two Canadian scientific observers were invited to the British GRAPPLE thermonuclear test series held between May and September 1957, but what they may have reported is unavailable.[109] The closest uniformed Canadians got to the new BLUE DANUBEs was when the test aircraft overflew Canada, something not recorded at the Cabinet level. Nine Valiants, twelve Canberras, and twenty-eight transports and three Shackleton MPAs staged through Goose Bay and Namao (Edmonton) headed to Malden Island in the Pacific. The aircraft spent thirty minutes on the ground at each site and five hours in transit, with practically no security precautions. The same operation was repeated in November for the GRAPPLE X shot. All four tests were thermonuclear weapons in BLUE DANUBE casings, dropped from operational Valiant bomber aircraft.[110]

As a consolation prize, the British invited Canadians to the SAPPHIRE (originally VOLCANO and later changed to ANTLER) test series in Australia in the fall of 1957. Canadian participation was comparatively small but included twelve DRB scientists, and two Army and three RCAF officers. The primary areas of interest were thermal and gamma measurements and decontamination techniques. The limited participation reflected a DRB-AWRE understanding that information collected and analyzed by AWRE would be made available to Canada through the normal channels.[111]

The objectives of Operation ANTLER included the development of "nuclear warheads, small in physical size and yield, for defensive use in surface-to-air guided weapons; to develop more efficient versions of the tactical aircraft bomb RED BEARD; and to increase scientific knowledge in order to produce smaller fission bombs as triggers for Megaton weapons."[112]

Once again, Maralinga was selected as the test site. There were three shots. The first, PIXIE, was a trigger for a thermonuclear bomb that had a yield of 1 kt. The second was a device called INDIGO HAMMER, which was designed for use in a surface-to-air missile (SAM) or as a thermonuclear weapon trigger. Fired from a tower, it yielded 6 kt. The finale, a balloon-suspended device, also a trigger, detonated at its expected 25 kt. Flying in S-55 Whirlwind helicopters, Canadian personnel assisted in the aerial survey portions of the tests.[113] In due course ANTLER test data was delivered to Canada and was distributed by the Joint Staff to its end users.[114]

ANTLER was not the last time Canadians would observe nuclear tests. General Charles Foulkes, the Chairman of the Canadian Chiefs of Staff Committee, would attend thermonuclear shots in the HARDTACK test series held at the Enewetok Proving Ground in 1958.[115] This, however, occurred after several developments and modifications to NATO strategy and information arrangements.

5

THERE WAS ONLY ONE CATCH:
DIEFENBAKER TAKES CONTROL, 1956–1957

"There was only one catch and that was Catch-22."
–JOSEPH HELLER, *CATCH-22*

"Why is it that the theoretical concept is not fulfilled in
practice? The barrier in question is the vast array of
factors, forces and conditions in national affairs that are
effected by war. No logical sequence could progress
through their innumerable twists and turns as though
it were a simple thread that linked two deductions.
Logic comes to a stop in this labyrinth; and those men
who habitually act, both in great and minor affairs, on
particular dominating impressions or feelings rather
than according to strict logic, are hardly aware of the
confused, inconsistent, and ambiguous situation in
which they find themselves."
–CLAUSEWITZ, *ON WAR*

Introduction

Canadian military nuclearization had taken a relatively linear path. The strategy
had been identified and accepted. Information on nuclear weapons effects and capabilities was acquired. The armed forces had studied this information and modified their doctrine to accommodate the new environment needed to operate on the
nuclear battlefield. The fourth step was, logically, to acquire nuclear weapons so
that those forces could be effective. The strategy itself was undergoing an evolution that would make the fourth part possible. Unfortunately the Liberal St. Laurent
government was unseated by the Progressive Conservative party led by John
Diefenbaker in 1957.

The change in government highlighted the problems of communicating national security policy from one government to another. What happens if a new government is not inclined to support the carefully constructed and expensive national
security policy, but at the same time has no alternative? This dilemma affected
Canada's efforts to develop the joint continental air defense command, NORAD:

this problem would have long term effects on Canada-US relations and on the defense of the strategic deterrent on which NATO as a whole relied. It also affected NATO's ability to implement its new strategy.

The North American Air Defense Command

The NORAD affair was the first of a series of problems in acquiring nuclear weapons for the Canadian forces. It set the tone in the relationship between the Canadian national security establishment and the Diefenbaker government. Since NORAD came about before and during the transition from the St. Laurent to the Diefenbaker government, it is necessary to have a clear understanding about what the NORAD problem was all about.

The NORAD affair has been examined and reexamined by many writers. The prevailing view is that an integrated Canadian-American air defense command for North America was an evil scheme concocted by the USAF and their Americanophile RCAF lapdogs (and subsequently promulgated by their lackey, Charles Foulkes), with the deliberate aims of subverting Canadian sovereignty and bringing Canada within the American economic orbit permanently. In this view, Foulkes bypassed the democratic process by pushing NORAD's acceptance by the new Diefenbaker government in the early and confused days of that government's tenure, without approval from the professional diplomats or the people of Canada.[1] Was this in fact the case?

An integrated North American air Defense system had been under development and was not some last-minute attempt by the military to manipulate the politicians. The RCAF Air Defence Command sent its first liaison officers to the USAF Air Defense Command in 1951 by the Military Cooperation Committee to coordinate the Basic Security Plan air defense annex. In 1953 the Joint Planning Committee concluded that some form of integrated Canadian-American air defense system was needed. In 1954, Air Vice-Marshal Slemon met with USAF Major General Chidlaw to draft a plan for a single commander of a projected North American air defense system. A joint RCAF-USAF air defense planning group met at CONAD headquarters in Colorado to coordinate planning and brainstorm integration.[2]

Roy Slemon believed that integration was necessary when he analyzed MC 48. At the same time, SAC reassessed its vulnerability and concluded that the air defense zone should be extended further north to provide better warning.[3] In February 1955, CONAD and RCAF Air Defence Command staffers briefed the Military Study Group on air defense problems. The combined RCAF-USAF team thought the "most effective organizational arrangement for air defense of North America was the integration of two air defense systems and the ultimate establishment of a combined command."[4] Slemon publicly stated that integration was "inevitable" and was subsequently dressed down by Ralph Campney. Campney did not, however, halt the RCAF-USAF talks. The proposal went to the US Joint Chiefs for consideration, who decided that it might not be acceptable to the Canadian government, given Campney's reaction. The Joint Chiefs conferred with the Canadian Chiefs, and the plan was sent to the Military Study Group (the Canadian Air Member at this point was Air Marshal C. R. Dunlap, later Chief of the Air Staff from 1962 to 1964) for deeper analysis, which took several months.[5]

By December 1956 the Military Study Group had tabled its air defense integration study. The members thought that a headquarters called ADCANUS (Air Defense, Canada-US) should be established in order to formalize the existing RCAF-USAF air defense commands' relationship. It should not necessarily be a command, but it should have operational control in wartime and develop plans and operating procedures in peacetime, much like a NATO command. ADCANUS should also be similar to a NATO headquarters in that the two air forces would retain command of their aircraft and missiles: they would conduct a transfer of authority in wartime, in the same way SACEUR and SACLANT handled their national forces in the transition from peace to war. ADCANUS would report to both the Canadian Chiefs and US Joint Chiefs.[6]

In January 1956, the Chiefs passed the plan to Campney and External Affairs for their views. After discussions with External Affairs, Campney directed Foulkes to clarify items of political interest with the US Joint Chiefs before bringing the paper to the Cabinet. These included: that the planning was capabilities planning and not requirements planning;[7] that there would be full Canadian participation in planning on a similar basis to that of NATO; that the commanders would report to the Chiefs of Staff of both countries; and that the deputy commander would be Canadian.[8]

Foulkes briefed the Chiefs, noting that:

these proposals will bring the control and planning functions of the air defence of North America into line with similar functions exercised in other NATO commands. The proposals will have the advantage of placing Canada in a position to take a more active part in air defence planning and to have greater control over planning at the staff level.[9]

The US Joint Chiefs approved the proposal in February 1957, while the Canadian Chiefs prepared to brief the Cabinet.[10]

Domestic factors revolving around the upcoming election prevented the proposal from reaching the Cabinet. As Foulkes recalled:

I prepared forty copies of the Cabinet defence paper which was approved by Campney and it went to Bryce [Secretary to the Cabinet] for distribution. . . . The Prime Minister called me in with Campney and it was a kind of conversation like this, "Well," he said to Campney, "we're coming back [after the election] aren't we and then we'll deal with this." And he said to me, "General is that going to upset you?" I said, "well, the only thing that worries me is that the [US JCS] have approved this and I am expecting any day to hear that the Secretary of Defense has approved it and it may be a bit difficult because as you know the [Americans] are not too good at keeping secrets." [St. Laurent] said "I don't feel like taking this on at the moment. Just hold your fire and wait until we come back."[11]

Foulkes amplified this statement, noting that "As Canada-United States relations could become a political issue, it was considered advisable not to have the paper approved until such time that it was not a political issue."[12] The Americans received the message loud and clear and deferred announcing the arrangement's existence for the time being.

The deferral went on for several months during the election campaign. Two days after the election, Foulkes sent a memo to the designated Minister of National Defence, Major General George R. Pearkes, VC. Pearkes had served in the Army during the First World War, receiving his Victoria Cross after being wounded leading his men during the Passchendaele offensive in 1917. Entering politics after the Second World War, he became the Conservative Party's defense critic in Parliament where, prior to Korea and the Canadian defense buildup, he attacked the King and later the St. Laurent government on its lackadaisical approach to defense policy. Later, a favored Pearkes target was 1 Air Division to Europe (he believed it should stay in Canada to provide air defense beyond the twelve squadrons already deployed). Pearkes and Foulkes knew each other intimately, as Foulkes had been a staff officer under Pearkes at the start of the Second World War.[13]

The situation reached a point where Foulkes told Pearkes:

> [It] might bring about quite a serious deterioration in Canada-US military relations and the matter may be given some publicity. It would further ap-pear difficult to expect another government to be able to deal with a com-plex military problem of this nature within a few days. It is therefore for consideration whether this matter could be approved subject to confirma-tion by the incoming government. It should be borne in mind that this pro-cedure would of course involve the incoming government in a joint press statement on a matter of policy to which it would only have a power of veto. On the other hand, to take no action would cause some doubts as to whether international agreements with Canada had continued validity.[14]

On 21 June, Pearkes became Minister of National Defence. Diefenbaker did not immediately appoint an External Affairs minister and thought that he, the Prime Minister, could fill both roles. Diefenbaker left abruptly for a Commonwealth con-ference, and Foulkes tried to see him before he flew off. Unable to do so, he passed the NORAD paper to Pearkes. When the delegation came home, Pearkes told Foulkes: "I talked it over with the P.M. and he thinks it's all right. You might well prepare whatever papers we need to get this thing discussed."[15] Foulkes talked to Bryce to arrange a Cabinet Defence Committee meeting to discuss it, but, after consulting Diefenbaker, Bryce told Foulkes: "There is going to be no committee." Diefenbaker told Bryce to tell Foulkes: "This government is going to take its own decisions and not on the prompting of these Liberal officials now."[16] In other words, Diefenbaker was not going to listen to the most experienced voice on defense issues in the gov-ernment because he was "tainted" by having too close contact with the policies of the previous Liberal government.

Foulkes recommended that Bryce get the Prime Minister to reconsider, since Parliament was due to open after the election and the Liberals, now led by Pearson would attack the new government on its apparent vacillation on defense policy and international treaties. Bryce did so and told Foulkes: "He'll have nothing to do with these advisors and he wants no meeting with advisors." Foulkes talked to Pearkes, who took the paper to Diefenbaker. He came back to Foulkes, threw it on the desk and said: "This is approved." Foulkes then inquired whether or not he could arrange a joint public release with the Americans.

The senior unelected official in External Affairs, Undersecretary of State Jules Leger, was on leave, and the third man in charge was out of the country dealing with the suicide of E. Herbert Norman, former Canadian ambassador to the Soviet Union.[17] The American ambassador to Canada called External Affairs to arrange the public announcement and got John Holmes, the acting undersecretary, on the phone. Holmes, who did not know about the past three years of work on NORAD panicked. He wondered where the agreement had come from. Eventually the proper arrangements for public release were made and NATO was secretly informed first. Pearkes and Charles E. Wilson, American Secretary of Defense, made the joint public announcement. NORAD was a bilateral arrangement, not a NATO one as later alleged, and basically followed the recommendations made in the ADCANUS proposal.[18]

In a curious twist, Diefenbaker met with US Secretary of State John Foster Dulles late in July 1957. Despite his private fulminations, the Prime Minister claimed that he had always been fully behind the idea of a Canada-US air defense command, since in his view "he had long been disturbed over the fact that Canada might have an inadequate or no voice at all in setting in motion actions which rendered war inevitable." There would be, he believed, "no time for either Congress or Parliament to act if the Soviets launched a surprise attack" and that "it was essential that there be a high-ranking [Canadian] officer in a senior position in the USAF headquarters where such a decision would presumably have to be reached."[19]

On 12 September 1957, NORAD was established at Ent AFB, Colorado. General Earle Partridge and Air Chief Marshal Roy Slemon were named as CinCNORAD and Deputy CinCNORAD, respectively. NORAD officially assumed operational control over all air defense forces in Canada and the United States. In peacetime, NORAD was responsible for "the development of plans and procedures to be used in war . . . [NORAD] will be responsible for the general pattern of training . . . in order to ensure the readiness of the forces and facilities in time of emergency."[20] In wartime, NORAD would be "responsible for the direction of air operations in accordance with the plans which have been agreed in peacetime."[21] Specific Terms of Reference were now needed for the commanders so that they could carry these responsibilities.[22]

Meanwhile, Diefenbaker appointed Sidney Smith as External Affairs minister. Formerly President of the University of Toronto, Smith had been a possible contender for the Conservative Party leadership, had impressive party credentials, but no foreign policy experience. He was apt to be "captured by the staff" at External Affairs, which in this case meant Jules Leger and Holmes. Smith, possibly acting on Holmes's recommendations, wondered why NORAD had not been handled the "proper way," that is, through a formal Exchange of Notes between governments and debate in the House of Commons. This was naive thinking to national security policy insiders. The St. Laurent government had made many defense arrangements without recourse to this formal method, like the 1951 Goose Bay SAC operations and storage agreement, and the 1956 MB-1 overflight agreement. Military command arrangements, including those within NATO, were not done in this formal fashion. Even though the commitment of forces to Europe was given Orders in Council, no Exchange of Notes existed between the United States and Canada or NATO and Canada promulgating the commitment of the Royal Canadian Navy to SACLANT. On the other hand, the St. Laurent government had followed the "proper way" in such matters as the Sound Surveillance System (SOSUS) for underwater listening and DEW Line systems established on Canadian soil. The reality of the situation was that, despite procedural bickering, NORAD formalized and fine-tuned an already existing close liaison between the RCAF Air Defence Command and the American continental defense commands. The only difference, which rapidly grew into a big difference, was that the commander wore an American uniform and the Deputy wore a Canadian uniform.[23]

External Affairs had been involved at every step of the way. It had representation on the Military Study Group, for example, and the Permanent Joint Board, the Military Cooperation Committee, as well as the Chiefs of Staff Committee. Foulkes liaised with Pearson frequently. How could Holmes say that External did not know what was going on over the past three years?[24]

When Leger returned, he and Smith learned that the Chiefs were examining the Terms of Reference for the NORAD commanders. If, Foulkes told Leger, they were to sort out the terms of reference, any exchange of notes had to be written in broad terms so that the Chiefs would have room to maneuver with the Americans. Smith wanted the issue handled by an interparliamentary Canada-US group, clearly a cumbersome undertaking. These developments occurred simultaneously with the Opposition attack on NORAD in the House of Commons. A full-blown "NORAD Treaty" would not be signed until 1958.[25]

Diefenbaker brought on the NORAD problem and he should have taken responsibility for it. His was the ultimate authority, and he was responsible for his subordinate's actions. He did not have to approve the August announcement, and he was given an opportunity to prevent it. He chose not to. He also chose not to pursue a detailed examination of the problem early on in his tenure as Prime Minister; he sloughed it off on a new and untrained subordinate. Perhaps Foulkes acted hastily in the matter, but Diefenbaker's brush-off was not called for. External Affairs was well aware of NORAD's development, so Foulkes was not pulling the wool over their eyes. Pearkes did not believe that he had been manipulated by Foulkes; he thought there was legitimate pressure from the Americans because they wanted the system up and running as soon as possible for operational/vulnerability reasons.[26] In sum, the negative attitudes generated among the protagonists were a portent of the future when the Canadian forces moved to acquire nuclear weapons.

The Diefenbaker Government:
Altering the Defense Policy Process

John G. Diefenbaker, a lawyer from Saskatchewan and a staunch monarchist, became a Member of Parliament in the 1940s. Diefenbaker was the Conservative Party's foreign affairs critic in Parliament and continually took shots at the St. Laurent government, particularly its financial and military "complicity" with the United States (American corporate investment in Canada had dramatically increased in the 1950s, as had cultural penetration). He was particularly vociferous after the 1956 Suez Crisis, slamming Pearson for abandoning and then backstabbing the British, and for allowing Nasser to dictate the terms of the United Nations deployment.[27]

John Diefenbaker was the antithesis of Louis St. Laurent. "Uncle Louie" was Catholic, French-Canadian, and dignified. "Dief the Chief" was Protestant, a Westerner, and histrionic (prompting the alternative nickname, "Dief the Actor"). A charismatic orator, Diefenbaker would appeal directly to the average Canadian's ingrained emotional distrust of the United States, a distrust that was aggravated by American investment in Canada and the proliferation of American bases and military forces operating from Canadian soil. St. Laurent could not counter this approach with cool rationalism.

There are two schools of thought on why the Liberals lost the 1957 election to Diefenbaker. One perspective argues that the Liberals were overconfident (they had been in power since 1935) and "afflicted with incurable arrogance, hubris, the quality of blind conceit that invites divine retribution" and lost the election.[28] An alternative position is that "the electorate got bored."[29]

St. Laurent's policy style relied on delegating tasks to a network of extremely competent and dedicated defense and foreign policy professionals, both elected and unelected. As with personality, Diefenbaker was St. Laurent's antithesis when it came to policy formulation and execution. Personality, more than any other factor, directly affected the course of Canadian strategic policy from 1957 to 1963.

Diefenbaker did not like the committee decision-making process. Consequently, there were fewer Cabinet Defence Committee meetings.[30] Under St. Laurent, the procedure involved a presentation by Foulkes, and then the Cabinet questioned him. Either they would accept the paper under discussion, or reject it and study it further. Under Diefenbaker, meetings were generally held only when complex issues were under discussion, and then their manner was not conducive to making a timely and wise decision. General Foulkes remarked:

> when Diefenbaker had a cabinet defence committee, it was against his better judgment . . . he wouldn't allow anybody to even explain the paper. He just came in like a prosecutor at court and went around the table and questioned people in the most objectionable manner. Whether he knew what was actually in the paper I never knew because he would never give anybody a chance to discuss [it].[31]

Even Air Chief Marshal Miller, who had a "quiet and retiring personality,"[32] had problems with Diefenbaker:

> Diefenbaker thought that all of the Chiefs of Staff were either Liberals, Liberal supporters, or Liberal sympathizers . . . whether they were Liberals or whether they were just experts in their fields that he was not too sure

about himself, and therefore had to be at the mercy of the experts and there-fore distrusted them or not, I don't know. I think there was quite a deal of both of it because Mr. Diefenbaker [was] not a man who trusts experts of any colour in fields that he himself [did] not know much about.[33]

Another factor in the friction between Diefenbaker and the military leadership was his war record. Diefenbaker had served in the First World War, not dishonor-ably by any stretch of the imagination. He had, however, apparently been compelled to enlist after he had tried various excuses for not participating. He was afraid, as most politicians are, that there would be long-term ramifications in the media if this were known and he always thought that some general would call up his service record and use it against him for political purposes.[34]

Diefenbaker also had problems dealing with other senior NATO leaders. Dur-ing the 1958 NATO Ministerial Meeting in Paris, Diefenbaker thought that he had been left off the seating plan. He told Foulkes to take him home because he did not want to be in a place where he was not invited (there was no seating plan for the head table, as a senior External Affairs official discovered). After dinner Foulkes then

found him standing in the corner all by himself and I said to him, "Now, Mr. Prime Minister, you seem to be alone. Now, I know all these NATO people because I have been in NATO for twelve years. Is there any one you'd like to meet? I know all these other politicians." "I don't want to meet anybody," he said, "first of all they sat me in a draught, then they sat me between a Pole . . . "I said "A Pole? There are no Poles here." "Well, they sat me between two people who couldn't speak English. I want to go home. Take me home." So I put him in my car . . . he said to me, "You know, you're the first general I ever wanted to speak to . . . I don't like generals." And I said, "what do you mean? Just as a group?" He said, "I don't like them. I don't like their thinking or anything else."[35]

Diefenbaker's behavior during the NATO meeting was worse. Leger was scared to death of the Prime Minister and didn't control his superior effectively. During a speech-making session, Diefenbaker suddenly demanded that Leger go "get Spaak" (NATO Secretary General Paul Henri Spaak) and inform him that he wanted to speak next. Spaak stood up and announced that, after the next three delegates were done (since they were scheduled first) "Mr. Diefenbawker" of Canada would speak next. This mispronouncement of Diefenbaker's name (it would also cause problems with Diefenbaker's relationship with John F. Kennedy later on) made Diefenbaker furious for the rest of the morning, and he wanted to leave as soon as possible. Without consulting his External Affairs briefs on the matter at hand, Diefenbaker voted for the NATO decision that was under discussion. This was the meeting in which NATO heads of government formally decided to accept nuclear weapons into their force structures and accept the NATO stockpile plan. The matter under discus-sion was the acceptance of the nuclear strike role for the RCAF's 1 Air Division.[36]

George Pearkes was Minister of National Defence. Pearkes has historically been portrayed as being afflicted with various degrees of senility (he was slow on the uptake in Parliament and his reasoning sometimes appeared convoluted).[37] This was probably not the case as anybody could easily become mentally and physically exhausted working for Diefenbaker. Some have charged that Pearkes was Foulkes's puppet, but this is also unfair. The two men had known each other for years, and Foulkes was somewhat deferential to Pearkes because of his rank and Victoria Cross. That said, Foulkes did wield a lot of influence with Pearkes, who consulted him on a daily basis.[38] If Pearkes was a Foulkes puppet, it was because he chose to be. Even though Pearkes was a general, Diefenbaker trusted him at times, probably because of his record as a defense policy critic.[39]

Pearkes did not think Diefenbaker's approach to defense policy "functioned very well."[40] Diefenbaker would "rather hear my opinion in his office rather than have one of the Chiefs express an opinion in a committee."[41] Pearkes generally thought that Campney and Foulkes had handled defense matters well during the previous government and did not seek radical change.

Diefenbaker viewed External Affairs with some suspicion. They had too many "Pearsonalities," in his view, and he was overly concerned about "the Pearson Cult in External."[42] Diefenbaker despised Norman Robertson, a Pearson contemporary who had served as Canada's High Commissioner in London during the Suez Crisis, as Canadian ambassador to the United States (1957–58), and as Undersecretary of State for External Affairs (the senior unelected official in the department 1958–1962).[43] US Ambassador Livingston Merchant noted "Norman Robertson's influence with his Minister [Howard Green] is almost negligible. It seems to me that he realizes this and while not exactly lethargic he certainly gives the impression of non-involvement in the big issues."[44] This state of affairs would change.

Diefenbaker preferred to deal with Basil Robinson, a diplomat who was appointed to a newly created position, "External Affairs liaison officer to the Prime Minister's Office." Robinson had been attached temporarily to the PMO when Diefenbaker was his own Secretary of State for External Affairs[45] and then kept on, probably because "the job had been set up so that the Prime Minister could avoid having to deal with Norman Robertson, whom he thoroughly dislikes."[46]

In terms of policy process, Jack Granatstein wrote that:

> Memoranda and papers from [External Affairs] came up through the Under Secretary [Robertson] to the Minister [Smith or Green]. . . . Most decisions were made by the Minister. But many had to go to the Prime Minister and these papers came into Robinson's hands. At his own insistence, Robinson dealt directly with Diefenbaker on these important or delicate questions. . . . The Prime Minister liked to give immediate answers and oral responses were the norm, something that required Robinson to make very sure he got the matter straight. . . . If possible, he talked over the subject with Robertson first. . . . There was unlimited room for misunderstanding here.[47]

The special Canadian-American exchange groups like the Military Study Group and the Canada-US Scientific Advisory Team fell into disuse (mostly due to the creation of NORAD) and were eventually disbanded between 1959 and 1961. The Permanent Joint Board and the Military Cooperation Committee remained in existence, but they became less influential under Diefenbaker. He preferred annual summit meetings with Eisenhower, of which there were two: Camp David in 1959 and Montebello in 1960.[48]

If continental matters of an urgent nature arose, the Canada-US Ministerial Committee on Joint Defense could handle them. Established on an ad hoc basis in 1958 after Eisenhower's visit to Canada, the Ministerial Committee consisted of the Secretary of State for External Affairs, Minister of National Defence, and the Minister of Finance. The American side included the Secretary of State, Secretary of Defense, and Secretary of the Treasury. The meetings alternated between the capitals, with the chairmanship going to the host. The PJBD and MCC now took their marching orders from the deliberations of the Ministerial Committee; they would theoretically investigate continental defense matters and monitor their implementation. The difference between the Ministerial Committee and the Permanent Joint Board "was one of status" (since the former included ministers, not civil servants).[49] The division of labor gave nuclear weapons issues, continental air defense issues, NATO long-range studies, and defense production sharing to the Ministerial Committee, while more mundane issues like employee benefits, disposal of surplus property, and the St. Lawrence Seaway were relegated to the Permanent Joint Board.[50] In effect, the Ministerial Committee was designed not only to limit contact between the Canadian and American militaries and foreign services, but to prevent them from implementing policy without ministerial oversight.

What of Diefenbaker's foreign policy priorities? Basil Robinson noted that Diefenbaker's "fear of Soviet power and of the potential spread of communism in Europe and the nonaligned regions of the world was coupled with an emotional commitment to "freedom," as exemplified by the Western democratic nations. He was thus a ready supporter of Canadian partnership in the NATO alliance."[51]

A monarchist, Diefenbaker thought Pearson had done the British wrong over Suez and wanted to "repair the relationship with London" and "enhance Canada's standing in the Commonwealth." Robinson asserted that Diefenbaker wanted to use the Commonwealth as a counterweight to American influence, but did not get into the specifics of such maneuvering. Essentially, Diefenbaker pandered to the so-called emerging nations through the Commonwealth medium. He was not overly impressed with the United Nations as a vehicle for change and initially viewed disarmament efforts as part of Cold War propaganda war, not as serious policy. The factor that overshadowed all aspects of Diefenbaker's foreign policy was his opposition to the St. Laurent government's trade policy with the Americans, which he viewed as extremely damaging to Canadian pride.[52]

Given the chaotic state of the Canadian national security policy formulation process under the Diefenbaker government, it is not surprising that those who understood strategic policy developed ways to maintain the complicated balance of NATO strategy, Canadian strategy, technological change, and force development. The awkwardly named body known as the Panel on the Economic Aspects of Defence Questions coordinated the financial aspects of the Canadian Mutual

Assistance Plan to NATO and the implications of NATO policy on force structure and Canadian financial policy.[53]

After the 1952 Lisbon meeting, NATO set up an annual review process by which (ideally) NATO commanders would assess what forces members had pledged to the commands and recommend changes. Members were not obligated to make those changes, but many took the annual review process as high-level informed advice, and did so. In Canada's case, SACEUR and SACLANT were consistently pleased with Canada's contribution and the process did not dramatically affect the course of Canadian policy prior to 1957–1958. The impact of the annual review process at the Cabinet level was minimal, because the issues were discussed in the Panel and the response was coordinated there before being folded into other policy decisions and then going to the Cabinet.[54]

The importance of the annual review to Canada increased significantly in 1957–58, because the new review involved MC 70, the plan to integrate nuclear weapons into NATO forces. Thus, with the inconsistent Cabinet Defence Committee meetings and the Diefenbaker style, the importance of the Panel in determining Canada's NATO policy, and thus Canadian strategic policy, increased.[55]

The structure of the Panel remained relatively consistent. It included Foulkes, Miller (Deputy Minister of National Defence and later Chief of the Defence Staff), Bryce (still the Clerk of the Privy Council Office), Zimmerman (who replaced Solandt as Chairman of the DRB); A. F. W. Plumtre (Deputy Minister of Finance); Robertson (or other External Affairs people like George Ignatieff, if the Undersecretary was away), and a member from the Bank of Canada (usually Louis Rasminski, the Deputy Governor).[56]

On the Allied front, NATO personalities were already well known to Foulkes. He had a long-standing relationship with Lauris Norstad, who became SACEUR in November 1956. Jerauld Wright, who had been SACLANT since 1954, was also a known quantity. Admiral Radford, the helpful US Joint Chiefs Chairman, was replaced by an equally helpful General Nathan F. Twining, USAF, in the summer of 1957.

The make up of the Chiefs changed by 1958. Admiral De Wolfe remained Chief of the Naval Staff until 1960, but Air Marshal Slemon moved on to become the Deputy CinCNORAD in Colorado. He was replaced with Air Marshal Hugh Campbell. The hard-working and capable Campbell was the Director of the Air Staff in London during the Second World War. While getting operational experience in the Middle East, Campbell's jeep ran over a mine, and he was sent back to Canada for convalescence, eventually becoming the Air Member for Personnel from 1945 to 1947. Campbell was a champion of Canadianization during the Second World War. Campbell pushed for better aircraft and Canadian command autonomy from the RAF leadership.[57] He was the Chairman of the Canadian Joint Staff Washington from 1949 to 1951, and then commanded 1 Air Division in Europe under Eisenhower.[58] He was then appointed Deputy Chief of Staff for Operations in SHAPE.[59] In other words, he had significant NATO connections and an understanding of what was going on in Europe. He was inclined to deal more with the Americans than, say, with the British.

Lieutenant General S. F. "Fin" Clark replaced Howard Graham as Chief of the General Staff in 1958. Clark, a Royal Canadian Signal Corps officer, had been Guy Simonds's Chief Signals Officer in II Canadian Corps in Northwest Europe during the Second World War.[60] Clark was a "perfectionist" who was also "energetic and innovative."[61] Clark had been Chairman of the Canadian Joint Staff in London and commanded Central Command in Ontario from 1956 to 1958 before assuming his duties as CGS.[62] Given his background in the Signal Corps, he was the man for carrying out Diefenbaker-era projects involving continuity of government bunkers (Project BRIDGE) and the reorganization of the Militia into a civil defense role. His experience in London and his wartime relationship with the Canadian National Military representative at SHAPE, General George Kitching, ensured that the brigade group in Germany was taken care of.

An ongoing Defence Research Board–RCAF squabble over information access produced continuing problems within DRB. Solandt's replacement, A. H. Zimmerman, was friendly and personable but he was not trusted by his staff. One member even wrote to Diefenbaker anonymously:

> although we are a body of expert scientists, we have as our leader and mouthpiece a man who is not a scientist and who is unable to give Science a proper influence on military judgement. . . . [Zimmerman] is a mining engineer, his doctor degree is only an honourary one, and his acquaintence with defence research before 1956 was due only to his being Mr. C. D. Howe's [Department of Defence Production] personal representative on the DRB. . . . We admire him as a man but we do not respect him as a scientist and we know that he does not speak up for our scientific conclusions in the Chiefs of Staff Committee.[63]

Such a letter would only have fuelled Diefenbaker's suspicions of the Chiefs and its advice on defense matters.

The lack of existing bipartisan defense policy-making mechanisms in the Canadian governmental structure during the 1950s produced some amount of suspicion on John Diefenbaker's part while he was in opposition to the St. Laurent government. In Canada the Opposition was frozen out of the process, unlike in the UK where the Opposition maintains a shadow Cabinet whose members are provided with classified briefings on relevant defense and foreign policy issues (Churchill's Cabinet even included some Opposition members during the Second World War). A combination of media-driven anxiety and the realities of nuclear war, mixed with the lack of detailed information emanating from the government (because of the secrecy provisions on intelligence and planning) probably were significant factors in the chasm of trust between Diefenbaker and the professional advisors in Defence and External. That relationship was about to be tested in the NATO forum.

MC 70, Minimum Force Requirements, and the NATO Nuclear Stockpile Question 1957–1958

Once the North Atlantic Council accepted MC 48/2 as a basis for planning, SHAPE and SACLANT planning staffs developed studies to incorporate nuclear weapons into NATO's forces. At the same time, the Americans informally passed on to External Affairs information that their nuclear weapons sharing policy would change. These weapons would be held in American custody and released to NATO members in an emergency. The Chiefs then reassessed service policy regarding nuclear weapons, Canadian strategy, and future Canadian force structure in March 1957.

On the air defense side, the RCAF was still trying to decide which weapon it would get for its interceptor aircraft: MB-1 or Sparrow. It was convinced that BOMARC was still essential to the air defense system. In Europe, it expressed interest in equipping 1 Air Division with atomic bombs if they became available, but thought that SHAPE should be approached first before establishing a definite requirement. The Canadian Army initiated an informal exchange program with the US Army. Canadian officers attended courses at the US Army Artillery School since it was interested in two weapons: the Honest John free-flight rocket and the Lacrosse guided missile. The RCN was keen to get Tartar surface-to-air missiles, nuclear torpedoes, and nuclear depth bombs. The Chiefs concluded that the systems desired by the Canadian forces were still under development and that they would wait until they were available in American service before making specific recommendations.[64]

In April 1957, the Americans informed NATO that several nuclear weapons systems would be made available to members: Honest John, the Matador long-range cruise missile; and the Nike surface-to-air missile. Nuclear warhead availability would be subject to changes in American law. This reflected a shift in American policy prompted by NATO's acceptance of nuclear deterrence in the 1954 and 1956 strategy discussions.[65]

By May 1957, however, SHAPE examined the 1957 annual review chapter on Canada and produced a paper on force goals that recommended, in part, changes to the Canadian forces committed to Europe. SHAPE wanted Canada to acquire Honest John for the Canadian division, and replace four of the twelve fighter squadrons with three squadrons of attack bombers and a strike bomber squadron, all equipped with F-100s. After some study, the Army had changed its mind and thought that it should have Lacrosse and Little John (an airportable version of the Honest John). SHAPE was going for standardization in the Central Region and was going with proven technology (the Americans had deployed Honest John in 1954, and the other two systems were under development). With regard to 1 Air Division, SHAPE backtracked. It wanted to reduce the number of conventional squadrons stationed in Europe and replace them with missiles. Slemon told the Chiefs that, in a pinch, he could reequip four squadrons of CF-86s with the appropriate bomb racks for the bomber/strike role, but if they took this on, it would be better to get new aircraft.[66]

The Chiefs also reassessed the two-phase war concept. They were concerned about cost as Diefenbaker was looking for cuts to pay for election promises. If new weapons were introduced, something had to be reduced. The Chief of the Naval Staff and Chief of the General Staff were adamant that their services required flexible forces that could handle conflicts short of nuclear war. Foulkes was concerned about not having the strategic lift to get the rest of the division to Germany in Phase I. Could the two brigade groups be converted to airportable brigade groups and money saved? Jules Leger from External Affairs remarked, "Any change in the allocation of the balance of the division to NATO might result in the unfortunate conclusion amongst European countries that Canada was reducing her NATO commitments."[67] Thinking then shifted to the Mobile Striking Force. The need to reduce enemy lodgments in North America was declining. Perhaps this issue should be reviewed. In fact, the whole concept of reserve forces should be reviewed to see what savings could be made. This would be a tough call, and it was deferred until General Norstad could sort out how he saw things shaping up in Europe.

Foulkes was curious about what SHAPE was up to: his interest was piqued by SHAPE's response to the Chief's musings. While preparing for the July 1957 Military Committee meeting, he spoke with General C. V. R. Schuyler, the SHAPE Chief of Staff. Through this point of contact, Foulkes acquired a draft of the SHAPE paper that was the basis of the MC 70 nuclear structure plan. He was able to leverage this from the review team, arguing that the recent election had caused confusion in defense policy and the Canadian Chiefs had to be prepared to answer questions on future thinking.[68]

The SHAPE review team was obliging and passed on their views on the future pattern of forces for 1960–62 in the Central Region. SHAPE wanted to retain the brigade group in Europe, but also wanted the Canadian Army to provide an Honest John battalion. SHAPE had planned for twenty-five non-US "Atomic Support Units" for the Central Region: Belgium and the Netherlands each were to provide two; France and the UK four each, and Germany twelve. In terms of corporal surface-to-surface missiles, the UK would provide two battalions, the Germans three, and the French one. Canada was not expected to contribute to the twenty-five-planned Nike missile battalions in the Central Region.[69]

On the air side, the SHAPE review team based its assumptions on SACEUR guidance which stated that:

> *all* NATO (ACE) strike and attack aircraft will have the capability of nuclear weapon delivery and that the . . . aircraft will, if possible, have an atomic delivery capability in addition to its ability to deliver conventional weapons. . . . All atomic strike and atomic-capable aircraft will be modern all-weather equipment and will wherever possible contain instrument bombing equipment which does not rely on external bombing aids.[70]

The SHAPE recommendation that caused Foulkes consternation involved the definition of roles. SHAPE wanted four day fighter, four all-weather fighter, three attack, and one strike squadrons. Strike aircraft were strictly nuclear delivery aircraft, while attack aircraft were to be nuclear-capable, but would have as their primary role "diversionary attacks against radar sites and other ground targets which can be destroyed with non-nuclear weapons." They were to be able to handle the nuclear role if necessary. If adopted, the SHAPE recommendation would "permit" Canada to provide 30 of 657 Strike aircraft and 28 of 583 attack aircraft that SHAPE needed to carry out its operations in the Central Region.[71]

Foulkes balked. The Chiefs did not want to introduce two new aircraft types in Europe in addition to the CF-86 and CF-100. The program support for two additional aircraft projects would be staggering, particularly if Canada would be providing only sixty aircraft. Canada had agreed to the NATO collective force concept. Expecting Canada to provide balanced forces would increase costs astronomically. It might even force Canada to accept mutual aid from the Americans, something Canada had not done so far, and was not palatable in the new political environment.

SACLANT, Admiral Jerauld Wright, also passed on his review team's thinking. He was impressed with the RCN and RCAF's existing contribution, but he wanted a second Canadian aircraft carrier, in addition to the already-programmed eighteen *Restigouche*-class escorts and thirty Argus maritime patrol aircraft.[72]

Foulkes was not happy with this state of affairs. SHAPE, SACLANT, and the Chiefs wrangled the entire summer of 1957 over force requirements: who was allowed to generate them, and who could impose them. Foulkes informed Jules Leger in a letter:

> I have now been advised that SHAPE considers MC 70 as a minimum force requirement study; for example, the strike role for air forces in particular has been allocated to all countries without previous discussion with these countries, and SHAPE is unwilling to delete from MC 70 the force tabs which have been defined for Canada since this would give rise to speculative discussion on the part of other countries. Further, they did not feel that SHAPE could be told by any country what that country's proposed force contributions in this particular plan should be. . . . These recommendations would cause serious embarrassment to the Government as financial and economic considerations may cause the Government to refuse to accept [them]. . . . This raises again the serious and dangerous procedure of allowing the Supreme Commanders or the Standing Group to state that the contribution that should be required by each country.[73]

In other words, Canada had to have the right to negotiate what it would provide NATO, not have its contribution imposed by SHAPE. There had to be give and take. To be fair, SHAPE was under a lot of pressure to provide some form of force structure that was both militarily viable and politically feasible. The acceptance procedure for NATO papers was slow and subject to the impact of national proclivities.

External Affairs emphatically agreed. Foulkes was able to get Norstad to withdraw the unacceptable portions of the Canada chapters. Due to some bureaucratic glitch, the original requirements made their way back into a paper that was being passed around NATO relating to MC 70, and passed around, incidentally, by Canada's NATO delegation. Foulkes was furious and had to start all over again.[74]

There was serious confusion regarding the relationship between the annual review process and MC 70. Some SHAPE planners thought they were the same thing, while others understood MC 70 to be an exercise to demonstrate to the council how a deterrent force in Europe *might* be put together, that is, demonstrate that it was possible and generally what it *might* consist of.[75] There was a possibility that the MC 70 problem was similar to the Regional Planning Group problem that produced Canada's land force commitment to Europe in 1951. Foulkes was not going to allow that one to happen again, and he saw the MC 70 process producing the same problem with 1 Air Division and the strike/attack role.[76]

In addition, the information flow problem on new nuclear weapons and delivery systems posed problems in the MC 70 process.[77] NATO confusion over basic defense issues during a period of acute anxiety (Sputnik was launched while all of this was happening) spurred SACEUR to solve the problem quickly.[78] Foulkes once again had to approach Norstad to sort out Canadian issues, and as a result, Norstad was somewhat indebted to Foulkes for heading off a diplomatic crisis that had in turn been initiated by the Canadian NATO delegation in Paris.[79] Getting fifteen nations to agree to a radical force structure plan was, of course, not an easy prospect, and doubts from one nation tended to spread to others rapidly like wildfire.

Diefenbaker then wanted a defense policy review so that he could be "brought up to speed" with an eye towards affecting "economies" in defense expenditures. Pearkes conducted the briefing in September 1957. Canada's aim was to provide a collective deterrent to aggression by providing certain forces to NATO. These forces were not balanced forces, since that would cost too much money. Rather, they were critical components of the collective deterrent system. The mainspring of the deterrent effort was the nuclear bombers from SAC and UK Bomber Command, protected by the air defense system in North America. Shield forces in Europe ensured the security of the NATO area there.[80]

Pearkes explained the MC 14/2 (revised) concept to Diefenbaker, emphasizing the two-phase concept of war. War would come with little or no warning, forces had to be ready in peacetime, and more thought had to be given to providing continuity of government and national survival. Canada was expected to contribute to the "containment and liquidation of such Soviet forces as were on NATO territory."[81]

Pearkes expressed doubts as to whether Canada could continue to meet its existing commitments and acquire nuclear weapons and delivery systems to upgrade those commitments. SACEUR had made recommendations and had been told that they were unacceptable. Therefore, the Minister of National Defence suggested areas in which economies could be made.[82]

First, the RCAF's auxiliary squadrons could be deleted, as could some naval reserve divisions. The entire militia was costing too much and should be altered. The CF-100/Sparrow version could be canceled. Finally, the Avro Arrow program could also be reviewed, but "any delay in reaching a decision would mean added costs . . . the US and the UK had urged Canada to proceed with this programme."[83] Diefenbaker took note of the briefing, with little comment.[84]

The Chiefs received the MC 70 draft in October 1957.[85] MC 70, "The Minimum Essential NATO Force Requirements 1958–1963," consisted of several parts. There was an analysis of the military situation from both SACEUR's and SACLANT's points of view. Another consisted of a discussion of the need to adapt new weapons into NATO's force structure, including Intermediate Range Ballistic Missiles (IRBMs). This section also included detailed force recommendations for each nation.[86]

The SACEUR section, based on MC 14/2 (revised) and MC 48/2, noted that forward defense of the NATO area was possible and politically necessary. Nuclear weapons were assumed to be available. The aim was to create a uniform line of nuclear and conventional forces opposite the Iron Curtain from Norway to Turkey.[87]

The Canadian joint planners thought that SACEUR's assessment was acceptable. Army forces in Europe should have a nuclear capability, though the recommended Honest John was really a corps-level weapon in Canadian thinking. Little John or Lacrosse was more suitable. Furthermore, the two other brigade groups in Canada should be airportable, with their equipment based in Europe to facilitate their arrival (this idea predated the American REFORGER concept by almost twelve years). As for the RCAF in Europe, the JPC saw the air defense role being completely taken over by the Europeans, and Canadian influence waning with the elimination of the role. The RCAF members of the Joint Planning Committee "consider[ed] that a transition to a strike role is the logical future of the RCAF in Europe."[88]

The SACLANT section, in terms of its conception of naval war under MC 14/ 2 (revised) was almost a carbon copy of the existing RCN/RCAF Concept of Maritime Operations, which portrayed three defensive zones extending out into the Atlantic with nuclear-armed anti-submarine forces operating to keep enemy missile launching submarines away from the coast. In the JPC view: "Satisfaction of SACLANT's requirement, therefore, would enhance the direct defense of North America as well as that of the SACLANT area,"[89] and was therefore acceptable, with two exceptions. SACLANT wanted Canada to acquire a second aircraft carrier. This, from the RCN's perspective, was not economically feasible and would curtail acquisition of the state-of-the art *Restigouche*-class anti-submarine destroyers. The RCN thought that helicopter-carrying destroyers, already under development in Canada, would be a better substitute and more flexible. Secondly, there was no way the RCAF could provide forty new maritime patrol aircraft by 1958.[90]

General Norstad was called on the carpet by the council at a special North Atlantic Council meeting in October 1957 and interrogated about the feasibility of MC 70 in light of the Sputnik event. He surprised the council by stating that MC 70 took into consideration the fact that the enemy would develop ballistic missiles. To British chagrin, MC 70 addressed the problems in developing a balanced force structure:

> [Norstad's] present study showed that we have the means to deal with less than ultimate war by the use of weapons not limited to conventional weapons but without resort to the full nuclear counter offensive. At same time, SACEUR said, it would be very difficult to prevent a limited war in Europe from becoming a general war; therefore it is important to prevent a limited war from starting. We must have the means of providing this deterrent.[91]

European North Atlantic Council members were skeptical. Despite the April announcement, would the Americans really provide the delivery systems and warheads to their NATO allies? Norstad had an answer to that, too:

> [the] availability of nuclear weapons . . . was beyond his competence, but he had strong views. . . . In spite of some currency difficulties, which he implied involved the USA, he was confident that there were ways of

meeting these requirements within the near future without too much difficulty. . . . He had formulated a proposal which he felt would not upset anyone's laws or restrictions. Essentially this is based upon existence of a NATO stockpile of atomic weapons which would not belong to any individual units and which would have a supply system to permit the weapons to be married up [with the delivery systems].[92]

It would take time to move through the NATO political system and, in Norstad's view, not be ready for the December NATO heads of government meeting. In the meantime, Canadian policy makers urged that there be "maximum consultation between SHAPE and SACLANT and the member governments followed by a full consideration of the Commanders' force recommendations."[93]

After the tussle between representatives from SHAPE, the Canadian Chiefs, and External Affairs over MC 70 requirements, Foulkes believed that Norstad should visit Canada and brief the Chiefs of Staff Committee. Norstad had spent time at Eagle Lake "fishing." He met with Deputy Minister Frank Miller to sort out what the brief should consist of.[94] Norstad eventually briefed the Prime Minister, probably because the lack of impact that had been made on Diefenbaker by the Chiefs in the Cabinet Defence Committee meeting in September.

The Panel assembled on 1 November to coordinate activities in relationship to the upcoming Norstad visit. To ensure that there was no misunderstanding, Foulkes and Leger laid out the chronology of the MC 70 problem and determined that, "Although the procedure used in circulating the country force allotments was perhaps objectionable, the harm or embarrassment caused by this procedure had already been done."[95] Defence and External Affairs, as departments, could now present a united front on the issue.

Pearkes and the Chiefs pre-briefed Diefenbaker the day before Norstad's arrival. Pearkes slowly explained problems that had been encountered in formulating MC 70 and that Norstad would probably make recommendations as to the future status of the Air Division. The Arrow could not be adapted for a nuclear strike, so Canada would have to acquire another aircraft if she chose to accept this role. The Army would need a surface-to-surface missile, but this could probably be acquired under the Mutual Aid Program. Foulkes interjected and pointed out that SACEUR would not speak to specific recommendations regarding Canadian forces unless directly questioned. The purpose behind the briefing was to outline SHAPE's thinking on patterns of war and force structuring to meet it.[96]

Pearkes and Foulkes noted: "The U.S. would probably offer to give to NATO atomic weapons and warheads to be placed under SACEUR for release when war came. This proposal was not entirely new."[97] They would probably ask whether or not the Europeans wanted IRBMs as well. Other members of the Cabinet wanted it noted that no decisions would be made in the meeting with SACEUR: it was for information purposes only.

In his Ottawa meeting with Diefenbaker, Norstad emphasized that the December meeting was probably going to be the most crucial one since NATO had been formed. The public display of will, a critical aspect of deterrence, would be on the line in Paris. NATO had to "create an atmosphere that we were moving forward." In

SACEUR's view, there were grave consequences "if any members of the Alliance, particularly the United States and Canada, materially reduced their contributions." He needed a nuclear stockpile and delivery systems. He also needed IRBMs in Europe. These were vital elements. When queried about what he thought about the air defense effort in North America, Norstad thought that more work needed to be done on an anti-ballistic missile system. Norstad did not discuss Canadian MC 70 issues.[98] He came away from the meeting with the belief that SHAPE "would continue to receive the Canadian Government's active support, which is so essential if NATO is to maintain its effectiveness."[99] Diefenbaker did not record his reaction or views on the matters at hand in his autobiography, nor did Basil Robinson.[100]

Canadian strategic policy makers wanted to ensure that Canada was prepared for the December 1957 NATO meeting. The item of primary interest was the nuclear stockpile proposal. The departments were less concerned with MC 70 or the IRBM issue (since they viewed them as a European-US problems). Consequently, the Panel met twice more to coordinate Canadian policy on the NATO stockpile before the Cabinet could formulate policy without professional advice.

Panel members understood several problems would arise in any discussion on NATO stockpiling. The first was control. The aim behind SACEUR's proposed procedures was to "ensure that these new weapons will not enable any NATO country to embark unilaterally on a nuclear war against any other power, or accidentally to provoke a situation which could lead to preventive or retaliatory action by a major power."[101]

These procedures were linked to the problem of responding to alternative and minor conventional threats to the NATO area. If NATO declared war, would SACEUR have full control over the weapons, or would some control be reserved by the North Atlantic Council?[102]

Secondly, once the stockpile plan was announced, there would be a violent reaction on the other side of the Iron Curtain, at least from a propaganda standpoint, which might also affect the nonaligned nations attitude towards NATO nations. This reaction could be countered by having the United States assure all that the provision of nuclear information and weapons would forestall NATO nations from embarking on new nuclear weapons programs (which they might use for their own unilateral purposes), and it would assure Europe that the United States was not abandoning it.[103]

The Panel agreed that the stockpiling concept was the best way to deal with these problems, and that the Canadian position in Paris should support it.[104] Bryce suggested that Canada go one step further. Foulkes had already noted that there was a Canada-US agreement to use nuclear weapons over Canadian territory in the event of war. Why not have the Prime Minister announce that Canada would accept the stockpiling of defensive ASW and air-to-air nuclear warheads in Canada *before* the NATO meeting to promote the program? Perhaps it would persuade reticent NATO members, like France, to go along with it. The Panel recommended the Cabinet discuss the matter.[105]

External Affairs was preoccupied with control. During the course of the discussion, Foulkes noted, "It was unrealistic to expect a military commander to wait for authority from the [NAC] or from governments to use nuclear weapons should a small incident develop quickly into a general war." SACEUR should be allowed to use nuclear weapons in certain situations. He would, "of course use whatever time was available to him for consulting with his political superiors."[106] The External people thought this was far too complicated a question to raise in December. The Panel agreed.[107]

The draft joint submission to the Cabinet (External Affairs and Defence) was written in simple language and for the most part reiterated material that the Prime Minister was familiar with. There could be no mistake as to what the issue was all about and what the professionals recommended. In effect, Canada had certain nuclear weapon requirements to upgrade her forces. If Canada did not get the weapons, the alternative was to increase conventional forces, which would be prohibitively expensive. Withdrawal from the NATO commitments was not an option. Canada did not need ballistic missiles. Storage, maintenance, and control over the warheads posed minor problems since

> Canadian requirements could be met from stockpiles in other NATO countries under the custody of SACEUR. . . . [RCN and RCAF needs] could be provided from stocks at a United States base in the United States or Canada which could be under the custody and control of SACLANT. . . . If however nuclear warheads should be required by Canadian air defence forces they would have to be stored at each RCAF fighter base in Canada under *nominal* custody of a United States officer. . . . Minor modifications to regulations would be needed to permit stockpiling of nuclear weapons in Canada for the use of Canadian forces or for use of United States air defence forces at Goose Bay, Labrador and Ernest Harmon Air Base.[108]

However, by early December the Panel withdrew its proposal to get the Prime Minister to announce stockpiling in Canada.[109] The reason was left unstated in the Panel minutes. In all probability, Foulkes and the other members recalled the developing political problems over the NORAD affair. The Americans by this time were starting to link the defensive weapons stockpiling issue with proposals involving SAC operations in Canada.[110] There was not enough time to examine the long-term political implications of all of these matters together. If the Panel pushed on the stockpile issue and drew Canada into other related agreements, it would have made the NORAD blow-up appear minor in comparison.

The Panel's elaborate preparation had no effect on Diefenbaker. Cabinet met on 12 December 1957 and barely considered the NATO heads of government meeting and the stockpile issue. It was the last item on the fifteen-point agenda.[111]

What of MC 70? Canadian policy makers agreed that MC 70 was not suitable for discussion at the December 1957 NATO meeting. The Americans believed that MC 70 was still evolving from the SACEUR and SACLANT requirement studies. The British still wanted changes to any document mentioning any action short of nuclear war.[112]

The December NATO meeting focused on ballistic missiles for NATO, and the stockpile issue was virtually a fait accompli. The only dissenter was Norway.

The British attempted to get MC 70 put onto the agenda, but were foiled by NATO Secretary General Paul Henri Spaak, who told the council that MC 70 would be ready in February 1958. Diefenbaker echoed this, ensuring that NATO members understood that future consultation would prevent unpleasant problems in force goals.[113] In effect, NATO accepted the stockpile plan and IRBM acquisition in principle, and the MC 70 odyssey continued into 1958.

The NAC analysis of MC 70 was scheduled "sometime" in early 1958. It disturbed Foulkes, who expressed concern to Leger. He was concerned that the NAC was not getting the proper advice from the Military Committee and was hell-bent on discussing MC 70 to meet an artificial deadline. The chiefs of staff in all member nations were bypassed by this process. In his view, "The implications of MC 70 to Canada may be of a considerable magnitude. Therefore, we should insist on adequate time for study of this paper by national authorities." Foulkes knew from the Canadian SHAPE representative, General Sparling, that there was considerable debate over limited war, and that SACLANT had made a new proposal that a peacetime anti-submarine barrier be established in the Atlantic. How could the Chiefs provide proper advice to External, which would be representing Canada in the council, if it had not had access to the current draft of MC 70 which was then under development based on, Foulkes presumed, the fall MC 70 minimum force studies that were themselves flawed from a Canadian point of view?[114]

When queried, Dana Wilgress in Paris agreed. Wilgress, however, attended the January NATO meeting without any instructions beyond "stall and wait for the final version of MC 70" (many NAC members thought that the meeting was a waste of time, since they had not had time to examine MC 70 yet either).[115] By the end of January 1958, a new version of MC 70 was discussed in the Panel.[116]

The British were far less strident on advocating the trip wire strategy as opposed to the shield strategy. This new position, in Leger's view, made acceptance of the strategy and threat section based on MC 14/2 (revised) and MC 48/2 easier. The new problem was that Part II (the minimum recommended forces) would now interfere with the 1958–1959 annual review process. This problem was similar to the one encountered in 1957, when most nations confused MC 70 with the 1957 annual review. The solution, Foulkes thought, would be to push for acceptance by the council of Part I and merge Part II with the annual review process that year. This, of course, was easier said than done, but Leger promised to try.[117]

The Chiefs examined MC 70 this time in preparation for the March 1958 Military Committee meeting in which Norstad would bring the members up to date on MC 70. Since Part II had not been redrafted, the Chiefs looked at Part I. On the whole, they thought the draft was acceptable. SHAPE thought that 1 Air Division should be reequipped "as a matter of urgency," but Canadian planners were cognizant of the political problems and wanted more pliable language. MC 70 Part I also stated that ballistic missiles had not really altered the NATO concept. The Chiefs believed that "if the developments made possible by the Sputniks increase the accuracy of missiles, this may well affect the whole concept of defense in Europe. We therefore consider that this statement is indefensible and appears to be too arrogant to insert."[118] There was some concern that there was not enough profile given to the

Canada-US Regional Planning Group or the relationship of the North American air defense system to NATO.

Once the draft force tables arrived, the Chiefs grew agitated over what they saw as inconsistencies between the force structure proposals and draft strategy in Part I. They thought that constructing a NATO nuclear strike force based on aircraft and static airfields was not consistent with the assertion that the Soviets held the initiative and would possess mobile nuclear missile launchers. Why should Canada spend a lot of money on a system that was vulnerable to a first strike? This troubling question would pose serious problems in the acceptance of the strike role for 1 Air Division in 1959.[119]

Norstad briefed the Military Committee in March 1958. SHAPE incorporated more information on CUSPRG and NORAD into MC 70, reiterating the same wording used in MC 14 back in 1951. As for the mobile missile versus static airfield problem, Foulkes's report was vague on this point, noting that it had been dealt with informally. The necessity of ensuring harmony between SACEUR's thinking and SACLANT's thinking was also addressed. There was more credence given to the nuclear missile–launching submarine threat, since this would directly affect NATO's ability to reinforce or conduct operations in Phase II. The most surprising thing Norstad revealed was that only eight and one-half of his eighteen divisions were up to standard.[120]

Once again, the problem of actions short of nuclear war reared its head. In a bizarre situation, there was a four-way debate over the definition of the following phrases: effective deterrent, hostile local action, incursion, and infiltration:

> The French wanted to take a strong line regarding the definition of "local hostile action." The British were frightened that this meant a type of limited war and was being used by the French to interfere with the British reduction of forces; and there is no doubt the further reduction of the UK forces had a great deal to do with this question. The United States . . . were opposed to a too precise definition of these terms and [suggested that they be deleted from the text]. The Germans took strong objection to any deletion, General [Adolf] Heusinger said that he was under strict instructions to have this matter of terms clearly laid out. . . . This stand was strongly supported by the Italians, the Danes, the Greeks, and the Turks and caused a deadlock. The Chairman did not handle the question well and at one stage wanted to send the paper to the [NAC] without reaching agreement. [Foulkes] objected to this procedure and pointed out that this would be the first time that the Military Committee had failed to reach agreement. . . .
>
> After a long discussion, a break was called and Norstad and [Foulkes] persuaded Heusinger to allow these statements to be removed so as not to delay the approval of the paper, but agreed that the Standing Group [would have to deal with specific language later].[121]

If this still did not satisfy West Germany, the council could deal with the language. Heusinger agreed, and the paper was passed on to the council. *They* ran into the language problem and the delay continued. It was nearly approved in April[122] and was accepted in its final form in June.[123] Eventually, the force structure numbers generated to support MC 70 were slightly recalculated after all NATO nations produced their input.[124]

The Atomic Information Problem Reasserts Itself

The decision taken by NATO to accept an integrated conventional/nuclear force structure and stockpile arrangements necessitated changes in the American Atomic Energy Act. Military planners needed accurate and current information on weapons, weapons effects, and available and planned delivery vehicles.

General Lauris Norstad pushed for an expanded NATO information sharing arrangement in April 1957 so that his integrated planning staff could work on MC 70. He wanted information on: the effective employment of nuclear weapons with regard to military targets; the effects of underwater atomic bursts against all types of ship targets; atomic weapons training aids for delivery vehicles such as Honest John, Matador, and F-84F; fall-out effects of megaton weapons for defensive planning; the size of the US arsenal of nuclear and thermonuclear weapons.[125]

SACEUR got the go-ahead for all of the items except the last one, since, in the US Joint Chiefs' view:

it is difficult to determine how the disclosure of the size of the entire U.S. stockpile would contribute appreciably to NATO defence plans. It is quite possible that if certain NATO allies were appraised of such sensitive information, they might be forced by internal political pressures to reduce their national military appropriations, rationalizing such actions on the size of the U.S. atomic arsenal.[126]

Norstad also pushed for the dissemination of nuclear targeting information to Allied Air Forces Central Region (AIRCENT) and the Allied Tactical Air Forces within ACE. If his forces were to meet the readiness requirements of MC 48/1 and MC 14/2 (revised), this information was critical. The JCS agreed with one proviso: American tactical targeting data that showed targets in West Germany was not to be released.[127] This move was a response to the political debate in West Germany over the "damage" caused by Ex CARTE BLANCHE. Leftist German newspapers decried nuclear weapons planning after the results of this exercise were leaked. The exercise indicated that a wide belt of West German territory would become irradiated in a Warsaw Pact-NATO confrontation.[128]

NATO nations needed more information if the stockpile plan was to work. Weapons effects information was one matter, nuclear weapons safety was another. The Allies needed both. The Eisenhower administration's policy was to release such information, pending changes to the Atomic Energy Act, but Congress was putting the brakes on the bill. One member even wanted legal restrictions on the yield of the weapons that might be deployed limited to 2 kt. This thinking, according to US JCS Chairman Nathan Twining, was "impractical and undesirable."[129] The main problem with amending the act was a highly complex series of issues involving the French government under Charles de Gaulle, however such a detailed discussion is beyond the scope of this study.

There were two distinct types of agreements. The first was between NATO and the United States; these would allow passage of information to NATO commanders and planning staffs. The second type was the bilateral agreement signed between a NATO nation and the United States. The bilateral agreements covered the same information as the NATO-US agreement. With the 1958 amendments to the Atomic Energy Act, the nature and scope of the information available to NATO members under bilateral means changed depending on what the national requirements were. For example, the British gained access to American nuclear weapons design and fabrication information when elements of the 144b portion of the act were lifted.[130]

The bilateral Canada-US information sharing agreement was not signed until 1959. There is no doubt that the domestic political situation on continental defense and NORAD was the primary factor, but there were legal issues involved. If American ships or submarines propelled by nuclear reactors entered Canadian ports, did the USN have to apply for an import permit for fissile material or not? This problem was also entangled with the issue of storing nuclear weapons for SAC at Goose Bay, which in turn was entangled with the larger problem of providing nuclear air defense weapons to both RCAF and USAF forces operating in Canada.[131] This, naturally, did not prevent the Chiefs or the services from obtaining information using informal methods and continuing their force development programs.

Conclusion

The problems in having the Diefenbaker government accept the NORAD agreement contrasted with the well-oiled national security policy-making apparatus created by the St. Laurent government. Though responsibility for a lack of continuity on air defense policy should rest on inadequate transition of power mechanisms, the effects of Diefenbaker's personality was a significant factor. These effects included his antimilitary attitude, his suspicion about the people in the Department of External Affairs, and his suspicion, and then outright rejection, of the government committee process. The NORAD affair unfortunately "confirmed" all of this to the new Prime Minister. This situation was a prescription for disaster.

It is clear that Diefenbaker, though briefed on Canadian national security policy, had little appreciation for the complex series of decisions that had been made to get the policy to the point where it was an effective part of realizing Canadian national aims of peace, security, and economic prosperity. In this sense Canadian strategic tradition was almost irrelevant to the Prime Minister. This gross lack of attention to detail would not bode well for Canadian national security policy. The only positive aspect of this lack of situational awareness was that existing national security policy-making processes could continue, albeit at a sub rosa level. There were men in the government, however, who knew that the lack of a policy was still a policy and would continually try to give that lack of policy better definition, even if the Prime Minister himself was not interested. One of these men was the new defense minister, George Pearkes. The stage was set for the next phase in the development of Canadian strategy and force structure: the debate in Canada over air defense.

6

IS POWER NOTHING WITHOUT CONTROL? CONTINENTAL DEFENSE PROBLEMS AND DOMESTIC POLITICS, 1957–1959

Power is nothing without control.
—PIRELLI TIRE COMMERCIAL

Sovereign: 1. Exercising or possessing supreme authority, jurisdiction, or power. 2. Free, independent, and in no way limited by external authority or influence. 3. Possessing supreme excellence or greatness; preeminent: paramount. 4. Superior in efficacy: potent.
—*FUNK AND WAGNALL'S CANADIAN COLLEGE DICTIONARY*, P. 1283.

Introduction

The main roadblock to achieving a full nuclear capability for Canadian forces was the continental defense gestalt. The Diefenbaker government was vulnerable in the domestic political arena. Her Majesty's Loyal Opposition, the Liberals led by Mike Pearson, were well informed on national security policy matters, and rapidly exploited the contradictions that their own policy in the previous government had created. The objective was the destruction of the Diefenbaker government and the reelection of the Liberals. The method used the emerging policy contradictions to convince the media and the public that Canada had abrogated her sovereignty to the United States. Because of security reasons the practical aspects of sovereignty and command/control were known only to the practitioners: a Canadian RCAF officer, Air Marshal Roy Slemon, commanded certain American nuclear-capable air defense forces as well as Canadian air Defense units in his capacity as Deputy Commander in Chief, NORAD.

Despite the rhetoric, important air defense projects were initiated under the Diefenbaker government, but the shattering of the jewel in the crown, the CF-105 Arrow with its planned nuclear capability, resulted in continuing attacks on what was perceived by the media to be an increasingly muddled national security policy.

The NORAD debates generated an environment in which the government became over-sensitized to criticism over sovereignty issues. The CF-105 Arrow and the BOMARC SAM systems represented significant contributions to creating a deterrent and protecting Canadian sovereignty. The lack of such contributions forced the Americans into a position of protecting Canada with their MB-1-equipped aircraft and BOMARC missiles. This seriously impinged on Canadian sovereignty.

It was increasingly clear that the Diefenbaker government did not understand the relationship between quality capable military forces, the ability to protect sovereignty through operational influence, and the ability to influence the Americans. Government officials made decisions based on domestic political prestige at the expense of such influence. Without nuclear-capable Canadian air defense forces, the United States, by default, had to take up the burden of continental air Defense with a consequential decline in Canadian sovereignty. This could have been avoided if Canada had simply asked the United States government for nuclear weapons: it is ironic that the policy of the Eisenhower administration was to give Canada nuclear weapons if so asked, without the usual American dual-key controls.

NORAD Redux

The Opposition firmly shoved NORAD under the parliamentary microscope from November 1957 to July 1958. There were two periods of intense debate, November–December 1957 and May–June 1958. In the first period, the Opposition prodded the Diefenbaker government into pursuing a more formal NORAD agreement, while in the second period, they turned around and bashed them for doing so. Both debates generated a series of unanswerable and arguably unsolvable questions.

Before embarking on a detailed examination of the debate and its implications, it is necessary to establish at the start that the Opposition developed a progressively sophisticated and coordinated attack on the government. This attack followed in the wake of the government's September 1957 NORAD announcement. It started out with less notable Opposition members, but former Cabinet members Paul Martin and Mike Pearson took the lead. The purpose was to generate nonconfidence in the government by pandering to the media through the medium of parliamentary debate.

The Opposition, however, pushed this process to extremes that eventually damaged allied confidence in the Canadian contribution to NATO deterrence. The main offspring of the debate was a series of issues regarding Canada's place in the world and her relationship to the United States. These issues were aggravated by the Opposition's shift of focus on nuclear weapons and led to obstructing the Canadian forces' ability to access the nuclear stockpile as the Diefenbaker government lumbered about trying to address the charges.

The Diefenbaker government was a minority government: this produced a certain sensitivity to any issue raised in Parliament by the Opposition. If the Diefenbaker government lost a vote of nonconfidence, its ability to accomplish its larger aims would be imperiled. It was in this environment that the debate was initially fought.

The initial engagement in October–November 1957 produced three questions. First, was the NORAD agreement discussed in the Cabinet, and had it been the subject of an Order in Council? This issue was aggravated by a media story in which General Partridge, USAF CONAD and CinCNORAD, mentioned that he did not need to consult the American President before ordering his forces into action. Second, could CinCNORAD commit Canadian forces to war? Third, was NORAD part of NATO? The government waffled on these questions while the Opposition proclaimed that NORAD was an "inscrutable and intangible arrangement" that might not even be legal. Pearkes tried to explain that NORAD was structured to produce plans and training in peace. When confronted as to whether NORAD could make the decision of when Canada went to war, Pearkes waffled even more.[1] This produced a further question: Who made the decision to go to war: CinCNORAD or Canada? Clearly this was a question of import to those who championed Canadian sovereignty.

The debate accelerated in November. In a parliamentary exchange between Pearson and Diefenbaker, Diefenbaker stated that NORAD was a bilateral arrangement within NATO's Canada-US Regional Planning Group. Pearson retorted that if this was the case, Dulles had made a public statement that General Partridge (CinCNORAD), an American general, could launch air Defense forces without presidential authorization. What was the role of the North Atlantic Council in this process if NORAD were part of NATO? Pearkes mumbled that the procedures established in Europe would apply in Canada. A *Time* magazine article that erroneously stated the "SAC bombers at NORAD" would be launched without delay in the event of an attack caused further consternation. The magazine's distortion was deliberately exploited by Pearson (knowing full well that SAC and NORAD were separate), who pressed again for information on the NATO-NORAD link. If NORAD used nuclear weapons, Pearson mused, would Canada be advised or consulted? Pearkes attempted to defuse this question by distinguishing between planning consultation pre-war and operational clearance during a war. Canada would be asked for clearance.[2]

This in turn produced more questions: What was the NORAD-NATO relationship? What was the relationship between SAC and NORAD? To what extent would Canada be consulted on the use of strategic nuclear weapons (as opposed to air defense weapons for NORAD)?

Diefenbaker shot back on all of this, stating that the Second World War Canada-US Ogdensburg agreement was a precedent for placing Canadian forces under American command. This agreement had been signed by a Liberal government in 1940, and NORAD was just a logical extrapolation of this policy. Paul Martin demanded more information on the predelegated authority given to Partridge, citing the *Time* article. He was cut off as his time was up. Pearson then took over, wanting to know how the 1957 agreement was reached legally, a question which Diefenbaker evaded. Pearson pressed this. Surely Parliament and thus the Canadian people should have access to the same information that the American Secretary of State was providing to the American public. Ogdensburg was a dodge. The attempt to portray NORAD as part of the CUSRPG was a dodge. Pearson went so far to state that the air defense of North America was not NATO-related at all, which as we have seen in previous chapters, was an outright lie. Pearson stated that he wished NORAD *were* part of NATO.[3] It would then be like NATO in its modus operandi, and it should receive the same legal treatment in Parliament that NATO had had in 1949. Why had this not happened? Parliament has the right to be informed. Perhaps NORAD was an interim measure and, if so, what was its nature? The government continued to waffle.[4] These were bold statements coming from the man who negotiated the 1950 Goose Bay nuclear storage arrangement, the 1952 SAC overflight arrangement, and the 1956/1957 MB-1 overflight arrangements, as well as someone with direct knowledge about the development of NORAD prior to June 1957, and who did not refer any of them to Parliament when he was Secretary of State for External Affairs.

By December 1957, the Diefenbaker government limply counterattacked. Pearkes announced that CinCNORAD's Terms of Reference were now under study and would be approved with the United States in 1958. In a belated attempt to respond, Pearkes noted that agreed-to Canadian-American air defense rules of engagement had existed since 1951 and had been approved by the St. Laurent government at the time. Pearkes then stated that this had been done to protect SAC and the industrial capacity of North America. This was a serious error on Pearkes's part: Was the air defense system designed to protect the Canadian population or the American SAC? If it were designed to protect the population, why should Canadian forces be under American command? Pearson continued, asserting that External Affairs had never been consulted on the NORAD issue, which was another untruth.

Pearkes, who had in the interim asked Foulkes to produce a chronology of NORAD's development, informed Pearson that External Affairs had, in fact, examined the issue as early as 1956.[5] Pearson backed off. Another Opposition member then queried the degree of civilian control over NORAD. If Norstad corresponded to the North Atlantic Council in Europe, what did Partridge correspond to in North America? What was the constitutional and legal basis for NORAD? Pearkes dodged once again, stating that NORAD was an "'interim' measure."[6]

The Opposition continued to harp on the lack of legal congruence between NORAD and NATO well into January 1958. The main line of argument was that SAC was not part of NATO. NORAD protected SAC and therefore NORAD could not be part of NATO. Diefenbaker continued to insist that NORAD was part of NATO. Pearkes continued to insist that NORAD was subordinate to the Canada-US Regional Planning Group. Pearson slammed the government, reading aloud from the *NATO Handbook* (a public document) which stated that the Canada-US Regional Planning Group (CUSRPG) was not even a command.[7]

We will recall at this point that the CUSRPG functioned as a "front organization" for the Permanent Joint Board on Defense/Military Cooperation Committee to feed sanitized continental defense information to NATO and give some appearance of coordination. Once the NATO commands SACEUR and SACLANT were formed and the regional planning groups discarded, CUSRPG soldiered on in limbo. At that point neither Canada nor the United States wanted to pass on detailed continental defense information and the Diefenbaker government was reaping what had been sown back then. It was a mistake for Diefenbaker's people to fall back on CUSRPG.

Pearkes countered stating that NORAD, if not part of NATO, still served as part of the NATO deterrent system. It could not be completely separated from NATO and even used procedures modeled on NATO ones. Pearson accepted this and then shifted his attack to the nature of the command. If Partridge was away, could Slemon command American forces? Would the Americans allow this? Pearkes did not waffle: Yes, Slemon could command Americans. Pearson was not mollified and demanded that Parliament should approve these "verbal, shaky" arrangements. There was not enough civilian control over these matters in his view. Pearkes shot back, asserting that civilian control was not a problem since Slemon reported to him and he reported to the Cabinet. What, Pearson argued, would happen if there were a crisis off Formosa with China and Partridge sent bombers to respond to it? What if he also alerted the air Defense system to respond to the crisis? This was another misrepresentation of the facts, which Pearkes pounced on after he talked to Foulkes.[8] SAC and NORAD were different, he stated, despite what an article in an American publication displayed by the Honorable Member from Algoma East claimed.[9]

Diefenbaker was in no position to respond to the series of complex questions that emerged in the first part of the NORAD debate. Why was this the case? The existing NORAD arrangements were still under development by the command, particularly since the bulk of the forces provided to NORAD were American and in turn came from the CONAD command. CONAD had US Army, US Navy, and US Air Force units assigned to it and sorting this out took time. Diefenbaker's haphazard approach to strategic policy and treatment of knowledgeable uniformed advisors was another barrier. Diefenbaker was unable to match Pearson's intimate knowledge of the issues and the experience it took to negotiate international agreements. Pearson, in fact, had an inside source either at External or Defense who was feeding him classified air defense planning information.[10] Unclassified information for use in the House of Commons was derived from ill-considered public statements made by American policy makers and commanders to the America media. Pearson was thus able to maintain pace with the developing situation and outmaneuver Diefenbaker.

Round two commenced after the government won a majority in the House of Commons in a March 1958 general election.[11] In May, Sidney Smith, who was now Secretary of State for External Affairs, announced that NORAD negotiations with the Americans were complete. These negotiations were initiated by Canada in November 1957 when the really strong Opposition questioning started. The Americans were only too happy to collaborate, and the formal process proceeded until May.[12]

In May 1958 Smith established in Parliament that NORAD was not part of NATO, though it was NATO-like in procedures and it did contribute to NATO. The issue of civilian control was addressed in the Terms of Reference for the NORAD commanders, though Smith thought that NORAD would report to the CUSRPG, the US Joint Chiefs, *and* the Canadian Chiefs. Pearson pressed Diefenbaker to bring the NORAD agreement into the House for debate, but Diefenbaker resisted. Pearson argued that it had not been considered in the Cabinet and thus had no legal basis. Diefenbaker retorted that the process was initiated under the St. Laurent government and they should know, since he was not allowed by law to view Cabinet minutes from the previous government. Pearson kept hammering away at the relationship to NATO. Paul Henri Spaak had announced publicly that NORAD was not part of NATO. Why was NORAD not part of NATO? Diefenbaker dodged this one.[13]

Diefenbaker regrouped on 10 June 1958 and produced an impassioned litany blaming the St. Laurent government for starting the NORAD process in the first place. In his view, the Liberals had given away political control of Canadian forces and breached Canadian sovereignty. The new agreement did not do so, he argued. NORAD was in line with NATO and in the spirit of previous Canadian-American arrangements. NORAD was there to protect SAC. Unfortunately, Diefenbaker segued into SAC matters. Pearson had given SAC permission for nuclear weapons over-flights seven years ago and made arrangements to station SAC tankers in Canada. Why were they continually questioning NORAD?[14]

This outburst prompted a reaction from Pearson that, in retrospect, confirms what the former External Affairs Minister's agenda really was. He had privately informed American colleagues that it was his intent to "seek to embarrass the government."[15] Pearson asserted that the Diefenbaker government was "inept." The NORAD matter was not considered in Cabinet and had no legal basis. If the Cabinet did not consider and approve matters, how exactly was this government being run? It took the government ten months to negotiate with the Americans on NORAD. This alone demonstrated incompetence in foreign affairs. There was still this waffling on the NATO-NORAD relationship. NORAD was really serious stuff for Canada, he went on, since SAC would operate under information provided by NORAD.[16]

Pearson wanted to know who exactly controlled the weapons. Could Canadians command American forces armed with certain weapons? Pearson was deliberately vague as to which weapons he was referring: SAC weapons carried over Canada, or MB-1 air defense overflights. Paul Martin chimed in. Could Partridge "push the button" without consulting Canada? Could Slemon? Martin was, of course, distorting the issue, since Partridge could not order SAC to launch, though information he provided would be used in that decision. The big problem was, how exactly did the West transition from peace to war and where did elected civilians fit into that process?[17]

This question could not be answered and Pearson once again changed tact. The United States would equip itself with air defense nuclear missiles to replace fighters. Canada, as far as he understood it, had no plans to do so and would be left behind. Would Canada have to keep pace and get nuclear missiles too? Furthermore, as he understood it, American law prevented foreign commanders from commanding American units equipped with nuclear weapons. The Deputy CinCNORAD was Canadian. If CinCNORAD was indisposed, would the command be left helpless? Pearkes waffled, stating that NORAD did not have command of the squadrons. The subordinate national commanders commanded their own forces. This, of course, was nonsense.[18]

Another Opposition member, Alan Mcnaughton, then attacked NORAD on sovereignty grounds, stating that "[Canada] has not had full sovereignty for so long that we can afford to give it away in bits and pieces. . . . political sovereignty is what the great powers tolerate." In his view, NORAD made Canada a junior partner in an alliance, while in NATO Canada was a full partner. In a nuclear war, Canada would become "another Belgium."[19] Sidney Smith was able to recover and respond to this.

NORAD was a "temporary delegation of sovereignty" in wartime. Diefenbaker went on the offensive, slamming the Opposition since it was "dangerous for any political party to arouse fear in the hearts of the people,"[20] a hypocritical statement for a man who campaigned in 1957 playing on the fear of Americanization in Canada.

By the end of June 1958, the government recovered the initiative in Parliament. Diefenbaker lashed back. It was the St. Laurent government who were in the process of giving away Canadian sovereignty when Diefenbaker was elected. The St. Laurent government produced the ambiguous NORAD plan, not the Diefenbaker government. The rhetoric continued to build and Diefenbaker remarked that "the Canadian people were shown a terrible bogeyman" that did not exist.[21]

Pearson shifted once again to the nuclear issue. Prompted by an article written by James Minifie, a CBC (Canadian Broadcasting Corporation) journalist who advocated Canadian neutralism,[22] Pearson formally requested information from the United States government on nuclear command and control laws. Minifie had previously reported that foreign commanders could not control American nuclear weapons. This alarmed the American embassy in Ottawa, which figured that Pearson wanted the information "presumably to see if he can find basis for renewed attempt to trip up the government on NORAD."[23] The American ambassador, Livingston Merchant, wanted the information for himself so that he could "protect US interests in this matter."[24] It does not appear that Pearson was able to secure what he wanted.

In another attempt to undermine the government's sovereignty credentials, Pearson asked the house in June 1958 why American squadrons had access to nuclear weapons and Canadian squadrons did not? Sidney Smith had stated publicly that nuclear weapons would not be stored in Canada. Pearson was again deliberately confusing the Goose Bay storage issue with media reports that there were negotiations under way to store USAF MB-1s at American bases in Canada. Why did Canada have to rely on American interceptors commanded by an American general to defend Canada? Could American legislation be changed to accommodate Canada? Would Parliament be consulted this time? Once again, the Diefenbaker government did not have the answers.

In the end, Parliament approved the NORAD agreement 200 to 8 in June 1958. The only dissenters were the members of the socialist Cooperative Commonwealth Federation. Passage of the agreement was not really in doubt since the Diefenbaker government held 207 of the 265 seats.[25]

Canadian media reaction to the whole affair was mixed. Most media outlets appeared to support the idea of NORAD, but were unhappy with the apparent inconsistencies of both the Opposition and government arguments.[26] It would take some time, but the larger questions would surface again and form the basis for further opposition attempts to harass the government on the nuclear weapons issue.

With respect to NORAD, the Canadian Chiefs, and the US Joint Chiefs closely followed developments as the debate progressed from November 1957 to May 1958. Slemon and Partridge had put their heads together and generated NORAD terms of reference, which were accepted by the Canadian Chiefs and the US Joint Chiefs in the spring of 1958.[27] These terms of reference, when distilled for public consumption, became the language used in the formal NORAD agreement in May 1958. It is important to note that there was little change in the wording and substance of the terms of reference between October 1957 and May 1958.[28] The parliamentary debate did not affect the terms of reference at all; it merely forced Diefenbaker to take the arrangement to Parliament, where the Opposition could have a crack at the government.

The terms of reference indicated that NORAD was a joint Canada-US command, and the commander and deputy commander were not to be of the same nationality. A headquarters and staff would be established called the North American Air Defense Command, it would have Canadian and American members and it would report to the Canadian Chiefs and the US Joint Chiefs. The NORAD commander would exercise operational control over the Mid-Canada Line, the DEW Line, and the air Defense forces in Alaska, Canada, and the continental United States. NORAD would develop plans and conduct exercises. Without explicitly referring to the command and control of nuclear weapons, the terms of reference noted that the Deputy Commander in Chief would have the same authority if the Commander in Chief was indisposed for any reason in all situations and cases.[29]

In other words, Air Marshal Roy Slemon had operational control of American nuclear air defense weapons when General Partridge was absent and if the American President had released the weapons. As Slemon noted,

> Initially Canada was not privy to the highly classified nuclear part of the business, and after we had been functioning for three months—it was US Eyes Only on practically all of this stuff—Pat Partridge got hold of me. He said, "Roy, I'm supposed to be the Commander in Chief of NORAD and you're supposed to be the Deputy Commander in Chief. When I go out on a trip, inspecting units or go away to have a little fun, you have the responsibility and the authority. I can't go away on these trips and have any peace of mind because you don't know what the hell goes on with respect to the weapons. So as of this minute you are privy to all that is necessary with respect to the nuclear weapons." He never referred that to Headquarters or anyone. He made the decision right then and there and the word was passed on. I got a concentrated education on all of these weapons from the staff. . . . He was never rebuked by his superiors. . . . It could have cost him his commission, because the security on those weapons is top. . . .
>
> So I was able to take on the task meaningfully and thank God; a couple of things happened that, if I hadn't had the knowledge, would have been rather difficult. . . . Partridge retired and General Lawrence Kuter became [CinCNORAD], a very clever, highly intelligent man, but not with the same sort of human understanding as Pat. But he, unfortunately, was sick about a third of the time, in the hospital and so on, so I was in the hot seat. . . . And Kuter retired and General Don Gerhart became [CinCNORAD] and I was his Deputy [too].[30]

The media gave great play to an interview conducted with Partridge by the *New York Times* in the fall of 1958. Partridge allegedly stated in a NORAD press briefing that he had predelegated authority to release and employ nuclear air Defense weapons if necessary. This article prompted harried communications between External Affairs and the State Department, probably generated by the lingering political sensitivity of the 1958 NORAD debates. The State Department investigated and the facts emerged. Partridge was double hatted in that he was CinCNORAD (the binational command) and CinCCONAD (the national commander of the American component of NORAD). CinCCONAD had been granted predelegation by President Eisenhower to "use nuclear weapons against hostile aircraft within the area of that Command," that is, over the continental United States and in adjacent waters. This authority was in fact predelegated all the way down to US Air Defense Division commanders in CONAD.[31]

Some members of the State Department wanted to bring in the Canadian ambassador and explain the details. Others noted that Eisenhower had given the authority that it "be held on a most restricted basis" within the US government only. The close-hold people won out but thought that the matter should be raised when the Canadian government requested access to nuclear air defense weapons in the future. The Canadian government was so informed.[32] Canadian planners rapidly figured out the nuances delineating CONAD and NORAD authority. Foulkes recommended to the government that any and all Canadian commanders at NORAD be granted predelegated release authority from Canada as well, so that there would be no misunderstanding.[33] However, they would not get this authority until 1964.

To sum up: Partridge had predelegated nuclear release for CONAD forces in the continental United States prior to and/or during the outbreak of war, as did his American subordinate commanders. Slemon could release them if Partridge or CinCCONAD were indisposed.

In any event, NORAD was formally established on 12 May 1958.[34] The problem for Canada was the need to improve RCAF air Defense forces to bring them into line with American air Defense forces so that there would be interoperability, continuity, and thus credibility in the combined air Defense system.

Genies Almost Out of the Bottle

By 1959 the Canadian air Defense system had not kept up with technological developments, which in turn had political effects on Canadian influence and sovereignty. There were the nine CF-100 squadrons with minimal capability against advanced bomber types and no replacement aircraft on the horizon. The BOMARCs would not be available until 1961 at the earliest, assuming that a nuclear weapons sharing agreement could be produced and signed. There was, however, a fine early warning system that was manned by both Canadian and American personnel. In terms of capability, RCAF Air Defence Command compared poorly with CONAD (see figure 6.1). The bulk of USAF air defense was nuclear-capable. The drawn out air defense debate in Canada appeared to leave the air Defense of Canadian air space in American hands, but this statement must be qualified. The USAF interceptor squadrons operating in Canada at this time, which included the 59th Fighter Interceptor Squadron at Goose Bay, the 61st FIS and 323rd FIS from Harmon AFB in Stephenville were not equipped with MB-1s, but their F-89J and F-102A aircraft were nuclear-capable, with the F-102A capable of carrying the GAR-11 nuclear-tipped Falcon.[35] The USAF ADC aircraft operating from bases in the "lower 48" did have MB-1, but could reach out only to the limit of their aircraft range, which covered only the southernmost regions of Canada. There was no depth save for those USAF squadrons based in Alaska; Keflavik, Iceland; and at Thule, Greenland. The Keflavik squadron had the conventional F-89C and would not get the nuclear-capable F-102A until 1962, while the Thule-based squadron had conventional F-86Ds until 1958, when nuclear-capable F-102As were deployed. The initial deployment date of MB-1 nuclear weapons to these squadrons is unclear: Certainly by 1962 all had access to MB-1 or GAR-11 in some capacity, be it readied weapon, dismantled systems on-site, or allocation of a stock of weapons to be flown in at some designated alert level.[36] See figures 6.2 and 6.3.[37]

There was, therefore, a critical need to improve the system until BOMARC could be fully deployed by 1961. There were several possibilities for how to accomplish this. The Newfoundland-based USAF squadrons could be equipped with MB-1. The MB-1 overflight agreement could be expanded. American interceptors equipped with MB-1s could deploy to Canadian bases at clearly defined alert levels. All of these avenues were at odds with the sovereignty problems established during the NORAD debates and each would encounter resistance when attempts were made to implement them.

The St. Laurent government had authorized the Chiefs in December 1956 to establish a formal arrangement so that MB-1-armed USAF ADC interceptors could fly over Canadian airspace and use nuclear weapons in an emergency. The MB-1s would only be used once a conventionally equipped interceptor clearly identified an incoming hostile aircraft. Any accidents involving MB-1s would be under RCAF jurisdiction pending the arrival of American clean-up teams. Finally, if the USAF wanted to station MB-1s in Canada, the government would be consulted first. The overflight agreement would be in effect until 1 July 1957, when the "emergency period ended" (that is, the Suez Crisis).[38]

During the 1956 Canadian-American discussions on the overflight agreement, some mention was made about permanently stationing MB-1s at USAF bases in Canada. As the RCAF representative understood it, the USAF did not plan to station MB-1s in Canada during the six-month period covered by the agreement, though plans existed to store them at two bases in the future. General Coiner (the USAF representative) implied that there were presidential restrictions on stationing MB-1s outside the continental United States, but that this might change by 1958.[39] This concern was driven by the belief that "Congress might see fit, in the event of [a nuclear accident] to outlaw the further use of atomic weapons inside the US; while NATO nations permitting the US to store and maintain atomic arms abroad would possibly abrogate these privilieges."[40]

The temporary Canadian Chiefs–USAF arrangement was formalized in February 1957. It had always been the intent of both parties that an exchange of notes through the Permanent Joint Board would produce an agreement, which took several weeks.[41] It was also delayed because Pearson was dealing with the United

Figure 6.1
CONTINENTAL INTERCEPTOR FORCES, 1958–1960

		1958	1959	1960
Missiles (US)	**BOMARC A (nuclear)**	nil	17	111
	BOMARC B (nuclear)	nil	nil	nil
	Nike Ajax (conventional)*	2844	2040	2088
	Nike Hercules (nuclear)*	96	912	1152
Aircraft (CDA)	**CF-100 (conventional)**	162	162	162
	CF-86 (conventional)	144	nil	nil
	Total:	306	162	162
Aircraft (US)	**F-89 (conventional)**	74 to 62	21	nil
	F-86 (conventional)	419 to 327	188 to 133	nil
	F89 (2X MB-1)	286 to 264	260 to 207	108
	F-102A (2X AIM-26 A)	627	611 to 482	480
	F-104 A (conventional)	51 to 100	86 to 90	90
	F-101B (2X MB-1)	nil	73 to 188	306
	F-106A (1X MB-1)	nil	18 to 97	100
	Total conventional:	544 to 489	295 to 244	90
	Total MB-1/AIM-26 A capable:	913 to 891	968 to 974	988

* assumes 12 missiles per battery.
Sources: Shaffel, *The Emerging Shield* p. 226; Knaack, *Post-World War II Fighters* pp. 159–173; Green *The First Line* pp. 343–387; Drendel, *VooDoo* p. 48; Kinzey, *F-89 Scorpion* pp. 12–13; Worley, *New Developments* pp. 24–34; Milberry, *The Avro CF-100 Canuck* p. 177; Milberry, *The Canadair Sabre* p. 368; NORAD Historical Office, "NORAD Resources Statistics Book 1958–1976."

Nations deployment to Suez at the time.[42] Meanwhile, American negotiators were hopeful that extensions to the agreement, perhaps even permanent ones, could be made and they believed that:

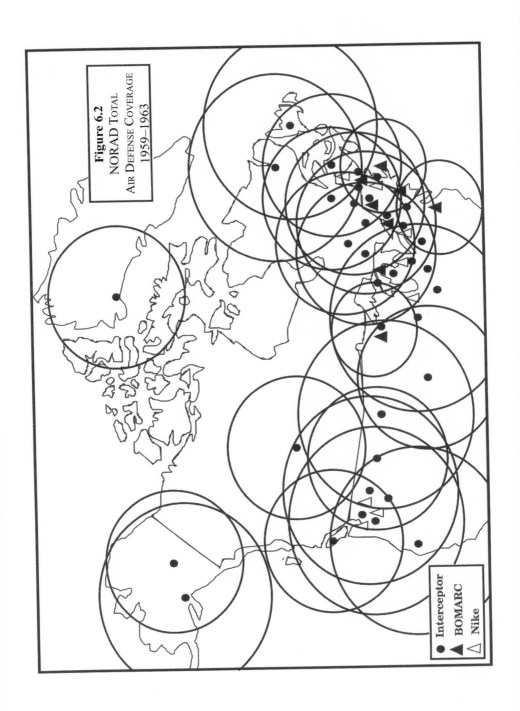

Figure 6.2
NORAD Total
Air Defense Coverage
1959–1963

- Interceptor
- ▲ BOMARC
- △ Nike

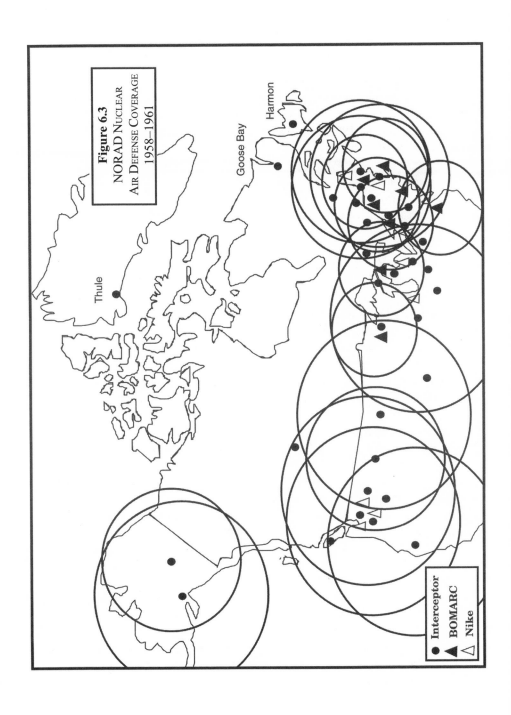

Figure 6.3
NORAD NUCLEAR
AIR DEFENSE COVERAGE
1958–1961

Thule

Goose Bay

Harmon

Interceptor
BOMARC
Nike

the successful conclusion of the . . . negotiations may well hinge on both our being prepared in the near future to make Canadian fighter aircraft compatible with our nuclear missiles and our readiness to provide Canada with some of those weapons. The legislative and other authority for us to do the latter is lacking at this time.[43]

One sticking point developed over allowing American nuclear-tipped surface-to-air missiles to attack targets over Canada. Phraseology covering this was removed at Canadian insistence, and the agreement remained MB-1-oriented.[44]

On 19 February 1957, the Canadian government accepted that USAF aircraft equipped with MB-1 could:

enter Canadian airspace only in the event of an air defense warning yellow or red is declared. In such an event, the USA planes will confine their activities in the main to Canadian territory bordering on the Great Lakes and extending northward to about 50 degrees north latitude . . . [aircraft armed with] MB-1 weapons . . . will be authorized by the Canadian Government to land at, or take off from, Canadian bases in the territory over which they have authority to operate.[45]

Note that this was a temporary emergency agreement that expired on 1 July 1957. By May the Americans were looking for a one-year extension to July 1958, with more modifications, though they saw this as another temporary delay until a more comprehensive agreement involving equipping RCAF aircraft with nuclear weapons could be worked out.[46] The Americans got their additional twelve months on 28 June 1957. It squeaked in under the wire just before Diefenbaker took office.[47]

The ongoing expansion of the air defense base system to protect SAC prompted the Americans to request a change in the MB-1 overflight agreement in January 1958. The only change was to extend the operating area to 54 degrees north latitude and to lower the level of alert necessary to send the aircraft over Canadian airspace.[48] The Diefenbaker government, now in power, in between NORAD debate rounds and running a general election, gave a hurried "yes," but wanted to emphasize that the new agreement would not involve "the equipment of the USAF squadrons at Goose Bay with the MB-1 Rocket, or the storage of the MB-1 rocket or of any other atomic or nuclear weapons in Canada."[49] As discussed earlier, the Americans had approached the Canadian delegation after the December 1957 NATO meeting in which the US-NATO stockpile proposal was announced. The Americans had indicated that a comprehensive agreement involving MB-1 storage, SAC storage, interceptor operations, and the integration of nuclear weapons into the Canadian forces should be considered.

Ignorant of the domestic political storm brewing in Canada over air defense and the lack of attention that could be directed by the Diefenbaker government to the detailed matters at hand, Assistant Secretary of Defense Mansfield Sprague urged State Department officials to pressure Canada to remove the language relating to MB-1 storage and equipping the American air Defense squadrons in Newfoundland with the weapons.[50] The pressure was not applied and the amendments to the MB-1 overflight agreement were accepted on 12 May 1958.[51] A further extension was granted by Canada for the period 1 July 1958 to 1 July 1959.[52]

The Air Defense System: 2 Steps Forward, 105 Back

Despite the public debate on NORAD, 1957 and 1958 were big years in the development of a nuclear capability for Canadian air defense forces and other projects designed to improve air Defense capability.

As discussed previously, the RCAF/DRB Combined Air Defence Study and the reappraisal of the AVRO Arrow development program concluded that Canada should pursue the acquisition of the BOMARC area defense missile, the Arrow-manned interceptor, and a point defense missile (either Nike B or Talos), which would constitute, with existing and additional radars, an air Defense system. All three weapons were to have nuclear warheads in order to obliterate incoming enemy bombers and/or render their nuclear bombs ineffective. BOMARC and the Arrow were under development and the point defense system acquisition was in some doubt because of cost and interservice problems.

In the United States, BOMARC and the SAGE computer were considered to be partner systems. General Earle Partridge, who was at the time head of USAF's Air Research and Development Command prior to his accession as CinCCONAD in 1954, was the driving force. He believed that a BOMARC/SAGE combination might, in the future, be able to bring down ICBMs as well as bombers.[53] In terms of operation, SAGE computers took incoming data from radar sites and converted it to digital form so it could be sent via telephone lines at high speed to combat control centers which would in turn direct intercept aircraft or missiles against enemy targets. In theory, targeting data from a given radar site could be fed directly to the BOMARC missile itself prior to or after launch, whereby the BOMARC's own pulse Doppler radar system would kick in and the missile would track and destroy the target.[54]

Both SAGE and BOMARC were technologically immature projects when the USAF and RCAF had them under consideration. Between February 1956 and September 1958, the planned number of BOMARC As dropped from forty squadrons of 120 missiles each to six with 28 missiles each. There were delays in construction, in equipment calibration, and problems when test missiles could not hit subsonic drones with a conventional warhead. Eventually, the IM-99 B or BOMARC B, with a solid-fuel motor and nuclear warhead, was chosen to supersede the A model. This produced further delays. Congress saw BOMARC and Nike-Hercules systems as a duplication of effort and wanted to cut funding to one or the other, which resulted in a compromise. Both systems would be acquired by the United States but on reduced scales.[55]

Canadian air defense planners participated in joint air Defense thinking through the mediums of the CONAD liaison staff,[56] the Canada-US Military Study Group, and the Military Cooperation Committee. USAF CONAD produced a "Continental Air Defense Objectives Plan 1956–66 (CADOP 56-66)" that had RCAF and DRB input. This was passed on to the MCC for discussion in February 1957 and formed the basis for BOMARC deployment planning in Canada. The threats considered included manned bombers, intercontinental cruise missiles, submarine-launched missiles, and ICBMs. The enemy would use electronic countermeasures and decoys to spoof the air Defense system. The threat would continue to be a multipurpose one and not shift totally to ICBMs. The targets would fall into five major areas with eight possible routes of attack (see figure 6.4); each would require multilayer defense. This would include long-range interceptors (F-101) and medium-range interceptors (CF-105 Arrow, F-102, and F-106) for a total of sixty-nine USAF and twelve RCAF squadrons,[57] long range missiles (BOMARC) for a total of forty USAF and two RCAF squadrons, plus short range missiles (Nike B or Talos), a total of ninety-five US Army missile battalions, with detachments in Canada to protect Goose Bay. There were to be two headquarters to command all of this, one in Canada (Trenton, Ontario) and one in the United States. Two of eight SAGE-equipped headquarters would be located in Canada; one at North Bay, Ontario, and the other at Calgary, Alberta.[58] The entire radar network south of the DEW Line and the Mid-Canada Line would have to be expanded and upgraded.[59]

Detailed information on BOMARC started to flow from Boeing Aircraft and the USAF early in 1957, while the RCAF wanted clarification on government policy regarding nuclear air defense weapons since the Arrow project was reaching a juncture where a decision had to made on how the aircraft would be equipped.[60] The RCAF was still juggling Sparrow II and Sparrow III, with MB-1 as the fallback position. After cancellation of Sparrow II, the RCAF was still keenly interested in acquiring a guided nuclear air-to-air weapon, including the planned Sparrow X, even if it would take time to arrange. Some RCAF analysts were skeptical about the CF-105's ability to accurately fire MB-1s in a hostile ECM (electronic countermeasures) environment and then escape the blast. Ideally, the RCAF wanted a nuclear-tipped Sparrow II or III with electronic counter-counter-measures on board. The "boffins" recommended that the RCAF acquire Sparrow II now, and get a nuclear version later.[61]

Each weapon required a different fire control system, however. Canada had the indigenous ASTRA system under development, which it was hoped could handle any or all of the potentially available air-to-air missiles. There were other fire control systems available, but they were American and thus tailored to American requirements. There were proprietary as well as sovereignty problems associated with buying "off the shelf." ASTRA had developmental problems that contributed to slowing down the whole Arrow program and increasing the cost. RCAF planners considered abandoning ASTRA to speed things up, which is what eventually happened. This left the Arrow saddled with the Hughes MA-1 fire control system, optimized for use with the Hughes Falcon missile, which at this point had no nuclear capability (an early nuclear warhead for the Falcon was canceled roughly at the same time as the USN canned the Sparrow II, though a nuclear version of the Falcon, the GAR-11, was eventually deployed in the 1960s). The fire control/missile system for the Arrow quickly became the bane of the entire program's existence even though the MA-1 could also handle MB-1 Genie.[62] The June 1957 election temporarily disrupted planning in all spheres even though "active consideration is being given to the MB-1 as an armament for the CF-105."[63]

138

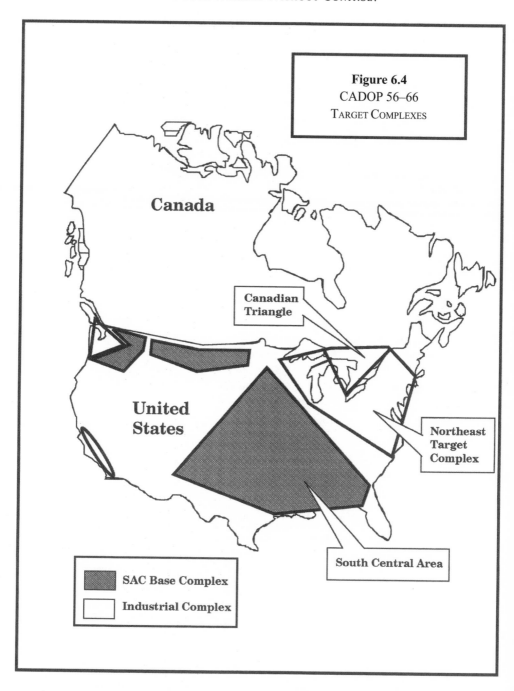

Figure 6.4
CADOP 56–66
TARGET COMPLEXES

Canada

Canadian Triangle

United States

Northeast Target Complex

South Central Area

SAC Base Complex

Industrial Complex

The Canadian air defense program was ambitious and expensive. Diefenbaker called the Cabinet Defence Committee together to review strategic policy and equipment expenditures in September 1957. Pearkes, having laid out the strategic concept and where each piece fit into it, noted that the future costs of upgrading the forces to meet the concept would be great. Therefore, he proposed, there were some areas in which economies could be made, mostly by cutting reserve forces. The Sparrow/ CF-100 program could also be eliminated. And the biggest cost was the Arrow program.[64]

The Chiefs reexamined the Arrow in October 1957. Foulkes was "gravely concerned with the delay in the CF-105 . . . [Unless the project was accelerated] it might appear that a great deal of money was being spent on an aircraft and its associated missile and ground environment which would be outmoded before it became fully operational."[65]

What was going on? Campbell and DRB chief Zimmerman noted the problems with the Sparrow II and III missile and that Sparrow II could not take a nuclear warhead at this time. It would cost more money to change over to a nuclear capability if Sparrow II was selected. This in turn affected the selection of an appropriate fire control system for the aircraft. Admiral De Wolfe questioned whether the aircraft would be needed in the ballistic missile age, while General Graham thought the whole program should be reassessed, perhaps even abandoning it altogether.[66] The Cabinet Defence Committee was informed, "in addition to Sparrow II, the Arrow will be capable of carrying an atomic air-to-air missile such as the Genie (MB-1) and will be so equipped should arrangements for the provision of this missile to Canada become possible."[67]

Campbell, supported by Foulkes, continually stressed to the Chiefs (and even to some RCAF "heretics" who favored BOMARC to the exclusion of manned aircraft) that missiles and manned aircraft were complementary systems. No one weapon could do everything under all conditions. Missiles would be volley-fired in the event of a mass raid and it might take up to a week to replenish and reload the sites. Missiles could not conduct reconnaissance missions or identify targets in peacetime. Finally, manned bombers would continue to form part of the threat even after the introduction of ballistic missiles.[68]

The RCAF heretics, Air Vice-Marshal Max Hendrick believed, were:

> conditioned on the assumption that our budget was going to be restricted and, therefore, we could not do the Arrow and the other things. This unnecessary restriction to our thinking has dominated a lot of the deliberations and influenced the recommendations unfairly in my view since the size of the budget is not for the Air Force to assume. We should state our requirements to meet the military problem and leave the Politician to decide how much money he will give us to meet the threat. . . . If you assume that you won't have enough money before you start there is no future except continual retreat as the Politician forces you to economize.[69]

The Cabinet eventually approved the acquisition of twenty-nine preproduction aircraft, noting that the Arrow was part of a system that included BOMARC, SAGE, and an expanded radar system. The Arrow's development would continue as well.[70] This approval coincided with the first major NORAD debate in the House of Commons.

By early December 1957, during the residual NORAD debates in the House of Commons, Campbell tabled proposals on BOMARC and SAGE in a Chiefs of Staff special meeting. BOMARC should go into North Bay, near the planned SAGE site (the Calgary SAGE site was abandoned due to cost and the perceived lack of enemy targets in western Canada) and near Ottawa. General Graham raised the issue of the ballistic missile threat. If this was going to supersede the bomber threat, why did Canada need an antibomber force? British strategic assessments indicated that this was where the Soviets would place their resources. Frank Miller, the Deputy Minister, countered, "if it were the intention of the United States to proceed with their present plans for the installation of BOMARC, failure of Canada to contribute her share of the overall plan would leave a gap in the defense that might place [Canada] in an almost untenable position."[71]

Either Canada had to establish BOMARC on her own territory (expensive), let the Americans build and control BOMARC on Canadian territory (not politically acceptable), or opt out completely (not morally acceptable). If the Americans continued to establish BOMARC sites on the periphery of the United States, these weapons would be used over Canadian airspace. The prospect of malfunctioning missiles carrying 10-kt-yield warheads falling into the Canadian industrial triangle from BOMARC bases in Michigan and New York was not palatable to Canadian planners.

The solution was to sound out the Americans on a cost-sharing arrangement to cover building Canadian BOMARC bases and equipping them with missiles.[72] The problem would be getting access to American nuclear warheads for the BOMARC and there appeared to be significant legal barriers.

It was at this point that the Americans proposed the NATO stockpile plan at the December 1957 NATO meeting in Paris. The Canadian delegation was informally approached by American representatives to discuss deploying nuclear air defense weapons to Canada both to support the USAF interceptor squadrons based in Canada and RCAF interceptors. They also indicated that the SAC storage agreement for Goose Bay should be included in a larger agreement.[73]

Formal discussions did not start until right after the NATO meeting in December 1958. State Department officials and General Herbert B. Loper, the Chairman of the Military Committee to the Atomic Energy Commission, met with Norman Robertson to discuss expanding the 1956–1957 MB-1 overflight arrangements that were due to expire 1 July 1958. The Americans felt that it was only fair to allow their closest ally access to similar weapons since this would benefit both parties. Specifically, Loper wanted to discuss the following: how to supply MB-1 rockets to RCAF interceptors, the provision of atomic warheads to any BOMARC units that might be established in Canada, and possible Canadian requirements for Nike-Hercules type weapons with atomic warheads.[74]

These items would, perhaps, be included with MB-1 storage plans for USAF interceptors in Canada. The US Navy was "prepared to undertake separate discussion with the Canadian Navy concerning an item of more urgency, namely, the introduction of nuclear anti-submarine devices at the leased base in Argentia."[75] Before any action was taken, however, the Americans insisted that it was imperative that Canadian views on these subjects were known before they made further plans at the military level. As an aside, the Americans also noted that they wanted to reexamine the SAC storage arrangement at Goose Bay.[76]

Norman Robertson was taken aback. What about the Atomic Energy Act and other restrictive American legislation regarding nuclear weapons? Loper assured Robertson "the limitations of present legislation required USA custody, but that this was one of the detailed matters which it was hoped to explore further."[77] As for SAC weapons, the USAF already had experience in dealing with the British on the same issue, and this could form the draft basis for an arrangement.

The Chiefs, minus Foulkes who was in Paris, eagerly examined the American policy change. They thought that the Goose Bay storage expansion was fine, since it enhanced the deterrent. It would have to go to the Cabinet. The stand-in External Affairs representative in the Chiefs of Staff Committee, J. J. McCardle, was skittish on SAC storage. He was concerned that there would be snowball effect whereby SAC would then want to place ICBM bases in Canada after getting SAC storage and then MB-1 storage. Nobody really wanted to deal with this issue at this time.[78]

In January 1958, the Cabinet approved further discussions with the Americans on both nuclear air defense weapons and SAC storage. The Chiefs asked for and got a USAF briefing team. Canadian requirements included MB-1s and BOMARC warheads for air Defense and nuclear antisubmarine weapons, while the Americans needed SAC and MB-1 storage at Goose Bay and Harmon, and nuclear antisubmarine weapons storage at Argentia.[79] Once the details of these requirements were established (safety, numbers, and delivery systems) then both countries could move forward to their Cabinets. Foulkes deemed this delay necessary since the RCAF had not determined which weapon would be mounted on the Arrow, the status of the CF-100/Sparrow upgrade, or the status of the BOMARC program.[80] It was put off until April 1958, when it was deferred yet again because of the pressing need to give attention to the air defense system. The Arrow, BOMARC, and the other supporting air defense programs occupied more than 75% of the Chiefs' and Cabinet Defence Committee's time from April to September 1958. The development and funding of each component of the air Defense system became more and more dependent on each other over time.

The Chiefs approached the whole air defense issue with caution. They did not want to be expendable scapegoats for politicians of either party if there were problems. They did not want to be accused of pushing the government into any arrangement or rushing any of the programs through. The government, on the other hand, "became intrigued by the possibility that the relatively cheap BOMARC offer by the United States might reduce, if not eliminate the need for [the CF-105]"[81] despite professional military input. After the 1957 NORAD debate, the government then "recoiled from having to reach a decision," given domestic political factors revolving around the budget deficit and increased unemployment in the Toronto area, where most AVRO Arrow contractors and subcontractors were located.[82] Another factor was Howard Green, who at this point was acting Minister of Defence Production. Green was "adamant that defense expenditures will be for items produced in Canada completely without regard either to the extra cost involved or to the delay which might prejudice the military posture. . . . Mr. Green is supported in this by Mr. Diefenbaker."[83]

This was a contradictory position for Green, since the Arrow was designed to fire nuclear-tipped missiles to protect Canada against aircraft carrying nuclear bombs. Green abhorred nuclear weapons. Clearly Green's calculus was geared towards political factors (employment, sovereignty) as opposed to moral ones in this case, or perhaps Green was deliberately sabotaging the entire air defense program by insisting that the fiscally impossible be achieved and hoping that the RCAF would back down.

There were other factors delaying the production of a final air defense plan early in 1958. If the Chiefs were to recommend that money be poured into SAGE, BOMARC, the CF-105, and an expanded radar system, this decision had to be based on a sound up-to-date threat assessment. Unfortunately, the American National Intelligence Estimate dealing with the bomber and missile threat, the NATO Standing Group's assessment, and the Canadian Joint Intelligence Committee views all differed, and this prevented the formulation of a combined Canadian-American threat estimate on which to base the joint air defense system plans. Would the Soviets continue to expand their bomber force along with expanding their missile force, or would the Soviet bomber force size plateau after 1960? In November 1957 the American threat NIE and the NATO Standing Group analysis thought that there would be expansion and improvement of the Soviet bomber force, while the Canadian Joint Intelligence Committee and joint planners thought it would plateau by 1960. The USAF agreed with the threat NIE, but thought that improvements would cease after 1962. However, the January 1958 NIE on the threat flip-flopped on this view and supported the Canadian position, which posed a problem in the Military Cooperation Committee.[84]

The NORAD intelligence staff also briefed RCAF planners. NORAD was at this time developing the North American Defense Objectives Plan (NADOP) for 1963. The January threat NIE assumed a number of things. It assumed that there would be warning so that SAC could get off the ground. It assumed that the United States would possess lots of ICBMs so that not all could be taken out in a mass raid by enemy ICBMs. The NIE assumed "a mass attack by manned bombers would throw away the initiative of surprise . . . and therefore they will consider this weapon as not worth continuing or exploring further."[85] Thus the enemy would not pursue manned bombers and would pursue ICBMs.

NORAD HQ disagreed. There was absolutely "no assurance whatsoever of a warning of an attack . . . a sneak attack by bombers is feasible and, therefore, likely to be followed by the mass attack."[86] NORAD planners believed that there was too much "fallacious thinking" going around which argued that a nuclear deterrent was enough to maintain the peace. The West had stated clearly that it would not attack first and thus nullified the first assumption. As for the second point:

> The second assumption was correct when only the west had nuclear power, but now that both sides have it in equal quantity an unprotected deterrent by itself (particularly when it is now open to surprise) is no protection whatever. This leads to the essential need for defense to support the offense.[87]

Consequently, NORAD's concept of operations revolved around fighting the air battle as far away from the targets. In terms of attack style, NORAD believed that up to 1960:

> the attack will be a manned attack by infiltration aimed at [SAC]. This will be followed within 8 to 24 hours by a mass raid over the North Pole of again manned bombers against both SAC bases and centres of population. . . . [in 1965] threat is envisaged as a surprise attack by ICBM's attacking primarily SAC bases and missile sites, followed again by a mass raid of manned bombers over the Pole.[88]

Both attacks would consist of bombers, electronic countermeasures support aircraft, and older or obsolete aircraft like the TU-4 acting as decoys. NORAD wanted a family of weapons to include long- and mid-range interceptor missiles, a long-range interceptor aircraft, medium-range SAMs (BOMARC and Nike Zeus), and an ABM (antiballistic missile) system (Nike Zeus).[89]

How much money should be allocated to the air Defense system and how much should go into research and development of an anti-ICBM system? The Chiefs were concerned enough about the matter to send a letter to US Director of Central Intelligence Allen Dulles requesting that the situation be resolved.[90]

In lieu of any American consensus, Canadian planners relied on Canadian Joint Intelligence Committee analysis produced in January 1958 in their review of the air defense situation. The joint planners were asked to answer the following questions: Does Canada need more radar cover in eastern Canada to exploit Canadian weapons and more in western Canada to exploit American weapons? Should SAGE be used in the Ottawa-North Bay region? Should BOMARC be used in the Ottawa-North Bay region?[91]

In terms of the threat, JIC determined that:

> The period between 1961 and about 1965 is one of transition during which the long-range ballistic missile threat will sharply increase. Long-range ballistic missiles will be suitable for attack on area targets, "soft" ICBM sites and SAC bases, but unsuitable for "hard" ICBM sites. Manned aircraft and submarine-launched missile attacks will continue to be employed, particularly the early part of the period . . . but the need to employ these weapons will progressively reduce.[92]

See figures 6.5 and 6.6.

Radars needed to be improved since the new enemy aircraft would have a ceiling of 50,000 feet, whereas the existing radar net was geared to 40,000 feet. The increased number and speed of enemy aircraft would overload the manual control system. Therefore SAGE was necessary. Better ground control radar stationed further north was required to exploit weapons like the BOMARC and manned interceptors equipped with guided missiles. More effective aerial weapons were necessary as well.[93]

The joint planners believed BOMARC had several advantages. It could be operational by 1961–62 along with SAGE. Since bombers would be part of the

Figure 6.5

Joint Planning Committee Bomber Threat Estimate, May 1958

Year:	TU-4 BULL	TU-16 BADGER	M4 BISON, TU-20 BEAR	Supersonic Bomber
1958	650	1100	100	nil
1959	500	1050	150	nil
1960	350	1000	195	10
1961	200	950	195	80
1962	nil	900	180	160
1963	nil	850	170	200
1964	nil	750	150	200
1965	nil	650	130	185
1966	nil	500	100	170
1967	nil	350	80	160

Source: DGHIST file 112.012 (D260), 14 May 58, "Report by the Joint Planning Committee to the COSC on the Review of Air Defence Against the Manned Bomber Threat."

threat until 1970, it would not be a temporary stopgap investment. The "B" version was suited to Canadian needs, that is, volley-firing ability (five per minute), a nuclear warhead, and the ability for a SAGE site to control seventy-five of the missiles simultaneously. Two sites in Canada would complete the chain that the Americans proposed and would provide added depth to protect SAC bases in the northeastern United States and would provide immediate area Defense for the Canadian industrial region of southern Ontario and Quebec. If the enemy developed a cruise missile for their bombers, BOMARC would be effective against them too.[94]

On the down side, BOMARC was limited in low-level intercepts by the lack of a Doppler seeker in the "A" model. More radars dedicated to low-level coverage would be needed. More critically, BOMARC used mid-course guidance provided by the radar network, which could be vulnerable to enemy jamming. BOMARC could, however, home in on significant electronic countermeasure transmissions and the provision of different types of ground radars would ensure that the enemy would be incapable of jamming them all.[95] Canada should, therefore, acquire SAGE, BOMARC, and better radars.

An independent Defence Research Board study supported the joint planners' report. Where the joint planners focused on the air Defense system, the DRB looked at the problem in light of SAC operations. The existing system (1958) was seen as

Figure 6.6

ACTUAL SOVIET STRATEGIC BOMBER THREAT TO NORTH AMERICA, 1955–1968

Type:	Variant:	Weapon:	Year:	Estimated Number:
TU-4 BULL		Gravity Bomb	1952	1000 (one-way missions, two-way with forward basing)
TU-16	BADGER A	Gravity Bomb	1954-1955	2000 (two-way mission with in-flight refuelling: limited number of tankers, many non-nuclear variants reduce number of available bombers)
	BADGER B	Missile Carrier	1961	
	BADGER C	Missile Carrier	?	
	BADGER D	Missile Carrier	1968	
TU-20	BEAR A	Gravity Bomb	1956	(1960- 48) (1964- 105)
	BEAR B	Missile Carrier	late 1950s	15
M-4	BISON A/B/C	Gravity Bomb	1955	(1961- 58)
M-50	BOUNDER	nil	1960?	supersonic B-58 equivalent never produced in qualtity
TU-22	BLINDER A	Gravity Bomb, Missile Carrier	1961	(1961-90)
	BLINDER B		1967	(1967-60) total TU-22: 150 plus 35 recce versions (two-way mission with in-flight refuelling and stand-off missile use)

Sources: Zaloga, *Target America: The Soviet Union and the Strategic Arms Race 1945–1964* (Novato: Presidio Press, 1993) pp. 251–275; Cochrane et al, *Soviet Nuclear Weapons* (Cambridge, Massachusetts: Ballinger Publishing Co., 1989) pp. 228–247; Bock, *TU-16 BADGER In Action* (New Carrollton, Texas: Squadron Signal Publications, 1990) pp. 6-8.

inadequate, and the DRB predicted that 30% to 50% of SAC bases would be destroyed within fifteen minutes of first warning by low level air attack and submarine-launched missiles. Mass bomber raids were "unlikely, unless preceded by a short warning attack to reduce retaliatory potential since the ready retaliatory force could destroy a high proportion of Russian targets unless so reduced."[96] Thus, sea-launched missiles and some bombers would open holes for larger raids and at the same time reduce SAC's immediate ability to reduce enemy follow-on attacks. To counter this, BOMARC should be used along with the Arrow, which was also compatible with SAGE. BOMARC was ten times better than the Arrow in terms of "kill potential," but the Arrow was necessary to provide depth to the missile line. Thus, all three improvements were necessary.[97]

The Chiefs considered these reports carefully in June 1958. The Army, temporarily represented by Major General George Kitching, started pushing for Nike Hercules acquisition to handle the low-level threat (see figure 6.7). Nike Hercules, they argued, was cheaper and more effective. It was already operational in the United States and it had a bigger nuclear warhead. BOMARC would not be available until the 1960s. More importantly, Nike Hercules could be upgraded to Nike Zeus, an antiballistic missile then under development in the United States. The Army did not believe that BOMARC would be able to handle the ICBM threat. The Nike Hercules, furthermore, would have a wider variety of nuclear warhead that could be used in different situations, whereas the BOMARC had only one type of warhead.[98]

Foulkes reiterated long-standing arguments about point defense and megaton-yield weapons and the potential demand by the population to extend expensive point defense protection to every population center across the country. According to Foulkes, this was exactly what happened to the Americans when they placed Nike Ajax around SAC bases and then were forced by public pressure to extend the same protection to major population centers. Recommendations for SAGE and BOMARC would go to the Prime Minister. As for the Arrow, further discussion would have to wait until the costs of the SAGE and BOMARC programs could be ascertained.[99]

The RCAF leadership viewed a classified USAF BOMARC film in July 1958. A surprisingly balanced product, the film highlighted the technical problems encountered in the program, which ones had been overcome, and which ones remained unresolved. It also showed a test of a conventional warhead, which only had an effective radius of sixty feet. Some thought that the "the film is a good one to show to the higher echelons." However, the Vice-Chief of the Air Staff, Air Vice-Marshal D. M. Smith, thought, "This is dangerous because it might lead to a re-examination of the Arrow."[100]

The ongoing Chiefs' debate on air defense produced an unwanted effect. The delays in the program, which in part were prompted by the air defense system reappraisal, triggered union and other forms of political pressure orchestrated by the AVRO company and directed at the Diefenbaker government. This "intense lobbying annoyed the Government, especially the Prime Minister, who suspected the military, particularly the [RCAF] of leaking information to [AVRO]."[101] This in turn led to a confrontation between Diefenbaker and the Chiefs, in which the Chiefs were dressed down verbally.[102]

Figure 6.7
BOMARC-NIKE HERCULES COMPARISON

	BOMARC "A"	BOMARC "B"	Nike Hercules
Target Types:	Manned Bombers	Manned Bombers and Cruise Missiles	Manned Bombers and Cruise Missiles
Range:	230 nm	420 nm	75 nm
Altitude:	65 000 feet	82 000 feet	90 000 feet
Speed:	Mach 2.5	Mach 2.3 to 2.7	Mach 2.7 to 3.5
Fuel Type:	Liquid	Solid	Solid
Warheads:	Nuclear: W 40 7-10 kt	Nuclear: W 40 7-10 kt	Conventional Nuclear: W 31 1-2 to 40 kt
In US Service:	1959	1961	1958

Sources: NORAD History Office, "NORAD Resources Statistics Book 1958–1976"; Hansen, U.S. Nuclear Weapons: The Secret History (New York: Orion Books, 1987) pp. 106–107; NAC RG 24 vol. 6158 file 0033.32 v.1, memo dated 27 September 1963, "Surface-to-air Missiles: BOMARC "B" vs. NIKE Hercules." FOIA USAF, Thomas W. Ray, "BOMARC and Nuclear Armament 1951–1963." ADC Historical Study No. 21.

This in turn produced even more caution on the part of the Chiefs. Foulkes then ordered that all air defense alternatives be placed on the table before he and Pearkes went to the Cabinet for a decision. These were:[103]

Plan A: Acquire 167 CF-105, two BOMARC sites, SAGE, and additional radar.
   Advantages: Flexible, better performance in an ECM environment.
   Disadvantages: Cost is $1.5 billion and this would leave no money for 1 Air Division reequipment or ABM projects.

Plan A1: Same as plan A, but without BOMARC. Saves money but reduces probability of kill versus bombers.

Plan B: Acquire 37 CF-105, arm them with MB-1, stop ASTRA/Sparrow development, and acquire SAGE and BOMARC.
   Advantages: Saves money, allows for nuclear weapons use by CF-105, allows money for 1 Air Division and ABM program.
   Disadvantages: Political problems re: AVRO.

Plan C: Cancel CF-105 program totally, acquire three BOMARC sites (one for the west coast), and acquire SAGE.
Advantages: Considerable savings; allows for 1 Air Division reequipment and ABM program.
Disadvantages: Inflexibility in an ECM environment. Creates political problem with regards to explaining away the $400 million sunk into the CF-105.

Plan D: Build 60 CF-105, persuade the USAF to buy 60 more for squadrons at Goose Bay,[104] and get SAGE and two BOMARC sites.
Advantages: Same as "A"
Disadvantages: Delay reequipping 1 Air Division and ABM program.

Foulkes stalked off to discuss the Arrow funding situation with the Panel on Economic Aspects of Defence Questions.[105] Pearkes, meanwhile, was able to get Diefenbaker to allow the Americans to expand and improve the ground control radar system and to enter into negotiations on SAGE. Diefenbaker wanted cost sharing with the United States on SAGE, however, which added another delay.[106]

The Chiefs reluctantly concluded that "military and economic considerations did not justify the continuation" of the Arrow on the scale originally envisioned. Pearkes then briefed the Cabinet Defence Committee on 15 August 1958.[107] This was an "acrimonious meeting" in which Canada's senior military leaders were "accused of not providing all the relevant information. It was alleged that the officials were holding back to cover up the shortcomings of the previous [government] in failing to curb the expansion [of the Arrow program]."[108]

Diefenbaker then forced Foulkes to "produce a dossier on the whole project showing complete documentation. . . . [it was] produced without delay but with some qualms about . . . furnishing confidential information of the previous administration. This was contrary to normal custom."[109]

In due course, the reasons were narrowed down to the costs of developing the Iroquois engine; the ASTRA/Sparrow system; and a reduced planned production run.[110] The original 1953 planned run of five hundred aircraft had been reduced to one hundred once the BOMARC was factored in to air defense requirements.[111] This was coupled with the lack of a vigorous AVRO and/or government marketing campaign to Commonwealth and NATO allies, which in turn contributed to a decrease in the number of aircraft to be built and thus increased cost.

Diefenbaker held several lengthy Cabinet debates on the Arrow in August and September. Note that Cabinet meetings did not include the Chiefs and that Pearkes represented the defense establishment's point of view without direct professional support. He told the Cabinet that manned bombers would continue to be a threat but the Chiefs thought that it would "be more economical to procure a fully developed interceptor of comparable performance in the US."[112] Discussions focused on SAGE and BOMARC, because of the potential cost-sharing agreements with the Americans and the fact that BOMARC would have a nuclear warhead and would be cheaper and more effective than the Arrow, both in manpower and cost. The Arrow, in Pearkes's view, should be abandoned. Other Cabinet members noted that if the

Arrow project were not abandoned, it would mean a $400 million increase in the defense budget for several years. They raised the specter of "increas[ed] taxes. . . . Adding it to the present overall rate of deficit would mean the wrecking of Canada's credit and the stimulation of inflation."[113]

There were, however, sovereignty issues at stake. If Canada became dependent on American air defense equipment, what would this mean in Parliament? Cabinet inexorably started to convince itself (despite three years of air defense planning that emphasized that fact that manned interceptors and missiles complemented each other) that BOMARC could replace the Arrow, that the threat would diminish, and that no replacement interceptor aircraft was required. There was, apparently, "an inclination to exaggerate the potential of the BOMARC (especially when armed with a nuclear warhead) . . . to soothe any uneasiness about the diminution of the air defense of Canada and to forestall any clamour about provision of an alternative interceptor aircraft."[114]

Unfortunately, the Cabinet continued to defer a decision on the Arrow due to AVRO, union, Opposition, and media clamor.[115] Under pressure to make a decision so that the other programs could get under way, the other issues were shunted to the Cabinet Defence Committee, which then approved SAGE and BOMARC acquisitions in October 1958.[116]

On 5 September 1958, Diefenbaker secretly conferred with Robert Bryce, who was at the time Secretary to the Cabinet and also sat on the Panel with Foulkes and the others. Bryce recommended to the Prime Minister that the Arrow be canceled, that Canada acquire BOMARC as well as forty to fifty F-106C interceptors from the United States and to "make available to the RCAF under arrangements similar to those in the United Kingdom, nuclear warheads for use on the BOMARC and air-to-air weapons to be used on the F-106C's."[117] Bryce also recommended that Diefenbaker should "[announce] forthwith that because of the improvement in missiles (both defensive and offensive) in recent years, and the changes in the size and nature of the bomber threat, we are introducing the BOMARC missile and proposing to introduce atomic warheads into Canadian air defense."[118]

Bryce changed his mind on the matter and thought that the Arrow was too expensive. He thought Pearkes was playing for time and delaying the inevitable. It is important to keep in mind that Bryce had a reputation in Ottawa for being an impartial economics wizard and this is probably why Diefenbaker sought his advice. Bryce examined the cost-benefit of the Arrow versus the BOMARC and, given the information that he had, saw the obvious course of action to him.[119]

Subsequently, the Panel explored cost-sharing arrangements on BOMARC/SAGE, thus behaving as though the Arrow was already canceled (Bryce chaired these discussions, and Foulkes was absent). The Panel members thought that Canada could build, maintain, and man the sites if the Americans provided the ground support equipment, missiles, and warheads. USAF "security regulations . . . with those missiles with atomic warheads" were unknown, and there might be "some restrictions on Canadian maintenance."[120] US Secretary of Defense Neil McElroy was approached directly, and responded within forty-eight hours that he thought this was a good plan, but did not have the authority to approve the American end of it. He would have to ask the President. The Panel came up with another incentive. Seaward extensions to the DEW Line would need a long-range, high-endurance aircraft. Perhaps Canada could trade an airborne warning and control system (AWACS) version of the Yukon transport aircraft for BOMARC support (this was discarded after some debate by the Americans).[121]

The Panel drew up a contingency plan that could form an umbrella that would share costs for all Canadian-American North American defense projects. The cancellation of the Arrow would remove the main Canadian-produced component in the air defense system. Canada was "in danger of slipping into much too high a degree of dependence on [the] United States in the development and production sphere."[122] Canadian industrial objectives, next to providing for the defense of the nation, were "high activity, properly diversified, and at economic rates." High cost and limited numbers posed a problem for purely Canadian systems. Integrated production was desirable, that is, components developed and produced in both nations, combined in one nation or the other, to produce a complete system. It was too late to do this with SAGE, BOMARC, and the radars now. Perhaps the first such project should be an ABM system. This should be done as rapidly as possible if the Arrow was canceled to prevent the loss of the industrial and technological base developed during the Arrow program.[123] These trends would have important implications for the decision to reequip 1 Air Division with the CF-104 strike aircraft later in 1959.

The USAF was amenable to accepting a cost-sharing formula for SAGE, BOMARC, and the radar system expansion. The package included seven heavy radars, forty-five "gap-filler" radars (to cover the low level gap), a SAGE command centre, links to SAGE from existing radars, and two thirty-missile BOMARC squadrons. Canada would cover one-third of the cost ($128.8 million U.S.) and the Americans would handle the other two-thirds ($249.2 million U.S.). Canada would cover construction and most of the manning, while the Americans would cover technical equipment.[124]

The MB-1 issue remained dormant until fall 1958. An extensive Cabinet discussion on MB-1s ensued on 15 October 1958, while the future of the Arrow program and BOMARC systems acquisition plans were examined. Pearkes placed several programs on the table. If Canada got BOMARC, she would need nuclear warheads for it. The MC 70 requirement for Lacrosse was, at this point, still under discussion, but it would need nuclear warheads, too. And the Arrow would need a nuclear warhead. American squadrons at Goose Bay and Harmon AFB needed MB-1 to be fully effective, and maritime forces needed nuclear antisubmarine weapons.[125]

Pearkes briefed the Cabinet on the NATO stockpile arrangements and controls. Nuclear warheads would be placed in SACEUR's and SACLANT's custody and released during wartime. CinCNORAD should also have custody if Canada got nuclear weapons for air defense:

> Although this procedure might appear cumbersome, there were advantages
> in not requesting special arrangements for the defense of North America.
> Ownership of the weapons would remain with the U.S. and hence the cost

could be expected to be borne by the U.S., at least until the time came to use the warheads.[126]

This reflected Foulkes's thinking on the matter.[127] Pearkes and Foulkes wanted to get on with negotiations that had been delayed since January, but because of the Diefenbaker policy process, only Pearkes could be in the Cabinet meeting.

Cabinet was agitated about the possibility that such negotiations would be leaked. It was, in their view, "highly desirable . . . [that] no information should reach the press."[128] The most pressing problem was the sovereignty issue. The cumulative effects of the NORAD debates were taking their toll. The custody plan would cause problems and it would be:

> desirable to impose conditions to preserve Canadian sovereignty so far as possible and ensure the proper use of these weapons. It would be highly distasteful to have these weapons stockpiled in Canada to be released only with the permission of the U.S. Such restrictions were understandable for offensive weapons but these were for the joint defense of North America. . . . in the proposed negotiations it should be said that they would be used in and over Canada only with the agreement of Canadian authorities.[129]

It is unclear from the minutes who was making this point. It was probably not Pearkes, though the statement, "The alternative to not coming to some agreement . . . was that Canadian forces would not be equipped with the best weapons available"[130] was probably his. Pearkes was instructed to allow the Chiefs to initiate negotiations provided they ensured that: "a minimum of other persons be informed of them; as much freedom as possible be obtained for Canadian use of these weapons; every effort be made to ensure that the Canadian government or its designated representatives would also have to authorize the use of these weapons in or over Canada by U.S. as well as by Canadian forces."[131]

Foulkes then met with General Loper of the Atomic Energy Commission and presented Canadian requirements for warheads. Loper thought that the current series of US-Italian agreements on custody and control of Jupiter ballistic missiles might be used as a basis for a future US-Canadian agreement. North America would be something different, though. The law stated:

> custody [was] to remain in American hands by which is meant that American citizens protect the weapon under conditions which would require the use of force by an outside party to gain access to the weapons. In the case of a single-seated aircraft, this would mean that the pilot would have to be an American citizen.[132]

Thus the agreement would have to deal with this after the law was changed. The best way, Loper explained, was to do another bilateral agreement with the appropriate language for training and information exchange once this other purely American step was done. Loper "felt that perhaps we should handle the problems of storage, transportation, and custody in Canada first, and leave the rather difficult problem of the release for use to later."[133]

Foulkes also asked about safety and salvage in the event of a crash in Canada. Loper passed on unclassified information and suggested that the RCAF follow up for classified information at some vague point in the future.

Foulkes, however:

> made the point that there were outstanding agreements requested by the Americans for the flight of MB-1's over Canada and for the storage of MB-1's at Goose Bay and indicated that consideration of these requests would be linked with adequate resolution of Canada's desire to have atomic [war]heads for its own defense. He pointed out that Canada could not accept the position where [her] armed forces were unfavourably armed vis a vis American forces doing the same task, ie: defending the United States. . . . the adequate resolution of Canada's ability to police its own country was related to the desire of the Americans to fly strategic missions over Canada and that if this were adequately resolved, the permission to make these flights might well be withdrawn.[134]

The message was clear: no nuclear warheads for Canada, no more SAC flights over Canada, and maybe no SAC storage at Goose Bay. Foulkes then told Loper that Canada did not want to own the weapons, since this would cost too much in the initial purchase and later when the weapons were upgraded and new ones introduced. Having the NATO commanders handle everything was better, since: "By using the NATO commander in his US role and having him arrange for the supply of these weapons to Canada, we had an American advocate to argue our case on operational grounds, who had direct access to Washington. Therefore, it was more likely to get results."[135] Presumably from men like John Diefenbaker and Howard Green.

Foulkes met with Nathan Twining, who assured Foulkes, "the Joint Chiefs and the [US] Air Force would lean over backwards to provide [for Canadian] requirements within the law."[136] Emergency plans for salvaging nuclear weapons in the event of an accident became an issue that Foulkes used. If there was no Canadian capability to handle salvage and there was a crash, this would mean that American teams would have to be brought into Canada. This was unacceptable for a sovereign nation. If this happened, Foulkes told Twining, the Prime Minister might prohibit SAC overflights altogether. This contributed to breaking loose more information on the weapons themselves and the establishment of RCAF nuclear weapon recovery teams.[137]

Eisenhower's National Security Council considered the matter of Canadian access to the nuclear stockpile throughout the fall of 1958. This examination was part of a larger discussion in the NSC that reflected American concern about their relationship with their northerly neighbor and the problems associated with defense issues:

> the Canadian Government is confronted with a dilemma. On the one hand, the Government has emphasized the rights of Canada as a sovereign power

and the relationship of defense production to Canadian industrial and scientific growth; on the other hand, it is faced with the economic reality that Canada does not have the resources to finance the more expensive weapons systems for modern Defense. [This] is exemplified by its recent decision to reduce drastically the production of the Canadian-developed CF-105 supersonic interceptor aircraft and to introduce into the Canadian air Defense system the U.S.-produced BOMARC missile in its stead. . . .[138] [Canada] can be expected to be sensitive over any future defense production sharing arrangement which create the impression that Canada will produce only minor components for joint defense projects. . . . Unless Canadian defense industries do remain healthy, the United States probably will not receive the same excellent cooperation in the joint defense effort that has prevailed in the past.[139]

Initially the NSC discussed ways of helping Canada increase cash flow such as reducing American restrictions on oil imports, or giving increased preferential treatment to Canadian Defense contractors and a better exchange of industrial information.[140] The American policy was unknown to the Canadians.

The Canada-US Committee on Joint Defense, consisting of Foulkes, Pearkes, Smith, Dulles, and US Secretary of Defense Neil McElroy, met on 15 December 1958 to discuss nuclear weapons for continental Defense. At this meeting, Pearkes and Smith tabled a draft statement that they planned to take to Diefenbaker so that he could make a statement in the House of Commons to keep the public informed. The purpose was to focus the discussions specifically on the nuclear weapons issue. In effect, the draft statement argued that nuclear weapons were necessary, not only for the defense of Europe, but for North America as well. Canada agreed that this was necessary, but so was "the importance of limiting the spread of nuclear weapons at the independent disposal of national governments,"[141] the continuing need for arms control negotiations, and the continuing need for collective security and deterrence. The main issue was control. NORAD would command nuclear air defense forces over Canada and release would be by mutual consent of the Canadian and American governments. Canadian nuclear weapons use in Europe would be subject to further negotiation with SACEUR.[142]

Dulles attempted to make a connection between defensive nuclear weapons stored in Canada and offensive SAC nuclear weapons stored in Canada. This was fobbed off by Smith, who told Dulles that this matter was not up for discussion at this time and should not have any bearing on defensive weapons acquisition by Canada. With regard to joint NORAD control over defensive nuclear use, McElroy had no problem, as long as the military commanders were consulted. There were some technical problems, however. If the planned American ICBMs were launched over Canadian territory, did the United States have to inform Canada first? McElroy considered ICBMs to be defensive weapons. Did Canada really want joint control over these? In reality, the Canadians were more concerned about MB-1 and BOMARC use instead.[143]

Both sides agreed that a public statement should be made, but detailed discussions on release procedures should start as soon as possible and nuclear information agreements should be promulgated so that they could be implemented. Dulles came away with the impression that "the meeting served more as scenery than as a place for substantive debate."[144]

In the wake of the Smith-McElroy meeting, the NSC concluded that Canada should be given defensive nuclear weapons without the restrictions the Americans planned to impose on its NATO allies. In an annex to the NSC 5822/1 dated 30 December 1958, the NSC recognized that "the early attainment of an operational nuclear delivery capability for Canadian continental defense forces would contribute significantly"[145] to the defense system. There were discussions already underway, and Canada would probably ask for access to nuclear weapons, but the NSC believed Canada did not have access to information needed to attach weapons to existing delivery vehicles, information to "assure the operability of the nuclear warhead and information necessary for safety in the employment of the weapons."[146] A new agreement was needed.

The NSC noted:

> whether or not the Canadians themselves request actual custody of and authority to use nuclear weapons, such custody and authority . . . will be required for optimum effectiveness if we are to assure a . . . fully effective continental defense posture . . . [this can only be met if] Canada has actual custody and authority to use the nuclear warheads in question. For example, if MB-1 rockets are provided, the Canadian forces should be allowed to carry the weapon aloft, in preparation for an attack, on the same basis that U.S. forces carry such a weapon. If nuclear anti-submarine weapons are provided, the warhead should be aboard the Canadian vessel and subject to procedures for use identical with those for U.S. vessels. In the case of any fast reacting air defense missiles systems the utility of the weapon would be degraded if involved bi-lateral procedures delayed weapon launching.[147]

Furthermore:

> It is considered that the transfer to Canada of custody and the authority to use nuclear weapons should be in accordance with agreed procedures for the expenditure of nuclear weapons by U.S. forces.[148]

There would be problems with the Atomic Energy Act and with the NATO allies, the NSC assumed. As for Canada, if NATO-type procedures were used, it would "carry an implication of distrust or a limitation on the partnership status envisioned under our continental defense arrangements. . . . Canada itself might not desire preferential treatment."[149]

The NSC initially thought Canadian forces should use American custodians, and that nuclear information dissemination should be expedited. Pending a change in the Atomic Energy Act, "It is in the U.S. security interest to transfer to Canada at an appropriate time the custody of nuclear components for continental defense. . . .

In no case should action be taken outside the Executive branch without prior knowledge that Canada desires such custody."[150]

The Canadian Chiefs wanted the government's authority to continue discussions on the matter of nuclear warhead access and storage. Cabinet met to examine the issue in December 1958 prior to the annual NATO meeting. Some members thought that the mere fact the only the President could release nuclear weapons infringed on Canadian sovereignty, though someone pointed out that, while it took Eisenhower to release weapons, their actual use by Canadian forces would be subject to Canadian control. This amounted to more hairsplitting on the control issue, which continued to ignore the fact that there might not be time to consider and then issue joint orders. The Americans still wanted to link defensive MB-1 storage with SAC storage. Cabinet was adamant that "It would be impossible to agree to the storage of offensive nuclear weapons at Goose Bay until Canadian forces were in the position of being able to use . . . modern defensive weapons as U.S. forces."[151]

In other words, SAC storage was hostage to Canadian access to MB-1s, nuclear depth bombs, and Honest John warheads. The possibility that the Americans might entertain transferring the custody of nuclear weapons to Canada did not occur to Canadian policy makers. Foulkes and Pearkes's previous beliefs that this would increase the already-strained defense budget negated any possibility of Canadian consideration of this course of action.

Canadian access to nuclear weapons was now subject to the legalities of a bilateral Canada-US agreement on nuclear information sharing. The Americans had already modified their Atomic Energy Act in July 1958 to allow for a wider distribution of information. Once the Americans backed off on the SAC storage and SAC overflight issues, the Diefenbaker government was amenable to signing the bilateral agreement. For all intents and purposes, the 1959 agreement was similar to the 1955 agreement. The only difference was that the appendix listing the types of information that would be made available would be expanded.[152] Delays on the agreement continued into 1959.

In January 1959, the USAF released MB-1 installation drawings to the RCAF, which then forwarded them to AVRO "to assist in the design of the MB-1 installation in the Arrow." Other material on the way included a study for equipping the CF-100 with MB-1.[153] Why was this done? Some of the RCAF leadership was still hopeful that something from the Arrow program could be salvaged. Any decision to cease production of the Arrow would still leave Canada with twenty-nine partially completed aircraft. There was no reason why these machines should be wantonly discarded. The RCAF was clearly hedging its bets. If the twenty-nine aircraft were retained, they could be equipped with the cheaper MB-1 system. If the Arrow was canceled, the CF-100 could carry MB-1 until a replacement aircraft was acquired. The CF-100 lacked the altitude to deal with some threats, but provision was made to modify the MG-2 fire control system to fire the MB-1 in a snap-up action. The USAF air defense squadrons had developed a snap-up maneuver employing the F-89J/MB-1 combination. The launching aircraft ascended at a sharp angle toward the target until the interceptor's ceiling had been reached and flipped the

MB-1 beyond the ceiling at the high-flying target. The CF-100 was capable of performing the maneuver.[154]

The Arrow affair came to a head in February 1959. The Chiefs met in no less than four special meetings to reconsider the air defense program. Campbell was increasingly concerned that if the Arrow did not go through, no provision had been made to acquire a replacement for the CF-100. He started to push for the American F-106 as its replacement; the F-108 was still under development (the F-108 was never completed). The DRB "boffins" were called in to give their views on the ballistic missile threat and the possibility of defending against them. They were pessimistic about the prospects of an effective ABM system, though they though the manned bomber threat would continue until at least the mid-1960s.[155]

Pearkes met with the Chiefs, who then told him that if the Arrow was canceled, alternative arrangements would have to be made with the Americans to protect Canada. Canada should acquire 100 to 150 American interceptors, allow the USAF ADC to occupy more than two bases in Canada, allow USAF interceptors to disperse to Canadian air bases, and make arrangements for USAF BOMARCs to operate in Canada. The CF-100s could handle BADGER but not BEAR or BISON aircraft. The initial enemy attack would consist of about 100 aircraft (BEAR, BADGER, and/or BISON) but there was no clear evidence that a Soviet supersonic bomber was in production. Pearkes interpreted this as a lessening of the manned bomber threat and therefore he believed the announcement of the Arrow cancellation could be based on this factor. Campbell tried to get Pearkes to go along with a replacement aircraft but to no avail. Pearkes sent the brief recommending canceling the Arrow to Diefenbaker without getting the Chiefs' consent.[156] This was done "in order to cover up this dissension among the Chiefs of Staff at a time when feeling was running high."[157] Attempting to use the sovereignty issue as a means to protect the Arrow had failed. Apparently some members of the Air Staff openly wept after the decision was made.

On 20 February 1959, Diefenbaker told the House of Commons that Arrow was dead and that Canada would, as a compensatory measure, discuss with the Americans provision for nuclear warheads for BOMARC and MB-1 Genies. The Arrow decision not only put 25,000 skilled aerospace workers on the street, damaged the industrial base, and caused further political problems, it killed Canada's only locally-designed and built nuclear delivery system.

Chief of the Air Staff, Air Marshal Hugh Campbell suggested the physical destruction of the Arrow aircraft at Malton in the spring of 1959. George Pearkes asked Campbell how the airframes would be disposed of and Campbell told him that they could be declared surplus or turned over to the Department of Defence Production and scrapped. Campbell was disinclined to recommending declaring the Arrows surplus since it "could lead to subsequent embarrassment, that is, airframe and engine could conceivably be placed on public view or even in fact used as a roadside stand. This, I am sure, you will agree is most undesireable."[158] D. A. Golden, Deputy Minister of Defense Production, and Pearkes concurred and ensured that the grim task was carried out.

The destruction not only included the existing aircraft but much of the paperwork generated by the program. Many observers at the time saw this as overkill and questioned why it was done.[159] It is likely that the overzealousness of the security forces in the round-up of the Arrow program can be attributed to the fact that there was a complete set of MB-1 Genie installation diagrams and manuals on the premises of AVRO Canada and that one of the aircraft was in the process of fitting the MA-1 fire control system which was capable of firing MB-1s. All of this material would have been highly classified American nuclear weapons design data and would have to have been secured to prevent it from falling into the wrong hands.

The political fallout from the Arrow cancellation joined the dust that was already lingering in the atmosphere from the NORAD debates. The Opposition had taken continual shots at the delays and cost of the Arrow program since 1957 and it got worse after 20 February.[160]

What did the end of the Arrow mean in relationship to the 1957–1958 NORAD debates? The lack of a manned interceptor would leave a hole in the defense system. SAC's vulnerability would increase, and its deterrent value decrease; therefore risk would increase. If USAF interceptors filled the hole, then this process was nullified, but this produced an additional problem. It would mean more American personnel and American bases on Canadian soil and more American aircraft flying overhead, which would add to the appearance that Canada could not participate in her own Defense and result in an even greater erosion of sovereignty. This is exactly what the Diefenbaker government had been elected in 1957 to *prevent* in the first place.

There was another aspect to the problem. With no manned interceptor squadrons, what could Canada contribute now to legitimize her equal partner status in NORAD? Sixty BOMARC missiles for which bases had not been built yet, or nuclear warhead agreements signed for yet? A SAGE command center that was not even under construction? Nine aging CF-100 squadrons was not enough "currency." There was, of course, the geographical contribution and the early warning system, but Canadian airspace needed to be patrolled and defended by Canadians. In other words, cancellation of the Arrow *exacerbated* the multitude of problems raised during the NORAD debate.

In the end, the Arrow was canceled because the Diefenbaker government would not allocate more money to the defense budget so that Canada could maintain a balanced force structure in Europe and North America.[161] As the Chief of the Air Staff noted in the aftermath, "they came in with an avowed intention of cutting military expenses and raising old age pensions, etc. and it all costs money . . . they are holding it at the present level dollar-wise and taking a chance of being under the wing . . . of the [United States]."[162] The bright light in the affair was that the reequipment of 1 Air Division could start. The unemployment ramifications were slightly alleviated when Canadair got the contract to build the CF-104 strike fighter in Canada, but the whole Arrow matter left a bad taste in everyone's mouth.

7

ENGINES FOR ARMAGEDDON: CANADIAN NUCLEAR FORCES AND NATO, 1957–1960

We don't make policy here, gentlemen. Elected
officials, civilians, do that. We are the instruments
of that policy, and although we are not at war, we
must act as though we are at war. We're the tip of
the spear and we'd best be sharp.

–Top Gun

Introduction

It was one thing to have a policy, another to have a policy and a strategy, and still something else to be able to execute that strategy to fulfill the objectives of the policy. The NATO wrangling over the MC 70 nuclear force plan never really went away, but something had to be done if NATO commanders were to have forces capable of deterring the Soviets. Once the Diefenbaker government agreed that MC 70 constituted a basis for Canadian force structuring, the armed services were free to explore how they would adapt. Note that the armed services had been primed for the better part of the 1950s and much groundwork had already been laid to accept nuclear weapons into the Canadian forces. The aim of this section is to provide an overview of the thinking that led the armed forces to select specific delivery systems. The reasoning in most cases was to retain Canadian saliency in the NATO and NORAD alliances as much as to provide an effective deterrent force.

MC 70 and Army Rocketry

The Army's centerpiece was the West Germany–based brigade group committed to SACEUR. The brigade group worked with I (British) Corps as part of the Northern Army Group (NORTHAG). Under MC 70, the Dutch, West German, British, Belgian, and Canadian units committed to NORTHAG were to be equipped with a variety of delivery systems. The original 1957 MC 70 recommendation to Canada regarding surface-to-surface missiles in Europe was one "Atomic Delivery Unit," a battalion consisting of two batteries each with four launchers. NATO planners wanted the Honest John unguided rocket throughout the Central Region since the weapon was a mature system, had been in service since 1954, and was reliable. At that time, the Honest John was considered a corps-level weapon. Since Canada did not possess a corps, the Canadian Chiefs believed that it was excessive to have a whole battalion, even for the division commitment of which only a brigade group was deployed in West Germany. In 1958, the commitment was tentatively switched to two Honest John and two Little John launchers, and then it changed again to two Little John and two Lacrosse launchers.[1] This change was probably the result of the possibility that the brigade group might change its role into the Central Region mobile reserve.

Little John and Lacrosse were still under development in 1958, but these two weapons appeared to suit the Army's needs for the foreseeable future. The Honest John was a large rocket mounted on a truck, with a number of other support vehicles. Little John and Lacrosse were airportable with a minimum of preparation. Lacrosse was mounted on the back of a truck, while Little John was trailer mounted and could even be transported by helicopter. Little John was a smaller version of the Honest John and, as such, was an unguided rocket. Lacrosse, on the other hand, was a guided missile. The US Army had plans to use both and was developing a family of conventional and nuclear warheads for both systems.[2] The Canadian Chiefs were able to convince the Cabinet to give approval to a Lacrosse purchase, and were permitted to also explore a Little John purchase. However, the Little John requirement evaporated when the decision was made to keep the brigade group in its original role in NORTHAG, rather than convert it to an airmobile formation. The requirement now became four Lacrosse launchers.[3]

Lacrosse ran into severe developmental difficulties in 1959. The US Army acquired eight battalions of the original version and canceled the improved version, which was the one the Canadian Army was interested in. Lacrosse, a command guided missile, was subject to enemy electronic countermeasures as well as interference from friendly radio sets: these were clearly not good characteristics for a weapon equipped with a nuclear warhead. In addition, only one missile could be controlled in the air at any one time within a given radius. These parameters were unacceptable if the weapons had to be volley fired. Finally, there were an unacceptable number of component failures, which reduced the weapon's serviceability.[4] The Canadian Army dropped Lacrosse.

Army planners looked to Honest John to fulfill the MC 70 requirement. How many launchers were required? SHAPE wanted four located in Europe. A number would be needed for training in Canada. A compromise produced six launchers: two in Canada and four in Europe with 115 rockets, which the planners believed would do for Phase I of a conflict. Cabinet approved the acquisition of Honest John with little discussion on 25 March 1960, probably because the nuclear capability of the system was downplayed throughout the process. 1 SSM (Surface-to-Surface Missile) Battery and 2 SSM (Training) Battery were formed in September 1960.[5]

Canadian Maritime Forces and Nuclear Antisubmarine Warfare

The RCN and RCAF created a concept of maritime operations to take into account the pattern of war developed in MC 48 and the evolving maritime force structure, which included surface ships, land- and carrier-based ASW aircraft, and a mix of conventional and nuclear ASW weapons. The adoption of MC 14/2 (revised) did not alter RCN/RCAF thinking, as the planners viewed MC 14/2 (revised) as a minor evolution of MC 48. The planners referred to both concepts as "MC 48" well into 1961. MC 70 requirements for the RCN/RCAF maritime forces did not have a great impact on the concept. Even the stockpile announcement was considered evolutionary to some extent, as Canadian maritime planners were well aware of American developments in nuclear antisubmarine warfare (ASW). The COSC authorized the RCAF and RCN to enter into "exploratory discussions" with their American counterparts in January 1958 to "determine the Canadian requirements for the use and storage of nuclear anti-submarine devices . . . and then discuss the possible requirements for the storage of American weapons in Canada and what opportunities there might be for joint storage."[6] External Affairs' only concern at this point was that the Canadian commanders ensure that safety precautions were adequate.[7]

New intelligence on Soviet capabilities entered the picture when the MCC submitted "MCC 600/2: Future Defence Analysis" to the Canadian Chiefs and US Joint Chiefs. MCC 600/2 argued that the Soviets would, by 1961, be able to maintain forty-one submarines in the Atlantic and sixteen in the Pacific Ocean in peacetime on stations off the coasts of North America. Eight of these would be nuclear powered. Most of these submarines would be equipped with nuclear mines, nuclear torpedoes, or nuclear guided missiles. They would be supported with covert minelayers (merchant ships equipped for this purpose) and long-range aircraft equipped with nuclear weapons. The Soviets were already equipped with a 500-mile-range cruise missile, and its range would extend to 1000 miles by 1961. The accuracy of this weapon would improve and targets would probably be SAC bases.[8] MCC 600/2 recommended that a large number of improvements were critical and that there be "provision for the employment of atomic weapons."[9] The Chiefs accepted this as a basis for planning and instructed Vice-Admiral De Wolfe to execute it.[10]

The RCN's 1958 Emergency Defence Plan (EDP) used MC 14/2 (revised) as its basis. The emergency plan recognized that SAC was the priority target, with industry, government, and population as secondary targets. Canada would have two or three hours warning from the DEW Line for a bomber attack, though submarines might be able to attack earlier. The EDP would be conducted "in the initial stages of a war and before SACLANT reassigns forces to other tasks."[11] In doing so, the RCN's primary task was the destruction of enemy submarines, followed by the destruction of incoming cruise missiles launched from both submarines and long-range aircraft, and the protection of Canadian ports from nuclear mines and torpedoes.[12]

Existing Canadian maritime forces would be deployed on the Atlantic coast to "prevent submarines from gaining advantageous missile-firing positions" for up to the first thirty days of the war.[13] There would be no time to mobilize the reserve fleet. At this time Pacific Command had initiated a relationship with USN forces on the west coast and had conducted antiguided missile submarine exercises in concert with them. These exercises incorporated the use of the Mk 90 "Betty" nuclear depth bomb from USN maritime patrol aircraft into exercise "play": the participating RCN units were indoctrinated with the safety distance and other employment techniques of that weapon.[14]

The maritime patrol aircraft fleet was under constant development during this time. The RCAF considered the P2V Neptunes to be interim aircraft. The replacement aircraft was the CP-107 Argus (though both types served side by side because of the Canadian commitment of forty MPAs to SACLANT under MC 70). The Argus was the most advanced and capable of this type of aircraft in NATO, and continued to be well into the 1960s. A four-engine aircraft, the design incorporated two huge bomb bays capable of carrying 8000 pounds of weapons. It had superior range and endurance to all existing NATO patrol aircraft. The Argus possessed sensor systems that included MAD (magnetic anomaly detection), LOFAR (low frequency analysis and recording) buoys, and explosive echo ranging. In terms of weapons, the Argus was originally designed to carry conventional Mk 54 depth bombs and Mk 30 and Mk 43 homing torpedoes. The aircraft's immense capacity, however, was well suited to cater to future technological developments. There were initially three Argus squadrons deployed in 1958 (all assigned to the east coast) for a total of thirty-three aircraft.[15]

With this new capability coming on-line and with the NATO stockpile announcement, it should come as no surprise that the RCAF produced more detailed requirements for nuclear ASW weapons. A report by the nuclear weapons requirements team in July 1958 determined that there were two types of USN nuclear depth charges, but more information was required on their comparative characteristics so that a choice could be made. For thirty days of operations in Phase I of a war, the team concluded that the RCAF would need 128 nuclear depth charges.[16]

American nuclear ASW capability had increased exponentially by 1958. All maritime patrol aircraft in USN service (S2F, P2V, P5M) were capable of using the Mk 90 "Betty" and the new Mk 101 "Lulu." The Mk 101 was a physically smaller weapon and thus could be adapted to a wider variety of platforms, like the Sikorsky HSS-1 and HSS-1N helicopters operating from USN ASW carriers. The "Lulu" had a W 34 warhead with a 10–15 kt yield and could be surface-burst against ships as well as against submarines.[17] The follow on to the Mk 101 was the Mk 105 "Hotpoint," deployed late in 1959. The Mk 90s were retired shortly after that. The Mk 105 was similar to the Mk 101 in yield but had a "cookie cutter" shock-absorbing nose and improved aerodynamic shape.[18]

Air Commodore W. W. Bean and Commodore Jeffry Brock were assigned to produce a joint Canadian requirement for nuclear weapons in a maritime setting. This requirement was produced in 1959, when the effects of the antinuclear weapons faction in the Cabinet were in ascendance. The authors noted at the beginning of the report, "Whilst present government policy precludes the use of special weapons, it is considered that the potential of these weapons is such that there is a requirement for their use by Canadian Maritime Forces."[19]

A conventional weapon was less effective against nuclear-propelled or fast, conventional submarines. Therefore, the report argued, kill probability could be increased by increasing the weapon's delivery accuracy, increasing the accuracy of the detection and fire control systems, or increasing the lethal radius of the weapon. With existing technological limitations in delivery and detection, the course of action was to increase the lethal radius, and this could be done only with a nuclear weapon.[20]

Notably, both planners believed that there might be limitations on nuclear ASW weapons use. It would be costly to rely solely on nuclear weapons. Tactical and geographical restrictions "precluded exclusive use." In terms of types of weapons, Brock and Bean thought that the ASROC stand-off missile with a nuclear warhead was "not suitable for retrofitting in RCN ships," but thought it might be incorporated in later designs. Of the two existing aerial nuclear depth bombs, the Mk 90 could be carried by the RCAF patrol aircraft, but not the RCN's Trackers or their planned helicopters. The Mk 101 could fulfill Canadian requirements since it could fit on all platforms.[21] Brock and Bean strongly recommended that the maritime forces pursue nuclear weapons acquisition.

The RCN was at this time finalizing its requirements for a new shipboard helicopter. Successful tests conducted with a platform mounted on the destroyer HMCS *Buckingham* convinced the RCN that large ASW helicopters carrying dunking sonar, torpedoes, and depth bombs could operate from destroyer-sized vessels.[22]

The new machine had to be able to operate independently from its parent ship, as well as in concert with it. It had to have the capability of "the carriage and release of one 1,200 lb weapon in lieu of two homing torpedoes."[23] The Mk 101 "Lulu" weighed 1200 pounds.[24] The only machine that met these requirements was the Sikorski HSS-1 Sea King, then under development in the United States for the USN. The RCN initiated procurement procedures late in 1961, ensuring that the special weapons capability was downplayed, and made plans to modify the *St. Laurent* and *Restigouche* classes of destroyers to accept the Sea King in the early 1960s.

USN-Canadian relations, already relatively close, grew closer still in 1959. In February of that year, Admiral Wright notified the JCS that, "The increasing threat of Russian submarine capability to launch guided missiles against the United States and the number of Russian submarines which threaten the shipping necessary to resupply our National and Allied Forces in Europe cannot be destroyed with the forces now available."[25]

Wright recommended that there was a "requirement to accelerate preparations to meet the submarine launched guided missile threat" that entailed increasing the peacetime operational readiness of the USN; the extension, integration, and improvement of the SOSUS underwater listening system; the installation of a barrier system in the GIUK (Greenland-Iceland-United Kingdom) Gap, and the "rapid procurement of proven ASW hardware,"[26] which presumably included nuclear ASW weapons.

More and better information on USN nuclear ASW requirements and capabilities was informally passed on to the RCN and RCAF. If Canada required nuclear antisubmarine weapons, the USN indicated that such weapons could be made available from their stocks, that is, Canada would not have to buy them. If Canada chose to base the weapons in Canada, storage facilities needed to be built, with the primary locations at Comox, British Columbia; Greenwood, Nova Scotia; and Summerside, Prince Edward Island. The Greenwood site would handle both RCAF and RCN weapons, while any RCAF MPA deployed to Torbay, Newfoundland, could conceivably draw on the USN storage site located on the leased base territory at Argentia. All of this was subject to government-level negotiations that foundered in 1959.[27]

The USN had already embarked on an extensive storage construction program to support its forces operating in the Atlantic. In 1958, there were three sites: Brunswick, Maine; Norfolk, Virginia; and Jacksonville, Florida. In 1959, the site at Argentia, Newfoundland, was completed, followed by Keflavik, Iceland, in 1960.[28] The Argentia site would, however, not contain assembled nuclear weapons before 1967:[29] it was another casualty of the Diefenbaker government's nuclear weapons policy.

1 Air Division, RCAF and the Nuclear Strike Role

1 Air Division commanders, after participating in several exercises, thought that the formation should shift to the nuclear strike role. In 1957 the RCAF leadership was in favor of replacing the CF-86 and CF-100 fighters with either the F-100 or F-104 for the strike and reconnaissance role. The 1958 version of the SACEUR minimum force study thought that four RCAF squadrons equipped with F-100s would be acceptable, but Foulkes and others were neither happy with the process by which this recommendation was generated, nor did they think that it was economically feasible to maintain four different types of aircraft in small numbers in Europe.

SHAPE could not wait for Canada to make up her mind on the matter and its planning for war in Europe continued to evolve. The basic concept of operations in ACE from 1957 to 1963 was the same as the one discussed in the Army section earlier, to whit: SACEUR's forces had to be able to survive the initial enemy attack, destroy the enemy's ability to use nuclear weapons, stop their land attack as far east as possible, and interdict their ability to continue offensive operations. SACEUR's 1958 Emergency Defence Plan included a revised aerial Atomic Strike Plan (ASP) that had three programs that corresponded to the basic concept of operations. These included a Scheduled Plan (nuclear delivery capability targets); Counter Radar Program (radar and control centers); and an Interdiction Program (mobility targets like bridges and rail junctions).[30] Most targets were "deep inside the Soviet sector" in East Germany, Czechoslovakia, and western Poland.[31]

The delivery vehicles for the 1958 ASP were mostly American F-100 and B-66 aircraft, plus Matador cruise missiles based in Germany, France, and the UK.[32] The British prepared to deploy a nuclear Canberra force but this would not be available before 1958. MC 70, if fully implemented, would relegate a significant proportion of these targets to other NATO air forces once they had been reequipped.[33]

In its deliberations over the 1958 NATO Annual Review, the Panel on the Economic Aspects of Defence Questions considered the future status of 1 Air Division. The Canadian chapter maintained that a mixed force was incompatible with Canada's policy of collective forces and that the matter was under continual study.[34] By August, the temporary External Affairs representative to the Panel, D. V. LePan, actually thought that 1 Air Division should be returned to Canada. Perhaps this would solve the problem. If, LePan reasoned, missiles would take over the air defense job, External Affairs might consider this to be an option, though the brigade group would have to stay to exert a Canadian presence in Europe. Foulkes was opposed to removal of 1 Air Division. The implementation of MC 70 in other NATO nations was not going well. Introducing this new variable into the mix would cause greater confusion and could put the whole deterrent effort in jeopardy. Canada could lead by making up her mind and implementing a positive course of action. Norstad was constantly pressuring Foulkes to do so. Foulkes thought the issue needed greater technical study by the RCAF and favored delaying tactics while this was done. As part of this effort, External Affairs should criticize the British and the French in the NAC for their intransigence on MC 70 to take the heat off Canada.[35]

The RCAF needed technical requirements from SACEUR as to roles and missions. It knew that the entire formation would have to be reequipped with one aircraft type and that type might have to serve multiple roles. If twelve strike/attack squadrons were more than what SACEUR needed, could the number of squadrons be reduced to save money?[36] The entire matter was complicated by the ongoing CF-105 Arrow problem. The CF-105 was unsuited to the strike/attack role, yet there was still a requirement for an interceptor for North American air defense. There might not be enough money for both the CF-105 and a new strike/attack aircraft. There was a dilemma: if Canada put money into the nuclear strike commitment and eliminated funds for the CF-105, this would mean that the USAF would have to defend Canadian airspace when the CF-100s wore out. This was politically unacceptable.[37]

The cancellation of the CF-105 Arrow sent shock waves throughout the Canadian strategic policy-making community. A vital but costly system had been eliminated. Though disappointing to the RCAF in the air defense field, it assisted in solving the 1 Air Division reequipment problem.

The matter was examined during the annual RCAF senior officers meeting in March 1959. Multiple factors propelled the RCAF in its decision. The first was cost. Pearkes addressed the gathering, stating that he had to come up with half a billion dollars for the program. He believed that the program was so vital that he wanted Norstad to come over and brief the Prime Minister on the nature of the requirement.[38] Chief of the Air Staff Campbell emphasized that any selection would be in part dictated by cost:

> [I know] what we want and I have SACEUR's agreement to accept what is needed. In June we hope to have a decision but I will not forecast that we have a decision. The fact that we are in this rather difficult period vis à vis ourselves and the public places demands on the part of the senior officers for the utmost effort and a display of untold leadership and it requires the backing of all the senior officers to transcend this period. . . . It is being done on an informal basis with the backing of the Minister.[39]

This undoubtedly was in reference to the demoralizing Arrow affair and the strain it placed on the RCAF-Government and personal relationships.

The second factor involved NATO, as Campbell elaborated:

> the business of re-equipping the Air Division is broader than the RCAF. It should be re-equipped because NATO is comprised of the Big Three and the remainder of the smaller nations and the smaller nations look to Canada

and if Canada does not see fit to re-equip, it will be looked upon as a dis-memberment of NATO and the politicians will not face up to that particular ditch . . . [the RCAF] is in a strong position, we have a recommendation from SACEUR for the role we should be going into—a strike role. . . . I am more optimistic than I was recently.[40]

Foulkes had a conversation with Norstad, the gist of which he conveyed to the RCAF senior officers:

Every time we talk to Norstad about this he is adamant. He would be very upset to see [the] Air Division or the Brigade leave. He maintains the Air Division and the Brigade are very good examples for the other people to follow, and it is to demonstrate to the other countries that countries besides the United States can keep its forces at a high state of readiness and make a proper contribution. If we started to make suggestions of withdrawal our first difficulty would be with Norstad and our second would be with the Council [NAC]. The French have just decided to take their Mediterranean Navy from outside NATO command and it has caused a lot of rumblings. But it would cause more rumblings if it looked like North America was going to pull out of NATO . . . things in NATO are perhaps shakier than they have ever been.[41]

To assist in decision making, Air Vice Marshal Larry Dunlap, who at the time was serving at SHAPE as the Deputy Chief of Staff, Operations, briefed the confer-ence on the nature of the SACEUR nuclear strike plan. Within a matter of hours after the go order, strike aircraft would range to a depth of several hundred miles deep into Warsaw Pact territory with the aim of "deny[ing] the enemy both tactical and strategic flexibility and mobility." The first phase of the ASP (not to be confused with Phase I of the MC 48 or 14/2 concepts) would be to go after rail, road, and communications systems.

The RCAF generated its operational characteristics for the future strike/attack aircraft by the beginning of April 1959. Dubbed the CF-111 on paper, the stated primary roles of the aircraft were:

a) The effective delivery by day or night of nuclear or high explosive stores from low or medium levels, not above 20000 feet, under visual or limited blind bombing conditions against pre-selected targets.

b) The effective delivery by day or night of nuclear or high explosive stores or a variety of air-to-ground weapons from low altitude under visual condi-tions against tactical targets of every description including armoured ve-hicles, troop concentrations, lines of communication, air fields, and targets of opportunity.[42]

Once Campbell had his ducks in a row, Foulkes arranged to have Norstad fly to Ottawa in May once again to address Diefenbaker and the Cabinet. In his view, Norstad stated:

In the past none of the allies had been better in quality than Canada and this quality adapted to the delivery of atomic weapons in the strike/attack role would be an important element in NATO's strength. The Canadian Air Division and the Brigade would, if the Canadian government agreed, have atomic weapons available to them under the same type of arrangements that applied in the case of the United Kingdom. Warheads would be made available on NATO authority in furtherance of NATO plans; they would be located on Canadian bases and guarded by Canadian servicemen; the "key to the cupboard" would be held by a United States officer, and maintenance would be done by a small group of United States personnel. These weapons could be used only if both Canada and the appropriate NATO authority, acting on behalf of the United States, agreed.[43]

It was not a formal Cabinet meeting, so no decision was taken. When the Cabinet next met on 19 June 1959, Pearkes reiterated the need to reequip 1 Air Division lest "the NATO Alliance would start to disintegrate."[44] Though the Cabinet agreed to the reequipment of the formation, it was their understanding that they were doing so on the belief that

The RCAF's role in Europe had been essentially defensive. With the new role proposed, it would change to the offense, the political implications of which should be very carefully considered particularly as it would be using nuclear weapons. To this it was pointed out that before the RCAF went into action, the first blow would have to be struck by the other side. The new role was really one of counter-attack.[45]

Cabinet did not, however, consider in detail what was meant by "the first blow." Pearkes took it to the Cabinet the same day for discussion and Canadair was given the green light to build the Canadian version of the F-104, now called the CF-104, in Canada. On 2 July 1959 Diefenbaker announced the decision to the House of Commons and later that month the Canadian representative to the NAC did the same.[46]

Pearkes's speech to the House of Commons elaborated on Diefenbaker's and was interesting in that it mentioned the need to contribute to the deterrent, but it did not note the fact that the CF-104 would be delivering nuclear weapons. He noted that there was "a need for aircraft which could penetrate the area between the combat zone and the Russian border for reconnaissance and for strikes on targets of opportunity such as advancing columns of troops."[47] Note that the reconnaissance role was placed ahead of the strike role in the speech. This statement was at variance with the aircraft requirement as explicitly described to Diefenbaker by Foulkes, Pearkes, and Norstad. One can only speculate about the origins of the language used in the statement, but Diefenbaker did not contradict it at the time, either formally or informally.

The selection of the aircraft was only part of the battle. All NATO members were having problems meeting the MC 70 minimum force requirements. The

European NATO air forces were under a lot of pressure by Norstad to get on with aircraft selection so that integrated strike planning could commence, which was in turn necessary so that the strategy could be implemented.

The West German Luftwaffe also selected the F-104 to fulfill its MC 70 requirement late in 1959. There is no direct evidence available that the RCAF's selection of the F-104 in June had a direct impact on this decision.[48] However, it should also be noted that there were strong connections between the RCAF and the fledgling Luftwaffe. The RCAF had trained most of the Luftwaffe's CF-86 pilots in the mid-1950s. The RCAF had an advisory group at the Luftwaffe's headquarters. The Luftwaffe also had extensive connections with Canadair, who supplied Sabres and spare parts. There were significant operational connections between the RCAF and the Luftwaffe in 4 ATAF, AIRCENT, and SHAPE once the West Germans came on board.[49] West German Defense Minister Franz Josef Strauss and the Chief of Staff of the Luftwaffe, Lieutenant-General Josef Kammhuber conferred with Pearkes, Foulkes, and the rest of the COSC in Ottawa in September 1959 on how to explore program coordination. The Germans selected the F-104 partly because of its multirole versatility, not cost.[50]

The combination of the RCAF and Luftwaffe F-104 selection, combined with Norstad's push for standardization and the willingness of the United States to supply some aircraft and spares under the MAP, significantly influenced the majority of NATO nations to go with the F-104. The Belgians, the Dutch, and the Italians were directly influenced by the Canadian and German decisions, which in turn also influenced Norway, Denmark, Greece, and Turkey.[51]

The Germans were intrigued with the F-104 and wanted a version designed to their specifications. Lockheed complied and created the F-104G to meet them.[52] The F-104G and the CF-104 differed in some respects. The avionics were different, and the CF-104 airframe was slightly larger. The CF-104 did not mount the M-61 20mm rotary cannon and thus could carry more fuel and had a longer range. The CF-104 had a better radar bombing system, the NASRR R 14A, while the F-104G had an earlier version. In other words, the CF-104 was optimized for the low-level nuclear strike role more so than the F-104G.[53]

This was a deliberate decision taken by Campbell, who briefed the Air Council on the CF-104 concept of operations. While, in his view, "the capability to carry conventional weapons could possibly be retained, no provision of this type stores should be contemplated"[54]; this was in direct contradiction to the April operational requirements. In case anybody on the Air Council did not understand, Campbell explicitly stated: "All AFHQ staffs concerned with the CF-104 program are to be made fully aware that the CF-104 and conventional weapons are incompatible and it would be militarily unsound to provide such a capability. Nuclear weapons [will] be planned for."[55]

Why would Campbell issue such instructions? The other services as well as the RCAF's Maritime Air Command were leery about accepting a totally nuclear force structure and all recognized the need for flexibility in weapons employment. Why should 1 Air Division be any different?

The answer was a combination of several things. The main factor was the ongoing nuclear weapons problem with the Diefenbaker government. By accepting the reequipment of 1 Air Division, they had accepted a nuclear commitment. This acceptance contradicted their stance on nuclear weapons and the air defense of North America and to some extent SAC operations. If 1 Air Division was a strictly nuclear force and there was no ambiguity or potential ambiguity with regards to the role, it would accentuate any appearance of a contradictory policy on nuclear weapons. Diefenbaker's people could not claim that the force was conventional or conventional-capable for political reasons, since it would be costly to re-role the pilots and aircraft. This would expose the existence of a contradictory policy.

There were two reasons why Campbell might want to do this. The reequipment of 1 Air Division was in part a political device to get other NATO members to stop procrastinating on MC 70, which in turn was a critical factor in ensuring that the deterrent concept was credible. If the government changed horses in midstream and declared that 1 Air Division was not a nuclear force, it would produce confusion within NATO and generate further uncertainty in the deterrent concept. The Soviets might take advantage of this.

The second reason is more personal. Campbell and other RCAF senior officers had served overseas in England during the Second World War. The predominant RCAF experience during that war was its extensive participation in the strategic bombing campaign as part of RAF Bomber Command. Many RCAF staff officers were trained at the RAF Staff College Bracknell and thus were indoctrinated in British airpower theory that emphasized Sir Hugh Viscount Trenchard's strategic bombing theories. The RCAF's attempt in 1951 to get three bomber squadrons as part of the NATO commitment (the Paris Plan) was foiled and the primary emphasis and allocation of resources was on fighters, radar, and air defense. The reequipment of 1 Air Division now gave the RCAF the opportunity to reestablish itself in the bombing role.[56]

The new role was progressively refined in conversations with AIRCENT. 1 Air Division's division of labor was "in conjunction with the other NATO air forces, the isolation of the European Combat Zone and the destruction of those enemy forces operating within SACEUR's tactical theatre of operations."[57] Targets would include airfields, missile sites, radars, and communication centers.[58]

AIRCENT was willing, by 1960, to discuss the special weapons that the NATO F-104 force might employ. SHAPE wanted to use the Mk 57 bomb that was then under development for use with the USAF's F-105 force.[59] A physically small weapon, the Mk 57 came in three variants with yields varying from 5 to 20 kt. It was designed as a "limited war" weapon for use against tactical targets like airfields. It could be delivered by helicopter (USN Sea Kings used it as a depth bomb), it could be parachute retarded, or it could be dropped with no retardation.[60] The RCAF was so enthusiastic about the small size that they asked SACEUR if the CF-104s could be equipped with more than one Mk 54. Norstad indicated that this would not be necessary.[61]

The RCAF was, of course, willing to go along with whatever weapons SACEUR wanted to mount on the aircraft. However, it did not stop them from some experimentation. The original operational requirement for the CF-104 stated that it should have the ability to carry and launch two air-to-surface weapons of an unspecified type. The best candidate was the Martin AGM-12D Bullpup with its W 45 warhead, ten-mile range, and 1.5 to 15 kt yield. Such a weapon could provide the CF-104 with a stand-off capability. As discussed earlier, Bullpup was probably a casualty of the nuclear weapons crisis in Canada, though the possible lack of the required accuracy and reliability vis-à-vis a gravity bomb may have been a factor given SHAPE's strict accuracy requirements. It also was a dual capable system, which would have disqualified it given Campbell's directive. The Air Council rejected the CF-104/Bullpup configuration.[62]

It would take longer for 1 Air Division to prepare itself for a nuclear delivery role. The Army and the maritime forces had, by 1960, delivery systems and operational thinking that put them ahead in the game, though both were stymied by the political problems with nuclear warhead access. Canadair had to build the CF-104, the RCAF had to train pilots and ground crew, and the aircraft had to be deployed to Europe before 1 Air Division could even worry about nuclear weapons access. This process would continue through 1963, but the foundations laid here with the selection for the aircraft and the role it would fulfill were prerequisites for achieving a nuclear strike capability.

All in all, Canadian forces committed to NATO roles and missions were progressing well by 1960. The main problem for the Diefenbaker government lay in the air defense of North America and its relationship to the USAF's Strategic Air Command.

8

ENTER THOR'S GAUNTLET, WIELDING A WRENCH: CANADIAN PROBLEMS WITH THE USAF STRATEGIC AIR COMMAND, 1958–1960

Desirable Characteristics of a Deterrent:
1. Frightening 2. Inexorable 3. Persuasive
4. Cheap 5. Nonaccident Prone
6. Controllable
–Herman Kahn, *On Thermonuclear War*

"Mr. President, about 35 minutes ago, General Jack Ripper, the commanding general of Burpelson Air Force Base, issued an order to the thirty-four B-52's of his wing, which were airborne at the time as part of a special exercise we were holding called Operation DROP-KICK. Now, it appears that the order called for the planes to attack their targets inside Russia. The planes are fully armed with nuclear weapons with an average load of 40 megatons each. . . . It is beginning to look like General Ripper exceeded his authority."
–*Dr. Strangelove or: How I Learned to Stop Worrying and Love the Bomb*

Introduction

The loss of the CF-105 Arrow forced a pause on the Diefenbaker government's attempts to grasp the relationship between Canadian sovereignty and Canada's forces. Effectively, government officials painted themselves into a political corner with no graceful exit. The raison d'être of the exercise, deterrence through the protection of SAC, now reared up. The new ballistic missile threat and its effects on SAC operations prompted the formation of a small cabal in External Affairs to portray such operations as dangerous, provocative activity that threatened the balance of power. These men not only advocated an arm's-length philosophy: they engaged in outright obstructionism. Canada shifted from making a positive contribution to NATO security through the defense of North America, to interfering with SAC activities and nuclear access agreements that in turn affected all of Canada's defense efforts in Europe, North America, and the Atlantic. The apparent issue involved SAC bomber alert consultation between Canada and the United States. The obstructionists wanted to both preserve Canadian sovereignty and rein in the Americans. What these men refused to understand was that technology overrode national sovereignty. There was just no time for drawn out consultation. The air defense and SAC deterrent system had to function as a whole. Canada could still use the intimate relationship for other purposes, but the fact remained that the main purpose of the exercise was to deter the Soviet Union by presenting an effective defense of the SAC bomber force.

Howard Green Enters the Cockpit and Takes Flight; Pearkes Prepares to Bail Out

Sidney Smith died on 17 March 1959, and Prime Minister Diefenbaker temporarily took over as Secretary of State for External Affairs. In the Cabinet, Diefenbaker stated that the planned nuclear agreement was not really an agreement at all since the wording was "imposed" by the Americans. He wanted to know what the US-UK agreement contained, as he had been reliably informed that the British would get access to more information than Canada. Pearkes soothed the Prime Minister, noting that the British were more advanced than Canada in nuclear weapon design and production and therefore were entitled to more information. The Canada-US agreement was tailored to Canadian requirements, established by Canadians. The expanded areas included information on new weapons and the delivery systems, safety features so that Canadian teams could recover weapons involved in accidents, a section permitting the transfer of non-nuclear components of nuclear weapons to Canada, and the easing of restrictions on discussing released information with other nations with bilateral arrangements with the United States.[1]

Diefenbaker wanted to wait and see what the US-UK agreement language consisted of. Fortunately, he was dissuaded from doing so, and the Prime Minister approved negotiations with the United States.[2] A. D. P. Heeney signed the documents on 22 May 1959.[3]

This was only one step in acquiring a Canadian nuclear capability. The American formula established for doing so included a multitude of agreements. The 1959 bilateral information-sharing agreement allowed Canada access to non-nuclear components, that is, delivery systems minus the attachment hardware and some electronic systems necessary for weapons arming and delivery. Then a government-to-government general agreement had to be signed to formally allow Canada to acquire these components, safety training from American sources, and actual access to stockpiled weapons under the custodial system. Once the government-to-government agreement was signed, the actual implementation of the three components was conducted by the signing of several service-to-service agreements. This was the formula in its ideal form.

The reality was that Canadian forces already possessed varying degrees of nuclear weapons training, safety, and tactical employment information. They already had American delivery systems, which had been acquired before the Americans modified their own versions to deliver nuclear weapons. Future Canadian delivery systems acquisition was already in progress, initiated based on certain information made available to Canadian planners.

Negotiations for the general agreement to follow the information agreement commenced more or less immediately, but then ran into a number of problems. Some of these problems related to a renewed MB-1 overflight agreement and the proposed MB-1 storage arrangements, while others related to SAC operations and consultations on alert declarations during crises.

NORAD HQ noted operational limitations in the interim MB-1 overflight agreements and sought to rectify them, while the Americans thought that a permanent agreement should be signed to replace the six-month renewable one, perhaps concurrent with the NORAD agreement. Specifically, the original agreements mentioned only the MB-1 weapon and there was no provision for technological change: if new weapons replaced MB-1, did the agreement apply to them too? Secondly, new interceptor aircraft were able to extend their range beyond the 54th Parallel. Finally, the USAF wanted to drop the alert level for nuclear overflights from Yellow or Red to the lower state of Air Defense Readiness, but only if declared by CinCNORAD, not CinCONAD.[4] Analysis demonstrated that there would not then be enough warning time to launch the interceptors if there was a surprise attack.

To facilitate the passage of the agreement, the Americans acknowledged that the interception rules of engagement for USAF interceptors over Canada would adhere to RCAF engagement rules and that:

> [the US] will continue to take the utmost precaution in designing nuclear air defense weapons . . . to insure a minimum possibility of public hazard when employment of such weapons is necessary. Representatives of the [RCAF] will continue to be thoroughly informed by the [USAF] concerning both storage and operational safety measures [and] will take measures to insure that the Canadian Government is immediately notified of any crash in Canadian territory.[5]

What appeared to Canadian and American defence and foreign policy cognoscenti to be a logical and prudent modification to an already-existing agreement was viewed differently by Canada's new Secretary of State for External Affairs.

Unable to handle the portfolio and his role as Prime Minister at the same time, Diefenbaker assigned Howard Green, who was at the time Minister for Public Works (and former Agricultural Minister), to the position in June 1959.[6] Like Diefenbaker, Green was a lawyer, a westerner (Vancouver, BC), a monarchist, anti-American, and a First World War veteran. Green apparently thought that God had put him on earth to use Canada's influence to rid the planet of nuclear weapons.[7] He was fixated on preventing nuclear testing to the detriment of his other responsibilities. In a conversation with US State Department officials, Canadian ambassador to the United States, A. D. P. Heeney, noted Green did not like "soldiers, weapons, or policemen." His counterparts remarked that "such an attitude made cooperation in the political-military field rather difficult, because agreement is occasionally needed on some positive project."[8]

Green was just as suspicious of military leaders (both Canadian and American) as Diefenbaker was and the two of them fed off of each other. For example, at the Montebello summit meeting between Diefenbaker and Eisenhower in 1960,

General Nathan Twining, Chairman of the JCS, inadvertently provoked Green in discussions over nuclear weapons' release procedures. Green's worst fears about the "lack" of civil-military control of nuclear weapons was "confirmed," and he continued to be "apprehensive over the possibility that the USAF and other elements of the armed forces carried on an existence rather independent of civilian control and were inclined to be trigger-happy."[9] Green's *Weltanschauung* interpreted the resumption of American nuclear tests after the moratorium as "evidence" that "the military and the AEC had triumphed over civilian opinion and that the United States under the present administration would be unreliable in the event of the sharpening of tension and might provoke a conflict."[10]

On the NATO front, Major General George Kitching remembered a meeting in Paris in which: "Green shook me by denigrating NATO and all it stood for, implying that we were a bunch of warmongers wasting taxpayers' money which could be better spent feeding the poor of third world countries. He went on to say that Canada's foreign policy was going to change; in future it would be to get to know and love and help the small countries of the world."[11]

Green was happy to run External Affairs in an almost antihierarchical fashion. He frequently jumped down several levels in the chain of command to directly imprint his vision, actions which caused Norman Robertson some consternation. Green also had a habit of categorically dismissing advice from the more experienced External personnel.[12]

External Affairs people were appalled at Green's personal behavior at NATO meetings. Allied delegations grew tired of being lectured by Green on various topics relating to disarmament. W. H. Barton, chief of External's Defence Liaison Division, noted, "Green is not at his best in meetings of this kind since he does not have a background of experience in diplomacy, does not have the same intellectual sophistication, and refuses to wear a hearing aid despite the need for one."[13]

Though not unbiased observers, Americans in the State Department thought that "the most dangerous Minister from the standpoint of the United States is Green, because of his strategic position, political ambitions, stubborn concern over Canadian sovereignty, and influence with Diefenbaker."[14] As the Diefenbaker era progressed, Pearkes lost ground to Green in the Cabinet and thus lost influence with Diefenbaker. There was considerable animosity directed by Green against Pearkes, particularly over nuclear weapons.

The new nuclear air defense weapons overflight agreement was stalled. American observers initially believed that it was not necessarily "motivated by a desire to take a stand opposite of the United States, but rather represented some fuzzy thinking on the part of Norman Robertson and possibly other high officials in External Affairs."[15] McElroy asked Pearkes what was going on, Pearkes asked Foulkes, and Foulkes discovered that the agreement was on Green's desk and remained unsigned. Foulkes thought that if Green continued to stall, he could get Bryce or Robertson to "expedite" it.[16] Foulkes did so, and the new arrangements were approved with some modification since Diefenbaker did not want the agreement signed concurrently with the NORAD agreement, for fear of Opposition criticism.[17] (Green also reluctantly approved some of the SAC overflight arrangements at the same time.)

A. D. P. Heeney, who replaced Norman Robertson as Canadian ambassador to the United States, recorded Green's response to a briefing on the status of the various nuclear weapons agreements, the Berlin situation, and NATO. Heeney informed Green the Americans had made a "conscious effort . . . to meet reasonable Canadian demands (Mr. Green injected that we should not expect them to meet requirements which were unreasonable). I believed that the senior members of the Administration were engaged in a genuine effort to restore Canadian confidence in the United States."[18] Green then:

> referred to the number of requests which were being received from the United States in defence matters (he had reference in particular to those relating to NORAD and SAC, overflights of US aircraft with special weapons, alerts, etc.). Mr. Green said that he felt that the United States should be "held down" in these matters, should not be given all they asked for. . . . He felt, particularly in view of the attitude which he had adopted in Opposition and in the recent elections, that he had a special responsibility to safeguard Canadian sovereignty.[19]

Heeney desperately tried to get Green to understand that these measures were taken as part of a joint defense effort. Canadian and American interests were the same on these matters since, he believed "it was true that Canadian sovereignty must be protected but surely it must be protected from the north as well as from the south. . . . I [told him that] in certain quarters he was regarded as being prejudiced against the United States or even anti-American."[20] This was to no avail and the situation got worse.

It is possible that Green was inspired by shifting French nuclear weapons policy. Charles de Gaulle's accession to power in January 1959 produced a firm policy statement in June: there would be no nuclear weapons stored in France unless they were under French control. The usual American custodial arrangements were not acceptable on French soil for sovereignty reasons (though acceptable for French forces stationed in Germany). Norstad promptly moved 250 USAF tactical aircraft to bases in Germany and the United Kingdom.[21]

Green influenced Diefenbaker on nuclear matters and harped on the sovereignty issues raised during the NORAD debates. During a meeting with US Secretary of State Christian Herter:

> The Prime Minister stated that his government faced a difficult problem from the viewpoint of both public opinion and the opposition parties in connection with the storage of nuclear weapons in Canada. He added that the lack of any Canadian share in the control of their storage or use was a great worry. [Limiting American overflights] was to strengthen the government's position in handling opposition questions.[22]

All three proposed storage arrangements were stalled well into the fall of 1959, as were modifications to SAC overflight operations made in response to the developing Berlin Crisis. According to one Canadian observer:

the situation is very awkward because Mr. Green says no to all American requests on principle and his External staff are helping him in this attitude. General Foulkes is very embarrassed by the attitude of Mr. Green. . . . Mr. Robertson [is] assisting in this attitude by presenting the requests in poor light and causes considerable pressure on national defence to get action.[23]

It is unclear what prompted Norman Robertson to contribute to this behavior. Robertson was cognizant of the direction of Canadian strategic policy and had supported it up to this point. There are several possibilities and they may have overlapped to produce a change in Robertson's views. According to Basil Robinson, Robertson attended classified briefings at NORAD and SAC in March 1959 that were blunt in describing the effects of a nuclear attack on North America. He "became visibly appalled and distressed," an effect that was probably exacerbated by SAC's activity during the 1958 Lebanon Crisis, the ongoing Berlin Crisis, and the possibility that an attack might actually occur.[24] Taken with Green's moral repugnance regarding nuclear weapons, this created a catalyst for obstruction. It is also possible that Robertson and Green positively viewed Charles de Gaulle's policy for dealing with the United States (refusal, obstruction, intransigence, and manipulation)[25] and sought to emulate it.

There is another possibility. Air Vice-Marshal Max Hendrick was convinced that Robertson was motivated by fear that the United States would deliberately or inadvertently provoke the Soviet Union into a nuclear confrontation. In June 1958, Foulkes informed Pearkes that SAC had initiated a series of Fail Safe flights in which SAC bombers were launched during periods of crisis on prearranged flight plans towards designated targets in the Soviet Union.[26] Once the bombers reached a predetermined point in airspace, they waited to receive further orders. Events that triggered Fail Safe flights included an increase "in the number of unknowns that appear in the air defence system [and/or] unusual activity on Soviet bomber bases or a Soviet long-range air force exercise."[27] At this point (1958), Fail Safe flights were not conducted over Canadian airspace:

> The United States has never asked for authority for one of these "Fail Safe" flights; nor would I anticipate that they would because these flights are sent off at very short notice and in contemplation of a possible strike. The United States is well aware that we would not grant authority for the use of Canadian air space on such a flight without full consultation with the Government. Therefore it is our conjecture that any of these flights which take place go in other directions than over Canadian territory. . . . any unexplained flights would be picked up by our early warning systems and we would soon hear about this situation.[28]

A related point was that Foulkes informed the RCAF leadership in March 1959 that "United States authorities" were so concerned about the possibility of the initiative resting with the Soviet Union "that they are looking at the forbidden preventative war approach" as a serious option.[29]

We probably should conclude that Robertson knew about SAC operations and general thinking. In addition to Fail Safe flights, SAC and even RAF Bomber Command conducted even more provocative activity that could have influenced Robertson's views. "Ferreting," or the deliberate aerial penetration of enemy territory to gather intelligence, was not a new activity in 1958.[30] However, between 1953 and 1959, General Curtis LeMay ordered SAC to conduct a series of operations to penetrate the Soviet air defense system. In one case, three groups each consisting of seven B-47 bombers and two RB-47 recce aircraft approached the Soviet Union. At the last minute, the B-47s peeled off and returned to base while the RB-47s dropped down and entered Soviet airspace to overfly the Kola Peninsula and gather photographic and signals intelligence.[31] In another reconnaissance series, Project HOMERUN, 146 RB-47 fights were conducted from Thule over the North Pole against the Soviet Union.[32] The Soviets were vocal in their opposition to such activity, and it is likely that Robertson knew about similar operations, since Canadian Signals Intelligence (SIGINT) facilities routinely monitored USAF Ferret flights departing Thule and Alaska.[33]

Conversely, Robertson should also have known about the frequent Soviet penetrations of NORAD's early warning systems.[34] External Affairs was informed of one particular case in which a TU-16 BADGER crashed at a Soviet Arctic drift ice station, right on the boundary line between Canadian and Soviet waters. RCAF Lancasters from 408th Squadron overflew the site several times (especially when the Soviets were engaged in recovering the aircraft) and brought back the West's first close-up, detailed pictures of this Soviet nuclear bomber type operating from a forward ice runway just outside Canadian territorial waters.[35]

The abortive 1959 NORAD Exercise SKY HAWK was the perfect example of a Robertson nightmare come true. It also produced further delays in nuclear weapons storage and overflight agreements. This exercise was to be a comprehensive test of NORAD and was called by CinCNORAD with Slemon's concurrence. It was to involve the entire NORAD area and all NORAD-assigned forces. SAC bombers would realistically penetrate the defense system and all nonmilitary air traffic was to be grounded for the duration of the exercise. This was necessary so that full jamming capabilities could be tested, jamming that would interfere with civilian air control systems. SKY HAWK would employ over 1500 fighter aircraft and all SAM units in North America. Joint Canadian-American planning started in January 1959, and the six-hour exercise was scheduled for October.[36]

There are no indications that SKY HAWK was deliberately structured to "signal" the Soviet Union over Berlin, and in fact the dates of the exercise were explicitly changed so as not to coincide with Sergei N. Khrushchev's visit to the United States.[37]

National Defence and Department of Transport had been coordinating with their American counterparts through NORAD for several months. Green suddenly claimed late in August that External Affairs had not been consulted (this only after a draft press release was forwarded to External from the US State Department on the prompting of the US Joint Chiefs), that the exercise was unnecessary, and that jamming would disrupt civil air traffic.[38] There had been some miscommunication between McElroy and Pearkes in early August (Pearkes did not fully understand the relationship between airborne jamming and the need to ground civilian aircraft), but this was a side issue. The State Department found it hard to believe that "the Canadian Cabinet bases its decision on a press statement that has not been approved for publication rather than the merits of the matter."[39]

The matter went to the Cabinet and the Prime Minister sought to cancel the exercise. Diefenbaker then called in the American ambassador, Richard B. Wigglesworth, who believed:

> [Diefenbaker] was much agitated and it was clear that his views were influenced by two factors. First of these was the late date at which he and other high officials heard of the project. . . . Second factor is that opposition criticism of NORAD has stressed the theme that military people, primarily US, make decisions which are shoved down the throats of Canadian civil officials.[40]

The situation was serious enough for Eisenhower to communicate with Diefenbaker directly. Eisenhower asked him to reconsider canceling the exercise and assured him it would not be provocative in light of the summit.[41] Diefenbaker replied that, from discussions with Green, he took the position that SKY HAWK was unduly disruptive and provocative and that it should be reduced in scale.[42] Diefenbaker was also concerned that the cancellation should be kept secret so that the Opposition would not use it against him.

It is clear that Robertson was influencing Green, Green was influencing Diefenbaker, and Diefenbaker was influenced indirectly by Pearson. Robertson was concerned about provocation, while Green was interested in obstructing the Americans. Diefenbaker was worried about being attacked by the Opposition. The upshot of the whole affair was that SKY HAWK was canceled, an even bigger rift appeared in Canadian-American relations, the Cabinet looked befuddled, and Foulkes personally tried to ensure that Norman Robertson was kept out of the loop on defense matters in the future.[43] NORAD could not effectively evaluate itself, which in turn produced operational uncertainty and possibly weakened its value as a component of the deterrent system. Livingston Merchant, now the Deputy Undersecretary of State, saw the episode as "one more manifestation of Canada's softer approach to the Communist world. A tough education job, therefore lies ahead to convince Canadian Cabinet leaders that we must deal with the Soviets from a position of strength."[44]

Despite the SKY HAWK debacle, CinCNORAD reopened negotiations for storing MB-1s for the USAF squadrons based at Goose Bay and Harmon AFBs in October 1959. The Chiefs discussed this in July (Robertson was present for all four meetings and continually pushed for minor rewording of the draft agreement at every opportunity, which delayed the proceedings),[45] but apparently were unable to make any headway in getting the item placed on the Cabinet's agenda in light of the SKY HAWK situation in August.

Cabinet approved, in principle only, the storage and use of the weapons and authorized detailed discussions on 22 September. By 2 October, a draft proposal was sent to State from External. The weapons would be air-to-air defensive weapons under CinCNORAD's control. Physical security would be joint, safeguards would be maximum, ownership would be American, and transport through Canadian airspace would be authorized by Canada. The weapons would only be deployed when authorized by both nations.[46]

Inexplicably, the State Department did not reply until January 1960.[47] By that point, the USAF informed the Canadian government that the Harmon and Goose Bay interceptor squadrons would probably be phased out by 1963.[48] It is highly likely that the Americans did not want to push on this matter for fear of aggravating the tense situation.

The US Navy, meanwhile, observed what was going on with regard to nuclear storage and discretely approached the Canadian Joint Staff Mission Washington to discuss storing nuclear antisubmarine weapons in Canada. SACLANT proposed that three sites be constructed in Canada (funded with NATO Common Infrastructure funds): two for Canadian use and one for joint Canadian-American-Netherlands use. Foulkes had previously inquired as to what American plans were for the proposed Argentia site so that he could work this into his discussions in Ottawa. He wanted to know more about how Commander in Chief Atlantic (CinCLANT) proposed to employ nuclear antisubmarine weapons before he approached the Cabinet and pushed for storage. The CinCLANT representatives balked, stating that the correct procedure was to have a general nation-to-nation bilateral agreement signed first, and then a service-to-service agreement between CinCLANT and the appropriate Canadian military authorities before this information could be passed on. These agreements had not been signed yet.[49]

Foulkes saw the general agreement as the key to solving several problems, not the least of those being the ability to equip Canadian forces with the nuclear warheads themselves. Consequently, he started pushing for this after the Camp David meeting in November 1959.[50]

The Camp David meeting originated in part by the State Department's desire to improve Canadian-American defense relations after the SKY HAWK affair. It believed that the situation:

> resulted largely from a breakdown in proper liaison between Canadian Military and political channels, it also revealed a lack of appreciation and understanding on the part of Canadian Cabinet Ministers, particularly Mr. Green and the Prime Minister. . . . it has become evident that they tend to look upon NORAD as another U.S.-commanded and U.S.-financed defense project in Canada as U.S. projects [rather than joint projects].[51]

Specifically, State predicted that the Canadian delegation was interested primarily in nuclear weapons issues, command and control issues, and the degree of civilian control over the American military, particularly SAC:

> there is a pervasive, if not articulated, concern that civil authority over joint United States-Canadian military undertakings needs more frequent

reaffirmation. This somewhat vague uneasiness apparently stems from two factors: 1) a misconception that in the United States professional military interests have a disproportionate voice in policy determination (they are not entirely persuaded that "preventive war" is ruled out by the Pentagon; they are disturbed by the frankness of the testimony of [US] military leaders before Congressional committees.[52]

External expected to have to deal with American requests for nuclear air-to-air weapons storage at Goose Bay and Harmon; nuclear ASW weapons storage at Argentia; and SAC storage at Goose Bay. External now believed that SAC storage should be approved, as should the other two, provided that removal of the weapons from storage for use was subject to joint Canadian-American control.[53]

Held on 8 and 9 November 1959, the Camp David meeting was the official second meeting of the Canada-United States Ministerial Committee on Joint Defense and as such included Green, Robertson, US Secretary of State Christian Herter, Pearkes, McElroy, Twining, Foulkes, and Hendrick.[54]

When discussions turned to air defense of North America, McElroy offered Pearkes American aircraft to replace the aging CF-100s. This was the genesis of the RCAF's acquisition of the CF-101 Voodoo nuclear-capable interceptor.[55] The thorny problems encountered with SKY HAWK were also raised, and Twining emphasized the critical need for military forces to train during peacetime so that they would be effective in wartime. Pearkes repeated concerns about the size of the exercise and Green was concerned that future air defense exercises involving SAC might provoke the Soviets. Twining noted, "that previous SAC [and NATO] exercises involving flying toward the Iron Curtain had caused no adverse comment."[56]

Green leapt on this. SKY HAWK, according to Green, was "almost a declaration of war as far as the Canadian public was concerned. . . . we do not believe that it is necessary to threaten the USSR."[57] Herter was shocked. This was just a defensive exercise to test NORAD, not a SAC provocation. McElroy chimed in, stating that "if we do not show that we were capable and ready to defend ourselves we were merely inviting a surprise attack." Norman Robertson believed that SKY HAWK would have scuttled any attempt to arrive at an accommodation with Khrushchev, a point to which Herter took great exception.[58]

Then there was the nuclear storage issue. McElroy wanted decisions made, since storage issues had dragged on for two years at this point. What exactly was Canada prepared to allow the United States to do? Green noted that Canada agreed to MB-1 storage in principle, and Pearkes noted that European sites for Canadian forces were no problem, they just had to be built. Both men agreed that nuclear antisubmarine weapons should be stored at Argentia. The question was, who released nuclear weapons for use from Canadian soil?[59]

Green then stated that Canadian approval was required to remove MB-1s at Goose Bay and Harmon, and that this had been agreed to in October. This was not the case. It became "apparent that because the proposed Canadian wording had not yet been studied fully . . . that the US secretaries were not aware of the Canadian opinion on the matter and it came as quite a shock to them."[60]

As for Argentia and antisubmarine weapons, some Canadian and American delegates thought that SACLANT should be the releasing authority if the weapons stored there were for use by NATO forces. Others thought this ran against Canadian sovereignty. They wanted a Canadian veto on the wartime deployment of nuclear antisubmarine weapons at Argentia to ships, be they American, Canadian, or other NATO ships. The Americans were not enthusiastic about this. McElroy and Green agreed to work out the details once the bilateral general agreement was signed. Foulkes thought that SACLANT's proposed nuclear ASW storage sites for Canadian naval forces at Summerside and Shearwater should be constructed, but without NATO Common Infrastructure money, which might confuse the control issue (NATO control versus Canadian/US control).[61]

The conversation shifted to SAC storage at Goose Bay. McElroy stated that these weapons were for a second wave attack and Foulkes backed him up on this. Green stated, "it had been very difficult for the Canadian Government to agree to the storage for defensive purposes, and that it was even harder to agree to storage for offensive purposes in the House of Commons."[62] Christian Herter was appalled at this:

> what was most likely to keep the peace [?]. . . . if we are going to move toward real disarmament and a relaxation of tension in the next few years, the USSR must continue to believe that a sudden attack by it on America could not possibly succeed. SAC was the force which prevented this possible success, because such at attack meant irreparable damage. . . . SAC, therefore, is a defensive force.[63]

Green did not want to reduce the effectiveness of the deterrent, "but he did not want it to be increased either. . . . it was difficult to explain to the Canadian people . . . U.S. arguments about the deterrent would justify the storage of anything in Canada."[64]

It is apparent from this exchange that Green's obstructionist attitude emanated from fear of domestic criticism. The Americans came away from the meeting believing "there is some agreement on broad principles but that a meeting of minds has not yet been reached."[65]

The lack of a meeting of minds jeopardized the development of the bilateral general nuclear agreement that was the linchpin for everything. Foulkes focused most of his effort on this after Camp David, in addition to solving the problems of MB-1 storage at Harmon and Goose Bay and antisubmarine weapon storage in Argentia. He recognized that the major stumbling blocks in the Cabinet centered on control and release issues with respect to storage. These were sovereignty issues that therefore had to be resolved before an umbrella agreement could be promulgated. In effect, Green, Diefenbaker, and Foulkes had each contributed to creating a confusing linkage between the two. Storage and release issues regarding American weapons for SAC bombers, USN maritime patrol aircraft, and USAF interceptors operating from bases in Canada were in fact separate from storage and release issues regarding American weapons stored in Canada destined for RCAF interceptors (manned and unmanned) and RCN and RCAF maritime patrol aircraft. Green did not recognize this distinction; he saw them all as impositions on Canadian sovereignty.

The proposed government-to-government general agreement was structured to allow Canada to acquire delivery system components (modifications for aircraft), safety training, and actual access to stockpiled weapons under the custodial system. This would then open the door for the detailed service-to-service agreements necessary to implement the general agreement. Foulkes had previously implied that continued SAC overflight authorization and possible SAC storage at Goose Bay were contingent on the Americans agreeing to develop the general agreement, which the Americans readily acquiesced to. On the other hand, the US Navy, in trying to get Argentia for nuclear ASW weapons storage, was informed by Foulkes that this was contingent on the provision of release, security, and safety information to Canada. The US Navy would not do so until the general agreement was signed. Green made no effort to solve the problem after the Camp David meeting.[66]

Foulkes, Hendrick, and Pearkes completed a draft general agreement early in December 1959. Americans would own the weapons and they were responsible for custody. Exact release procedures would be subject to the service-to-service agreements and would vary depending on the type of employment. Safeguards, transport, and salvage would be subject to service-to-service arrangements.[67]

In terms of Canadian access to warheads based in Canada, Canada would be responsible for providing land, construction, external security of the warheads while they were moved through Canada, and the provision of signal facilities. CinCNORAD and SACLANT would consult with Canada to select a location. A similar arrangement was to be implemented in Europe, with SACEUR serving as the executive agent and NATO Common Infrastructure funds paying for the storage sites.[68]

Pearkes attempted to get Green to sign it and take the matter up in Cabinet. Green failed to do so and Pearkes indicated to Diefenbaker that he was no longer interested in continuing to be Canada's Defence Minister.[69]

Canada and SAC Support: The Diefenbaker Government, 1957–1960

The Diefenbaker government was reticent to provide support to SAC. The first stumbling block was the sovereignty issue. Procedures established under the St. Laurent government were satisfactory; that is, the Canadian government could say yes or no and SAC would probably behave accordingly. However, SAC wanted more flexibility in a crisis, and this related to the second point of contention. The Goose Bay storage site, we will recall, was a Pearsonian tool to lever advanced warning of pending SAC operations in addition to its sovereignty function. The American government had to consult Canada prior to using Goose Bay for SAC strike operations. The same went for the "Z" procedure. If SAC were allowed to circumvent consultation, Canada theoretically had no warning and no nominal control over its airspace and facilities. This in turn was linked to the inflammatory NORAD alerting issues and control over air defense operations over Canada. The big question was, who decided when Canada went to war: Ottawa, Washington, or both? How was it to be done? Would Washington trust Ottawa with the information if the United States chose to act unilaterally in a crisis?

The answer depended on whether the Soviets struck first or not. Some Canadian policy makers were circumspect about the actual degree of American civilian authority over SAC and NORAD. In a crisis situation, Pearson (when he was External Affairs minister) wanted to exercise a small degree of influence over the Americans, using SAC storage and overflights, and force some consultation that might in turn lead to other constructive diplomatic activity. On the other hand, Diefenbaker and Green wanted to inhibit American activity in Canada in peacetime to fend off domestic political attacks regarding sovereignty. Norman Robertson wanted to reduce the scale and frequency of what he believed to be deliberate American provocation in the dangerous brinkmanship game of the Cold War. All four Canadian policy makers were unwilling to confront the real issue: time obviated sovereignty in the nuclear age.

This unwillingness led Canadian policy makers deeper into a quagmire as technological change produced new piecemeal defense agreements and altered existing ones. These fell into several broad areas: early warning, alert readiness and consultation, and SAC coordination with NORAD. Diefenbaker and many of his civilian advisors were never able to conceive the pieces as comprising a deterrent system, a gestalt. Consequently, their approach was haphazard and at times contradictory. Sometimes it helped SAC, at other times it hindered it.

Analysis of SAC's operational readiness in the wake of the Suez Crisis produced changes in SAC planning which in turn affected the XYZ procedures. In practice the actual SAC alerting procedure was rudimentary and did not react quickly enough. It was geared to a "bolt from the blue" event, not a gradual crisis. SAC wanted the ability to phase its operations during a crisis which meant that it wanted to draw nuclear weapons from the stockpile earlier, deploy to advance bases, and narrow the strike plan selection at various stages. SAC's Reflex Action and Ground Alert programs were an outgrowth of the projected ICBM threat. SAC instituted one-third ground alert for all of its North American–based bombers and conducted its first Reflex Action (ten B-47s flown with their nuclear weapons to French Morocco on forty-five-day rotations) in 1957.[70] The Reflex Action aircraft were on ground alert, but based much closer to the Soviet Union to afford quicker reaction time. Reflex Action aircraft, particularly those stationed in the United Kingdom, had to transverse Canadian airspace. Note that XYZ overflights did not just involve SAC bombers carrying bombs. At this point SAC was establishing Jupiter and Thor ballistic missile bases to support NATO. These weapons and their components were transported by C-124 Globemaster transports through Canadian airspace and all had to be cleared diplomatically under the Y procedure.[71]

Consequently, SAC believed that Y overflight clearance took too long (two to seven days), and this restricted their ability to react in a crisis situation. Use of the Z procedure for such activity was a problem as "there would be risk that the Canadians would believe that we had ordered a strike."[72] SAC wanted another overflight category in addition to the existing XYZ ones and went so far as to speed up SAC–State Department communications by instituting the code name STARGAZE on a priority telephone system. STARGAZE was a code name to initiate rapid consultation with the Canadian embassy. Attempts to go further than this were scuttled by the June 1957 election.[73] Continued efforts to change the XYZ procedures in 1958 got bogged down when the Americans attempted to link SAC storage and overflights with MB-1 storage and overflights.[74]

The discussion over SAC refueling facilities in Canada was revived after the Sputnik launch in the fall of 1957. The institution in SAC of a one-third ground alert posture preceded Sputnik, but the decreased SAC reaction time against a potential ICBM threat gave some impetus to the project. After some wrangling, the Cabinet approved the construction of SAC refueling facilities at Frobisher Bay, Cold Lake, Namao, and Churchill.[75]

Initially the plan was to have the facilities constructed and ready for use in the event of war. The KC-97 tankers would take off from their bases at some early alert stage and prepare to support the bombers from the northern bases when those bombers launched. This thinking changed after Sputnik:[76]

> As a result, the USAF now considers that their main retaliatory capability rests with *the SAC bomber force based on this continent*. A missile attack could be made on these SAC bases [overseas] with as little as 15 minutes warning. Hence, to maintain an effective deterrent, the USAF must have the capability to launch a significant portion of their bomber force with 15 minutes from time of warning. As the success of the bomber operation is dependent on aerial refueling, this means that the tanker aircraft must also be on a similar alert basis. . . . this new 15 minute alert status, known as Reflex Alert, has made necessary greater dispersal of bombers and tankers in peacetime.[77]

Foulkes briefly considered the possibility that the RCAF might acquire the tanker aircraft and conduct the aerial refueling missions over Canadian airspace for SAC, but this idea was rejected, probably due to the political problems with blatant Canadian involvement with SAC.[78] By April 1958, SAC wanted to base six tankers and station 250 personnel at each base, and then establish Nike missile defenses at all four sites. These six tankers would be located at each base on immediate readiness, with a build-up of an additional fourteen tankers if war appeared imminent.[79] The six aircraft, either KC-97s or KC-135s, would rotate every seven days from their parent units (Frobisher could not handle KC-135s). Once war started, the twenty tankers at each base would each conduct five sorties "within a minimum of 72 hours to a maximum of 15 days."[80]

There was one catch. The new SAC requirements for providing missile defense of the four bases caused serious problems for Canada. The increase in American personnel permanently stationed in Canada for the tanker bases was enough of a sovereignty problem, let alone introducing even more people to man missile sites. Second, the placement of missile defense manned by Americans posed problems similar to those of stationing MB-1-equipped interceptors at Goose Bay and Harmon. Third, if Canadians were to man the missile sites, this would prompt the Canadian public to call for point defense of all population centers in the country, something the government could not afford. Fourth, there would be command and control issues regarding NORAD, another sore point at this time. Pearkes instructed the Canadian Joint Staff Mission Washington to tell Twining that the missile defense component would have to be removed from the draft agreement.[81] CinCNORAD concurred with this and the matter was dropped. The agreement was signed in June 1958.[82]

The Sputnik scare also produced SAC Operational Plan (OPLAN) 10-59, the Hostile Action Evacuation Plan. In the event of attack, SAC would disperse its bombers from its bases to a variety of civil airports, disused military bases, and even interstate highways. Some aircraft would merely orbit over a particular point in space. The open, vast expanses of Canadian airspace beckoned SAC planners who needed as much airspace as possible for these maneuvers. Liaising directly with the RCAF, orbit areas were established and emergency diversion bases assigned.[83] 8th Air Force's ground alert B-52 bombers would disperse to Gander Airport, Newfoundland; Summerside, Prince Edward Island; Greenwood, Nova Scotia; Torbay, Newfoundland, and Argentia, Newfoundland.

All of this had to be coordinated with NORAD. There was great concern that the air defense system might misidentify inbound KC-97 tankers as TU-4 BULLs or orbiting B-47s as TU-16 BADGERs. SAC evacuation would "be ordered concurrent with or subsequent to declaration of Air Raid Warning Red."[84] The RCAF used this plan to justify the arrangement as a service-to-service arrangement and the matter was not passed on to the diplomats for exchange of notes.[85]

Warning Systems

Though Sputnik was not the primary catalyst for its creation, the Soviet space launch accelerated the development of a ballistic missile defense (BMD) system. As with the air defense system, the proposed BMD system would primarily be designed to protect SAC by providing NORAD with early warning information and by establishing an active defense of SAC bases. The existing Canadian defense effort was strained financially just handling antibomber defenses, and an independent Canadian BMD system was out of the question. Finances did not prohibit Canada from contributing significantly to the American BMD program, however.

The best-known system was the Ballistic Missile Early Warning System (BMEWS). The possibility of radar detection of ballistic missiles was raised in 1955 in a USAF study and virtually unlimited funds were provided by Congress to design and build such a system. Three BMEWS radar sites, each with their distinctive "golf ball" radar domes, were eventually constructed between 1958 and 1963. They were located at Clear, Alaska; Thule, Greenland; and Fylingdales Moor, United Kingdom.[86]

DRB participated in significant aspects of BMEWS research and in fact DRB made BMD a research priority in 1957. For example, DRB opened the Prince Albert Radar Laboratory (PARL) at Prince Albert, Saskatchewan, in 1959. PARL's purpose was to work closely with MIT's Lincoln Laboratory in studying the effects of Aurora Borealis and other phenomenon like high altitude nuclear weapons effects on BMEWS radar systems. BMEWS was positioned to monitor the polar region, which was considered the most likely avenue of Soviet ICBM attack. The effects of natural phenomena on the planned BMEWS radar systems were unknown.[87] It turned out that the technical problems were serious and PARL contributed to solving them.[88]

The Thule and Clear BMEWS sites were USAF-manned. BMEWS information flowed to the NORAD combat operations center in Colorado, to SAC HQ in Omaha, and to the Pentagon.[89] The information flow from the Thule and Clear sites, however, had to physically go through Canada, and this necessitated yet another Canadian-American agreement. Permission was given by the Cabinet for the USAF to install four communications systems, two at each site for redundancy.[90]

BMEWS was estimated to give NORAD fifteen minutes warning of a Soviet ICBM launch. This short time was created by the inability of the BMEWS radar beams to conform to the earth's curvature, which effectively allowed warning some time after launch instead of immediately. This limitation was well understood by the American planners, who were searching for other means to supplement BMEWS and gain more warning time.

The solution lay in outer space. Placement of a satellite in geosynchronous orbit between the edge of the BMEWS effective range and the Soviet launch areas would provide that extension. The question then revolved around the type of sensor to attach to the satellite. The Americans were already engaged in deploying the CORONA photo reconnaissance system. CORONA, however, utilized a capsule to deliver its product and the delay in acquiring and interpreting the data was not compatible with an early warning function.[91]

ARPA or the Advanced Research Projects Agency, the rough American equivalent to the DRB, was contracted by the USAF to develop a missile defense alarm system (MIDAS). The selected detection method would be infrared.[92] DRB was in the forefront of infrared technology at this time. In addition to PARL, part of the DRB satellite tracking activity established in 1958 included the use of five ground stations across Canada utilizing infrared systems to track orbiting satellites.[93] DRB was approached to contribute in MIDAS's development and testing.

The theory behind MIDAS was that Soviet ICBMs would emit a hot plume of gas during the immediate launch and boost phases. A satellite with the appropriate equipment should be able to detect the plumes and report directly to NORAD through the BMEWS site's communications systems (and thus through Canadian communications systems).[94] It would provide an additional fifteen minutes warning for a total of thirty minutes.

A MIDAS test vehicle was successfully launched from Cape Canaveral in May 1960, but teething problems and the devaluation of the missile-gap delayed the project into the mid-1960s.[95] Both BMEWS and MIDAS were critical to intercepting ICBMs, but the ability to "hit a bullet with a bullet" was a long way off. They would, however, have contributed to SAC's survival in the event of a Soviet missile attack.

With the BMEWS and MIDAS systems in varying stages of development in the late 1950s, some alternate means had to be found to provide early warning beyond the DEW Line so that SAC would not be caught on the ground. The preferred method of long-range early warning was SIGINT. Canada-United Kingdom-United States (CANUKUS) SIGINT collection, dissemination, and exchange formed the first line of early warning. It is not a coincidence that Canada established a SIGINT facility at the northernmost tip of Baffin Island in the 1950s. Named after HMS *Alert*, a Royal Navy sailing vessel that explored the area in 1875, Canadian Army Signal Station (CASS) Alert was constructed in 1958. Alert was one of several Canadian SIGINT stations, but it was probably the most important because of its location. In addition to their peacetime intelligence gathering functions, Alert's primary function was to provide early warning of a Soviet bomber (and later missile) attack by monitoring Soviet Long Range Aviation's transmissions. CASS Alert had a high-power transmitter and a back-up teletype machine that relayed information directly to Ottawa.[96]

The Problems of Alert Consultation

Possessing a strategic nuclear deterrent, early warning systems, and defensive measures was useless without a readiness and alert system. The problem in 1958–1959 was that this issue was continually deferred, particularly in NATO circles, because of its potential divisiveness. War was, under MC 14/2 (revised), a more or less instant thing, and any concept that accepted a gradual increase in tension and measures less than total was still under debate.

Prior to the creation of the American Defense Condition (DEFCON) system and the formal acceptance of the NATO Alert System (both in 1959), Canadian defense planners had to deal with a number of separate national alerting systems. As the need to decrease reaction time became greater throughout the decade, contradictions and ambiguities emerged. This was compounded by Canadian policy makers' increased awareness of the linkage between alerting and authorizing the use of Canadian forces and sovereignty. It was further compounded by the link between the air defense and antisubmarine weapons and SAC's activities prior to and during war.

The problem was raised prior to 1955 when the RCAF and USAF were developing the air defense annexes to the Canada-US Basic Security Plan and trying to ensure the proper degree of interoperability for USAF air defense squadrons under Canadian operational control. The Canadian-American air defense alerting system consisted of the following levels: Air Defense Warning White, Air Defense Readiness, Air Defense Warning Yellow, Air Defense Warning Red, and Military Emergency.[97]

There was also an Air Defence Preparedness level that preceded Readiness. Air Defense Readiness alerted the air defense system, Yellow indicated that attack was possible, Red that it was imminent, and White was used to "de-cock" the system. All of these levels could be implemented by subunits of USAF Air Defense Command. Military Emergency, on the other hand, was an American level and could be implemented only by the President, Congress, the US Joint Chiefs, or the commander of USAF Air Defense Command.[98] This presumably allowed the President to authorize the AEC to release nuclear weapons to SAC and SAC would then carry out its missions.[99]

The Canadian national alerting system was instituted in 1955. If an emergency developed, the Cabinet was to be informed immediately. Cabinet could then call for one of three stages:

1.   Simple Alert: Initiated on receipt of credible information indicating definite preparations to attack NATO. Implement measures short of mobilization.
2.   Reinforced Alert: Initiated when there are conclusive indications that the outbreak of hostilities is imminent. Ready the services for imminent war and mobilize.
3.   General Alert: Initiated when an overt act of aggression takes place in the NATO Area. Execute war plans.[100]

These would not necessarily be called in sequence and, as would become apparent during the 1962 Cuban Missile Crisis, they did not "absolve Ministers and senior officers from taking the initiative."[101]

On the NATO side of the house, SACEUR had been developing an alert system since 1952 (the MC 67 series). This planned system had two complementary components: the Formal NATO Alert System and the ACE Counter Surprise Military Alert System (CSMAS). The Formal Alert System was under continual debate from 1953 to 1959. It had three levels: Simple Alert, Reinforced Alert, and General Alert, which were based on the Canadian national alert system. The Counter Surprise system was created by SACEUR and accepted by the Defense Committee in 1956. It also had three levels: Military Vigilance, State Orange, and State Scarlet. Military Vigilance was called to get existing forces up to the highest state of preparedness short of movement, State Orange indicated that an attack was due in one hour, while State Scarlet indicated an attack was due in minutes. SACEUR had the authority to implement these measures for his existing earmarked forces, whereas the Formal system was supposed to be declared by the North Atlantic Council. SACLANT initially had no alert system.[102] The Formal system remained unratified before 1959.

By 1957, the Americans created a special system for gaining authority to change alert levels. If a Military Emergency were declared, the US Joint Chiefs would hold an emergency telephone conference and then dispatch JCS Emergency Action Messages. These messages were prerecorded requests that would be sent to the President requesting various actions. On presidential response, the JCS would send the appropriate action message. For example, MRF 2A requested the transfer of atomic weapons from the AEC to SAC; MRF 4A was presidential authority to actually use atomic weapons. MRF 10A instructed American units to carry out the Canada-US Emergency Defense Plan. (It is not clear how the President or JCS were supposed to get Canadian concurrence to activate the Canada-US Emergency Defense Plan, but it was probably by telephone and/or through the Canadian Joint Staff Mission Washington or Canadian embassy.) In a no-notice test, held in May 1957, it took fourteen minutes to get the JCS together and another thirteen minutes to get the US Joint Chiefs to make a decision. It took a further four minutes to get USAF Air Defense Command on the line and another minute for it to send its alert orders. It took fifteen minutes to do all of this in a later exercise that year.[103]

It is an inescapable fact that the mechanisms designed in the early to mid-1950s for alerting national forces and joint commands were loosely connected and not interoperable. In addition to the changing threat, one catalyst for change was an ABC agreement initiated in 1956 when St. Laurent was in power that led to an abortive bilateral Canadian-American attempt at an agreement in 1958.

Back when he was Secretary of State for External Affairs, Pearson wanted to ensure that there was a formal arrangement to exchange intelligence information between the two countries if there were indications that there might be an attack against North America, and that there would be formal consultation between Canada and the United States at the Chiefs and State-External levels—not at a lower command level—prior to the declaration of an alert and before war actually started.[104]

The agreement bogged down on language. What exactly was an alert? Was it a SAC alert? An air defense alert? A civil defense alert? The Americans were unsure and suspected that Canada wanted to know when SAC was alerted. Heeney, then Canada's ambassador, tried to clarify. The alert referred to was an air defense alert. If there was time, diplomatic channels should be used. If there was no time, the Chiefs level should be used. The Americans had no problem with intelligence information sharing, but they wanted to consult with the British.[105] The British quickly agreed, and the ABC nations established continuous twenty-four-hour communication channels to pass alert intelligence to each other. They were not interested in North American alert arrangements.[106] Similar arrangements were made between CONAD (and later NORAD), SAC, and SHAPE. If either SHAPE or CONAD declared an air defense warning, all four commands (including RCAF Air Defence Command) were informed instantly.[107]

The dialogue continued throughout 1957. In essence, the Canadian position revolved around

> the concern motivated by fear [that] declaration of a national emergency before consultation with all implies re: full readiness of continental defense forces might involve Canada automatically in a war which in its origins Canada might believe contrary [to] its interest. Hence arises Canada's interest in early high-level consultations before [the] situation deteriorated to a point where US under imminent risk of attack which would of course bring Canada in.[108]

As with other matters, the June 1957 election delayed action on the consultation and intelligence agreement. With the advent of the Diefenbaker government, the NORAD debates in the fall of 1957, and the rearing of the sovereignty issues, the alert consultation agreement took on a different importance.

Diefenbaker's Cabinet had approved the bilateral intelligence and consultation agreement earlier in April 1958. That agreement was the final version of the agreement drafted back in early 1957. In effect:

> In a situation in which either Government concludes that alert measures are necessary or desirable . . . the two Governments agree to consult through

the diplomatic channel and through the respective Chiefs of Staff. . . . Such consultation will precede the institution of alert measures by either Government except in the following extreme circumstances: if either Government considers an attack on North America to be imminent or probably in a matter of hours rather than days, consultation might, of necessity, coincide with or even follow the institution of separate alert measures. . . . If either Government is impelled by the time factor to take alert measures before initiating consultation, it agrees to immediately inform the other . . . as soon as possible.[109]

Physical mechanisms for Canadian-American consultation generated in the wake of the agreement included the establishment of the so-called Gold Telephone between the Prime Minister and the President. Another mechanism was the Joint Chiefs of Staff Alerting Network (JCSAN). The JCSAN was a special conference call in which American CinCs in command of nuclear weapons could be connected in fifteen seconds. Provision was made to allow the President of the United States and the Prime Minister of Canada to participate if the connections could be made. Notably, if the conference call was cut off in an emergency at certain defense readiness conditions, some CinCs were permitted to conduct predelegated release of nuclear weapons.[110]

Another factor prompting closer consultation was Eisenhower's willingness to use SAC activities for signaling purposes during crisis situations. One case was the 1958 Lebanon Crisis. After a coup in Syria in July 1958 and in response to other unstable situations in the Middle East, American and British military forces were requested by Lebanon and Jordan to forestall possible Soviet encroachment in the region. Additional measures, recommended by General Twining, included deploying SAC tankers to forward bases and alerting eleven hundred SAC bombers. Diefenbaker concurred, according to secondary sources, stating that these measures should not be concealed from the Soviets.[111]

In reality, however, a senior RCAF officer brought a locked briefcase to Pearkes: it contained the SAC overflight request. Keeping his back to the RCAF officer and looking out the window, Pearkes wondered aloud if his secretary would use the "Minister of National Defence" signature stamp on the document, presumably so he could say, if he were questioned, that he hadn't actually seen the documents.[112]

When SAC was alerted for the Lebanon situation in 1958, CinCNORAD placed NORAD on an increased alert level (the exact level is unknown),[113] a fact that was subsequently announced to the media by NORAD HQ.[114] Pearson, while Opposition leader, immediately attacked Diefenbaker in the House of Commons. One observer noted that this was done with an: "obvious motivation for publicity. . . . [the concern was] that Canada through its defense arrangements with United States might be drawn into perilous situation by action of United States in which Canada did not participate or about which Canada was not consulted."[115]

Diefenbaker was furious and stated that he had not been consulted and that the first he heard of it was in the newspapers. This was a simplification of events. Eisenhower had, in fact, telephoned Diefenbaker a full day before the

Marine landings took place in Lebanon to inform him of the operation. Diefenbaker simply did not make the connection between the landing operation, nascent SAC support of it, and the protection of the deterrent, or alternately, Eisenhower inferred too little from the conversation.[116]

Behind the scenes, Twining called Foulkes and asked him to come down to Washington immediately so that he could be briefed prior to commencement of the Lebanon operation. Foulkes had a Cabinet Defence Committee meeting and did not think he could get away, so "reading between the lines, and at the same time we had somebody in CIA so we had a complete flow of intelligence coming," Foulkes dispatched a representative to meet with Twining, who in turn wanted to raise the readiness state of the air defense system and deploy SAC bombers and bombs to Goose Bay since there was a possibility the Soviets might respond with military force. Foulkes then met with the Chiefs (with Robert Bryce as well as Jules Leger from External present), who all agreed that an increased state of readiness was acceptable as long as it was kept secret. A SAC deployment to Goose Bay beyond the existing measures, however, needed further discussion.[117]

The JCS Chairman concurred, stating he was about to brief Eisenhower and he had some doubts as to whether Eisenhower would go for the nondeployment to Goose Bay. Foulkes asked Twining to have President Eisenhower call Prime Minister Diefenbaker on the matters at hand. Twining told Foulkes that there already were some discussions between the two men, but promised to confirm with the President. Bryce assured Foulkes that he would pass this on to Diefenbaker too. Foulkes then tasked Canadian signals intelligence resources to monitor the Americans so that he would know when the alert level should be raised. When the Americans recalled their personnel from leave, Foulkes called Bryce to confirm that Diefenbaker had been informed and consulted (Pearkes was accompanying Princess Margaret on a royal visit and could not be reached). In any event, none of Diefenbaker's advisors informed him of the situation. Bryce, Foulkes, Pearkes, and others were called in by Diefenbaker and subjected to a tantrum in which the Prime Minister yelled questions like, "Who's running this country? Who's the Prime Minister? I never get told, I have to learn these things over the radio!"[118]

Apparently, consultation on NORAD alert had taken place at the State-External level and at the military level through the Canadian Joint Staff Mission Washington. Diefenbaker was not told by Smith or any of the External staff, or by Pearkes. Despite this and according to CinCNORAD's terms of reference, Partridge was empowered to raise the alert level if he believed it was necessary, or if he consulted with the Chiefs level, or if they ordered him to. Partridge decided to do what was prudent given the situation and informed the appropriate Canadian officials.[119] The situation so perturbed Diefenbaker that he later attempted to alter CinCNORAD's terms of reference to limit him to alerting NORAD for training purposes or "in the event of an unacceptably large number of unidentified aircraft within the warning system."[120] The Lebanon Crisis merely added to the discomfort that the Diefenbaker government was experiencing over NORAD.

The alert and readiness situation was not helped by the existence of several different alert systems and the ambiguous NORAD-NATO relationship

Unfortunately, attempts to rationalize an alert system that could serve multiple purposes was complicated by the Berlin Crisis in 1958–1959.

Khrushchev presented the West with an ultimatum in November 1958: get out of Berlin or suffer unspecified consequences. This action was in part brought on by NATO's and, more importantly, by West Germany's acceptance of the MC 70 nuclear force integration plan. The Soviets were determined to apply pressure to West Germany and force the rest of the West to accept East Germany as a sovereign state. In December 1958, the Joint Planning Committee was, on Foulkes's instructions, to prepare several prealert states of readiness for Canadian forces. They were to be created with two things in mind: "any measures adopted should be such that they did not come unnecessarily to public notice on implementation and that they would not cause the enemy to believe that an attack was imminent."[121] The measures should be compatible with SACEUR and NORAD alert levels and measures, and exercises should be held frequently to disguise the nature of the levels. The word "mobilization" was now obsolete because it connoted too much and should be replaced with "Emergency Defence Plans."[122]

The JPC produced the Canadian Forces States of Increased Military Vigilance. These states were structured to alert Canadian national forces "during a period of international tension prior to the declaration of an Alert by the Canadian Government."[123] There were two phases: a "Discrete Phase" and a "Ready Phase," which would be called by the Chiefs. During the Discrete Phase, the services would review their emergency plans, place ships on four hour's notice to move, place ships on assigned stations, disperse logistic facilities, increase intelligence and communications facility readiness, and repair all unserviceable aircraft. The Ready Phase canceled leaves, increased security measures at facilities, deployed alternate and mobile headquarters, topped up ships and aircraft with weapons and fuel, provided for minesweeping operations, alerted standby battalions for deployment, and brought some units up to wartime strength. The increased states of military vigilance were structured to be implemented prior to the existing Simple-Reinforced-General alert system in Canada, which could only be implemented on the Cabinet's approval.[124] The Chiefs approved the two new phases in July 1959. It does not appear to have been referred to Cabinet for approval.[125]

Canada, therefore, had a five-stage national alert system: Discrete, Ready, Simple, Reinforced, and General. Ready and Simple overlapped in reality, but one part was called by the Chiefs and the other by the government. The Canadian system now had to be coordinated with NATO, NORAD, and the Americans.

NATO had not yet ratified MC 67/1, the NATO Formal Alert System (Simple, Reinforced, General), though the Counter Surprise Military Alert System (Military Vigilance, State Orange, State Scarlet) was in existence, and State Orange was changed to provide thirty-six hour's notice of an attack. SACLANT was prepared to use the Formal Alert System if and when it was ratified. NORAD had, by this point in 1959, produced an expanded alert system that built on the existing CAN-US air defense alert system. It included the following levels: Normal Readiness, Increased Readiness (conditions 1 through 4), Maximum Readiness (Air Defense Readiness and Air Defense Emergency), and Air Defense Warnings (Red, Yellow, and White).[126] Air

Defense Emergency now alerted the Civil Defense and Emergency Measures Organization in the United States and Canada in addition to the air defense forces.

By April 1959, the powers with forces in Berlin, France, Britain, and the United States formed a planning group called LIVE OAK to produce a catalog of plans to respond to whatever level of aggression the Soviets used against Berlin and its road, rail, and air communications. LIVE OAK was a non-NATO organization, though SACEUR was double-hated as its head, and it was co-located at SHAPE. Foulkes understood that LIVE OAK was structured to develop and implement plans that would precede and could even precipitate a full-scale MC 14/2 (revised)–pattern conflict with the enemy. If LIVE OAK initiated some level or levels of response to an incident, this might accelerate or escalate the situation rapidly. Therefore, he wanted an expanded link or understanding between NORAD and SHAPE/LIVE OAK.[127]

Foulkes consulted with Twining. Twining himself was agitated at the situation, and the JCS was concerned that "appropriate steps should be taken now to ensure that the military forces assigned to NORAD will be properly prepared against possible enemy action against North America, which could result from a rapidly deteriorating situation in Berlin."[128] And, of course, SAC alert was predicated on NORAD early warning. State then approached External on the matter, and the Canadian embassy was briefed on LIVE OAK. Canadian policy makers wanted a clearer definition as to what constituted denial of access before they agreed to any increased state of readiness for NORAD.[129]

The real problem was External's view that the NORAD terms of reference that allowed CinCNORAD to alert NORAD to certain levels should be changed, as the Lebanon situation had demonstrated. External felt left out and wanted some say in the matter regardless of the time factor. Robertson was, as discussed in the last chapter, afraid that alert stages could produce precipitative action on the part of SAC or the Soviets. In effect, the External officials thought they should have the ability to influence every aspect of Canada's fate in a world in which actions taken in minutes could save or destroy millions of people. The JCS were appalled by this stance and resisted it.[130]

At the same time, however, LIVE OAK and SHAPE could not reach concurrence about what exactly constituted denial of access.[131] Was SACEUR required to take the matter to the NAC if denial occurred or not? Was LIVE OAK part of NATO or not? Was Berlin part of the NATO Area or not? If LIVE OAK implemented a measure that resulted in local retaliation by the enemy, and NORAD were already alerted, could a misinterpreted Soviet action or activity in the Arctic prompt SAC to launch?

In the end, State and External agreed that the NORAD terms of reference would not be changed, but that:

> CinCNORAD is not in a position to assess all the political factors available to both [governments]; therefore, it will be the responsibility of the Chiefs of Staff of Canada and the United States, in consultation with their respective political authorities, to reach agreement for increasing states of

readiness of NORAD during periods of international tension where factors of overriding political significance are involved. In these circumstances, parallel consultations will be carried on between the political authorities . . . prior to reaching such an agreement.[132]

It is important that the diplomats made a distinction between an increase of international tension resulting in an attack and a sudden attack by an enemy. In a period in which there was supposedly no tension, NORAD could alert his forces at will if he thought it was necessary. In a period of tension, he had to consult with the Canadian Chiefs of Staff and US Joint Chiefs while External and State talked to each other and determined whether or not an alert was actually warranted or "allowed."

While this diplomatic wrangle was in progress, the JCS noted that its own alerting process was cumbersome. By November 1959 all American commands had their alert levels rationalized into the DEFCON system.[133] NORAD readily adopted the DEFCON system, which produced a situation whereby Canadian military planners were faced with an easier compatibility situation and Canadian diplomats were confronted with an even closer and inexorable link between NORAD and SAC. The DEFCON system, when aligned with the NATO and Canadian systems, looked like figure 8.1.

Figure 8.1

RELATIONSHIP OF ALLIED ALERT SYSTEMS TO CANADIAN ALERT SYSTEM

International Situation	U.S./NORAD	NATO	Canada
Peacetime, Cold War, Normal	DEFCON 5	--------------------	----------------------------
Delicate or Strained International Relations	DEFCON 4* DEFCON 3	Military Vigilance Counter Surprise Military Alert System	Discrete Phase Ready Phase
Reliable information that Enemy preparing to attack	DEFCON 2	Simple Alert	Simple Alert
Definite and Conclusive indications that hostilities are imminent	DEFCON 1	Reinforced Alert	Reinforced Alert
Hostilities have commenced	NORAD Air Defence Emergency (US): Defense Emergency	General Alert	General Alert

* SAC was always at DEFCON 4 in 'peacetime'.

CinCNORAD, CinCCONAD, or any other American unified or specified command commander[134] could request that the DEFCON be changed in his own area of responsibility and then the JCS would convene an Emergency Telephone Conference (JCS ETC) on the JCSAN to formalize the change and consult on further measures. The JCS ETC was similar to the previously described Emergency Action Message system.

1. Conference telephone call, roll call.

2. Situation briefing by Commander declaring an emergency condition.

3. a. Notify the President, commands, and agencies.

    b. Determine whether the Canada-US Emergency Defense Plan has been placed in effect.

4. Intelligence brief by J-2.

5. Consideration on which Emergency Messages to send, which would include:

    EM-1: situation and action messages to US CinCs.

    EM-1A: situation and action messages to major NATO commanders.

    EM-2: request US Secretary of Defense (SECDEF) to contact the President and request national emergency. If SECDEF not available, Chairman of JCS will contact President.

    EM-2A: if President not contactable, contact Congress.

    EM-3: if President approves in response to EM-2, EM-3A (war message) is sent by JCS to all CinCs.

    EM-4: if President approves in response to EM-2 (concurrence of Prime Minister of the United Kingdom is required) and the situation is that of general war, EM-4A (use of UK bases) is sent.

    EM-5: if presidential approval is granted in response to EM-2, JCS sends EM-5A (atomic weapons for specified Allies).

    EM-6: the EM-6A (CinCLANT and CinCEUR transfer of authority to SACLANT and SACEUR).[135]

Item 3b is somewhat ambiguous and its position in the sequence curious. It presumably meant Canadian and American Chiefs of Staff consultation as to what Canada was doing *prior* to JCS contacting the President to declare an alert, since the implementation of the Canada-US Emergency Defense Plan required consultation between the US Joint Chiefs and the Canadian Chiefs. The US Joint Chiefs communications system had a dedicated high frequency radio link with Ottawa. Only the other American unified commands and NATO commands had equivalent high priority on communications.[136] Canada, we can reasonably conclude, was scheduled to be consulted prior to American manipulation of its own DEFCONS and the release of nuclear weapons to Canadian forces. It should be noted that CinCNORAD had the ability to alert his assigned forces all the way up to DEFCON 1 without consultation. If External thought it could use consultation on air defense alerts to influence SAC's activities, it was wrong. It could try to veto Canadian participation in an air defense alert, which in turn made SAC more vulnerable and decreased its deterrence value, which in turn increased the likelihood of precipitous action by the enemy. Alerting military forces in the nuclear age was a military affair that was made even more dangerous with this sort of meddling. There was simply no time for diplomats to become involved in the process.

The major problem remained the lack of a compatible means of consultation between the Prime Minister and the Chiefs so that alert measures and consultation could be implemented effectively. This problem would never be solved and, as we will see, it contributed to the nuclear crisis that unseated the Diefenbaker government.

SAC Overflights and Canada

The Soviet ICBM threat produced a number of challenges for SAC. One of these was the acceleration of the USAF's ICBM program. Between 1958 and 1966, thirteen Atlas and six Titan squadrons were constructed and activated in the continental United States. A number of them were located close to the Canadian border (Plattsburg AFB, New York, and Fairchild AFB, Washington State, were two).[137] The projected ballistic flight paths of the missiles overflew Canadian airspace on their way to the Soviet Union. Did SAC have to get Canadian clearance using the Z procedure before launching them?

The USAF routinely kept the RCAF informed about ICBM development. Foulkes and Slemon were even briefed as to what the planned targets for the Atlas missiles were. The ICBMs, Chief of the Air Staff Campbell was informed, would not overfly major Canadian population centers. Some debris from the boosters might land on Canadian soil, but it would be minor. These discussions were not passed on to External Affairs. Foulkes thought that there was no need to generate yet another written agreement that would limit SAC's activity.[138]

The XYZ procedures would, however, require some modification for another SAC response to Sputnik. By 1958 CinCSAC was allowed to launch the ground alert aircraft (which eventually totaled one-third of the SAC bomber fleet) without direct orders from the President or the JCS. These positive control launch or "Fail Safe" flights could be undertaken by CinCSAC if he felt that a Soviet attack was imminent. The bombers would return to base at the Positive Control Turn Around Point unless CinCSAC issued the "go-code" on the SHORT ORDER High Frequency communications system after he had received permission from the President.[139] This system was not deemed to be the final answer to the ICBM threat, however. It still took some time to get the ground alert bombers off the ground in an emergency.

SAC initiated Exercise HEADSTART in September 1958, which was designed to validate Airborne Alert, a concept by which a certain number of SAC bombers equipped with nuclear weapons were kept continuously in the air using airborne refueling and rotated with other bombers over time. The HEADSTART tests were conducted over Canada using B-52 bombers based at Loring AFB, Maine. Phase I, held in September, used unarmed bombers cleared using the X procedure. Phase II, scheduled for October 1958, would carry nuclear weapons. Since four bomber flights per day at six-hour intervals (in addition to tanker support sorties) were necessary to conduct the tests, SAC wanted an extended Y procedure to cover the entire test period.[140]

The Canadian embassy made it clear that Canada was opposed in principle "to grant[ing] blanket clearances over an extended period for the overflight of Canada by SAC aircraft."[141] However, if the service-to-service requests were made under the Y procedure and Pearkes agreed, then HEADSTART Phase II was acceptable. The overflights continued without incident.

Validating Airborne Alert was only part of establishing an actual Airborne Alert capability. Air and ground crews for the tankers and bombers had to be trained in the techniques and this was the impetus for the SAC Airborne Alert Indoctrination Training Program code-named STEEL TRAP. Ambassador Heeney was informed in February 1959 that SAC would conduct a six-month training exercise that would include 1436 aircraft, many of which would be equipped with nuclear weapons. All communications and weapons safety systems needed to be checked and crews qualified. A significant portion of the indoctrination force would overfly Canada. SAC wanted to clear with the RCAF each batch of flights thirty days before they were conducted. Was this feasible? A lot was riding on the Airborne Alert program, and it would dramatically enhance the deterrent.[142]

An on-going exercise of this magnitude was not an easy pill for the Diefenbaker government to swallow, even before Howard Green became the External Affairs Minister. Norman Robertson was perturbed about STEEL TRAP as he "was particularly concerned with the large number of planes involved in the exercise and couldn't help wondering whether the increase in scope over previous exercises wasn't related to the Berlin situation and the increased world tension."[143]

Even though State Department officials assured Robertson that this was not the case, the matter still had to go to Ottawa. Diefenbaker was directly involved. He stood to be convinced that STEEL TRAP was not another Lebanon-like "provocation." Heeney was briefed by the Americans on the establishment of LIVE OAK and the formulation of Berlin contingency plans as well as their relationship to SAC:

> the information given to him on a most restricted basis concerning the development of our contingency planning with respect to Berlin had been the decisive element in the Prime Minister's approval. The anxiety of the Canadian Government remains, however, lest future actions on our part as the crisis unfolds mistakenly lead the Soviet Government to calculate that we are planning to take preemptive action.[144]

As with other agreements, there was to be absolutely no publicity given on the matter. The US Department of Defense (DOD) was severe in its handling of a near-leak perpetrated by USAF public affairs people, reminding them that "the matter of nuclear overflights of Canada by SAC is a highly sensitive subject in Canada and one of important political significance to the Canadian Government."[145]

STEEL TRAP had Canadian clearance for four months before renewal. Diefenbaker inserted a caveat into the arrangement in that "circumstances might arise which would necessitate further consideration by the Canadian Government of the desirability of particular overflights and which could justify the suspension of the flights over Canadian territory."[146] The exercise was a massive undertaking that, in the end, involved moving 4232 nuclear weapons between July 1959 and June 1960, many of them over Canada. The majority of the weapons involved in STEEL TRAP were the Mk 39 and Mk 36 mod 2 weapons. B-52s involved in STEEL TRAP carried either two Mk 15/39s (yield: 9 to 10 megatons) or one Mk 36 (yield: 9 to 10 megatons).[147]

The existing XYZ procedures were too restrictive to deal with post–STEEL TRAP airborne alert operations. Foulkes wanted a three-to-six-month period with service-to-service clearance for individual flights. The USAF wanted to eliminate the X clearance so that overflights with non-nuclear components could become routine flights. It also wanted overflight clearances to last a six-month period and even attempted to make linkages between overflights and SAC storage and MB-1 storage.[148]

By this point Green was External Affairs Minister, and the USAF ran into a brick wall on changing the XYZ procedures. The Americans continued to equate SAC overflights with MB-1 overflight arrangements and SAC storage in hopes of getting a single agreement to cover all of these things. It appears that Green did not attempt to block the STEEL TRAP extension during the fall of 1959 in the wake of the SKY HAWK debacle[149] but the matter remained static well into 1961.[150]

SAC's first Airborne Alert Plan, code-named KEEN AXE, kicked off in January 1961. It appears that KEEN AXE consisted of one route to, from, and around Alaska.[151] Even though Howard Green made no more attempts to interfere with SAC overflights, Secretary of Defense Robert S. McNamara directed SAC to establish a contingency plan called CHROME DOME that added two new routes: Greenland and the Mediterranean (see figure 8.2). This was done "to preclude the overflight clearance problem with Canada."[152] McNamara believed that the President should not have to be concerned with overflight clearance in an emergency and took steps to limit those debilitating effects on SAC's ability to strike at the heart of the Soviet Union. By 1966 or earlier, the Greenland route was changed to overfly Canadian airspace.[153] The number of bombers overflying Canada varied according to the level of international tension.

The debate over SAC operations, air defense, and alert consultation was not merely related to Canadian sovereignty. The External cabal's willingness to pursue obstruction directly affected Canada's carefully thought-out force structure and strategy by affecting Canada's ability to pursue access to the nuclear weapons necessary to carry that strategy out. This led directly to the nuclear weapons crisis that would eventually jeopardize Canada's security, damage Canada's reputation with her closest allies in NATO, and finally unseat the Diefenbaker government in 1963.

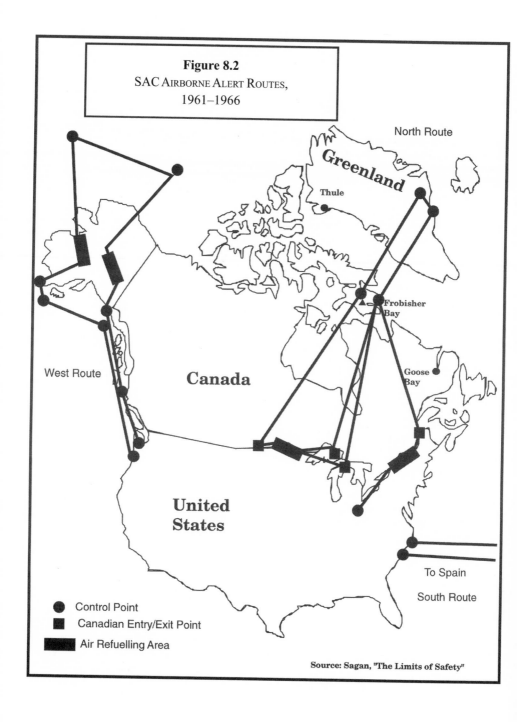

Figure 8.2
SAC AIRBORNE ALERT ROUTES,
1961–1966

North Route

Greenland

Thule

Frobisher
Bay

West Route

Canada

Goose
Bay

United
States

To Spain

South Route

● Control Point
■ Canadian Entry/Exit Point
▬ Air Refuelling Area

Source: Sagan, "The Limits of Safety"

9

CANADA'S NUCLEAR CRISIS, PART I: A YEAR OF TRANSITION, 1960

The human element appears to have failed us here.
–Dr. Strangelove or: How I Learned to Stop
Worrying and Love the Bomb

So are they all, all honourable men.
–Julius Caesar

Introduction

Canada's ability to implement her defense responsibilities was blocked. On the surface, the block consisted of linkage between Canadian access to the American nuclear stockpile and various American projects involving Canada (SAC and MB-1 overflights and SAC and MB-1 storage). Beneath this lay three layers of fear coupled with a misunderstanding. Some Canadian policy makers were afraid of domestic political opposition, some of the Americans, and the rest of the Soviets. The first two groups of policy makers possessed an inability to recognize the problems posed by time, space, and political consultation, which were in turn related to the sovereignty questions produced by the NORAD debates.

Though the 1963 election was decisive in breaking this deadlock, the years immediately before were rife with danger as East and West grappled with two serious crises: the Berlin Crisis in 1961 and the Cuban Missile Crisis in 1962. The situation was complicated by evolving NATO strategy and the need for Canadian national security policy to change to accommodate it during the crises.

This change was subject to dramatic interpersonal dynamics. The main pillar of continuity in Canadian strategic policy making, Charles Foulkes, retired, while Defense Minister George Pearkes resigned. This produced the usual disarray in any changeover, but Pearkes's replacement, Douglas Harkness, was a strong personality who would not tolerate Howard Green's de Gaullist tendencies and Diefenbaker's unwillingness to support Canada's allies. At another level, the ascension of John F. Kennedy to the presidency in the United States generated friction when Kennedy and Prime Minister John Diefenbaker clashed at the personal level. The inability of the Diefenbaker government to adequately deal with all these challenges undermined Canadian-American-NATO relations and also undermined NATO's ability to protect its primary deterrent, SAC. Skillful political maneuvering on the part of Opposition leader Mike Pearson ultimately used the lack of Canadian access to nuclear warheads to generate a lack of confidence in the Diefenbaker government, which would result in its demise in April 1963.

1960: A Year of Transition

Charles Foulkes, tired of the internal debate over nuclear negotiations with the United States and appalled by the shabby and vindictive treatment meted out to the outgoing RCMP Commissioner by the Prime Minister, announced that he would retire after thirty-five years of service.[1] Pearkes was not happy about the prospect of losing Foulkes. In a Cabinet meeting, he noted that the retirement should be announced in the House, and Diefenbaker had no problem with this initially, though he thought that it "should be made known in the House of Commons prior to the expected debate on defense matters, to avoid giving the mistaken impression that the retirement occurred because of differences of opinion."[2]

In a stunning reversal, however, Diefenbaker announced to the House that Foulkes was being kept on "for some months in a desire to bring about a continuance in completion of the negotiations which are taking place in the military field."[3] Foulkes, who had planned to retire in January 1960, found himself pressed back into service by the Prime Minister. Behind the scenes, however, Pearkes selected the Deputy Minister of National Defence and former Air Marshal Frank Miller to replace Foulkes. Diefenbaker did not want Miller, and Foulkes said he would stay on only if Miller became Chairman of the COSC after him.[4] Consequently, Foulkes stayed on until May.

It is worthwhile, then, to provide insight into Foulkes's evolving strategic *Weltanschauung,* as it was undoubtedly transmitted to Miller. Foulkes saw MC 14/2 (revised) as the dominant Canadian strategic concept, with its two-phase pattern of war and Shield and Sword pattern of forces. Foulkes recognized that "So successful have our endeavours in deterring aggression in NATO been, that Soviet policy appears now to be directing its attention to other more sensitive areas."[5] Canada and NATO had to have the ability to respond in a conventional fashion on NATO's periphery. This could be a Korea-like operation or a UN Suez-like operation. In other words, Canada had to maintain a flexible force structure.

This new situation did not, however, distract Foulkes from the most important issue, which was the changing dynamics of nuclear warfare. He believed that the offense was in the ascendancy because of the ballistic missile, though a mixed threat would still be in existence for some years to come. More importantly, he noted that:

> so great an advantage lies with he who takes the initiative and makes the first strike, and already some doubts are being raised as to whether what is left after the first attack will provide a sufficient deterrent to persuade the Soviet Union that the retaliation is unbearable. Some United States authorities are so concerned about this aspect that they are looking at the forbidden preventative war approach.[6]

He was concerned about Berlin, which was "a most explosive situation and one which is going to have to be carefully watched or we might stumble into the war that none of us wants." The Berlin Crisis was primarily about West Germany's acquisition of nuclear weapons. However, given the existing state of affairs, was the West "prepared to go to war over who stamps a visa? . . . Can we use limited force in East Germany without risking a major war?"[7]

In the event that either preventative war or escalation over Berlin produced nuclear attack against North America, Foulkes strongly advocated that, in addition to the existing NATO and UN forces, Canada needed a comprehensive effort to mitigate the effects of a nuclear attack. Canada needed access to the American nuclear stockpile. To contribute to the Shield and Sword, Canada needed BOMARC and MB-1 warheads, nuclear ASW systems, and missiles and bombs for the forces stationed in Europe.[8]

Canada signed a bilateral nuclear information sharing agreement in March 1959. A second government-to-government agreement between Canada and the United States was necessary before Canadian forces had access to advanced safety training, arming mechanisms, and the nuclear stockpile. This second agreement remained unsigned into 1960, though Foulkes, Hendrick, and Pearkes produced a draft in December 1959.

On 4 January 1960, Diefenbaker asked Pearkes to provide him with a written report examining the status of BOMARC; acquisition of a new interceptor, the CF-104 strike aircraft; and the "present position regarding the acquisition and control of atomic warheads" in Canada and in Europe.[9] Pearkes informed the Prime Minister that on 13 July 1959, the RCAF and the USAF agreed to the detailed implementation plan for BOMARC/SAGE and construction started on 14 December 1959. Unfortunately, Pearkes noted in the memo, "The BOMARC 'B' when installed will be capable of utilizing either a high explosive or a nuclear warhead" (a statement which was erroneous and would cause problems later).[10] Pearkes also erred by stating that the decision to acquire the CF-104 strike aircraft was made in August 1958 (it was made in August 1959), and that the Chiefs were asked in 1958 to determine which interceptor aircraft should replace the Arrow and had not yet made a decision.

Information on acquisition and control was included in a follow-up to the 4 January request. In it, Pearkes noted, "the full effect of modern weapons both as a deterrent and as a defense, should the deterrent fail, cannot be achieved without the employment of nuclear warheads." As for NATO policy, the 1957 NATO meeting confirmed that nuclear weapons were officially part of the NATO deterrent system and that the Americans would provide a nuclear stockpile that would be released by the American President.[11]

As for the effects of these policies on Canada, Pearkes noted that storage would be required in Canada for SACLANT, SAC, and NORAD forces and for the Air Division and 4 Brigade in Europe. SACLANT, SACEUR, and CinCNORAD were the releasing authorities for the weapons. At this point, Pearkes explicitly stated: "No nuclear weapons are at present stored in Canada," though the Americans were still pressing for MB-1 storage at Harmon and Goose Bay air bases; nuclear torpedo and depth charge storage at Argentia; strategic nuclear weapons at Goose Bay; and "as soon as the BOMARC becomes operational . . . there will be a Canadian require-ment for the storage of nuclear warheads."[12]

The custody of, as opposed to the control of, nuclear weapons in Canada was still a debatable issue. The Americans, Pearkes believed, wanted sole custody over the weapons, while Pearkes wanted joint custody; that is, two rings of defenses around each storage site (US on the inside, Canada on the outside). Pearkes stated that release should be from the American President to the Canadian Prime Minister and then to the Canadian forces at the Prime Minister's discretion. SAC weapons based in Canada should also be a joint release matter. Things were more vague in Europe: "Canadian forces operating in Europe under [SACEUR] would be autho-rized only to use nuclear warheads under conditions agreed to between Canada and [SACEUR]."[13] Pearkes also included the December 1959 draft agreement.

All of this was in preparation for three lengthy Cabinet meetings in January 1960, which were preparation for a House of Commons debate. Diefenbaker told the Cabinet that storage and acquisition of the weapons was acceptable on the basic principle that "there would be no use of these weapons without the consent of the Canadian Government." He wanted this made clear, as he intended to protect him-self in the debate from charges of throwing away Canadian sovereignty. (This went back to the open wound generated by the NORAD debates in 1957–1958.) Conse-quently, Pearkes was to redraft the government-to-government agreement to make this absolutely clear.[14]

Foulkes and Bryce handled the redraft, and the matter came before Cabinet on 14 January.[15] Green, however, interrupted the process, claiming that there would be "widespread repercussions" as there was still American control over the weapons. Diefenbaker uncharacteristically stated:

> most statements on defense policy had been rather foggy and that the Cana-dian people were becoming aroused over what appeared to be a confused situation. . . . the policies of the USSR still constituted a threat to peace. . . . It was absolutely necessary that the Cabinet be quite clear in its attitude towards nuclear weapons for the Canadian forces and that [Diefenbaker] be in a position to make a clear statement on the matter.[16]

Green, Pearkes, and others were to draft a statement for Diefenbaker to use in the House. Back in Cabinet on 15 January, Diefenbaker confirmed that Canada should have joint custody (the dual key concept) and joint release authority over the weap-ons. In the Cabinet discussion, views swung to both extremes. Some members wanted total Canadian control over the weapons (custody and release with no American say so); others thought that there should be no weapons for Canadian forces at all. In the end, the House statement was redrafted.[17]

Diefenbaker presented the statement on 18 January 1960:

> Canada's stand might be summarized in this way: Eventually Canadian forces may require certain nuclear weapons if Canadian forces are to be kept effective. For example, the BOMARC anti-aircraft missile to be

effective would require nuclear warheads. It is the belief of the Government too that there should be no increase in the number of countries manufacturing nuclear weapons. . . . if obtained, they will be obtained from the [US]. . . . negotiations are proceeding with the United States in order that the necessary weapons can be made available for Canadian units if and when they are required. . . . arrangements for the safeguarding and security of all such weapons in Canada will be subject to Canadian approval. . . . I want to make it abundantly clear that nuclear weapons will not be used by the Canadian forces except as the Canadian Government decides.[18]

This was an explicit statement of Canadian nuclear policy, though some have interpreted it as "ambiguous."[19] The Opposition did not make much of the statement at the time and flagrantly ignored it in their subsequent attacks on the government over the nuclear weapons issue. On 9 February, Diefenbaker reiterated in the House what he had said in January, adding: "If and when Canada does acquire nuclear weapons" it would be done "with our obligations under the North Atlantic Treaty," firmly linking nuclearization with NATO.[20]

Voodoo Economics

Most of February 1960 was devoted to making headway on a replacement for the CF-100. General Lawrence S. Kuter, who replaced Earle Partridge as CinCNORAD, presided over the development of the 1961–1965 NORAD Objectives Plan in late 1959. The NADOP was then dispatched to the COSC for approval. With Canadian staff input at NORAD HQ in the wake of the Camp David meeting in 1959, Kuter proposed that USAF F-101B Voodoo interceptors be transferred to the RCAF to replace the CF-100s and that Canada take a third BOMARC base with another thirty missiles.[21]

The third BOMARC site was out. The provision for it was based on American intelligence estimates that indicated there would be a greater number of Soviet supersonic aircraft in their arsenal than the Canadian analysts believed. The need for an interceptor aircraft, however, was another matter altogether. The CF-104, though based on an interceptor aircraft, was not suited to Canadian safety requirements for operation over Northern Canada.[22] The CF-104 could not carry and fire a nuclear-tipped air defense missile, and it could not handle SAGE direction. Nor could the CF-100, which did not have the ceiling necessary for a high-level intercept and could not interact with SAGE.[23]

Why not just leave the manned intercept mission to the American squadrons at Thule, Goose Bay, and Harmon air bases? This was not acceptable, asserted Foulkes, because of sovereignty, the same implications that had not been taken into account with the cancellation of the Arrow. How would Canada pay for a new interceptor? Most of the money devoted to the RCAF was being poured into the CF-104, BOMARC/SAGE, and Canadian Air Defence Integration (CADIN) programs. Chief of the Air Staff Campbell's staff generated a proposal (probably with NORAD collusion) by which Canada would take over eleven of the American-manned PINETREE radars in exchange for sixty-six F-101Bs.[24]

This proposal was then brought before the Cabinet. Pearkes revealed that the USAF offered to release some of its long-range interceptors (F-101Bs) from areas that could be covered with the shorter-ranged F-102s. Pearkes made it abundantly clear ("Having a greater operational capacity than the CF-100 and being capable of carrying a nuclear air-to-air missile") that the Voodoo was the best, most capable, and cheapest choice. There was an extended Cabinet debate. The primary sticking point was the Cabinet's fear of the Liberals, who they assumed would use this arrangement to bash the government on sovereignty grounds. Some even proposed acquiring more BOMARCs, which they believed was more politically palatable. In the end, because they were afraid of criticism, the Cabinet chose to defer the F-101B Voodoo acquisition decision and with it any hope of Canada's contributing significantly to protecting her airspace and alliance prerogatives in NORAD.[25]

The RCAF leadership used the break in the action to convene its annual Air Officers Commanding conference in March 1960. Unlike previous conferences, this one was devoted to brainstorming. What was the probable course of events that would affect the RCAF? How should a response be formulated and implemented?

The RCAF leadership noted that the dominant strategic concept would continue to be MC 14/2 (revised), which the 1960 RCAF Emergency Defence Plan was in accordance with. The biggest problem identified by the RCAF planners was their belief that the Canadian national alert system "might not be able to react quickly enough" and as a result the planners created four RCAF "readiness states" which corresponded to the existing national alert levels. The RCAF commanders had the ability to alert their forces to correspond to the NATO and NORAD systems without getting governmental-level permission. In effect, the RCAF subverted not only the officially approved Simple-Reinforced-General system, but the Chiefs of Staff Committee–developed (and not ratified by Cabinet or any other responsible governmental body) Discrete and Ready levels.[26]

One of the most important themes in the meetings was a response to the ICBM threat and the place of it in the RCAF's concept of operations. An indigenous Canadian antiballistic missile system was out of the question because of cost. After consultation with the Americans in 1960, the RCAF was told that Canada could provide valuable assistance in testing components of an American antiballistic missile program or Canada could contribute directly to the deterrent either by stationing ICBMs on Canadian soil or by providing three nuclear-powered submarines capable of firing Polaris. Canada could use its geography to assist in dispersing the American deterrent to reduce its vulnerability. Active defense was deemed to be "an extremely doubtful proposition" since it could be flooded with masses of cheap missiles. But then the question was, how much deterrent was enough? The commanders also discussed the problems with what they perceived to be an American over-reliance on city targeting. What if the Soviets evacuated their cities?[27]

In terms of maritime operations, the RCAF leadership was convinced that the submarine threat would continue to pose problems no matter what the future pattern of war was since "if there is such a thing as a second phase [MC 14/2 (revised)] the submarine will . . . take part in that phase also. You have the fact of the submarine being used as a diplomatic weapon in a period of tension."[28] This in turn led to a discussion of rules of engagement. They were concerned about American proposals to declare a five-hundred-mile limit within which unidentified submarines "would be considered a threat against North America" and presumably be attacked.[29]

In terms of the future, Air Vice-Marshal Clare Annis from Air Material Command believed, "Containment has failed. It [has failed] in the Middle East, the Caribbean, etc. Consequently, the other big thing which will fail is defense by defensive methods. It will fail during the 60s. . . . The new situation is that the USSR is on the loose, with no known methods of stopping this economic and political expansion. . . . I feel that our government is skirting at the fringes of neutralism. This is not winning any respect from the US. . . . [W]e fought to have and to hold atomic forces and we seem to be on the breakthrough of having achieved this at long last. . . . If deterrents fail we must get in and help the Americans in their offensive methods. . . . I think we need to get into the offensive role [in NATO]."

Some of the more radical ideas came from Air Commodore F. S. Carpenter. Carpenter had been a Catalina ASW squadron commander in the Second World War and commanded Transport Command. Transport Command was heavily into UN peacekeeping operations, which influenced his thinking.[30]

Carpenter predicted that, in terms of influence, "[Canadian] real estate would be relatively unimportant to the Americans because of the increased range of their missiles."[31] In terms of peripheral areas, "A total war should only come about through miscalculation or in some situation in which it cannot be contained. This should be the basis for our planning." In other words, "We have considerable prestige in the world because of the integrity of [Canadians] and because the world recognizes that we have no territorial ambitions. . . . We should endeavour to make the fullest use of this esteem."[32]

Furthermore, "We should admit that we have no large offensive capability and that we should, in fact, go along with what is likely to be the most probable policy of our government—that we should not have atomic weapons. . . . the basis for our forces in the future should be a kind of combat police force . . . [operating] in a disarmament inspection role."[33] These views were deemed to be heresy. "We should not have in our inventory any offensive atomic weapons. There is no advantage to Canada in having atomic weapons, or even the West having them and we should discourage other countries from having them."[34]

Campbell had, in anticipation of the annual conference, tasked Air Commodore W. A. Orr to put together an ad hoc team examining similar issues. Campbell craftily had Orr give his briefing *after* the air commanders had expressed their views. In his summary, Orr stated, "Our importance to the United States decreases in the defense of the United States—that we should maintain our position in the overall alliance to which we belong by making at least an equal contribution, and this naturally turned to offensive contribution. . . . we really [must] make this NATO force into a hard-hitting offensive force."[35]

Air Vice-Marshal Max Hendrick, fresh off the plane from Washington, DC, and no doubt frustrated with the nuclear agreement negotiating process noted:

Canada [is] in the position of not pulling her weight. . . . We are very proud of our capability and believe that the Canadian people respect us for our [nuclear] capability, but we are allowing our critics to go unanswered. . . . But we have allies outside in city suits who I think will speak for us if we were to inspire them in the right way. . . . Let us give the party line to our friends, even to the extent of writing articles they can cite; in other words, have a fifth column outside on our behalf. . . .

Arguing with the Government [using] logic is useless; and I don't think we should try it. Therefore, we come to a poker game. . . . We have got to be a little more devious in selling, less honest perhaps. If we become useless to the United States our bargaining power will become useless. They are very friendly and co-operative people but they are also realists and we can only use our nuisance value for so much.[36]

Carpenter had a serious problem with this approach:

There was kind of a suggestion that came up a couple of times within these four walls that in spite of what the public in Canada want or think they want, or in spite of what the Canadian Government may want or think they want that we should be devoting a good deal of our effort to chart something that the Government might want or the public might want. Surely this kind of thing cannot be right. I think we should try to educate the public on what the facts are. . . . It is necessary with a public such as ours which is rather detached from the realities of world affairs.[37]

At some point after the conferences, Air Chief Marshal Campbell discretely reached out for Wing Commander William Lee from the RCAF public relations organization and instructed him to develop a plan to get the RCAF's message across to the public via friendly media sources. Harkness knew about this but did not want Campbell to tell him about the details.[38]

Letters from some of these conference attendees reached the Prime Minister. For example, Kenneth Andras, who had served with Slemon in Bomber Command during the Second World War and was now a high-powered stock exchange investor in Toronto, sent an extremely detailed and technically accurate memorandum on NORAD, SAC, and nuclear air defense weapons to Diefenbaker.[39]

Though nuclear issues were not predominant in the April 1960 Canada-US Foreign Ministers Meeting held in Washington, Green was told that the BOMARC program was running into funding problems. The American Senate had withheld funding on the basis that the project was getting out of control, with too much money spent on too many missile test failures. An American Senator named Chavez even publicly stated, "the United States was trying to impose on the poor Canadians a missile that is so bad we cannot use it."[40]

Foulkes had had enough and retired in May 1960. He then flew to Washington and vented to his former wartime superior, President Eisenhower. When queried on why he retired, Foulkes told the President he was tired of trying to combat the "excessive confidence" in disarmament and the unwarranted "feeling that too much money was being spent on defense."[41] Foulkes and Ike were in agreement that American isolationism was dangerous if Canada reduced her NATO commitments. "The difficulty," Foulkes stated, "is not with the people but with the government." Green's insistence that NATO adopt a no-first-use policy undermined the deterrent. NATO needed nuclear weapons *and* a conventional build up. Eisenhower reiterated his previous thoughts on the unacceptable state of affairs in Congress regarding the restrictions on the release of nuclear weapons information to NATO allies. Foulkes agreed, but thought that Congressional statements on BOMARC were extremely "embarrassing" for those trying to implement the existing air defense agreements. Eisenhower ended the discussion by telling Foulkes that the United States should go so far as to provide Canada with Polaris and Minuteman missiles for an independent Canadian deterrent.[42]

Just prior to this meeting, Francis Gary Powers climbed into the cockpit of his Lockheed U-2 reconnaissance aircraft, took off, photographed the Tyuratam Cosmodrome and the Chelyabrinsk nuclear facility, and then was shot down by an SA-2 GUIDELINE antiaircraft missile near Sverdlovsk. This did not dramatically affect the proceedings of the NATO Ministerial Meeting in Istanbul, but it cast a pall over the planned Eisenhower-Khrushchev summit. On 15 May, Khrushchev met with Charles de Gaulle in Paris and demanded that Eisenhower issue an apology or the summit would not proceed. US Secretary of Defense Thomas Gates requested and received permission to place US national forces at an increased state of readiness. NORAD was not alerted, but CONAD was. Twenty-four hours later, Pearkes informed the Cabinet that he learned about this action but had not been consulted. Air Vice-Marshal Roy Slemon, Deputy CinCNORAD, informed Air Marshal Campbell that the US JCS ordered increased readiness for US CONAD forces. Campbell then informed Pearkes. Pearkes and other Canadian officials later learned that this was a no-notice ten-hour communications exercise and that air defense units were not moved.[43]

The Soviet news service broadcasted that Canada was "complicit" in the "crime" since Canada allowed U-2s to operate from Canadian bases. Pearkes had to explain to the Cabinet that U-2s did overfly Canada but did not operate or refuel from Canadian bases.[44] Diefenbaker was convinced that putting off Exercise SKY SHIELD had averted provocation, but the U-2 incident demonstrated to him that aerial activities were inherently provocative. After this pseudo-alert and the lack of consultation, Diefenbaker concluded that the U-2 was a deliberate American military provocation in that "most senior U.S. air force officers appeared to prefer a war in 1960 or 1961 and to believe that the U.S. could not win a war beginning in 1962 or later."[45] This was a serious accusation but it was kept in Cabinet.

Jules Leger returned to Canada from Paris late in May to provide Canadian policy makers with his views on NATO in the wake of the collapsed Paris Summit. Leger and Miller chose to use the almost-defunct Panel for this discussion. The real crux of the problem, in Leger's view, was the place of Germany in the postwar world and more immediately, Berlin. The German role, in turn, was related to NATO's implementation of MC 70, particularly the provision of ballistic missiles for SACEUR. There were spin-off problems. First, NATO commanders in Europe were concerned about the CF-104 program. There was a possibility that Canada might be the only middle power to provide aircraft for SACEUR's deterrent. The Danes and the Norwegians were wavering and might not accept nuclear weapons, but the Belgians and Dutch probably would. The French problem had not changed.[46] Leger implied that positive Canadian movement on nuclear weapons negotiations with the United States would have a unifying effect within NATO.

Miller told the Panel that no movement was likely in the near future:

> This was somewhat worrying, because it was difficult to explain in Parliament a defense programme which contemplated the purchase of such weapons carriers . . . when the decision to provide nuclear warheads for these weapons had not yet been taken.[47]

Leger also noted that Canada's conventional forces in Europe, 4 Brigade, were a very valuable contribution. Norstad was increasingly

> concerned about the need to strengthen the conventional forces in the shield. He was impressed less now by the danger of a massive attack on Western Europe than by the danger of increasing involvement of the shield forces in a conflict resulting from the lack of political settlements in Germany. General Norstad considered that it was essential to have strong conventional forces to contain the first wave of a small scale attack; he would wish to avoid using tactical nuclear weapons until he had to deal with the second, or larger, wave.[48]

There were other considerations causing problems, particularly NATO allies' mention that Canada's "emphasis on disarmament in recent months had been too strong and some concern had been expressed that our defense contribution might fall off."[49] The government would, however, have to contend with criticism emanating from closer to home.

In Washington, public statements by congressmen and lack of liaison between the State Department and the Pentagon regarding BOMARC's value and how much money, if any, was going to be spent on it caused concern in Ottawa. Before the whole affair could blow up into another SKY HAWK–like problem, Pearkes "has so handled himself that the anticipated attack here has to date been somewhat blunted."[50] In other words, Pearkes gracefully showed a great deal of understanding and did not make public hay out of the situation.

In its premeeting analysis, the National Security Council was apprised of the situation. Canada requested this meeting, believing "that [US leaders] are in fact abandoning continental defense and putting all [their] emphasis on [their] retaliatory capability. The Canadians feel lost between the United States and the USSR in this situation."[51] The main sticking point was BOMARC and its funding problems. The NSC staffers (erroneously) believed that Canada had given up the Arrow for the BOMARC and (correctly) believed that Canada thought the United States was reneging on an agreement. The NSC believed, however, that funding would be restored. A Canadian initiative was on the table: Canada would buy sixty-six F-101B Voodoos in exchange for a USAF purchase of thirty-five Yukon long-range transport aircraft from Canada. The American policy was that Canada really did not have to pay for the F-101Bs; they would be provided under the Mutual Assistance Plan (MAP) or a similar project. Canadian pride was in the way, as well as self-interest since Canada never had accepted defense "welfare" and still needed to maintain her aircraft industry. Eisenhower wanted a position that he could take to Diefenbaker to solve this, noting: "Diefenbaker was not difficult to deal with if he were kept informed in advance, even though he was inclined to make impetuous statements and then refuse to modify them if they turned out to be wrong."[52]

The Canadian and American delegations, which included Christian Herter, Livingston Merchant, and future SACEUR, General Andrew L. Goodpaster, on the American side and Robinson, Bryce, and Heeney on the Canadian, discussed the Open Skies concept and economic matters. On the defense side, Herter informed the Canadians that he had Robert Bowie working on a ten-year NATO planning exercise. Canada was invited to participate in the process. BOMARC also was discussed and the President informed the Prime Minister that funds would be made available for the completion of the project no matter what Congress said publicly. As for the F-101B, Diefenbaker gave his assent to talks with the US Department of Defense.[53]

In Ottawa, the government was taking heat from the Special Committee on Defence Expenditures (SCODE). The situation was exacerbated by the lack of unclassified information and the Opposition's willful manipulation of the facts to embarrass the government. The main problem was that there were several types of negotiations, all of which were inextricably linked. There were the SAC and MB-1 storage and overflight negotiations; there were the two Canadian-American/NATO information sharing agreements (1954 and 1959); there was the general government-to-government agreement; and then there had to be several service-to-service agreements for each specific weapons system. All of these were secret agreements. No details could be released *despite* the obviously politically embarrassing delays perpetuated by Green and others. What appeared to the media and to the Opposition (which was far too reliant at this stage on the media interpretation of things) as inconsistencies and stalling techniques were, in fact, mostly legitimate negotiation problems and technical details.

What exactly did the SCODE experience contribute to the nuclear weapons debate? Almost all of the larger questions regarding Canada and nuclear weapons that the Opposition and the media would ask in the next two and half years were already well established in 1960 through the efforts of Hellyer and Pearkes. The Special Committee on Defence Expenditures discussions also generated many dangerous perceptions about strategy, release, and use. In the end, the Opposition was able to continue and expand upon the doubts and fears generated during the NORAD debates three years previous. The fact was there was a public Canadian government policy on nuclear weapons. Was it a clearly defined and articulated one? No. Was it an appropriate one given the times? No. But there was a policy and the policy was: "Wait."

The Nuclear Disarmament Dimension in 1960

The question of whether there was any hope of reducing or eliminating nuclear weapons tantalized certain policy makers and External Affairs departments throughout the nuclear weapons debate in Canada. There was a great deal of confusion not only within the bureaucracy but in the public mind about the relationship between defensive nuclear weapons in Canada, offensive nuclear weapons in Europe, and the activities of SAC, when it came to the emotional desire to rid humanity of weapons of mass destruction. These issues frequently intruded at critical junctures and interweaved themselves with the policy-making process.

Disarmament activities pursued by the St. Laurent government were coordinated with those of other NATO countries; that is, disarmament was not likely and the aim was to derive the maximum propaganda benefit by portraying aggressive Soviet behavior as the problem. Most disarmament efforts in the 1950s revolved around the Open Skies proposal and the push for an atmospheric nuclear weapons test ban treaty.[54]

In September 1959, Canada joined nine other nations[55] to form the Ten Nation Committee on Disarmament that had as its objective to "promote general and complete disarmament under a system of international control."[56] The U-2 affair disrupted the committee's deliberations and the Soviets walked out.

Canada's primary representative to the committee was General E. L. M. Burns, who commanded the UN observer force in the Middle East. "Tommy" Burns, probably the most intellectual and most published general Canada ever produced, suffered from having a personality like a "cold fish" and being far too "dour" in his outlook on life.[57] Having fought in the First and Second World Wars, eventually commanding a corps in Italy, Burns had experience in war that lent him credibility that most arms control and disarmament people could only dream of. Burns was out of the mainstream Army/DND policy-making community [commanding United Nations Truce Supervisory Operation (UNTSO) in the Middle East was not the Army's plum assignment: 4 Brigade in NATO was] and was a high profile UN personality with the right connections (like Secretary General Dag Hammarskjöld and his special assistant, Ralph Bunche). It is probably for these reasons that Norman Robertson, in his capacity of Undersecretary of State for External Affairs, appointed Burns to act as Canada's ambassador for disarmament in 1959. In early 1960, Burns formulated new principles that formed the basis of Canadian disarmament policy during the Diefenbaker years: these, in turn, were picked up by Howard Green in his crusade for nuclear disarmament.[58] In effect, then, Burns influenced Robertson, Robertson influenced Green, and, as we have seen, Green increasingly influenced Diefenbaker over time.

What exactly were Burns's views? He believed that, first, while nuclear weapons were not inherently more or less moral than any other weapon, their use in a strategic sense was outright murder. Second, the arms race would inevitably get out of control and result in a nuclear war. Finally, nuclear war was so destructive that it went beyond morality. Burns was convinced that deterrence could fail and would fail unless some restraints were placed on the entire process. In effect, like his American counterparts Generals Maxwell D. Taylor and James M. Gavin, Burns believed that the declared American policy of so-called Massive Retaliation was bankrupt.[59]

The details of the DND–External Affairs relationship with regard to disarmament are beyond the scope of this study and are covered in other works. Suffice it to say, the COSC and JPC frequently provided Burns and External Affairs with the military view on specific aspects of disarmament. The COSC particularly took a dim view of the disarmament effort, referring to it as "very loose thinking."[60] Foulkes thought that disarmament activities were "dangerous on strategic grounds and impractical on technical grounds."[61]

Despite the Soviet walkout, Burns prepared a plan which encouraged the creation of a nuclear-free zone in the NATO and Warsaw Pact areas.[62] "Minimal deterrence," that is, SAC and its Soviet counterpart, would remain outside the zone with no missiles in Europe. While this plan was under debate in Geneva, Burns informed Robertson that if Canadian efforts were to succeed, Canadian defense policy and Canadian disarmament policy must be compatible, that is, to set an example Canada should not accept nuclear weapons.[63] There is a strong possibility that this, in addition to Robertson's existing views on nuclear weapons was the second step in delaying the government-to-government agreement and other storage negotiations with the United States in 1960, in addition to Green's policy of "holding down" the Americans.

Another important event was the tabling of the Irish Resolution in the UN General Assembly in June 1960. The terms of this resolution were that existing nuclear powers had to declare a moratorium on nuclear weapons proliferation, and non-nuclear weapons states should be required to declare that they would not acquire them.[64] There was no distinction between defensive tactical nuclear weapons and strategic offensive nuclear weapons, which, as one could surmise, would cause some confusion. As Legault and Fortmann note in their study *Diplomacy of Hope*:

> Canada, as a member of NATO and NORAD, faced the prospect of being accused of duplicity or hypocrisy by voting [for] the Irish Resolution while simultaneously equipping her forces with nuclear weapons.[65]

The debate over the Irish Resolution, both in Canada and in the UN, would continue throughout 1960. Robertson wrote to Diefenbaker urging him to get the Cabinet to vote yes for the resolution, but the Cabinet refused and wanted to abstain. DND, instead of rejecting the Irish Resolution outright, recommended that the wording "acquire" be altered to "acquire control of" nuclear weapons. Green ordered that the Canadian delegation to the UN *not* be informed of the Cabinet's decision to abstain. Denmark, Norway, and Iceland, the only other NATO governments that had expressed any interest in signing the resolution, had been ordered by their governments to follow Canada's lead. The Canadian delegation voted yes, that is, that Canada would not acquire *control* of nuclear weapons. The Irish Resolution passed in the UN General Assembly in December 1960.[66]

This scheme posed new and severe contradictions for the Diefenbaker government. Control over the nuclear weapons stationed in Canada for Canadian forces was necessary from a sovereignty standpoint, and currently was the cornerstone of the government's position in its discussions with the Americans. The Liberals were hounding the government on the control issue. Was there something motivating Green beyond sheer abstract horror of nuclear weapons use? Arthur H. Dean, an American representative in nuclear disarmament talks at this time, noted cryptically, "Too many statesmen, with an eye on the Nobel Peace Prize, come forward with proposals that hit the front page but are both unrealistic and dangerous."[67] A later analysis of Canada's UN activity suggested that Green "is very nearly obsessed with the need to demonstrate 'Canadian initiatives' in the UN arena."[68]

We must therefore consider the possibility that Green was motivated by a craving to bring home a Nobel Peace Prize for the Conservative Party and the Diefenbaker government in order to match Mike Pearson's Nobel Peace Prize for his part in resolving the 1956 Suez Crisis.

The Montebello Meeting, June–July 1960: More Voodoo

Just prior to the Montebello meeting, Howard Green produced for the Cabinet a summary of the status of the nuclear weapons negotiations that he had previously claimed in the House were not happening. In effect, there were five issues: MB-1 storage at Harmon and Goose Bay; ASW storage at Argentia; SAC storage at Goose Bay; "the possible acquisition of nuclear warheads for Canadian use in Canada, especially for BOMARC"; and "the possible acquisition of nuclear weapons for Canadian use in Europe."[69]

So far, the Cabinet had agreed to MB-1 storage, but the Americans had yet to reply to Canadian insistence that control would be joint. This was ridiculous, since the weapons would be under NORAD control when released from the sites, which in effect constituted joint control and use. The real sticking point was that the original lease agreement with the Americans (circa 1942), was that the RCAF commander be permitted access to all parts of the base which, in External Affairs' view, included any nuclear storage site. Clearly, this was a delay tactic instigated perhaps by Green and/or Robertson.

As for nuclear antisubmarine weapons storage, Green insisted that removal of any stored weapons to American ships from the Argentia should be subject to Canadian assent. No progress had been made in this area, and no progress had been made on SAC storage, for indeterminate reasons.[70]

BOMARC, Honest John, and CF-104 agreements were, in Green's view, stalled because of his perceived conflict between American law and "Canadian Ministers' wishes regarding control over release from storage and for use."[71] This was nonsense. The only minister who had a problem with this was Green. By presenting this to the Cabinet as policy, Green kept the other members confused and neatly placed the blame for the delays of the government-to-government agreement on the Americans. Why Pearkes did not call him out for this distortion of the situation remains a mystery.

The second meeting of the Canada-US Ministerial Meeting on Joint Defense met in the Seigniory Club at Montebello, Quebec, on 12-13 July 1960. Though the

Montebello meeting focused on defense issues, the American and Canadian delegations conducted a "tour d'horizon" which included the prickly problem of Cuba, the best American response to Castro's inflammatory anti-American rhetoric, and Soviet arms flow to his island. In essence, Norman Robertson and Howard Green did not approve of American economic sanctions. This issue would pose problems in the Canadian-American relationship later in 1962.[72]

There was inconclusive discussion regarding BOMARC, with Green asking again if the manned bomber was still a threat. Secretary of Defense Gates revealed the existence of the Hound Dog cruise missile and the planned Skybolt stand-off missile, both which would be carried by bombers: the Soviets would eventually have their versions. "Did Canada still want to acquire manned interceptors from the United States?" asked Gates, who told the Canadian delegation that the price could be discussed later. Green, who should have known better given his knowledge of the CF-105 decision, told Gates that it was a political problem now, and indicated that he and the Canadian people did not and do not understand why two years previously they had been told that manned bombers were no longer a threat. Now the Canadian people had to be told that bombers were still a threat and that manned interceptors were necessary. Pearkes intervened: "We did not cancel the CF-105 because there was no bomber threat but because there was a lesser bomber threat and we got the BOMARC in lieu of more airplanes to look after this,"[73] a statement which contradicted the Arrow program process in 1958, but was congruent with his answers in public forums.

Livingston Merchant wanted to sort out the MB-1 storage agreement. Green said that he "would check on these matters."[74] Gates then pressed on nuclear ASW storage at Argentia, SAC storage at Goose Bay, and storage for weapons in Europe. The reason why there had been no movement on the Argentia agreement, according to Green, was the problem of control. There was no agreement similar to the MB-1 overflight agreement for the forces storing and using the planned Argentia storage site. Some form of agreement had to be worked out first. Green also noted, "He had no control over the use of the weapon once it has been put on the ship and therefore the problem is control of release to the ship or of loading."[75]

Green was curious about what arrangements the Americans had with the Germans regarding custody and control. Perhaps these could serve as a model for a Canadian-American agreement. Green was told that the Germans controlled the use of the weapon and the Americans controlled the release of the weapon to the Germans. The NATO alert procedures were also part of this. The German government had to agree to the assignment of particular forces to SACEUR in an emergency (since SACEUR did not "own" forces in peacetime) and that the declaration of an alert, which could trigger release of weapons from SACEUR's control to German forces control, was affected at the NAC level. It was possible that if weapons were located in a third country, that country might, in fact, exercise a veto over their use from that territory. The discussants were clearly referring to France.[76]

The American delegation instructed Green on the steps necessary to get access, that is, the stockpile, government, and service agreement process. Green, of course, already knew this and was stalling. Pearkes urged Green to get on with it, but Green replied, "He was in no hurry whatsoever." Gates pressed on. Was MB-1 storage at Goose Bay and Harmon acceptable? Green said yes, but SAC storage, Argentia, and Canadian forces in Europe would be subject to further discussion. Gates urged Green to visit a base in Europe to see how it was done. As an aside, Gates informed Green that the Bowie team was still working on its long-range NATO plan. Did Green want the team to send a draft of the exercise to Canada for constructive comment prior to its tabling in Paris? Green was not particularly interested in this and shifted to law of the sea issues. In doing so, Green spurned an invitation for Canada to participate in a project that had the potential to influence the future of NATO strategy.[77]

The Montebello meeting accomplished little. The Americans were bending over backwards to accommodate the Diefenbaker government and, once again, Canada was vacillating. The Americans were confused, particularly when Green digressed at length about a minor legal case in the middle of a discussion on world security policy. Ambassador Heeney thought Green's behavior at Montebello was "unconscionable."[78]

Diefenbaker was summarily informed about the Montebello deliberations. Another American press story caused him agitation. Despite assurances to the contrary, Diefenbaker read that BOMARCs could be released and fired only on the orders of the American President, which naturally flew in the face of what Green had been told at Montebello regarding the German arrangements. The Prime Minister's inability to accept what his ministers had told him over a mere press story provoked a long diatribe in Cabinet:

> Canada would decide if the warheads would be used and, that the reason for the length in the negotiations on the acquisition of warheads for Canada's forces was to ensure that the Government did not intend to have control over their use in the hands of the U.S. If Canada were to agree now to the proposed arrangements for interceptor aircraft at Goose Bay and Harmon Field in respect to the MB-1 defensive weapons, it might be that the Government would lose some bargaining power over warheads for Canadian forces.[79]

This statement clearly demonstrates that Diefenbaker was moving into a world of unreality on this issue. Only six months before, Pearkes had briefed the Prime Minister on Canadian control and custody policy. The Americans had not challenged this policy and, in fact, were ready to acquiesce to it to get on with the negotiations. Green had injected a red herring with the Argentia release issue, but again, as Pearkes had already stated, there was a Canadian policy in which the Americans were ready to acquiesce. Either Diefenbaker forgot or someone had planted some doubt in his mind on the issue and he was stalling.

This confusion also affected the F-101B Voodoo acquisition. In a series of flip-flops, the Cabinet met six times and even went so far as to make a decision to acquire the Voodoos on 9 August. Three days later, the Cabinet rescinded the decision. The main arguments against acquisition were political (related to politically embarrassing questions over the Arrow cancellation); media oriented (the Americans revealed at Montebello that they had only five ICBMs operational in 1960, while the *Washington Post* claimed that there were more); financial (there was no agreement on trading Yukons for Voodoos); and even irrational (Pearson came out in favor of interceptor acquisition, therefore the Conservative Party had to come out against them.)[80]

The Opposition was not idle. In August 1960, Pearson and Hellyer went on the offensive in the House of Commons. In what amounted to a virtual Liberal policy statement on nuclear weapons, Pearson stated that American control over nuclear weapons release was an infringement on Canadian sovereignty and that negotiations to acquire nuclear weapons for Canada jeopardized disarmament negotiations. The CF-104 nuclear strike role was not good for Canada, as the bases were vulnerable to missile attack; it was an offensive role, and the French probably would not allow the RCAF to operate from its bases in France. Air defense of North America was "hopeless." Interceptors were required for a sovereignty identification role only. Nuclear antisubmarine weapons were not effective. What NATO really needed were more conventional forces in Europe. This would be the approved Liberal Party defense platform by January 1961.[81]

Secretary of State Christian Herter requested a meeting with Howard Green in September 1960. Accompanied by A. D. P. Heeney, Green was ominously informed by Herter that he "had been receiving disquieting reports . . . [of] antipathy and antagonism towards the U.S. . . . it would be a sad case if Canada and the U.S. were unable to get along together."[82] What were the root causes of the problem? How could Herter and Green solve them? Green explained that it was not as bad as Herter thought, that this criticism had always been part of the relationship. The trouble was mostly economic in nature, Green asserted, and related to the high level of American investment in Canada.[83]

The American record of that meeting stated:

Canadians were not nearly so worried about the Russians as were the Americans. . . . [I]n Canada there was no support at all for increased military expenditure. . . . Mr. Green said that there was among Canadians a widespread feeling that nuclear war must be avoided. The U.S. Defense Department were thought by some to be courting such disaster by provocative words and actions. The U-2 incident profoundly shocked Canadians. ["Because it was spying," asked Herter, "or because we admitted it?"] [Green] said that . . . the Government were opposed the spread of nuclear military capabilities. His own personal view was that Canadian forces . . . should not be armed with [them]. He thought this was a position which would be widely shared in Canada.[84]

This exchange provides more insight into Green's (and to some respect even Norman Robertson's) thinking than it does into actual Canadian nuclear weapons policy or what the Canadian people actually thought.

Developments in NATO Strategy: 1960

Howard Green's squandering of an opportunity to comment on American views for future NATO strategy should not be underestimated. In NATO, 1960 was a turbulent year. This turbulence was caused fundamentally by the old but continuing problems over who controlled the nuclear deterrent and what the appropriate balance between conventional and nuclear forces should be. Eisenhower was concerned, as he did not like the United States dominating NATO strategy and planning. He did not like allies believing they were "secondary in their role."[85]

In essence, the study "The North Atlantic Nations Tasks for the 1960's," better known as the Bowie Report after its author, confronted these problems. Robert R. Bowie from Harvard University believed the increased Soviet nuclear capability in Europe posed problems for the deterrent; the Soviets were making significant gains outside the NATO area; and there was dissension within NATO about how to handle these two problems.[86]

NATO strategy in the 1960s had to: "(a) enhance the non-nuclear capability of Shield forces to resist attack by Soviet ready forces and substantially lessen their dependence on nuclear weapons. (b) enable NATO to mount nuclear retaliation against larger threats without a US veto."[87]

To counter Soviet moves outside the defined NATO area, Bowie recommended that NATO nations increase trade, financial, and technical aid to the Third World. Notably: "The Atlantic nations should seek to enhance UN capabilities for maintaining peace and order in less developed countries. They should be prepared to earmark contingents or transport facilities for use by future United Nations forces."[88] Which was the course Canada had embarked on as early as 1956 and had even discussed internally since 1955 (see chapter 2).

Bowie briefed the President in August 1960. The Bowie Report did not go into detail in a number of critical areas. One of these was the relationship between conventional operations and nuclear operations. When queried by Eisenhower, Bowie "did not think there could be a stage of conflict between the non-nuclear and all-out strategic attack—in other words, there can be no war limited to tactical nuclear war in Europe."[89] Eisenhower heartily agreed. The main problem, Eisenhower mused, was the nuclear component. The problems were "not with the Europeans but [with] Congress, which strives to keep in its own hands the details of military foreign policy. . . . the Joint Committee on Atomic Energy is unconstitutional in its functions."[90] In other words, the system of bilateral nuclear agreements imposed by Congress did more to cause dissension within NATO than any other factor.

Further discussions between Eisenhower, Norstad, and Bowie revealed that there was concurrence on these issues.[91] The problem was arriving at a consensus in the US Joint Chiefs before moving the matter over to NATO. The US Joint Chiefs were asked to discuss the feasibility of either "an increased deterrence to aggression regardless of its nature or scale, or a flexibility of response, in the event that deterrence fails."[92] This consensus was never achieved during the Eisenhower administration.[93]

Nevertheless, SACEUR directed the formal creation of the ACE Mobile Force (Land) and ACE Mobile Force (Air) in 1960. These multinational formations would be equipped with nuclear and conventional units and be capable of rapid deployment to threatened NATO areas in the event of international tension and prepared to resist all forms of intimidation.[94] Thus, AMF(L), AMF(A), and the LIVE OAK organization formed the backbone of a NATO flexible response capability in the face of attempts to retain a purely nuclear response to aggression. Canadian planners were well aware of these developments, even though their political leadership did not fully understand them. The Chairman of the COSC, Air Marshal Frank Miller, even received an advanced draft of the Bowie Report that was passed around the almost defunct Panel in October 1960.[95] Norstad continued his push for a NATO nuclear force and increased conventional forces, which formed the backdrop of Canadian deliberations over force structuring and the nuclear issue.

Force Structure and Continuing Negotiations: August–December 1960

Toward the end of August 1960, the Permanent Joint Board met at Camp Gagetown, New Brunswick, for its first substantial discussion of continental defense issues in three years. The Americans pleaded with the Canadians to find a solution to the MB-1 storage problem. Dana Wilgress, the Canadian chairman for this meeting, had to insist, "The questions of storage of nuclear weapons in Canada for United States forces and of acquisition of nuclear weapons by Canadian forces had given rise to serious political problems for the Canadian Government."[96] Wilgress would do his best to stimulate some activity in Ottawa.

The RCAF was concerned about the lack of service-to-service agreements. Its leadership knew that it would take a great deal of time to train its people in the specifics of nuclear weapons use and for making the technical modifications to the delivery systems. Out of the blue, on 26 August 1960, Air Chief Marshal Campbell told his staff that the Minister of National Defence had informed the Chiefs "that all planning is to proceed on the assumption that Canadian Forces will be provided with necessary nuclear weapons at the appropriate time."[97] There are no indications that the matter even went to the Chiefs for discussion, as there was no meeting between 11 August and 1 September. NATO was pressing for a decision on Honest John and CF-104 storage facilities and so were the Americans for North America.[98] It is possible that Pearkes caved in and issued the instruction.

As a consequence, Pearkes authorized Miller to start negotiations with the Germans to construct two Special Ammunition Storage Sites at the existing Canadian bases in Germany: Zweibrücken and Baden-Soellingen. The RCAF bases in France would not initiate similar activity "due to the negative French attitude to the presence of other than French nuclear weapons on French territory."[99] A site for the Army's Honest John warheads was also authorized.

What was the status of Canada's nuclear delivery systems at this time? The RCN's nuclear antisubmarine platforms were in the best shape. The Tracker contractor, DeHaviland Aircraft, had asked the USN through the appropriate channels for drawings of nuclear ASW weapons so that it could construct dummies for fitting purposes. This had been approved. By May 1960, the RCN and RCAF had asked the USN for training pamphlets dealing with bombing and arming systems for the

Mk 101 Lulu. They even went so far as to ask for a Mk 102 practice "shape" to train on.[100] DeHaviland determined that a special hoisting lug was required and drawings for this were also acquired. By September 1960, a report noted, "the trial installation of the subject store has now been completed,"[101] that is, a CS2F had been successfully modified to carry, but not deliver, a Mk 101 Lulu. The RCN then went back and asked the USN for ground support equipment, which included bomb trolleys and hoists. Work on the project stopped in October, pending government approval. The RCN determined that, though it wanted all CS2F and future ASW helicopters modified to carry the Mk 101, there would be no further action until "the policy regarding these weapons has been clarified."[102] Nothing appears to have been done to the Argus and Neptune patrol aircraft at this point.

BOMARC was having serious developmental problems in the United States and encountered a hostile environment in Congress, but presidential intervention had opened more funds for the missile's development. Unfortunately, in June 1960 a BOMARC A missile with a nuclear warhead attached melted down in a fire at McGuire AFB in New Jersey, which posed political problems for the program. Internal USAF reports also noted, "The ability of the IM99 [Interceptor Missile 99, the technical designation for the BOMARC] to operate as planned in an Electronic Countermeasures environment has not yet been established," and "the ability of the missile to operate in all types of weather" had not been demonstrated.[103] On the plus side, the B model, which Canada was acquiring, hit targets five out of thirteen times. One B actually hit a supersonic Regulus missile at 35,000 feet at a range of 148 miles. It would take until 1963, however, to fully test the BOMARC B.[104]

In Canada, the RCAF established the 446 SAM and 447 SAM Squadrons located at North Bay, Ontario, and LaMacaza, Quebec, respectively, and started training personnel for them. By the end of October 1960, the North Bay site was 65% complete, and LaMacaza was 10% complete.[105]

As for the CF-104, Canadair still had to test fly its first aircraft. Still, the RCAF was actively engaged in requesting ballistic training shapes resembling the Mk 28 and Mk 43 nuclear weapons for training purposes and for future flight testing. One device, called the BDU8B, was an expendable lead shot- and concrete-filled representation of a nuclear weapon. The RCAF also contracted with GE to use its IBM 650 computer to compute bomb delivery profiles.[106] Additionally, the Air Council instructed the commander of 1 Air Division to "make arrangements . . . to draw on USAF(E[urope]) depot stocks for nuclear, conventional, and Sidewinder missiles as required."[107]

As for the Honest John units, 1 SSM Battery was formed on 15 September 1960, at Picton, Ontario, with 2 SSM (Training) Battery forming at Camp Shilo, Manitoba, shortly thereafter. Their equipment, less nuclear warheads, arrived in early 1961, and the crews feverishly began their intensive training activities without access to nuclear weapons data.[108]

This left the ongoing Voodoo saga. On 21 September, the Cabinet finally agreed to present a "swap" proposal to the United States. The Americans would purchase the Yukon transport aircraft and give Canada the Voodoos. Canada would, in turn, pay for the operating costs for five PINETREE radars that were manned by the

RCAF but paid for by the Americans. Canada would pay for one-third of the cost of the F-101B spares.[109]

At the end of September, Eisenhower and Diefenbaker met in New York for the deliberations of the UN General Assembly. Diefenbaker told Eisenhower, "Communist propaganda had caused an upsurge of concern over US domination of Canada and this had been growing dangerously in the last three months."[110] Consequently, Canada would take over part of the PINETREE Line in exchange for F-101Bs. Eisenhower was perplexed. He had "not previously heard of this new alternative," but thought it was acceptable. Diefenbaker noted there had been adverse reaction to selling CL-44s to the United States (which was not the case) and this alternative, which cost Canada more, would result in producing a more effective defense more quickly.[111] According to Finance Minister Donald Fleming, Eisenhower delayed immediate action on the agreement, thinking that it could be handled after the 1960 election, which delayed the acquisition even further.[112]

On 12 October 1960, Douglas Harkness replaced George Pearkes as Minister of National Defence. Harkness was determined to solve the nuclear negotiation situation as rapidly as possible. The most levelheaded man ever to hold the Defense portfolio, Harkness had a great deal of personal integrity. He was an artillery officer and veteran of the Second World War, having commanded an M-10 self-propelled antitank unit in the Mediterranean and northwest Europe. Harkness won the George Cross for bravery when his transport ship was sunk in July 1943.[113] Also a westerner (Calgary, Alberta), Harkness had known Pearkes since the 1930s, when Pearkes had been a staff officer with Military District 13 (Alberta).[114] Fellow Cabinet member Donald Fleming thought Harkness "was tough, abrasive and courageous."[115] He was certainly nobody's puppet and nobody's fool.

Harkness could be acerbic with softheaded and ill-informed constituents, and frequently he expressed his views on strategic policy to them. For example, when a constituent who opposed nuclear weapons acquisition wrote Harkness and threatened not to vote for him, Harkness wrote back telling him: "While I appreciate your well-warranted concern on this subject, I should like to emphasize that I have never been deterred from following the course I consider right by fear of losing votes."[116] Harkness was not a man to be trifled with, particularly when it came to defense issues.

What was the status of the nuclear agreements when Harkness came on board? Pearkes asked Green on 21 September to formally exchange notes with the Americans on the MB-1 storage issue. Green had still not sent the exchange of notes to the Cabinet for further discussion. As for nuclear antisubmarine weapons, SAC storage, and the government-to-government agreement for Canadian acquisition, Green argued that the MB-1 storage agreement must be signed first before any consideration would be given to the other matters. The Chiefs had prepared suitable draft agreements, but these had not been passed on to the Cabinet pending Green's exchange of notes with the Americans.[117]

Harkness asked for and was given a detailed brief of the Canadian services' position on nuclear weapons requirements. Canada's Europe-based forces needed weapons ranging from fractional-kiloton-yield to multihundred-kiloton-yield weapons. The CF-104s, he was told, would use tactical nuclear weapons in a strike role, as "the CF-104 aircraft armed with conventional high explosive bombs would be an impotent weapon in a theatre committed to a nuclear strategy."[118] Air defense weapons would include BOMARC B and MB-1 Genies, which needed nuclear warheads to increase the probability of kill and to "kill" the bomb inside the bomber with radiation. Harkness was told, accurately, that no conventional warhead was planned for the BOMARC B. As for nuclear ASW weapons, Canada wanted nuclear depth bombs for Tracker maritime patrol aircraft and the future antisubmarine helicopter, as well as an antisubmarine missile for future ships. The Argus and Neptune maritime patrol aircraft "with minor modifications . . . could be equipped to carry nuclear depth charges."[119]

In another abrupt move, Diefenbaker announced in a 25 November speech that no decision would be made on the nuclear agreements unless there was significant progress in nuclear disarmament talks. This was a change from the more cautionary wait-and-see approach taken earlier in the year by Green in the House of Commons. Diefenbaker also noted, as an aside, Canada would not "in any event consider nuclear weapons until, as a sovereign nation, we have equality in control, a joint control."[120]

Pearson then made several alarmist speeches claiming that if Canada acquired nuclear weapons, she would be joining "the Nuclear Club," a rather misleading statement. Joint control, Pearson added, was merely an illusion of sovereignty.[121] This added even more to the Diefenbaker government's caution on the issue.

The Joint Staff was asked (by either Miller, Harkness, or both) its opinion and to develop arguments demonstrating that Canada had already made a commitment to equipping her NATO-tasked forces with nuclear weapons. The Joint Staff took the issue all the way back to December 1954 with the establishment of MC 48 as the driving event. The December 1956 NATO Ministerial Meeting and the December 1957 NATO Heads of Governments Meeting merely confirmed the fact that Canada had committed her forces to a nuclear strategy in Europe. These decision, when combined, "gave rise to the following requirements for tactical nuclear weapons":

> (a) Nuclear depth charges are required by naval and maritime air forces to offset their limited ability to locate submarines accurately. The much larger lethal area of these weapons would significantly increase the NATO antisubmarine capability.
>
> (b) Nuclear missiles and artillery are required for direct support of NATO land forces in Europe down to battalion level. . . . The addition of these weapons to NATO's present armament are essential to compensate for the overwhelming superiority of the Soviet land and tactical air forces.
>
> (c) Nuclear-armed air strike forces are required in Europe to counter-attack the enemy's atomic capability and to assist in retarding the advance of numerically superior enemy forces.[122]

In sum, the Joint Staff concluded that Canada had a "strong presumptive policy"[123] commitment to NATO in that she accepted NATO strategy at all times in

THE QUINTESSENTIAL COLD WAR THREAT FROM THE AIR: A SOVIET BOMBER AIRCRAFT CARRYING NUCLEAR WEAPONS. HERE A TUPOLEV BEAR IS INTERCEPTED BY A CANADIAN CF-101 VOODOO. (CF PHOTO)

. . . AND AT SEA. SOVIET SUBMARINES LIKE THIS NUCLEAR-POWERED MISSILE-LAUNCHING HOTEL CLASS AND AGI INTELLIGENCE GATHERING "TRAWLERS" REGULARLY INFILTRATED CANADIAN WATERS AND WERE TARGETED FOR DESTRUCTION WITH NUCLEAR WEAPONS BY CANADIAN MARITIME FORCES IN THE EVENT OF WAR. (CF PHOTO)

THE TWO MEN MOST RESPONSIBLE FOR CANADIAN NUCLEARIZATION DURING THE COLD WAR WERE LIEUTENANT GENERAL CHARLES FOULKES, THE CHAIRMAN OF THE CHIEFS OF STAFF COMMITTEE; MIKE PEARSON, UNDERSECRETARY OF STATE FOR EXTERNAL AFFAIRS AND LATER PRIME MINISTER; LED BY MINISTER BROOKE CLAXTON. (CF PHOTO)

JOHN DIEFENBAKER'S LACK OF LEADERSHIP ON NUCLEAR WEAPONS ACCESS AGREEMENTS AND HIS TENDENCY TO VACILLATE UNDER PRESSURE DEGRADED NORTH AMERICA'S DEFENSIVE POSTURE DURING BOTH THE BERLIN CRISIS IN 1961 AND THE CUBAN MISSILE CRISIS IN 1962. (CF PHOTO)

THE MAN WHO SAVED THE DAY IN OCTOBER 1962: MINISTER OF NATIONAL DEFENCE GEORGE HARKNESS, SEEN HERE MEETING WITH DEPUTY COMMANDER IN CHIEF OF NORAD AIR MARSHAL ROY SLEMON AND GENERAL EARL PARTRIDGE. HARKNESS BYPASSED THE PRIME MINISTER AND AUTHORIZED ALERTING CANADA'S FORCES. (CF PHOTO)

A CF-101 VOODOO FIRING A PRACTICE MB-1. (CF PHOTO)

An MB-1 Genie, later re-designated AIR-2A, being handled by Canadian loading crews. (CF Photo)

CANADIAN CF-101 VOODOOS WERE KEPT ON 15 MINUTES ALERT IN QRF SITES LIKE THIS ONE AT FOUR FACILITIES ACROSS CANADA. (CF PHOTO)

THE NUMBER 1 WEAPON: AN MK 28 BOMB ATTACHED TO A CF-104 STARFIGHTER AIRFRAME. (CF PHOTO)

THE NUMBER 2 WEAPON: AN MK 43 BOMB IN MOUNTING TRIALS ATTACHED TO A CF-104 IN ORDER TO CHECK GROUND CLEARANCE. (CF PHOTO)

THE NUMBER 3 WEAPON: AN MK 57 BOMB OR SHAPE UNDERGOING TRIALS ON THE CF-104 AIRFRAME (CF-PHOTO)

1 Air Division Quick Reaction Force sites in Europe and their CF-104 aircraft were prepared to execute SACEUR's nuclear strike plans on an almost no-notice basis. (434 Squadron History)

CF-104 pilots were trained in parachute-retarded deliver of the Mk 28 and Mk 43. This involved the delivery of "shapes" or weighted bomb casings at the Primrose Lake Air Weapons Range in Alberta. (434 Squadron History)

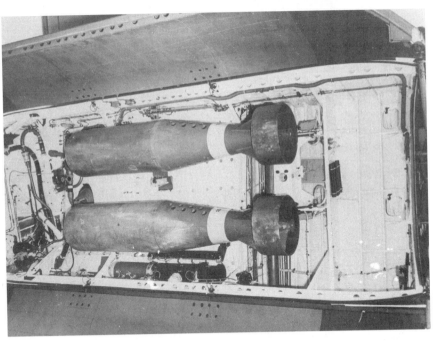

CANADIAN ANTISUBMARINE FORCES RELIED ON AMERICAN-SUPPLIED LULU NUCLEAR DEPTH BOMBS. (NATIONAL ATOMIC MUSEUM)

THE RCAF'S P2V NEPTUNE WAS THE FIRST CANADIAN MARITIME PATROL AIRCRAFT MODIFIED FOR NUCLEAR DEPTH BOMB DELIVERY IN 1961–62 (CF PHOTO)

CANADIAN-BUILT RCAF ARGUS MARITIME PATROL AIRCRAFT WERE MODIFIED FOR NUCLEAR
DEPTH BOMB DELIVERY JUST BEFORE THE CUBAN MISSILE CRISIS IN 1962. (CF PHOTO)

A NUMBER OF ROYAL CANADIAN NAVY CS2F TRACKERS WERE MODIFIED ON AN
EMERGENCY BASIS IN 1961 FOR NUCLEAR DEPTH BOMB DELIVERY DURING THE BERLIN
CRISIS. (CF PHOTO)

RCN SEA KING HELICOPTERS WERE WIRED FOR NUCLEAR DEPTH BOMB USE, AND STOWAGE SPACES IN CANADIAN DESTROYERS LIKE HMCS *ASSINIBOINE* WERE EARMARKED TO RECEIVE THE WEAPONS IN AN EMERGENCY. (CF PHOTO)

A BOMARC SURFACE-TO-AIR MISSILE CARRYING A W-40 NUCLEAR WARHEAD IS RAISED TO ITS FIRING POSITION FROM ITS "COFFIN" LAUNCHER. (CF PHOTO)

BASED OUTSIDE OF NORTH BAY, ONTARIO, AND AT LAMACAZA, QUEBEC, CANADIAN BOMARC SQUADRONS EACH HAD 28 BOMARC MISSILES CONNECTED TO THE SAGE SYSTEM. (CF PHOTO)

RARE PHOTOS CAPTURING THE ARRIVAL OF W-40 WARHEADS AT NORTH BAY. THE USAF USED C-124 GLOBEMASTERS FOR THIS TASK. (*ROUNDEL*)

THE CANADIAN ARMY RECEIVED SIX HONEST JOHN LAUNCH VEHICLES, FOUR OF WHICH
WERE DEPLOYED TO WEST GERMANY WITH 4 CANADIAN INFANTRY BRIGADE GROUP AS
PART OF NATO'S DETERRENT FORCES. (CF PHOTO)

ROYAL AIR FORCE VALIANT BOMBERS, SPECIALLY EQUIPPED FOR TESTS IN AUSTRALIA AND
CHRISTMAS ISLAND, TRANSITED OVER CANADA CARRYING BLUE DANUBE WEAPONS LIKE
THIS ONE. (RAF PHOTO)

FOR THE FIRST HALF OF THE COLD WAR, CANADA'S POLICY WAS TO SUPPORT THE WEST'S PRIMARY NUCLEAR DETERRENT FORCE, THE USAF'S STRATEGIC AIR COMMAND. HERE A CF-100 CANUCK INTERCEPTOR ESCORTS A SAC B-47 THROUGH CANADIAN AIRSPACE. (CF PHOTO)

THE MASSIVE AIR BASE AT GOOSE BAY, LABRADOR, REGULARLY HOSTED SAC AIRCRAFT LIKE THIS B-36. GOOSE BAY ALSO HAD A FACILITY TO STORE SAC'S NUCLEAR WEAPONS TO BE USED AGAINST THE SOVIET UNION. (CF PHOTO)

THE USAF ALSO DEPLOYED TWO SQUADRONS OF F-102 INTERCEPTORS TO BASES IN
CANADA. THE F-102 WAS EQUIPPED WITH A NUCLEAR-TIPPED VERSION OF THE FALCON AIR-
TO-AIR MISSILE, THOUGH NEGOTIATIONS ON STORAGE RIGHTS DRAGGED ON FOR YEARS
BETWEEN THE NORAD PARTNERS. (CF PHOTO)

SAC'S NORTHERN TANKER FORCE, CONSISTING OF KC-97 AERIAL REFUELING AIRCRAFT
BASED AT SEVERAL DISCRETE LOCATIONS IN CANADA, WERE MAINTAINED ON SIOP ALERT
TO SUPPORT SAC B-47'S IN THEIR MISSION TO BOMB THE SOVIET UNION. (CF PHOTO)

Canada built numerous radar and signals intercept sites across the north that fed the joint Canadian-American air defence system. These systems, like RCAF Station Falconbridge, provided the warning necessary to disperse and protect SAC's increasingly vulnerable aircraft. (CF Photo)

the past, had committed CF-104 aircraft to the nuclear strike role, and had committed an Honest John unit to fulfill MC 70 requirements. Copies of this study were passed on to External Affairs.

In an attempt to break the deadlock, Robert Bryce arranged a meeting between Frank Miller and Norman Robertson on 30 November to develop recommendations to the government on nuclear weapons issues. The three agreed that the MB-1 storage agreement would "proceed without delay," that negotiations for the specific weapons systems already publicly announced would start, and that "physical preparations for nuclear weapons and training could continue."[124] There were two caveats to all of this, both inserted at Robertson's insistence. First, the phrase "when and if needed" was inserted into the recommendations regarding the systems agreements. Second, nuclear weapons acquisition "was subject to the progress on disarmament and arms control."[125]

The first addition was an artful piece of diplomatic speak. It could be read a number of ways. Taken in one way, the government-to-government agreement could now be negotiated, as could the service-to-service agreements, everything short of actually bringing the warheads into Canada. Or, the government-to-government agreement could be signed to permit the service-to-service agreements to be signed "when and if needed." Or, the government-to-government agreement would be signed "when and if" the Canadian government determined that nuclear weapons were necessary. Why Miller even agreed to this is unknown, but it is likely that Miller figured he could creatively interpret this language for the forces' benefit.

These recommendations, which in part were based on the Joint Staff study, were then formulated with some modification into a memorandum for Cabinet. It was understood that Canada was committed to equipping her forces in Europe and the BOMARC squadrons with nuclear weapons and that this was all based on NATO strategy that Canada also accepted. An additional matter was also raised in the memorandum, that of the SACEUR ballistic missile force that was due for discussion later that month at the NATO Ministerial Meeting. In addition to sorting out the nuclear weapons problems specific to Canada, the government also had to formulate a policy on the planned multilateral force that was assumed to consist of one hundred Polaris missiles, based on the Bowie Report's recommendations.[126]

As for control issues, the memo recommended a dual-key system for NORAD-committed weapons based in Canada, "whereby each nation has a veto on the use of the weapons."[127] NATO control was more problematic and undergoing evolution. The most pressing matter, though, was the lack of direction by the government on warhead acquisition, since "The absence of a decision to implement such a policy is becoming increasingly difficult to justify both in principle and in the light of the funds being expended on the nuclear carriers."[128] In sum, the Diefenbaker Cabinet had to make a decision and make it soon since the interval between now and completion of the systems and facilities was decreasing rapidly. With Robertson's added language, the memo read:

> It is proposed that the Canadian Government should proceed now with the
> necessary international negotiations to enable Canadian forces to be in a

position to acquire, when and if they need them, those nuclear weapons which it has already been announced that the Canadian forces would be equipped to use (ie: the CF-104, the BOMARC and the Honest John) and also, possibly, weapons for anti-submarine warfare and for fighter aircraft in North America. . . . It would be clearly understood and stated that Canadian action in acquiring, holding, or using nuclear weapons and means of their delivery would be subject to any measures or disarmament or arms control agreed between East and West.[129]

Prior to the Cabinet meeting, Robertson sent a copy of the memo along with his comments to Howard Green. In essence, Robertson told Green, "it would be inconsistent and hypocritical for us at the same time to adopt policies which can only have the effect of compounding the nuclear problem."[130] There was a new American government (John F. Kennedy had just been elected), and Robertson informed Green it might seek accommodation with the Soviets. This was an inaccurate assessment on Robertson's part given the combative nature of the Kennedy presidential campaign rhetoric regarding the so-called missile gap. In Robertson's view, the Americans should not be allowed to store nuclear weapons in Canada since this would have "great symbolic importance," and, since equipping Canadian forces would soon follow, it would interfere with the prospects for disarmament.[131] In other words, Robertson deliberately undermined his agreement with Miller.

The actual extent of Robertson's faith in disarmament talks is unknown but appears, if this was not a calculated position to manipulate Green, to be part of a response to his fears about nuclear war that arose back in 1959. The imposition of his opinion on the matter and the means by which he molded Howard Green's less-than-sophisticated approach to the nuclear issue are, in retrospect, reprehensible. Robertson knew what Canada's defense policy was and how it was linked to NATO strategic concepts, since he had participated in these discussions years ago. He knew that billions of taxpayer dollars were being spent to provide Canada's contribution to the deterrent and the direct defense of his country. He was a senior, unelected, civil servant. His job was not to create policy for the government if the government had decided that the policy was to be deliberately vague.

Despite Robertson's efforts, the Cabinet decided on 6 December 1960 to start negotiations with the Americans for the acquisition of nuclear weapons for Canadian forces subject to "the acceptance of joint controls."[132] Canadian forces should train for their use and facilities should be constructed. In a reversal, the Cabinet decided the MB-1 and other American storage issues should not be resolved until the acquisition and joint control issues were sorted out. Cabinet affirmed that "Canadian Ministers should recognize that the Government has agreed, at the meeting in December 1957 and at other times, and is morally bound, to supply Canadian forces under NATO command equipped and ready to use nuclear weapons if and when they are necessary."[133]

Canada would also vote in favor of the Irish Resolution in the UN: the Cabinet did not recognize that doing so was at variance with the previous decisions in this meeting; that is, that by voting for the Irish Resolution, Canada was committing herself in the United Nations not to acquire control of nuclear weapons, the very thing that External Affairs was demanding Canada should have before Americans could store nuclear weapons in Canada and Canadian forces could have access to the stockpile! In addition to Green's and Robertson's manipulation of the situation, Harkness had not been informed about alterations to the wording of the Irish Resolution, or he would have fought it upon becoming Minister. Miller should have informed him about the relationship of the Irish Resolution to the nuclear weapons problem.

The nuclear weapons issue also came up in the Panel's deliberations over preparations for the December NATO Ministerial Meeting. The main protagonists in this discussion were Bryce, Miller, and Robertson. Bryce informed the Panel about the Cabinet meeting's conclusion: "Canada would continue to make preparations for our NATO forces to be suitably equipped and trained so as to be ready to use nuclear weapons. Canada would not . . . make any commitments on the question of the proposed NATO nuclear deterrent force."[134] Miller wanted to make it clear that the purpose underlying the American proposal to provide medium range ballistic missiles (MRBMs) to NATO was twofold: first, it was to allay European concerns that Europe would not have a nuclear deterrent if the Americans became isolationist, and second, to prevent nuclear proliferation. The same motives underlay the original 1958 stockpile plan, and as a consequence, the Canadian CF-104 force. However, Miller noted, NATO plans were not compatible with Canadian nuclear disarmament policy. This had to be sorted out before any more forward movement could be made.[135]

Robertson was horrified about the MRBM proposal. He believed it:

> would raise doubts as to whether the NATO powers seriously wanted disarmament and the abolition of nuclear weapons. Moreover, it would seem that the introduction of a battery of MRBM's that could eliminate the cities of Eastern Europe represented a significant shift in the present balance of power in Europe. We did not know what forces the Soviet Union had in Eastern Europe but it did not seem they had given nuclear weapons to their satellites.[136]

Robertson's inappropriate comparison between the captive nations and the free world notwithstanding, Bryce and Miller were dismayed. The Soviets had, in fact, deployed missiles to Eastern Europe. They had overwhelming conventional forces. Disarmament would be achieved only, Miller emphasized, if the West maintained a balance of military power and negotiated from a position of strength. MRBMs were needed for military, as well as political reasons. NATO had to counter Soviet deployments to maintain the balance. The real question was one of how joint control should be exercised.

Robertson then revealed that he thought American custody was better for Europe, since "It was impossible to ensure against a coup d'etat in some country which might put an irresponsible government into possession of nuclear weapons." His main concern was Germany: "It was essential to recognize that Germany had some major political discontents about which some German Government in the future might want to take action."[137] An interesting but hypocritical statement from the man who opposed joint control of nuclear weapons with the Americans in Canada on sovereignty grounds.

This discussion prompted Miller to study the custody and control issue further in terms of how it affected Canada. In a brief for Harkness, Miller informed the Minister that there was far too much misunderstanding on the control issue both by the Opposition and in the Cabinet. The American position had remained constant:

> Any proposal that has ever been made by the United States envisioned sharing the control. In essence the United States maintain the right to see that atomic weapons are not used until such time as it is decided by the President that an emergency of sufficient gravity exists to justify the release of the nuclear weapons both to the American and to the Allied forces. Thereafter it is entirely up to the force to whom the weapons are released to decide whether or not they will fire them.[138]

In other words, those who were upset about the issue of joint control were arguing a nonissue, unless they favored complete, unilateral control and custody of nuclear weapons by Canada.

Miller then explained each system. BOMARC had its warhead attached while on alert. The orders to release BOMARC would come through NORAD to the control center, and then a separate Canadian order would be required to launch. As for Honest John and the CF-104s, Harkness was told, "the Canadian Government can arrange that under no circumstances could these weapons be used without their prior concurrence."[139] But most importantly, Miller also emphasized that there already was some degree of control exerted through Canadian representation on all of the NATO and NORAD staffs, which were integral to the planning process and release process. Therefore, there already were mechanisms in place to exert control.

All of this appeared moot when Canada voted in favor of the Irish Resolution and committed itself in the UN not to acquire control over nuclear weapons.

Conclusion

The progression in the nuclear weapons crisis reached its next level in 1960. Whereas the previous stance revolved around Green's predilections over sovereignty issues in 1959, the situation was exacerbated by the introduction of disarmament negotiations, which were pushed by Robertson and Burns, as well as Green. The inability of the Prime Minister to see that there was a drastic contradiction in Canadian policy and correct it was itself exacerbated by the turnover in the defense team over the course of the year and by opposition attacks. Before the new defense team (Harkness and Miller) could come to grips with the situation, Green and Robertson committed Canada to a contradictory policy without informing Cabinet or the Prime Minister of the possible implications, something even Burns had warned Robertson about. Certainly there was little or no appreciation on the part of Robertson and Green about the financial and human effort required to develop and train a force structure and the lead times required for such activity. Rapid changes of course were not feasible in such a technologically and doctrinally complex environment. Robertson's fear of provocation and his consequent attempts to thwart Canadian defense policy must rank highly in the myriad of causes of the nuclear crisis.

The fact that the Soviet Union constituted a serious threat to NATO was still secondary in Diefenbaker's mind to the perceived political "threat" from the Opposition. The situation would only get worse with John F. Kennedy's accession to power in the United States in 1961.

10

CANADA'S NUCLEAR CRISIS, PART II: FRUSTRATING INCREMENTALISM, 1961

"I couldn't have called him a son of a bitch.
I didn't know he was one at the time!"
–QUOTE ATTRIBUTED TO JOHN F. KENNEDY

"I didn't think Diefenbaker was a son of a bitch.
I thought he was a prick."
–ACTUAL QUOTE BY JOHN F. KENNEDY
(BESCHLOSS, *THE CRISIS YEARS*)

Introduction

The second phase of Canada's nuclear weapons crisis was marked in many ways by the antagonism between John Diefenbaker and John F. Kennedy. This clash of personalities drastically magnified attempts by the disarmament proponents in the Canadian government to prevent Canadian forces from acquiring nuclear weapons. International tension, ratcheted up with the erection of the Berlin Wall in August 1961, did not alleviate this problem. NATO strategy continued to evolve while Chairman of the Chiefs of Staff Committee Air Marshal Miller formulated a Canadian strategic concept to keep pace with it. At the same time, the armed forces utilized their informal relationships with their American counterparts to move closer to acquiring a nuclear capability.

The Continuing Nuclear Debate: January–February 1961

Douglas Harkness tried to get Howard Green to have the draft government-to-government nuclear agreement signed early in January 1961. This version presented the control issue in a vague fashion: Harkness stated control could be dealt with in each service-to-service agreement on a case-by-case basis depending on the weapon system. The objective was to get the process moving. Green delayed yet again, stating he would ask "the officials of my Department, who are concerned with this question, to examine this draft and let me have their comments."[1]

While Harkness waited for Green's reply, the RCAF was inching forward. The first eight CF-104 instructors trained at Nellis AFB in Nevada during the spring of 1961.[2] Training "shapes" were being procured for the newly stood up CF-104 Operational Training Unit (OTU), while a small number of RCAF training officers received clearances to acquire some nuclear weapons data from the USAF so that the training syllabus could be written. A cadre of RCAF armorers were prepared with the relevant data so that the cadre could be filled out rapidly in an emergency. Special Ammunition Storage (SAS) facilities were also under construction. As for BOMARC, the RCAF was able to load personnel onto joint Boeing-USAF nuclear weapons safety courses.[3] The USAF and the RCAF even started to negotiate the draft BOMARC service-to-service agreement wording in preparation for the day that the government-to-government agreement was signed. A Neptune maritime patrol aircraft was prototyped for Mk 101 carriage as part of a plan to provide technical experience so that the Argus fleet could be equipped with a similar capability. Unfortunately training and other aspects necessary to develop a cadre nuclear capability in Maritime Air Command (MAC) were blocked by the USN, which insisted on a formal service-to-service agreement before proceeding further.[4]

A new player joined the antinuclear weapons side of the Canadian policy-making team in January 1961: George Ignatieff. A Russian-born émigré, Ignatieff was Canada's ambassador to Yugoslavia in the 1950s. He was then Assistant Undersecretary of State for External Affairs in 1961. Ignatieff was nominally Norman Robertson's deputy. In reality, Diefenbaker wanted Ignatieff to be his special advisor on national defense and nuclear affairs. As Ignatieff put it: "Diefenbaker wanted clear, black and white position statements, the kind of arguments a lawyer could use to win his case."[5] Diefenbaker told Ignatieff that he felt misled about the BOMARC, particularly in terms of the A (conventional and nuclear) and B (nuclear only) models. He thought the RCAF had maneuvered him into acquiring the B model, and he blamed Air Marshal Campbell for this confusion. Ignatieff's answer to this was to offer two options: either accept nuclear warheads or do not accept them. Diefenbaker had in one briefing "attacked Campbell so viciously that . . . [Harkness] finally intervened and said that this kind of abuse of a senior Air Force officer was unacceptable."[6]

Ignatieff and Robertson decided early in 1961 to coordinate their antinuclear activities. It was easy to convince Green, but the Prime Minister still required work. Ignatieff talked frequently with Robertson during this period and the two of them devised a formula that they knew the Americans would never accept. In essence, it followed the similar line imposed by Robertson already, that is, Canada must have joint control over the weapons and acceptance of nuclear weapons would be contingent on the success of the (stalled) disarmament talks. In Ignatieff's words, this was a "holding action," a delay not meant to survive detailed scrutiny. They specifically played to Green's growing fears about radioactive fallout.[7]

On another front, the Liberals formulated a detailed defense policy platform in January 1961. It was based on the following precepts:

1. No nuclear weapons either under separate Canadian control or under joint US-Canadian control.
2. NATO must build up its conventional forces.

3. Any NATO nuclear deterrent must be under joint NATO control.
4. Tactical nuclear weapons should not be given to individual NATO members.
5. Canada should withdraw from BOMARC and interceptor commitments; Canada should just be involved in warning functions.
6. Canada will commit her land, sea, and air forces to supporting UN police and peacekeeping activities.[8]

Pearson followed this up in a 27 January speech in which he stated that his opposition to nuclear weapons revolved around the sovereignty issue:

> [I]f we do acquire [nuclear weapons], the U.S. Government should not determine—as it can now—whether Canadian forces can or cannot use them in defence. At present, a Canadian officer in charge of such weapons could not order their use without the approval of an American authority. This situation is not altered by the fact that the Canadian authorities can also refuse to carry out a U.S. order to use them.[9]

This statement contained a number of erroneous assumptions. It assumed that Canada had no say in the process by which nuclear weapons were authorized; that is, Pearson discounted the substantial Canadian presence on the NORAD planning and operational staffs and elsewhere. As with other previous statements made during the NORAD and SCODE debates, there was no appreciation of time and space. The only response to Pearson's statement was either to affirm the dual key system and then be accused of throwing away Canadian sovereignty or to discard nuclear weapons altogether, which was the aim of the Liberal policy statement in the first place. Even though Pearson lacked the classified information on nuclear release processes and predelegation of authority, his argument was flawed since it posed only two alternatives when in fact there were others. Pearson was slowly boxing in Diefenbaker on the nuclear weapons issue.

An even more fractious and public split opened up in the Diefenbaker Cabinet early in February. Howard Green had made several supportive public speeches to Canadian antinuclear groups. The press heard a rumor that Harkness had encouraged RCN reserve officers at a mess function to counter the antinuclear movements. This hit the papers and quickly became a cause célèbre.[10] When the smoke cleared, it was apparent a journalist who was not even at the function had misquoted Harkness. One citizen even wrote Harkness accusing him of implying that "such men as Howard Green, [and] Lester Pearson . . . are motivated by subversive thoughts."[11] In fact, Harkness had not used names and merely stated his "opposition to neutralism and pacifism as expounded by those who advocate unilateral disarmament."[12]

When accused of not following government policy by citizens or the media, Harkness consistently argued that he did not oppose genuine disarmament efforts. He did believe, however: "that until such agreement can be reached and as long as there are those who believe in the use of force to achieve their aims, we must maintain our defences and contribute to the common endeavor to prevent the outbreak of war."[13]

February 1961 Gallup polls bore out Harkness's view. When asked if nuclear weapons made war more or less likely, 56% of those polled said that they made it less likely, with 25% believing that it made war more likely. In terms of the percentage of the population favoring Canadian acquisition of nuclear weapons, 45% were in favor, 34% had no opinion, and 21% were opposed. This information was passed on to the Prime Minister.[14]

General Loper and Air Vice-Marshal Hendrick continued their attempts to solve the nuclear weapons agreement impasse in February 1961. Loper raised the matter of the planned Skybolt, a bomber-launched stand off missile. If the USAF were equipped with such a system, was a new agreement with Canada necessary to fly and launch such weapons from Canadian airspace?[15] If so, Loper proposed that a formal treaty handling all aspects of nuclear weapons be formulated between the two countries. This would "escape the restrictions of the Atomic Energy Act of 1958."[16] If the Senate ratified it, it would override any previous restrictions. This had not been attempted with any other ally before and might work.

Loper thought that the treaty would include joint control by both governments; custody by Canadian forces; "As much maintenance by Canadians as we wish to assume"; bomb disposal information; and "any other aspects of Canadian sovereignty which may be of special concern to us."[17] If Canada wanted to try, Loper added, the State Department should be asked directly. Unfortunately, this potential solution would soon be submerged in a personality clash.

First Clash: The Prime Minister Versus the President

The accession of John Fitzgerald Kennedy to the presidency in 1961 altered the already fragile Canadian-American relationship. No two men could have been more dissimilar than John Diefenbaker and John Kennedy. Journalist Knowlton Nash, who covered Washington for the CBC in the early 1960s, masterfully captured this in his work *Kennedy and Diefenbaker*. Diefenbaker had an obsessive dislike of Americans and feared rejection by Kennedy, while Kennedy had a complete lack of knowledge and interest in Canada and feared failure. Diefenbaker was an "aging, suspicious prairie populist," and Kennedy was a "youthful, quick-witted Boston sophisticate."[18] Kennedy was "a realist masquerading as a romantic," while Diefenbaker was a "messianic nationalist."[19] Monarchist Diefenbaker thought that Kennedy's father Joseph betrayed the British during the Second World War, while new world Irish-American scion Kennedy arrogantly thought Canada was a "child nation." Diefenbaker was courtly with women, while Kennedy behaved like a pig toward them.

Their first meeting on 8 February was a disaster. Kennedy asked Dean Rusk, his Secretary of State, to find out how Diefenbaker's name was pronounced. Rusk asked Foy Kohler, his Assistant Secretary for European Affairs who told Rusk that it was a German name and thus pronounced "Diefen-bawker." The new President used this pronunciation in his speech, to the Prime Minister's horror. The worst was yet to come. In their coverage of the event, ABC News used "Diefenbacon," the *Washington Post* called him "Diffenbaker," United Press thought it was "Fifenbaker," while a State Department release called him "Diefenbacker." These were all major affronts to Canada and the Prime Minister had to be dissuaded from lodging an official protest through diplomatic channels.[20] Little was accomplished at this first meeting.

This inauspicious beginning prompted both Diefenbaker and Kennedy to lay the groundwork for another meeting in February 1961.[21] Diefenbaker wanted to discuss a wide variety of issues with the American President, while the Americans were primarily interested in sorting out the defense relationship. As Dean Rusk noted:

> The Government's tendency to procrastinate and its defensive reaction to criticism of Canada's defence position has tended to confuse the public and helped spawn some neutralist and semi-pacifist groups. . . . Should this general situation continue over a long period, a drift toward a kind of unconscious neutralism could develop with a concommitment loosening of defense ties with the United States. . . . Loss or diminution of use of Canadian air space and real estate and the contributions of the Canadian military. Particularly the RCAF and Royal Canadian Navy, would be intolerable, particularly in times of crisis.[22]

Rusk established a cordial relationship with Canadian Ambassador A. D. P. Heeney. Rusk was a quick study and absorbed Heeney's perspective that the two largest problems in the Canada-US relationship revolved around defense and economics, and that both were intertwined with sovereignty and nationalism. In addition, Rusk looked forward to fishing trips in Canada and, with them, the opportunity to carry out informal discussions.[23]

Air Marshal Miller, meanwhile, wondered if the Loper proposal had any chance of succeeding. The Chairman also explored another option: could the United States legally make nuclear weapons available to Canada without an agreement? Clearly he thought there was a possibility that American nuclear warheads could be moved to Canadian bases in an emergency, attached to the aircraft, and launched under NORAD command. A legal analysis indicated the Atomic Energy Act of 1958 did not prohibited this. Was it operationally feasible, however? This would require further study.[24]

At the same time Miller continued to deal with Bryce and Robertson in preparation for the Diefenbaker-Kennedy meeting. Miller informed both that the issue over control was chimeric, that all proposals that had been made in the past "envisioned sharing control."[25] Canada still retained the right to determine whether her forces would actually use the weapons once they had been released. Was there any conceivable situation whereby Canada would need the weapons and NORAD would not release them?

Robertson did not reply. Instead, he prepared a paper for the Privy Council that indicated that there would be problems in "develop[ing] acceptable formulae to provide for the joint responsibility . . . to exercise controls through consultations in situations likely to give rise to the use of nuclear weapons."[26] Miller disagreed with this part of the paper and thought that it should be removed before presentation to the Cabinet. What this section does reveal is that Robertson was linking, at least in his mind, joint control over nuclear weapons and the problems with consultation. It is possible that Robertson was trying to use this issue to exert influence over what he viewed to be the American tendency towards provocative activity and precipitative action during times of crisis.

This sort of sophisticated diplomatic maneuvering remained outside of Diefenbaker's grasp of the issues, and Robertson did not attempt to enlighten either the Prime Minister or Green. In Cabinet, Diefenbaker stated that one of his objectives at the meeting would be to determine "how far President Kennedy would go in the direction of joint control over the use of nuclear arms if located in Canada."[27] Analysis conducted for the Cabinet also indicated that Canada's accession to the Irish Resolution in the UN did not, in fact, "prevent the government of Canada from obtaining nuclear weapons from the United States at this time."[28] The existing policy, that is, the January 1960 statement, would remain the public policy and this was reaffirmed in a speech on 17 February.[29]

Green accompanied Diefenbaker on the February 1961 flight down to Washington, where he took the entire two hours to harangue the Prime Minister on nuclear weapons and disarmament.[30] The actual meeting itself included Diefenbaker, Green, Heeney, Rusk, and Merchant. No military or defense department personnel were present. Most of the meeting revolved around the ongoing Congo and Laos issues and what role China might be playing in world tension. Diefenbaker suddenly launched into a defense of Canada trading with Cuba and China. Canada, he indicated, resented American interference in these sovereign matters. While on this subject, Diefenbaker asserted that Canadians "welcome[d] the President every week via TV into [their] living rooms but that Canadian news gets less treatment in the United States than that from a 'banana republic.'"[31]

As for nuclear weapons, Diefenbaker told Kennedy, "The Canadian Government will not decide at the present time whether or not Canadian forces should be equipped with nuclear weapons."[32] The reason for this was the ongoing disarmament negotiations. If a decision was made, Canada would insist on "joint custody and joint control." Kennedy wondered if the existing formula as established with the British was acceptable; that is, the dual key system. Diefenbaker thought this was the proper formula. With regard to storage, Canada would insist on joint control over MB-1, SAC, and ASW storage. However, these arrangements would not be made until the decision had been made to accept nuclear weapons for Canadian forces or not.[33]

It may appear mystifying to see such a nonissue repeatedly brought up for discussion by such high-level people. We must remember, however, that there had been a change in the American administration, and the Kennedy people were not fully conversant with the details. That said, there is a clear inconsistency in Diefenbaker's attitude to what constituted joint custody and control. The Canadian defense people had never altered their perspective, nor had the Americans. Both of these parties maintained that joint custody and control was acceptable. The vacillators were Robertson, Green, Ignatieff, and the Prime Minister.

After the meeting, Bryce informed Harkness that the MB-1 storage agreement negotiations should continue, as should the nuclear depth bomb storage arrangements, but they were to be conducted on the assumption that joint control was necessary, that is, the Canadian government had to agree to release the weapons from their storage sites in an emergency. The antisubmarine weapons agreement should be processed through NATO and the MB-1s through NORAD. This much was passed to the Cabinet, and Diefenbaker confirmed that he had accepted the dual key formula for control and custody.[34] A distorted version leaked to the media, which concluded that an agreement had been reached on nuclear weapons. Diefenbaker then publicly denied that an agreement had been reached, but he did not clarify the difference between American storage for their forces and storage for Canadian forces. The Prime Minister's action added to the public confusion on the nuclear issue.[35]

As for the continuing F-101B acquisition situation, the Yukon transport sale to the United States was off. The Americans instead proposed to fund 70% of the cost of F-104Gs that would be given to NATO nations under the Mutual Assistance Plan. Canada would pay for the other 30%, would take over eleven instead of five PINETREE radar sites, and then receive sixty-six F-101B interceptors. Cabinet was informed that this was a bargain and served many political as well as military purposes. Canada needed an interceptor. The Liberal defense policy platform discounted the requirement for an interceptor, so now the heat was off in terms of Opposition backlash for acquiring a CF-105 replacement. Cabinet was also informed, "The F-101B was capable of being armed with either conventional or nuclear weapons but the choice on this subject would be for decision later. The aircraft would in normal course be delivered with conventional air-to-air missiles and not with nuclear missiles. No doors should be closed at this time."[36]

The Americans chose not to force the issue of nuclear armament for the CF-101. Militarily, they were concerned that transferring USAF F-101Bs to the RCAF without nuclear armament would reduce the number of effective interceptors available to NORAD.[37] On 2 March 1961, the Cabinet agreed to acquire F-101B Voodoo interceptors, though the announcement would not be made for another five months.[38]

The Evolving Strategy

While the Canada-US debate continued, MC 14/2 (revised) remained NATO and Canada's strategic concept. The ambiguities contained in that document, combined with questions on how to handle the Berlin Crisis and the NATO MRBM deterrent problem did, however, produce some thoughtful questioning early in 1961 that affected the evolving Canadian strategic concept.

Once again, the British were in the forefront of the reexamination of NATO strategy. In essence, the British asked two questions. First, now that the Soviets had deployed tactical nuclear weapons in quality to support their overwhelming conventional superiority in Europe, was MC 14/2 (revised) obsolete? Second, to what extent and under what conditions should NATO plan for Phase II of an MC 14/2 (revised) pattern of war, and did this have to change as well? As before, the British were desperately concerned about their financial situation and the accompanying problems of finding the right conventional/nuclear force balance.[39]

In their analysis, the British had loosened up slightly in their opposition to operations short of nuclear war in the NATO area. They now argued that MC 14/2 (revised) was in fact flexible enough to accommodate "general war or local hostile actions," but they still argued "there is no concept of limited war in Europe."[40] They noted that Norstad had been playing around with the pause concept and they were interested in this since "[it] seems desirable to examine whether the strategy can be adapted so as to provide for whatever degree of force, not excluding nuclear weapons, might be required to induce an aggressor to abandon his aggression while, at the same time, minimizing the risk of precipitating all-out nuclear war."[41]

Nuclear weapons were still required, though, in three cases: (1) after the pause had taken place, and the enemy continued his aggression; (2) in support of strategic nuclear forces; and (3) after strategic nuclear forces had been used. The NATO battlefield still needed to be isolated from enemy reinforcement in all cases, which contributed to maintaining the integrity of the NATO area generally.[42]

The American perspective on the British views was based on the belief that MC 14/2 (revised) was sufficiently "broad and flexible" in its wording to handle all of these problems. It was merely a question of how SACEUR chose to interpret MC 14/2 (revised). The US JCS was concerned that too stringent interpretation, "particularly with respect to the threshold of nuclear employment, would undoubtedly serve to alert the Soviets as to specific Alliance intent and thereby facilitate Soviet planning."[43] Norstad was capable of introducing a pause concept without altering NATO's strategic concept since it was "already implicit in the NATO strategy." The biggest problem with formal adoption of a new concept was, in the American view, "letting it appear that the Allies fear the consequences of general nuclear war more that the Soviets fear them."[44]

The actual definition of the pause concept produced some uncertainty. Norstad originally noted in a public speech in 1960 that NATO Shield forces should, "at a minimum, be able to force a pause and, during this break, to establish clearly that the action is aggression . . . we should not use more force than is necessary."[45] Many observers had assumed that NATO forces were either conventionally trained and equipped or tactical nuclear forces. They did not understand that NATO forces in the Central Region were dual-capable in many respects, that tactical nuclear weapons complemented conventional weapons. SACEUR rated his forces capable of forcing a pause of some duration, but incapable of resisting the enemy on conventional terms for a protracted period.[46]

There was, of course, a great deal of public and private speculation about how long the "pause" actually was supposed to be. Norstad clarified his earlier thinking, stating publicly:

> I have mentioned the rather interesting subject of the pause and spoken of forcing a break in a dangerous continuity of action. "Pause" in the sense used here to mean a break, but a break which cannot be defined in precise terms of time, space, or strength of forces involved. I have never in my own mind related it to a period of time. The important objective is to provide an interval for decision and then to force a conscious decision to be made. This may mean minutes, hours or days. I would like to emphasize that the concept of the pause does not relieve us of the responsibility for taking all

necessary steps, using all necessary means, to deny an aggressor the occupation of any NATO territory.[47]

Which of course meant maintaining a strong nuclear deterrent at all levels. Note that Norstad recognized the political problems that were developing in NATO nuclear consultation. The pause presumably was as much for NATO to make a decision as to force the Soviets to reconsider theirs. On the whole, Norstad thought that the British questions were a healthy thing, in line with the objectives of the Bowie Report. NATO needed more conventional forces, better nuclear forces, and more control over the nuclear forces. It was not a question of reducing one for the other.[48]

Canadian military planners were skeptical about the pause concept and viewed peripheral conventional operations as ad hoc affairs that could be handled with special, conventional stand-by forces. Consequently, the reappraisal of NATO strategy did not have an immediate impact on the new 1961 Canadian concept of operations that continued to be based on MC 14/2 (revised).

The Chiefs requested and the Joint Planning Committee delivered a formal Canadian strategic concept entitled "CSC Paper 2(61): The Concept of the Employment of the Canadian Armed Forces in the Event of Unlimited Nuclear War." It was accepted in mid-March 1961. In effect, CSC Paper 2(61) was designed to focus Canadian thinking on what Canadian planners viewed to be the most likely course of action in the event of war with the Soviet Union in the early 1960s.[49]

Canadian defense policy continued to be to prevent the outbreak of war and to provide for the security of Canada if deterrence failed. Canada continued to rely on collective security and in doing so "helps formulate and subscribes to the collective strategic concepts of NATO."[50] Consequently, MC 14/2 (revised) was the underpinning of CSC Paper 2(61).

In addition to the Sword and Shield, NATO had to have the ability to deal with "local incidents and incursions which if left unchecked, might develop into major war."[51] As for North American defense, the Canadian concept included provisions for protecting SAC and National Survival (continuity of government, reentry and rescue operations, decentralization).

If the Soviets initiated strategic nuclear warfare, Canadian planners assumed the Soviets would "[preserve] their country from destruction by first attempting to destroy all nuclear offensive power ranged against them before it could be used."[52] Surprise would be the order of the day, and "further preparation and deployment of Soviet Bloc forces beyond that which had occurred as a result of the international situation would be kept to a minimum to avoid compromise of the initial attack."[53] The Soviets would then initiate a mass attack against Europe. In other words, CSC Paper 2(61) recognized that an attack might result from an international incident or protracted international tension of some kind, but, like MC 14/2 (revised), it did not provide any detail or scenario. It specifically discounted the possibility that the Soviets would launch a massed conventional attack against Europe.

CSC Paper 2(61) assumed no strategic warning. There would be two to three hours warning of a bomber attack, and seven to twenty minutes warning of an ICBM attack. In terms of targeting, CSC Paper 2(61) assumed that SAC bases in the United

States would bear the weight of enemy weapons. Weapons might not be targeted against Canada in the best case, though fallout would cover portions of the country. In the worst-case scenario, Canadian cities would be directly attacked. The difference lay in how quickly Canada could transition from peace to war. The elements of this process included ready and alert air and ASW defense forces in being and the actual alert system itself.[54]

In effect, CSC Paper 2(61) was a worst-case outlook and placed great emphasis on immediately ready forces in North America and virtually ignored Phase II forces. Phase II was beyond definition and impossible to plan for in military terms. Existing military forces in Phase II would be involved in national survival operations, while the Phase I forces were designed to limit the damage to Canada itself. Canadian forces in Europe were to preserve the integrity of the NATO area in the event of war during Phase I. Their fate in Phase II was not discussed.[55]

CSC Paper 2(61) generally served as an umbrella for service-specific thinking in 1961, though the services were not forced by the Chiefs to use it as a blueprint for service planning.

The Army was not overly challenged with the conceptual aspects of NATO strategic musings in 1961. The need for mass mobilization of several divisions did not exist under CSC Paper 2(61), but there was a requirement to man national attack warning and fallout reporting centers, rescue operations (reentry operations), and to provide aid to civil power tasks to maintain law and order after a nuclear attack. Few organizational changes were required, and the equipment necessary for these new missions was not expensive.[56] Army planners did not, however, make a link between NATO trends shifting back toward more conventional operations and the need to create or maintain the potential for a larger Canadian Army based on mobilization with the appropriate equipment. Army planners assumed, like the JPC, that the most likely course of action in the early 1960s would be a catastrophic nuclear war and planned accordingly.[57]

The RCN initiated a comprehensive policy review in 1961 that in some ways diverged from the tenets of CSC Paper 2(61). Admiral Herbert Rayner, the new Chief of the Naval Service, asked Rear Admiral Jeffry Brock to lead the Ad Hoc Committee on Naval Objectives in determining what the purposes, roles, tasks, and composition of the RCN should be over the next twenty-five years. This study, known as the Brock Report, provides insight into RCN thinking at this time.[58]

The Brock Report contributors closely followed the nuclear debate in Canada and strategic musings in NATO. Both streams found their way into the study. Disarmament and arms control were excised from consideration immediately: "Experience suggests that disarmament negotiations are likely to be in a large measure a manifestation of the Cold War rather than a means of ameliorating it."[59] The international situation was locked into a "self-enforcing nuclear impasse" now that the Soviets had secure retaliatory forces. This made a mass attack against Canadian cities improbable but "will tend to increase the feasibility of limited war."[60]

The big questions were: Will tactical and defensive nuclear weapons be used in limited war or not? Will tactical and defensive nuclear weapons use lead to strategic nuclear weapons use? The committee thought:

[it] appears unsound to assume that any use of nuclear weapons in limited war would inevitably lead to more widespread use of such weapons and, hence, by a process termed "escalation", result in all-out nuclear war. In effect, such an assumption denies the concept of limited war itself, which means that war aims are limited, ie: a war for something less than absolute surrender. . . . any limited war involving the United States and the Soviet Union, directly or indirectly, could only be entered into with the clear prior knowledge of the existence on both sides of secure retaliatory forces. . . . [I]t is not really a question of what types of weapons are used but rather a failure to appreciate the political consequences of a resort to force. It is also contrary to the facts of the Korean War and the Suez Crisis.[61]

Consequently,

in future the cutting edge of policy is likely to depend increasingly on non-nuclear weapons and forces, since they will be the only kind of military forces which can rationally be employed to support policy in the more probable situations. Tactical nuclear weapons will have an essential role as a deterrent to enemy use of such weapons, though there will be great and increasing reluctance to initiated use of them.[62]

However, the committee concluded that it was "militarily unsound" to create a strictly conventional force structure:

[to] be fully effective [Canadian maritime forces] should follow training, equipment and fitting policies which would give them the known capability to participate, if and when required, in engagements involving the use of nuclear weapons. *This does not mean that they must have nuclear weapons in their possession in time of peace, provided adequate arrangements have been made for emergency situations.*[63] (Italics added.)

On the air side, the annual RCAF "meeting of minds" allowed the RCAF leadership to discuss strategic matters informally.[64] The question of whether the ICBM would replace manned bombers in the near-term was put to rest by "a breakthrough in intelligence" that produced "virtual unanimity among all intelligence agencies as to the size of the Soviet ICBM force." This had to be CORONA satellite imagery, new intelligence that demonstrated "the build up of these weapons had been much slower than was previously estimated on the basis of very tenuous evidence."[65]

Air defense issues notwithstanding, Air Marshal Larry Dunlap held center stage because of his proximity to SACEUR, who, as we will recall was wrestling with the NATO nuclear force problem, and because the RCAF leadership was concerned about the Canadian CF-104 force in light of the nuclear weapons debate.

Dunlap had been briefed on targeting plans at SHAPE and informed the conference attendees that any ballistic missile force that fell under SACEUR's command involved "target planning that is specifically related to military objectives which are of direct concern to [ACE]," that is, the missiles would be used against Soviet airfields and missile bases (some of which were in the western Soviet Union) and not against cities. Dunlap noted, "You can question whether they are tactical or strategic. We don't any longer use those words because they are too confusing. . . . they would be employed against targets from which the enemy would take off and attack [ACE]."[66] As enemy delivery means gained greater range, they were moved further east. NATO aircraft could reach only so far, which increased the need for NATO ballistic missiles. The deepest targets that could affect ACE would have to be handled by SAC and RAF Bomber Command. SACEUR had to have the ability to react quickly, Dunlap emphasized. CF-104s, therefore, were still critical.

The biggest problem, according to Dunlap, was the consultative process which in his view:

> would take far too long. . . . One of things considered and which is perhaps a step forward is that perhaps in time of peace nations would agree to a delegation of authority to perhaps the Secretary-General or to SACEUR to cover specific situations which can be foreseen in advance. For example, one of the perhaps simplest of the situations is when an aggressor does make an attack and does use weapons, and there is no doubt he is launching an atomic war and has launched weapons. . . . The ones which are more difficult are the ones in which there is more tie associated with, and perhaps one can resolve them by consultative means on the outbreak of hostilities. . . . The Council members are studying that line of approach.[67]

There was not going to be any easy solution in the near future.

As for the Canadian CF-104 force, the RCAF leadership expressed concern about its place in NATO planning. What happened if the Government did not agree to accept nuclear weapons for it? Would this throw off SHAPE planning? Sites had to be constructed, crews had to be trained. Air Vice-Marshal L. E. "Larry" Wray noted: "The Americans, of course, are most helpful in any way they can be, but because of a lack of a Canada-US agreement, we can only go so far."[68] Harkness, who attended this session, reassured Wray that "I think this matter will be settled in the near future. In the meantime, I think we can go ahead on the assumption this is going to happen. . . . [T]his is on the assumption that these weapons are going to come into use in the forces and come into use with nuclear warheads."[69]

As for NATO strategic change, none of the conference members thought that the "pause" concept would be accepted as NATO strategy any time soon. Dunlap reiterated that NATO strategic policy was to defend the NATO area as far forward as possible, using all methods available.[70]

Dunlap also told the Minister:

> May I stress that this strategic guidance was subscribed to by Canada and its substance was fully understood by the departments of the governments strictly concerned, namely Defence and External Affairs. Not only was this

strategic guidance subscribed to but so were the policies and implementing programmes.[71]

In other words, the government knew what the commitments entailed. Dunlap inadvertently put on a lecturing tone in what clearly reflected SACEUR's concerns:

> Cabinet in supporting [the CF-104 acquisition] were aware of the mounting role of strike aircraft. How then could there be any doubt in the minds of the Canadian Cabinet in the environment of atomic weapons? That strategy relies on nuclear weapons both for deterrence and for defence, although limiting its uses to situations which so warrant. Until our force structure in support thereof is radically changed, there is no alternative. . . . [T]hat this ammunition happens to be atomic is no excuse for leaving our forces without the means of fulfilling their roles and missions.[72]

The RCAF leadership questioned Dunlap on custody, control, and release arrangements in NATO. Campbell wanted to know if the nuclear weapons would be released and attached to the CF-104s at a particular stage in the alert process. Dunlap told him the weapons were attached in peacetime and the CF-104 force as a whole would be placed under SACEUR's command upon declaration of Reinforced Alert. The North Atlantic Council was the authorizing authority to change the alert level to Reinforced Alert at this time.[73]

The French problem, Dunlap enlightened his listeners, despite public pronouncements, was unrelated to sovereignty. De Gaulle was "endeavoring to get U.S. provision of information on the manufacture of atomic weapons. They weren't getting anyplace and they dug their heels in. . . . This was a bargaining position."[74] This left Canada "holding the bag," because Canada was the only non-US member with forces and bases in France that needed nuclear weapons. There were plans in the works to deploy nuclear weapons from Germany and the UK by air to temporary sites at bases in France at certain levels of alert. This idea, in addition to the Brock Report's concept of "fitted for but not with" nuclear ASW weapons, percolated in Air Marshal Miller's mind and would bear fruit later on in the course of the nuclear weapon debate in Canada.

The conference members addressed the matter of 1 Air Division vulnerability, which had been raised during the SCODE deliberations and in previous RCAF meetings. NATO planners believed, in a scenario in which the enemy struck first and there was some warning, dispersed CF-86 and CF-100 interceptor aircraft might be held on the ground between thirty-five minutes to five hours. Even though "fallout would cover practically all of Europe" except parts of Spain, there was enough decontamination capability to ensure continuous operations for the fighter force. Once the CF-104 was introduced, however, the Canadian bases jumped to the top of the enemy's priority target list. Air Officer Commanding (AOC) 1 Air Division bluntly stated: "We don't think we will get too much warning. We are well within range of their surface-to-surface missiles. . . . [T]he time-to-impact area is very tight."[75] Existing NATO missiles were retaliatory. Unless something was done to counter the enemy missile capability, vulnerability would continue. Wray wanted more deployment airfields and he wanted them prestocked for at least seven days, a plan that included dispersed nuclear weapons.[76]

NATO air commanders were also starting to come to grips with reconnaissance requirements. The introduction of an NATO ballistic missile system, no matter where it came from, increased the need for more aircraft to conduct poststrike reconnaissance. With CF-104 strike aircraft, the pilot conducted his own reconnaissance. Missiles could not report back. Therefore, NATO air planners were intrigued with having the two planned squadrons of RCAF CF-104s equipped for such duties.[77]

RCAF commanders wanted the two reconnaissance squadrons to have access to dispersed nuclear weapons and predelegated authority to use them after the war had started. However, Commander of 4 ATAF was not allowed to release nuclear weapons for targets of opportunity. There were too many problems with custody, control, and release, since "it is a difficult one to sell both in military and political area[s] because in effect it means that you are delegating . . . right down to the level of the chap in the aircraft."

As for limited war issues, Air Commodore Carpenter weighed in as he had in 1960. In his view not enough was being done to develop conventional capability to handle peripheral operations. He suggested that the RCAF had demonstrated its reluctance during the deployment of the UN force to the Belgian Congo. In the RCAF, Carpenter asserted, "the ability to fight limited wars may vastly increase in importance . . . [We must] design our forces because we are so small that we have some degree of flexibility [in this area]."[78]

At the end of March 1961, President Kennedy announced to Congress the future direction of American NATO policy, based on discussions with SACEUR and the President's national security advisors. There were three objectives:

"1) American forces should be designed to deter any deliberate nuclear attack on the United States or its allies, as well as to reduce the danger of accidental nuclear war.
2) The United States requires a more flexible array of forces with which to respond to threats at all levels . . . and increase our ability to confine our response to non-nuclear weapons.
3) U.S. military forces would be subject to ultimate civilian control and command at all times . . . including all decisions relating to the use of nuclear weapons, or the escalation of a small war into a large one."[79]

The announcement confirmed speculation about what the future of NATO strategy should look like. Implementing it, however, was easier said than done. It became more and more difficult to explain to the public the need to improve nuclear forces and at the same time increase conventional forces when for years the public had been told that nuclear weapons made up for conventional force deficiencies. The nuances were contained in how the forces would be used and this was not open to public scrutiny.

Second Clash: Harkness Versus Green, the President Versus the Prime Minister

The run-up to the second Kennedy-Diefenbaker meeting consisted of another Harkness-Green skirmish. Harkness reminded Green on 1 March that "considerable time had elapsed" and a decision had to be made soon, since the delivery system's "operational dates approach."[80] With no formal reply from Green, Bryce attempted to broker another meeting between the two men. Bryce also attempted to establish what the existing situation was before this meeting took place so that Green and Harkness could agree to disagree. Essentially, MB-1 storage at Harmon and Goose Bay was acceptable assuming the Americans agreed to joint custody, control, and release authority. As for Argentia, NATO would determine release but custody would be joint. If BOMARC warheads and nuclear warheads for Canadian interceptors were deemed necessary, joint custody and control would be necessary. A new wrinkle had been added, according to Bryce: all negotiations had to be wrapped up in a "package deal." There would be no individual agreements.[81]

Green finally replied a month later to Harkness's 30 December 1960 draft government-to-government agreement. This would not do, asserted Green. Where were the service-to-service sections for each system? How could Canada sign the agreement without knowing exactly what Canada was agreeing to? Green demanded that release procedures for each weapon be included in the general agreement, since "this is my understanding that this is what the Prime Minister had in mind" when he talked to Kennedy.[82] Green recommended that Miller meet with Robertson to handle the redraft. This constituted yet another delay tactic on the part of Green and Robertson.

Miller presented Robertson with the already-established formula, which consisted of a general government-to-government agreement and several service-to-service agreements which would be worked out at the command level (that is, 1 Air Division would deal with USAFE, Commander Canadian Atlantic Sub-area [COMCANLANT] with CinCLANT, etc.). Robertson told Miller, "such an approach will not be acceptable with [External Affairs] nor . . . to the Government as a whole."[83] In other words, Robertson wanted a whole series of government-to-government agreements, with External Affairs negotiating directly with the American command concerned. This was unacceptable to Miller and the military commanders.

Harkness had an acrimonious meeting with Green on 3 May. Harkness told Green this "whole cloth" approach was not acceptable at all. He would not have External Affairs interfering with National Defence business. Harkness forced Green to agree to present the government-to-government agreement in Cabinet without the service-to-service agreements grafted on, and to drop the External Affairs concept of negotiating with the American commands.[84] Green, reluctantly, would go along, but stressed, "A decision to enter negotiations could not be considered a decision to accept nuclear weapons, but only as a wish to be in a position to do so if necessary."[85] The matter was brought to the Prime Minister's attention on 5 May. He made note of it but took no action to resolve the issue after Green told him acceptance of the "dual key" system would prejudice the ongoing disarmament talks.[86] Green then backed off from his agreement with Harkness to submit the general government-to-government agreement to Cabinet.[87]

The Kennedy-Diefenbaker meeting was rapidly approaching. In a letter to Diefenbaker, Harkness informed him:

> There is no real difference in opinion concerning the content of the general agreement. . . . I do feel that to include the supplementary [ie: service-to-service] agreements formally as part of the general agreement may well be unnecessarily cumbersome in regard to subsequent changes that may be desired in the detailed arrangements . . . my main concern being that we get on with the negotiations. We shall very shortly be in a position of having weapons systems in situ which will be complete except that warheads will not be immediately available if required.[88]

This statement was not made lightly. Harkness had consulted Miller to find out how much time was required to achieve a nuclear capability. Due dates for BOMARC were July 1962 for North Bay and December 1962 for La Macaza, while the first CF-104s were supposed to arrive in West Germany in December 1962. The Honest Johns were supposed to be in Europe in early 1962. Ground and aircrews had to be trained in new technologies and procedures, and the lack of the service-to-service agreements, let alone access to nuclear weapons themselves, was producing barriers.[89] Some of these barriers were overcome using informal techniques. For example, Mk 28 and Mk 43 "shapes" were not supposed to be released to Canada without the service-to-service agreement, so the RCAF built their own and took them to the American Armed Forces Special Weapons Project for certification, which subsequently approved them for use.[90]

RCAF planners noted with satisfaction, "a great deal has been accomplished by close liaison with the USAF. This liaison is enabling us to engineer into the [CF-104] the capability of carrying nuclear weapons. It is enabling us also to begin the preparations of safety studies, loading and delivery hand books."[91] The ASW aircraft were all ready for modification, and the Honest John battery was reaching the point where it only needed access to the warheads.

It was still not enough. The outstanding areas in which Canada could not proceed without the nuclear agreements included construction of special ammunition storage sites, alert facilities, assembly and maintenance buildings, as well as installation of special release and control communications, training of personnel for protection, handling and use of nuclear weapons, incorporation in the weapon carrier of an approved capability for the carriage and release of nuclear weapons, and finally provision of facilities and administrative support for US custodial detachments on Canadian bases.[92]

The draft general government-to-government agreement was the same as the one dated 30 December 1960, which was virtually identical to the one Foulkes, Pearkes, and Hendrick had produced back in December 1959.[93] The supplementary agreements, however, were the result of intense External-Defence negotiation and would form the basis not only for the actual service-to-service agreements, but Canadian thinking on custody, control, and release procedures over the next three years.

The American position on custody, which the draft supplementary agreements emphasized, was defined as "the control of property, the control of access to, and the control of weapons employment prior to the release of the weapon for operational use."[94] It was designed so that a deliberate act of force would be necessary for an enemy to gain access to the weapons themselves. There were three additional elements: "ownership, accountability, and actual possession."[95] The first two were never passed on to the non-US user: the user was responsible for the third once released to that country by the American President or his designated representative. Non-US control was also exercised at the alliance command level that created and approved the employment plans. External Affairs, the Opposition, and the Prime Minister did not understand these important factors during the nuclear weapon debates. Notably,

> control over operational use of the weapon and the release of the weapon for operational use is exercised by the Canadian Government . . . [which was entitled] to exercise this control in any way it wishes and to place restrictions or conditions . . . on weapons employment. At this point, there is neither negative or positive control from the US and the weapon is not, therefore, under joint control.[96]

BOMARC would have an "enabling device which will necessitate a physical key which action by one designated Canadian officer and an independent physical key switch action by one designated US officer" located at the SAGE command centre at North Bay. The Americans would have a communications line to the nearest CONAD command that could release the weapons. Both Canada and the United States would have to authorize CinCNORAD to increase his state of readiness to the point whereby CinCNORAD could release the weapons to Canada for use authorization if the enemy struck.[97]

Unlike other systems in which the warheads were mated with the delivery system after some alert level had been reached, the BOMARC would have its warhead attached all the time. Out of the 318 men in a BOMARC squadron, 30 were American custodians responsible for logistically maintaining the warheads. The RCAF would be responsible for the security of the BOMARC base.[98]

The situation for the CF-104 force and the Honest John missiles was different from the BOMARCs in the draft agreement. The Americans would release the bombs for the CF-104s on order from the American President or his representative to the RCAF, which would then place the planes under SACEUR's operational control. Then SACEUR had to get permission from NATO authorities and Canada to employ the CF-104 force. This could get complicated:

> If the [NAC] should decide to authorize SACEUR to declare a Simple or higher state of alert, the two Governments [Canada and the US] shall determine whether such a decision shall be deemed to constitute authorization

for SACEUR to employ the nuclear weapons at any time when in his judgment such action is required. In the absence of such a decision by the [NAC], should either Government be of the opinion that the situation warrants the removal of the nuclear weapons from storage and/or their use, they will consult. . . . Should the determination be affirmative, the approval thereby given will be deemed to constitute authority for SACEUR . . . to employ them [subject to the Chief of Staff Committee's approval].[99]

Whether this cumbersome process could function in a rapidly deteriorating situation was left open for discussion and not addressed in the agreement.

As for nuclear ASW weapons, they would be stored at Greenwood, Nova Scotia (for both RCAF and RCN use); Summerside, Prince Edward Island; Comox, British Columbia; and Torbay, Newfoundland (for RCAF use and onboard RCN ships at sea). All sites would have USN custodial personnel. Some weapons would be designated for CUSRPG use, and other for SACLANT use. SACLANT would release the weapons to the RCAF and RCN through the American custodial personnel on the East Coast, and US Commander in Chief Pacific (USCinCPAC) would release to Canadian Commander Maritime Forces Pacific (CANCOMARPAC) on the West Coast.[100]

All of this detail served multiple purposes. First, it staved off External Affair's insistence that more technical detail be included. Second, the detail also served to educate the Prime Minister about the specifics of what actually constituted joint control, custody, and release. Third, it clarified for all who were involved what was actually required to achieve a nuclear capability in a way that the Opposition and the media did not and could not understand.

There was one problem. Since the decision to acquire the F-101B was still under discussion and had not been formally accepted by the Americans, it was not included in the supplementary section. Harkness asked Miller about alternative armament for the Voodoo back in April and had been told that the F-101 could carry either two MB-1 and two GAR 1D (or 2A) Falcons or just two Falcons. The Falcon was, as we have seen, a conventional weapon and of lesser effectiveness. Harkness prepared a letter to ask External Affairs to add the F-101B/MB-1 combination to the supplementary agreements, but apparently did not send it, fearing it would be used as a device to delay the whole agreement again.[101] This would come back to haunt the defense people in the future.

The Americans were also concerned about the lack of the nuclear agreement, but increasingly saw it as part of a larger neutralist direction taken by Howard Green. For example, Green told the NATO Ministerial Meeting at Oslo in May that as far as he was concerned, Canada was between the two superpowers and had a duty to reduce the tension between them.[102] In another case, one week before Kennedy was to visit Ottawa, Green publicly rebuked the United States and insisted that she "stop pushing Cuba around." Ambassador Heeney was called into the State Department by a baffled American staff and asked about this. Heeney was "appalled" by Green's behavior.[103]

Livingston Merchant, the American ambassador to Canada, had several private conversations with "the majority of Cabinet, the top hierarchy in External, Mike Pearson . . . and a handful of diplomatic colleagues." Merchant was shocked "that anti-Americanism has gone wide and deep," and that "Cabinet and Mike Pearson have become genuinely concerned that anti-Americanism and talk of neutralism—talk which they have positively encouraged—was going so far as seriously to endanger Canadian national interests." Harkness had demonstrated "courage and conviction," but Merchant was "fearful that Diefenbaker will refuse to reach a decision on [nuclear] weapons for Canada until after the next election. Green's influence is still strong."[104]

Merchant went so far as to meet with Diefenbaker prior to Kennedy's May 1961 Ottawa visit in an effort to circumvent Howard Green. The discussion quickly focused on nuclear weapons. Did the Prime Minister realize that the PINETREE-Voodoo arrangement was predicated on the need for the aircraft to be equipped with nuclear weapons? How could Canada negotiate in good faith for this delivery system if she would not sign the general agreement? Did acceptance of the F-101Bs mean that Canada was about to sign the agreement?

> Diefenbaker told Merchant that he understood American wishes, but had "genuine concern" about Canadian opinion. . . . First, there were strong divisions among the public—and not all opponents were "communists and bums." Second, [External Affairs] was "riddled with wishful thinkers who believed that the Soviets would be propitiated and disarmament prospects improved if only Canada did nothing to provoke [them]. . . . Diefenbaker said that this was a ridiculous view and that cabinet would reach a decision quickly.[105]

Despite all efforts, Diefenbaker-Kennedy personality problems overrode the implementation of the nuclear weapons agreements. The stringent security arrangements set up just prior to the visit produced friction between US Secret Service agents and the Royal Canadian Mounted Police. These "affronts" paled in comparison to Kennedy's use of French in a speech made once he stepped off Air Force One at RCAF Station Uplands on 16 May. Not only was Kennedy's French better than Diefenbaker's fractured mumblings in Canada's other official language, Kennedy once again referred to "Prime Minister Diefen-bawker" and even called Canada, "Canader."[106] To make matters worse, Olive Diefenbaker did not get on well with Jacqueline Kennedy. Olive was a University of Saskatchewan graduate, a high school teacher, and vocational guidance instructor who was frugal. Jackie, on the other hand, was a socialite who was a product of "Vassar, the Sorbonne, [and] Manhattan High Society."[107]

The Kennedy-Diefenbaker discussions involved five topic areas: Cuba, Canada and the Organization of American States (OAS), NATO and nuclear weapons, NATO and Berlin, and the F-101B deal. No military or foreign policy advisors, save the two ambassadors, were present. Diefenbaker retracted Green's statements on Cuba. He wanted to know if the Soviets had placed nuclear weapons in Cuba. Kennedy assured the Prime Minister this had not yet happened, but if the Cubans tried to expand elsewhere in Central America, the Americans would intervene. Kennedy also thought Cuba could be used as a counterweight if the Soviets blockaded or interfered with Berlin traffic. No matter what action the United States took, Kennedy assured Diefenbaker, he would consult Canada first.[108] As for the OAS, Kennedy wanted Canada to join it so that the Americans could have another friendly ally and reduce trade to Cuba. Diefenbaker fobbed this off and discussed Cuban cigars.[109]

The discussion shifted to NATO and nuclear weapons. Kennedy was all for increasing NATO's conventional capability and was concerned about the independent French deterrent. Diefenbaker was opposed to the French deterrent and told Kennedy that there had been "an upsurge of feeling about nuclear weapons" in Canada. There was too much antinuclear weapons mail being sent to him, apparently. This affected Canadian acquisition and storage of nuclear weapons. It was conceivable that, under joint control, storage might be feasible in the future, but "it just could not be done at this time. In fact, he doubted whether he could carry his own Cabinet with him on the issue."[110] Kennedy asserted that if the antinuclear movement in Canada prevailed, it would make Canada neutral in the Cold War. The Prime Minister said that he "would make an effort to change public opinion."[111]

Diefenbaker was being deceptive in this conversation. As we have seen, Canadian public opinion was overwhelmingly in favor of nuclear weapons. Most of the Cabinet members were also favorably inclined, despite Green's machinations. Diefenbaker had already vacillated on the issue of joint control time and again. He now agreed to it, but was vague about when it would be implemented.

Finally, the discussions came to the F-101B swap. Canada was ready to get on with the deal. There was, however, a snag in the American camp:

> in order to be in a position to defend offshore procurement in Canada of $200 million worth of F-104G's in the face of a depressed aircraft industry in the United States and a balance of payments problem, it was essential to be able to demonstrate that the air defenses of both countries were being improved with the transfer of the F-101B's to the RCAF. . . . to make the transfer of these fighters currently in the USAF inventory and currently equipped with nuclear-tipped rockets would result in a degradation rather than an improvement of our air defense if they were armed with conventional rockets.[112]

It is clear from this change in American policy that Merchant (possibly in consultation with Harkness and others) wanted to use the F-104G Mutual Assistance Plan deal and the F-101B Voodoo deal as leverage to get on with the nuclear weapons agreements; that is, the aircraft needed MB-1s to be fully effective, the USAF was stripping its squadrons to provide Canada with interceptors, either sign the agreement or the Mutual Assistance contract might be restructured.

Diefenbaker fell back on the alleged public opinion problem he had with nuclear weapons and promised to alleviate it. He also "hoped that the aircraft arrangement could proceed without awaiting a governmental decision on the matter of nuclear weapons for Canada." Kennedy "again expressed perplexity at the fact that the difficulties were so great for Canada in taking this step."[113]

The personality factor came back into play. Kennedy spent an inordinate period of time with Mike Pearson at a cocktail party, an affront that did not go unnoticed by Diefenbaker. Worse, a Diefenbaker staffer found a memo to the President (penned by Walt W. Rostow) in a garbage can. Titled, "What We Want from the Ottawa Trip," the memo constantly referred to the need for Kennedy "to push" Diefenbaker/Canada on the Organization of American States (OAS), on Laos, and on Latin America. That was bad enough, but apparently someone had scribbled what looked like "SOB" in the margin next to Diefenbaker's name (it was probably "OAS"). Basil Robinson recommended that the Prime Minister return it immediately. An enraged Diefenbaker wanted to lodge a diplomatic protest, but was dissuaded from this action. Diefenbaker put the memo in his safe and would later attempt to use it to blackmail Kennedy. Kennedy was, in his eyes, "a callow young man."[114] In the words of Robert F. Kennedy, "my brother really hated John Diefenbaker. He thought him a contemptible old fool. . . . My brother really hated only two men in all his Presidency. One was Sukarno and the other was Diefenbaker."[115]

The matter of the "push memo" illustrates the Canadian-American cultural gap as much as the Diefenbaker-Kennedy personality clash. In Canada, "push" has more ugly and forcible connotations than it does in the United States. In Canadian parlance, the word "press" would be used in similar circumstances. This misunderstanding was not a minor one, as it had sovereignty implications. It played right to Diefenbaker's increasingly suspicious perception of the United States and it appeared to him that it was now a personal issue. Diefenbaker *was* Canada, and he had been personally slighted yet again; therefore Canada was slighted.

As for the F-101B deal, Cabinet quickly saw the political benefits that would accrue from not only providing a manned interceptor, but from the F-104G MAP arrangement. Orders totaling $200 million would be placed in Canada, of which Canada would put up $50 million, the Americans $150 million. In return for this $50 million and taking over eleven PINETREE sites, Canada got a manned interceptor and support for almost nothing, and "direct employment for [7,000 to 8,000] persons for three years and an equal quantity of employment would be generated indirectly."[116]

Ambassador Heeney met with McNamara's people at the Pentagon, and memoranda of understanding (MOUs) were exchanged. Cabinet met yet again to discuss how to handle the issue publicly. Nuclear weapons were not mentioned in relation to the F-101B acquisition, but the Prime Minister would note the Voodoo was nuclear-capable if asked. The aim of the public statement would be to play up the jobs angle. There was still residual concern about the Opposition taking the government to task for the cancellation of the Arrow, but the Cabinet agreed to the proposal and finally approved it on 9 June 1961.[117] There was nary a peep from the Opposition when Diefenbaker announced that Canada would acquire the F-101B Voodoo interceptor as part of Canada's contribution to NORAD.

On 24 July 1961, Douglas Harkness accepted the formal handover of the first

CF-101B Voodoo at RCAF station Uplands, Ottawa. Emphasizing that the deal symbolized the Canada-US defense partnership, the Minister of National Defence told his audience: "NORAD must be capable of providing defence for the retaliatory forces of Strategic Air Command and for the industrial and highly populated centres of Canada and the United States our air defence must be sufficiently strong to convince a potential aggressor that in an attack upon us with bombers he would suffer prohibitive losses in exchange for highly uncertain gains."[118]

The Berlin Crisis: August–September 1961

The ongoing Berlin Crisis spiked once again in August 1961 with the erection of the Berlin Wall. The Diefenbaker government's response to the Berlin Crisis highlighted both the problems in signing the general government-to-government nuclear agreement and the impact of rapidly evolving NATO strategy on Canadian strategic policy.

The "pause" concept discussed earlier in 1961 was supplemented by other important thinking that would lead to alterations in NATO strategy. Khrushchev's threats over Berlin reached new levels of bellicosity in March and April 1961. American policy makers, specifically Dean Acheson and Robert McNamara, were increasingly concerned about how to respond to the various types of force that the Soviets could use against Berlin. Norstad's LIVE OAK organization was deficient in some ways, since it was purely military in nature and structured to deal with small-scale access blockages. Acheson and McNamara wanted a series of political and economic measures, and an expanded list of military measures now, including the incorporation of nuclear weapons use, increasing NATO conventional forces, and increased SAC readiness. The question was: at what point did LIVE OAK–like activities transition into conventional, tactical nuclear, and strategic nuclear war in NATO's Central Region, and how should the allies, including Canada, be consulted?[119]

The Cabinet discussed this question and others late in July 1961. Diefenbaker, though not specifically referring to strategic intelligence, told the Cabinet that Khrushchev "was now starting to drink again and speak more freely. . . . [He] seemed to think he had superiority over the United States in missiles and nuclear weapons."[120] The Soviet Premier was "challenged at home and by China and must show progress [on] Berlin and the German situation." The East Germans might even try on their own to take over West Berlin. Ambassador Merchant had informed Canada that they were considering instituting measures like calling up Army and Navy reserves to move six divisions to Germany. Canada had to decide on a response and soon. Additionally, Canada also had to make a decision on MB-1 storage and the general government-to-government agreement. These negotiations might take two months, according to Howard Green, and they should be started "now."[121]

Green thought Canada should push for economic sanctions against the Soviets and perhaps deploy a second and maybe even a third brigade group to Europe alongside 4 Canadian Infantry Brigade. French action against Bizerte, Tunisia, was the moral equivalent of Soviet action against Berlin, according to Green.[122] He also thought that the UN should mediate over Berlin and in Algeria. As for nuclear weapons for Canada, Green once again emphasized that acquisition would imperil disarmament talks and would be a provocative move in this time of crisis: "He hoped that

Cabinet would not rush in to approve Canada becoming a nuclear power. . . . It was an issue that might determine whether or not Montreal, Toronto, Hamilton, Ottawa, Vancouver, and other Canadian cities might be blotted off the map . . . [It] was the future of Canadian civilization."[123]

Harkness then weighed in. The issue was not some moral equivalency between Algeria and Germany. Khrushchev's objective was to break up NATO. If NATO did not stand up to the enemy in Berlin, West Germany might leave NATO, reunify, and go neutral, or worse, come under Soviet domination. The United Nations "could not have much effect" and such propositions "had no relationship to reality." Defensive nuclear weapons for Canadian forces were not multimegaton hydrogen bombs. There was no comparison. BOMARCs could not start a war: they were defensive weapons. Diefenbaker tentatively agreed, but Green insisted that joint control infringed on Canadian sovereignty. Diefenbaker thought that the MB-1 agreement, which in his mind had been "held up as a trading point," should continue now as a step towards signing the general agreement.[124]

Green again raised the specter of Armageddon. Merchant, he told the Cabinet, "had left him with the distinct impression that they were now set for nuclear war." Harkness challenged Green on this point. Canada, then, should have the most effective air defense she could get in the time available.[125] This meant accelerating the F-101B program, arming them with MB-1s, and allowing the Americans to store and use MB-1s from Harmon and Goose Bay.

Harkness was satisfied enough by the Cabinet meeting that he had Deputy Minister Willis Armstrong contact Miller to arrange to meet with Robertson to sort out some minor changes to the draft general agreement prior to it going to Cabinet for final approval. After waiting four days, Robertson informed Miller that Green was going on vacation and that he had not yet examined the supplementary agreements at length.[126]

On 3 August, Kennedy sent Diefenbaker a message. In order to provide the best united front possible in the course of the Berlin Crisis and to protect SAC, Kennedy noted:

> There is . . . an aspect of our continental defense which, for reasons which we both understand, is imperfect. This is the lack of orderly arrangements for insuring that the RCAF as well as the USAF should be possessed of nuclear weapons to respond to any attack across the Pole. . . . It would now only be prudent to renew with vigor our efforts to conclude negotiations. . . . I recognize that this is not an easy matter for you, but I do believe that we cannot achieve a successful negotiating position on Germany and Berlin until we have taken every reasonable step to strengthen our military security.[127]

The Prime Minister did not reply for ten days. During this interval, the Soviets started to reinforce the Group of Soviet Forces Germany, which increased the tension once NATO intelligence people assessed and disseminated this information.[128] Miller was having further problems with Robertson, who had altered the wording of the draft agreement so that American responsibilities regarding custody were not defined. The detail that existed in the former draft regarding the release procedure for the warheads was excised. Since this was the point in American law on which these agreements were based, the new draft was unacceptable. Miller promptly informed Harkness.[129] Diefenbaker finally called Kennedy and promised that he would have Harkness and Green expedite the nuclear weapons agreement.[130]

In the interim Dean Rusk prepared a classified speech for the North Atlantic Council, which was transmitted verbatim to Canada one week prior to its presentation.[131] Rusk called for linkage between LIVE OAK and NATO. Berlin contingency measures were risky given the state of the Shield forces in the Central Region. Consequently, there had to be closer coordination between the two activities. Allied Command Europe had to be at a higher state of alert before any LIVE OAK measures could be implemented. NATO, therefore, "must also be prepared across a spectrum of military operations,"[132] which could include the reinforcement of Europe, the deployment of the ACE Mobile forces, movement of the Shield forces to their Emergency Defense Plan positions, the conduct of another Berlin airlift, the harassment of East Bloc shipping, the conduct of small- and medium-scale probes down the Berlin access routes, and finally the use of nuclear weapons in limited demonstrations, direct nuclear support of probes, or even large-scale use against bases in the USSR.[133]

The Joint Staff completed some anticipatory planning starting on 3 August, but the Rusk speech gave more impetus to these proceedings. Canada should at the outset reinforce 4 Brigade in West Germany with an additional eight hundred men to bring it up to war establishment strength. Second, 3 Canadian Infantry Brigade should prepare to deploy to West Germany. Third, 1 SSM Battery should take its Honest John rockets and launch equipment and deploy to join 4 Brigade in 1961 rather than in 1962. Perhaps a "buck shee" arrangement could be made with the British to access their Honest John warhead stockpile in the British Army of the Rhine (BAOR). Finally, the Army recommended accelerating the National Survival program and the strategic materials stockpile program in anticipation of nuclear attack.[134]

Diefenbaker then gave a speech at Halifax, Nova Scotia, in which he declared those who thought Canada should withdraw from NATO if forced to accept nuclear weapons were "dangerous to the survival of freedom itself. . . . Would you, faced with the overwhelming power of Soviet might in East Germany close to West Berlin with large divisions fully armed, place in the hands of those who guard the portals of freedom nothing but bows and arrows?"[135]

Another long Cabinet meeting on Berlin followed on 17 August. Green pressed for a UN peacekeeping force for Berlin and thought Canada "should not just fall in line with the Americans by taking actions which would tend to add to the atmosphere of threat." Green also discussed the Rusk speech in the NAC. He wanted the Cabinet to allow him to talk to Rusk and get him to back off on Berlin contingency planning since it was too provocative, in his view.[136]

Harkness countered Green's pacifism. Canada needed to sign the general nuclear agreement. That was the best way that Canada could prepare for the crisis, next to dispatching more forces to Europe. The situation was dire. The Chiefs believed that the Soviets would not necessarily go to war over Berlin, "but that war could occur nevertheless, particularly if there was a revolt in East Germany and if West German forces were tempted to move in and help."[137] National Survival measures should also be accelerated. Cabinet would only agree to reinforcing 4 Brigade, to studying the deployment of 3 Brigade to Germany and to implementing National Survival measures.[138]

As for nuclear weapons, Green finally submitted the draft agreement to Cabinet on 22 August. After a detailed briefing on the agreement itself, Cabinet members would only agree to "give further consideration to the matter" at a future meeting."[139]

The next day, the Cabinet conducted an extended meeting on the draft agreement. Diefenbaker was now concerned "that if negotiations were started with the U.S. the fact that they were taking place would almost certainly become known and would be interpreted as meaning that Canada had taken a decision in principle to obtain stockpiles of nuclear warheads."[140]

The Prime Minister was convinced that nuclear weapons would be acceptable for Canada's NATO forces but he was concerned about opposition backlash over nuclear weapons in Canada. Diefenbaker wanted deniability. In other words, negotiations were not supposed to imply that Canada would actually get nuclear warheads for its systems in Canada. The Prime Minister was, therefore, prepared to bargain in bad faith with the Americans because of his fear of Pearson and the Liberals. Cabinet delayed a decision yet again, and then again on 25 August.[141]

Canada committed to accepting nuclear weapons and her strategic policy, alliances, and forces were carefully structured to use them to deter and, if deterrence failed, limit the damage that could be wrought on Canada and her allies by the Soviet's use of nuclear weapons. All Canadian decision makers involved in strategic policy, elected and unelected, knew this to be true. The perspective voiced by Green, Robertson, and others flew in the face of all this, not to mention what the Canadian people (as opposed to the Liberal Party, the media, and the academics) actually wanted. To undermine the protection of the Canadian people, against their wishes and especially during the Berlin Crisis, was morally wrong. It is unfortunate that Prime Minister John Diefenbaker was complicit in this effort for his personal, self-interested objectives.

Green's views on arms control and disarmament were shattered on 22 August 1961, when the Soviet Union embarked upon an aggressive atmospheric nuclear test program. The Soviets conducted fifty nuclear shots between 22 August and 30 October; the last one conducted in the Arctic totaled approximately 59 megatons. Radioactive fallout drifted over Canada.[142] NATO forces in Europe even embarked on some civil defense measures in the face of noticeable increased fallout from these tests. The Americans soon joined in with Operation NOUGAT, which, unlike Soviet tests, consisted mostly of "clean" underground shots.[143] Rather than railing against Soviet nuclear saber rattling, Diefenbaker was angry about the lack of consultation with Canada and NATO on the American test program. Diefenbaker now swung in Green's direction on the nuclear weapons negotiations issue. The Prime Minister announced in Cabinet that if the Americans did not accede to joint control, the deal was off. Nobody bothered to tell the Americans.[144]

All of Canada's planned nuclear delivery systems had to have nuclear weapons to be effective and in no way were to "be compared with such strategic nuclear weapons as are maintained by the United Kingdom, the United States, and the Soviet Union."[145] There were real, quantifiable threats, as Douglas Harkness pointed out: "the situation is much the same as that of a man living in a lonely cabin in the woods who fears he may be attacked by a bear. He does not wait until the bear actually attacks him to buy a rifle, but secures it beforehand and has it ready in the event of need."[146]

Paul Hellyer, oblivious of events, argued in the House that ICBMs made air defense measures useless and "We continue to believe that it is not worth while to put Canada into the atomic club."[147] Canada's priority, in his view, should be on building up NATO's conventional forces and "if atomic weapons of the defensive type are required . . . in NATO, we would not object to Canadian forces being so equipped if these weapons came under NATO collective control."[148] Pearson also shifted gears in a House speech on 14 September, arguing that the only sure way to maintain peace was through SAC and the ability to protect that deterrent. Then, during a 15 September House debate, Pearson argued that joint control made Canada a member of the so-called nuclear club and it also interfered with disarmament negotiations. Canada should, perhaps, restrict herself to the warning function or "birdwatching" as it was condescendingly called by the government. Now it was the Opposition's turn to be vague, contradictory, and obscure on the nuclear weapons issue.[149] In response, Harkness gave Pearson a blast: "We would warn the Americans that the enemy was coming, we would tell him who he is, we would fix and track him, but then we would virtuously withdraw and let the Americans do the killing. This is a solution worthy of Pontius Pilate, not of a Lester B. Pearson and his associates."[150]

A serious problem now developed in the NAC. Not all LIVE OAK nations wanted close coordination with NATO defense planning in the Central Region. At the same time some NATO member nations were not impressed with what appeared to them to be a "big three" device to control when NATO went to war over Berlin. The American ambassador to NATO, Thomas Finletter, warned Washington that if there was no consultation among France, the UK, and the United States with the rest of the Alliance, NATO "might even fall apart." Finletter "learned in strictest confidence [that] Canada, Italy, and the Netherlands are countries which have expressed dissatisfaction . . . and have implied that if the matter is not corrected they cannot be counted on."[151] The Belgians then joined the revolt. The net result of the application of this pressure over the next two years was to focus more attention on developing a true flexible response strategy for NATO that would directly affect Canadian strategic policy and force structure in 1963 and 1964.

Inching Towards a Canadian Nuclear Capability: June–December 1961

The process of equipping the Canadian forces with nuclear delivery systems progressed slowly throughout the last half of 1961. There was much to do, and the RCAF in particular exploited its formal and informal relationships with the USAF and the USN to the maximum. In particular, the RCAF used the existing nuclear weapons information sharing agreements to maximum effect and the Americans even bent the rules at times.[152]

The first Canadair CF-104 flew on 14 June 1961, but 6 Operational Strike-Reconnaissance Training Unit (later changed to 6 OTU) at Cold Lake, Alberta, would not receive its first single seat CF-104 until September. The first dual-seat CF-104D aircraft did not arrive until January 1962. Prior to training at Cold Lake, the first RCAF CF-104 pilots were sent on course to Chatham, New Brunswick, where they started flying CF-86 Sabres in low-level "profile" navigation missions against the many covered bridges in that province.[153] One area that caused problems was the delivery method. NATO authorities would not tell the RCAF how the weapons were to be delivered, so the RCAF training personnel built all three methods (retarded, toss, and dive), into the curriculum basing this on some sanitized USAF F-104C and F-105 manuals that had been acquired through the Canadian Joint Staff Mission Washington.[154]

Another holdup relating to the lack of government decision on nuclear weapons involved the communications arrangements for the storage sites at Zweibrücken and Baden-Soellingen. If the government wanted a separate release channel from Ottawa, in addition to the American and NATO channels, this would require modification to the buildings, antenna parks, trunk lines, and headquarters. Arrangements would also have to made with the West Germans, who owned the land. Plans were drawn up for this capability just in case the government demanded it.[155]

1 Air Division staff and RCAF staff officers at SHAPE, AIRCENT, and 4 ATAF had conducted an intense information gathering campaign throughout 1961 with the aim of being as prepared as possible without the actual service-to-service agreement necessary to achieve a full nuclear capability. This included the formulation of a complete checklist of information. The planners wanted to know about USAFE OPLAN NR 143-59, the nuclear strike plan; how the lock wires and seals on the arming systems worked; what the safety criteria were for aircraft on Quick Reaction Alert (QRA); how the crews and pilots would be evaluated; how communications might function. Not all of this information was provided by USAFE and 4 ATAF.[156]

It was not enough to just acquire aircraft and train air and ground crews. 1 Air Division planners learned that there were more than eight hundred targets within 4 ATAF's area of responsibility alone, half of which were strike targets and half of which were reconnaissance targets. 1 Air Division needed an expanded intelligence organization to handle the Canadian portion of this load, whatever this proportion might be. Since pilots would be tasked to handle multiple targets, the staff figured that they needed to be familiar with at least 4000 separate targets.[157] By May, Air Marshal Campbell told Harkness, "a great deal has been accomplished by close liaison with the USAF. This liaison is enabling us to engineer into the aircraft the capability of carrying nuclear weapons. It is enabling us also to begin the preparation of safety studies, loading, and delivery hand book."[158]

The CF-101 work-up was easier in many ways. The sixty-six aircraft, fifty-six singles and ten dual trainers, had previously belonged to USAF CONAD squadrons (most of which were located in the southern United States) that were disbanded so that Canada could receive them. In 1961 the RCAF cadre pilots attended ground school at Otis AFB and then did flight training at Hamilton AFB. There they learned the workings and tactical employment of the GAR-II Falcon and, to a lesser extent, the MB-1 Genie. The course was hampered by the security clearance problem, though two navigators were "accidentally" loaded on a USAF course in which certain information on how the MB-1 was to be operationally employed was made available to them. The pilots learned the recommended escape maneuver (placing the belly of the aircraft to the blast). All of the crews were given a combat ready check by the USAF staff. None of the crew members were told outright at the time what the exact yield of the MB-1 was. Upon graduation this RCAF cadre went to Namao, Alberta, to train Canadian CF-101 crews and passed on all of this information throughout the fall of 1961.[159]

There was also movement on the nuclear ASW front. At some point in 1961, a US Navy mobile training team was sent to Canada under the auspices of the Joint Atomic Information Exchange Group to conduct a four-day course on nuclear weapons safety and aircraft compatibility with the Mk 101 NDB (nuclear depth bomb) for both the RCAF and RCN.[160] The RCN then established Project SNOWFLAKE to see what exactly was needed to rewire the CS2F Trackers to carry armament circuits for NDBs.[161] Liaison was established between the RCN and the US Navy Naval Weapons Evaluation Facility (NWEF) at Kirtland AFB, New Mexico, to schedule weapons compatibility trials. As with the CF-101 training, there were a number of information blocks. The NWEF would release only information that had already been released under the 1955 and 1959 information-sharing agreements. If the RCN wanted more nuclear weapons restricted data information, a formal application had to made through the AFSWP.[162]

An RCAF team traveled to Kirtland AFB, New Mexico, in September to visit the NWEF in order to examine the possibilities of modifying the RCAF's P2V7 Neptune for Mk 101 nuclear weapons delivery. All the NWEF needed was a Neptune wiring diagram from the RCAF, as the RCAF Neptune's electric system for releasing conventional ASW weapons were slightly different from USN Neptunes. From this the NWEF could give the RCAF the appropriate standards for the safety and release system. The NWEF was even willing to certify the weapon-loading equipment, but the RCAF had not brought this with them.[163]

By October 1961, the RCAF realized that the task of transforming the RCAF to accept nuclear weapons was much larger than had been anticipated and could no longer continue on an ad hoc, delivery system basis. The technological complexity of the CF-104, in addition to the stringent safety requirements demanded by the USAF in the carriage of nuclear weapons, posed staff and coordination problems. The situation was different from the BOMARC and CF-101 systems, since they had already been designed to use nuclear weapons and had all of the appropriate safety systems built into their design and maintenance procedures. The problems with the nuclear ASW program straddled both extremes, since the P2V2 Neptune was an American-built aircraft, and the Americans had already modified theirs to carry NDBs, while the Argus was a Canadian aircraft that had no such modification as yet. MAC had a Neptune at Kirtland, and it had been modified for Mk 101 delivery, but the entire installation for the Mk 101 had to be designed from the ground up.[164]

There was still no movement in Cabinet on the general agreement by October 1961. The first BOMARC missiles started to arrive in Canada on 19 October (though they were without warheads and they would not be placed in their launch shelters until December), while 1 SSM Battery was prepared to launch a rocket with a dummy warhead for the benefit of Canadian policy makers to prove that they were ready. NATO allies in Europe wanted to know how much space 1 SSM Battery needed for nuclear storage and communications systems. These events prompted Harkness to prepare yet another plea to Cabinet to sign the agreement.[165] However, Norman Robertson was somehow able to prevent the topic from being added to the Cabinet's agenda.[166]

At the same time the Joint Staff was asked, with RCAF help, to prepare a working paper that could be attached to the Cabinet memo. This paper was in part structured to refute all of the antinuclear weapons arguments that had so far been raised. It was an extremely blunt piece of staff work:

> Through her participation in NATO, Canada is committed politically and militarily to a nuclear defence strategy and cannot shirk her defence responsibilities while expecting a full voice in the Alliance. To reject nuclear weapons for her own armed forces, while supporting a nuclear strategy, can only weaken the Alliance and prejudice Canada's stature in the eyes of the other nations of the world.[167]

For those who believed that Canada would be the first middle power to join the so-called nuclear club, the Joint Staff pointed out that membership was restricted to those nations with an independent strategic capability. Joint control did not count, and Canada would have joint control. In fact, Italy and Turkey, by their acceptance of Jupiter IRBMs, predated Canada in acquiring joint control of nuclear weapons. The proposition that the Soviets would now give nuclear weapons to the Warsaw Pact satellite nations on the basis that Canada was now acquiring them was equally wrong as "Soviet behavior would indicate that the USSR needs no such excuse to dictate what armament it will provide . . . it will be because of military necessity."[168]

Speculation that Canada's acquisition of nuclear weapons would increase the threat of nuclear war was unsupported. To the contrary, "if North America were to come under attack, it is most unlikely that Canada would be spared because she did not possess them."[169]

The disarmament arguments were the easiest ones to refute, according to the Joint Staff, as "such an approach is difficult to reconcile with Canada's sales of Uranium"[170] to Canadian allies, which reached at one point 50% of the material the Americans needed for their stockpile.

The most spurious argument against Canadian nuclear weapons acquisition was "if Canada adopts nuclear weapons, she may forfeit her influence with the 'uncommitted nations' and with it their ability to act as peacemaker." The Joint Staff pointed out that the *Soviets* had not lost any influence with the so-called uncommitted nations by her possession of a nuclear stockpile. Canada's "greatest ability to exert influence undoubtedly lies in her partnerships in NATO and NORAD, where she has a voice and influence far greater than her national stature would suggest. By shirking from meeting her NATO and NORAD commitments to adopt nuclear weapons, she can only prejudice this voice and influence."[171]

In a memo to the Joint Staff, Miller gloomily told them: "I do not want this paper distributed. It reads too much like a propaganda blurb for atomic weapons. I do not know what it can accomplish."[172] In retrospect it should have been leaked through the RCAF to its supporters to have any dramatic effect.

The Army had not been lax on the introduction of Honest John into its force structure. The equipment was delivered in July 1961 and included twenty-four practice rockets equipped with a spotting charge. There were no plans to acquire conventional high-explosive warheads for either battery and it was well understood within the Army and elsewhere that it was strictly a nuclear delivery system. Throughout the summer of 1961, Commander 4 Brigade entered into discussions on Special Ammunition Storage and access with HQ US Army Europe. The Americans would discuss only administrative facilities for the custodial staff: "HQ USAREUR will not participate in further discussions in the absence of a satisfactory bilateral agreement between Canada and the US on the use and control of nuclear warheads."[173] All was not lost, however. 4 Brigade HQ privately discussed warhead access with HQ BAOR, with which, as we will recall, 4 CIB worked extremely closely. Perhaps the British could be persuaded to develop an "understanding"?

1 SSM Battery at this point was "not technically trained on the arming procedures associated with nuclear warheads," though it had been able to acquire a nuclear warhead training simulator device in preparation for this advanced training and was capable of performing all of the other actions necessary to launch and tactically employ Honest Johns. The British arrangement with USAREUR was that their Honest John warheads were stored in sites that had British security teams and American warhead custodians. The British transported the warheads to the firing sites upon release and the American team armed the warheads there. In other words, even though there was no formal arrangement for Canadian-designated warheads from the warhead stockpile allocated to BAOR, there remained the possibility that in an emergency, warheads could be made available to 1 SSM Battery in Europe.[174]

BAOR and 4 CIB had already established, on approval by the West German government, a Special Ammunition Storage Site would be constructed at Hemer within the 4 CIB garrison area. Canada and the UK would share construction costs. Until such time as Canada signed its bilateral agreements, the site would house warheads and rocket motors for 50 Medium Regiment, Royal Artillery. Once the agreements were signed, then Canadian-designated warheads and rocket motors would be moved into the site or a portion of those warheads already in the site would be designated as 4 CIB–tasked. Until the site was actually built in 1964, warheads and rocket motors were available from a number of other British SAS sites located at Dortmund, Muenster, and Ludenscheid.[175]

Harkness went to Cabinet twice in November 1961 to demand a decision on the general agreement. The missiles were starting to arrive at the BOMARC site at

North Bay, and 1 SSM Battery was about to leave for Europe. These units would be useless without nuclear warheads. When asked, Harkness told Cabinet that conventional warheads might be made available, but they would have to be produced and this could take six months. The weapons would not be effective even with conventional warheads, since the plans and concept of operations on which their acquisition was predicated required nuclear warheads. No decision was reached on 21 November (Diefenbaker even ordered the Cabinet Secretary to leave the room and no notes were taken). Harkness returned on 30 November and told the Cabinet that a recent Gallup poll concluded that 61% of Canadians were in favor of nuclear weapons acquisition, 8% had no opinion, and 31% were against. How could the Cabinet continue to stall on this matter when the people were in favor of these defensive measures? No decision was reached.[176]

The CF-101 interceptors were delivered to Canada throughout the fall of 1961. The first squadron, 425 (Alouette) Squadron, converted at Namao, Alberta, in October and served as the operational conversion unit. Between October 1961 and March 1962, five CF-100 squadrons underwent operational conversion at Namao prior to deploying to Comox, Ottawa, North Bay, and Bagotville.[177]

Detailed construction information for the SAS sites was not supposed to be passed on in the absence of the general government-to-government and service-to-service agreements. However, the USAF had bent the rules for some of this information so that BOMARC site construction could progress. Campbell wanted to get similar information for the CF-101 sites, but progress was slow in the fall and "entirely in the hands of the USAF and dependent on their cooperation and goodwill." By December, the information was in the hands of the architects, and the sites had been selected.[178]

The RCN quietly continued with Project SNOWFLAKE. On 7 December two RCN CS2F Trackers from development squadron VX-10 flew to Kirtland AFB "to carry out the clearance drop test of a simulated nuclear depth bomb. The drop was successful and the CS2F was given a clean bill of health allowing the modifications to be subsequently incorporated into additional Trackers."[179] On the same day, the third and fourth BOMARC missiles belonging to 446 SAM Squadron were placed in their launch shelters at the North Bay BOMARC base.[180]

The battle for the general agreement continued, with Hugh Campbell expressing private concern that External Affairs meddling in the matter of custody and control might imperil the ability of the defense forces in getting timely authorization for their use, assuming that the agreements were not scuttled completely.[181] Harkness was forced to add the CF-101/MB-1 section to the Robertson-proposed supplemental agreements, which once again gave Robertson and Green an excuse to delay the process.[182]

The release of another Gallup poll result in December 1961 indicated two-thirds of the Canadian people supported nuclear weapons acquisition.[183]

Conclusion

The ongoing struggle over the Canada-US government-to-government nuclear agreement remained polarized, with Douglas Harkness and Air Marshal Frank Miller on one side and Howard Green and Norman Robertson (supported by George Ignatieff) on the other. Green and Robertson introduced deliberate delay tactics that aggravated the situation. The Prime Minister was in the middle, but was leaning in Green and Robertson's direction. This lean was accentuated due in equal parts to fear of Opposition criticism in the House of Commons and to the unnecessary Kennedy-Diefenbaker personality conflict, which permeated all aspects of the Canada-US relationship. Green can be blamed for the disunited front presented by the Diefenbaker government since he behaved as though Canada was a neutral, nonaligned nation, while at the same time Canada acquired the nuclear-capable CF-101B interceptor aircraft to replace the aging CF-100 fleet.

The Berlin Crisis, however, indicated the need for a wide spectrum of responses to Soviet belligerency and that such measures could be put into action only with a secure strategic nuclear deterrent. By procrastinating on the nuclear agreement, Canada was unable to contribute to the protection of this deterrent. NATO strategy continued to evolve during this period with an emphasis on more conventional forces and better nuclear forces. Strategic conceptual musings focused on the pause concept. Canada's force structure was generally in a good position to deal with any proposed changes to NATO's strategy, but her ability to fight a protracted conventional war had deteriorated dramatically with unwillingness of the Diefenbaker government to pay for it.

Once again, we are confronted with the growing divergence between Canada's long established, realistic, and acceptable national security policy and the behavior of Howard Green and his supporters. It was not realistic to seriously arrest the momentum of the existing national security policy. There was a real threat. Canada had made commitments. Canada had to remain militarily capable to carry these commitments out, not merely for prestige reasons, but for the legitimate security objectives consonant with those commitments. Too much money, manpower, industrial resources, and diplomatic effort was invested in Canada's contribution to NATO and NORAD. Too many Canadians were gainfully employed. Green and Robertson refused to accept this reality and thought they could do an about-face by resorting to manipulative bureaucratic methods and ignoring the interests of the Canadian people. Deliberately blocking acceptance of the nuclear agreements during the Berlin Crisis was the height of folly. The situation would only get worse in 1962 with the advent of a new crisis.

11

DODGING THE NUCLEAR BULLET: CANADA AND THE CUBAN MISSILE CRISIS, 1962–1963

Oh Superman, where are you now?
When everything's gone wrong somehow
The men of steel, men of power,
Well, they're losing control by the hour.
–GENESIS, *LAND OF CONFUSION*

There are no dangerous weapons; there are
only dangerous men.
–ROBERT HEINLEIN, *STARSHIP TROOPERS*

Introduction

The third act in the nuclear weapons crisis drama was its climax. Canadian-American relations plunged into a tailspin, assisted by John Diefenbaker and John F. Kennedy's estrangement. The ongoing antinuclear machinations emanating from External Affairs interfered with the formal accession to a nuclear weapons–sharing arrangement between the two countries, while the armed forces continued their informal and incremental approach to achieving a nuclear capability. The complex interplay among personalities, technology, and strategic policy brought out the worst political crisis in Canadian history as Nikita Khrushchev and John F. Kennedy squared off over Cuba and threatened to launch the world on the path to Armageddon. After the world pulled back from the brink, Mike Pearson and the Opposition counterattacked and knocked down the rotting structure that was the Diefenbaker government that they had successfully undermined over the past four years.

Developments in Early 1962

The Progressive Conservatives were suffering from internal division in 1962. There was a significant "dump Dief" camp that believed that a future election would finish off the party if Diefenbaker remained in control. The Prime Minister called for a snap election in June 1962 to stave off opposition from within his own party's ranks, and to shore up the government in the House. It was against this backdrop that the next phase of the nuclear crisis played out.[1]

The RCAF toyed with the idea that, in the absence of a formal government-to-government agreement guaranteeing Canadian access to nuclear warheads, some form of "understanding" could be arranged with the Americans so that a portion of the stockpile could be delivered to Canadian units in an emergency. At some undetermined point in 1962, the USN established one such understanding with regard to providing nuclear depth bombs to RCN and RCAF maritime forces in an emergency.[2]

In January 1962, Air Marshal Campbell privately expressed his concern to his staff:

> somebody might mention to the Minister [Harkness] the possibility of nuclear warheads for both the BOMARCS and the MB-1s remaining in storage at selected points in the [United States] to be available for deployment to Canada under emergency conditions only. We all know that there would be an unacceptable time requirement . . . but the CAS wishes it to be spelled out.[3]

In other words, the RCAF did not want a possible emergency standby plan serving as a solution to a political problem.

Unfortunately for the RCAF, Robertson, Green, and Ignatieff got wind of the standby concept and sent a memo outlining it to Diefenbaker in January.[4] Bob Bryce refused to support External's proposal and even cautioned the Prime Minister against considering it, let alone publicly discussing it.[5] Diefenbaker then gave a press conference on 24 February in which he baldly stated nuclear weapons could be made available to Canadian delivery systems within half an hour to an hour of an alert. This speech was repeated in the House of Commons two days later. When queried by the Opposition about the lack of a formal agreement, the Prime Minister argued it was an acceptable course of action, since in his view, the American law demanding joint control was unacceptable, and until it was changed a standby system had to suffice. This was somewhat misleading.[6]

The Americans were nothing short of "astonished."[7] No such arrangement existed, and even if it were formally agreed to, estimates implied that it would take at least fifteen hours to move the weapons to Canada. It was merely one possibility under examination by the RCAF. In State's view, the speech:

> stem[med] from [a] compound of ignorance of [a] complex subject, profound reluctance [to] face up to [a] disagreeable subject, [an] unfortunate propensity [to] point to [the] US as immovable stumbling block and heat of the moment in lively parliamentary exchange with Pearson for whom he feels [a] positive emotional dislike. . . . [the] liberal opposition despite its own less than forthright stand on nuclear weapons, will not let the matter lie and will seek daily to probe this soft spot.[8]

On 28 February Diefenbaker denied in the House that such an arrangement existed. He then went on to emphasize that such an arrangement *should* exist.

Professor Douglas LePan, formerly of External Affairs, came out publicly against the scheme. He argued that such a stance would undermine the deterrent value of the weapons.[9]

Sensing an opening, and with that opening the possibility to generate movement on the government-to-government agreement, Dean Rusk went public in a news conference. If Canada wanted nuclear weapons, Canada must decide for herself. Custody must be in American hands, but the United States was willing to work out joint control issues with Canada. Rusk emphasized that the United States was willing to discuss the matter "at any time."[10] Ambassador Livingston Merchant then met with Diefenbaker, who implied that negotiations might in fact proceed.[11]

The Opposition in the House then subjected Minister of National Defence Douglas Harkness "to an intense prolonged grilling" on nuclear weapons. Pearson, Hellyer, and Martin all took turns lambasting the government for not living up to its NATO responsibilities. This time the attack was based on the government's alleged reneging on providing nuclear warheads for the CF-104 strike force. Harkness "put on an impressive display of evasive tactics during the four hour discussion" and declared, accurately, that the point was moot since the CF-104s would not be shipped to Europe for some time. Pearson then hit upon the one-hour standby "non-arrangement," asserting that this plan was "preposterous." Harkness, of course, could not comment in any case as there was no such arrangement or agreement.[12]

The chasm between Diefenbaker and Kennedy then reached new depths. Diefenbaker's gracious congratulations regarding John Glenn's orbital flight received no official acknowledgment or reply from the White House.[13] The entire affair took a disturbing turn when Diefenbaker summoned Livingston Merchant for a tirade that Merchant described as a situation in which Diefenbaker "was excited to a degree disturbing in a leader of an important country, and closer to hysteria that I have ever seen him."[14] The Liberals were making full use of the Kennedy-Pearson meeting. Kennedy, in the Prime Minister's view, was deliberately interfering in Canadian affairs. Diefenbaker then pulled out the infamous May 1961 "push memo" from his special safe. The Canadian public, he believed, would go crazy when they were informed that the Americans were prepared to "push" Canada in many ways. He was now "forced" to use it in the election campaign to counter the Opposition.[15]

Merchant was horrified. At first he lied to the Prime Minister, telling him Kennedy had a great deal of respect for him. He urged him not to reveal the contents of the memo as it "had no official status and was not intended for Canadian eyes." There would be a "backlash," and the Prime Minister would be forced to explain how he came by the memo in the first place. As a last ditch effort, Merchant than played the NATO card:

> Finally I said that the Prime Minister bore a heavy responsibility as an ally of the United States and as a member of the Free World coalition. Domestic elections could be divisive in any country. I thought he should give sober historic thought before he responded as he intended to the capitalization of his political rival on an incident that was innocent and certainly not intended as intervention.[16]

Merchant was disturbed by the encounter. He informed the State Department:

> Given Canadian sensibilities and apprehensions of American influence, it
> is in our interest neither to intervene in Canadian domestic elections nor to
> give the appearance of doing so. Were we to intervene and be successful,
> our candidate would be labeled as a running dog of the United States and
> inhibited from acting along lines agreeable to us.[17]

The ambassador recommended that Kennedy arrange a visit with Diefenbaker
to solve this one. The President of the United States exploded, referred to the Prime
Minister of Canada as "a prick, a fucker, a shit," and refused to have any further
personal communications with the man.[18]

NATO Strategy and the Ministerial Meeting at Athens, April–May 1962

While the leaders' relationship broke down, NATO strategy talks in Athens assumed
new importance to Canadian strategic policy in many ways. NATO was trying to
redefine strategy without declaring that it was, in fact, doing so, and Canadian analysis
of the meeting provides us with insight into this process, as well as American strategy that affected Canadian interests and nuclear weapons. MC 14/2 (revised) remained the dominant expression of NATO strategy in 1962. The most important
challenge was the revolt in NAC after the Berlin Crisis, led by Canada over the
tripartite domination of NATO strategic policy.

A dedicated NATO activist, Secretary General Dirk Stikker ensured that the
main strategic issues did not remain on the back burner in the NATO forum. Stikker
was not in favor of challenging MC 14/2 (revised) at this point since it would undermine NATO unity in what was then a perpetual crisis over Berlin. He did favor, as
General Norstad did, increasing conventional forces and moving them forward to
the Iron Curtain from the Weser-Lech line. Stikker was concerned that, without a
formal understanding between NATO and the United States, American nuclear support remained uncertain in a crisis that did not meet the pattern of MC 14/2 (revised). American provision of more and better nuclear weapons information would
go a long way toward reducing the unease.[19]

To this end the NATO Defense Committee generated two studies on NATO
strategy by the end of February and passed them on to member states for discussion.[20] NATO countries were asked to consider increasing conventional forces; that
a pause concept might be incorporated into emergency defense planning in ACE;
that NATO might make "discriminate use of nuclear weapons" in order to prevent
escalation to strategic nuclear war; and the possibility that NATO could fight a protracted large-scale conventional war to contain an enemy attack.[21]

These ideas reflected a number of problems. The first was the ongoing issue
of a graduated response to Berlin incidents and the possibility of escalation to strategic nuclear war. Second, the West German population and its leaders felt increasingly exposed in that the defense of the Weser-Lech line did not guarantee the

security of the eastern-most portion of the country: this had domestic political repercussions that could be exploited by the enemy.[22]

Other issues affecting Canadian strategic policy were raised at this time. The British advocated the creation of a "NATO Peacetime Nuclear Administrative Committee." This was the genesis of the NATO Nuclear Planning Group which emerged later in the 1960s. The aim was to give the European NATO members "a greater sense of participation in the whole range of NATO military planning," that is, nuclear weapons planning. It would have an advisory function, not a command function. It would handle liaison and coordination between SACLANT and SACEUR and assess Soviet nuclear planning.[23] If such a committee was formed, the CF-104 strike force would therefore allow Canada access to more corridors of influence within the alliance.

George Ignatieff had by this time replaced Jules Leger, who suffered a heart attack, as Canada's ambassador to NATO.[24] Ignatieff and the External Affairs staff produced a detailed examination of the direction in which they believed American and NATO strategy was heading and what it meant for Canada. The External study asserted that there really was no new direction in Kennedy's strategic policy, that it was merely "a clarification, a sharpening up and a franker facing of major issues. . . . Some new phrases have appeared in the American vocabulary but these do not represent new ideas."[25] In essence, the Kennedy administration was merely emphasizing adherence to the existing *conventional* MC 70 goals with some fine-tuning regarding theatre nuclear forces command and control. The real problem, and it was not a new one, was the dispute between the UK and the US regarding what constituted the "correct" balance of conventional and nuclear forces and how the nuclear forces would be used (incrementally or all at once).[26]

The External staff argued that the new interpretation of American strategic thinking with regard to NATO was not something that was to be imposed on Europe to ensure American dominance. Rather, "the effect of nearly exclusive reliance upon US nuclear striking power is to saddle the US government with an appalling responsibility and to place at risk in every minor crisis the cities and population of North America."[27] In other words, the Americans should not be expected to have the onus placed entirely on them by the Europeans. On the other hand, the staffers were convinced the Americans and British were concerned about the West Germany having too high a proportion of the conventional forces in Europe (with its corresponding effects on who controlled operational strategy in the Central Region) and having in the future a perhaps less friendly West German government with access to long-range nuclear weapons capable of striking the Soviet Union, weapons that might not be under NATO control.[28]

There were vital Canadian interests at stake in the resolution of the NATO strategy question. These included:

1. The political solidarity of NATO and its vulnerability to external threats and pressures;
2. The distribution of power within the Alliance, and specifically the avoidance of a German preponderance or a German nuclear weapons program;

3.   The political health and vitality of the North Atlantic Community, including its ability to formulate and pursue constructive policies in fields apart from defence.[29]

Canada could not remain aloof from the strategy debate. If the British and Germans were successful in getting NATO to implement an "all or nothing strategy" and war occurred, "withdrawal from NATO would not relieve Canada in any material degree from the possibly disastrous consequences" of a nuclear war. It might be embarrassing if Canada was asked to contribute more conventional forces, but that was easier to live with.

As for the nuclear command and control issue, the Canadian stance was that the Americans should have sole custody and even control of nuclear warheads tasked to NATO. The Europeans should be encouraged to accept this, despite the Canadian position on the joint control and custody issue for weapons in North America. External Affairs was not in favor of the NATO MRBM program and was convinced that American Polaris submarines assigned to SACEUR could do the job just as well.[30]

Canada's ability to influence all of these debates was constrained, however:

> The present unresolved status of the nuclear weapons issue in Canada clearly represents a serious restriction upon Canada's ability to pursue a constructive role in accordance with Canadian interests in the great strategic debate within NATO. This is likely to be true with the passage of time and as the debate enters a more decisive phase. . . . Canada is exposed to the charge that she has failed to live up to the commitment accepted at the 1957 Heads of Government meeting. This must be expected to reduce Canada's prestige and influence in the complex and difficult negotiations which lie ahead. In a general sense, Canada's stand on nuclear weapons invites the charge that Canada is indifferent to the security requirements of her Allies. . . . More specifically it deprives Canada of two potent arguments:
> (a) The North American commitment to NATO is beyond question;
> (b) Joint stockpiling arrangements are a feasible alternative to the establishment of independent nuclear deterrents.[31]

Without a nuclear-armed CF-104 force, Honest Johns, and significant conventional forces stationed in Europe, Canada had little credibility and influence in the NAC. This would threaten Canadian influence in the short term and Canadian security in the long term.

The next move in the strategic debate involved Norstad. In the revised Emergency Defense Plan in April 1962, Norstad incorporated the pause concept, but not as it had previously been understood. He now officially recognized there would be some form of preliminary conventional phase prior to Phase I of MC 14/2 (revised), but he distinguished between LIVE-OAK–type operations and an enemy attack on the Central Region. The pause would therefore come between a LIVE OAK probe encounter and an enemy attack on West Germany. The pause was that point in time when NATO reinforced its forward positions and the Soviets reconsidered escalating the probe incident to attack the Central Region. The West Germans were not at all happy with this interpretation.[32]

Under the terms of the defense plan, NATO retained the right to initiate nuclear weapons use at any level or phase of a conflict, including any run up to Phase I. If the Soviets attempted any form of attack against NATO territory, be it conventional, tactical nuclear, theatre nuclear, or strategic nuclear, SACEUR was not prevented by any political constraints in the use of nuclear weapons to limit or stop these aggressions.[33]

There were several other important changes to the SACEUR defense plan that affected Canadian forces stationed in Europe. The EDP altered the priorities in the SACEUR nuclear strike plan. The destruction of enemy nuclear delivery systems remained paramount, but the interdiction program was dropped to one level below destruction of enemy troop concentrations. Greater emphasis was placed on armed strike reconnaissance against targets of opportunity using nuclear weapons. Nuclear weapons, which to this point could already be used against targets in neutral countries only with SACEUR's express approval, now required approval only if the weapons used were larger than 10 kilotons. As for command and control, SACEUR retained predelegated authority for selective nuclear weapons use (either singly or in small numbers) in any context short of general war; that is, he or she could use them in LIVE OAK–type situations or on the flanks if it were deemed necessary.[34]

Unfortunately, the Canadian Chiefs' minutes dealing with preliminary Athens deliberations and NATO strategy are missing, and the External Affairs records are not accessible for this time. Canadian policy makers had access to the constant reports sent back to Ottawa by George Ignatieff and A. D. P. Heeney, who was still Canada's ambassador in Washington. Cabinet was fully briefed on the issues by Harkness and Green on 24 April 1962.[35]

Historical analyses of the Athens meeting in May 1962 have focused attention on Robert McNamara's speech in which he laid out the Kennedy administration's defense policy. McNamara's points included his belief that NATO's nuclear forces were adequate; that the Soviets would not initiate nuclear weapons if the West remained superior in this regard; that NATO needed and was capable of supporting a conventional force buildup; that NATO should adopt a new strategy centered on flexible responses to Soviet actions and capabilities; and that NATO needed increased political control of nuclear weapons so that a flexible response strategy could actually be implemented.[36]

The real accomplishment of the Athens meeting was not merely some new openness on the tenets of broad American strategy. NATO adopted the "Athens Guidelines," which represented alliance agreement on nuclear weapons use by NATO forces. Summed up,

> In effect nuclear weapons could be used if the Soviets used nuclear weapons in the NATO area, but only on a scale proportional to that employed by the Soviets. If the Soviets attacked with conventional forces, NATO could use tactical nuclear weapons if necessary, and then only on a scale appropriate to the circumstances. Any other situation requiring nuclear weapons use would be considered on a case-by-case basis.[37]

The Americans also stated they were prepared to consider some confidence-building measures within NATO:

> Procedures should be instituted under which we would share information about our nuclear forces and consult about basic plans and arrangements for their use in the NAC and the Standing Group-Military Committee. Although we should withhold highly sensitive operational information concerning sorties, commitments, time on target, penetration tactics and the like, we can and should provide a considerable body of information including targeting policy, nuclear force strengths, analysis of force capabilities, some intelligence on Soviet Bloc strengths.[38]

This also included:

> (i) advance delegation to some person or group of authority to order use of the MRBM Force (*in conjunction with other nuclear forces available to NATO*) in the clearly specified contingency of unmistakable large scale nuclear attack on NATO
>
> (ii) Agreement that the decision to order use of the force in other contingencies should be based on a prearranged system of voting in the NAC, which a majority of our allies will almost certainly wish to provide for voting by unanimity or by a group including the U.S.[39] (Italics added.)

There was virtually no movement on the NATO ballistic missile issue.

The Canadian media and the Opposition had no inkling of what Athens was all about. They instead focused on a sanitized version of the McNamara speech, which McNamara presented at Ann Arbor, Michigan, in June.[40] Canadian media interpretation of this event argued that the supposedly new emphasis on a conventional force buildup meant Canada did not need to arm the CF-104 force with nuclear weapons. This was a misperception of events, which the Opposition immediately used in the House to attack the government yet again on the nuclear issue.[41]

Norman Robertson then asked Frank Miller whether or not the CF-104 force could be exclusively equipped with conventional weapons instead of nuclear weapons. Miller, sensing a trap, stonewalled Robertson and would not provide him with a definite answer.[42]

The next challenge to the CF-104 force came from within the ranks of the RCAF. In July 1961 Campbell established a Special Studies Group (SSG) to determine what the RCAF should look like in the 1970s. The SSG was headed by Air Commodore Fred Carpenter. Most of the SSG's work between its formation and June 1962 did not have a direct relationship to the ongoing nuclear debate in Canada. As we have seen in previous chapters, Carpenter had, for the past two years, pressed for the RCAF to adopt a force structure emphasizing peripheral and conventional operations. Carpenter now used the McNamara speech at Ann Arbor as a launch pad to attack the CF-104 force.[43]

As before, Carpenter asserted that the Cold War stalemate moved the East-West conflict into the peripheral regions. It was in these regions that the Cold War would be won or lost. Canada could gain more influence in the world "by adopting and applying such a policy of flexibility" and make a real contribution to "her own and her allies' security and freedom."[44] Carpenter wanted to base large numbers of tactical conventional fighters in Canada and deploy them to Europe and/or the peripheral areas as required. Now was the time to make this decision, not in the 1970s, since in Carpenter's view NATO strategy was shifting toward conventional operations, and he erroneously believed the Canadian electorate was against nuclear weapons. Carpenter asserted but did not prove that the CF-104 force was so vulnerable that it was useless. Reducing the maritime patrol squadrons could also produce savings, since, again in Carpenter's view, "The USSR is not likely to devote a major share of its resources in the development of a Polaris strike system" (note that the first YANKEE-class nuclear powered ballistic missile–carrying submarines, or SSBNs, were deployed five years later in 1967).[45]

Campbell recognized that Carpenter's assertions were incorrect, based on faulty presumptions, and did not reflect the prevailing opinion within the RCAF. The Chief of the Air Staff disbanded the Special Studies Group before it could cause further damage.[46]

The 1962 Election

Nuclear weapons were an insignificant issue in the 1962 campaign. Pearson routinely accused the government of "procrastination and indecision" on the matter and when asked to ante up by the government in the House, generally evaded the issue.[47] The Opposition did, however, modify its platform. Pearson was quoted in the media saying he believed, "We should have a defence policy which will not require Canada to become a nuclear power in the sense of making, or using, or securing nuclear weapons for her forces and which would be under national control . . . or by having our soil used on a nuclear base under the national control of any other country."[48]

Pearson canvassed Paul Hellyer, Douglas LePan, and Walter Gordon for input into a hastily formed defense platform for the election. In effect, the platform asserted "There is no protection against missile attack whether intercontinental, or intermediate from aircraft, surface ships or submarines. The only defence now is the prevention of attack by deterrence, based on the certainty of immediate and annihilative retaliation." Canada's only role should be surveillance, detection, and air refueling. BOMARCs were "useless without nuclear warheads" and "should be scrapped."[49]

Pearson asserted acquisition of nuclear weapons by Canada would not add "in any substantial way to our own or to collective defence." It would also "weaken our advocacy at the UN and elsewhere of the limitation of membership in the nuclear 'club.'" There should be no nuclear weapons in Canadian hands and none under any joint control system. It was only in this way that Canada could limit nuclear weapons from falling into the hands of Japan, West Germany, China, and Cuba. Pearson waffled, however, noting, "they should be made available to Canadian forces in NATO for defensive tactical purposes, if they are under NATO, and not national, control."[50] Overall, Canada should devote most of her resources to a "permanent international police force" and increase the RCAF's transport capability to lift an assigned Army brigade group for this purpose. Antisubmarine vessels were "out of date and of no use whatsoever against atomic submarines."[51]

Air Marshal Wilf Curtis, who had by this time retired from the RCAF, was unimpressed with Pearson's rhetoric. The nuclear arms issue should not become an election issue, in Curtis's view, as it was vital Canada be defended against a real threat.[52] Pearson wrote back to explain his waffling position on the matter:

> I have tried to recognize the particular difficulty of putting forward a defi-
> nite defence policy in any dogmatic and final way, in the absence of one
> from the Government. I have done this by qualifying my views. . . . So far
> as nuclear weapons are concerned I have tried to avoid being final and
> dogmatic (and have gotten into a good deal of political trouble as a result)
> and have been careful in my choice of words. . . . I have said that our policy
> should not "require" us to use nuclear weapons, which is of course less
> definite that to say we will *never* use nuclear warheads in any circum-
> stances.[53]

It was exactly this sort of obfuscation that got the Diefenbaker government into hot water on the issue.

The campaign itself remained unfettered by the nuclear issue. Diefenbaker chose to pull out the usual anti-American rhetoric and even implied that Kennedy was deliberately destabilizing Canada. In the end, the Conservatives lost ground in Parliament. They retained 116 seats, while the Liberals got 100; Social Credit, 30; and the New Democratic Party (NDP), 19.[54]

Force Development to September 1962

The armed forces continued their incremental moves towards achieving a nuclear capability throughout 1962. There were no significant attempts to get the govern-ment-to-government agreement signed prior to October. The RCAF's 446 and 447 SAM squadrons accepted their first BOMARC missiles without warheads. A USAF evaluation of 446 Squadron stated it "exceeded the individual and unit training requirements in all training areas. . . . the RCAF squadron actually achieved an unprecedented 110% of these programmed training requirements."[55] The 446 Squad-ron was well on its way to achieving its aim of having eighteen missiles operational (again, without warheads) by the set target date of 1 March 1962.[56] The 447 Squad-ron at LaMacaza was another matter. A Treasury Board problem with construction funds delayed completion. Consequently, the first ten missiles were not fully in-stalled and checked out until 14 September which in turn delayed the SAGE-BOMARC connection tests.[57]

Nevertheless, there were still several pieces of the puzzle missing. In an aide memoir the Vice Chief explained to Campbell that there were seven steps needed to achieve a nuclear capability: the government-to-government agreement; the ser-vice-to-service agreements (technical arrangements for warhead security, storage, handling, and maintenance); the actual implementation of these arrangements; a USAF Initial Capability Inspection (ICI) to ensure that the installations were done properly; the delivery and installation of the warheads themselves; the establishment of formal release procedures; and a Final Capability Inspection by the USAF.[58]

Smith noted, however, the CADIN agreement in the late 1950s was being used to acquire "certain detailed technical arrangements," which included the construction, training, installation, and checking of most of the equipment at the North Bay site. The 446 Squadron even passed its ICI on 1 March 1962. The site was, in all respects, ready to receive the warheads and install them. Smith told Campbell, "in an emergency, installation and check out of the warheads at each site could be done in seven days."[59] The actual operational release procedures would take some time, perhaps three months, and it probably could be done concurrently (with informal USAF help) with the negotiation of the government-to-government agreement.[60]

The construction of the Northern NORAD Region HQ Combat Centre at North Bay was completed in August 1962. It would, however, take another eight months before the huge underground facility was equipped with a SAGE computer and have it attached to the BOMARC bases.[61] This meant that Canadian BOMARCs would have to be temporarily attached to SAGE sites in the United States.

As for developing a nuclear capability for the CF-101B Voodoo, several RCAF teams from the armaments engineering branch visited the United States early in 1962 to determine where exactly the RCAF stood. In essence, the same steps necessary to give BOMARC a nuclear capability were applied to the CF-101B/MB-1 combination.[62]

RCAF officers were surprised to learn that a follow-on weapon to the MB-1 was under development. The MMB-1, as it was called, was conceived as a dual-capable weapon; that is, it could be equipped with a conventional or nuclear warhead. It was not ready yet. The Canadian officers also "ascertained that a conventional head did exist for the MB-1 but the USAF personnel regarded this combination as hopelessly ineffective."[63]

The exact MB-1 weapons effects information still could not be released by the Air Force Special Weapons Center at Albuquerque to the RCAF without the government-to-government agreement.[64] A status report to Campbell noted:

> although a specific Governmental agreement would normally be the first of the above series of actions leading to the acquisition of nuclear weapons, the implications of our recent procurement of the CF-101B's and the cooperation of the USAF has made it possible to make some progress in developing the necessary technical arrangements.[65]

This cooperation included the USAF's sending a "proposed manual" of safety and release procedures to the RCAF through Air Vice-Marshal Max Hendrick. All service parties agreed this constituted a "pseudo-technical agreement," while at the same time the USAF wanted the RCAF to know that a government-to-government agreement was necessary before the safety and release procedures became "operative."[66] Hendrick's people in Washington spared no effort to collect open source information from the USAF, who even downgraded and declassified material for them.[67] By mid-1962, the RCAF had sited the alert and storage facilities, acquired the ground support equipment, and established security arrangements. Planners predicted that the Quick Reaction Alert sites could be completed by December 1962 and the storage sites by the spring of 1963. Notably, "it is anticipated that most of the details of the security and communications facilities which will be required by the USAF can be obtained even in the absence of a Governmental agreement."[68]

The status of the CF-104 Starfighter force was much different. The aircraft were still being built, and 6 OTU was still training pilots to fly low-level missions. The necessary steps to have a nuclear capability were slightly different from the BOMARC and CF-101B/MB-1 units. Instead of an ICI, NATO units had to pass an Operational Readiness Inspection (ORI) before nuclear weapons could be delivered. Then NATO authorities had to conduct a tactical evaluation before the squadrons could be assigned for duty.[69]

As with the other systems, informal relationships between the RCAF and USAF facilitated information passage. Training the CF-104 force pilot was, in the end, dependent on information on the weapons that the force would employ. As we saw in the last chapter, enough information was available for the RCAF to build its own practice drop "shapes" and have them certified by American authorities at Sandia. By March 1962, the RCAF was able to confirm that the CF-104s would initially employ the Mk 28 Mod-1 nuclear weapon.[70]

The RCAF, RCN, and USN wrestled with the problems imposed by the lack of the agreements throughout 1962. The draft service-to-service agreements wording had originally omitted the possibility that nuclear antisubmarine weapons might be placed on board RCN ships exclusive of the aircraft carrier. The new plan to retrofit several St. Laurents with helicopter decks and acquire and operate Sea King antisubmarine helicopters from them prompted a change in the wording.[71]

Another problem existed in developing release authority and command relationships. All of the government-level negotiations regarding maritime nuclear weapons that had been conducted since 1959 revolved around the use of SACLANT as the releasing authority for the weapons to Canada. Forces on the Pacific coast, which was not technically part of SACLANT's area, were left out. How would the USN release nuclear antisubmarine weapons to Canadian naval forces? There was no easy answer in 1962, but Admiral Rayner approved a proposal to allow release of nuclear antisubmarine weapons to east and west coast Canadian maritime force commanders "on or prior to the Simple Alert stage" after consultation with American commanders.[72] This was to be inserted into the government-to-government agreement draft prior to negotiations with the Americans.

On the positive side, the RCN and the RCAF made a joint agreement in March 1962 with the USN "for the purposes of exchanging information on the subject."[73] This agreement was probably similar in nature and status to the pseudo technical agreement between the USAF and the RCAF regarding CF-101B information. The RCN also placed a liaison officer in the RCAF Special Weapons Branch of the Directorate of Armament Engineering to ensure information flow.[74] The RCAF/RCN/USN arrangement allowed Canada to send personnel to USN nuclear weapons courses held in Norfolk. These included two officers from the armament directorate and two complete P2V2 Neptune loading crews, one from station Comox and one from station Summerside. The course was called the "ASW Special Weapons Loading Course."[75] These men then served as a training cadre for their respective home stations.

As for the hardware, a number of Neptunes were modified to accept Mk 101 and Mk 57 nuclear depth bombs and prepared for a Pre-Operational Safety Study that was to be held in October 1962.[76] By August, "as a result of the pre-initial safety study, action was initiated to prototype two Argus aircraft which will embody the modifications and equipment recommended." Once these modifications were accepted by the USN in October 1962, "fleet modification would be authorized."[77] In September 1962, a joint USN team from the Naval Weapons Evaluation Facility in New Mexico conducted a tour of the Canadair Argus plant in Quebec, RCAF Station Summerside, and an RCN Tracker squadron.[78] In the words of one memo: "The RCAF/RCN/USN nuclear programs appear to have reached the point where some formality with the USN should be introduced."[79]

Air Marshal Hugh Campbell grew agitated in August 1962 over the lack of progress on the formal agreements and solicited opinions from his senior staff officers. Air Commodore E. M. Reyno, the Deputy Vice-Chief of the Air Staff (VCAS), suggested the RCAF press the Minister to ignore all other systems save the CF-101B/MB-1 and BOMARC. The other weapons could be added "subsequently" in the ill-defined future.[80]

Reyno thought the RCAF's public relations campaign should tell the Canadian people the truth: BOMARCs and MB-1s were by no means offensive weapons; the only way to destroy an enemy bomber was to cook the nuclear weapons it carried while inbound over the North; and air defense was a critical component to add credibility to the deterrent against war. "People are laughing at us now because we have carriers but no weapons," and this was not good for morale, let alone protection.[81]

Pressure was starting to build from NORAD and the Permanent Joint Board. In a letter to Harkness, Campbell stated, "twice in the past year and a half CinCNORAD has pleaded that we attempt to get approval for air defence weapons even if for no others."[82] If Campbell could not get all of the nuclear weapons the RCAF required for its tasks, perhaps he could get the Minister to prioritize the air defense systems since they bore a clear and direct relationship to Canadian defense. He informed Harkness about the advanced stages of capability in the air defense systems (Voodoo and BOMARC) despite the lack of a formal agreement. However, Campbell cautioned the Minister about the emergency availability conceptual thinking that was still making the rounds in Ottawa. This thinking was, in Campbell's professional view, impractical and according to the USAF, "planning emergency transportation of nuclear weapons to forward locations in Canada is not an effective answer to the problem."[83] Either Canada signed the agreement, or the CF-101Bs and BOMARCs should be returned to the United States and the Americans allowed to defend Canadian airspace.[84]

This letter accompanied one written by Air Chief Marshal Frank Miller. Miller laid out the reasons why maintaining stockpiles of MB-1s and W 40 warheads for the BOMARCs in the United States for airlift to Canada in an emergency was not acceptable. The Americans maintained only two special transport squadrons to move nuclear weapons, and their aircraft were specially fitted for this task. Therefore, the RCAF would have to move the warheads.[85] Eight RCAF C-130 transports would have to be modified and their crews would be needed on constant standby in order to pick up and deliver the W 40s to the two BOMARC bases. This tied up those transports twenty-four hours a day, seven days a week. It took two hours for each armament crew to mate each warhead to each airframe. There were only two such crews per base. If the mating time were to be reduced to ten hours (for the twenty-eight missiles at each base), six more armament teams per base were required. Thus, "these crews would have to work without relief for a period of ten hours which exceeds the safety criteria for loading crews." More Americans in the custodial detachments would be required to supplement the loading crews. More ground vehicles were required. More accommodation was required. In short, the entire BOMARC base would have to be redesigned, which would cost a lot of money and take even longer to implement over the long term.[86]

There were other reasons on which Campbell did not elaborate. These included the possibility that weather could interfere with the transport operation; that there might be a danger of moving the warheads by air in a hostile environment; that the time to mate the W 40s with the BOMARC missile airframe precluded immediate use in a situation where NORAD had two hours warning; and that actions taken to load nuclear weapons in haste would increase the probability of an accident during a crisis situation.[87]

It is probable that Miller leaned to the lengthy time necessary to prepare the BOMARCs to make his point instead of focusing on attaching MB-1s to CF-101s in an emergency. This would have been an easier proposition. The CF-101B crews knew how to employ the weapon. Attaching a large rocket to an aircraft designed to accept it takes minutes and required less special training than mating a W 40 to a complex BOMARC airframe. In a dire emergency RCAF CF-101Bs could even fly down to USAF bases, upload MB-1s and conduct operations. Factors that militated against this approach revolved around weather and warning time. Such a scheme would have produced too much uncertainty for NORAD planners who were schooled in applying numbers of delivery systems and weapons versus inbound targets and determining probabilities of kill.

For comparative purposes, USAF's Air Defense Command employed an aerial dispersion concept for its interceptor squadrons that was similar to the emergency deployment concept favored by Norman Robertson and examined by the RCAF earlier in 1962. For example, a similar method was employed in the USAF ADC northeast air Defense sector covering New England. At the Air Defense Readiness (or DEFCON 2) level of alert, MB-1s were transported from a depot at Wurtsmith AFB to Griffiths AFB by C-119 aircraft four hundred miles away. Alternative arrangements included flying the interceptor aircraft from the squadrons at Griffiths to Wurtsmith, picking up MB-1s, and then deploying to dispersal airfields (local and civilian airports).[88] In terms of numbers, each American F-101 squadron was assigned 148 MB-1s, while F-106A squadrons had 107.[89]

Harkness wrote Diefenbaker late in August laying out the nature of the problem. A PJBD meeting determined that it would, in fact, take fifteen hours to deliver nuclear warheads to Canadian air defense forces. The Prime Minister's response is unrecorded.[90]

Note the provision of nuclear antisubmarine weapons using a similar method was not integrated into these discussions. An emergency standby plan was in the process of development with the USN concurrent with these discussions. It is probable that the RCAF leadership did not want the feasibility of the emergency standby plan leak out, though a plan involving ASW weapons was qualitatively different from any similar proposed plan involving air defense weapons. This would pose problems in the future.

Canada, Nuclear Weapons, and the Cuban Missile Crisis: September–October 1962

At a March 1962 dinner the new Assistant Undersecretary for External Affairs, Ross Campbell, had a conversation with Rufus Smith, the Counselor to the American embassy in Ottawa. Campbell remarked that Canadian defense policy "was a mess" and was told in turn by Smith that Canada's position in NATO was compromised. Campbell pointedly responded, "Oh, come now, you know that when the chips are down we'll be with you." Smith stated he "thought the chips *were* down."[91] The Americans were about to learn how far down the chips actually were, and how much support Canada would actually give them in a dire emergency.

Cuban Defense Minister Raul Castro met with Nikita Khrushchev in July 1962 and consummated a mutual defense pact. Later that month American intelligence sources indicated that Soviet merchant ship movements in the Black Sea were destined for Cuba. By August, the Central Intelligence Agency informed the President that the Soviets might try to place nuclear weapons in Cuba to "counterbalance" NATO missile deployments in Turkey. American reconnaissance flights in late August revealed that there were Soviet surface-to-air missile sites under construction on the island. On 4 September, Kennedy issued a public statement warning against any attempt to establish nuclear bases in Cuba.[92]

Coincidentally, the Canadian armed forces participated in a NATO-wide command post exercise (CPX), FALLEX 62, throughout September as the crisis was building. Designed to "test the ability of NATO and National Commands and organizations to operate efficiently under conditions of transition from peace to war involving nuclear attack,"[93] FALLEX 62 had been planned since May 1962 and preparations for Canadian participation had been underway since then.[94] The Canadian forces therefore got a dry run through the alert systems immediately prior to the outbreak of the crisis in October.

As we have seen, Canada was involved in several alerting systems, none of which were interoperable. The primary device that spelled out Canadian commanders' and leaders' activities during each phase of an alert was called the War Book. Each government department and each armed service had one. The first of these was issued in 1955, and revisions were made through the years. Previous exercises highlighted numerous "detail" problems and the current edition had been revised but not promulgated just prior to FALLEX 62. FALLEX 62 used a draft for the purposes of the exercise.[95]

While FALLEX 62 was in progress, the first Soviet ship carrying Medium-Range Ballistic Missiles, the *Omsk*, arrived in Cuba, followed by the *Poltava* with eight more on 15 September. On 21 September, the Canadian Joint Intelligence Committee received intelligence from American sources that the situation was getting worse. Mike Pearson started asking questions about Canadian policy towards Cuba in the House of Commons on 28 September. For the first six days in October, Robert McNamara met with Admiral Robert Dennison, CinCLANT/SACLANT, and ordered him to prepare for a blockade. This increased CinCLANT's state of readiness on 6 October. By 11 October, CANCOMARLANT, Rear Admiral K. L. Dyer, decided to increase the range and frequency of his maritime patrol aircraft missions over the Canadian area on his own initiative.[96]

Douglas Harkness once again tried to get the government-to-government agreement onto the Cabinet agenda for discussion. This was prompted by the imminent deployment of the first CF-104s to Europe and appears to have been unrelated to the growing crisis. Norman Robertson was able to influence Howard Green into delaying any such discussion, citing ambiguities in the current draft. Robertson then bureaucratically sabotaged the entire endeavor by suggesting "an interdepartmental working group" was needed to "thrash out the details."[97] Finance Minister Donald Fleming now:

> was beginning to entertain suspicions that Dief was attracted by the idea of making a moral issue out of the [nuclear] question and visualizing himself as leading what would be pictured as a crusade for peace. This role could be purchased only at the cost of breaking faith with NATO and the United States, and irresponsibly adopting a "holier than thou" attitude while sheltering ourselves behind the American nuclear deterrent.[98]

A USAF proposal to give another twenty-two F-101B Voodoos to the RCAF was also scrapped.[99]

On 14 October, American U-2s photographed the construction of Soviet ballistic missile sites in Cuba. The next day, the National Photographic Interpretation Center in Washington confirmed this and informed McNamara. McGeorge Bundy informed John F. Kennedy on the sixteenth, which in turn prompted six more U-2 flights. These revealed that SS-4 MRBM missiles were in Cuba and sites for SS-5 IRBMs were under construction.[100]

Soviet plan ANADYR was designed to install twenty-four SS-4 SANDAL and twelve SS-5 SKEAN nuclear missile launchers in Cuba with the express purpose of threatening SAC bases. The SS-4 had a range of 1250 miles and could carry warheads up to 16 megatons in yield (such a test was conducted successfully in 1961). The SS-5 had a 2500-mile range and was believed to carry a 3 or 5 megaton-yield warhead. For targeting purposes, the SS-4 force could reach Washington, DC, and at least fifteen SAC bomber and ICBM bases, while the SS-5 could reach any target in North America, including all Canadian population centers and military bases. CIA analysis confirmed most of these facts on 16 October.[101]

The actual specifics of the Soviet nuclear deployment to Cuba was not known for many years. It included thirty-six SS-4 missiles and thirty-six nuclear warheads for them (yields between 200 and 700 kt). It also included six free-fall bombs of an unknown yield for the IL-28 BEAGLE light bombers, as well as ninety-six tactical nuclear weapons for the FROG SSMs and the KOMAR missile patrol boat cruise missiles. Twenty-four more warheads of 800 kt yield were sent to Cuba in anticipation of the SS-5 deployment, but were not unloaded from their transport ships.[102]

Soviet missiles stationed in Cuba equipped with high-yield nuclear warheads invalidated all NORAD war planning assumptions and force structures. The precious twenty-two-minute warning for ballistic missile attack and two to three hours warning for bomber attack would be cut down to single digit minutes. On the plus side, the SS-4 was liquid fueled, which could take up to eight hours to prepare and provide more warning time if a close watch was kept. Coordinated with a missile launching submarine attack, the ballistic missile force in Cuba was an extremely serious threat that had to be countered at all costs. At another level, threatening the alliance's main deterrent and North American cities might persuade the United States to not respond with SAC and other forces if the Soviets assaulted Berlin and/or Western Europe with overwhelming conventional strength.

The same day the SS-5 information was brought back, an RCAF Argus made its first submarine contact three hundred miles southeast of Halifax. The target was heading for the Op BEARTRAP area, which was the area that Canadian maritime commanders assumed Soviet missile-launching submarines would enter to shoot at SAC bases in New England. US Navy Admirals Taylor and Koch, from CinCLANT, arrived discreetly at CANCOMARLANT's headquarters in Halifax for discussions, the nature of which still remain secret.[103]

Another American U-2 overflight on 20 October discovered the existence of a nuclear storage facility near an MRBM site. Other intelligence information indicated that twenty of the forty planned Soviet nuclear warheads were on Cuban soil. While this was happening, RCAF and USN aircraft discovered a Soviet ZULU-class missile submarine refueling on the surface from a Soviet oiler northwest of the Azores.[104] If the Soviets intended to attack North America with their bomber force, Canadian and American planners had assumed many years before that such an attack would be coordinated and even preceded by a missile submarine attack against military targets. The presence of even one of these submarines gave a sense of urgency to Canadian military planners. What Canadian and American commanders did not realize at this point was that the Soviets had actually deployed eleven attack and seven missile submarines into the western Atlantic over the course of the past two months, specifically to support the Cuban operation.[105] SACLANT, Admiral Robert Dennison, considered any placement of Soviet submarines close to the East Coast to be an "extremely provocative move" and planned to act accordingly.[106]

Intense internal American discussions on courses of action followed. The prevailing response was to impose the blockade around Cuba. John McCone, Director of Central Intelligence, realized that the Cuban problem could not remain delinked from the Berlin problem. Thus, any American action over Cuba would involve NATO, since the Soviets might provoke another Berlin crisis to balance the Cuban crisis.

Consequently, McCone suggested that the West's position would be stronger if NATO allies were on side: "The president felt that [Harold] Macmillan, de Gaulle, Adenauer, and Diefenbaker should be made personally aware of the crisis details in advance of his address to the nation."[107]

Rusk suggested that Livingston Merchant, who had recently retired from foreign service, should brief the Canadian Prime Minister. Merchant was reached while watching a college football game at Princeton and proceeded with great haste to Washington. He then got on a plane and flew to Ottawa late on the night of 21 October.[108] Ivan White, who was temporarily in charge of the American embassy in Ottawa, let Bob Bryce know that Merchant would be arriving with something critical, though White did not tell Bryce what it was. At the same time, an External Affairs representative who was in Washington attending an intelligence conference unrelated to Cuba noticed that most of the American members kept getting called away. Eventually the Americans broke down and explained in general terms what was going on. This information was passed back to Norman Robertson. The Prime Minister was then informed, also in general terms, that there would be a showdown over Cuba.[109]

Douglas Harkness was not informed that Merchant was in town until 1000 hours on 22 October. A meeting with Diefenbaker, Green, Bryce, and Miller was not scheduled until 1700 hours, one hour before Kennedy was to make his speech on international television.[110]

22 October was a long day in every capital. In Moscow the KGB arrested Oleg Penkovsky, who performed feats of espionage and had alerted the West about Soviet intentions. Fidel Castro mobilized his people against an American invasion. Dean Acheson flew to Paris and briefed Charles de Gaulle, while David Bruce briefed Harold Macmillan in London. The USAF and Turkish armed forces made the first fifteen Jupiter missiles operational. By 1300 hours, CinCCONAD jumped the gun and alerted USAF Air Defense Command. This alert allowed him to place nuclear-armed interceptors on fifteen minute alert. Sixty-six F-101Bs, 64 F-106As and 31 F-102As, for a total of 161 nuclear-armed interceptors, flew to sixteen dispersal bases (nonmilitary and municipal airfields) within the continental United States.[111]

Air Marshal Roy Slemon then called the VCAS, Air Vice-Marshal Clare Annis, from NORAD HQ. CinCNORAD was asking permission, through Slemon, to arm the USAF Air Defense Command squadrons at Harmon AFB and Goose Bay with nuclear weapons; to increase the level of alert for RCAF Air Defence Command CF-101B and the BOMARC squadron at North Bay; and to disperse some of the USAF ADC interceptor force to airfields in Canada.[112] The inclusion of the BOMARC squadron in this list of requests is interesting given that there were no warheads, nuclear or otherwise, attached to the BOMARC airframes, since there was no nuclear weapons agreement between the two countries yet. Nothing could be done until the Prime Minister had received the intelligence briefing.

Merchant, White, William Tidwell (the CIA briefing officer), and the Ottawa CIA chief of station, Rolfe Kingsley, met with Harkness, Green, and Diefenbaker in the East Bloc's Council Chamber. The Americans produced blown up U-2 overflight photos, explained what was happening in Cuba, "outlined the actions which were to be taken," that is, the American blockade and invasion plans, and provided a copy of Kennedy's evening speech. Harkness asked about what stages of alert the American military foresaw in the near future and was told that they did not know exactly how things would progress.[113]

Harkness thought that the blockade would lead to a naval conflict, "which might be more likely to produce a general war than a direct landing in Cuba." In his view, "only a landing would definitely and finally clean up the situation."[114] Diefenbaker declared "the evidence [of Soviet missiles] was overwhelming."[115] The Prime Minister also told Merchant that "the best diplomatic efforts will be necessary to resolve the crisis" and pledged Canadian support in the UN. Diefenbaker also instructed Merchant to inform Kennedy that Canada would participate in a UN mission to observe the removal of the missiles if there was a diplomatic breakthrough. Canada would also deny her airspace to Soviet Bloc aircraft.[116] It appears as though this was Norman Robertson's idea, which he thought up earlier in the day after some of his External people informed him what was happening in Washington.[117] Basil Robinson noted in retrospect, "it is not hard to imagine the lights that must have flashed on in Diefenbaker's mind at this reminder of an occasion when Pearson himself had gilded his reputation and been rewarded with the Nobel Peace Prize."[118]

Finally, Diefenbaker "stated that in the event of a missile attack on the United States from Cuba, Canada would live up to its responsibilities under the NATO and NORAD Agreements."[119]

Diefenbaker recounted in his 1977 memoirs:

> [Merchant's] purpose was to convey President Kennedy's demand that my government should give carte blanche in support of unilateral action by the United States. Specifically, President Kennedy, through Mr. Merchant (as well as through service channels) requested that we immediately and publicly place the Canadian NORAD component on maximum alert. I considered it unacceptable that every agreed requirement for consultation between our two countries should be ignored.[120]

Diefenbaker claims that he then called Kennedy on the telephone:

> I asked him why he had not raised United States forces to a level of maximum alert. He said that this would cause international repercussions, but if Canada did so, it would not have the same effect. I told him that our defence forces were alerted and would be ready if a real crisis developed. . . . When the President again raised the question of a national alert in Canada, I asked, "When were we consulted?" He brusquely replied, "You weren't," as if consultation in North American defence was of no importance to him.[121]

Prime Minister Diefenbaker's version of events bears little resemblance to reality. The Kennedy-Diefenbaker telephone conversation actually took place the next day (Tuesday, 23 October). Diefenbaker could not have called Kennedy sometime after 1700 hours that day, because Kennedy was preparing for the speech he was about to make to the world at 1800 hours. Canadian forces were not yet at any level of alert, and American forces *were already* on alert. Under the terms of the alert consultation agreement, the Merchant/Tidwell briefing certainly constituted some form of consultation. It was certainly more consultation than Eisenhower gave Diefenbaker in the Lebanon and other crises where air defense forces were alerted. No other participant in the meeting noted that Diefenbaker gave any indication of displeasure with the state of affairs during or immediately after the briefing.

Kennedy gave his speech at 1800 hours, 22 October 1962. The US Joint Chiefs told the State Department that the United States armed forces would be at DEFCON 3 by 1900 hours. One eighth of the SAC B-52 force was placed on airborne alert, while 183 B-47s and their associated tankers dispersed to thirty-three airfields. ICBM crews were alerted and the USN Polaris submarine force dispersed to stations at sea. In addition to the already-alerted air defense forces, twenty-two more nuclear-armed interceptors were placed in the air in the south off Cuba.[122]

The US Joint Chiefs then asked SACEUR, General Lauris Norstad, to increase NATO's alert level in Europe. There was some confusion as some American forces in Europe were automatically alerted through the American system, and Norstad, being a NATO commander, did not have control over them. Norstad communicated with the British Prime Minister Harold Macmillan, who thought that any NATO mobilization over Cuba would repeat the same mistakes as the 1914 mobilization that helped precipitate the First World War. Norstad concurred. After consultation between Norstad and Kennedy, Norstad "was explicitly authorized to use his discretion."[123]

At 1900 hours, Air Marshal Frank Miller entered Douglas Harkness's office and informed him that the Americans had gone to DEFCON 3. He then asked if he could bring Canadian forces up to Ready state. Harkness said to go ahead and do it. Miller, however, noted that the new War Book which authorized the Minister of National Defence to authorize this action had not been accepted by the Cabinet and that the old War Book had problems with it. They both agreed that the Prime Minister should be informed and asked if this was acceptable activity.[124]

This was the first mistake. The original War Book, as we saw in chapter 8, explicitly stated that the Minister of National Defence and senior military officers had the leeway to use their initiative. It also stated that the Chiefs could move the forces to Discreet state, but that the Minister of National Defence could put the forces at Ready. It required Cabinet approval to move through Simple, Reinforced, and General levels. Harkness should have just ordered Ready (the equivalent of DEFCON 3).

Harkness then called Diefenbaker, and the two men met at once in the Centre Block of the Parliament buildings:

> I gave him the information I had received and told him the course of action I proposed and asked his agreement. He was loath to give this and said it should be a Cabinet decision. Whilst we were still arguing the matter, Howard Green arrived at the office. I explained the situation to him and to my surprise he agreed to the action I proposed. However, the Prime

Minister was insistent that authority should be given by the full Cabinet in the morning and would not call a special Cabinet meeting that night as the House was sitting.[125]

Harkness was aghast. The Americans had B-52s in the air and wanted to disperse tankers and MB-1s to the USAF air defense squadrons in Canada. Canada was pledged to defend North America. What was Diefenbaker playing at?

The Minister of National Defence returned to a waiting Frank Miller and:

> discussed what action we could take, without declaring a formal alert, which would put us in a position of maximum readiness. . . . I ordered immediately full manning [of the service emergency headquarters], intelligence and communications centres, warning orders to the Commands and manning of their communications.[126]

Kennedy, meanwhile, received word through Rusk of Diefenbaker's pledge to support a UN disarmament initiative and inspection in Cuba if it were necessary. Diefenbaker had made such a pledge public in the House of Commons later that evening after seeing Harkness. According to CIA briefer William Tidwell, "The Kennedy brothers appear to have taken offense at this, feeling that Diefenbaker was questioning the integrity of the United States." Tidwell noted rapidly that this was a misunderstanding and "tried to correct the impression, but I was too junior to make such an impression."[127]

On Tuesday, 23 October, the blockade went into effect, and the USN and USAF conducted multiple low-level reconnaissance flights over Cuba.

Deputy CinCNORAD Air Vice Marshal Roy Slemon called RCAF HQ operations center and reminded Annis and Hendrick that NORAD was at DEFCON 3. CinCNORAD had instructed him to make three requests of the Chiefs. The first two were to put the RCAF Air Defence Command to DEFCON 3 equivalent and disperse the CF-101B force. The third item was "that NORAD should be allowed to bring in nuclear weapons if necessary into Canada and start the arming process."[128] Frank Miller then entered the operations center and was briefed on the requests. Miller then went to see Diefenbaker, Green, and Harkness, who all "just bowed away from the question of nuclear tips." Miller then called Slemon and said that some other method was required to get the ball rolling on nuclear armament. Miller called Slemon and told him that he thought that CinCNORAD should ask the Canadian government to arm its F-102s at Goose Bay with nuclear Falcons. In minutes NORAD HQ made a formal request to Miller to do so.[129]

The Chiefs met with Harkness early in the morning and confirmed American intelligence reports with Canadian sources. In this meeting, in which no formal notes were taken, Harkness, Air Marshal Miller, Admiral Rayner, General Walsh, and Air Vice-Marshal Campbell examined "the steps which could be taken to put [Canadian forces] in the same state of readiness as the U.S. forces, and what was required at each subsequent stage."[130]

If Harkness and the Chiefs were following the War Book (either the pre-1962 or draft edition) and they wanted to enact the Discreet *and* Ready states (DEFCON 4 and 3 equivalent) and then Simple Alert (DEFCON 2 equivalent) at the national level, this would have entailed the following actions.

For a Discreet State of Military Vigilance, the Chiefs could ask the Minister for permission, or the Chiefs could individually declare the state and then inform the Minister. Basically, Discreet allowed the Chiefs to examine and confirm plans for: emissions controls, communications system expansion, troop movements, and the protection of National Defence facilities. Each service was then to inform its commands, man emergency headquarters, increase the staffing at existing headquarters in preparation for advancement into the formal alert system (Simple, Reinforced, General), tighten security at facilities, and restrict leave.[131]

The Chiefs were also authorized to "examine and start progressively executing emergency defence plan and mobilization plan to the extent indicated by the gravity of the emergency."[132] As for the service commanders, they were authorized to deploy naval forces, implement National Survival plans, and examine with CinCNORAD the control of air traffic.[133]

For the Ready State of Military Vigilance, the state that Harkness wanted to move to in order to conform with DEFCON 3, the Chiefs had to request a state change to the Minister. Each service Chief was then to concentrate overseas reinforcements and make preparations to transport them, prepare to clear military hospitals, disperse logistic stocks from potential target areas, while the Minister was to advise Cabinet in preparation to implement Simple Alert formally. The Navy and Army had a number of administrative tasks to complete. The RCAF was to confirm that air control measures were ready to be implemented. At Simple Alert, reserve units were to be called up and moved, while the CNS and CAS implemented their War Books and permitted their commands to implement lower-level instructions.[134]

The RCAF Emergency Defence Plan assumed the alert states would change when the NORAD DEFCON alerts changed and that RCAF actions would respond accordingly. For example, RCAF exercises prior to the Cuban Missile Crisis assumed that within one hour of declaration of the Ready state, the Chiefs would ask Cabinet permission to allow the deployment of nuclear weapons from the United States to Canadian units using the standby procedure.[135] The timing and detailed actions for this stage were unclear given the existing government policy on nuclear weapons and probably were the reasons why the DND War Book was under revision at the time of the crisis.

Harkness and the Chiefs now had to compress the Discreet and Ready stages as rapidly as possible. He then instructed the Chiefs "to have all preparations made to issue orders on these and other numerous matters as soon as I telephoned from Cabinet that the alert had been authorized."[136] "These other matters" probably referred to Slemon's request to disperse USAF air defense fighters to Canadian airfields and to allow nuclear weapons to be brought to Harmon and Goose Bay for the American squadrons there. It might also have referred to SAC's desire to disperse tanker aircraft to the bases in northern Canada, to increase the readiness for the B-47 force, and to allow for more SAC B-52 overflights, since SAC had dramatically increased the number of bombers on Airborne Alert. Again, there does not appear to be any indication that these measures were incorporated into the 1962 edition of the DND War Book.

At the same time, Annis and Campbell discussed the possibility of using the situation to get the Americans to arm the BOMARC squadrons, which would make the overall nuclear issue a fait accompli. Annis was concerned "the Americans might react much more broadly" and rock the boat (translation: if the response was too formal, the government might actually consider it in Cabinet and block it). Slemon, unaware of the discussion, then called and informed them, "we've been thinking of this question of what would be the fastest way if we were to put [nuclear] tips on your weapons up there."[137] Slemon thought the best way was to have the Voodoos fly to American bases and upload there. In his view to move them to Canadian bases "would take a great deal of work because the key problem would be the training of the technicians." Hendrick thought this might be a great opportunity to crash-train RCAF technicians on the MB-1s, but Annis shot this idea down as excessive given the political circumstances.[138]

As for the BOMARCs, the NORAD staff believed "within six days of any starting time they could have a half squadron capability and within nine days the BOMARC squadron could be fully operational with nuclear tips."[139] Hendrick also thought they should dust off the planned service-to-service agreement and get the Americans to sign it while the pressure was on, presumably so that the RCAF could use this as a lever with the Diefenbaker government on the nuclear weapons issue:

> I was told again that the Chairman has been so busy looking for a probe that maybe there might be some success and there seems to be a feeling that any boat rocking at this time may be dangerous if we started acting as though we knew the Government was going to give authorization to bring nuclear tips into the country. . . . So we are very much here being held down with the iron hand.[140]

Harkness was able to get Diefenbaker to call a Cabinet meeting, which met at 1030 hours. Cabinet agreed that National Survival measures should be placed in effect, that is, the emergency regional headquarters should be manned and their communications checked. As for alerting the Canadian forces, most of what was said that day has been deleted from the historical record. Harkness informed the Cabinet that NORAD was at DEFCON 3. The American forces were all at this stage, including the squadrons at Goose Bay and Harmon. CinCNORAD was asking Canada to increase the stage of alert for the air defense forces to conform to DEFCON 3, that is, Ready stage. A heated discussion ensued. There was no movement on the nuclear weapons issue.[141]

A number of Cabinet ministers wanted to see what the British position was and follow suit while at the same time claiming they did not want Canada "stampeded" into any action by the United States. On the plus side, Harkness was able to get Cabinet to convene the Cabinet Defence Committee (which had not met in years) to sort out some of the War Book inconsistencies.[142] On the whole, though, "The Prime Minister argued against [the alert] on the grounds that it would unduly alarm the people. . . . [H]e and I came to some fairly hot words, but he refused to agree to the alert chiefly, I think, because of a pathological hatred of taking a hard decision."[143]

Douglas Harkness then went back to the Chiefs and:

ordered them to put into effect all of the precautions we had discussed in the morning, but in as quiet and unobtrusive way as possible. . . . Everything was ordered to go ahead as though we were on alert. These measures accomplished the majority of the purposes of an alert, ie: to get into a state of preparedness to meet an attack. . . . I did not tell the Prime Minister or any other members of the Cabinet of the steps I had taken, but I did keep him informed throughout the day and evening of intelligence reports which came in.[144]

Harold Macmillan sent a message to Diefenbaker later on 23 October urging him not to declare an alert, in order "to avoid any provocative action."[145] Macmillan also thought that the matter should be handled in the UN. George Ignatieff reported back that he was "isolated" in the North Atlantic Council because Canada had not come forward with explicit support for American actions over Cuba as the rest of NATO had.[146]

President Kennedy called Diefenbaker in the afternoon. He asked Diefenbaker to raise the Canadian air defense alert level to correspond with DEFCON 3 as a precaution and also asked for a pledge of Canadian support in the UN. This time, however, Diefenbaker thought he was being ordered around by Kennedy and refused to acknowledge that he would authorize either action. Taking the easy way out, the Prime Minister heatedly told Kennedy he would have to take it up with Cabinet. That day, Diefenbaker announced in the House that the United States had not seen fit to consult with Canada about the Cuban situation.[147]

A combination of personal ambition, vanity, potential glory, perceived American arrogance, and overreliance on the British prerogative convinced John Diefenbaker not allow a formal alert of Canadian defense forces so that they could prepare to repel a threat that existed and was building. Coupled with Robertson's and Green's three-year delay tactic on the nuclear agreement, none of Canada's continental defense systems were equipped at this point in the crisis to carry out their duties as part of the NORAD alliance system.

Despite this state of affairs, Air Defence Command's chief of staff, Air Commodore A. Chester Hull, received instructions from his superior, Air Vice-Marshal Max Hendrick. Hull was to call Air Defence Command unit commanding officers and tell them to "do all things associated with a certain defence condition." This translated to: "make all preparations necessary to receive nuclear warheads in the air defence forces."[148]

The situation in Europe, however, was somewhat different, and Ottawa was not well informed about what was happening with the Canadian forces stationed there. 1 Air Division was in the midst of deploying its CF-104 aircraft to Europe in Operation RHO DELTA, and the squadrons would not be activated for several weeks.[149] 4 Brigade, on the other hand, was combat ready and prepared to fight in the defense of the Central Region. Brigadier Mike Dare assured that the brigade's war plans were integrated with I (British) Corps and that 1 SSM Battery could contribute:

> The whole of [NORTHAG] was on alert and the American custodial attachment attached to us immediately did so, although they were not ordered by their central command. They had independent release for atomic warheads if circumstances required it. . . . The young man in charge of the American detachment moved his men to the storage area, ready to respond.[150]

The brigade was then alerted and "bugged out" to its survival areas. It eventually deployed with live ammunition to its Emergency Defence Plan positions. At the same time Major General Jean V. Allard, the Canadian in command of the 4th British Division, prepared a multinational force under the auspices of LIVE OAK in preparation for a move down the Helmstedt approach to Berlin. Certain USAFE nuclear units were alerted through the American chain of command, but SACEUR did not authorize an alert of his nuclear forces until 25 October. At that point 163 American, West German, and British nuclear delivery aircraft were alerted.[151]

As for Canada's maritime forces, Admiral Dyer once again increased his surveillance patrols and gained another submarine contact five hundred miles southeast of Halifax. Maritime Air Command commanders were personally and informally told to increase their state of readiness. Dyer continued to chafe as he wanted to send the fleet to sea and disperse his logistics force, but the Chief of the Naval Staff, Admiral Rayner, was not prepared to go that far yet.[152]

By Wednesday, 24 October, Harkness was finally able to push Diefenbaker into holding another Cabinet meeting so that the Canadian forces could be moved up to Ready state. The first meeting at 0930 ended inconclusively. A number of ministers were persuaded by the Macmillan argument that an alert would precipitate war.[153]

Diefenbaker had more discussions with the British and appeared to have been relying more and more on the British High Commissioner's opinion rather than on Canadian military and political leaders. The British High Commissioner "pointed out that it was difficult to classify weapons strictly as offensive and defensive." Diefenbaker was further irked by the State Department's use of aerial photographs in a UN meeting and with the media. In Diefenbaker's mind, this was privileged information; he had been manipulated by Kennedy and not actually consulted. The Cabinet meeting shifted to a discussion of Canadian military dependents in Europe rather than a discussion of how to reinforce the units in Europe.[154]

Harkness was beside himself:

> This proved to be a long and unpleasant meeting at which members of the Cabinet were asked for their individual opinions. Most favoured the alert. The meeting was about to end inconclusively when I made a final effort with a rather angry outburst that we were failing in our responsibilities to

the nation and *must* act, which produced an outburst from the Prime Minister to the effect that he would not be forced into any such action.[155]

Miller hunted down Harkness and informed him that SAC and CinCLANT had gone to DEFCON 2. General Power, CinCSAC, issued his orders *en clair* to his command both to reassure them and to send a message to the Soviets. Harkness then went to Diefenbaker's office and told him Canada could not delay any longer. He replied "in an agitated way, 'all right, go ahead.'"[156] There were limitations, however. Only RCAF Air Defence Command could increase its state to Ready.[157] This was done at 1334 hours, and CinCNORAD was informed, almost one and half days after the rest of NORAD had gone on alert. CF-101Bs were now placed on fifteen minutes alert.

The RCN was concerned that it was not included in the alert, particularly since USCinCLANT had deployed ten diesel submarines and seventeen P2V Neptunes to Argentia in preparation for the establishment of a sea-air barrier in accordance with defense plans. The Naval Board instructed that the HMCS *Bonaventure* task group which was visiting Portsmouth, United Kingdom, to return home. A Canadian destroyer escort force engaged in a joint exercise with the USN was instructed to refuel at San Francisco. The force stopped to help the USN hunt a submarine contact. The RCN implemented most of required actions for a Military Vigilance Ready alert level without actually declaring it. Admiral Dyer then activated his wartime command structure in Halifax and decided to establish the RCN Defence Plan as the basis of his command's activities.[158]

As discussed in previous chapters, the bulk of the RCN CS2F Tracker fleet had been modified for nuclear depth bomb delivery. During the crisis:

> L.Cdr. Shel Rowell therefore felt obligated to so inform [HMCS] Shearwater [Commanding Officer] Capt. Ted Edwards (surprise), which in itself was a bit of a bombshell since apparently the subject had never been previously discussed. Rear Admiral Dyer, on being informed was similarly caught off guard. The outcome, after consultation with the USN, was a contingency plan to disperse the six modified Trackers to Yarmouth NS, with the crews standing by to await further orders. The proposed plan was to fly the aircraft to either Quonset Point or Norfolk Naval Air Station, where they would be employed as necessary by the USN should the crisis escalate to the point where nuclear depth bombs were authorized for use. Such authorization under the "Rules of Engagement" was normally only given if a missile carrying submarine came within range of the continent and gave an indication that it was preparing to launch its missiles.[159]

The reason for such a move, as we will see later in the crisis, was dictated by the fact that most of the USN's antisubmarine barrier forces on the East Coast were shifted south to conduct the blockade, thus stripping the northeast seaboard of protection against enemy submarines.

With RCAF Air Defence Command finally at the same level of alert as the rest of NORAD, CinCNORAD, General J. K. Gerhart, was able to inform Miller of what had been happening and to express some concerns. Gerhart had dispersed most of his interceptors and had run into some problems: "(1) Canadian bases for dispersal were not available because of the restrictions on overflying Canada with nuclear weapons until declaration of DEFCON 1 or higher. (2) Lack of operating facilities and heated storage at many dispersal bases to assure proper handling of nuclear weapons."[160]

The unexpected redeployment of USAF interceptors to cover the southeast of the United States placed a strain on the forces covering the northwest and northeast. The strain was so great that CinCNORAD considered asking the JCS to reduce the state of alert for the air defense forces, something he did not want to do given the threat. Gerhardt desperately needed the RCAF squadrons to relieve this pressure.[161]

It was probably at this point that W 40 warheads were flown to the BOMARC base at North Bay, attached to the airframes and a dual key system jury-rigged. The LaMacaza BOMARC site was not as close to a state of readiness as North Bay, and it appears that the W 40s for it were kept just across the border at Plattsburg AFB in New York. MB-1 rockets were apparently not deployed to Canadian bases, though it appears that USAF security force custodians and technicians were sent to the CF-101B bases in preparation for an emergency deployment of MB-1s to them. In some cases, temporary special ammunition storage facilities were designated and guarded by RCAF and USAF security personnel. The USAF already had MB-1s and W 40s identified for emergency movement to Canada.[162]

That night, Howard Green was interviewed on television and claimed that NORAD was not involved in the current crisis. He then told the interviewer that the United States had not made any requests of Canada to support it in the crisis.[163] Both statements were falsehoods and served to confuse the issue even further in the public mind.

Cabinet met yet again on 25 October. This time they approved a temporary amendment to the DND War Book that required the Minister to get the Prime Minister's approval before implementing the Ready state of alert, which amounted to closing the door after the horse had bolted.[164] Diefenbaker then got up in the House, indicated that the crisis was still in effect, and committed Canada to resolving it in the UN. Paul Hellyer then asked Harkness whether the BOMARCs had been armed with nuclear warheads, and Harkness replied that they had not yet been so armed.[165]

Behind the scenes, the Kennedy administration was examining a proposal with the Soviets to trade off Soviet missiles in Cuba for the NATO-assigned American Jupiter missiles based in Turkey that had just been made operational. There was no consultation with the NATO allies on this effort. On 26 October, CinCLANT was informed that there were problems in activating the Argentia-Azores barrier force because of a shortage of Mk 43 aerial torpedoes. Five hundred of these had to be borrowed from the RCAF.[166]

The crisis nearly spun out of control on 27 October. The CIA informed the President that the SS-4 missiles on the island were operational. At the same time, a U-2 was shot down over Cuba. Another U-2 strayed off course into Soviet airspace and had to be escorted back by USAF air defense interceptors armed with nuclear weapons in the face of Soviet air defense forces alert.[167]

In the Atlantic, the American commander of the ASW Defense Forces Vice-Admiral E. Taylor, asked Canadian maritime forces to assist him in two ways. The reduced number of available USN patrol aircraft (many had been hived off to assist with the blockade, including all of his long range P3 Orions) prompted CinCLANT to ask CANCOMARLANT to add Argus patrol aircraft to the eastern-most portion of the barrier extending southeast from Newfoundland. Second, the lack of American ASW resources had left a hole in the defenses of the northeast seaboard of the United States. Could Canada assist? Taylor in fact wanted to place the barrier up at the GIUK Gap but was not allowed to do so.[168]

The next day the Georges Bank barrier extending south from Nova Scotia was in place. This move essentially corresponded with the BEARTRAP zone south of Nova Scotia and included four surface destroyer groups, Argus patrol aircraft, and Tracker aircraft operating inshore and maintaining surveillance on the substantial Soviet "fishing fleet" in the area. Several RCN frigates backed up the Argentia barrier.[169]

While Khrushchev stopped his ships in their tracks on 29 October, his submarines kept bearing down on the eastern coast of North America. A situation report from CANCOMARLANT (Dyer) dated 30 October noted there were twelve submarine contacts in his areas of responsibility made by either SOSUS, surface ship, or patrol aircraft, with five more unknowns being actively persecuted by antisubmarine forces.[170]

At this point COMASWFORLANT asked CANCOMARLANT to allocate Argus patrol aircraft to the Bravo 2 Sierra patrol. The exact nature of the B2S patrol cannot be confirmed from the available documents. It was not part of the Argentia barrier operation, it did not conduct fishing fleet or replenishment ship surveillance, and it did not participate in RCN/RCAF operations on the Georges Banks.[171] Vice-Chief of the Air Staff Clare Annis discussed the mission at RCAF HQ, who opposed it, and the actual assignment of Argus aircraft to the patrol was not approved on 31 October.[172] Yet by 2 November one Argus was continuously assigned to the B2S patrol for a twenty-four-hour period. This patrol happened again on 6–7 November.[173]

We know that in August 1962 several Argus aircraft were rewired to handle nuclear depth bombs. There was a shortage of USN patrol aircraft as evidenced by the contingency plan to move the six nuclear-capable RCN Trackers to the United States to cover the northeast approaches and by the requests for Argus aircraft to assist in the Argentia barrier operation. Clare Annis, who was skittish about the MB-1 deployment, was also skittish about the B2S patrol. Other RCAF officers thought positive actions regarding nuclear weapons during the crisis would have a positive effect on establishing the government-to-government agreement and formalizing the nuclear relationship. We know there was an emergency standby arrangement established between the USN and the RCAF to provide nuclear depth bombs to RCAF maritime forces from the storage site at NAS Brunswick, Maine.

As for the American side of things, SACLANT Admiral Robert Dennison was a dedicated "NATOist" and had the same predelegated authority that SACEUR had to make preparations and to use nuclear weapons for defensive purposes in an emergency.[174] Additionally, the USN's Chief of Naval Operations, Admiral George W. Anderson, had a penchant for keeping details of naval nuclear planning out of the hands of the Secretary of Defense and other officials.[175]

When Anderson was Commander, 6th Fleet, he would discuss his actual intentions in a crisis only orally with his staff. Nothing was sent back to Washington. Note also that Anderson had a great deal of respect for Canada and particularly the RCN. Anderson had served on the PJBD and the MCC in the 1940s and 1950s when most of the joint defense planning was done and personally knew all of the Canadian commanders involved.

It is logical to conclude that the B2S patrol involved some form of ground and air alert involving nuclear depth bombs. It is also logical to conclude that the Argus was a "goalie" of sorts, in place to destroy any Soviet missile-launching submarine operating in the Bay of Fundy that eluded the other two barriers. As we have seen, there were certain positions from which such a submarine could attack several SAC bases, let alone New York City and Boston. The nature of Soviet submarine behavior and locations during this time probably prompted the B2S alert on those days. It is notable that Admiral Taylor went out of his way to thank CANCOMARLANT in a secret message: "Your assistance in support of the ASW barrier and the Bravo two sierra patrol are of particular value. The cooperation shown in coordinating forces in this key area is another example of the importance of our common plans for readiness."[176] Indeed, at some point during the crisis, a number of additional nuclear depth bombs were delivered to Greenwood, Nova Scotia. Rumors persist to this day that a number of Argus and Neptune aircraft were in fact uploaded with these weapons and that some flew patrols to the outer edges of the sea-air barrier because the long range of the Argus's exceeded the operating range of the US Navy Neptunes based at Argentia.[177]

Douglas Harkness was finally able to get Cabinet to discuss the nuclear issue in a 30 October meeting. The previous day, Pearson asked the government in the House about what arrangements had been made. The government was increasingly vulnerable on this point. Harkness revealed, without going into details, that there were standby arrangements for nuclear weapons delivery to Canada in an emergency. It was only a temporary measure and limited to the Cuban emergency. It was important that a permanent government-to-government agreement exist, and negotiations for it had to start as soon as possible. In a complete turnaround, Diefenbaker stated "He thought it would be necessary to proceed with the negotiations but on the understanding that if there was any leak . . . they would stop forthwith."[178]

According to the Cabinet minutes, there was a "lengthy discussion." The debate moved back and forth between those who thought that the emergency standby arrangements should become the content of the government-to-government agreement and those who recognized that this was not a feasible long-term arrangement. In the end, those favoring the formalization of the emergency standby arrangements succeeded in their efforts. Harkness, Green, and Gordon Churchill were authorized to initiate negotiations.[179]

The Cuban Missile Crisis was now in a holding pattern as high-level moves continued over the relationship between the NATO-tasked Jupiters in Turkey and the Soviet MRBMs in Cuba. On 31 October, however, 30th NORAD region alerted its BOMARCs and scrambled its nuclear-armed interceptors when the Mid-Canada Line reported that two unidentified aircraft had penetrated Canadian airspace. Nothing was found and the reason for the tracks was never discovered.[180]

Negotiations over the MRBM withdrawal got hung up when the Americans insisted that the IL-28 BEAGLE bombers also be withdrawn. Soviet ships were turning around, and the MRBM sites were bulldozed, but the submarines and their support ships remained on station throughout November. By 13 November, however, there was movement on the IL-28 issue and the sub air barrier was terminated. On 17 November, the dispersed USAF air defense nuclear-armed interceptors returned to their home bases and on the twenty-seventh, RCAF Air Defence Command stood down.[181]

Nuclear Negotiations, the NATO Ministerial Meeting, and the Nassau Agreement: November–December 1962

The events and issues regarding nuclear weapons and NATO strategy discussed in the last two months of 1962 were not decisive things unto themselves. They basically contributed to the makeup of the weapons that would be used and the terrain over which the 1963 Canadian election campaign would be fought.

In early November, Harkness, Green, and Gordon Churchill arranged a meeting with Ivan White from the American embassy and asked for a formal American negotiating team to resolve the nuclear weapons impasse. A team consisting of White, a USAF general, and a State Department representative arrived within days. There was no problem with sorting out the NATO end of things. The Canadians, including Green, had no problem with the by now standard section dealing with Canadian access to the stockpile assigned to SACEUR. The biggest problem was access to nuclear weapons for the continental defense forces.[182]

Prior to the talks dealing with the continental defense forces, Harkness maintained close communication with Air Marshal Larry Dunlap, who replaced Campbell as the Chief of the Air Staff, and Air Vice-Marshal Roy Slemon at NORAD. Harkness wanted a detailed assessment of the steps and timing necessary to implement a formal emergency standby plan.

Slemon sent a detailed analysis, which almost forty years later unfortunately remains heavily redacted. Slemon appears to have based his argument against the emergency standby approach on the warning time and reaction time by the air defense forces. We know from other sources that submarine-launched missiles could impact within fifteen minutes of launch, that ICBMs would be detected fifteen minutes after launch and that the total flight time was between twenty-two and thirty minutes; and that the other radar systems gave NORAD two to three hours' warning of a bomber attack.

All three systems would be used against North America in combination. Therefore, to take the two-hour bomber warning time and argue that MB-1s could be picked up, delivered, and attached in time for use was unreasonable under attack.

The same went for the BOMARC warheads. In light of the problems encountered during the Cuban Missile Crisis, Dunlap told Harkness and Green that:

> At some stage in the period of rising tension, a decision would have to be arrived at by the Canadian Government to *request* the nuclear warheads— this in turn to be followed by an approach to the United States—this in turn, by the issuance of instructions by the [deleted]. . . . (How much time *is* required for a decision to invite the United States to send nuclear weapons to Canada? You *are far better judges* of that than I. Let me merely say that, *under certain circumstances of the day or night* [deleted] then to that you must add your estimate of the time for a decision.[183]

The whole process just took far too long given the threat. Using this system in a protracted crisis was also out since the Cabinet could not make up its mind in time and would not delegate authority to the military commanders.

The Canada-US negotiating group explored several methods all of which revolved around the existing emergency standby approach. One method, discussed earlier in this chapter, involved having transport aircraft on standby fly down to American bases, pick up warheads, return to bases, attach them, and prepare to use. The same arguments used within the RCAF against this approach were used in the Canadian-American discussions. These were the problems associated with weather, the short warning, and the long time needed to mate BOMARC warheads to their airframes. The group concluded:

> any such plan was impractical and far too costly and the only purpose it would serve would be to enable the Canadian Government to say no nuclear weapons were being held on Canadian soil. This, however, appeared to be Howard Green's chief objective and he insisted on going over the times, men involved, and all the other details at great length, evidently with the hope of convincing himself and others that it was a workable scheme.[184]

One member of the negotiating group raised the possibility that, perhaps, certain essential parts for the weapons themselves could be removed and stored in the United States, deployed to Canada in an emergency, and inserted by trained technicians. The Americans went home to explore this avenue.[185]

Later in November the Americans came back to Ottawa with a number of "missing essential part" concepts. Apparently, one of these schemes reduced the delivery and insertion time to one hour.[186] This improvement did not, however, overcome the problems with getting the government to ask for the delivery promptly in the midst of a crisis or in a situation where the precrisis period produced ambiguity.

Another aspect, which does not appear to have been raised in detail, was the physical danger of inserting an essential part of a nuclear weapon under duress. We are assuming here that the essential part referred to is the "physics package," the actual core of the weapon. Nuclear weapons, like any other type of explosive, are susceptible to electrical fields and discharges. The delivery casings were rigorously tested to ensure that things like static electricity did not interfere with the arming or detonating systems. The weapons were designed to be sealed in a ready state and attached to their carrier before they were used (in the case of the MB-1 or the Mk 101) or to be an integral part of the carrier at all times (like the W 40 on the BOMARC). The weapons are unsealed only when they are undergoing maintenance, and then such maintenance is undertaken in a special facility devoid of electrical and other interferences. Having a nuclear weapon maintenance technician, as opposed to the more numerous aircraft armorers, fumble with a multikiloton physics package on a dark, cold, and wet runway at 0400 hours with the pressure of enemy inbound nuclear weapons on his mind, after having been awoken and flown several hundred miles in a propeller-driven transport aircraft, was a prescription for disaster.

Harkness then tried to get Diefenbaker to sign the government-to-government agreement late in November so that the NATO forces could sign their respective technical agreements. Diefenbaker refused and said that it would all have to be signed and announced at once. Furthermore, Diefenbaker added, why not sign the agreement and then call for a snap election? This move would theoretically allow the people to decide. Some Cabinet members thought that, yes, there should be an election, but the nuclear weapons issue should not be the main focus of it.[187]

The genesis for future alterations in the Liberal Party's defense platform for the 1963 election and Canadian defense policy initially involved a tour of NATO Parliamentarians. An annual event, each member sent a bipartisan group of elected officials to Paris for briefings and networking. In late November 1962 Paul Hellyer, accompanied by the portly, impulsive, but astute thirty-eight year-old Judy LaMarsh, the Member of Parliament from Niagara Falls (herself an Army veteran), flew to Europe. Hellyer and LaMarsh had an agenda: to collect "up-to-date information about [Canada's] role in collective security"[188] for use as political ammunition.

LaMarsh and Hellyer quickly learned from Air Vice-Marshal Larry Wray that the Air Division was useless without nuclear weapons.[189] None of the 4 Brigade people "would tell us whether their warheads were filled with sand, were empty shams, or were operative warheads."[190] LaMarsh met General Norstad at "one of the interminable receptions":

> Over a drink, I opened a discussion of the failure of our Canadian personnel to be armed for their accepted responsibilities. I remember his long, green-gray eyes widening with surprise at being so verbally assaulted, and by a women at that. He quietly confirmed that this was true and that it was a matter of considerable concern. . . . Next day, in great secrecy, so that External Affairs would not get wind of it, an appointment was arranged for Paul Hellyer to meet with Norstad for a private interview. . . . Our information proved right: Diefenbaker had led us, and our allies, up the well-known creek and left us there without a paddle.[191]

On the flight home, LaMarsh and Hellyer discussed what to do. They both concluded "It led to no honourable alternative but a change in our non-nuclear policy to accept the responsibilities." Hellyer then molded the information into a memo for Pearson and both met with Pearson, who "didn't react very well."[192]

Hellyer's memo included the substance of the current NATO strategy debate, namely that conventional forces needed to be built-up and that the theatre nuclear forces needed to be improved and under non-American control. Without a flexible force structure, Norstad noted, "We are subjecting ourselves to unnecessary risk." The Air Division and 4 Brigade were critical to SHAPE's plans since both were manned by extremely competent and dedicated personnel who set an example. In the case of the Air Division, there was no other alternative but to use nuclear weapons; they were a key part of SACEUR's strike force and there was no replacement for them. In fact, Norstad told Hellyer, Canada's influence in NATO would dissipate if the Air Division were removed or if it was incapable of fulfilling its role. It was that high profile.[193]

Hellyer concluded by stating "we must uphold the honour and integrity of the nation" and "the great majority of the Canadian people would want their country to fulfill its obligations." There was no choice but to establish a platform calling for accession to the government-to-government agreement.[194] Pearson took all of this under advisement for the time being.

Part of this advisement process included extensive briefings by Charles Foulkes. Foulkes had run as an MP in the last election, but was defeated. It did not prevent Pearson from relying on Foulkes's advice on NATO and the nuclear issue. After all, Pearson had been in opposition since 1957 and had not had access to the important decisions made from then until 1960.

Foulkes produced several detailed briefings. The most important of these confirmed for Pearson the fact that there was a nuclear commitment implicit in Canada's acceptance of MC 48 and MC 14/2 (revised), an explicit one in signing the NATO stockpile and information sharing agreements, and, most particularly, in the acceptance of the CF-104 strike role. As for BOMARC, there was "never any intention" on the part of Canada or the United States of arming it with a conventional warhead.[195] Noting in another extensive briefing that nuclear weapons were a "complicated and complex subject, which is discussed in an atmosphere of prejudice, emotion, and misunderstanding," Foulkes walked through the precepts of deterrent strategy and explained how each Canadian contribution, conventional as well as nuclear, fit into this. He also outlined the custody and control problem and the dual key solution.[196] Pearson now had a clear understanding of the complexities of the relationship between nuclear weapons and conventional forces in the NATO and NORAD structures, and of the desperate need for timely warhead access.

Dean Rusk noted in a telegram that the 13–15 December 1962 NATO Ministerial Meeting was "marked by an almost intolerable serenity."[197] It was readily apparent that NATO members agreed with an American State Department assessment that "the Cuban crisis demonstrated the value of a broad spectrum of power . . . which permitted the application of a carefully measured response sufficient to deal with imminent danger without triggering a nuclear response."[198] Most of the potential outrage which had been anticipated from the Italians and Turks over the removal of the Jupiter IRBMs had been muted with promises to allocate Polaris submarines to SACEUR and the beefing up of the South European Task Force, a joint NATO nuclear command based in Italy.[199] It was a bit of a lull before another storm that would erupt in 1963 over multilateral NATO nuclear arrangements.

Green, Harkness, McNamara, and Rusk, however, privately discussed the continental nuclear issue in Paris amongst the NATO meetings. There was little movement on the issue, though the Americans at this point still thought that the "missing essential piece" plan was still workable. A press release was issued stating everything was in order and Canada was fulfilling her commitments to NATO.[200] This would cause problems later in January 1963.

A key event in the ongoing NATO nuclear weapons saga was the Anglo-American meeting between Kennedy and Macmillan at Nassau in the Bahamas from 18 to 21 December 1962. Though the details of the Skybolt/Polaris affair are beyond the scope of this work,[201] the Nassau Meeting had some later bearing on Diefenbaker's nuclear weapons policy in the 1963 election campaign. According to one observer, the Nassau Agreement was "an achievement in ambiguity."[202] In essence, the Americans were going to give the British Polaris missiles and technical assistance so that the British could eventually replace the V-bomber force with SSBNs. The ambiguity lay in whether or not the British had, in fact, committed the new Polaris force to NATO or would keep it for national purposes.[203] This compromise was necessary because the British needed the appearance of an independent strategic nuclear force, while the Americans did not want the French, and more especially the West Germans, having independent deterrents.

Canadian analysis distinguished between an Inter-Allied Nuclear Force (IANF) concept and the Multilateral Force (MLF) concept, both of which were discussed at the meeting. Britain advocated the IANF. The IANF would be a composite force consisting of portions of UK Bomber Command, USAF SAC, three USN Polaris-carrying SSBNs, and the existing theatre and tactical nuclear forces already in Europe, including RCAF 1 Air Division. SHAPE would select the targets. Release of the IANF would be a higher-level NATO responsibility, not an American one. The MLF, on the other hand, now had evolved into a grouping of American and British Polaris-carrying SSBNs, and a mix-manned surface fleet carrying Polaris missiles. Again, as with the IANF, SHAPE would handle targeting and NATO would control release. External Affairs and National Defence both consistently favored the IANF concept.[204]

Diefenbaker had originally invited Macmillan to Ottawa, but the British Prime Minister countered with an offer to have a meeting in Nassau after the other affairs were disposed of. Macmillan was even successful in bribing Kennedy to have lunch with Diefenbaker. Diefenbaker told Kennedy at some point that movement had to be made on formalizing the standby arrangement. Out of courtesy, Macmillan briefed Diefenbaker on the contents of the Nassau Agreement.[205] It would cause problems in 1963.

Polls taken in November and December consistently indicated that at least 60% of the Canadian people favored acquiring nuclear weapons.[206]

12

CLOSE TO THE APEX: THE PEARSON GOVERNMENT, NUCLEAR WEAPONS, AND NATIONAL SECURITY POLICY, 1963–1964

That One's Country Ought to be Defended,
Whether With Shame or Glory, By
Whatever Means Possible
—MACHIAVELLI, *THE PRINCE*

Introduction

The accession of Mike Pearson's Liberal government to power in April 1963 produced dramatic changes in Canadian national security strategy. Canada was now able to formally access the nuclear stockpile, complete all the modifications to the delivery systems, and effectively contribute to the defense of North America and Western Europe. Canadian roles and missions were not dramatically altered during the course of this process. This process, however, produced a question that no one in the Pearson government would or could answer: What exactly is the nature of the relationship between the armed forces and national aims?

The lack of a defined answer and dynamic means of implementing it generated in the successor Trudeau government in 1968, questioning over the fundamental *existence* of the armed forces, while at the same time the forces became a truly effective instrument *if* the government chose to use it (either in peacetime in an alliance context or in wartime in a conflict context). Put another way, Canada now had a force structure designed to implement her strategic policy. That strategic policy, however, was gradually moving away from the use of armed forces (in peacetime as well as wartime) as a key instrument in the conduct of national policy.

In effect, the Pearson government deliberately laid the foundations for denuclearization while at the same time accepting nuclear weapons into Canada's force structure. This chapter will examine the Pearson national security policy-making apparatus and process, the signing of the nuclear weapons agreements with the United States, and the background behind the 1964 Defense White Paper.

The 1963 Campaign: Diefenbaker Self-Destructs

The starter pistol for the 1963 phase of Canada's nuclear weapons crisis was inadvertently fired by General Lauris Norstad. Norstad retired, which entitled him to undertake a good-bye tour of NATO members. In reality, differences between Norstad and Kennedy's civilian national security advisors over NATO strategy as well as Kennedy's handling of the 1961 Berlin Crisis prompted the retirement. In essence, Norstad was considered by the Kennedy administration to be too pro-European in his outlook on NATO issues.[1] Apparently, SACEUR had virtually been accused of being a traitor by some of McNamara's younger "whiz kids" in the Pentagon corridors. The proud Norstad could put up with only so much of this for so long after all he had done to preserve the peace. General Lyman M. Lemnitzer replaced him.

Norstad flew to Ottawa and gave a speech on 3 January 1963. The speech itself was short and gave homage to Canada's NATO troops and to the idea of NATO. The question and answer period with the media following the speech proved to be politically explosive for the Diefenbaker government:

> Q: General, do you consider that Canada has committed itself to provide its Starfighter squadron in Europe with tactical nuclear weapons?

> A: . . . my answer to that is yes. This has been a commitment that was made, the continuation of a commitment that existed before. . . .

> Q: Does it mean sir that if Canada does not accept nuclear weapons for these aeroplanes that she is not actually fulfilling her NATO commitments?

> A: I believe that is right.[2]

Fundamentally, the media and the Opposition were confused by the process and relationship between the need for a bilateral agreement, training, and actually having access to the nuclear warheads. This information was secret, as it should have been. The media treated the answers as black and white issues; that is, in their thinking Canada should not have acquired CF-104 strike aircraft unless Canada had signed the government-to-government and then the service-to-service agreements. They could not understand the nature of the gray area in which the RCAF had operated by pushing the limits of the earlier nuclear information agreements. They could not understand the reluctance of the Diefenbaker government to sign the agreements. They could not accept ambiguity.

Judy LaMarsh noted "all hell broke loose."[3] With the press in full storm ("Norstad's NATO Warning Puts Government on the Spot" was the headline in the *Ottawa Citizen*), the Norstad visit was perceived by Prime Minister Diefenbaker as a Kennedy plot to dictate policy to Canada and to undermine the elected government by providing ammunition to the Opposition.[4] Norstad, however, was a firm supporter of NATO, a levelheaded strategist, and a friend of Canada. To assert that Norstad was following the orders of the amorphous, evil, manipulative Pentagon or the White House flies in the face of the reason he was retiring: the Kennedy people wanted him out.

By early January, Robert McNamara sent word to Harkness that the "missing essential piece" standby approach discussed in the wake of the Cuban crisis was not workable.[5] Diefenbaker shifted into evasive mode, would not talk about signing the agreement, and then called an election. As Harkness noted: "[Diefenbaker's] intrigue and hypocrisy on the [nuclear arms question] are apparent as is the fact that he looked at it almost from the partisan political point of view rather than from that of the security of the country and of our obligations in defence to NATO and NORAD."[6]

On the other side of the House, Hellyer and LaMarsh considered resigning if the Liberal Party did not adopt a new defense policy. Mike Pearson, meanwhile, carefully considered the Hellyer memorandum.[7] After extensive private discussions with contacts in NATO, the UN, and Washington, he relented. LaMarsh noted:

> His daughter later told me that she thought this was the single most difficult decision he had had to take and that it caused him much personal anguish. I have no doubt it is true. It was probably the first time he had to wrestle down his own strong views in formulating a policy for the country. No leader can reverse a public stand with any ease, especially when it means a battle against his own deeply held convictions. But he did it. . . . It seems to me too bad he didn't do it more often. And none of us foresaw the events to follow.[8]

There were, of course, pragmatic political reasons for changing the Liberal Party defense platform. One party member reminded Pearson in a 3 January letter that he was:

> almost equally concerned *as a practical politician* about retaining the support of the armed forces without which we cannot win an election. For (with dependents) close to a quarter of a million voters are involved and, like other voters, most of them are primarily concerned with their livelihood. And that quarter million voters in places like Chatham N.B., North Bay, etc etc. not to mention larger places like Halifax are highly sensitive. . . . Then there are veterans with pride in the three services. . . . [I]t is because I believe this is the one subject on which a wrong course could sink our prospects without a trace that I have written so emphatically.[9]

It is difficult to believe that purely moral and honor-oriented considerations were the only ones at play in Pearson's mind when he made the decision to flip-flop the Liberal defense policy platform. The polls clearly demonstrated what Canadians believed. In January 1963, 57.8% thought that Canada should have nuclear weapons in Canada (34.3% said no and 7.9% had no opinion). As for nuclear weapons for Canada's NATO forces, 67.2% said yes, 24.7% no, and 8.1% undecided. More tellingly, when asked whether Canadian defense policy should be in agreement on major issues with the United States, a whopping 77.8% said yes, 16% no. Pearson was well aware of these figures in January 1963.[10]

On 12 January 1963, Mike Pearson gave a speech at a luncheon of the York-Scarborough Liberal Association. This speech formed the basis of future Canadian defense policy and served as another shot at the Diefenbaker government's lack of movement on the issues. Most importantly, Pearson tentatively renounced his destabilization policy: "An Opposition has a duty not to exploit defence for purely partisan reasons. I certainly accept that obligation for myself."[11]

The overall framework of the new platform included the following points:

1. The prevention of war cannot mean the sacrifice of freedom. We must have peace *and* freedom.
2. Defense policy must be designed to prevent war by ensuring that the price of aggression will be too high to be borne by the aggressor.
3. Deterrent and defensive force is necessary to preserve peace; every country has an obligation to do what it can, even in the nuclear age, to defend its own territory.
4. No country can defend itself alone; the only security lies in collective action.
5. In dealing with our friends, we must assume that a change of government would not normally mean a sudden and unilateral renunciation of treaty obligations. Our friends have the same right to assume that the commitments of Canada are the commitment of the nation.[12]

Canada, therefore, had a commitment to provide CF-104s and Honest Johns to NATO and BOMARCs and nuclear interceptors to NORAD. These commitments could not be changed through nonaction and obfuscation. Emergency standby arrangements were unacceptable. Any changes had to be negotiated and discussed. Notably, Pearson leaned on the authority provided by Norstad's speech.

In addition to the framework, Pearson provided a checklist of actions that he though the government should undertake:

1. A special committee in the House should be formed to reexamine all aspects of Canadian defence policy.
2. Canada should sign the nuclear weapons agreements with the United States and action should be undertaken to equip Canadian forces with nuclear weapons.
3. Canada should press NATO for collective control of nuclear weapons within NATO and oppose independent nuclear deterrents.
4. Canada should support the strengthening of NATO's conventional forces.
5. Canada should continue to support early warning systems.
6. Canada's defence policy should be geared to its industrial structure. We should not try to do a little of everything.
7. Canada's defence forces, whether stationed in this country or Europe, should be so organized, trained and equipped as to be able to intervene wherever and whenever required for UN, NATO, or Canadian territorial operations, especially in UN Peace Preservation operations.[13]

There were caveats. Canada's new defense policy, after its examination by the house, "must not hinder or minimize Canada's influence for peace at the UN." This contradicted a statement later in the speech that said "[Canada] must do nothing to weaken continental or NATO collective policy and action."[14] One other controversial aspect, thrown in at the end, was: "The three Canadian defence services should be fully integrated for maximum efficiency and economy, both in operation and administration."[15] Though this would not necessary affect Canadian nuclear policy in a direct sense, it would forever alter the structure and ethic of the Canadian armed forces. In a follow-up television interview, Pearson reiterated aspects of the new platform for a national audience.[16]

Pearson's flip-flop was not without cost. He lost the support of the small but growing left-leaning francophone elements within the Liberal Party, as well as many anglophone academics who generally were Liberal Party supporters. The most potentially influential person who responded negatively to the new policy was Pierre Elliot Trudeau, future Prime Minister, who caustically referred to Pearson as the "defrocked priest of peace" after the Scarborough speech. In a rather acerbic editorial, Trudeau concluded (without evidence) that "les hipsters" in the Kennedy administration in Washington had collaborated with Pearson to unseat the Diefenbaker government.[17] Trudeau's views would have a delayed and negative effect on defense policy later in the decade.

Diefenbaker gathered his political organizers and instructed them to oppose the Pearson defense platform at all costs and to "delay any decision on acquiring the warheads."[18] This ended the ongoing discussions with the Americans.

More internal discussions within the Conservative Party occurred when Harkness attempted to get the party leadership to implement a platform supporting nuclear weapons acquisition. Diefenbaker blocked this, and Harkness told his wife in private that he would resign if this state of affairs continued. Harkness threatened to resign in a 20 January Cabinet meeting. Some members made conciliatory moves, urging Harkness not to take precipitous action. The next day, Diefenbaker acceded to Opposition demands that a defense debate take place in the House.[19]

The Prime Minister also accepted, under duress, the formation of a special Cabinet committee to examine the nuclear weapons issue. This special committee included Harkness, Green, Fleming, and Churchill. It had ten meetings in two days, during which the four men met in Donald Fleming's office and pulled out every classified Canadian, American, and NATO document and public statement ever produced on the nuclear weapons issue. Even after the assembly of an impressively detailed chronology that clearly demonstrated there were several nuclear commitments, Green asserted that this was not convincing enough evidence. He held this position until the other three forced him to sign a summary of the special committee's findings.[20]

This summary was massaged for Green's benefit, but not too much. The key to the whole argument was the CF-104 force. It was clear this commitment, taken in 1959, included nuclear use obligations. Green was able to get the committee to state that the Nassau Agreement and the ongoing Multilateral Force debate in NATO placed the commitment under "some doubt." Canada, therefore, should clarify this commitment. If NATO said to arm, then Canada should arm the force with nuclear weapons. The same went for the Honest John battery. Training to work with and employ nuclear weapons was already in progress, and it should continue. As for NORAD, negotiations would continue, "with a view to ensuring the highest degree of availability for Canada."[21]

According to Donald Fleming:

> Doug and I proceeded to meet Dief in his little office at the house at 7:30 p.m. . . . . Before we had even opened our mouths it was plain to me that he was in a truculent and very impatient mood. . . . . He said in preemptory tones, "Come to the point. What have you done?" With satisfaction, I said, "We have reached agreement," and handed him a copy still expecting his commendation for it. Instead, after quickly glancing over it he angrily flung it down on the desk and said, "I won't have it!" He repeated the words. There was nothing else for me and Doug to do than say good night.[22]

The House defense debate occurred on 25 January. Diefenbaker contributed a long, evasive, rambling speech. It is not worth going into the details here; suffice it to say it incorporated elements of the special Cabinet committee conclusions, babble about disarmament and the Nassau agreement, the MLF and Polaris, and incoherent statements about CF-101Bs. The speech was all interspaced with judicious quotes and misquotes from Hansard and media sources. There was no logic or organization to the speech.[23]

Pearson then went on to deliver a reasoned argument. A strong Canadian identity did not mean isolationism, Pearson said, and isolationism meant "immaturity." There were real problems with American economic penetration, but these were divorced from the exigencies of legitimate defense measures that had to be taken in the face of a real totalitarian threat. Canada had NATO and NORAD commitments, and she had to live up to them.[24]

After the debate Douglas Harkness realized the perception generated in the media was that Diefenbaker's speech was antinuclear. It forced Harkness's hand. The next day he issued a press statement to "clarify" the Prime Minister's remarks. This press release was fundamentally the same document that the special Cabinet committee had generated.[25]

Diefenbaker called Harkness on the carpet and said: "This is terrible! You've ruined everything! Why did you do it? You had no right to make such a statement!" The Prime Minister stormed out of the room. It was, Harkness noted, "a very unpleasant five minutes."[26]

It was now time for the Americans to interfere. William Tyler from the American embassy, in a communication with George W. Ball, Undersecretary of State, gave his analysis of the situation. The nuclear issue was "beclouded" by the speech and was "misleading" in its references to Nassau. "Prompt action" was necessary to "clarify the record and to sweep away the confusion which Diefenbaker's statement can cause in Canadian minds."[27]

The American press release was issued the next day and touched off a firestorm in the House and in the Canadian media. In it, the State Department stated clearly that the BOMARC B was designed to protect Canadian cities and US SAC bases. It could carry only a nuclear warhead. The two governments had agreed to the program in 1958. After the Cuban Missile Crisis the two countries started negotiations for nuclear warheads access that was "exploratory in nature." No acceptable solution had been found. Nassau had nothing to do with continental defense and little to do with Canada. Canadian acquisition of these warheads did not in any way constitute Canada's joining the "nuclear club."[28]

This release contradicted statements by the Prime Minister, Green, and in some cases, even Pearkes back during the Senate hearings of 1960. Harkness was appalled. It was, in his view, "a very foolish move which was bound to be resented in Canada as an attempt to interfere in a very controversial political question."[29] The Cabinet now attempted to respond. Diefenbaker maniacally asserted: "We now have an election issue!" to his horrified colleagues, who then attempted to dissuade him of this fantasy. Pearson demanded Harkness's resignation in the House and Diefenbaker instructed Harkness not to discuss the issue publicly. Secretary of State Dean Rusk recovered and, after being chewed out by a furious John Kennedy, had the State Department issue a public quasi-apology on 1 February.[30]

Diefenbaker then recalled Canada's ambassador to the United States, Charles Ritchie. He taunted Pearson and claimed that the Opposition leader was collaborating with the Americans to unseat the government, a charge that Pearson was forced to deny in the House.[31]

Lieutenant Colonel, The Honourable Douglas Harkness, PC, GM, ED, MP, was finally at the end of the rope:

> I had come to the conclusion that the intransigence of the Prime Minister and his complete preoccupation with maintaining his own position as Prime Minister, together with his disregard for the interests of the country and the party were such that he could no longer be trusted with the welfare of the country and must go. Several ministers to whom I spoke along this line agreed, and I told them I was now absolutely firm in my decision to resign unless he did so.[32]

On 4 February, he resigned in a legendary and vicious Cabinet session. On his way out the door, Douglas Harkness was called a traitor by Gordon Churchill and the pious Howard Green.[33]

The most blistering but correct analysis came from American Ambassador W. Walton Butterworth, who told Rusk in a cable that:

> In view our patient tolerance of unrealistic Canadian view of external world past half dozen years, witness [government of Canada] foot dragging in vital matter continental defence and pretentious posturing in various international arenas, our sudden dose of cold water naturally produced immediate cry of shock and outrage. Traditional psychopathic accusations of unwarranted US interference in Canadian domestic affairs, while vehement, are subsiding quickly. . . . For past four or five years we have—doubtless correctly—tolerated essentially neurotic Canadian view of world and Canadian role. . . . [Diefenbaker is] determined to carry on in dream world as long as possible. . . . He is [an] undependable, unscrupulous political animal at bay and we are ones who boxed him in. . . . We should be less the accoucher of Canada's illusions.[34]

On 5 February 1963, after a sustained attack by Diefenbaker on the Pentagon and the State Department, the government lost a vote of nonconfidence (142 to 111) in the House of Commons. Parliament was dissolved, and the 1963 election campaign was on. As Canadian ambassador to the United States Charles Ritchie put it: "I consider . . . [Diefenbaker's] disappearance a deliverance; there should be prayers of thanksgiving in the churches. And these sentiments do not come from a Liberal."[35]

Cabinet met before the election to discuss the nuclear weapons issue one last time. Gordon Churchill replaced Harkness as the de facto Defence Minister. Green was now in full control and initiated another round of discussions with the Americans. This time, however, the Americans were sick to death of the situation and "indicated that the U.S. government would not be prepared to enter into an arrangement including the storage in the U.S. of the nuclear warheads for possible use by Canada."[36] Nevertheless, Diefenbaker "expressed the hope that the negotiations would continue and would achieve success."[37]

Then Harkness went to the media and declared that the "missing essential piece" scheme was not feasible. If only to spite Harkness, the Prime Minister attempted to get the Americans to sign an agreement to this effect, but they were not playing ball. He then went to the House of Commons and gave a rousing speech claiming that Canada had been deceived, that the BOMARC was in fact capable of using conventional as well as nuclear warheads. The NORAD public affairs section then sent out a press release noting the differences between the BOMARC A and B models and the fact that Canada had agreed to get the B, which could in fact only use nuclear warheads. When confronted with this, Diefenbaker "smiled mysteriously and answered, "Ah, but I have the press release," which turned out to be a fact sheet dated 1958. Diefenbaker's behavior grew more and more bizarre. He then told the House that only six hundred of the twelve hundred USAF ADC interceptors carried nuclear weapons. The State Department then complained that he was releasing classified information, to which Diefenbaker responded that the United States was trying to treat Canada like Guatemala. The media had a field day.[38]

The situation was aggravated further by US Secretary of Defense Robert McNamara's testimony to the House Military Appropriations Subcommittee. In a discussion regarding the relative merits of the BOMARC system and how much money should be spent on it, McNamara included in his testimony his belief that:" At the very least [the BOMARCs] would cause the Soviets to target missiles against them and thereby increase their missile requirements or draw missiles onto these BOMARC targets than would be otherwise available for other targets."[39]

This was surely an insensitive statement to make given the politically charged atmosphere in Ottawa, a gaffe of the highest order. Diefenbaker then used the McNamara statements to pummel Pearson in the House, which lead to conspiracy theories emanating from the Prime Minister about American influence and manipulation. The American State and Defense Departments were extremely perturbed, noting, "It would be most unwise to exacerbate the matter further by release of more testimony," and that it "could have adverse repercussions on United States interests."[40]

The BOMARC issue dominated the entire last week of the election campaign and the media unrelentingly slammed anybody who remotely had anything to do with BOMARCs.[41]

It all came to an end, mercifully, on 8 April 1963, when John G. Diefenbaker's government was barely defeated at the polls by the Liberal Party led by Lester B. "Mike" Pearson. The rein of Dief the Chief was over, and Canada could now make good on her international commitments.

Strategic Policy Process and Personalities in the Pearson Regime

Pearson's cabinet established its objectives after being sworn in on 22 April 1963. Domestically, these included radical changes to the social security structure in Canada and a reexamination of Quebec's standing within Confederation. The priority, however, was to improve relations with the United States and United Kingdom and thus "restore Canada's responsibilities in international political and economic circles as a leader in search of peace, security, prosperity, and the elimination of poverty in the Third World."[42]

The team that would carry this out, the Cabinet, consisted of twenty-six people. Unlike the Diefenbaker or St. Laurent Cabinets, no less than eight of Pearson's Cabinet were ex-civil servants, which Mitchell Sharp, the Minister of Trade and Commerce (and later Secretary of State for External Affairs under Trudeau in 1968), pointed out "was not particularly healthy [for] the political process in Canada."[43] This arrangement sometimes set non-ex-civil service Cabinet members at odds with what they saw as an inner circle. The latter group included Bud Drury, former Deputy Minister of National Defence who was now in charge of industry, Jack Pickersgill (Secretary of State) and others. Pearson would have to be cautious, since his government was a minority government, and key parliamentarians had to be kept on a short leash in Ottawa in case of snap votes in the House.

Cabinet business under Pearson was rather informal. Paul Martin, Secretary of State for External Affairs thought Pearson was "a pleasant man who ran a relaxed regime."[44] The Prime Minister decided what the consensus was and used his "sense of humour and boyishness [which] served him well in Cabinet. He could dissipate tensions by a witty off hand comment or an anecdote,"[45] which usually related to Pearson's baseball obsession. Mitchell Sharp thought: "Pearson's pragmatism and diplomacy were reflected in his handling of the Cabinet and the Caucus; he was reluctant to take a clear position when there was dissent."[46] Pearson did not dominate, he mediated.

There were caveats. Martin wanted the Cabinet to pay more attention to foreign affairs, but Pearson told him: "Don't encourage that or we'll never get through our agenda."[47] Sharp noted, "Foreign policy, for example, was seldom discussed in Pearson's cabinet. Pearson and the Secretary of State of External Affairs, Paul Martin, made the decisions."[48] In fact, Pearson established intercabinet committees for several domestic policy functions. Normally, bills would be discussed by the committees, then taken to the Cabinet, and then to the House. There was a Cabinet committee for External Affairs and Defence but it rarely met, probably because

Pearson revived the Cabinet Defence Committee instead.[49] The Panel on the Economic Aspects of Defence Questions was considered a dangerous instrument and not resuscitated under Pearson.

Four men handled strategic policy. The first was Pearson. Paul Martin was second. A lawyer representing Windsor in the House of Commons, Martin had served under St. Laurent when he was Secretary of State for External Affairs in the Mackenzie King government. He was one of the original five Canadian delegates to the United Nations in 1945, but then served as Health and Welfare Minister. A foreign affairs enthusiast, Martin believed that NATO was the cornerstone of Canadian foreign policy, since "for a country like Canada, the danger of great power domination was to some extent lessened by our continuous participation in a common forum."[50] In his view, "Canada's soldiers in Europe gave us leverage in the [North Atlantic] Council, so NATO's collective military strength gave the West a formidable stake at the bargaining table."[51] His chief antagonist in the cabinet thought Martin was an indecisive man who "seemed to seek a mild and non-controversial solution which, in the long run, weakened his position." Apparently Martin's "circumlocutory style could be very amusing."[52]

That antagonist was Walter Gordon, Minister of Finance. A chartered accountant from Toronto, he first met Pearson in 1934, when Gordon was a witness on a Royal Commission studying Canadian economic policy. He served in a wide variety of capacities dealing with economics during the Second World War in the King government and later on in the St. Laurent government. He was a senior Liberal Party strategist and wielded immense political influence. An economic nationalist, the only difference between Diefenbaker's approach and Gordon's approach to Canadian-American relations was a slightly lesser degree of suspicion on Gordon's part. As for defense matters, his view was: "The whole idea of spending a great deal more money on defence was nonsensical, both because I failed to see what Canada could gain or accomplish by having a larger or better-equipped military establishment and because I felt the money could be spent in better ways."[53] Canada, in his view, had completed its mission in Europe and should withdraw now that the European's were back on their economic feet twenty years after the war. He thought that Paul Hellyer, Minister of National Defence, was as "strange, serious, enigmatic" as his ideas on national defense.[54]

Part of the problem with regard to Gordon's convoluted economic policy making revolved around the advice he took from two "investment executives from Toronto [who] continued to be paid by their firms, and a tax specialist studying for his Master's degree at Harvard." This "gradually estranged Walter Gordon from his permanent officials."[55]

Paul Hellyer was now unleashed onto the scene with his carefully constructed agenda. As one observer noted in retrospect:

> There appeared to be no doubt in the mind of Mr. Hellyer, that his mandate from the government on being appointed Minister, was the eventual unification of the Armed Services. He set about it with determination and personal energy, so much so, that to many in the department it seemed to be

prompted more by political ambition and to eventually achieve a higher cabinet appointment and perhaps ultimately Prime Minister.[56]

Hellyer, wary of being captured by the staff in another 1957 NORAD–like situation, refused to sign anything or make any decisions during the first thirty days of his tenure as Minister of National Defence.[57]

The uniformed defense team did not change at this point: Air Chief Marshal Frank Miller, Admiral Herbert Rayner, General Geoffrey Walsh, and Air Marshal Larry Dunlap remained at their posts until mid-1964. As for External Affairs, the chain-smoking Norman Robertson, who had known Paul Martin for thirty years, continued as the Undersecretary until early 1964 when he had a cancerous lung removed. Marcel Cadieux replaced him, but only after Pearson and Robertson had a falling out.[58] Cadieux was "a staunch opponent of Communism" and a firm supporter of NATO.[59] Robert Bryce moved from Cabinet Secretary to Deputy Minister of Finance. The Clerk of the Privy Council now was Maurice Lamontange, who would exert influence on Pearson's domestic agenda toward Quebec, which affected strategic policy.

Domestic considerations regarding Quebec formed a large portion of the backdrop to policy making at this time. The long-standing and corrupt French Canadian political establishment in Quebec collapsed under its own weight in the early 1960s. This power vacuum was filled by an increased ethnic consciousness and a moderate-left provincial government. There were those who thought this government was too moderate and, in the wake of the Front de liberation Nationale (FLN) success in Algeria and Castro in Cuba, world revolution was imminent and Quebec was destined to be an independent socialist state. The government understood Quebec separatism threatened Canada's continued existence and set about ensuring that it did not happen. Then bombs started to go off in Montreal, and military armories were raided by the shadowy Front de Liberation du Quebec (FLQ). One FLQ action unit even planned to seize the LaMacaza BOMARC base in April 1965, but was thwarted before it could do so.[60]

The overall Pearson plan in the wake of the 1963 election, dubbed "Sixty Days of Decision," was nearly stillborn when a crisis over the federal budget emerged in May 1963. Walter Gordon's budget, which was not reviewed by the Cabinet or the Prime Minister, announced that Canada would implement massive trade protectionism. The main target was the United States with its preponderance of economic and cultural power. There were some heated scenes between Gordon and American Ambassador Walton Butterworth, who Gordon thought was "a prototype for the 'Ugly American' type of [US] diplomat."[61] Though this spat was by no means as serious as the nuclear weapons crisis, the undertones affected the Canadian-American relationship throughout the period.

Out of the Starting Blocks: Preliminaries to the Canada-US Nuclear Weapons Agreements, May 1963

Pearson dove headlong into the nuclear question on 1 May 1963, when he convened the Cabinet Defence Committee. The last time the CDC had met was in October

1962, and then only briefly, and before that in January 1961. In this meeting, Hellyer reviewed the status of the nuclear arrangements. The premise that the BOMARCs, CF-101Bs, Honest Johns, and CF-104s were ineffective without nuclear weapons was immediately agreed to, as well as that RCN and RCAF ASW aircraft should continue to be "adapted to use nuclear depth charges in order to meet a prospective requirement."[62]

Martin explained the relationship among the government-to-government agreement, the service-to-service agreements, and the nuclear information agreements. He confirmed that emergency standby arrangements existed to supply Canadian continental defense systems with warheads. Accordingly, Martin stated, "The initiative rested with the Canadian government. The question of nuclear weapons for the CF-104's must be decided if Canada is to be able to participate fully in NATO."[63]

The main issue was the projected obsolescence of the systems and whether NATO strategic concepts would militate against nuclear acquisition. Miller and Hellyer noted that BOMARC would be in service in the United States until at least 1966, and it was too late to get Nike Hercules. There was still a substantial bomber threat, and this threat would exist into the late 1960s. As for the CF-104 force, these aircraft were programmed into SHAPE's force planning, and the next review would not take place until 1969. No good purpose could be served by delaying their arming with nuclear weapons. Pearson queried Miller as to whether the Voodoo force needed nuclear weapons to fulfill its role. Miller explained the mechanics of nuclear air-to-air weapons.[64]

The Cabinet Defence Committee met again on 7 May to discuss the issue further. Martin continued with his chronology of nuclear weapons agreements. The only weapons not discussed publicly, he noted, were the nuclear antisubmarine weapons. The government might take some Conservative heat in the House on the other systems, but discussion of nuclear ASW weapons could be kept to a minimum. The biggest problem, Martin noted, was a growing dispute with the Americans. The American position on weapons release involved the predelegation issue. They thought that SACEUR, SACLANT, and CinCNORAD should continue to have predelegated use authority in certain restrictive circumstances. The emerging Canadian position, championed by External Affairs, was that the American president should have release authority, but only after intergovernmental consultation, where practical. Miller thought that a dual-key system for defensive weapons was "ridiculous," since those systems had to be able to react quickly. Dual-key, in his view, was acceptable for offensive systems. The Cabinet concluded, "For political reasons . . . it was important that the principle of dual control be embodied in the agreement. The Government would almost certainly be asked in parliament about the control of the weapons and must be able to give assurances that the right of the Canadian Government to authorize use had been protected in the agreement."[65]

Pearson asked whether the government-to-government agreement would have to be modified if Canada joined the NATO MLF. Miller told him no, that the MLF was a separate issue. What about the MB-1 storage agreement? Did the American squadrons stationed in Canada have MB-1s yet? Despite the request during the Cuban Missile Crisis, Miller told him, such permission was not given, though a plan to disperse USAF fighters equipped with MB-1s to nine Canadian airfields in an emergency was currently under consideration. As for SAC overflights, Miller assured the Prime Minister that there were twelve such flights per day over Canada carrying nuclear weapons on airborne alert.[66] (The SAC airborne alert flights were ended after a B-52 crash near Thule, Greenland, in 1968.)

The matters then went to Cabinet for lengthy discussion. The Cabinet Defence Committee report recommended that negotiations be undertaken immediately with the United States to acquire nuclear warheads, and that perhaps the Prime Minister should raise the issue in his upcoming meeting with the President at Hyannisport. The Canadian negotiating team was to ensure "no action is being contemplated by the United States, in respect to its own air defence forces, which might be construed as seriously discrediting any action taken by the Canadian Government to meet the requirements of its own air defence forces . . . particularly in regard to the BOMARC B missiles."[67]

Pearson was concerned about domestic political reaction. In this case, he proposed initiating negotiations with the Americans, giving a public explanation for the policy (though the government-to-government and service-to-service agreements would remain classified), and then allowing for debate in the House. If there were serious problems in the House, the service-to-service agreements would not be immediately signed. In his view, "The matter had been the subject of too much public debate to permit the governments simply to arrange for the stockpiling of the warheads and then present it as a *fait accompli*."[68] Pearson was now worried, as John Diefenbaker had been between 1957 and 1961, about the domestic political ramifications of a situation that was created long before the Liberal government came to power.

The Prime Minister was also concerned about coordinating the agreements with the election-promised open committee on defense policy, which was scheduled to start in June 1963. It might be desirable to delay a parliamentary debate until after the first round of committee hearings, or even artificially slow down the negotiating process with the Americans.[69] Pearson was already starting to have second thoughts and to follow John Diefenbaker's path of indecision and political ramifications.

Hellyer righted this rapidly by reminding the Prime Minister:

> the important argument in favour of honouring Canadian nuclear commitments was political: to re-establish confidence in Canada among the Allies and reopen lines of communication. The consequence of a failure to do this could be far-reaching; it might, for example, jeopardize extensive sales to the United States of the Caribou II [tactical transport aircraft designed and built in Canada], or lead to the withdrawal of U.S. concessions on the importation of Canadian oil.[70]

Cabinet members were primarily concerned with the custody and control arrangements. They agreed that the standard agreement was acceptable; that is, custody and ownership was an American affair, while the external security of the sites in Canada was a Canadian affair; that US forces would not use warheads designated for Canadian forces; and finally, that "the warheads would be released from U.S. custody by the President and the proposed agreement would require, here practical, prior intergovernmental consultation."[71]

Cabinet was briefed in detail on the annexes for each delivery system (Honest John, BOMARC, CF-104, nuclear antisubmarine weapons, and CF-101B/MB-1s). There was some questioning about the inclusion of the nuclear depth bombs, since there was "no formal commitment" made by Canada to accept these weapons. The government, some believed, had pledged to the Canadian public that the existing commitments would be met. This was not an existing commitment; therefore inclusion of it "would be at variance with that pledge,"[72] and by inference, cause problems with the Opposition if and when it became publicly known.

Hellyer countered, stating, "a number of Canadian antisubmarine aircraft had already been modified to permit the use of these weapons and he had had military advice that it would be soon impossible to carry out Canada's anti-submarine role without nuclear weapons."[73]

Inclusion of nuclear ASW weapons in the government-to-government agreement did not imply that the service-to-service agreement regarding nuclear antisubmarine weapons would in fact be signed. As Hellyer noted:

> continued expenditures on the adaptation of aircraft to permit them to use these weapons without taking even the preliminary steps towards making the weapons available would expose the government to the criticism that had been leveled at its predecessor. Several Ministers said that it was not so much a question of honouring commitments but of defending Canada by whatever means was necessary.[74]

Nuclear depth bombs remained in limbo for the time being.

Pearson was ready to discuss the matter with Kennedy, and he wanted Cabinet's concurrence. He was concerned about the effects of the Skybolt affair in the UK and did not want a similar thing happening to Canada's nuclear systems. The Prime Minister put off any discussion on MB-1 storage for the USAF air defense squadrons until after the Hyannisport meeting.[75]

Pearson flew down to Hyannisport on 10 May 1963 for discussions with President Kennedy. He told Kennedy a diplomatic note would be sent outlining the interest in Canada's continuing the nuclear negotiations for the Honest John, CF-104, CF-101B, and BOMARC warheads. There would be minor modifications to the language for domestic consumption. Pearson wanted Kennedy's assurance that neither he nor McNamara would "pull a Skybolt" on Canada. He also noted, "He wished commitments had not been made in [the] first place but this was water over the dam."[76] Nevertheless, Kennedy had to realize that close consultation was critical, since "the importance of the Canadian air contribution in Europe . . . was second in importance only to that of the United States."[77]

Kennedy was delighted and proceeded to brief Pearson on the status of the Nassau Agreement and the NATO MLF. What was Canada's position? Could Canada come aboard? The President emphasized that the MLF was politically significant regarding European unity and Germany's place within Europe. Pearson did not think that Canada would participate directly and did not support the idea of the MLF, since it was militarily dubious. He was more interested in the Inter-Allied Nuclear Force and the role Canada could play in that with its existing forces in Europe.[78] As the State Department noted, the "general atmosphere [of the] talks was excellent with Pearson giving repeated evidence of his determination [to] create and sustain cordial and frank relationship between two countries whose destiny [was] closely linked by history as well as geography, while maintaining Canadian identity and defending Canadian interests."[79]

Cabinet met in a follow-up session after the Hyannisport meeting. The debate over a nuclear ASW annex continued. Hellyer was of the opinion that it should be included, but Martin made a strong case for the potential political fallout that could occur in Parliament if an "additional" nuclear system were introduced at this supposedly late date. Hellyer again pointed out that the RCAF and RCN maritime forces were useless without these weapons and strenuously pressed for noninclusive language to be included in the agreement so that obsolescence of specific systems would not prohibit their replacement in the future. Pearson refused to accept this perspective and cabinet agreed only to the BOMARC, Honest John, CF-104, and CF-101B systems.[80] Pearson's stance was consistent with his belief that Canada should not have nuclear weapons and would eventually divest itself of them, perhaps after the special parliamentary defense committee concluded later in 1963. He essentially opted for rust out and did not leave any opening for replacement.

Pearson also told Cabinet that Kennedy had placed the issue of USAF ADC nuclear weapons storage at a lower priority in his discussions. Thus it did not have to be addressed at this time. According to minutes of that meeting, neither leader actually brought up this issue, so Pearson's motive for this statement in Cabinet is unknown.[81] Perhaps it was used to facilitate acceptance of the four warhead types.

The matter of SAC operations in Canada became increasingly irrelevant in 1963. Robert McNamara decided that the increase in deployed USAF ICBMs justified an accelerated reduction in the B-47/KC-97 force. The PJBD was informed about this decision, which would end Northern Tanker Force operations at Fort Churchill, Frobisher Bay, in 1963 and possibly at Namao and Cold Lake in 1964. No movement was taken on this on Kennedy's order during the 1963 election campaign. After consultation with the Canadian government, the USAF announced the withdrawal in August 1963.[82]

NATO Ministerial Meeting in Ottawa and the MLF: May 1963

The Diefenbaker government's flawed nuclear weapons policy prevented it from participating in the NATO MLF debate. The prevailing External Affairs' view was that the MLF or something like it should exist, with the express purpose of reining in perceived West German desires for nuclear weapons. This was an unfounded concern given West Germany's acceptance of MC 70 and the arming of its forces with nuclear weapons in 1959–1960. At the same time, however, External's leadership (Robertson and Green) eschewed participation in an MLF and even had ensured that any potential Canadian contribution to the Nassau-proposed Inter-Allied

NATO nuclear force with the CF-104 units was muted by the lack of access to the nuclear weapons stockpile. At the same time, NATO was undergoing a profound schism, as de Gaulle continued with his noncooperation doctrine.[83] Canada's contradictory nuclear policy excluded any hope of influencing the process in NATO with regard to the MLF and the French split. It was left to Pearson's government to pick up the pieces.

External Affairs provided Pearson with its earlier analysis of the IANF versus the MLF and their relationship to the Nassau Agreement.[84] In addition, External Affairs (Ross Campbell and Basil Robinson representing), Defence, and the Chiefs had received a briefing by an American MLF team back in November 1962. (The Diefenbaker government had expressed no interest in it at the time.) This briefing basically laid out what the MLF was and what planners were hoping Canada could contribute to.

The MLF concept had by this point stabilized into twenty-five special ships with each ship carrying eight ballistic missiles. The entire force would consist of mixed-manned crews totaling seventy-five hundred men drawn from NATO countries. It was a military as well as political force in that the purposes were to counter the Soviet missiles in Western Russia, to forestall independent nuclear proliferation within NATO, and to provide smaller NATO nations with a say in nuclear weapons use, free of bilateral relationships with the United States. Targeting and control would reside in SACEUR, perhaps with a special deputy to handle the MLF.[85]

Miller convened the Chiefs twice in May 1963 to discuss the MLF so they could provide advice to Cabinet for the upcoming NATO Ministerial Meeting to be held in Ottawa. Miller determined the IANF was really "conceived as a pilot scheme to lead to the MLF." Admiral Rayner was opposed to MLF since he thought Canadian participation would be drawn from the RCN. There was not enough manpower and it would detract from other commitments.[86]

On the other hand, if Canada contributed to the MLF, more influence within NATO would accrue:

> It is quite probable that Canada must be prepared to declare "in" or "out" in the comparatively near future. In this regard, it is incumbent upon the Canadian military authorities to do everything within their means to ensure that our future NATO undertakings are not cast into the limbo of uncertainty which until recently surrounded our nuclear capable forces under NATO command. Canadian participation in the Multilateral Force in more than nominal terms is important in preserving the NATO nature of the undertaking and thus in avoiding any connotation that American scraps are being thrown to placate European dogs.[87]

After Cabinet discussion, Pearson believed "Canada had no role to play in such a force."[88] Hellyer agreed, as he understood that the MLF's purpose was to constrain West Germany, not provide NATO with MRBMs. Martin, though a believer in the MLF, thought the CF-104 force could provide enough Canadian influence in NATO through the IANF instead: France would probably veto the MLF anyway. Canadian participation in the MLF would, however, be valuable later when the CF-104s became obsolete. Pearson sought to move the discussion away from any consideration of a future Canadian nuclear role in NATO.[89] Cabinet agreed the Prime Minister would draft the Canadian position for the NATO Ministerial Meeting and he would "make certain that the wording did not bind the government to an indefinite extension of a nuclear role."[90] Martin remained unconvinced. He thought a lack of Canadian support to the MLF would jeopardize nuclear weapons acquisition agreements with the Americans.[91]

By 20 May, Cabinet was still debating the MLF issue. A media report criticizing the government on the acceptance of a nuclear role for the CF-104 force and its relationship to the MLF had generated doubts in Pearson's mind. After going over NATO documents, he was now firmly convinced that Canada indeed had a commitment to arm the CF-104s with nuclear weapons. If an IANF were established, the CF-104 force would be placed under its command. As for the MLF, the Canadian delegation would "confine itself to noting any progress report that might be tabled at this meeting, while saying nothing that would prejudice U.S. attempts to gain support for this proposal."[92]

Briefly, business considered at the Ottawa NATO Ministerial Meeting on 22–24 May 1963 ranged from out of area problems, to Anglo-French economic problems, to cries for a conventional force buildup. On the nuclear front, NATO ratified plans for an expanded nuclear information agreement that would build on the 1954 and 1958 agreements.[93]

The MLF discussion did not go well and reached a point where Dirk Stikker and Kennedy had a private chat. The negative French position on MLF was based on what Stikker referred to as the "de Gaulle syllogism": "a great country must have nuclear weapons. France is a great country, therefore France must have nuclear weapons" in an unfettered way.[94] If this were not done, France would continue to foment distrust in NATO by declaring that North America had given up on Europe. Kennedy "remarked it was unfortunate that with people like Pearson, [Ludwig] Erhard, [Joseph] Luns, [Amintore] Fanfani and [Aldo] Moro as national leaders, all committed to cooperate within the Atlantic Alliance, one man could block the flow of history."[95]

In the end, the NAC generated a compromise. There would be no separate IANF for SACEUR, though the British committed their V-bomber force and the Americans committed several Polaris missile-launching submarines to SACEUR. SACEUR would also create a special nuclear deputy. Most importantly, there would be "arrangements for broader participation by non-Americans in nuclear activities at SHAPE and in Omaha."[96] This referred to the Joint Strategic Target Planning Staff (JSTPS), the link between NATO nuclear planning and American targeting. Eventually the MLF project was dropped by the Lyndon B. Johnson Administration as being politically unworkable.[97]

The decision to limit Canadian participation in the MLF, though positive in the long run, should not be seen as insightful on Pearson's part. He was primarily concerned with things other than NATO influence, specifically, domestic politics.

What it did produce, again by accident, was an increase in the bargaining power of the CF-104 force in NATO circles, assuming Canadian policy makers chose to use it.

End Game: The Government-to-Government Agreement Is Signed, August 1963

Problems relating to the release of nuclear warheads were placed before the chiefs in July 1963. In the COSC view, SACEUR and CinCNORAD "should have the authority to use nuclear warheads without further specific authority from the governments concerned in response to an unexpected and unmistakable large scale enemy attack."[98]

There would be time for consultation in other situations, however. The chiefs thought this was acceptable given the provisions of the Athens Agreement. In the NORAD situation, high-level consultation was desirable before NORAD was placed on DEFCON 1, "which would then constitute approval for CinCNORAD to use nuclear weapons as he subsequently required."[99] There were still concerns about the omission of nuclear ASW weapons from the agreement, but action on these would not be taken until the other agreements were finalized. The BOMARC, CF-101B, CF-104, and Honest John agreements were all approved by the Americans and were about to go to cabinet.[100]

Paul Martin presented Cabinet with the final agreement package on 18 July. It dealt with the four systems and did not address USAF air defense nuclear weapons storage at Goose Bay and Harmon. The Americans agreed at this point to remove the long-standing linkage between the two matters. Another draft agreement for these and the Argentia ASW site would be submitted later.[101]

Political considerations still affected the timing of the signing. Secretary of State Jack Pickersgill thought introduction of the agreement into the House for debate in July would seriously interfere with other important debates, like the budget debate, which would be divisive. Then there was the vital federal-provincial conference, which involved elements of the Quebec question. Attempting to sneak in the nuclear agreement was not conceivable given its volatility with the Opposition. Additionally, some Cabinet members did not believe they had enough time to examine the agreements. Pearson therefore put it off for another week.[102]

President Kennedy had by this point delegated signing authority to Walton Butterworth, the American ambassador. He was leaving town, which delayed the signing again. Then atmospheric test ban negotiations appeared to be on the verge of a breakthrough. This was not considered to be congruent with an announcement that Canada would obtain nuclear warheads.[103]

The Cabinet Defence Committee met on 2 August to assess the situation. The only sticking point was a small bit of wording. Both countries now had to authorize weapons use, not just the United States. This meant that the Prime Minister consulted with the President, and each separately informed his national units. The Canadian units in Canada would then await the Prime Minister's release order after the American custodial detachment had received word via national means. This was all incorporated at the last minute.[104]

After some procedural delays involving the wording of the joint public announcement and more minor debate over storage in Canada for non-Canadian units, the Cabinet finally met on 16 August to finalize things prior to a noon press conference. Pearson was emphatic that every effort be made to ensure the signing was portrayed as the culmination of three years of work and not some new scheme. He was still afraid of Opposition and Soviet criticism, given the proximity in time to the atmospheric test ban treaty. The announcement was made.[105] On 29 August 1963, Air Marshal Dunlap ordered his subordinate commanders to carry it out, pointedly punctuating the time lag:

> In line with the Cabinet decision of 6 Dec 1960 and the government-to-government agreement concerning the acquisition of nuclear weapons which was announced by the Prime Minister on 16 August 1963, you are to proceed to implement all necessary actions to provide a full operational capability for the BOMARC, CF-101B and CF-104 weapons systems at the earliest possible date.[106]

There was relief and euphoria, particularly within RCAF headquarters. There was a possibility, however, that the ongoing strategic policy reassessment might still wipe out what had been achieved. Consequently, many waited with bated breath for the next eight months while that drama played itself out. The rest hurried to complete the final arrangements necessary.

Cabinet still had some cleaning up to do, particularly with regard to the Goose Bay, Harmon, and Argentia storage issues which were still pending. Pearson argued there were no logical grounds on which the air-to-air weapons storage could be refused now that the RCAF had the same weapons. The SAC storage issue was another matter. As for the nuclear ASW weapons, the Argentia storage arrangement could wait until Canadian naval policy was reexamined in the fall. Paul Martin was then authorized to sign the USAF ADC air-to-air weapons storage agreement. The release of the weapons from American sites to the USAF interceptors was governed by the same regulations governing the RCAF CF-101B squadrons and, in an emergency, would have been released at the Reinforced Alert level (American DEFCON 1).[107]

At the highest level, Pearson was briefed on the functioning of the "hot line" between Ottawa and Washington, DC. Journalist Peter Newman noted Pearson maintained a laconic attitude toward it:

> Diefenbaker had always kept in full view as a symbol of his power the red telephone that connectes the Prime Minister of Canada directly with the President of the United States. . . . Pearson not only removed the instrument from his desk, but hid it so carelessly that one morning during the winter of 1964 when it rang, he couldn't find it. Paul Martin was in the PM's office at the time. The two men heard the NORAD phone buzzing, couldn't locate it, and began to chase each other around the room like a pair of Keystone Kops. "My God," said Martin, "do you realize this could mean war?" "No," Pearson puffed, "they can't start a war if we don't answer that

phone." The instrument was finally located behind a curtain and the caller—who wanted to know if "Charlie" was there—turned out, by incredible coincidence, to have both the wrong number and accidental access to one of the world's most private hot lines.[108]

NATO Nuclear Strategy and the Special Committee on Defense: October–November 1963

The public defense forum chugged along in the fall of 1963. After much verbal fencing between the government's representatives and the committee, Paul Hellyer arranged to have SCOD visit NATO where SCOD members were treated to several confidential briefings. Secretary General Dirk Stikker informed the committee that any withdrawal of Canadian forces from Europe "would have a disastrous effect" on NATO's forward strategy, as "NATO feels that the Soviet Union should be faced with a strong cohesion of allied forces and any withdrawal of the Canadian forces would certainly seriously affect this cohesion."[109] What about removal of forces to Canada and return in an emergency? Stikker would "consider any such move to be disastrous. If Canada were to withdraw [her] forces, it might help those people who have the idea [to do so]. Please don't help them."[110] The diplomatic Stikker was, of course, referring to the British.

What about converting Europe-based forces to a mobile reserve? This was not feasible either, since "any withdrawal of forces [from the Central Region] is going to harm our military posture," that is, forward defense. This was different, of course, from the concept of the AMF(L). Canada could make an important contribution to this multinational force, but not from her forces already stationed in Europe. Stikker reiterated his point: "My feeling is that the need for the presence of Canadian forces in the centre of Europe is absolutely essential and that it would be disastrous to withdraw now."[111]

As a follow-up to Stikker's comments, George Ignatieff fielded questions on the NATO force development process. In doing so, he cleared away many misconceptions, particularly that force requirements were imposed on Canada. He explained the process by which NATO asked for the CF-104 force. Ignatieff also touched on the conventional-nuclear force balance and emphasized that both types of forces were critical to the success of the operation. NATO had always been and would in the foreseeable future be based on a nuclear strategy. Nothing could be done to alter this as long as the Soviets retained their current posture in Europe.[112]

As for the CF-104 force, some committee members wanted to know if it could be changed to a conventional strike force. Ignatieff explained yet again that the CF-104 force was an integral part of the deterrent that had been programmed into the force structure many years ago. If Canada withdrew from the role, there was no immediate way to fill it, that is, cover all the targets assigned to the force. Removing a large chunk of the NATO deterrent would not positively affect Soviet behavior in the slightest, Ignatieff added.[113]

Some suggested that Denmark, Norway, and Iceland had refused nuclear weapons without affecting their defense posture. Why could Canada not accept a similar posture? Why was Canada under pressure to accept nuclear weapons and these NATO members were not? It was simple, remarked Ignatieff. Iceland had no armed forces, and the other two nations were peripheral ones. The region requiring the main defensive effort was the Central Region, the one to which Canada was committed with stationed forces.[114] Canada, of course, was not Iceland, Norway, or Denmark. She was a middle power with immense resources and disproportionate influence. This was lost on some of the more small-minded members of the committee.

The SCOD members were then treated to an amazingly frank SHAPE briefing on the threat and SHAPE strategy, as well as a Q and A session with SACEUR, General Lyman Lemnitzer. The relationship between local aggression and full-scale attack was laid out, as was the concept of forward defense. Local aggression would be dealt with by the conventional forces right on the Iron Curtain and by the mobile forces on the northern and southern flanks. Nuclear weapons were available for all contingencies. If there were a large scale attack on NATO, SACEUR would launch "a nuclear counter offensive against Russia with external nuclear forces . . . and engage in an air land and sea battle in the [ACE area] to prevent the enemy surface forces from taking possession of allied territories."[115]

In the event of general nuclear war:

> SACEUR's nuclear means would be used in the following manner: on one hand, at the SACEUR's level and started directly by him, a large-scale offensive comprising an immediate attack on all enemy military objectives from which the nuclear offensive against Europe started. This counter offensive at the SACEUR's level, would be carried out by all the fighter bombers, the bombers, and the devices on alert which constitute the quick reaction alert force. In addition to this a priori nuclear plan of the SACEUR which would take care of the automatic launching of an attack against the previously established objectives, each regional command would carry out nuclear plans, which we refer to as regional priority nuclear plans, against the objective directly threatening the operations of the regional command, together with various regional plans which are anti-nuclear plans for the nuclear vectors aimed at that region.
>
> On the other hand, a nuclear prohibition plan or plans aimed at slowing down the enemy land and air forces or destroying his communications and logistics. A nuclear plan of land fighting for the purpose of supporting the land forces with the help of nuclear fires applied on the enemy land forces and finally a naval battle plan to keep communication zones free.[116]

It did not get much clearer than this without reference to the actual plans and targets. Any more questions about the efficacy of limited nuclear war were moot ones at this point. SACEUR clearly believed weapons could be used selectively and at sea without risk of escalation.

What did SACEUR think about Canadian withdrawal in whole or in part? Lemnitzer thought that the "Canadian contribution is very important. . . . I would like to see it maintained."[117] As for the CF-104 force and its possible conversion to conventional means, SACEUR was not in favor of this. It was too important in conduct of the nuclear strike program.

He was able to shed light on the release of nuclear weapons, however. In an unambiguous attack situation, Lemnitzer hinted, he could use whatever force he thought necessary to deal with it. For anything less than that, he had to consult the NAC, which he optimistically thought would rapidly grant him whatever he believed was needed for the given situation. If that failed, he hinted, he would put on his American hat and ask the President. In general, however, the problem remained "unresolved" for the time being and required further study.[118]

The most important briefing the committee received, next to SACEUR's, was from the West Germans. The German briefing team, led by Franz Kraph from the German foreign ministry and Colonels Jahne, Hopfgarten, and Neubert from the defense ministry, presented an exposition of the crushing threat the Soviets produced, the critical West Germany domestic political need for forward defense, and NATO's critical military need for the same. More importantly, they briefed the Canadian SCOD on MC 14/2 (revised) and the MC 48 series. This had never been done before. For the first time, the committee could see the framework of Canadian strategic policy. Their reaction was, however, unrecorded.[119]

In response to questions about escalation (conventional-tactical, nuclear-strategic, nuclear), Colonel Jahne explained that the nuclear use concept in forward defense was based on the selective use of nuclear weapons in the border regions. This was a nuclear firebreak designed to "move the enemy to break off its offensive action or make plain to him that there is a chance of escalation and therefore all out war." The German view was that selective nuclear release could be decided upon quickly and was in McNamara's hands at the moment for discussion. Jahne was referring to MC 100/1, the strategic concept that was designed to replace MC 14/2 (revised), but was never ratified because of French intransigence.[120]

As for the Canadian forces, Colonel Hopfgarten stated:

> It is our view that the forces of our nations which are stationed along the Iron Curtain should be equipped with organic nuclear devices as laid down [in MC 70]. I would not think that it would be useful if, let's say, the Canadian Brigade were divested of such weapons and would have to fight shoulder to shoulder with units that are equipped with nuclear devices.[121]

The same held true for the CF-104 forces.

It is clear from the transcripts that the SCOD members behaved in a less childish fashion than their predecessors on their European junket, both in terms of the questions they asked and their personal behavior while at NATO's headquarters. The fact that the media were not present probably contributed to this. The entire series of briefings served the same function as a bucket of ice cold water dashed in their faces. This was reflected in their final report.

The SCOD final report was released in December 1963. It was based on all of the meetings and briefings, was broken down functionally, and then there was a series of recommendations on defense policy generally:

NATO:
1. The Brigade Group and the Air Division should remain in Europe.
2. The possibility of CF-104 dual capability should be examined.
3. The Brigade Group needs armored personnel carriers and helicopters.
4. The Honest Johns should be allocated to a higher level of command.
5. ASW forces were still necessary.

NORAD:
1. Canada should remain part of NORAD.
2. The bomber threat was diminishing, but Canada still has a requirement to defend against them using BOMARCs and Voodoos.[122]

As for recommendations regarding defense policy, the SCOD members were unanimous in stating: "Canadian defence policy should not slavishly follow the policy of any other country." The best course of action was the one that had been taken all along: hybrid conventional-nuclear forces in Europe, antisubmarine forces in the Atlantic, air defense forces in North America, and UN forces to stamp out brushfire wars before they got out of control.[123]

The SIOP, the JSTPS, and NATO

NATO targeting and employment of nuclear forces, and thus Canadian nuclear forces, was affected by American strategic nuclear weapons employment policy, which evolved during the course of the Diefenbaker-Pearson handover. The most important development in this regard was the creation of the Joint Strategic Target Planning Staff in Omaha, Nebraska, in 1960. Colocated with SAC headquarters, the two-hundred-man JSTPS was the culmination of a lack of nuclear planning coordination among the American CinCs and services and the development of the Polaris submarine-launched ballistic missile (SLBM) system. The JSTPS was structured to create a database of targets (the National Strategic Target List or NSTL) and then generate a coordinated nuclear strike plan for SAC's missiles and bombers and the USN's SSBNs. Representatives from the joint commands worldwide provided representatives to the JSTPS to ensure that the regional nuclear use plans from the CinCs were properly coordinated with the master strike plan known as the Singly Integrated Operational Plan (SIOP).[124]

The SIOP underwent three major changes prior to 1964. The first was SIOP-62 created in 1960 during the last half of the Eisenhower administration. SIOP-62 was based on 2600 separate targets inside the USSR, China, and some Communist satellite countries selected from the 4100-target NSTL. One thousand fifty nuclear weapons were to be used within the first twenty-four hours. Targeting priority included Soviet nuclear capability (including 150 bomber bases); military and governmental command and control; and 50% of the industrial floor space in the Soviet Union (200 targets). There were also a projected 160 air defense suppression targets.[125] It should be noted that SIOP-62 was not specifically structured for retaliation to a Soviet attack or the preemption of one.[126] SIOP-62 had as many as sixteen attack options, all of which were based on the level of alert achieved by American and Soviet forces when the decision was made to launch. There were some withholding options against the Warsaw Pact countries exclusive of their air defense systems. There was, however, massive criticism directed against SIOP-62, particularly from the USN because of the high levels of damage and subsequent radiation that would result from any of the options.[127]

General Maxwell Taylor provided his critical views on SIOP-62 to President Kennedy during the 1961 Berlin Crisis. Taylor was concerned that the airborne Alert Force, if directed to attack counterforce targets as it was supposed to, reduced the flexibility of the other options, since the only flexibility in the plan was to withhold strikes as opposed to retargeting them. Attack should be restricted to the Soviet Union and not the other countries. This would increase flexibility. The main problem Taylor noted was that SIOP-62 assumed the Soviets would attack urban-industrial targets in the United States and not conduct an initial counterforce attack. There was a fear in the planners' minds that any other type of plan would result in SAC's targeting enemy cities in response to a Soviet attack on North America. SAC was loath to do this and chose options that allowed it to not confront this moral dilemma. As such SIOP-62 was an inflexible "blunt instrument."[128]

In June 1962 the JSTPS completed SIOP-63. Unlike its predecessor, SIOP-63 emphasized flexibility and provided for a controlled response to a general nuclear war in line with the Kennedy administration's stance of flexible response.[129] SIOP-63 had five attack options, "some designed for preemptive execution, others for retaliation." These target options were cumulative, not inclusive. The first two options could be selected in a preemptive attack if the Soviets were preparing to attack the United States or her allies. The other three were retaliatory attacks. SIOP-63 separated the Warsaw Pact nations and China as target sets and separated Soviet nuclear forces from bases located near cities. Portions of the American strategic force were to be held in reserve for "intrawar deterrence" purposes, and in some options certain enemy command and control/government facilities could be withheld to "permit a negotiated settlement."[130]

SIOP-63's first option was broadly interpreted as a counterforce plan, that is, to strip away Soviet strategic forces in a preemptive strike to limit damage to the West. Even if such an attack achieved its aims, planners estimated there could be between 88 million to 195 million American and European dead. SIOP-64 was not too different from SIOP-63. It went into effect in 1963 and remained so until SIOP-4 was implemented on 1 July 1966.[131]

The early SIOPs were virtually divorced from the regional nuclear planning undertaken by the American CinCs. As CinCSAC General Thomas Power noted, the JSTPS provided "packaged plans to the President" and included a "wide choice of options to meet any contingency and affords him complete flexibility." Power also noted, however, "It should be emphasized that all this applied only to the initial counterstrike in a general nuclear war,"[132] not in a regional conflict in Europe. In other words, a regional nuclear war in Europe was not directly connected to employment of the SIOP. They were separate processes that were coordinated, but one did not inevitably lead to the other. Some anomalies existed. For example, SIOP-62 targeted one hundred of the MRBM/IRBM sites (each site had four missiles in an unprotected launch facility), which theoretically were a SACEUR responsibility.[133] Even by late 1963 there was some concern, since "the number of [ACE] targets which would be attacked by theatre nuclear forces and would not have to be scheduled for attack by our Strategic Retaliatory Forces is uncertain."[134]

Late in 1964, however, US Secretary of Defense Robert McNamara ordered General Lyman Lemnitzer not to use NATO nuclear forces independently from SAC, which led to a horrendous argument between the two men. Lemnitzer's view, the correct one, was "that having the ambiguity of the use of nuclear weapons was the thing that gave us the deterrent we needed."[135] Linking NATO's European forces too closely with the strategic response from SAC would, in fact, limit options, not create them.

This argument was kept secret because of the obvious implications for NATO's independence and unity. When Paul Hellyer found out about it and queried McNamara about it at the December 1964 NATO Ministerial Meeting, McNamara erroneously told him all of SACEUR's targets were covered by multiple SAC strikes anyway and theatre nuclear forces in Europe were redundant. This led Hellyer to believe that 1 Air Division was redundant and bolstered his argument with Air Marshal Miller that the formation should have a conventional capability (this aspect is discussed later in this chapter).[136]

The targeting methodology employed by the JSTPS was similar to that employed by SHAPE in its nuclear planning. All American intelligence sources flowed into the JSTPS. Planning was undertaken based on the statistical probability needed to destroy a given target; that is, several nuclear weapons and even several delivery vehicles were allocated per target to ensure that there was at least a 90% probability of destroying that target if it was a nuclear weapon target, and 75% to 90% if it was any other sort of target. The number of weapons employed could range between one and four. A consequence was that some effects of a nuclear weapon (blast, shock, and electro-magnetic pulse) were emphasized over other effects (immediate radiation, fire, and fallout). The SIOP coordinated the time on target for each delivery vehicle. The probability of each delivery vehicle getting off the ground and reaching the target was also factored in. Cities themselves were not targeted though the actual installations in a given city or around it were. The SIOP also coordinated penetration routes to avoid fratricide. The SIOP was developed on predictability and began to be tooled to ICBM and SLBM use. Weapons systems that were "variable," like aircraft carriers, were less likely to be employed in initial strikes and formed a follow-on or residual capability.[137]

Closer coordination between the SIOP and SACEUR's regional planning was initiated in 1961. This coordination cell consisted of American officers assigned to SACEUR. They came from AIRCENT (USAF) and STRIKFORSOUTH (USN). There was a senior representative and two clerks.[138] One of the first things the SACEUR liaison staff undertook was to deconflict some SACEUR and SAC targets. Another arrangement was made between SACEUR and SAC to cover targets that he could not reach because he had a paltry MRBM capability, since the MLF was still under discussion, and there was a shortage of NATO strike capability.[139]

The JSTPS was on a high level of operational influence, directly linked with the decision to employ nuclear weapons by the American President and his delegated commanders: this was the place in which targets inside the Soviet Union were selected. Note that there was no non-American NATO representation at the JSTPS in 1960, 1961, and 1962. The NATO Ministerial Meeting in Athens (discussed in chapter 11) produced a new attitude in which American policy makers fostered confidence-building measures within the alliance which included more information sharing on doctrine, planning, and targeting policy. The Nassau Agreement reiterated this. The 1963 Ottawa Ministerial Meeting produced the decision to allow SACEUR to form a SHAPE liaison staff consisting of non-American NATO staff officers and assign it to the JSTPS. This was all directly related to maintaining NATO unity.[140]

The initial increment from SHAPE was originally brought in with the ultimate aim of expanding it, if and when the MLF or ANF concepts were fully implemented. Neither of these ideas was implemented, as we have seen, so the SHAPE increment stayed small. The first four members were Italian, West German, British, and French. Several administrative personnel were also dispatched. They arrived between October 1963 and July 1964 and reported to the Deputy Director of the JSTPS. There were also three American SHAPE liaison officers who represented SACEUR in his USCinCEUR capacity. The senior representative sat on the policy committee and had voting rights on it.[141] The lack of Canadian representation at this point probably reflected the fact that 1 Air Division had still not been issued its targets.

It is not surprising that the non-American SHAPE element did not have access to everything. It is more surprising that the American SHAPE element was in a similar situation. The non-Americans had access to the whole of SAC HQ, but they were required to have American JSTPS escorts if they visited the Command Post, the Air Intelligence Room, and the Operations Planning Room.[142] The American SHAPE group was not allowed access to all data in the SIOP process. They could not evaluate SAC intelligence and did not have access to the SIOP itself, though this may have changed over time.[143]

What exactly the non-American SHAPE group did in the SIOP process is unknown, but was probably related to deconflicting SHAPE targets and SAC targets. Information flowed one way. The SHAPE people probably explained SHAPE's targeting rationale to the JSTPS people, and the JSTPS people handled the discrepancies within their compartment and presented SHAPE with the solution.

What sorts of conflict could occur? There was no geographical line drawn between SACEUR's and CinCSAC's area of responsibility on the European land mass. As noted earlier, SACEUR's plans and the SIOP were not connected and some overlap occurred. SACEUR did not target anything that could reach North America: this was a SAC, UK Bomber Command, and/or USN responsibility. Any Soviet ground-based nuclear system located in Eastern Europe or the Soviet Union that could reach Great Britain was also covered by SAC, UK Bomber Command (prior to V-Force's assignment to SACEUR in 1963), the Royal Navy's SLBM systems, or the USN SLBM systems. This was intended to protect the USN forward-deployed SSBN facility at Holy Loch Scotland as well as the SAC and RAF bomber bases in East Anglia. The same went for the USN SSBN facility located at Rota, Spain.[144]

On the other hand, SACEUR planned on having the ability to cover the Soviet MRBM/IRBM fields in western Russia, exclusive of SAC resources. As noted in earlier chapters, this was why Norstad originally wanted IRBMs for NATO. Had the MLF existed, this is probably what they would have been targeted on. The probability is high that SACEUR's four dedicated USN SSBNs operating in the eastern Mediterranean were targeted on these sites. This will be discussed in more detail in the next chapter. SACLANT would be pounding the Soviet naval bases in the Kola Peninsula with his nuclear-armed aircraft operating from STRIKEFLEETLANT. These also required some coordination, though SACLANT had his own representation on the JSTPS through his USCinCLANTFLEET staff.[145]

As to the matter of Canadian representation at SAC HQ and the JSTPS, there were a small number of Canadian officers assigned to the JSTPS between 1964 and 1972. In some cases they were part of the SHAPE increment because of the percentage of nuclear strike resources provided by Canada in Europe and in others they were part of a NORAD liaison detachment. NORAD of course had to closely coordinate with SAC since inbound empty KC-97 and KC-135 tankers could be mistaken for inbound Soviet bomber aircraft.[146]

In terms of operational influence, visible Canadian representation was prestigious, but not as practical as operational influence exerted at SHAPE, AIRCENT, and 4 ATAF. This is partly because of the lack of control of the JSTPS over any operational forces (the JSTPS exerted influence on SAC and the USN, but did not control those forces), and partly because of the fact that the influence was probably limited to deconflicting SACEUR's regional plans and the SIOP. Despite all of the foregoing, the procedures employed to create the SIOP influenced the procedures used to target the star of Canada's saliency show, the CF-104 force in Europe.

13

DELIVERING THE BOMB:
CANADA GOES NUCLEAR

"RCAF Bombers to Carry One
Megaton H-Weapons."
–SAULT DAILY STAR, 16 APRIL 1963

Introduction

Forty years after acquiring a nuclear capability and twenty years after relinquishing it, a strong sense of cultural denial on the matter remains in Canada. Indeed, security and disinformation campaigns of the day and subsequent governments' tendency to play down nuclearization have succeeded too well: most Canadians (and for that matter, most Americans) are unaware of how extensive Canada's nuclear capability actually was. Many people who served in the three services in the 1960s still adhere to the fiction and assert "Canada didn't have nuclear weapons," and, when pressed, cite the dual-key access arrangements and American ownership of the warheads to argue their point. Other younger members of the armed forces refuse to believe Canada had such a capability. These arguments are moot and disingenuous. They are based on a false Canadian belief in moral superiority over the United States, which was cultivated in the 1970s.

RCAF documents of the day, for example, refer to things like "the CF-104/ Mk-28 weapons system." There was no distinction, in Canada's doctrinal employment of nuclear weapons, between the weapons carrier and what it dropped. Indeed there was a symbiotic relationship between a Canadian-built, -manned, and -commanded aircraft and an American-built and -controlled nuclear bomb. It is not just a matter of capability: there is the matter of intent. At the moment of truth, a Canadian pilot had to fly the aircraft and press the right buttons to ensure the target was eliminated: it was not an American hand in that aircraft. If a Canadian pilot had to do so, he was an expression of Canadian national will and nobody else's. Canada and her military personnel were not reluctant nuclear warriors. They were quite prepared, no matter what some claim in retrospect, to launch their aircraft and deliver their nuclear munitions.

This chapter details each Canadian nuclear system to explain how this symbiosis worked: how the weapons were made available, the numbers, and how they were to be employed in the NORAD and NATO strategic and operational contexts.

The full magnitude of Canada's nuclear involvement, ready to fight nearly fifteen years after the first Soviet nuclear test, is laid bare here. This is the climax of the Canadian nuclear weapons story.

ACE and Theater Nuclear Warfighting: 1964–1970

1 Air Division's place in SACEUR's Nuclear Strike Plans for the 1960s can be determined by a process of elimination. SHAPE had two types of attacks to contend with and the staff produced several sets of plans. The first type was a general nuclear war based on a massive Soviet conventional and/or theater nuclear strike preparations against Europe or a Soviet strategic attack on North America. The other was an escalatory situation produced by circumstances less than general nuclear war, a situation like Berlin or Cuba or Soviet pressure on, say, Turkey or Norway.

The first instance contained several plans: (1) General Strike Plan (GSP): immediate use of NATO forces on QRA against enemy theater-wide nuclear forces; (2) Regional Priority Nuclear Strike Program: against conventional/tactical nuclear forces in specified command areas; (3) Regional Anti-Nuclear Strike Program in specified command areas; (4) Nuclear Prohibition Plan to interdict the enemy logistical structure theater-wide; (5) Tactical Strike Program: land fighting plan to tactically support the land forces; and (6) naval battle plan.[1]

The second instance involved the selective release of nuclear weapons. This included the "shot across the bow" (like BERCON BRAVO), limited Berlin support provisions, operations on NATO flanks, limited use to effect a pause at the border in the Central Region, or even the placement of atomic demolition munitions (ADMs) in border areas to deter enemy attack.

The events that would trigger each response varied. If, for example, signals intelligence sources detected Soviet preparations to massively launch missiles against NATO in a preemptive strike before a ground attack (it would take one to three hours since they were liquid-propelled and had to be fueled) this was a sufficient indicator to launch the QRA forces and implement the regional nuclear plans with the follow-on forces. If the Soviets made preparations to launch a conventional land attack supported with tactical nuclear weapons, this too would take time to prepare, perhaps eight to forty-eight hours. It would prompt implementation of the regional antinuclear and interdiction plans, and the QRA force could be held for signs that the enemy theater nuclear force was preparing to launch before the QRA force itself was launched. Soviet conventional moves against the flanks would be met with the ACE Mobile Forces first. If it were determined that these were limited operations not related to the Central Region, selective nuclear use could be employed at SACEUR's discretion. One of SACEUR's roles in this process was to "exercise direct control over the selection of targets."[2]

SACEUR's area of responsibility was not strictly geographical, since he was permitted to target those enemy forces that posed a direct threat to NATO. Conversely, SAC was authorized to target anything that could reach North America and/or threaten non-NATO tasked strategic forces. (See figure 13.1.)

SACLANT's STRIKEFLEETLANT British and American nuclear-equipped aircraft carriers and CinCLANT's Polaris-equipped submarines would, in conjunction with SAC, destroy targets in the Kola Peninsula. These targets included naval

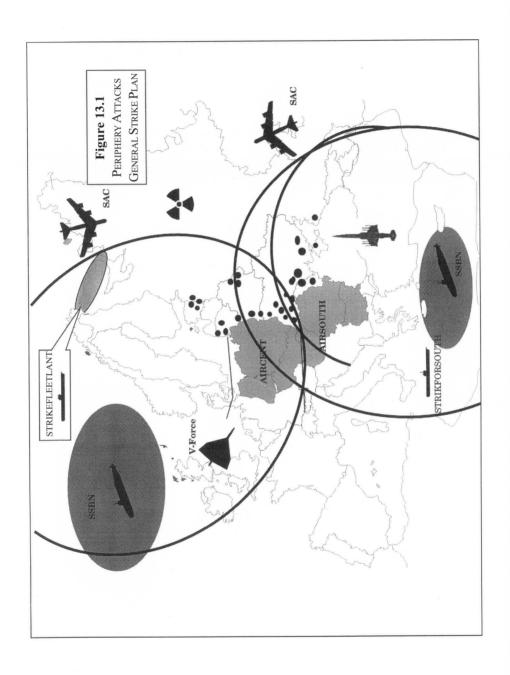

Figure 13.1
PERIPHERY ATTACKS
GENERAL STRIKE PLAN

aviation bomber bases (aircraft equipped with nuclear cruise missiles); submarine repair and construction facilities; and command centers for the Soviet submarine missile force. These attacks were coordinated with SAC in the JSTPS in Omaha. Generally, these operations were not a NATO responsibility unless the Soviets used ground and tactical nuclear forces against Norway, in which case ACE mobile forces would deploy, and perhaps Norwegian F-104s would receive nuclear weapons from outside Norwegian territory. In any event, attacking the Kola Peninsula limited damage that could be wrought against North America as well as Europe.

The Norwegian government eschewed stationing foreign forces on its soil and declined to accept nuclear weapons into its force structure. This eliminated a necessary means to cover Soviet threats emanating from the northern Soviet Union. It appears that Norway's air force planned to equip two F-104Gs with nuclear weapons, but this was never implemented.[3]

The most direct nuclear threat against ACE was the Soviet MRBM, IRBM, BADGER, and BLINDER bomber bases located in the western Soviet Union. In 1965 there were two hundred fixed missile sites, most of which were unprotected and concentrated.[4] There were two hundred airfields in the western Soviet Union capable of handling bombers that could range to the United Kingdom (Western analysts assumed Soviet bomber dispersal at various levels of alert).[5]

The IRBM/MRBM sites were the ones that Norstad originally wanted covered by a NATO IRBM force in the late 1950s, and as the MLF project evolved, these targets also justified the 200-missile request. Prior to 1964, these targets were covered by 60 RAF Thor IRBMs, 30 Jupiter IRBMs in Italy, and 15 in Turkey for a total of 105, all under dual-key control.[6] SACEUR also had the services (until 1969) of 144 TM-76A Mace ground-launched cruise missiles. These weapons belonged to the USAF and were based in southern Germany from 1959 to 1968. They had an 1100-mile range and could reach the Soviet MRBM/IRBM missile fields. Maces were based in hardened shelters and carried a 1 MT warhead.[7]

The United States dedicated five Polaris-equipped submarines to SACEUR in May 1962. These included 16 Polaris missiles each for a total of 80 Polaris A-1 and A-2 SLBMs equipped with W47 800-kt warheads. These were replaced by the Polaris A-3 in 1964 which had two Mk 58 warheads each yielding 200 kt (this was an MRV, not a MIRV: the two warheads would hit the same target and therefore increase the probability of a kill).[8] In 1965 there were 20 SSBNs operating from Holy Loch, Scotland and Rota, Spain, with 8 operating the eastern Mediterranean and 12 off Norway. Thirteen were committed to continuous alert, 5 of them targeted by NATO SACEUR and 5 targeted by US CinCEUR.[9]

RAF Bomber Command also dedicated three Valiant bomber squadrons (24 aircraft) to SACEUR between 1961 and 1965 to provide additional coverage. Each aircraft carried two bombs, originally Mk 28 and then Mk 43 armed for the 1 MT–yield range. This provided coverage for an additional 48 targets. SAC provided overlapping coverage on some 24–48 targets.[10] Until 1963 SAC assigned 20 B-47s targets in the western Soviet Union while SACEUR provided 52 Mk 28 bombs from his assigned stockpile for those bombers.[11]

In 1963 SACEUR had approximately 429 weapons to cover the Soviet systems located in the western Soviet Union. This changed, however, once the Jupiters and Thors were removed and the B-47s retired. After the Nassau Agreement and the 1963 NATO Ministerial Meeting, RAF Bomber Command was tasked to SACEUR. The Medium Bomber Force (MBF) consisted of 9 Vulcan and 4 Victor squadrons for a total of 104 aircraft. Sixty-four aircraft were equipped for multiple bomb carriage (usually two weapons) and 36–40 were equipped with the Blue Steel standoff missile (1 to 1.6 MT), which had a range of one hundred miles. This was in addition to the Valiant force, which was subsequently withdrawn in 1965 due to aircraft wear.[12] The MBF could theoretically cover 168 targets alone.

The Greeks operated two F-104 squadrons in the nuclear strike role (36 aircraft) starting in 1964.[13] The Turks eventually built up to 4 F-104 nuclear strike squadrons (72 aircraft).[14] These aircraft had the range to reach a number of targets in the southeast Soviet Union, though a proportion would have been dedicated to countering Soviet nuclear-equipped tactical aircraft and other Warsaw Pact forces (Bulgarian and Rumanian), conventional forces that would have been employed against them. If one assumed 4 QRA aircraft per squadron for a total of 24 F-104s, this could be legitimately added to the general strike plan total. Therefore, by 1965, SACEUR could target approximately 416 targets with his NATO-dedicated forces and approximately 80 more with additional Polaris-equipped SLBMs for a grand total of 496 targets in the western Soviet Union that could threaten NATO, 200 of which were the fixed missile sites.

As for regional strike plans on the southern flank, NATO STRIKFORSOUTH (basically the USN 6th Fleet), 5 ATAF (Italy) and 1 ATAF (eastern Mediterranean) would have employed nuclear strike aircraft to support Italy, Greece, and Turkey. Italy would eventually deploy two F-104 nuclear strike squadrons later in the 1960s, while in an emergency three squadrons of USAF F-100Ds would deploy to Italy from Spain and use prestocked nuclear weapons. This totaled twelve USAF and Italian QRA aircraft plus a variable number of carrier-based aircraft. Usually there were four QRA aircraft per carrier, and there could be two or three USN carriers in the Mediterranean at any given time.[15]

What of the critical Central Region (see figures 13.2 and 13.3)? The full buildup of the MC 70 strike force lasted from 1963 to 1966. (For the USAF forces assigned to AIRCENT, it was a continuous process.) Figure 13.2 depicts the buildup of purely nuclear strike dedicated aircraft to 1966, while figure 13.3 shows the forces breakdown between 2 ATAF and 4 ATAF. The predominant aircraft type was the F-104G in Belgian, Dutch, and West German service. British forces used the Canberra twin-engined bomber, the French operated the F-100D, while the Americans used F-100Ds and F-105s. Canada operated the CF-104.

A major changeover occurred in 1966. The French pulled their forces from NATO command. This included the Lahr- and Bremgarten-based F-100D squadrons from the French 1 CATAC (Commandement Aerien Tactiques) which were part of 4 ATAF's nuclear strike force equipped with American nuclear weapons. The Americans and the West Germans also phased in the Pershing 1 nuclear missile system, which was placed on continuous QRA. The RAF provided four Canberra squadrons in Germany and two more in the UK: all were trained in Low Altitude Bombing

Figure 13.2
CENTRAL REGION NUCLEAR STRIKE FORCE BUILDUP, 1963–1968

	1963	1964	1965	1966	1967	1968
West Germany F-104G	36 combat 12 reserve (2 Sqns)	+72 combat +12 reserve (4 Sqns)	+36 combat +12 reserve (2 Sqns)	+36 combat +12 reserve (2 Sqns)		
Pershing 1a				32		
France F-100D	68				(-68) (removed)	
Belgium F-104G		36 (2 Sqns)				
Netherlands F104G		18 (1 Sqn)	+18 (1 Sqn)			
CANADA CF-104	(no nucs) 108 (6 Sqns) 36 (2 Sqns Strike/Recce)	108 (6 Sqns) 36 (2 Sqns Strike/Recce)			+12 (CF-104D)	
United Kingdom Canberra	48+24 (4 Sqn's in Germany, 2 in UK)					
United States F-100D F-105 F-4 Pershing 1a	108 72	(partial	phase (phase out)	out) (-72) 108 24	108	

System (LABS) and were equipped with a mix of American and British nuclear weapons. USAF Europe also started to convert from F-105 to the F-4 Phantom.[16]

Taking 1966 as the peak year, there were 240 dedicated nuclear strike aircraft in 2 ATAF and 520 in 4 ATAF. There were an additional 56 Pershings on call, most of which were based in southern Germany (the 4 ATAF region). In 1967, this ostensibly dropped to 486 aircraft with the French withdrawal. 1 Air Division, however, developed a supplemental follow-on force (Project ABALONE, which will be

Figure 13.3
NUCLEAR STRIKE RESOURCES: 2 ATAF VS. 4 ATAF, 1966–1967

2 ATAF			4 ATAF		
West Germany			West Germany		
	4x sqn F-104G (72 combat, 24 reserve)	72		6x sqn F-104G (108 combat, 36 reserve) Pershing 1a	108 32
Belgium	2x sqn F-104G	36	Canada	6x sqn CF-104 (+36 recce, 12 CF-104D follow-on force)	108 (48)
Netherlands	2x sqn F-104G	36	France	2x sqn F-100D (withdrawn end 1966)	68
United Kingdom			United States		
	4x sqn Canberra 2x sqn Canberra (UK based)	48 24		6x sqn F-4 6x sqn F-100D Pershing 1a	74 74 24
Total:	216 240(with follow on)		Total:	512 (Fr incl) 444 (no Fr) 528 (with follow-on)	

discussed later) of 12 more aircraft to bring the Canadian total to 120 CF-104s or 23% of 4 ATAF's nuclear delivery means, 24% of 4 ATAF available aircraft, and 15% of the total nuclear delivery capability in AIRCENT. The West German totals are somewhat inflated. Generally each of the five wings had 36 combat-ready strike aircraft with 12 more in reserve that could have been used as part of a follow-on force.[17]

The American numbers require some explanation. A 1964 study from the US Secretary of Defense's office examining the ratio of nuclear strike to conventional attack forces claims that there were 441 USAF aircraft dedicated to nuclear strike operations with 4 ATAF. This is misleading, as are the other figures for Canadian and Dutch resources.[18] In 1965, there were six F-105 squadrons and nine F-100D squadrons in USAFE. There were three F-100D squadrons (or one wing) each in Spain, West Germany, and the UK. (The UK-based squadrons, which also included a number of F-100C day fighter squadrons, were the ones that evacuated France in 1959.) The F-100D squadrons were all dedicated to nuclear strike, but only four of the six F-105 squadrons were similarly equipped because of changing American thinking regarding flexible response. The other two F-105 units were conventionally equipped. The Spain-based F-100Ds were not part of 4 ATAF; they deployed to Italy and Turkey, picked up nuclear weapons in those countries, and were part of the

NATO AFSOUTH regional plan. The F-4 Phantom phased into service starting in 1965–1966 until there were ten squadrons by 1970. Not all of these aircraft were nuclear-strike dedicated: six squadrons were conventionally equipped. Therefore, a consistent figure of 200 USAF nuclear strike aircraft dedicated to the Central Region between 1964 and 1970 appears acceptable.[19]

These are strictly numbers of dedicated nuclear strike aircraft and do not represent the total capability. There is the matter of the nuclear weapons themselves. A 1964 study conducted for the US Secretary of Defense states there were nine airfields in the Central Region with non-US NATO nuclear strike aircraft operating from them, but operating with US nuclear weapons, and there were 250 nuclear weapons located at these bases, or 27 weapons per base.[20] By deduction, these bases were Lahr and Bremgarten (France); Norvenich, Lechfeld, and Memmingen (West Germany); Volkel (Netherlands); Kleine Brogel (Belgium); and Baden-Soellingen and Zweibrücken (Canada). Note that this was less than halfway through the AIRCENT buildup schedule.

The exact US stockpile figures for SACEUR are at present unavailable. However, Robert McNamara noted in a 1967 speech that there were 7000 American nuclear weapons *in Europe* (it is unclear whether this included *at sea* weapons supporting Europe), and in 1968 Clark Clifford stated that it increased to 7200. By 1975 this had dropped back to 7000. One estimate of the break down concludes that 21% were defensive weapons (ADMs, SAMs and ASW weapons) or 1470. This leaves 5530 offensive weapons: 1935 aircraft bombs, 1714 missiles, and 1880 artillery-delivered shells.[21] Note that the 1975 figures represent a relative "end state" of the 1960s buildup and are included for comparative purposes.

If we take the 1975 figure of 1935 aircraft-delivered bombs and divide it by the number of dedicated nuclear strike squadrons within ACE in 1966 (47), we get 41 bombs per squadron. If we take the figure of 1500 aircraft bombs from the 1958 estimate presented by the then-SACEUR General Norstad, and divide it by the number of squadrons, we get a figure of 31.9 weapons per squadron. In general terms, then, each Canadian squadron had between 31 and 41 weapons assigned. With six RCAF squadrons dedicated to the strike role, this gives us a bracket of 186 and 246 weapons allocated to 1 Air Division, or 8% and 13% of the aircraft-deliverable stockpile in the whole of ACE (not just the Central Region). For 4 ATAF, in 1967 there were eighteen squadrons and between 558 and 738 weapons. With six RCAF squadrons this gives a figure of 33% in both cases of the percentage of Canadian-delivered weapons in 4 ATAF. (All of the forgoing is, of course, only a rough estimate for comparative purposes, as the stockpile was constantly subject to change through maintenance.) Not bad for a so-called "middle power."

In a general war situation the implementation of the General Strike Plan would have entailed use of those forces in Europe assigned to QRA or Victor Alert first and then follow-on forces within thirty minutes. The QRA forces consisted of ready and loaded aircraft on fifteen minutes standby, twenty-four hours a day, seven days a week. Generally, the ACE standard for QRA was four aircraft per squadron. It was generally considered burdensome but necessary duty by Canadian pilots. However, it imposed a great strain on all manner of resources. The issue went all the way to the

Minister of National Defence, and an arrangement was worked out with SHAPE. Because of the strange Canadian basing system, Canadian squadrons would allocate two aircraft on QRA per squadron for a total of twelve aircraft at Zweibrücken and Baden-Soellingen.[22] Immediately available forces for the 1966 ACE GSP in the Central Region (2 ATAF and 4 ATAF) included approximately 176 aircraft and 56 Pershing missiles (for comparative purposes, the number of aircraft on QRA in the Central Region during the Cuban Missile Crisis in 1962 was 59).[23] In a general war situation the objective of the QRA would have been to preempt enemy nuclear forces in range of NATO bases. Priority targets included enemy long-range nuclear delivery means and their command and control system. It is possible that some Central Region QRA forces would have hit portions of the enemy air defense system to clear a path for the V-Force and the Mace cruise missiles on their way to the MRBM/IRBM sites in the western Soviet Union. The follow-on force then would implement a combination of the other four regional plans to take advantage of the QRA strikes.

The specifics of the regional plans remain unavailable. It is possible, however, to partially reconstruct the target systems in Eastern Europe for the Central Region plans. As noted earlier, there were four categories of planning in addition to the General Strike Plan. These could be implemented alongside it in total or in a selective mode independent of the GSP, depending on what the situation warranted and what SACEUR wanted. Figures 13.4 to 13.7 depict the four target systems in general terms. Note that Austria, a neutral nation, is included in the Nuclear Prohibition Plan. The exact amount of overlap and the various options between the four plans and the GSP are unknown and therefore the target systems should be taken as approximate. RCAF intelligence planners estimated at one point there were four hundred strike and four hundred recce targets in the 4 ATAF area of responsibility alone, including eighty airfields.[24]

As for the Regional Anti-Nuclear Strike Plan, there were 119 estimated fighter and bomber bases with 5000+ foot runways out of 152 with 4000+ foot runways. There were 47 more that required supporting equipment and there were 68 sod runways.[25] In some cases, 2 ATAF targets were covered with 4 ATAF resources for redundancy.[26]

1 Air Division and ACE's Central Region 1964–1969

1 Air Division's role was to "contribute to the isolation of the European combat zone and the destruction of enemy forces operating within SACEUR's tactical theater of operations."[27] 1 Air Division's structure was in a state of continuous flux between 1964, when the formation received its nuclear weapons, to December 1971, when it relinquished the nuclear strike role. The most stable period ran from 1964 to 1968.

De Gaulle's prohibition of American nuclear weapons on French soil altered the original concept of operations. Initially, there were to be eight squadrons in the strike/attack role for a total of 144 aircraft: four squadrons in France at Marville and Grostenquin and four in West Germany at Zweibrücken and Baden-Soellingen. A small number of aircraft from each wing were to have the ability to mount the Vinten VICOM reconnaissance camera pod and conduct pre- and poststrike recce. To get

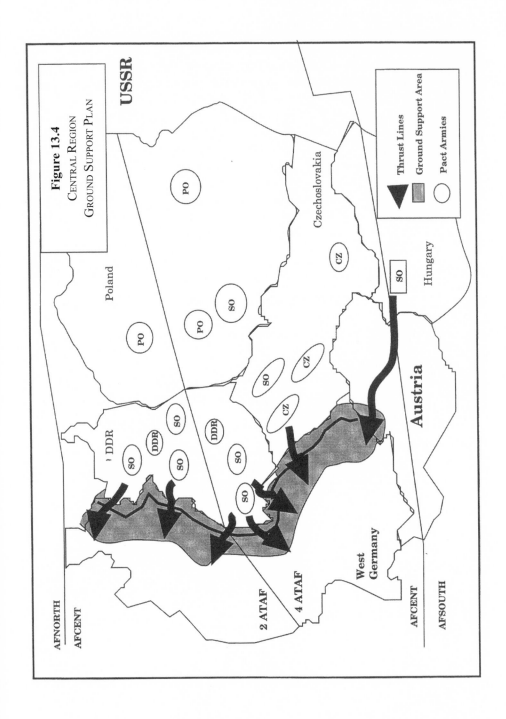

Figure 13.4
CENTRAL REGION
GROUND SUPPORT PLAN

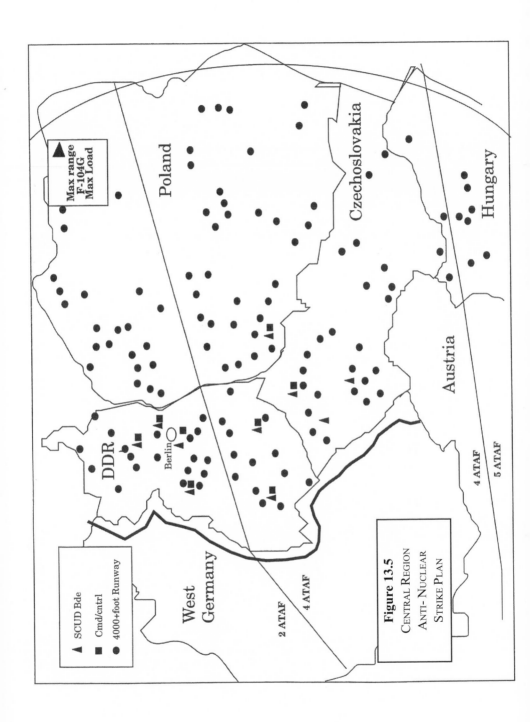

Figure 13.5
CENTRAL REGION
ANTI- NUCLEAR
STRIKE PLAN

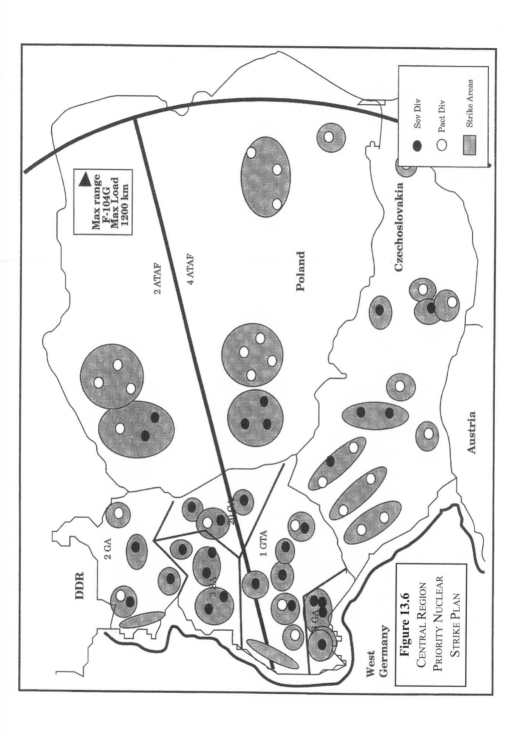

Figure 13.6
CENTRAL REGION
PRIORITY NUCLEAR
STRIKE PLAN

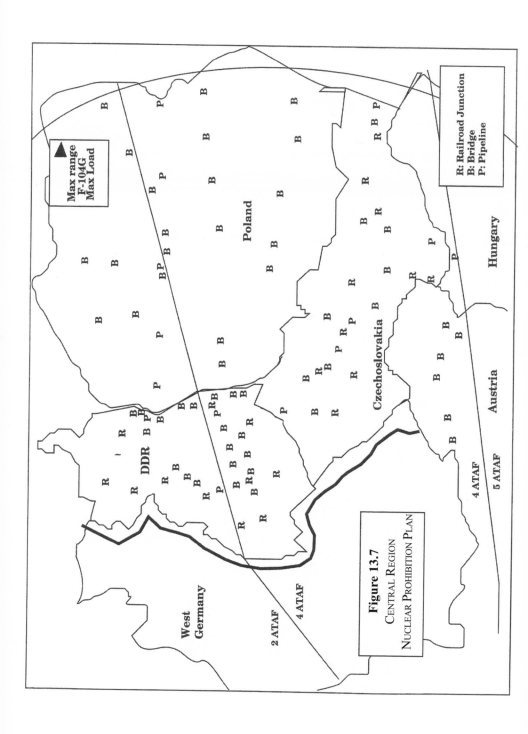

Figure 13.7
CENTRAL REGION
NUCLEAR PROHIBITION PLAN

R: Railroad Junction
B: Bridge
P: Pipeline

Max range
F-104G
Max Load

West
Germany

DDR

Poland

Czechoslovakia

Hungary

Austria

2 ATAF

4 ATAF

4 ATAF

4 ATAF

5 ATAF

around the basing situation in France, the two squadrons at Marville, 439 and 441 Squadrons (1 Wing), became dedicated recce squadrons, while 421 and 430 squadrons at 2 Wing moved to Zweibrücken and Baden-Soellingen, respectively.[28] This was a less than ideal situation in that dense packing of six squadrons on two bases posed an unacceptable concentration of forces. The dispersal concept that existed during the Sabre days was revived. Bertrix and another two sites were resurveyed for dispersed nuclear operations.

In 1966 de Gaulle ordered all non-French units out of France. This prompted the withdrawal of 1 CATAC and its two F-100D squadrons at Lahr and Bremgarten. Canada's cabinet of Defence Staff, General J. V. Allard, met with the redoubtable French General Jacques Massu in the wine cellar of the 1 CATAC mess in Lahr. Over a great many drinks, the two generals agreed to swap Marville for Lahr.[29] This took place in mid-1967. By 1968, with the Trudeau government in power, two Strike squadrons were disbanded leaving four. In 1969, Zweibrücken was closed as an "economy measure," and two more strike squadrons were struck off strength. 1 Air Division ended its nuclear strike days as 1 Canadian Air Group in December 1971.[30]

That, however, was in the future. The peak operating years for 1 Air Division were from 1964 to 1969, and for that brief time the formation provided the highest quality nuclear strike force in ACE. For example, the never-ending Operational Readiness Inspections and tactical evaluations honed Canadian expertise to a fine edge. On one no-notice ORI, 1 Air Division scored 100%. When the American nuclear safety experts at Sandia base in New Mexico heard about this, they conducted another no-notice exercise, which was passed again at 100%. More Americans arrived to study Canadian procedures and training, and as a result the whole F-104 nuclear weapons safety syllabus was rewritten. This apparently caused a certain amount of angst within the USAFE nuclear strike squadrons.[31] In April 1964 the SAS sites were ready, but the QRA areas were not completed, since they were awaiting communications equipment. The first nuclear weapons arrived at Baden-Soellingen and Zweibrücken in June 1964.[32]

Canada's CF-104 force used several types of nuclear weapons. The most ubiquitous nuclear weapon in non-American NATO air forces was the thermonuclear Mk 28. In Canadian service, the Mk 28 was known as the No. 1 Weapon and it came in two variants: the EX which was a free-fall weapon and the RE which was parachute retarded. There were four yield variants: 70 kt, 350 kt, 1.1 MT and 1.45 MT. The weapon could be fused for air or ground burst. Some MK 28s had hardened tips to improve penetration capability.[33]

The No. 2 Weapon was the Mk 43. Designed initially for the B-58 Hustler supersonic bomber, the Mk 43 was adapted to the F-105D, F-104, F-5, and F-15 aircraft. This weapon was also a thermonuclear weapon with a 1 MT yield. There were two versions: the Mod 0 which had an impact spike so that the weapon could penetrate into a hard surface without bouncing off, and the Mod 1, which was an airburst version. The Mk 43 saw comparatively limited service with 1 Air Division. In 1966 CF-104s were restricted in carrying the Mk 43 because of problems with the Lockheed bomb rack (which was mounted on some CF-104s) and the weapon mounting.[34]

The No. 3 Weapon was the Mk 57. The Mk 57 was designed for subgeneral war operations and as such had a lower yield: 15 to 20 kt. This weapon was configurable for use as an aircraft bomb or a nuclear depth bomb. It could be fused for airburst, ground burst, or underwater burst. In 1965 the USAF approved safety rules for the CF-104/Mk 57 combination and the weapons arrived in 1966.[35] Project ABALONE was related to the Mk 57 weapon deployment. Between 1964 and 1965, sixteen CF-104Ds, the two-seat trainer version of the CF-104, were modified to the Mk 57 weapons. The Mk 28 and Mk 43 were too large to carry, as the D version was lower slung. Several of the aircraft went to Sandia, and the combination was certified as a nuclear delivery system. The ABALONE aircraft were slated for a follow-on force in Europe. They would be employed after the QRA and main force follow on aircraft were launched. This was a residual capability of almost squadron strength and added between twelve and sixteen aircraft to the existing six-squadron capability. In a subgeneral war context, it was a significant capability to possess.[36]

The CF-104 force also had access to a number of Mk 61 weapons in 1970–1971. This bomb had four selectable yields, three of which were between 100 and 500 kt and a fourth that was about 10 kt. The yield was selectable prior to take off in the early versions: later versions deployed after Canada left the strike field could have their yield altered in flight, thus increasing the flexibility of the system.[37]

The characteristics of the weapons in question reveal their potential uses. Mk 28s equipped with the penetrating cap suggest a fixed, underground hard-protected target like a command bunker, while impact spike-equipped Mk 43s suggest an antiairfield role. The Mk 57, with its small yield, was more suitable for ground support operations in the Regional Priority Strike or Tactical Strike Programs or in a selected release mission in a conflict short of general strike. Standard Mk 28s and Mk 43s were considered general purpose and could be used against anything, including troop staging areas, railway marshaling yards, and bridges. The introduction of the Mk 61, given its kt-yields, appears to be part of a trend to move away from the massive damage and fallout that would be generated by the use of MT-yield weapons in Europe.

Safety rules similar to those of the CF-101 force were followed in 1 Air Division. This included "no-lone zones" and "nuclear access areas." These included the weapon and the center line bomb rack, the cockpit of a weapon loaded aircraft, and the code and PAL safes. Several instruments in the cockpit had a small lead seal to ensure their integrity. The American custodians came from the USAF's 7232 Munitions Maintenance Group's 306 Munitions Maintenance Squadron.[38]

Pilot training for nuclear weapons delivery was intense. Pilots completed a low-level navigation mission course at Chatham, New Brunswick, using CF-86s without shapes. The targets were the many covered bridges scattered throughout the province. No information on nuclear weapons was provided on this course. Upon assignment to 6 OTU at Cold Lake, two RCAF pilot instructors were the nuclear weapons specialists who were trained at Luke AFB in the United States. There was an additional USAF pilot exchange officer as part of 6 OTU at any one time.[39]

RCAF CF-104 pilots were:

introduced to the external physical characteristics of the two weapons to which Canada had access [in 1965]. We were not provided with any detail of how the trigger or atomic explosive mechanisms were assembled or of how they were configured within the weapon casings. The pilots actually had literally no need to know. . . . We received a pretty detailed series of lectures on weapons effects. It was in effect a short course in what now would be called weaponeering. In the main, all our pre-planned European targets had been weaponeered and our main responsibility was to fly the route. . . . We were instructed on the delivery parameters for the weapons and what would happen if the weapons were delivered outside of those parameters. . . . By the time the course finished, we knew what settings had to be manually set into the weapons, and how to set them in. We were given instruction on how the weapons were physically mated to the aircraft.[40]

1 Air Division target planning was a compartmentalized process: even the Air Officer Commanding 1 Air Division did not know where all the targets were. Air Commodore Reg Lane, AOC 1 Air Division in the late 1960s, did not want to know too much as there was a constant danger of kidnapping by hostile intelligence services.[41] Each base had a targeting committee. The preplanned (i.e.: nonselective release) SHAPE Priority Targets were provided by SHAPE through 4 ATAF. Then the Wing intelligence staff "weaponeered" or conducted delivery planning and tactics based on the characteristics of the weapon and the target. Air Division HQ at Metz approved the planning (not the targets), and then the planning went to 4 ATAF, to SHAPE, and then to the JSTPS in Omaha to ensure deconfliction. For the QRA mission each pilot had one priority target and one follow-on target (non-QRA related but not selective release: supposed to be launched within thirty minutes of QRA launch). These missions were "flown" by the pilots in simulators first, and then the delivery plans were justified to the target committee.[42] Selective nuclear release target planning was different given its opportunistic nature. Pilots and weaponeers could have between one to five hours to plan, depending on the situation. There was no preplanning other than an intelligence estimate in a folder.[43]

The types of targets assigned to Canadian pilots varied as much as the four target complexes depicted. In general terms, however, SACEUR assigned 1 Air Division to his highest priority targets in the general strike plan. This was a decision based on the extremely high quality and training of the force. The highest priority targets included command centers and operational headquarters.[44]

The command and control mechanism used to unleash 1 Air Division, that is, initiate what was referred to as the "stockpile to target sequence," was equally complex. Canada assigned 1 Air Division to SACEUR, who then delegated operational control to 4 ATAF. 4 ATAF had a high concentration of Canadian staff officers in the operations sections, with few administrative slots. Canada gained more slots once the French withdrew in 1966.[45] Once SACEUR secured his release authority from the NAC and/or the president or initiated a predelegated response, he would order the Supreme Headquarters Operations Centre (SHOC) to send the employment message via the Supreme Commander Alert Reporting System

(SCARS) code-named FAST CAT (known by Canadians as "Quick Pussy"). Installed in 1966 FAST CAT was "designed to provide the current status of the [QRA] forces, as well as to permit the instantaneous alert and release of selected nuclear delivery units assigned tasks under SACEUR's Nuclear Strike Plan."[46] This system skipped AIRCENT and 4 ATAF in the process, so the SHOC was directly connected to the strike squadrons and missile units. Prior to 1966, the messages went through 4 ATAF. At the same time, SACEUR in his CinCEUR capacity transmitted the same message via another secure US crypto teletype to the custodial detachments at each base.[47] Either message, properly authenticated, was valid. Only one was required for release to occur.[48]

Two types of employment messages existed: one for R-Hour and one for S-Hour. R-Hour release messages were for general nuclear war, while S-Hour messages directed selective release "under conditions of aggression less than general war."[49] R-Hour messages were sent in the clear, over all available US and NATO communications systems.[50] The US Alert Duty Officer, the RCAF Operations Duty Officer, and the US Custodial Agent in charge of the QRA safe authenticated the message or messages, which included an enabling code-word. The Custodial Agent then removed the permissive action link (PAL) codes from the safe and delivered them to the pilots on QRA.[51] At the same time, the squadron operations officers also received the SACEUR strike directive and authenticated this prior to launch. The safe in which the PAL cards was kept was a no-lone zone, as was a second safe containing the authentication-enabling code words. These safes were guarded by American personnel who did not have access to the safes.[52] The custodial detachment would use a special device attached to the weapon to enable it and remove the device, the aircraft would take off, and the pilot would arm the weapon using the PAL code that he received on the ground. He would then enter the four-digit code into a device in the cockpit while in the air.

In times of gradually increasing tension, the NATO Alert System prescribed the alert posture of the squadrons. At Military Vigilance (DEFCON 3) the "maximum number of delivery aircraft will be placed on QRA." The minimum requirement was that the existing QRA force be doubled. At Simple and Reinforced Alert, enough aircraft to cover "all strikes in SACEUR's Scheduled and Regional Priority Programs" were to be placed on alert. During State Orange and State Scarlet (the Countersurprise Military System) the maximum number of existing aircraft were to be placed on alert.[53] In Canadian parlance, the mass upload was called a Gyppo Line (a slang reference to the 1967 Six Day War when the Arab air forces were caught unprepared on the ground, wing tip to wing tip) on the taxiways.[54] A chain or vehicular barrier would be used to prevent the aircraft from taxi-ing and unauthorized launch.

In times of protracted tension, it was possible for 1 Air Division to implement a dispersal plan. This would only be done at the direction of SACEUR, and then only after he, in his CinCEUR capacity, authorized peacetime weapon movement. The problem with using CF-104s in such a plan was the single-place configuration of the aircraft. If a CF-104 took off with a nuclear weapon on board, this violated the no-lone zone rules. Therefore, if dispersal were ordered, non-US transport aircraft could be used to move weapons to the dispersal site, but only with American custodial personnel on board. The weapons would be in a disenabled state.[55]

Once released, CF-104s had about fifteen minutes flight time to the Iron Curtain. The approaches were at supersonic speed and very low to avoid antiaircraft systems. CF-104 pilots had two possible acquisition modes: visual and radar. The NASRR ranging radar could function in any weather, unlike some other national nuclear strike forces. There were three possible delivery modes: Low Angle Drogue Delivery (LADD), Low Altitude Bombing System (LABS or toss bombing ballistic delivery), and level delivery.[56]

Canadian pilots used LADD and level delivery since the LABS maneuver was inaccurate and made the aircraft more vulnerable to antiaircraft fire. For a LADD delivery, the pilot would penetrate the area at 200 to 300 feet, climb and release the weapon at 1400 feet. The weapon was dropped by a release timer that had been set by the pilot on the way in and the parachute deployed. If the parachute did not deploy, the weapon would not work. This was another type of fail-safe system called an Environmental Sensing Mechanism (ESM). Bomb activation was dependent on acceleration and gravity. The entire procedure resulted in a Circular Error Probable (CEP) for a LADD delivery of 800 feet. The level delivery mission involved a weapon equipped with a lay-down spike. The pitot boom on the CF-104 was used as a sight in this case. This was a low altitude, high-speed mission using a retarded weapon. The purpose was to stick the spike in either fresh turf or asphalt. A CEP of 50 feet was possible. In both cases escape maneuvers were fast, close to the ground at less than half of the height of burst of the weapon.[57]

All of the foregoing is not meant to suggest that the entire NATO release and employment system was flawless. It never could be. One serious problem was that the NATO command, control, and communications system, though adequate to handle the general strike plan and some initial stages of the regional priority plans, was vulnerable in a conflict fought with conventional forces and sub-kt nuclear weapons after a period of protracted tension and buildup. It probably could not have survived a complete, 100% total surprise attack. This was aggravated by the lack of a BMEWS-like ICBM detection system covering the entire NATO area. (Fylingdales was fairly effective in this regard but did not cover the Southern Region). In 1964, ACE had not yet completed its primary war headquarters bunker system, and thus its command and control facilities were soft.[58] The system was heavily reliant on SIGINT to provide warning for launch. Another serious problem was the exponential increase in the Soviet missile-launching submarine deployment in the Atlantic throughout the 1960s.

On the other hand, SHAPE emphasized dispersal in time of crisis, mobile headquarters elements, and their associated communications systems. As we have seen in previous chapters, SACEUR had a continuous communications link with NORAD for air defense and ballistic missile warning information. Headquarters within ACE also embarked on a hardening program throughout the 1960s, while SACEUR maintained four EC-135 aircraft as airborne command posts (code-named SILK PURSE) operating from bases in the UK.[59]

Minister of National Defence Paul Hellyer was somewhat curious about how

1 Air Division functioned. When he inquired about the weapon yields, Hellyer was told that they were adjustable and nothing more: "It was only when I demanded, point blank, to see the figures, that I was told the bombs were capable of yields ranging from a few kilotons to something in excess of two megatons."[60]

Hellyer also asked for a list of the targets and found that "in the event of all out nuclear war the same village could have been incinerated two, three, or possibly more times (I'm not sure what the upper limit was)." Hellyer wondered, "whether or not someone can be deader than dead."[61] Apparently, even Air Marshal Dunlap was initially unaware of the exact yields in 1963.[62]

These perspectives, as well as conversations with Robert McNamara and the changing NATO strategic concept, contributed to Hellyer's push to incorporate a conventional capability into the Air Division. Another factor was a detailed report the Canadian High Commissioner in London sent to the Prime Minister about the state of the Air Division and its lack of a conventional capability compared to the other NATO allies.[63]

In 1964, the existing conventional capability was in the form of the two recce squadrons. In 1966 there were sixteen recce squadrons in the Central Region. 2 ATAF had one Dutch and two West German RF-104 squadrons and four RAF Canberra recce squadrons. 4 ATAF possessed two West German RF-104 squadrons, five American RF-4 squadrons, and two CF-104 squadrons.[64] In terms of total recce resources, this gave Canada 12% for the Central Region and 22% in 4 ATAF.

SHAPE recce requirements were integral to the general strike and regional priority plans. These requirements included: (1) to determine new threat to Allied forces in Central Europe, particularly nuclear threats; (2) prestrike and poststrike recce; and (3) recce of friendly forces.[65]

Recce forces were flexible and would be used in the full spectrum of conflict. They carried a photo-recce pod external to the aircraft that could be removed. Canadian recce pilots had a reputation for overflying topless beaches in the Mediterranean, to the delight of the photo-interpreters. On a more serious note, RCAF recce flights in peacetime usually took place at altitude along the Iron Curtain. The cameras in the VICOM pod could range deeply into Czechoslovakia and East Germany for a substantial oblique distance.[66]

SHAPE also contemplated an armed strike-reconnaissance task in addition to these existing tasks. Planners thought that all recce aircraft should be nuclear-capable. In the general strike scenario as well as the regional priority plans, it would be advantageous for recce aircraft to carry nuclear weapons, perhaps the Mk 57, to take out targets of opportunity. These could include mobile missile launchers that had escaped attack on their central bases. Weapons with a low yield, again like the Mk 57, would be perfect for this task and could use airburst mode to destroy "fleeting targets."[67] It is this requirement that led to maintaining 1 Air Division CF-104 recce squadrons with the appropriate electrical circuitry and training to use nuclear weapons.

As we have seen in previous chapters, the concept of equipping 1 Air Division with conventional weapons was a long-standing issue, and the RCAF continuously resisted this move because of the concern that the government might incrementally reduce the nuclear capability over time. This led to several acrimonious conversations between Air Marshal Miller and Hellyer. In the end Hellyer and Miller agreed that the squadrons were to possess a conventional capability, but not at the expense of the nuclear delivery mission. This decision was made in early February 1965. Two million dollars was allocated to the project, which went towards the purchase of cluster bombs and napalm.[68]

There were several technical problems with this project. The electrical system in the CF-104 was optimized for nuclear weapons delivery and as such had been tested and certified by Sandia as being electrically safe to conduct this mission. The standards for nuclear certification were extremely high, since any anomalies in the electrical system could affect the ability to arm and drop the bomb or the ability to prevent a nuclear accident caused by TREE or other electrical effects. Alterations were expressly forbidden by the service-to-service and safety agreements. If alterations were made, the new electrical configuration of the aircraft had to be recertified by Sandia. In late 1966, the armaments were acquired. By 1967, approximately 20% of the six CF-104 strike squadrons were electrically reconfigured for the new weapons.[69] Unfortunately, the CF-104 was not exactly optimized for close support operations. It had a small wing area and was not maneuverable at low level, since it was designed for maximum speed. In short, it was not really suitable for conventional missions.

At first glance, the entire aerial nuclear strike force available to SACEUR was seen to be vulnerable to a bolt from the blue Soviet MRBM/IRBM strike. As we have noted, however, SACEUR was prepared to preempt such a move if his SIGINT and other intelligence systems indicated this was about to happen. He also possessed the forces to carry this out. If an escalatory situation short of general war occurred, dispersal options were available, though crowding was a greater problem. This was a direct result of France's decision to opt out and prohibit NATO air operations from its air base network, which had been constructed in part using NATO common infrastructure and a great deal of additional Canadian money. The defense critics had raised the question of Air Division vulnerability back during the SCODE hearings in 1960 and later, but the military could not divulge the facts of the situation as it would undermine the deterrent and make the world safe for conventional warfare.

In terms of contributing to NATO's nascent deterrent aspects, 3 Wing at Bade-Soellingen was adjacent to the Soviet Military Liaison Mission (SMLM) located at Baden-Baden. Those at SMLM were essentially uniformed spies. This "liaison arrangement" dated back to the Second World War but had evolved into a cat and mouse game. The Soviets had SOXMIS in the British sectors of NORTHAG, while SMLM-B was in Baden-Baden and SMLM-F was located in Frankfurt. Most of the Soviet "liaison officers" belonged to Spetsnaz (Soviet Special Forces), which would be the units targeting NATO facilities in wartime. There were corresponding British (BRIXMIS), French, and American liaison missions that operated from Potsdam in East Germany.[70]

The SMLM-B detachment had a natural curiosity about NATO nuclear operations. SMLM-Bs were deliberately not harassed when they observed (from a discrete distance) certain operational readiness inspections and tactical evaluations conducted at Baden-Soellingen. SMLM-B also had an SIGINT capability that was "permitted" at times to listen in. There can be no doubt that the Soviets rated 1 Air Division as a particularly formidable strike force.[71]

If SACEUR was unable to target the significant number of targets covered by 1 Air Division, his nuclear strike plans were moot instruments in both peace and war. He would have required even more American resources allocated to a region in which the preponderance of American military power was huge; this would have only added to the inferiority complex among the European nations. Consequently, 1 Air Division performed a critical psychological role in addition to its important military functions.

The Air Defense System: NORAD, Command and Control, and Forces

In order to understand the relationship between nuclear weapons, command and control, and operational influence, it is necessary to explain NORAD's organization and order of battle for the 1960s. There were six NORAD regions in 1966 (see figure 13.8), each divided into several divisions, and each division had several sectors. The sectors roughly corresponded to the airspace controlled by the SAGE computer installations (called Direction Centers or DCs) or manual control centers. Northern NORAD Region (NNR), with its headquarters at North Bay, Ontario, and associated SAGE DC, was commanded by a Canadian officer, while the other five were commanded by Americans. The Air Officer Commanding RCAF ADC (Canadian Forces ADC after 1964) was "double hatted" as the NNR Commander. Note that three NORAD regions commanded by Americans covered portions of Canadian airspace, while NNR covered part of Maine. As we have seen, the nuclear weapons overflight arrangements made in 1958 allowed for the use of USAF ADC interceptors over Canadian airspace. This entitled RCAF/CF ADC to participate in mix-manning those American DCs, Control Centers, and Sector headquarters dealing with Canadian airspace, which amounted to five hundred RCAF officers and men. Conversely, some USAF ADC personnel were stationed at North Bay.[72]

NORAD's CONAD component commanders at the division and even sector level retained predelegated defensive nuclear weapons release along the lines discussed in previous chapters.[73] This, for example, included the Bangor BOMARC site and the Maine-based USAF F-101 squadrons that came under NNR command in wartime. The Goose Bay and Harmon-based F-102A squadrons, though equipped with nuclear weapons, required Canadian governmental permission to allow withdrawal of their weapons from storage before use.

The proportion of RCAF ADC fighting forces to USAF ADC fighting forces had changed since the 1950s and actually worked to Canada's advantage as the 1960s progressed and obsolete portions of the American system were deactivated. For example, all Nike-Ajax missiles were deactivated by 1965 and not replaced. USAF BOMARC As were all gone by 1965 as well.[74] In 1966, Canada operated four CF-101B combat squadrons (and a training squadron that could be pressed into combat use in an emergency), while the USAF ADC had fifteen F-101B squadrons

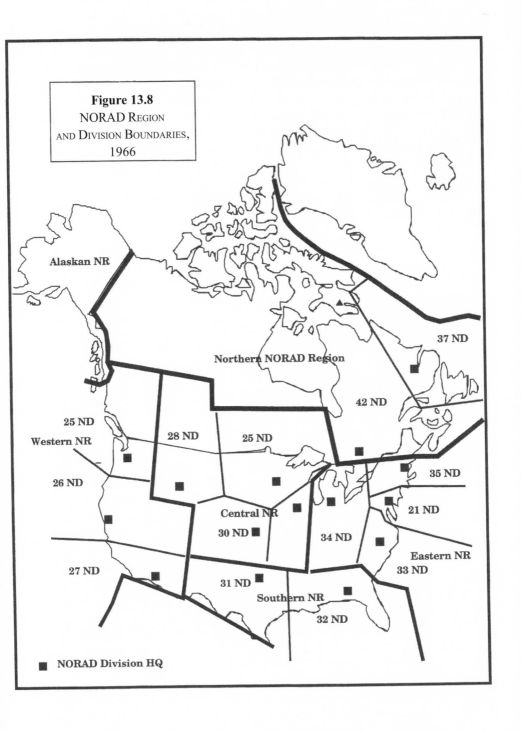

Figure 13.8
NORAD REGION
AND DIVISION BOUNDARIES,
1966

Alaskan NR

37 ND

Northern NORAD Region

42 ND

25 ND

Western NR

28 ND   25 ND

35 ND

26 ND

Central NR   21 ND

30 ND   34 ND

Eastern NR

27 ND   33 ND

31 ND

Southern NR

32 ND

■ **NORAD Division HQ**

and thirty-three other squadrons equipped with F-102A and F-106 interceptors. As for BOMARCs, there were 235 NORAD-dedicated missiles, 56 Canadian and 179 American. There were also 121 American Nike Hercules.[75]

All BOMARC and Nike Hercules missiles and more than half of the USAF ADC manned interceptor force were equipped with air-to-air nuclear weapons. All Canadian units had nuclear weapons. In 1966 NORAD had a total of 982 fighters and 356 surface-to-air missiles. Assuming that there were 3150 MB-1s, 2000 AIM-26As,[76] and 235 BOMARC W 40s, this gave NORAD a possible 5000 nuclear air defense weapons and 1250 delivery platforms for use against the bomber and cruise missile threat, which amounted to 150 to 200 bombers and 150 cruise missiles (sublaunched), a four to one ratio. There was no defense against the ICBM or SLBM except preemption since the antiballistic missile program in the United States bedeviled economists, politicians, and scientists alike throughout the 1960s. Fortunately, Soviet missiles were not accurate or overly reliable in this time frame.

Canadian CF-101B Voodoo/AIR-2A Weapon System

The most straightforward component of the air defense force relating to nuclear weapons was the CF-101B force. The concept of operations for the interceptors revolved around peacetime stationing at Comox, North Bay, and Bagotville with wartime dispersal to Val d'Or (a rather austere operating location in northern Quebec) and Chatham on DEFCON 3.[77] Special Ammunition Storage sites were now required for all of these bases save North Bay. North Bay had the NNR HQ, the 446 SAM BOMARC Squadron, and the SAGE center. Keeping a CF-101B squadron there created an unacceptable target.

The CF-101B technical agreements were signed in October 1963. The Air Staff projected the squadrons would have nuclear weapons on alert by 1 January 1965.[78] Until all the proper arrangements were made and the weapons delivered, Air Vice-Marshal Max Hendrick ensured the emergency availability procedures were maintained. These procedures were refined and included a plan to disperse eighteen USAF ADC F-101s, each carrying two MB-1s to Chatham, Bagotville, and North Bay on DEFCON 1, either to transfer the weapons to RCAF aircraft or to operate from those bases if the CF-101Bs had not received their weapons (the airlift relied on Air National Guard resources which were not as reliable as they could have been in an emergency). Hendrick noted:

> it was agreed between General [Arthur C.] Aghan and Air Marshal [T. S.W.] Harvey that in the event of a real flap, aircraft would deploy north loaded and south unloaded and if time permitted there could be a ferry service using fighters to lift the weapons, dependent solely on the ground handling equipment available on the Canadian bases. This plan would be a hip pocket plan and not in writing.[79]

The service-to-service agreements for the CF-101B/AIR-2 weapons system were signed in October 1963. The MB-1 designation was dropped and AIR-2A for Air Intercept Rocket became the new terminology.[80]

By August 1964, the SAS and QRA facilities for the CF-101B squadrons were almost finished. In October 1964, four fifty-man detachments from the USAF 425 Munitions Maintenance Squadron based at Ent Air Force Base in Colorado arrived in Canada at Comox, Val d'Or, Bagotville, and Chatham. Once they had settled in, several huge USAF C-124 Globemaster transport aircraft arrived and off-loaded the first AIR-2A rockets for the Canadian squadrons.[81]

Each squadron maintained four aircraft on peacetime QRA: two armed with conventional Falcons on five-minute alert, which would be scrambled first to identify, and two armed with AIR-2As, which followed on order if the targets were hostile. In the event of a mass raid, the procedure was different, and the interceptors lined up at the SAS site to receive their weapons and take off. The weapons would be released only on concurrence of the Prime Minister and the President, but in practice CinCNORAD had authorization to release in the event of a surprise attack. If an AIR-2A equipped aircraft intercepted a target and it was in the process of a hostile act, that is, dropping bombs, the aircraft commander could destroy the aircraft. The USAF custodial detachment maintained its own communications and off-line crypto verification system to NORAD HQ, probably to the CONAD component.[82]

The outer bays of the AIR-2A-armed aircraft in alert barns were double locked. The aircraft captain and the American custodian retained the keys. These areas were "no-lone zones," which meant that the two-man rule applied at all times, including maintenance and preflight checks (apparently it was difficult to climb into the cockpit while at the same time keeping both hands in the air and visible at all times). All armament switches were sealed with lead seals and wire, the trigger itself had a sealed trigger pin and there were two circuit breakers in the rear cockpit.[83]

The custodial detachments from the 425th MMS did all the maintenance on the W 25 warheads as well as the internal security to the SAS site compound. The RCAF armorers then mated the warhead to the rocket assembly, the two groups tested it and then jointly moved the weapon to the QRA aircraft after the aircraft had been inspected and a check made of the armament release switches. In a load situation, one American custodian was assigned to each weapon, while the RCAF provided the load crews and the bulk of the security for the operation.[84]

The Canadian BOMARC CIM-10B Weapon System

The BOMARC CIM-10B (the designation was changed from IM-99B to CIM-10B by 1965) situation was far more complex both from technological and procedural standpoints than the AIR-2A-equipped CF-101Bs. The service-to-service agreements were signed in October 1963 at the same time as the CF-101B agreements. There were two Canadian and seven American BOMARC squadrons in 1965. Of the original nine USAF BOMARC squadrons, two were deactivated in December 1964. One of these was the 30th Air Defense Missile Squadron at Dow AFB, Maine, assigned to the Canadian-commanded Northern NORAD Region.[85]

The two Canadian squadrons, without warheads, were assigned to the Commander of the Ottawa NORAD Sector for operational control on 1 October. Prior to that, from March 1963, 446 Squadron sent status data to the Sault Ste. Marie Sector, while 447 sent to the Bangor Sector. This corresponded with the temporary installation of data cables between the sites and the two SAGE control centers. Before the W 40 warheads could be delivered, however, 446 and 447 SAM Squadrons had to pass additional Initial Capability Inspections that were completed in November and December 1963, respectively. The planned arrival dates for the warheads were 10 November 1963 for 446 Squadron at North Bay and 20 December for 447 Squadron at LaMacaza.[86]

On 3 January 1964, the initial delivery of warheads took place late at night. USAF C-124 transports declaring they carried "hot cargo" to the control towers landed at RCAF Station North Bay and the runway adjacent to 447 Squadron at LaMacaza. The W 40 warheads were secured by 425th MMS detachment 1 at North Bay and detachment 2 at LaMacaza and then transported by trucks out to the BOMARC sites.[87] This amounted to thirty warheads at each site: twenty-eight operational and two spares.

External Affairs was caught unawares. Frank Miller called Ross Campbell to inform him of the situation. External Affairs had been foot dragging on the exact release procedures and the government had not approved any as yet. Interim release procedures were critical now that Canada had the weapons and was expected to use them to participate in the defense of the nation. Miller sent the interim procedures to Pearson, and they were subsequently approved.[88]

These interim arrangements were based on American procedures and worked out by Air Vice-Marshal Hendrick (Air Defence Command), General Gerhardt (USAF), Minister of National Defence Hellyer, and Chairman of the Chiefs of Staff Committee Miller. Once release was received by CinCNORAD from the president (in whatever form, including predelegated authority), CinCNORAD "would consult, to the limit commensurate with the tactical situation, with COSC and JCS prior to employing nuclear weapons."[89] CinCCONAD (who was also CinCNORAD) sent a release message to the US Warhead Release Officer on duty at the Ottawa NORAD Sector Headquarters who had "exclusive access to the single US BOMARC interlock key." (See Figure 13.9.) This key was not to be turned until the American officer authenticated the release message. Canadian release authorization "will be by CinCNORAD only." An authorization message would be passed from NORAD HQ through NNR HQ to the Canadian release officer on duty at the Ottawa NORAD Sector, who had exclusive access to his safety interlock key. This message was then authenticated. Both officers turned their keys and the process would be repeated at the Interceptor Missile Squadron Operations Centers (IMSOCs) located at each squadron by the custodians and the operations officers.[90]

It appears there was some agreement among Canadian policy makers to allow for a form of Canadian predelegation. In a briefing paper Hellyer stated: "CinCNORAD must also have received authorization from the Prime Minister or his authorized representative to release the weapons-carriers for use by Canadian forces assigned to NORAD."[91]

This authorized representative was probably the Commander of the NNR (whose Canadian "hat" was Air Officer Commanding Air Defence Command) in

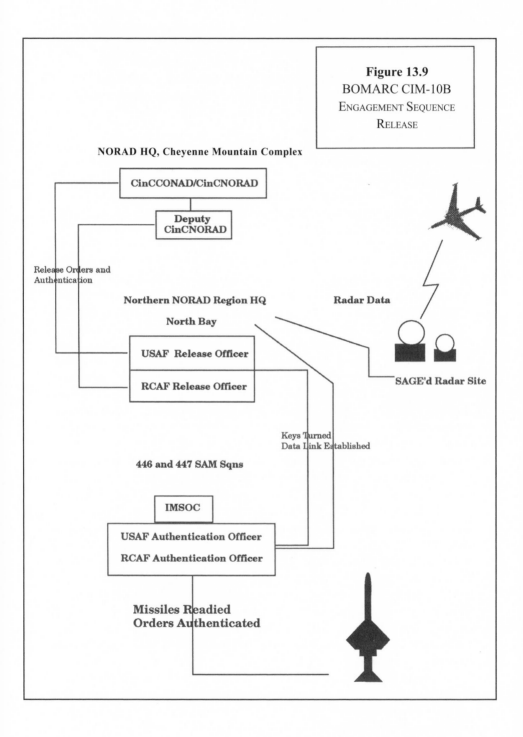

Figure 13.9
BOMARC CIM-10B
ENGAGEMENT SEQUENCE
RELEASE

NORAD HQ, Cheyenne Mountain Complex

CinCCONAD/CinCNORAD

Deputy
CinCNORAD

Release Orders and
Authentication

Northern NORAD Region HQ   **Radar Data**

North Bay

USAF Release Officer

RCAF Release Officer

SAGE'd Radar Site

Keys Turned
Data Link Established

446 and 447 SAM Sqns

IMSOC

USAF Authentication Officer

RCAF Authentication Officer

**Missiles Readied
Orders Authenticated**

this case Air Vice-Marshal Hendricks. The NNR was by this time conveniently colocated with NNR's SAGE computer in a deep underground site outside of North Bay.

The BOMARC CIM-10B could be launched in thirty seconds. The W 40 warhead had a "low altitude self-destruction system . . . ordinarily set between 7000 and 10000 feet altitude to protect ground personnel from atomic scorching." The W40 was "armed during the terminal phase . . . then fired from an influence fuse" when it was within 3000 feet of the target."[92]

The Maritime Forces and Nuclear Weapons, 1964–1967

The matter of nuclear weapons for Canadian maritime forces was more complex than attaching W 40s and W 25s to existing air defense aircraft or even loading Mk 101 Lulus onto Argus and Tracker aircraft. The main problem was the undecided nature of NATO strategy and the relationship of naval forces to it, as much as Mike Pearson's opposition to adding another annex to the nuclear agreement in fear of domestic political repercussions.

The effects of the White Paper process in and the continuous evolution of NATO strategy in 1963 posed serious problems for RCN planners seeking to create a stable force structure and trying to determine the place of nuclear weapons in it in 1964. In mid-1963, Herbert Rayner asked the Assistant CNS for Air and Warfare, Commodore A. B. Fraser-Harris, for his opinions on what the future fleet should look like and what missions it should carry out. Fraser-Harris thought the Soviets would eventually acquire an SLBM capability and this would render existing planning centered on countering the close-in missile submarine threat obsolete. Fraser-Harris also thought a stabilized deterrent system would make conventional war in Europe unlikely, and therefore convoy operations and ASW support to them was equally unlikely, though he allowed for the possibility "that a war initially limited in nature, might escalate to a stage at which it involved conventional warfare in Europe and thus the defence of shipping in the North Atlantic within the framework of conventional war."[93]

Fraser-Harris thought the most likely contingency was a limited war in a peripheral or Third World theater. If Canada was going to get involved in such operations, the RCN needed an improved air defense capability, general purpose frigates, and troop transports: "It is, therefore, believed that the [RCN] should strongly support any move that may be made to break out from the confines of NATO Force Goals as they now stand and to re-equip the forces of Canada with the prime objective of supporting Canadian interests in the future."[94] Fraser-Harris did not elaborate on what those interests were. Essentially, his views were similar to those of Air Commodore Fred Carpenter, the former commander of Air Transport Command who previously championed UN operations over NATO operations.

In November 1963, the Director of Operational Research (Navy), J. S. Vigder, visited Washington with Dr. Sutherland of the DRB in a fact-finding trip related to the Ad Hoc Committee on Defence. Though the information gathered was not incorporated in the Ad Hoc Committee report in detail, a report was passed to all members of the RCN leadership.[95]

Vigder relayed the American views on the future of ASW. The advent of ABM system development in the United States led some USN thinkers to place less emphasis on the close in ASW mission. More emphasis would be placed in the future on "defence of task forces, amphibious operations, and convoys. The prospect of fighting a convoy war in the north Atlantic ("Battle of the Atlantic") was considered a distinct possibility either *with or without a land war in Europe*."[96] In other words, a pure naval battle was possible within a flexible response concept, while at the same time the strategic nuclear forces canceled each other out.

For example, American planners thought a future Cuba-like situation could result in the Soviets' blockading Western Europe by sea. This meant that a wide range of conventional and tactical nuclear options had to available to respond flexibly. The USN was planning to build more escorts equipped with the ASROC system. ASROC would be retrofitted to older escorts to increase their ASW effectiveness and the ASROC would have a dual capability (conventional and nuclear). Some American planners thought "The introduction of nuclear weapons into a sea battle would favour the [submarine] more than the ASW forces."[97]

Rayner asked his staff to take all of these factors into consideration and come up with a credible plan. The recommendations of the 1961 Brock Report were beyond reach due to cost. What could be done?

In essence, a number of RCN planners believed "The idea of providing flexible general purpose forces in Canada can be supported," and "Specialized forces either on a national scale or within the Navy alone reduce the possibility of proper contribution in the future."[98] The 1960s force structure was not alterable at this point, and the existing missions (counter-missile submarine, shipping protection, and Army support operations) could be carried out with it. Twenty destroyers with helicopters, the carrier with Trackers and helicopters, eight general purpose frigates (GPF) and twelve other ASW ships were adequate. The GPFs was the only missing piece. The main threat would continue to be the submarine, but "there is no non-nuclear weapon system in sight that can destroy a submarine when launched at long range from an inaccurate datum."[99] Translation: nuclear ASW weapons were still required.

RCN planners were initially unaware of the 1963 Cabinet decision omitting nuclear ASW weapons and continued to examine storage requirements. Storage of weapons dedicated for patrol aircraft use was no problem: The planned HMCS *Shearwater* site would function like CF-101B bases in terms of custodial and release arrangements. The problem was storing them aboard ships. The RCN planners believed it was too expensive to keep nuclear ASW weapons and an associated USN custodial detachment aboard the destroyers during peacetime. The best plan was to keep the warheads at Shearwater and at Comox. Once released, they could be moved by helicopter to the ASW ships. The planners thought the USN would have no major issues here since "there is no doubt that the USN wishes the RCN to have these weapons, as emphasized by the assistance they have given the programme so far."[100]

As for the Argus and Neptune fleets, probable storage sites still included Comox, Greenwood, Summerside, and Torbay (wartime dispersal). No funds were allocated in 1964 for SAS site construction for ASW weapons at these bases.

The RCN and RCAF got together, at Hellyer's insistence, in February 1964 to explore the nuclear ASW issue and make recommendations to him so that the Minister could take the matter to Cabinet. Keep in mind Hellyer favored nuclear ASW acquisition, as evidenced by the Cabinet discussions on the matter in 1963. The main point of divergence between the two services was that the RCAF thought there should be two separate annexes: one for the land-based aircraft and another for the ships.[101] RCAF motives for this are unclear but probably were related to interservice rivalry as the RCAF continued to believe the Trackers and Sea Kings should belong to them.[102]

Essentially, the papers explained that nuclear ASW weapons were necessary because of problems in target localization and the need for an absolutely high probability of kill with regard to nuclear missile launching submarines. The new Soviet nuclear-powered attack submarines were too fast for the existing conventional weapons and this provided an additional rationale for aerial-delivered nuclear depth bombs. Until better conventional weapons like the planned Mk 46 torpedo were deployed, nuclear ASW weapons were the best method to deal with the threat. On the down side, there would be time delays in approving nuclear weapons use and deploying them to ships outside of helicopter range of land station HMCS *Shearwater* outside of Halifax. There might even be problems from some countries that would not allow nuclear-armed Canadian ships and aircraft to enter ports or airfields.[103]

The RCN and RCAF also explored the possibility of using the existing emergency standby arrangements if the government would not go for the other alternatives. This meant that transport aircraft would have to be kept on standby to move nuclear ASW weapons from NAS Brunswick, Maine, and NAS Argentia (if and when storage was approved from that site by the Canadian government) to Shearwater and the other bases.[104]

There were two major recommendation made by the RCN/RCAF study. The first was "that nuclear anti-submarine weapons be obtained for the Canadian Maritime Forces as soon as possible," and second "that immediate steps be taken to establish permanent special weapons storage facilities in Canadian ships and at Canadian maritime operating bases."[105]

The matter then went to the COSC for discussion. Miller noted the political problems with adding another annex to the nuclear weapons agreement. Admiral Rayner and Air Vice-Marshal Annis (Dunlap was away) stressed the operational necessity for nuclear ASW weapons since better conventional weapons would not be available before 1968, if then at all. The Chairman of the DRB, Zimmerman, chimed in to support the papers. Miller, however, clung to the political problem:

> it would be necessary to clearly establish a pressing requirement for these weapons if government approval is to be obtained for their acquisition. If the need is less pressing it might be easier to seek government approval to equip our maritime forces to take the weapons but to rely on US storage in peacetime.[106]

As for storage, Rayner suggested the process would be easier if permission could be given to construct the SAS sites. As for the ships, "space is already provided in the modernized *St. Laurent*-class destroyers, the *Mackenzie*-class destroyers, the two new *Nipigon* DDH's, HMCS *Bonaventure* and HMCS *Provider*, although alterations to accommodate the weapons have not yet been completed."[107]

Clare Annis, who was against nuclear ASW weapons, noted the RCAF had not yet approached the USN on accessing the USN stockpile located in the United States, which was not the case as we have seen. This could be done, and storage in Canada would not be necessary. In his view, only the Argus, Neptunes, and shore-based Trackers should use nuclear ASW weapons. Having them aboard ship was too unwieldy. Miller jumped on this thin reed of support and took the easy way out. The Americans should be assured that the matter was being given "serious consideration" by the Canadian government and that Canadian nuclear ASW weapons acquisition should be related to the discussions over the use of Argentia as a storage site. In effect, Miller vacillated on the issue and told Hellyer that there was "some doubt" about the need for the weapons given conventional weapons developments.[108]

In terms of forces, the RCAF provided thirty-three Argus and twenty-one Neptunes deployed as before. As for the RCN, the bulk of the ships and aircraft were on the Atlantic coast. Most of the Trackers were either on the carrier or at HMCS *Shearwater*, though there was a detachment located near Victoria on the West Coast. Several *St. Laurent* DDEs were converted to helicopter destroyers (DDH), each carrying one Sea King ASW helicopter. There were nine of these. Two more DDHs were building (the *Nipigon* and *Annapolis*, a separate class). In addition to the carrier HMCS *Bonaventure*, there were seven DDEs and five other ocean escorts. Pacific Command consisted of five DDEs and seven ocean escorts. Three *Oberon* SSKs were building.[109] With the exception of the fixed-wing aircraft, none of the other RCN ships or aircraft were equipped or certified to use nuclear weapons.

Drawing on the draft 1964 White Paper and several other recommendations, Admiral Rayner established a working group to examine future force structure. The eight-man group led by Commodore H. G. Burchell produced the "Study on Size and Shape of The Royal Canadian Navy 1964–1974." Rayner instructed them to determine what force structure was required if "the Navy is to be primarily effective for ASW and also have a capability for U.N. Peacekeeping Operations and Limited War."[110]

The working group undertook their task with some initial hesitancy, since they were "aware that broad, strategic studies are now being undertaken within NATO which might well change the force requirements of the Major NATO Commander and, consequently, the Force Goals of the RCN. . . . The NATO study is not, however, expected to decrease the requirement for conventional forces and might well specify an increased requirement."[111]

The working group agreed that the priority of RCN tasks included:[112]

1.   to defend sea lines of communications through control, escort and convoy of shipping;
2.   to detect, locate, and destroy enemy submarines;
3.   to contribute to early warning of attack launched from over, on, or under the sea;

4.   to transport, land and support Canadian Army contingents as required;

5.   to provide mobile command and base facilities for external undertakings.

To do all of this, the RCN should deploy five groups of forces: four in the Atlantic and one in the Pacific. In a shift back to the 1950s, the working group recommended the first ASW Group, a light aircraft carrier and seven *St. Laurent* DDHs "equipped with a full range of anti-submarine armament" (read: nuclear ASW weapons), be assigned to EASTLANT. A second ASW group consisting of a Landing Platform Helicopter (LPH, based on the USN's *Iwo Jima*-class), seven *Restigouche* and two *Mackenzie* DDHs would remain in WESTLANT under CANCOMARLANT's direction. Three *Oberon* submarines would be passed to SACLANT to operate as part of a larger barrier force, probably in the GIUK Gap or in the Norwegian Sea. The Mobile Logistic Force would be retained under national control. The Pacific group would be assigned to CUSRPG. It would consist of an LPH, four *Mackenzie*-class DDEs, three or so new guided missile destroyers, and one submarine. The aircraft carrier needed new fighters. The best bet was the compact A4E Skyhawk, which was suitable both for intercept and ground support.[113]

This was an extremely flexible force structure. The LPHs could be used for peripheral operations, either NATO or UN *and* could function as ASW platforms in a general war. If Canada acquired them, however, extensive modifications would have to be made. The USN's *Iwo Jima* as originally built did not have NBCD protection (prewetting and a citadel) and was not considered robust enough for North Atlantic weather.[114]

The 1964 Pearson government budget did not allow for LPH, A4E, and a guided missile destroyer.[115] Canada was left with a defense policy that was not reconciled to her force structure or her defense budget. As we will recall, the 1964 White Paper asserted that a maritime force in being was a necessary contribution to the deterrent, that is, priority three, behind UN intervention operations (priority two) and forces for Europe (priority one). With Hellyer unable to get any movement on nuclear ASW weapons from the prime minister, Canada possessed a naval force structure that was marginally effective in general nuclear war in the counter-SSBN role and (without special USN help) had no means to support or even carry ground troops to NATO's peripheral areas or on UN operations without stripping away dedicated ASW capability from her NATO commitments.

A 1967 reassessment of Canada's maritime forces confirmed this state of affairs and also reemphasized the main threat at sea. The CDS at this time was now General Jean Victor Allard, and he wanted to know what the proper balance was between the "requirements of flexibility, at the same time appreciating the importance of maintaining watch on prepositioned submarines in the seaward approaches."[116]

"The Russians," the study noted, "for the first time in their history have embarked upon a maritime strategy." In addition to Soviet surface deployments in the Mediterranean and in the Indian Ocean, there was a new dangerous threat confronting Canada. The new threat to North America (though predicted earlier in the decade) from the sea was the nuclear-powered ballistic missile submarine equipped with eight or more 1000- to 2000-mile-range missiles. Intelligence estimates predicted that the Soviets would have ten SSBNs on continuous patrol in the Atlantic and eight in the Pacific. Three of the eighteen SSBNs would be on patrol in Canadian areas of responsibility: one in the Pacific and two in the Atlantic. Prior to the outbreak of hostilities, the Soviets would surge their remaining missile submarines through the Norwegian Sea and five might arrive in the Canadian Atlantic sub area. Some might be used immediately and others would be used later, perhaps in a third strike after aerial reconnaissance. Soviet cruise missile submarines would be reoriented against NATO surface groups and not used against land targets.[117]

Allard's staff argued they "were unable to foresee organized attacks against shipping before a nuclear exchange occurs."[118]

Canada could opt out of participating in the maritime defense of North America. If she did, however:

> there can be no doubt that the US would feel compelled, for reasons of her own protection, to move into what we have hitherto regarded as areas of primary Canadian interest specifically our East and West approaches. . . . The forces that we provide for continental deterrence are more important to the interest of Canada than the fact that some SLBM's would likely be targeted on Canadian installations should the deterrence fail Our contribution to this defence is a relatively easy, and at the same time essential way of maintaining our sovereignty as a nation with pride and dignity.[119]

This echoed the same arguments deployed back in the 1950s when the air defense system was under debate. By not acquiring nuclear powered submarines, Canada effectively ceded the conduct of counter-SSBN operations to the United States in the same way she ceded antiballistic missile defense.

The Americans were not interested in waiting for Canadian concurrence or participation. They constructed a counter-SSBN force that would operate as far forward as possible based on new nuclear-powered attack submarines. American planners thought they would have between two and four days warning time provided by the SOSUS system off Norway and Iceland before Soviet missile launching submarines would be in position to fire.[120]

Close-in ASW forces were still necessary, but the Americans were hedging their bets on the thirteen *Permit*-class and thirty-seven *Sturgeon*-class attack submarines. All were equipped with SUBROC. SUBROC was a stand-off nuclear ASW homing torpedo with a range of twenty-five to thirty-five miles. It carried a W 55 nuclear warhead that had a 1 to 5 kt yield. Some SSNs also carried ASTOR, a nuclear torpedo with a warhead similar to that of the Mk 101 Lulu.[121]

The 1950s dilemma regarding the operational employment of Canada's maritime forces had come full circle. What proportion of these forces should be dedicated to close-in defense against submarines (either attack or missile launchers), and what proportion should operate in the GIUK Gap or even in the Norwegian Sea? It was not enough to assume that Soviet SSBNs would operate at the maximum limit of their missile range (1500–2000 miles). Some would be in close, as would the attack submarines that carried nuclear torpedoes. For the 1964–1967 period, it did not matter since the threat did not change. However, the first Soviet YANKEE I SSBN deployments in 1968 brought the question to the fore.

The 1967 CDS study made a number of material recommendations. Only one of these involved nuclear delivery systems. This recommendation was to upgrade four *Restigouche*-class DDEs. The favored weapon was the RUR-5A ASROC (AntiSubmarine ROCket), a weapon in extensive use by eleven nations including the USN. ASROC came in two versions, conventional and nuclear. It was a ship-launched rocket-boosted homing torpedo with an approximate range of six to ten miles. The nuclear version had a W 44 warhead with a 1 kt yield.[122] Four ships, HMCS *Gatineau*, *Kootenay*, *Restigouche*, and *Terra Nova*, had the pepperbox-like launcher fitted between 1969 and 1970.[123] Canadian launchers were capable of storing and launching nuclear-tipped ASROC without modification, though W 44–equipped RUR-5A were never stored onboard the four Canadian ships. Maritime command officers on the Combat Officer Course were trained in the weapons effects and use of the RUR-5A in tactical situations.[124] Emergency standby arrangements probably existed to deliver W 44s to Canadian ships in wartime in the same way Canadian patrol aircraft could access the USN stockpile.

The Army and NATO's Central Region

Unlike 1 Air Division, the Army's NATO commitments in the 1960s remained geared to participate in any level of conflict in the NATO area. The trend, however, was clearly toward reducing the nuclear component of these contributions. The effects of changing NATO strategy on 4 Canadian Mechanized Brigade (4 CMBG) were significant. 4 CMBG remained part of I (British) Corps in Northern Army Group.[125] How did SHAPE planning translate to NORTHAG reality? As with 1 Air Division, there were two sorts of planning circumstances. The first was a general war and the other included operations less than general war. General war planning was straight-forward. Upon receipt of warning, the West German, Canadian, British, Dutch, and Belgian land forces would cycle through the NATO Alert System, deploy to their assembly areas with their conventional and nuclear systems (the American custodian detachments were structured to accompany the formations they were attached to and bring their nuclear warheads with them), and then move into their assigned defensive positions, which were dispersed to prevent presenting a mass target. At some point in this process, twelve Atomic Demolition Munition engineer teams would pick up ADMs from the American custodians at the SAS site at Muenster and deploy by helicopter to the border.[126]

While the theater nuclear QRA forces pounded Soviet missile sites, airbases, and command posts, Warsaw Pact land forces would be massing for an attack along several routes. The lead elements would hit the ADMs, which would explode with a yield between 1 and 15 kt and, in turn, create a irradiated denial zone. The follow on echelons would pile up and the Honest John, Corporal, and Sergeant missiles would rain nuclear destruction on them while the enemy was still in East Germany. At the same time, elements of 2 ATAF's nuclear strike force in a regional priority nuclear strike program would be picking off the Warsaw Pact's second operational echelon with nuclear weapons, while deep nuclear strikes from 2 ATAF and 4 ATAF in a nuclear prohibition plan eliminated rail yards, bridges, aqueducts, and other communications targets to prevent the second strategic echelon from moving forward. Any enemy forces that made it through gaps in the coverage would then encounter NORTHAG forces arrayed in front of and behind the Weser River obstacle. They would then have to run a gauntlet of nuclear fire brought down by the remaining Honest John rockets and the nuclear-capable tube artillery integral with all NORTHAG divisions. Conventional forces would channel enemy attacks into killing zones and nuclear weapons would be used again. The immediate zone of destruction remained between the thirty kilometers between the border and the Weser River.[127] This destruction would, of course, have included the West German civilian population in this region.

Things were a bit dicier in a situation less than general war. Other than the Berlin contingency plans, NORTHAG possessed no established plan for operations without nuclear weapons in the 1960s. Any such situation requiring conventional response would have been based on the existing Emergency Defence Plan, but without nuclear weapons. The nature of the communications system and the low level deployment of nuclear weapons would have militated against any form of selective release in the event of a mass conventional attack. The best that SACEUR could do would be to deploy his land forces to their assembly areas or even their defensive positions as a deterrent. Despite MC 100/1 and all the rhetoric about flexible response, NORTHAG and 2 ATAF did not have the conventional forces required to halt a conventional attack indefinitely. They could, however, have imposed some significant delay for political negotiations, but this would leave them vulnerable to a Soviet surprise nuclear attack since both sides' theater nuclear forces would be alert and ready instead of the scenario of a slow build up in which NATO preempted Soviet theater nuclear weapons use. NATO planners felt that they might be able to impose a twenty-four, maybe even a seventy-two-hour conventional delay before moving to nuclear weapons.[128] In situations short of a mass conventional attack, NORTHAG conventional forces could probably have defended against any two of the six Soviet Armies (Corps in NATO terminology) in East Germany.

The Honest John capability was afforded its long deserved legitimacy in 1963 when the Pearson government signed the government-to-government agreement. This allowed service-to-service arrangements to be made with the US Army in Europe. By 1964 the Hemer SAS site was completed, 1 SSM Battery passed its nuclear safety inspection and was formally certified as a nuclear delivery unit. This act was almost a formality. The 69th US Army Missile Detachment was the custodial unit assigned to 4 CMBG.[129]

1 SSM Battery retained sixteen rocket bodies and sixteen warheads as their first line systems, four per launcher.[130] The Hemer site was divided into a rocket section and a warhead section. The warhead section was controlled by the custodial detachment under security, release, and safety conditions similar to the CF-101 and CF-104 bases. I (British) Corps retained final say over nuclear weapon employment. The Canadian Honest Johns were a corps resource. Once the warheads were released to the ground forces from the custodial detachment, who received their

instructions from their independent communications system, the general launch authorization orders came from the Corps HQ through SACEUR's designated Nuclear Release Officer (who was at least some of the time a Canadian major).[131]

The W 31 warheads were equipped with a mechanical combination lock PAL. The warhead had a variable yield (2, 20, and 40 kt) with three separate fuses, that is, the warheads were not like Mk 61s that could have their yield changed at will immediately prior to use. One fuse or the other was inserted while in the SAS site. In the case of the W 31s assigned to I (British) Corps, they retained the M-421 fuse which allowed the warhead to yield 20 kt. The custodial detachment collected the PAL codes upon receipt of the authenticated release order and followed 1 SSM Battery in their warhead transport trucks to the launch positions near the Iron Curtain. The warheads were tested prior to mounting on the rocket body. A key was then inserted to enable to selector socket. I (British) Corps' W 31s were usually set for airburst. The warhead was then bolted to the rocket, the safety plugs removed, and the firing plug inserted. The weapon was now ready for use.[132]

I (British) Corps deployed sixteen Honest John launchers and twelve 8-inch self-propelled artillery pieces capable of firing nuclear shells like the W 33 (5 to 10 kt).[133] The 8-inch guns were a divisional resource. Four of the sixteen Honest Johns were provided by 1 SSM battery or 25% of the corps capability.[134]

The matter of an Honest John replacement for NATO forces was raised by West Germany and the United Kingdom as early as 1966. There were serious concerns about range and survivability as well as age. The planned American replacement was the Lance missile system. Lance would be superior to Honest John in every way. It had twice the range and was a guided weapon. It was more mobile (it was on a tracked launcher instead of four trucks) and one version could even be transported by helicopter. Its planned W 70 warhead had five yields ranging between 1 and 100 kt. The first American Lance units would deploy in 1972 with the United Kingdom, West Germany, Belgium, Italy, and the Netherlands following suit later. The changing political climate in Canada, however, militated against Lance acquisition for 4 CMBG.[135]

This left the twenty-four-gun M-109 regiment. The M-109 carried a 155mm gun that was nuclear-capable. American nuclear shells for the 155mm included the Mk 48, first deployed in 1964. It had a yield of approximately 0.1 kt.[136]

NATO planners developed an emergency capability for non-nuclear certified Canadian and West German M-109 SP gun regiments. Canadian gunners and staffs were trained in nuclear fire planning as a matter of course. Firing tables and data were kept under lock and key at 4 CMBG HQ but there were no warheads stored with 4 CMBG and there was no custodial detachment. In the event of war, American field detachments equipped with secure communications and nuclear shells were prepared to augment allied M-109 units if nuclear artillery shells were released by SACEUR and the CENTAG General Defence Plan called for their use. This would only occur once 4 CMBG was deployed to its assembly area or once the battle had started. The Canadian Army, therefore, retained some semblance of nuclear weapons involvement well into the 1980s.[137]

14

CONCLUSION

The main argument of this study is that Canadian national security policy and the place of nuclear weapons in it during the Cold War forced Canadian policy makers to transcend Canadian foreign policy methods and objectives. It also forced Canada to take a position of increased importance on the world stage. The pillars of Canada's strategic tradition (saliency, alliance warfare, forward defense, and operational influence) affected the formulation of national security policy by influencing the means by which it was implemented.

The question of why Canada created a force structure (that is, one of the means of implementing Canada's national security policy) capable of using nuclear weapons and participating in nuclear war if necessary has two answers: Canada sought to influence her enemies and her allies.

Influencing the Enemy: The Threat/Deterrence Problem
Let us deal with the enemies first. Canadian national security policy throughout the period in question was directed toward preventing a war that would affect the freedom, prosperity, and even the continued existence of the Canadian people. This is not merely melodramatic rhetoric given the quantified potential effects of megaton-yield nuclear weapons use against, say, Toronto, Vancouver, or Montreal. The nature of such a war was increasingly intertwined with probable nuclear weapons use directed against Canada and her allies either as the result of a bolt from the blue surprise attack against North America and/or Europe, by miscalculation during a crisis, or as the result of a response to conventional attack on Europe by the enemy. The only likely enemies capable of conducting such a war against Canadian interests during this period were the Soviet Union and the Warsaw Pact nations.

Canadian national security policy throughout the 1951–1972 period rested on the imperative to deter the Soviet Union from initiating a war against Canada and her allies. The means by which deterrence was to be achieved was always under debate both in an alliance sense and a national sense. In the end, however, Canadian policy makers consistently concluded that the best means by which the enemy could be deterred was to contribute to the defense of North America and Europe through the deployment of high quality military forces equipped with conventional and nuclear weapons operating within an integrated alliance military system, and to participate in peripheral brush fire operations that could affect the integrity of NATO.

This manifested itself in two ways. First it entailed the protection of the main NATO deterrent, USAF's Strategic Air Command, and the protection of the industrial-mobilization base in North America by both air defense and antisubmarine warfare forces. Second, this also entailed providing land and air forward defense forces situated in the NATO area, specifically, Allied Command Europe's Central Region. Canadian forces deployed to these regions were equipped with both conventional and nuclear weapons so they could effectively fulfill their commitments to the deterrent system. These commitments were undertaken as extensions of Canada's strategic traditions, namely alliance warfare and forward defense. The difference this time was that Canada sought to prevent war from occurring, whereas Canada's strategic traditions had developed from wartime experiences that were based on responding to totalitarian threats after war had been initiated.

To what extent did Canada's national security policy influence the Soviet Union and the Warsaw Pact nations not to attack Canada and her NATO allies? The answer to that question is related to how well deterrence worked as a whole, given the nature of Canada's military commitments within the context of the deterrent system. Many people, citizens and scholars alike, debate the efficacy of the NATO deterrent system. The primary argument against deterrence in this debate revolves around the assumption that successful deterrence cannot conclusively be proven. Therefore we cannot know if deterrence worked or not.

There were several ways in which the enemy could extend his influence to Canada. The first was through espionage and subversion. Analysis of this is beyond the scope of this work, but there were extensive enemy activities in Canada during the Cold War. The second was through military means. The enemy could use them to threaten, bully, intimidate, or even directly assault Canada's closest cultural and economic allies in Europe and in North America. The enemy could use subversion first, then "invite" military forces into newly Finlandized areas (like the case of Czechoslovakia in 1948). Irrational Soviet leaders could have initiated a surprise nuclear attack on North America to eliminate the United States as a factor and then invade Europe. The possibilities were boundless, and given the actual capability to carry them out coupled with a shocking lack of honesty in their track record of dealing with the Western allies, the Soviets just could not be trusted to behave.

We know the Soviets and the Warsaw Pact countries had offensive plans specifically and carefully constructed to invade Europe. We know they had the forces to do so and these forces were also specifically constructed to invade the NATO area. We know the enemy conducted a massive espionage and subversion effort specifically to prepare for an invasion. We know they extensively trained to invade the NATO area. Yet it did not happen. What stopped them from invading?

The lack of will on the Soviet leadership's part prevented them from attacking the NATO area with military forces. At some point or points during the Cold War, the Soviet leadership chose not to "flip the switch." If the existence of NATO's military forces ever contributed to a decision or decisions made by the Soviet leadership not to initiate military action against NATO, we can conclude that those forces contributed to deterring an attack on NATO. Therefore, we may conclude that deterrence succeeded in its objectives, and that Canadian forces, which were part of this deterrent effort, contributed to the success of the deterrent. At this point, however, no such study on the Soviet leadership has been made.

How did Canadian leaders view the threat and how to deter it? Attempting to go beyond an open-ended view of deterrence is not a useful proposition. We could, for example, pigeonhole Canadian civilian policy makers' perceptions of deterrence into something resembling Patrick Morgan's idea of Immediate Deterrence or General Deterrence or by some other deterrent models generated by Herman Kahn.[1] This would not contribute greatly to this discussion, as it would amount to an ex post facto labeling exercise. St. Laurent's and Pearson's, let alone John Diefenbaker's, thinking on the matter did not appear to be fueled by such abstractions. The men of these three governments examined philosophically saw Soviet totalitarianism as a different but even more frightening version of the fascism that Canada successfully fought against in the Second World War. They were content to leave it at that. It is important to note that these views were not overly influenced by the threat estimates provided to them by military personnel. These estimates merely provided information on how the threat to Canadian interests specifically manifested itself.

The primary exception was Norman Robertson during the Diefenbaker period, who believed threats to Canadian security came from American overzealousness in what he viewed as provocative activity on the part of Strategic Air Command, and from West Germany's interest in acquiring a nuclear delivery capability under the auspices of NATO. In a way, he predated the dominant thinking of the Trudeau policy makers relating to the concept of mutual stability of the deterrence system.

After Pearson, the government of Pierre Elliott Trudeau consisted of policy makers who did not have the First or Second World Wars as formative personal experiences. They had no real personal contact with or appreciation for the effects of totalitarianism on individual freedom and values. Unlike earlier policy makers, they were influenced to some extent by bloodless strategic modeling. Certain Canadian elements of the deterrent system deemed destabilizing (like 1 Air Division and the ASW forces) were eventually removed so that they could not function as influence tools within the alliance.

Some Trudeau-era policy makers even openly questioned the existence of the threat, while at the same time they conversely argued that the threat was so massive it could not be defended against, since such a defense was too expensive. Therefore, somebody else would have to defend Canada, while at the same time Canadians could pretend the threat did not exist.

As for Canada's professional military leadership, the vast majority were convinced of the efficacy of the deterrent system and were more concerned with the practical aspects of generating and maintaining a force structure that could contribute to the larger deterrent effort than the inner workings of theoretical deterrence. Notably, the idea that the vulnerability of the CF-104 force to IRBM attack might force an early launch of SACEUR's nuclear strike forces, which in turn produced instability (as defined by Allison et al.) actually was interpreted by Canadian military leaders as a positive effect, since such uncertainty added to the ambiguity of the deterrent and promoted stability in Europe.

In terms of threat estimates, Canada's military leadership was laudably skeptical about allied attempts to manipulate some intelligence information for domestic political purposes, particularly when this spilled over into alliance strategy formulation: this *despite* Canada's modest efforts to produce intelligence and her heavy reliance on allies' intelligence. For example, Canadians did not agree with British arguments in 1956–57 that were constructed to justify a British conventional force drawdown in Europe. Similarly, Canadian military personnel did not believe a bomber gap existed, though they knew there was still a bomber threat and planned for it with the appropriate resources. It was not a case that either the threat existed or it did not. Even though Canada was somewhat dependent on American and British intelligence estimates, prudent Canadian analysis was conducted, and realistic conclusions were used in the formulation of Canadian national security policy. The air defense system is a case in point.

Influencing the Allies: Protecting Canadian Interests

The question of *how well* Canada's military forces contributed to the deterrent effort is more murky. There is the question of the credibility of the deterrent effort and the balance between achieving that credibility and how much a nation is willing to pay to contribute to it. NATO had to present forces capable of carrying out assertions that the NATO area would be defended. Those forces had to come from somewhere, and they had to be capable of fighting a war to keep the peace.

Canada's military forces, created by Canadian national security policy, were part of the deterrent effort. Yet they were also used to influence Canada's allies. How well did Canadian policy makers handle this aspect of national security policy? To answer this question, it is necessary to review national security policy under successive Canadian governments in the light of:

1. The definition of Canadian interests by the policy makers and how those interests were to be protected.
2. The relationship between the civilian policy makers and the professional military leadership in this process.
3. The ability of the Canadian armed forces to respond to Canadian interests.

The St. Laurent Government: 1948–1957

The St. Laurent government's definition of Canadian interests included national unity, the rule of law in international affairs, political liberty, the values of Christian civilization, and an acceptance by Canada of international responsibilities. The means by which these interests were to be protected was Canada's participation in NATO. The actual extent of Canadian military participation and relationship to those interests, however, was ill defined. Charles Foulkes set out to influence NATO's structure, a project in which he succeeded, but this was not enough "definition."

The lack of an appropriate military response to Korea exposed the weaknesses of not having ready military forces to protect Canadian interests. It also exposed existing weaknesses in the Canadian national security policy-making structure. At the same time, the United States sought to establish Strategic Air Command facilities in Canada to increase the effectiveness of the nuclear deterrent. A new Canadian interest emerged. There was concern on Pearson's part that the Americans might initiate nuclear weapons use without consulting allies. By establishing special criteria over the use of the Goose Bay facilities, Pearson wanted to use this leverage to protect Canadian interests.

The problems in responding to the Korean and NATO commitments drove Canada's leadership to alter the way in which business was conducted. The most important move was the creation of the Chiefs of Staff Committee and the Panel on the Economic Aspects of Defence Questions. The ubiquitous presence of General Charles Foulkes afforded unprecedented continuity and coordination of Canadian national security policy. It allowed long-term interests to be articulated and protected.

Thus, by 1951, NATO and the Canada-US relationship were expressions of the best way to protect Canadian interests. They both fit within the Canadian strategic traditions of alliance warfare and forward defense. New Canadian interests emerged, however. In Europe, the primary interest was to protect the NATO area from Soviet expansionism. The main vehicles for this were NATO military forces and the NATO strategic concept, which provided a framework for the implementation of deterrence and war fighting. Canada had an interest in ensuring the Americans and the British did not dominate the strategy process. The method by which Canadian interests were protected was through direct participation in the strategy formulation process. This fit with all three Canadian strategic traditions.

On the other side of the Atlantic, Canada's interest was defined as protecting North America from air attack. Though a debate emerged over whether the bulk of the protection should go to SAC or the industrial-mobilization base, another long-standing Canadian interest required better definition: sovereignty. A perception developed that too many Americans visibly defending Canadian interests could be confused with Americans defending American interests at Canada's expense. This was counterproductive in the domestic political arena. Another interest included Pearson's concern that the United States might shift into some form of isolation, a "fortress America" mentality, which in turn would affect Canada's overseas interests in ensuring that NATO was strong. The method used to protect Canadian interests here included participation in the strategy process. This could be done only if Canada contributed effectively to the air defense system by contributing effective forces. The St. Laurent government understood this and responded accordingly.

By 1953–54, the ability of Canadian national security policy makers to respond to change was excellent. The service chiefs consisted of a group of far-sighted men involved at all levels of the process. The civil-military relationship had greatly improved and was cooperative and coordinated. Personal relationships facilitated the effort.

The best way to protect all Canadian national security interests was to accept an overall NATO strategic concept that addressed all aspects of these interests. The result was MC 48, a strategy that was a nuclear strategy with nuclear implications for Canada's future force structure. During the debate over MC 48, a Canadian interest developed in ensuring nuclear weapons release and use was not merely the prerogative of SACEUR (an American officer), as well as ensuring the British did not dominate the process and dictate the force structure. Once again, the Canadian method was to actively participate in the process, access of which was based on the Canadian military contribution to NATO. The results of Canada's input in MC 48 were mixed: the strategy covered Canadian interests in that it detailed how Canadian forces would be employed in Europe and North America, but the debate over release of nuclear weapons and the wording injected by the Canadian delegation increased MC 48's ambiguity on the matter, which would pose problems for NATO strategy later on.

In a similar vein, Canada was able to protect her interests during the debate over the evolutionary strategy, MC 14/2 (revised). The British wanted to decrease conventional forces and increase their strategic nuclear forces. They also wanted no emphasis on conventional operations in the NATO area. They therefore pressed for a new NATO strategic concept. This affected Canadian interests in a number of ways.

First, Canadian policy makers understood that NATO had to respond to peripheral and small conventional threats to the NATO area so these threats did not escalate to general nuclear war. Coupled with this was the realization that strategic nuclear weapons use could not deter all forms of Soviet activity. Secondly, reduction of the British conventional presence in West Germany (though it would increase the ratio of Canadian to British forces and increase Canadian operational influence and saliency) would force Canada to spend more money to increase her land. This would affect the balance in the Canadian defense program, with possible detrimental affects on the North American air defense program, which was related to sovereignty. In the case of MC 14/2 (revised), Canadian pressure for ambiguity was directed toward producing flexibility in NATO strategy. Once again, participation allowed Canadian influence to be exercised.

Canada now had to modify its force structure so that it could participate in alliance operations within the context of MC 14/2 (revised). The aspects of a force structure necessary to participate included having the ability to operate in an environment in which nuclear weapons were used and the ability of the Canadian forces to use them. If Canada did not have them, her forces would be second-class and thus not salient.

As for the services, the Royal Canadian Navy had a defined area of command that allowed participation at all levels of the alliance strategy process in the Atlantic (SACLANT). The RCN and the RCAF had high quality ASW forces able to operate in a nuclear environment. A defined Canadian interest, in addition to direct defense and deterrence of the enemy, was sovereignty. As with the air defense forces, Canada could not be seen to turn over defense to the United States. Eventually, the RCN realized that effectiveness would eventually rest on nuclear ASW weapons use to protect the SAC and industrial-mobilization bases from missile-launching submarines.

The Army realized early on that ground forces had to have both a conventional and a nuclear capability to respond to different threats. Therefore both capabilities had to be built into the force structure. Canada's land forces in Europe were high quality forces and were salient because of their proportion to allied forces and because of where they were positioned.

The RCAF in Europe was a conventional fighter force dedicated to protecting SACEUR's nuclear capability. It was a salient force because of its numbers, its high quality, and its role. As for the RCAF in Canada, its air defense forces had the ability to detect and intercept an air attack against the continent. It had significant numbers and capability in addition to geography (between the USSR and the USA) as salient factors. Its relative military autonomy was protected in that it reported directly to Canada's military leaders as opposed to an alliance command. As with the naval forces, the RCAF recognized the threat would increase in capability and the air defense forces had to be able to meet that capability. Therefore, nuclear antiaircraft weapons would eventually be needed. They would include the BOMARC and the planned nuclear-capable CF-105 Arrow interceptor. On the whole, the armed forces reacted well during the St. Laurent years to the changing strategy.

The Diefenbaker Government: 1957–1963

Two initial problems relating to Canadian interests dominated the first years of the Diefenbaker government: the Canadian response to MC 70 and the NORAD agreement. Acceptance of the NATO strategic concept MC 14/2 (revised) by Canada accelerated the need to ensure Canadian forces remained capable of participating effectively in the deterrent system. The American stockpile agreement cleared the path. In their haste to create an integrated conventional-tactical nuclear force structure in NATO, the Standing Group and SHAPE attempted to impose a certain force structure on Canada. Canada had enough influence to oppose this and then develop a force structure that suited Canadian interests and capabilities.

General Lauris Norstad recognized Canada was a valuable and influential ally within the NATO structure. Canadian attitudes were critical indicators of allied thinking, and he also believed that Canadian moves influenced other NATO allies. General Foulkes performed a valuable mediation role within the Military Committee. Finally, Norstad also thought if Canada reduced her NATO commitments, others might do the same. These views were understood by Canadian policy makers and were accurate reflections of the status of Canadian influence.

The best example was the decision to convert 1 Air Division to a nuclear strike force. The quality of Canadian pilots influenced SHAPE to press for such a conversion. NATO standardization, necessary to save money and increase efficiency, was facilitated by Canada's (and to some extent West Germany's) selection of the F-104 as 1 Air Division's strike aircraft. This prompted other allies, particularly the Belgians, the Dutch, and the Italians, to acquire a similar aircraft, while the Norwegians, Danes, Greeks, and Turks followed suit later. It paved the way for these allies to accept the nuclear strike role as well. A spin-off benefit was the economic harvest reaped by Canadian companies and the subsequent employment of Canadians.

The NORAD situation was more problematic. The ability to protect Canadian interests via the use of an integrated air defense system was called into question by the opposition party. Spurious charges were made against NORAD that revolved around the question of who decides when Canada goes to war: Canada or the United States? The NORAD debates implied the Americans would misuse Canadian air defense forces. Another problem was that American aircraft equipped with nuclear air defense weapons were protecting Canada, and there was no comparable Canadian capability; therefore Canadian sovereignty was called into question.

The Diefenbaker government could not, however, avoid the fact that without up-to-date air defense weapons, Canada had by default to turn over the protection of Canadian airspace to the United States. A lesser capability would be a token capability. Canada's military leaders knew nuclear air defense weapons were necessary to protect Canadian sovereignty. However, the elimination of the nuclear-capable CF-105 Arrow ceded even more control of Canadian sovereignty interests to the Americans. Human pride and domestic political politics conspired to delay acquisition of a new nuclear-capable interceptor. This was a serious loss of influence.

Then there was the SAC problem. The question of the definition of Canadian interests revolved around who determined when Canada went to war and, to a lesser extent, peacetime sovereignty. Rather than viewing NORAD as Canadian participation in the strategic warning process, Diefenbaker chose to view it as an American imposition on Canada. The 1958 Lebanon Crisis alert and the miscommunication regarding consultation aggravated this problem. A further irritant involved External Affairs, whose personnel were trying to find means by which they could influence the American alert system and use this as a tool to "brake" American "overzealousness" for "provocative" action. This was the wrong way to approach the problem and indicates there was a lack of recognition that technology made sovereignty obsolete. Similarly, the Diefenbaker government's attempt to withhold SAC's use of Goose Bay highlighted the ineffectiveness of denial as an influence tool.

The entire nuclear warhead custody and control problem could have been solved in 1959 once the Americans entangled the nuclear storage arrangements with command control and acquisition arrangements. This allowed Foulkes to exert Canadian influence, in this case geographical influence relating to SAC storage and overflights, on the Americans, who at that time were willing to be influenced to the point of giving American nuclear weapons to Canada. Miscommunication prevented this solution from emerging and it was lost by 1960.

Canadian interests were not protected during the debate over control and custody of nuclear warheads since the process delayed the achievement of an effective military force structure. This was a false sovereignty issue, partly the result of Diefenbaker's twisted worldview, partly because of red herring manipulation by Norman Robertson. Canadian interests were not in fact threatened by the dual-key system. Canadian interests were not protected during the Berlin Crisis in 1961. Again, Diefenbaker, Green, and Robertson disallowed a Canadian force structure capable of efficiently participating in the defense of North America. By disallowing an effective force structure, Canadian sovereignty was in effect given over to the Americans.

Yet at the same time Leger and Ignatieff were still able to exert residual

Canadian influence in the NATO forum. They forced the British, French, and Americans to "NATO-ize" the LIVE OAK contingency planning. This helped propel the acceptance of flexibility in NATO planning and in turn protected the Canadian strategic tradition of alliance warfare, a vital Canadian interest.

Attempts by Howard Green to develop a "new" Canadian interest,[2] disarmament, were imposed by Green without coordination. They cut across existing Canadian national security policy interests and produced a situation in which Canadian interests were no longer clear to Canadian policy makers or Canada's allies. For example, the acceptance by Green of the Irish Resolution hampered Canada's ability to negotiate with the Americans the command and control arrangements for the nuclear warheads that were, in turn, necessary to have an effective Canadian force structure and deterrent posture. Similarly, Robertson's opposition to the NATO MRBM program enhanced the confusion about what Canadian interests were and called into question Canada's commitment to the nuclear CF-104 force into which Canada had just influenced several European NATO members to buy.

The problems generated by the Diefenbaker-Kennedy confrontation made the formulation and protection of Canadian interests almost irrelevant to Diefenbaker. Consequently, several serious issues were left on the shoulder of the road. Vital Canadian interests, as developed during the MC 48, MC 14/2 (revised), and MC 70 debates, were at stake in the 1962 flexible response debate within NATO. Other Canadian NATO interests also included the solidarity of NATO in the face of the existing threat and to ensure there was no preponderance of German power within NATO. Canadian diplomats found themselves constrained because nuclear warhead acquisition had not proceeded, and because Canada did not have the ability to participate with effective forces and thus meet the commitments she made to NATO. It was a serious blow to Canadian credibility. The year 1962 marked the decline of Canadian influence on NATO strategic policy formulation.

A worse situation was the Canadian response to the Cuban Missile Crisis in 1962. Not alerting Canadian forces during the crisis did not positively influence American behavior. It made the Americans feel even more vulnerable. Canadian interests during the crisis were not defined by the Prime Minister beyond the unrealistic expectations that Canada would decide when Canada would go to war in the face of ballistic missile attack by the Soviet Union. Canada's interests by default had to be defined by Harkness and the military leadership. The lack of definition drove Canada's military leaders to take steps to protect Canada's vital interests (the protection of North America) by BOMARC warhead movement to Canada, MB-1 standby arrangements, and nuclear ASW loading. These men had no choice but to take these measures given the gravity of the situation. What exactly is to be done with a democratically elected leader who will not make a decision during a crisis in which the survival of the Canadian people is at stake? This was an unprecedented problem that had to be overcome quickly.

Diefenbaker, Green, and Robertson share the blame for not taking measures to protect Canadian interests. These men, in effect, defined their individual self-interests as Canadian interests and acted accordingly. In his quest for international recognition as a peacemaker, Green utilized obstructionist tactics that ultimately undermined Canada's credibility and thus her ability to influence her allies. Robertson imposed his own views on what Canadian interests were, which involved de Gaullist tactics to stop what he believed to be American "provocation." These measures, in turn, were directed toward blocking the nuclear weapons agreements that were necessary so that Canadian forces could participate in their stated mission: to protect Canadian interests overseas and at home. In Diefenbaker's case, his self-interest was related to his personal inadequacy, his ego, and his inability to effectively deal with his prime antagonists, Pearson and Kennedy.

The armed forces' ability to respond to Canadian interests during the Diefenbaker period was mixed. Canada's senior elected ministers of National Defence and the professional soldiers, sailors, and airmen were at a loss as to how to react appropriately to the vagaries of John Diefenbaker's erratic behavior. Foulkes and Miller, and even Pearkes and Harkness knew that Canada's ability to protect herself as part of the alliance was of paramount Canadian interest. The informal measures taken by the RCN, Army, and RCAF to incrementally improve their posture with regard to accepting nuclear weapons into the force structure should not be portrayed as renegade Strangelovian behavior undertaken by uniformed warmongers. It is clear that these men had the best interests of the country at heart and responded the best they could, given the circumstances. It was simply not acceptable to allow the Prime Minister to decide on his own that Canadians should not be protected in a deadly nuclear confrontation because his ego was bruised.

The force structure was generally incapable of carrying out Canadian interests if war had started. The decision to scrap the CF-105 and then delay a manned interceptor replacement while delaying a decision regarding access to BOMARC warheads meant the United States took over protecting Canadian sovereignty. The informal emergency measures taken to provide Canada with a nuclear defense capability were not enough to compensate, though Canada squeaked by in October 1962.

In terms of protecting Canada's Cold War interests short of protection from annihilation, the fact that the military forces were actively pursuing nuclear and non-nuclear improvements contributed to maintaining Canada's credibility and influence in alliance circles. This was a wasting asset, however, and Canada was called out on it in October 1962. As for the air defense system, Diefenbaker would have been in a stronger position when dealing with John Kennedy if Canada was fully capable of meeting her air defense commitments. Kennedy could afford to be dismissive of the Canadian Prime Minister. Intransigence with no capability is a poor substitute for having an actual capability and then denying the benefits of that capability to an antagonist who needs it. Geography was not enough.

The Pearson Government: 1963–1967

Pearson's government was elected in 1963 partially to right the imbalance created by the previous government. This entailed the immediate establishment of concrete Canadian national security interests to replace the amorphous ones of the Diefenbaker government. This was relatively simple, since it required shifting Pearson's self-interested goals (reelection) and then using this concrete platform to implement them. These interests were defined as repairing the Canada-US relationship and restoring

Canadian influence and prestige worldwide. In addition, the Pearson government formulated another Canadian interest, national unity, in response to Quebec separatism as manifested by the FLQ's revolutionary terrorism.

The immediate means of protecting Canadian interests involved examining, modifying, and then signing the Canada-US government-to-government agreement on nuclear weapons access. This grouping of agreements established the command and control arrangements necessary to protect Canadian sovereignty.

By this point in 1963, the inexorable march of American and Soviet strategic nuclear forces toward acquiring massive ICBM and SLBM capabilities produced the elimination of the B-47/KC-97 bomber force and reductions in the B-52-KC-135 force. The Goose Bay nuclear storage and the Northern Tanker Force operating bases ceased to be relevant indicators of American intentions in wartime and thus leverage tools in an alliance context to the Canadian government.

In Europe, the partially formed Canadian interest formulated by Norman Robertson that related to constraining a preponderance of West German power within NATO was given some attention. Under Pearson, the Chiefs and External Affairs thought Canadian participation in the MLF would be a valuable means of exerting influence within NATO. Pearson and Hellyer, however, were more intrigued with the Inter-Allied Nuclear Force idea, since the existing CF-104 force manifested through 1 Air Division would provide as much influence and was already in place. Canada was instrumental in supporting the idea of a NATO nuclear force coordinated with SAC, but Canadian interests were defined as maintaining operational influence over 1 Air Division as opposed to using Canadian positions on the newly created Joint Strategic Target Planning Staff to push Canadian views on NATO nuclear strategy in a variety of fora. The formation of the Nuclear Planning Group provided Canada with an appropriate venue in this regard. Canadian participation on the JSTPS did, however, represent the ultimate level of operational influence and provided Canada with saliency.

Denuclearization

Another factor affecting Canadian interests was Pearson's election promise to re-evaluate Canadian national security policy. Such a potential redefinition of Canadian interests was carried out through the Special Committee on Defence, the 1963 Ad Hoc Committee on Defense, Canada's analysis of a new NATO strategic concept, and ultimately by the 1964 White Paper process.

The public and internal forums provided even more confirmation of the relationship between Canadian interests and military forces. In bald language, the committee stated that maintaining effective forces that could contribute to the alliance was critical to maintaining influence with Canada's allies and for supporting intra-alliance diplomacy that involved nonmilitary aspects. If Canada did not protect her sovereignty and her interests, her alliance influence would decrease and perhaps even her national unity. If Canada was to define new interests outside of her traditional European and North American–based ones, a whole new force structure would also be required. On the air defense side, everyone recognized there would be a decrease in emphasis on air defense in the 1970s, which in turn might affect Canada's ability to influence the United States in a number of areas like trade policy. For the time being, however, NORAD was salient, and it contributed to propping up sagging Canadian prestige in NATO.

The Ad Hoc Committee and the 1964 White Paper also noted Canada had, in 1963–64, an unprecedented chance to influence NATO strategic policy now that it was once again in flux. The 1964 White Paper reiterated that the ratification and implementation of Flexible Response was of great and long-term Canadian interest, since it was the most promising way of preventing general nuclear war. It also indicated that Canada's forces should contribute in a positive manner to Flexible Response. They should be updated and remain capable of operations in a nuclear as well as a conventional environment. The main flaws of the 1964 White Paper in pursuing these aims were the lack of emphasis placed on rebuilding the logistics system (which was geared for nuclear war) and complete inattention to the plight of the seriously depleted and demoralized reserve forces. There were also concerns that replacement of 1 Air Division's nuclear strike aircraft with conventional attack aircraft could reduce saliency.

Canada's ability to recreate her force structure to carry out policies that would protect Canadian interests was called into question after 1964, however. There were many reasons for this. First of all, the Pearson government's national security policy-making process was flawed in that Pearson did not properly coordinate the fiscal aspects of national security policy with those of his Finance Minister. Consequently, this produced a Canadian national security policy that could not be fully implemented with a force structure commensurate with the strategy. This, in turn, was aggravated by the changes to the national security policy-making process by Hellyer.

The cumulative effect of these changes was to reduce drastically the ability of the professional military leadership to influence that process. The effect of this on the civil-military relationship was devastating over the long term. What had started out as a cordial relationship in the wake of the animosity generated by John Diefenbaker shifted into what eventually amounted to bitter resentment by the services at the cavalier treatment of their leaders by Hellyer. This had the effect of further alienating the two factions in the midst of a crucial NATO strategic reappraisal.

By 1966–67, the Pearson government redefined Canadian interests around the national unity imperative. The main drivers here were FLQ terrorism, de Gaulle's tactless behavior during Expo 67, and the effects of Walter Gordon's mismanagement of the Canadian economy. At the same time, Canada was embroiled in a series of international crises that were either outside the NATO Area or on its periphery: ongoing unrest in Cyprus, the war in Vietnam, and the Six Day War in 1967. In effect, the Pearson government turned away from NATO problems in the Central Region. Though Canada had influenced the creation of the Harmel Report as a means to solving the problem of France's place within the NATO structure, there was almost no apparent effective Canadian influence exercised over the formulation of the MC 14/3 strategic concept or the creation of NATO's Nuclear Planning Group, which were the eventual solutions to years of problems relating to nuclear weapons and conventional force balance. If there was any influence exercised, it was not to the same degree as Canadian influence exerted during the MC 48, MC 14/2 (revised), or MC 70 debates.

Canada's force structure was, however, now capable of fulfilling the roles and missions to which Canada committed herself. The Honest Johns and CF-104s, along with 4 Brigade and the ACE Mobile Force commitment, assured effective Canadian participation in the deterrent system in Europe both in conventional and nuclear terms. Even 1 Air Division developed a nascent conventional capability. The air defense forces were finally capable of countering the bomber threat. Land and air transport forces continued to be committed to UN operations on a case-by-case basis. As before, Canada's forces maintained their relative military autonomy through Canadian participation in integrated alliance headquarters and through technical command and control means in terms of nuclear air defense weapons.

We must consider the possibility that Canada's shift towards isolationism influenced, to some extent, European NATO members' unwillingness not to build up their conventional forces to support the MC 14/3 strategy, known as Flexible Response, which was ratified in 1967. It is possible that Canada could have played a role in making MC 14/3 a realistic strategy in the same way that Canada's acceptance of the CF-104 nuclear strike role influenced Europeans to commit to similar missions. The primary Canadian interest that continued during the first Pierre Trudeau period (1968–72) was the focus on national unity to contain and eliminate Quebec separatism. The chosen methods were economic growth generated by the search for new markets and moderate economic nationalism to keep United States cultural and economic influence at arm's length. National sovereignty was also posited as a Canadian interest. Prime Minister Trudeau does not appear to have seen these interests as relevant to Canada's existing national security policy as it related to nuclear weapons.

In two national security policy reassessment studies, STAFFEUR (1969) and the Rationale for Defence Forces (1968), however, professionals noted the best way to influence the United States and France was to maintain Canadian participation in NATO to counterbalance their power. The lack of interest in national security policy, however, was evident in the Trudeau government's reaction to the 1968 Czech Crisis. The government was more concerned about getting NATO to accept Canadian force cuts than dealing with an alarming crisis that threatened NATO and thus Canadian interests. Even SACEUR's request for more conventional Canadian forces was left unheeded. In effect, the ability of military forces to help Canada apply influence was completely discarded by the Trudeau government, since some in that government believed participation in NATO did not positively affect trade policy between Canada and Europe. This highlights the unrealistic expectations on the part of the Trudeau government regarding the influence they wished to wield. It was an either-or proposition for them: either influence is total, or it does not exist.

Ironically, the "nonalignment," that is, neutrality option, explored during the Trudeau years, confirmed effective military forces would be necessary to enforce Canadian sovereignty if Canada was not part of a collective security arrangement. This, in turn, would exacerbate existing Canadian economic problems. Ironically, Canada would also need an independent nuclear weapons program to produce the weapons needed to guarantee Canadian sovereignty. Canada could not be neutral and independent without effective military forces. Therefore, Canadian interests, economic and military, were best served by remaining part of NATO, where Canada could get an almost free ride if her leaders chose to do so.

Maintaining the so-called mutually stable deterrence system was floated about as a possible Canadian interest, though it was not formally accepted as such. This thinking prompted calls for the elimination of "provocative" force structures, particularly 1 Air Division and the ASW forces. Not coincidentally, 1 Air Division was Canada's most salient force.

The force structure implications of the MC 14/3 strategic concept were understood by the Trudeau policy makers. Unfortunately, Flexible Response was rejected as unworkable and too expensive. The alternative, reliance on nuclear weapons, was considered too dangerous. Nonparticipation was, as we have seen, not an option. The consequence was the reduction of the force structure so that it was economically maintainable but incapable of seriously contributing to the deterrent, in essence a token force.

This contradictory national security policy proceeded since the national security process, already weak under Pearson, broke down completely. The Privy Council Office/Prime Minister's Office, the turmoil within the Department of National Defence and the Canadian Armed Forces, marginalization of professional military advice, coupled with the prospect of unelected civilian advisors supplanting elected representatives and professionals, ensured this would happen. The nonpaper presented in 1969 was the final nail in the coffin of the national security policy process and was a triumph of the amateurs over the professionals.

What of the military's ability to respond to Canadian interests? By 1972, the armed forces were incapable of responding to Canadian interests as defined over the previous twenty years. Without nuclear weapons, they could not participate in a general war either to protect Europe or protect North America. There was some capability with the CF-101B/AIR-2A combination, but there was no ABM system. The maritime forces were not allowed to target enemy missile submarines, and without nuclear ASW weapons or improved conventional ASW weapons, would be incapable of doing so in any case.

Canada could participate in "signaling" with the ACE Mobile Force and STANAVFORLANT in the NATO area, but 4 Brigade's ability to fight beyond three days in a small blocking operation was nonexistent. The Canada-based brigades were slashed and their equipment was decrepit. There was no airlift or sealift to move them. There were a large number of CF-5 light attack aircraft, but the ability to move them to Europe on short notice did not exist, and their operational effectiveness was questionable. The small number of CF-104s remaining in Europe (now converted to conventional operations) had decreased lethality in the new conventional environment. The only missions the armed forces were capable of conducting were an aid of the civil power operations to assist the police in containing terrorism in Quebec and to provide some limited coastal surveillance. The capability to conduct peripheral conventional UN operations remained, but the Trudeau government did not favor such operations.

None of these roles had any saliency in NATO, and since the Prime Minister did not regard influence in NATO as useful, the entire system was left to decay. The Trudeau government, in effect, relinquished Canada's hard-won seat at the table and justified it by asserting that the threat to Canadian interests was not imposing enough to warrant deployed effective military forces. In doing so, the level of Canadian international prestige and eventually her self-respect plummeted and then mingled with the nascent colonial inferiority complex that nestled deep within the mentalité of the Canadian populace. This low-level anger was then directed against the United States.

As US Air Force C-141 Starlifter transports arrived nocturnally at Canadian bases in 1972 to strip Canada of her hard-fought nuclear capability, leaving only the Genie air-to-air rockets attached to the CF-101 Voodoos in place until 1984, the Trudeau government set about pursuing its fantasies about catering to the Third World and trying to reduce Canadian reliance on the United States and Europe. It took until 1977 when the West Germans threatened the Trudeau government with a "No tanks, No trade" policy that the Trudeau government finally woke up to the realities of alliance politics. By then it was too late.

Summation: The Nature of Canadian Influence

In general terms, many who have written about Canadian national security policy have been influenced by the emotional aspects of the apparent Canadian subservience to a dominant United States. The sources of this visceral reaction range from abhorrence of American involvement in Vietnam, to the flood of American culture overflowing unchecked into Canada. Clearly, these are expressions of an insecure, postcolonial national mentalité without an anchor to hold on to.

In addition, many people still choose to believe the Cold War was initiated by the United States, the Soviet Union operated in a purely defensive mode, the threat was exaggerated merely for American economic purposes, and NATO is strictly an American tool to execute a malevolent worldwide economic agenda. If one adheres to this perspective, it follows that no country can influence the United States (let alone Canada), and that the national interests of American allies do not exist. This perspective, conversely, assumes that total freedom from American domination involves the ability of a nation to make decisions in complete isolation and completely free from outside influence. In other words, Canada is completely under American control, but it should have the ability to completely control its own destiny. This is an unrealistic proposition rooted in the revolutionary rhetoric of the 1960s. Influence is not a zero-sum game.

Canadian aims were not grandiose ones. Canadian policy makers merely wanted peace, freedom, and economic prosperity for the Canadian people. These aims appear mundane when compared to the flashy crusade-like expressions of American containment policy emphasizing democratization and capitalization. They may appear boring when compared to the exciting fervor gripping the 1960s' Third World revolutionary "movements." They appear violent when compared to providing passive idealistic aid to the Third World. Canada's national security policy aims were, however, realistic and morally acceptable ones.

At the next level, Canadian national aims within NATO revolved around selecting the best strategic concept to meet the threat and by implementing measures to protect Canadian forces from misuse. The fact that Canadian national security policy aims at times coincided with American national security policy aims does not conclusively prove Canada was duped or manipulated, and does not prove Canada was an American satellite. This was demonstrated time and time again by Canada's participation in the NATO strategic process (MC 48, MC 14/2 (revised), and MC 70) and the NORAD arrangements. Canadian policy makers developed a sophisticated understanding of the implications of a purely nuclear weapons-based strategy and strove for positive change. Canada had a choice and chose to exhibit behavior consistent with her interests.

At times, Canada even manipulated NATO allies for Canadian national purposes. Examples include the nuclear weapons effects information-gathering program, the creation of informal nuclear capability in the early 1960s, and the F-104G program.

It is true that missile technology did call into question some aspects of national sovereignty. This should, however, not be deemed a purely American imposition, given the size and strength of the Soviet nuclear forces and the uncontrollable factor of geographical proximity to the United States. Canada could either choose to participate in her defense or turn it over to the Americans. Independent air and missile defenses were not economically feasible, and denying Canadians protection was not morally feasible. The balance struck between the two did produce reliance on American technology and decisions relating to BOMARC and ABM systems. This does not demonstrate complete Canadian reliance on the American whim: It demonstrates the ineffectiveness of the government of the day in ensuring that Canadian interests were protected through vigorous participation in and lobbying for these programs.

Canada used a combination of approaches to exert influence. There were strategic, technical, and operational special relationships among Canada's armed forces and those of the United States, Britain, and West Germany. The most important one, however, was between the USAF and the RCAF. Canada's civilian policy makers did treat American influence as one of many influences during their deliberations over national security policy and not always as the dominant one. The Diefenbaker government adopted obstructionist tactics in an effort to pressure the Americans. The approach involving participation and the use of geography as influence tools was used extensively in the debates over the air defense system.

The problem for Canada in this case was that using these methods required a robust national security policy-making apparatus that had long-term interests as the basis for its activity as well as effective military input. Canada started to create one, but it was marginalized and eventually dismantled over the period in question. This ensured the critical understanding of the relationship between operational forces and national interests could not be communicated by the professional military representatives to the unelected, civilian bureaucracy and the elected civilian officials.[3] The purpose of the armed forces was called into question, and there was no adequate reply, which resulted in their dismantlement.

In the end, the 1951–1968 period marked the peak of Canadian global influence during this nation's short history. The 1950s and 1960s was a period of unprecedented international involvement to which, it is safe to say, Canada made a positive contribution. It is unfortunate that the Canadian government chose to retreat from this prominent position and seek virtual anonymity. Trudeau indeed succeeded in making Canada the largest of the small rather than the smallest of the large. As General Sir John Hackett once put it,

> This was Canada's opportunity to emerge out of the nursery. There was an acceptance among some supportive people that it was incumbent upon Canada to accept the invitation to the top table and bloody well stay there . . . one of the sadnessess within my *Weltanshauung* was that Canada has never taken the place it deserves in the councils of the world.

NOTES

Abbreviations

CIIA	Canadian Institute for International Affairs, Toronto
CISS	Canadian Institute of Strategic Studies
DDEL	Dwight D. Eisenhower Library
DDRS	Declassified Documents Reference System microfilm
DGHIST	Director General, History, Ottawa
DSP	Defense Support Program
FOIA	Freedom of Information Act
FRUS	*Foreign Relations of the United States*
LBJL	Lyndon B. Johnson Library
MG	manuscript group
MGFA	Militargeschichliches Forshungsamt
NAC	National Archives of Canada
NSA	National Security Archive
POEADQ	Panel on Economic Aspects of Defence Questions
PRO	Public Record Office, Kew
Raymont Study	"Report on the Organization and Procedures Designed to Develop Canadian Defence Policy, and on the Provenance of Documents and Records Compiled by Colonel R.L. Raymont and Placed in the Custody of the Director of History, Department of National Defence, and other sources, dealing with the Formulation of Canadian Defence Policy Since World War II"
RG	record group
SCOND	Standing Committee on National Defence
U of T Archives	University of Toronto Archives
US DOD	U.S. Department of Defense
US DOS	U.S. Department of State
USASK	University of Saskatchewan
USN OA	U.S. Navy Operational Archive
USNARA	United States National Archives and Records Administration
UVIC	University of Victoria Archives

Preface

1. Chong-Pin Lin, *China's Nuclear Weapons Strategy: Tradition Within Evolution* (Toronto: Lexington Books, 1988), 8.
2. As discussed in Charles P. Stacey, *Canada and the Age of Conflict Vol. 1: 1867–1921* (Toronto: University of Toronto Press, 1984) and *Canada and the Age of Conflict Vol. 2: 1921–1948* (Toronto: University of Toronto Press, 1981).

3. See Brian Loring Villa, *Unauthorized Action: Mountbatten and the Dieppe Raid* (Toronto: Oxford University Press, 1989); William Carter, *Anglo-Canadian Wartime Relations, 1939–1945: RAF Bomber Command and No. 6 (Canadian) Group* (New York: Garland Publishing, 1991); C. P. Stacey, *Official History of the Canadian Army in the Second World War Vol. 1 Six Years of War: The Army in Canada, Britain, and the Pacific* (Ottawa: Queen's Printer, 1957).

Chapter 1

1. See Denis Smith, *Diplomacy of Fear: Canada and the Cold War 1941–1948* (Toronto: University of Toronto Press, 1988), chap. 3.

2. John W. Holmes, *The Shaping of the Peace: Canada and the Search for World Order 1943–1957*, vol. 1 (Toronto: University of Toronto Press, 1979), chap. 7; Andrew Richter, "Canadian Defence Policy in a Changing Global Environment, 1945–1952," *CISS McNaughton Papers* (Winter 1995/96); James Eayrs, *In Defence of Canada: Peacemaking and Deterrence* (Toronto: University of Toronto Press, 1972), chap. 5; Robert Bothwell and William Kilbourn, *C.D. Howe: A Biography* (Toronto: McClelland and Stewart, 1979), 212–214.

3. Judy Lamarsh, *Memoirs of a Bird in a Gilded Cage* (Toronto: McClelland and Stewart, 1968), 5–6.

4. John English, *Shadow of Heaven: The Life of Lester Pearson; Volume One 1897–1948* (London: Vintage UK, 1989), 2, 43–45.

5. Ibid.

6. English, *Shadow of Heaven*, 321.

7. Douglas Bland, *The Administration of Defence Policy in Canada, 1947 to 1985* (Kingston: Ronald P. Frye, 1987), 149, 151; David Jay Bercuson, *True Patriot: The Life of Brooke Claxton 1898–1960* (Toronto: University of Toronto Press, 1993), chap. 9.

8. NAC, MG 32 (B5), untitled memoir, Brooke Claxton Papers, 941.

9. DGHIST, 82/820, "A Brief History of the Canada–United States Permanent Joint Board on Defence, 1940–1960"; NAC, MG 30, AGL *McNaughton Papers*, vol. 288 file 1-8-1, 14 December 1945, "Memorandum on Continued Collaboration between U.S. and Canada."

10. NAC, RG 24 vol. 21287 csc. 1652:1 pt. 1., 29 November 1946, COSC JPC, "Progress Report No. 1," plus organizational diagram.

11. For an extended discussion of St. Laurent's role in domestic politics, see Dale C. Thomson, *Louis St Laurent, Canadian* (Toronto: MacMillan of Canada, 1967), chaps. 8 and 9.

12. George Ignatieff, *The Making of a Peacemonger: The Memoirs of George Ignatieff* (Toronto: University of Toronto Press, 1985), 110.

13. Lester B. Pearson, *Mike: The Memoirs of the Rt. Hon. Lester B. Pearson* (Toronto: University of Toronto Press, 1972), 2:25.

14. Ibid., 26.

15. NAC, RG 24 vol. 21287 csc. 1652:1 pt. 12, "Memo to the Cabinet Defence Committee: Canada-U.S. Basic Security Plan Implementation Programme—Fiscal Year 1948–49," n.d.; 17 October 1952, "Report by the U.S. Section, Canada-U.S. MCC to the Canadian Section: Analysis of Functions of the Canada-U.S. Military Cooperation Committee."

16. See NAC, RG 24 vol. 21287 csc. 1652:1 pt. 3, 24 June 1949, ACAI 5/2. "Probable Courses of Action Against Canada, the United States and areas Adjacent thereto, 1 Jan 1957." One plan from the U.S. JCS PINCHER series, DEERLAND, and portions of it resemble the CUSBSP. See *The JCS 1946–53 Part 2: The JCS and the Soviet Union* (University Publications of America, microfilm), 30 September 1947, JWPC, "Strategic Study of the Northeastern Approaches to the North American Continent, Short Title: DEERLAND." See also DGHIST, 112.3M2 (D125), 26 November 1946, memo

from DCGS(A), "Defence Policy: General Considerations: Joint Planning with the United States."

17. Charles Foulkes, "The Complications of Continental Defence," in Livingston T. Merchant, ed., *Neighbors Taken for Granted: Canada and the United States* (New York: Frederick Praeger, 1966), 101–133.

18. NAC, MG 32 (B5), untitled memoir, Claxton Papers, 825.

19. Ibid., 823, 825–826, 978–979; see also John Bryden, *Best Kept Secret: Canadian Secret Intelligence in the Second World War* (Toronto: Lester Publishing, 1993), chaps. 12 and 13; R. MacGregor Dawson, *The Government of Canada* (Toronto: University of Toronto Press, 1952), 290. The Joint Intelligence Committee files remain closed.

20. John Bryden, *Deadly Allies: Canada's Secret War 1937–1947* (Toronto: McClelland and Stewart, 1989), chap. 9.

21. Claxton memoir, 964.

22. DGHIST, Charles Foulkes Papers (Raymont Collection Series VI), 24 June 1969, Paper given by Foulkes at National Defence College, "The Evolution of Canadian Defence Policy," 12–14.

23. DGHIST, 193.013 D8, files of the JPC. See for example, 14 June 1952, "UK JPS Work Projects." There are a large number of such exchanges in the JPC files. See Sean M. Maloney, *Securing Command of the Sea: NATO Naval Planning 1948–1954* (Annapolis, MD: Naval Institute Press, 1995), chap. 3.

24. Claxton memoir, 959.

25. PRO DEFE, 6/11, 14 October 1949, British JPS, "JPS and ABC Meeting."

26. Pearson, *Mike*, 2:43; NAC, RG 2 18 vol. 60 C-10-9-M, 14 September 1948, "Record of Discussions at 46th Meeting of the Cabinet Defence Committee."

27. John English, *The Worldly Years: The Life of Lester B. Pearson; Volume Two 1949–1972* (Toronto: Random House of Canada, 1993), 13–15.

28. Pearson, *Mike*, 2:55–56.

29. James Eayrs, *In Defence of Canada: Growing Up Allied* (Toronto: University of Toronto, 1980), chaps. 2 and 3; see also Escott Reid, *Time of Fear and Hope: The Making of the North Atlantic Treaty, 1947–1949* (Toronto: McClelland and Stewart, 1977).

30. David Jay Bercuson, *True Patriot: The Life of Brooke Claxton 1898–1960* (Toronto: University of Toronto Press, 1993), chap. 9.

31. See for example, NAC, RG2 box 244 C-10-9-M, Cabinet Defence Committee Minutes, 18 May 1949 to 22 December 1949.

32. NAC, RG 2 series 18 vol. 243 C-10-9-D, 18 July 1950, JIC "The Imminence of War"; "Crisis 1951: A Maclean's World Report," *Maclean's*, February 1951.

33. Herbert Fairlie Wood, *Strange Battleground: The Official History of the Canadian Army in Korea* (Ottawa: Queen's Printer, 1966), 12–13.

34. USNARA, RG 59 box 2773, 611.42/8-2150, Aug 21, 1950, memo to Acheson from Bonbright, "Appointment with Ambassador Woodward."

35. Ibid., 20; NAC, RG 2 sec. 18 C-10-9-M, Cabinet Defence Committee, 65th Meeting, 19 July 1950.

36. Wood, *Strange Battleground*, 23–24.

37. See Carl G. Rennie's "The Mobilization of Manpower for the Canadian Army During the Korean War, 1950–1951," MA thesis, Royal Military College, 1982.

38. Maloney, *Securing Command of the Sea*, chap. 3.

39. DGHIST, Canadian Chiefs of Staff Committee Minutes, meeting 455, 11 January 1950; DGHIST, file 82/196 vol. 8, 12 September 1950, "MCC Planning"; *Records of the JCS Part II: 1946–53 Europe and NATO* (UPA microfilm), 22 November 1949, memo, U.S. Section, CUSRPG to JCS, "Organization for CUSRPG Planning." COSC minutes,

specifically those in file 1308 of the Raymont Collection, 9 July 1954, 565th meeting; note that certain ACAIs were "expurgated" for use by the CUSRPG.

40. NAC, RG 2 series 18, vol. 243 C-10-9, Cabinet Defence Committee meetings, 23 November 1949, 22 December 1949, 1 December 1950.

41. NAC, RG 2 series 18, vol. 243 C-10-9, Cabinet Defence Committee meetings, 12 October 1950, 3 November 1950, 1 December 1950; Claxton memoir, 1266.

42. DGHIST, Raymont Collection, file 183, 27 September 1950, Foulkes to Claxton, "The Concept of the Integrated Force"; NAC, RG 2 series 18, file C-10-9-M, Cabinet Defence Committee meetings, 7 September 1951, 2 October 1951.

43. DGHIST, file 73/596, 26 April 1951, "Canadian Contribution to the Integrated Force (Europe)"; file 410.B27.042 (D1), "Operation PANDA."

44. DGHIST, Raymont Collection, file 192, 18 October 1951, Order in Council.

45. DGHIST, file 86/40, 20 June 1951, "Summary of the Paris Plan to Accelerate NATO Air Force Programme."

46. Claxton memoir, 1290.

47. Larry Milberry, *The Canadair Sabre* (Toronto: CANAV Books, 1986), 13; Grieg Stewart, *Shutting Down the National Dream: A.V. Roe and the Tragedy of the AVRO Arrow* (Toronto: McGraw Hill Ryerson, 1988), 59–60.

48. Milberry, *Canadair Sabre*, 16.

49. Ibid., 256, 285, 315.

50. NAC, RG 24 vol. 20710 csc. 232, 21 October 1959, memo for the Cabinet Defence Committee, "The Deployment of Nuclear Weapons to the Existing Storage Facilities at United States Leased Portion, Goose Bay Air Base"; NAC, MG 32 B 19 vol. 27 file 42–66 vol. 1, memo Foulkes to Pearkes, 15 November 1957; DGHIST, The Raymont Study, 38–39; NAC, RG 25 vol. 4501 file 50030-L-40 pt. 1, 24 October 1950, memo to Pearson, "Comments on Mr. Claxton's Memorandum of October 23 to Cabinet." See also Robert S. Norris, William M. Arkin, and William Burr, "Appendix B Deployments by Country, 1951–1977," *Bulletin of the Atomic Scientists* 55, no. 6 (1999): 66–67.

51. USNARA, RG 59 box 3174, 14 June 1951, memcon, "Possibilities of War with the Soviet Union 1951–52: Use of Atomic Weapons"; 27 July 1951, memcon, "Possibilities of War with the Soviet Union 1951–52: Use of Atomic Weapons."

52. DGHIST, Raymont Study, 38–39.

53. NAC, RG 24 vol. 29711 csc. 2-3-2 D9.2, 27 December 1950, memo for the Cabinet, "Expansion of the Defence Programme."

54. *Report of the Department of National Defence for the Fiscal Year Ending March 31 1949* (Ottawa: Queen's Printer, 1949), 108; *Report of the Department of National Defence for the Fiscal Year Ending March 31 1952* (Ottawa: Queen's Printer, 1952), 118.

55. DGHIST, uncataloged Raymont Collection, biographical questionnaire, Charles Foulkes, 19 July 1945.

56. Tony Foster, *Meeting of Generals* (Toronto: Methuen, 1986), 84–85; see also C. P. Stacey, *Official History of the Canadian Army in the Second World War Volume III: The Victory Campaign* (Ottawa: Queen's Printer, 1960).

57. Bercuson, *True Patriot*, chaps. 9 and 10; Eayrs, *In Defence of Canada: Growing Up Allied*, chap. 3.

58. DGHIST, Raymont Collection, See "Report on the Organization and Procedures Designed to Develop Canadian Defence Policy, and on the Provenance of Documents and Records Compiled by Colonel R.L. Raymont and Placed in the Custody of the Director of History, Department of National Defence, and other sources, dealing with the Formulation of Canadian Defence Policy Since World War II" [hereafter "Raymont Study"]. Brooke Claxton was also on very good terms with Gruenther: Claxton used to send

Gruenther cheese from Cooke's Old World Shop in Kingston, Ontario. Gruenther spoke several times at National Defence College Kingston and his wife developed an attachment to Stilton cheese. See DDEL, Gruenther Papers, Brooke Claxton folder, 2 May 1953, letter from Gruetnher to Claxton.

59. J. L. Granatstein, *The Generals: The Canadian Army's Senior Commanders in the Second World War* (Toronto: Stoddart Publishing, 1993), 177.

60. *Report of the Department of National Defence for the Fiscal Year Ending March 31 1951* (Ottawa: Queen's Printer, 1951), 9; Douglas L. Bland, *The Military Committee of the North Atlantic Alliance: A Study of Structure and Strategy* (New York: Praeger, 1991), chap. 6; Bercuson, *True Patriot*, 222–224.

61. Dominick Graham, *The Price of Command: A Biography of General Guy Simonds* (Toronto: Stoddart, 1993), 244.

62. DGHIST, Raymont Collection, file 1072, Chairman of the Chiefs of Staff Terms of Reference book.

63. Claxton memoir, 1231.

64. DGHIST, Raymont Collection, file 762, June 1963, "Canadian Defence Organization."

65. Ibid.

66. See NAC, RG 49 (DDP) vol. 708 file 247-5 vols. 1–4 for Panel on the Economic Aspects of Defence Questions material from the 1950s.

67. DGHIST, Raymont Study, 46–47.

Chapter 2

1. See Tony German, *The Sea is at Our Gates* (Toronto: McClelland and Stewart, 1991), 76, 82–85, 200–209.

2. See Dominck Graham's biography of Simonds, *The Price of Command* and J. L. Granatstein's, *Generals*, chap. 6.

3. *The Canadian Who's Who: A Biographical Directory of Notable Living Men and Women Vol. X 1964–1966* (Toronto: Trans-Canada Press, 1966), 245; Brereton Greenhous et al., *The Crucible of War 1939–1945: The Official History of the Royal Canadian Air Force Vol. III* (Toronto: University of Toronto Press, 1994), 52, 95–96, 110–111.

4. W. A. B. Douglas, *The Creation of a National Air Force: The Official History of the Royal Canadian Air Force* (Toronto: University of Toronto Press, 1986), 2:92; Greenhous et al., *Crucible of War*, 915–917.

5. For a detailed description of SHAPE's deficiencies, see NAC, RG 25 vol. 4533 file 50030-AB-40 pt. 3, 25 August 1952, memo for the Minister, "SACEUR's Report to the Standing Group on the Status of Forces in his Command"; 25 August 1952, "Review of SACEUR's Status Report to Standing Group, 12 July 1952–SHAPE 723/52."

6. NAC, MG 30 E 144, vol. 1 file, NATO Canadian Ambassador to Prime Minister Correspondence, Notes, memoranda 1952, 1953, 30 July 1952, letter A. D. P. Heeney to L. B. Pearson.

7. Alan Macmillan and John Baylis, *Nuclear History Program Occasional Paper 8: A Reassessment of the British Global Strategy Paper of 1952* (College Park: University of Maryland Center for International and Security Studies, 1994), 30–31.

8. DGHIST, "The Raymont Study," 132–133; NSA, memo Foulkes to Claxton, 15 September 1952, "Notes on Discussion with General Bradley held in Washington on 10 September 1952."

9. NAC, RG 24 vol. 20710 csc. 232, 7 October 1952, memo to the Cabinet Defence Committee, "Canadian Comments on UK View on Global Strategy and Defence Policy."

10. NAC, RG 25 vol. 4903 file 50115-P-40 pt. 2, 9 October 1952, Extract from Cabinet Defence Committee Meeting."

11. NAC, RG 2 vol. 2651, 15 October 1952, Cabinet Conclusions.

12. Document released by SHAPE Historian, 9 December 1952, North Atlantic Military Committee, "Decision on MC 14/1: A Report by the Standing Group on Strategic Guidance."

13. Ibid.

14. Ibid.

15. NAC, RG 25 vol. 4495 file 50030-E-1-40 pt. 1, Oct 7, 1952, Joint Intelligence Committee, "Strategic Guidance"; 8 October 1952, Report by the Joint Planning Committee to the Chiefs of Staff Committee, "Strategic Guidance"; 1 December 1952, memo for Defence Liaison, "NATO December Ministerial Meeting."

16. U.S. Joint Chiefs of Staff, *Records of the Joint Chiefs of Staff, Part 2 1946–53: The United States* (Bethesda, MD: University Publications of America, 1979), reel II, Joint Intelligence Committee, "USSR Long-Range Bombing Capabilities," 17 April 1950; NAC, RG 24 acc 83-4/167 vol. 8067 file NSTS 112070-15-1 vol. 1, 11 December 1947, memo to the Canadian Section of the Military Cooperation Committee, "Implementation Measures, Canada-U.S. Basic Security Plan."

17. Joseph T. Jockel, *No Boundaries Upstairs: Canada, The United States and the Origins of North American Air Defence, 1945–1958* (Vancouver: UBC Press, 1987), 61–64; Kenneth Schaffel, *The Emerging Shield: The Air Force and the Evolution of Continental Air Defence 1945–1960* (Washington, DC: Office of Air Force History, 1991), 172–174.

18. NAC, RG 24 vol. 4220 file 756-181-267-2, 10 December 1952, MIT Lincoln Laboratory, "Summer Study Group."

19. In essence, this would become what we know today as AWACS.

20. NAC, RG 24 vol. 4220 file 756-181-267-2, 17 September 1952, G. R. Lindsey, "Report on Summer Study on Air Defence Problems held by Project LINCOLN."

21. Ibid.

22. Ibid.; Schaffel, *Emerging Shield*, 197–201.

23. FOIA, USAF Air Defence Command, "Historical Study No. 30: Interceptor Missiles in Air Defence 1944–1964," February 1965; A. J. Bacevich, *The Pentomic Era: The U.S. Army Between Korea and Vietnam* (Washington, DC: NDU Press, 1986), 77–80; USNARA, RG 59 box 2880, U.S. State Department, "Fact Sheet: Guided Missiles and Rockets," 22 June 1959; BOMARC information was given to the RCAF by the USAF through the CJSM Washington in September 1952. DGHIST, file 79/429, VCAS, "Divisional Items of Interest Week Ending 18th Sep 52."

24. FOIA, USAF, Thomas W. Ray, "BOMARC and Nuclear Armamant 1951–1963," ADC Historical Study no. 21.

25. Chuck Hansen, *U.S. Nuclear Weapons: The Secret History* (New York: Orion Books, 1988), 176–177.

26. NAC, RG 24 vol. 4220 file 756-181-267-2, 17 September 1952, G. R. Lindsey, "Report on Summer Study on Air Defence Problems held by Project LINCOLN."

27. Jockel, *No Boundaries Upstairs*, 70.

28. U.S. DOS, *FRUS, 1952–1954 Volume VI Western Canada and Europe Part II* (Washington, DC: Government Printing Office, 1986), 2047–2048, memo Perkins to Matthews, "Difficulties encountered in obtaining Canadian Government approval for U.S. or joint Defence projects in Canada," 14 November 1952.

29. Schaffel, *Emerging Shield*, 193.

30. DGHIST, file 193.013 (D9) JIC 52/1, "The Threat to North America"; DGHIST, Raymont Collection, file 631, 19 August 1958, Chairman Chiefs of Staff (Foulkes) "Report on the Development of the CF-105 Aircraft and Associated Weapons System, 1952–1958"; see also Richard Organ et al., *Avro Arrow: The Story of the Avro Arrow from Its Evolution to Its Extinction* (Erin, Ontario: Boston Mills Press, 1980), 11–17.

31. DGHIST, Raymont Collection, file 11, 19 August 1958, "Review of Sparrow 2 Consid-

erations"; Raymont Collection, file 631, 19 August 1958, "Report on the Development of the CF105 Aircraft and Associated Weapon System."

32. Ronald Cole et al., *The History of the Unified Command Plan 1946–1993* (Washington, DC: Joint History Office), 23–24; DGHIST, "Raymont Study," 116–117; DGHIST, file 79/24, 31 August 1953, Air Vice Marshal F. R. Miller, "Report of the Second Meeting of the Canada-U.S. Military Study Group"; NAC, RG 24 vol. 112 file 096 107.4 vol. 1, 14 December 1953, memo from G/C E. M. Reyno to CPlansI, "CUSSAT."

33. DGHIST, file 193.009 (D53), 6 February 1953, AVM Miller, "Project COUNTER-CHANGE: Experimental Early Warning Radar Sites in the Arctic."

34. Ibid.

35. Schaffel, *Emerging Shield*, 193.

36. DGHIST, 73/1223 file 1330, 6 October 1953, Cabinet Defence Committee 95th meeting; 3 November 1953, Cabinet Defence Committee 96th meeting; NAC, RG 2 vol. 2651, 4 November 1953, Cabinet Conclusions. See also DDRS, 1978, frame 153 A and B, 20 October 1953, JCS, "Decision on JCS 1899/69, Interim Report by the Canadian-U.S. Military Study Group."

37. USN OA, Arthur W. Radford Papers, "Personal Log"; USNARA, RG 218 file 381-Continental Defence (1953–1954), letter MCC to Radford, "Status of Canada-U.S. Force Requirements Planning," 20 October 1953; memo Radford to SECDEF, 17 October 1953; memo Radford to Service Chiefs, "Continental Defence," 16 October 1953.

38. USNARA, RG 59 box 3174, 711.5611/10-2253, "Informal Views on and Actions of the United States Relative to Continental Defence Missions," 21 October 1953.

39. DGHIST, Raymont Collection, uncataloged, 4 January 1954, memo Foulkes to Chiefs, "Statement by the U.S. Representative at the December 1953 Meeting of the NATO Military Committee."

40. Ibid.

41. For a discussion of NSC 162/2, see Robert Allen Wampler, "Ambiguous Legacy: The United States, Great Britain, and the Foundations of NATO Strategy, 1948–1957," (PhD diss., Harvard University, 1991), 519–522.

42. NAC, RG 25 vol. 4903 file 50115-P-40 pt. 2, 24 March 1954, memo from W. H. Wershof to the Minister, "United States Defence Policy."

43. NAC, RG 25 vol. 4903 file 50115-P-40 pt. 2, 8 March 1954, "Extract of Notes by General Foulkes on Conversations Held in Washington on March 8, 1954."

44. NAC, RG 25 vol. 4903 file 50115-P-40 pt. 2, 22 January 1954, Heeney to Pearson, "United States Defence Policy."

45. NAC, RG 25 vol. 4903 file 50115-P-40 pt. 2, 9 February 1954, JPC, "A Study of Recent Changes and Trends in United States Defence Policy and the Implications It Might Have on Canadian Defence Policy."

46. NAC, RG 25 vol. 4903 file 50115-P-40 pt. 2, 5 February 1954, memo Wilgress to Pearson, "Implications of United States Strategy."

47. DGHIST, file 112.3M2.009 (D260), 15 June 1954, JPC, "United States Defence Policy and the Possible Implications for Canadian Defence Policy."

48. Ibid.

49. NAC, RG 25 vol. 4903 file 50115-P-40 pt. 2, 2 February 1954, memo to the Prime Minister from Pearson, "United States Defence Policy."

50. DGHIST, Raymont Collection, file 1308, 9 July 1954, COSC, minutes of the 565th meeting.

51. Wampler, "Ambiguous Legacy," 522; DGHIST, Raymont Collection, uncataloged, 5 May 1954, message Canadian delegation to NATO Paris to Undersecretary of State for External Affairs, "Meeting of Council with Standing Group."

52. DGHIST, Raymont Collection, uncataloged, 20 April 1954, note Drury to Foulkes.

53. NAC, RG 25 vol. 4533 file 50030-AB-40 pt. 4, 25 March 1954, message from Wilgress to Pearson, "Briefing at SHAPE."

54. Wampler, "Ambiguous Legacy," 609–618.

55. DGHIST, Raymont Collection, uncataloged, "Brief for Discussions with General Whiteley, 7–8 Jun 54."

56. Ibid.

57. DGHIST, Raymont Collection, uncataloged, "Report of General Foulkes on His Discussion with the Standing Group on 7 Jun 54."

58. Ibid.

59. DGHIST, Raymont Collection, uncataloged, 30 June 1954, letter Foulkes to MacKay.

60. DDEL, Gruenther Papers, "Foulkes, Charles" folder, 15 June 1954, letter Gruenther to Foulkes.

61. DGHIST, Raymont Collection, file 1330, Cabinet Defence Committee special meeting, 10 June 1954.

62. Ibid.

63. DGHIST, Raymont Collection, file 1330, Cabinet Defence Committee special meeting, 13 October 1954.

64. Ibid.

65. J. W. Pickersgill, *My Years with St. Laurent* (Toronto: University of Toronto Press, 1975), 217; *The Canadian Who's Who Vol. X 1964–1966*, 161.

66. DGHIST, Raymont Study, 164.

67. DGHIST, Raymont Collection, file 1330, Chiefs of Staff Committee minutes, 30 July 1954.

68. DGHIST, file 193.013 (D13), 27 October 1954, JPC "Semi-Annual Review of Intelligence."

69. Ibid.

70. Allan M. Winkler, *Life Under A Cloud: American Anxiety About the Atom* (New York: Oxford University Press, 1993), 93–96.

71. DGHIST, file 193.013 (D13), 27 October 1954, JPC, "Implications to the Canadian Defence Programme of a Possible Enemy Use of Megaton Nuclear Weapons."

72. Ibid.

73. Ibid.

74. Ibid.

75. NAC, RG 24 acc 83-84/49 vol. 4175 file 1930-106-1 pt. 1, 11 September 1956, memo DWD, "Canadian Army Requirements for Nuclear Weapons."

76. Ibid.

77. DGHIST, Raymont Collection, file 1330, Cabinet Defence Committee 100th meeting, 25 June 1954; DGHIST, Raymont Collection, file 1308, COSC, 564th meeting, 28 June 1954.

78. DGHIST, Raymont Collection, file 1330, Cabinet Defence Committee, 101st meeting, 12 November 1954.

79. NAC, RG 25 vol. 4903 file 5011-P-40 pt. 3, 2 July 1954, despatch to ADP Heeney from Pearson, "United States Defence Policy and Possible Implications for Canadian Defence Policy."

80. JCS Joint History Office, *The History of the Unified Command Plan 1946–1993*, 16–17.

81. Lydus H. Buss, "CONAD Historical Reference Paper No. 1: U.S. Air Defence in the Northeast 1940–1957," (Ent AFB, CO: HQ Air Defence Command, 1957), 16–18.

82. Note that the army possessed several 90mm antiaircraft gun batteries. These were deployed under the CUSRPG commitment, particularly around the locks at Sault St. Marie.

83. DGHIST, file 193.013 (D16), 27 October 1954, memo to COSC from Air Marshal Slemon, Chief of the Air Staff, "Air Defence Planning Policy."

84. DGHIST, file 193.013 (D16), 9 November 1954, 21/54 meeting of the JPC, "Air Defence Planning Policy: First Priority Target System for Air Defence."

85. DGHIST, file 193.013 (D16), 23 November 1954, 22/54 meeting of the JPC, "Air Defence Planning Policy: First Priority Target System for Air Defence"; 23/54 meeting of the JPC, "Air Defence Planning Policy: First Priority Target System for Air Defence."

86. DGHIST, Raymont Collection, file 1308, COSC, 569th meeting, 3 November 1954.

87. Ibid.

88. Ibid.

89. Ibid.

90. Ibid.

91. Ibid.

92. Ibid.

93. DGHIST, Raymont Collection, file 1329, Cabinet Defence Committee meeting, 12 November 1954.

94. Wampler, "Ambiguous Legacy," 619–622.

95. Document released by SHAPE Historian, North Atlantic Military Committee, 22 November 1954, "Decision on MC 48: A Report by the Military Committee on the Most Effective Pattern of NATO Military Strength for the Next Few Years."

96. Ibid.

97. Ibid.

98. Ibid.

99. Ibid.

100. DGHIST, Raymont Collection, uncataloged, 5 November 1954, "Service Comments—SACEUR and SACLANT Capabilities Studies and IPT Reports."

101. Ibid.

102. DGHIST, Raymont Collection, uncataloged, 24 November 1954, message Raymont to Cooper.

103. Ibid.

104. DGHIST, Raymont Collection, uncataloged, 24 November 1954, message Permanent Representative to NATO to Secretary of State for External Affairs, "The New Look."

105. DGHIST, Raymont Collection, uncataloged, 29 November 1954, memo Foulkes to Campney.

106. DGHIST, Raymont Collection, uncataloged, 22 November 1954, "Report by the Chairman of the Chiefs of Staff Committee on the Main Items Discussed at the Meeting of the Military Committee of the North Atlantic Treaty Organization."

107. Ibid.

108. DGHIST, Raymont Collection, uncataloged, 6 December 1954, memo Rogers to Foulkes; 4 December 1954, message High Commissioner for the United Kingdom, Ottawa from the Secretary of State for Commonwealth Relations.

109. Ibid.

110. DGHIST, Raymont Collection, uncataloged, 12 December 1954, "British Seek Check on Atom Warfare," *London Times*; 6 December 1954, message Permanent Representative to the NAC to Secretary of State for External Affairs.

111. DGHIST, Raymont Collection, uncataloged, 9 December 1954, Charles Foulkes, "Notes for Discussions on MC 48 Final."

112. Ibid.

113. DGHIST, Raymont Collection, uncataloged, 11 December 1954, message Secretary of State for External Affairs to CANAC, "Action to be Taken on MC 48."

114. DGHIST, Raymont Collection, uncataloged, 12 December 1954, message CANAC Paris to CCOS.

115. DGHIST, Raymont Collection, uncataloged, 22 December 1954, "Note on Negotiations for Approval of MC 48."

116. DGHIST, Raymont Collection, uncataloged, 13 December 1954, message CANAC Paris to CCOS Ottawa.

117. DGHIST, Raymont Collection, uncataloged, 13 December 1954, "Brief for the Ministerial Meeting of the North Atlantic Council, Paris, December 1954."

118. Ibid.

119. Ibid.

120. DGHIST, Raymont Collection, uncataloged, 14 December 1954, message Secretary of State for External Affairs to CANAC; 14 December 1954, "Statement by General Charles Foulkes at Second Session NATO Military Committee"; 15 December 1954, message Secretary of State for External Affairs to CANAC."

121. DGHIST, Raymont Study, 134–135.

122. DGHIST, Raymont Collection, uncataloged, 11 January 1955, letter Foulkes to Solandt.

123. See DGHIST, file 87/47, R. L. Raymont, "The Evolution of the Structure of the Department of National Defence, 1945–68: Report to the Task Force on Review of Unification of the Canadian Armed Forces—30 November 1979"; NAC, RG 25 vol. 4495 file 50030-E-1-40 pt. 1, 26 March 1955, "The Strategic Concept of the Nuclear Deterrent."

124. NAC, RG 25 vol. 4495 file 50030-E-1-40 pt. 1, 26 March 1955, "The Strategic Concept of the Nuclear Deterrent."

125. Ibid.

126. Ibid.

127. Ibid.

128. DGHIST, Raymont Collection, file 1308A, COSC, Special Meeting, 18 February 1955.

129. For the best work on the senior civil servants from the period, see J. L. Granatstein's *The Ottawa Men: The Civil Service Mandarins, 1935–1957* (Toronto: Oxford University Press, 1982).

130. DGHIST, Raymont Collection, file 1308A, COSC, Special Meeting, 18 February 1955.

131. Ibid.

132. NAC, RG 25 vol. 4499 file 50030-K-40 pt. 4, n.d., POEADQ, ED 6–56, "Memorandum on the Canadian Reply to ARQ(56)."

133. NAC, RG 25 vol. 4499 file 50030-K-40 pt. 3, 23 November 1955, memo to POEADQ from Foulkes, "Priorities within NATO."

134. DGHIST, Raymont Collection, uncataloged, 15 April 1955, memo Drury to Foulkes.

135. Department of National Defence, *Canada's Defence Programme 1955–56* (Ottawa: Queen's Printer, 1955).

136. Ibid., and Vernon Kronenberg, *All Together Now: The Organization of the Department of National Defence in Canada 1964–1972* (Toronto: Canadian Institute of International Affairs, 1973), 23.

137. NAC, RG 25 vol. 4499 file 50030-K-40 pt. 3, 23 November 1955, memo to POEADQ from Foulkes, "Priorities within NATO"; 11 October 1955, extracts from summary record of a meeting of the North Atlantic Council, held on the subject of future NATO common infrastructure policy.

138. NAC, RG 25 vol. 4499 file 50030-K-40 pt. 3, 11 October 1955, extracts from summary record of a meeting of the North Atlantic Council, held on the subject of future NATO common infrastructure policy.

139. USN OA, SPD box 317, file A-14, memo Director SPD to CNO, "Implications of British Emphasis on Civil Defence," 14 November 1955.

140. NAC, RG 25 vol. 4499 file 50030-K-40 pt. 3, POEADQ, 38th meeting, 15 November 1955.

Chapter 3

1. NSA, State Department memo, "Consultations with Canadians and British on Overflights and Storage of Non-Nuclear Components and Non-Consultation with France on Storage of Components in Morocco," 17 June 1952.

2. USNARA, RG 59 box 3219, memo Willoughby to Merchant, "Proposed Revision of XYZ Procedures," 17 March 1959.

3. USNARA, RG 59 box 3219, memcon Tovell and Farley, "Authorization for Emergency Landing During SAC Overflights of Canada," 24 December 1957.

4. Hansen, *U.S. Nuclear Weapons*, 122–141.

5. NSA, State Department memo, "Consultations with Canadians and British on Overflights and Storage of Non-Nuclear Components and Non-Consultation with France on Storage of Components in Morocco," 17 June 1952.

6. DGHIST, Raymont Collection, file 1329, 24 January 1955, Cabinet Defence Committee, 103rd meeting.

7. Ibid.

8. Ibid.

9. Norman Polmar, ed., *Strategic Air Command: People, Aircraft, and Missiles* (Baltimore, MD: Nautical and Aviation Publishing, 1979), 38–40.

10. DGHIST, Raymont Collection, file 1085, 9 April 1956, RCAF aide memoir, "USAF Operating Requirement in Canada—SAC Tanker Bases."

11. DGHIST, Raymont Collection, file 1085, 28 March 1956, letter to AVM C. R. Dunlap, RCAF from Maj. Gen. J. E. Briggs, USAF.

12. Ibid.

13. DGHIST, Raymont Collection, file 1085, 1 June 1956, message CJS(W) to COSC, "USAF Tanker Base Requirements in Canada."

14. DGHIST, Raymont Collection, file 1085, 4 June 1956, memo Slemon to Foulkes, "U.S. Application for Preliminary Surveys for SAC Tanker Bases in Northern Canada"; 4 June 1956, memo Foulkes to Campney, "USAF Military Operating Requirement in Canada SAC Staging Bases"; 15 June 1956, memo Slemon to Foulkes, "USAF SAC Requirement for Tanker Bases in Canada."

15. DGHIST, Raymont Collection, file 1085, 11 June 1956, memo to CPlansI, "Briefing on SAC Tanker Base Requirements in Canada."

16. Ibid.

17. Ibid.

18. DGHIST, Raymont Collection, file 1331, 13 June 1956, Cabinet Defence Committee, 110th meeting.

19. DGHIST, Raymont Collection, file 1085, 18 June 1956, memcon Foulkes and Twining, "USAF Operating Requirements: Tanker Bases in Canada."

20. Ibid.

21. DGHIST, Raymont Collection, file 1085, 22 November 1956, memo R. M. Macdonnell to Air Commodore Lister, "USAF Requirement for SAC Tanker Bases in Canada."

22. Polmar, *Strategic Air Command*, 44–45.

23. DGHIST, Raymont Collection, file 1308, 29 November 1956, COSC 602nd meeting; U.S. DOS, *FRUS 1958–1960 Volume VII Part 1: Western European Integration and Security; Canada* (Washington, DC: GPO, 1993), 734; "NSC 5822/1: Certain Aspects of U.S. Relations with Canada," 30 December 1958.

24. DGHIST, Raymont Collection, file 1331, 6–7 February 1957, Cabinet Defence Committee, 113th meeting; file 1085, 28 January 1957, memo to CDC, "U.S. Air Force Request for Tanker Base Facilities in Canada"; file 1308, 11 January 1957, COSC 603nd meeting.

25. USNARA, RG 59 box 3219, memo, "SAC Overflight of Canada," 1 October 1956.

26. USNARA, RG 59 box 3219, memo to file, "Canada-Overflight," 19 November 1956; memo to file, "Canadian XYZ Procedures—Operations ROADBLOCK and PINEGROVE," November 8, 1956; memo to file, "Operation ROADBLOCK and Operation PINEGROVE," 20 November 1956.

27. See Milberry, *Canadair Sabre*, 368 and Milberry, *Avro CF-100* (Toronto: CANAV Books, 1986), 189.

28. FOIA, NORAD History Office, "Air Defence Aircraft Chart: Dec 1950 to Dec 1959."

29. DGHIST, file 423.009 (D14), 16 June 1955, memo to CStaffO, "Canada-USA Emergency Air Defence Plan CANUSEADP 2–55"; DGHIST, file 73/770, 1 April 1957, Lydus H. Buss, "U.S. Air Defence in the Northeast 1940–1957: CONAD Historical Reference Paper No. 1."

30. Bill Green, *The First Line: Air Defence in the Northeast 1952 to 1960* (Fairview, PA: Wonderhorse Publications, 1994), 207–208, 293.

31. NAC, RG 24 vol. 17828 file 840-1050012, AOC Conference, January 1955, "The RCAF Position in Relation to Continental Air Defence."

32. Ibid.

33. Ibid.

34. Ibid.

35. DGHIST, Raymont Collection, file 1308, 11 February 1955, COSC 574th meeting.

36. DGHIST, Raymont Collection, file 1329, 3 March 1955, Cabinet Defence Committee, 104th meeting.

37. Ibid.

38. Ibid.

39. Ibid.

40. NAC, RG 24 vol. 20711 file 2-3-2 pt. 5, 4 November 1955, memo to the Cabinet Defence Committee, "Reappraisal of the CF-105 Development Programme."

41. DGHIST, Raymont Collection, file 1329, 3 March 1955, Cabinet Defence Committee, 104th meeting.

42. DGHIST, Raymont Collection, file 1329, 27 September 1955, Cabinet Defence Committee, 106th meeting.

43. Ibid.

44. Ibid.

45. It is a voluminous study. See NAC, RG 24 vol. 2071 file 2-3-2 pt. 5, 4 November 1955, "Report by the Working Group to the Ad Hoc Interdepartmental Committee for the Reappraisal of the CF-105 Development Programme."

46. DGHIST, Raymont Collection, file 1308, 1 November 1955, COSC 584th meeting. It should be noted here that the typed minutes of the COSC meeting state 50 thermonuclear bombs and 1000/950 bombers, but someone inexplicably penciled in 100 for "successfully delivered thermonuclear bombs," 600 attacking bombers, and 500 to be destroyed enroute.

47. Ibid.

48. Ibid.

49. Ibid.

50. NAC, RG 24 vol. 2071 file 2-3-2 pt. 5, 4 November 1955, "Report by the Working Group to the Ad Hoc Interdepartmental Committee for the Reappraisal of the CF-105 Development Programme."

51. DGHIST, Raymont Collection, file 1308, 1 November 1955, COSC 584th meeting.

52. NAC, RG 24 vol. 2071 file 2-3-2 pt. 5, 4 November 1955, "Report by the Working Group to the Ad Hoc Interdepartmental Committee for the Reappraisal of the CF-105 Development Programme."

53. Ibid.

54. Note that the TU-4 BULL, of which there were estimated to be twelve hundred examples was not included since it was a one-way aircraft and was superseded by the other types. The BADGER really was a one-way aircraft as well, though the Soviets were working on air-to-air refueling techniques with it. See NAC, RG 24 vol. 2071 file 2-3-2 pt. 5, 4 November 1955, "Report by the Working Group to the Ad Hoc Interdepartmental Committee for the Reappraisal of the CF-105 Development Programme."

55. NAC, RG 24 vol. 2071 file 2-3-2 pt. 5, 4 November 1955, "Report by the Working Group to the Ad Hoc Interdepartmental Committee for the Reappraisal of the CF-105 Development Programme."

56. DGHIST, Raymont Collection, file 1329, 17 November 1955, Cabinet Defence Committee, 108th meeting.

57. U of T Archives, O. M. Solandt Papers, B93-0041/033, 7 March 1956, "Intercontinental Precedes Effective Defence," *Ottawa Citizen*.

58. DGHIST, Max Hendrick Papers, Daily Dairy, 24 May 1956.

59. U of T Archives, O. M. Solandt Papers, B93-0041/033, 7 March 1956, "Intercontinental Precedes Effective Defence," *Ottawa Citizen*.

60. Ibid.

61. For information on VELVET GLOVE, see D. J. Goodspeed, *DRB: A History of the Defence Research Board of Canada* (Ottawa: Queen's Printer, 1958), 129–133; DGHIST, file 79/429 vol. 5, VCAS, "Divisional Items of Interest Week Ending 22nd Jan 53"; VCAS, "Divisional Items of Interest Week Ending 12th Feb 53"; DGHIST, file 79/429 vol. 7, VCAS, "Divisional Items of Interest Week Ending 16 Jun 55."

62. NAC, RG 24 acc 83-84/49 vol. 4175 file 1930-106-1 pt. 1, 14 September 1955, memo Abrams to Slemon, "Atomic Warheads."

63. ATI, 23 December 1955, memo Cameron to Slemon, "Request for Atomic Information."

64. NAC, RG 24 vol. 2071 file 2-3-2 pt. 5, 4 November 1955, "Report by the Working Group to the Ad Hoc Interdepartmental Committee for the Reappraisal of the CF-105 Development Programme."

65. Hansen, *U.S. Nuclear Weapons*, 106, 178; DGHIST, Hendrick Papers, diary, 30 November 1956.

66. DGHIST, Raymont Collection, file 1308, 3 October 1956, COSC special meeting.

67. USNARA, RG 59 box 3219, memo to files, "Proposal to Canada Concerning the Use of Nuclear Air-to-Air Weapons," 19 November 1956; memo to files, "Proposed Use of Air-to-Air Nuclear Missiles Over Canada," 23 November 1956; keep in mind that Operation PLUMBBOB was several months away, and the RCAF had not yet been invited to watch Shot JOHN.

68. See Bert Kinzey, *F-89 Scorpion* (Waukesha, WI: Detail and Scale, 1992), 12–13. See also Green, *First Line*, 329, 342, 362. The American State Department was not informed (it had no real need to know); it believed that the first MB-1 deployments occurred in January 1957. Consequently, State Department documents reflect this idea. See USNARA, RG 59, memo to Dulles from Elbrick, "Proposed Agreement Permitting Use of Air-to-Air Nuclear Missiles Over Canada," 17 January 1957.

69. DGHIST, Raymont Collection, file 1308, 21 November 1956, COSC special meeting.

70. Ibid.

71. DGHIST, Raymont Collection, file 1331, 19 December 1956, Cabinet Defence Committee, 112th meeting.

72. Ibid.

73. Ibid.

74. USNARA, RG 59, message State to Amembassy Ottawa, 15 February 1957; State to U.S. Information Agency, 18 February 1957; Embassy, Ottawa to State, "Canadian

Statement Regarding United States Announcement on Deployment of Air Defence Nuclear Weapons," 26 February 1957; message Ottawa to State, 21 February 1957.

75. DGHIST, Raymont Collection, file 1309A, 9 and 11 January 1957, COSC minutes of the 603rd meeting.

76. See Bacevich, *The Pentomic Era*.

77. DGHIST, file 423.009 (D14), 29 April 1955, AHQ, "Combined Air Defence Study."

78. DGHIST, file 423.009 (D14), 10 August 1955, "Anti-Aircraft Defence of Canada: Visit of VCGS to Air Defence Command, RCAF, 2 August 1955"; 26 July 1955, AHQ, "AA Conference at ADC."

79. DGHIST, Raymont Collection, file 1308, 21 February 1956, COSC minutes of the 589th meeting.

80. DGHIST, Raymont Collection, file 1308, 13 January 1956, COSC minutes of the 587th meeting.

81. FOIA USAF, Ray, "BOMARC and Nuclear Armamant."

82. Hansen, *U.S. Nuclear Weapons*, 186–187; Norman Friedman, *The Postwar Naval Revolution* (Annapolis, MD: Naval Institute Press, 1989), 52, 58.

83. NAC, RG 24 vol. 2071 file 2-3-2 pt. 5, 4 November 1955, "Report by the Working Group to the Ad Hoc Interdepartmental Committee for the Reappraisal of the CF-105 Development Programme."

84. DGHIST, file 423.009 (D14), 22 October 1955, AHQ, "CONAD Planning."

85. There had been some discussion about Canadian-British collaboration in 1946 after the McMahon Act was passed.

86. NAC, RG 24 acc 83-84/49 vol. 4175 file 1930-106-1 pt. 1, 11 September 1956, DWD/DARTY, "Canadian Army Requirements for Nuclear Weapons." See also Flags A through D, 25 January 1955, JSWPC, "Atomic Energy Programme in Canada"; 5 November 1954, JSWPC "Possible Canadian Requirements for Nuclear Warheads"; n.d., "Proposed Canadian Army Equipment Requirements Nuclear Weapons Systems"; n.d., "Development of Nuclear Weapons."

87. Ibid.

88. Frank Barnaby, *How to Build an Atomic Bomb and Other Weapons of Mass Destruction* (New York: Nation Books, 2004), 18.

89. NAC, RG 24 acc 83-84/49 vol. 4175 file 1930-106-1 pt. 1, 11 September 1956, DWD/DARTY, "Canadian Army Requirements for Nuclear Weapons" and Flags A–D.

90. Ibid.

91. NAC, RG 25 vol. 4499 file 50030-K-40 pt. 3, 25 November 1955, POEADQ, 39th meeting; RG 25 vol. 4495 file 50030-E-1-40 pt. 1, 17 July 1956, memo Foulkes to Pearson, "Note on Reappraisal of the Military Requirements of NATO."

92. NAC, RG 25 vol. 4495 file 50030-E-1-40 pt. 1, 17 July 1956, memo Foulkes to Pearson, "Note on Reappraisal of the Military Requirements of NATO."

93. NAC, RG 2 vol. 1852 file Jan–Mar 1957, 14 February 1957, Cabinet Conclusions.

94. See Wampler, "Ambiguous Legacy," chap. 11.

95. NAC, RG 25 vol. 4495 file 50030-E-1-40 pt. 1, 17 July 1956, memo Foulkes to Pearson, "Note on Reappraisal of the Military Requirements of NATO."

96. Miller was an Air Vice Marshal who was asked to replace Bud Drury as Deputy Minister of National Defence. Since this was a political position, he had to retire and don a civilian suit. Later, he was called to be the first Chief of the Defence Staff and he put his uniform back on to become Air Chief Marshal Miller in 1964.

97. NAC, RG 25 vol. 4499 file 50030-K-40 pt. 3, 25 November 1955, POEADQ, 39th meeting.

98. NSA, 27 August 1956, memo Edwin Martin to Robert Bowie.

99. DDRS, 1977 frame 355C, memcon Radford, Taylor, Goodpaster, and Eisenhower, 24 May 1956.

100. NSA, memo MacArthur to Dulles, "Review of NATO Military Strategy," 27 July 1956.

101. USN OA, Radford Papers, box 3 log: 30 March–30 September 1956, memorandum for the record, 20 September 1956.

102. PRO DEFE, 6 file 37, 28 September 1956, Joint Planning Staff, "Overall Strategic Concept for the Defence of the North Atlantic Area."

103. NAC, RG 25 vol. 4495 file 50030-E-1-40, 9 October 1956, memo Ignatieff to Canadian NATO Delegation, "Overall Strategic Concept for the Defence of the NATO Area."

104. NAC, RG 25 vol. 4495 file 50030-E-1-40, 9 October 1956, "Comments on IPT 131/20 of 15 Sep 56: Overall Strategic Concept for the Defence of the North Atlantic Treaty Organization Area."

105. An ad hoc group drawn from the NATO permanent representatives liaising with the military committee and the standing group.

106. NAC, RG 25 vol. 4495 file 50030-E-1-40, 9 October 1956, "Comments on IPT 131/20 of 15 Sep 56: Overall Strategic Concept for the Defence of the North Atlantic Treaty Organization Area."

107. NAC, RG 25 vol. 4495 file 50030-E-1-40, 5 October 1956, memo Leger to Foulkes.

108. DGHIST, Raymont Collection, file 1308A, COSC, 25 October 1956, 599th meeting.

109. DGHIST, memo donated to DGHIST by Robert B. Bryce, "Statement by the Canadian Representative to the NATO Military Committee, 18 October 1956."

110. Maloney, *War Without Battles: Canada's NATO Brigade in Germany, 1951–1993* (Toronto: McGraw-Hill Ryerson, 1997), 126–129; NAC, RG 25 vol. 4495 file 50030-E-1-40, 9 October 1956, "Comments on IPT 131/20 of 15 Sep 56: Overall Strategic Concept for the Defence of the North Atlantic Treaty Organization Area."

111. NAC, RG 25 vol. 4495 file 50030-E-1-40, 24 October 1956, message NATO Paris to External, "Military Committee Meeting Oct 1956"; 30 October 1956, COSC to members, "Overall Concept for the Defence of the North Atlantic Treaty Organization."

112. This was not the first time the British had attempted such a maneuver. These problems were factors influencing the SACLANT decision in 1952 and the makeup of the NATO naval command structure. See Maloney, *Securing Command of the Sea*, for a full appraisal of the situation prior to 1956.

113. Maloney, *War Without Battles*, 106–108; Maloney, "First Time Unto the Breach . . . "

114. NAC, RG 25 vol. 4499 file 50030-K-40 pt. 4, 22 November 1956, message Paris to External, "NATO Military Reappraisal."

115. NAC, RG 49 vol. 708 file 247-5, vol. 4 pt. 2, 28 November 1956, POEADQ, 45th meeting.

116. NAC, RG 2 vol. 5775 file 5 November–19 December 1956, 19 December 1956, Cabinet Conclusions.

117. DGHIST, Raymont Collection, uncataloged, NATO Military Committee, 23 May 1957, "Final Decision on MC 14/2 (Revised): A Report by the Military Committee on Overall Strategic Concept for the Defence of the North Atlantic Treaty Organization Area."

118. Ibid.

119. Ibid.

120. Ibid.

121. Ibid.

122. Ibid.

123. Ibid.

124. The COSC, particularly Slemon, had contributed to the formulation of MC 14/2's North America section. See RG 25 vol. 4495 file 50030-E-1-40 pt. 1, 9 October 1956,

Foulkes to COSC, "Overall Strategic Concept for the Defence of the North Atlantic Treaty Organization Area."

125. DGHIST, Raymont Collection, uncataloged, NATO Military Committee, 23 May 1957, "Final Decision on MC 14/2 (Revised): A Report by the Military Committee on Overall Strategic Concept for the Defence of the North Atlantic Treaty Organization Area."

126. Ibid.

127. NAC, RG 25 vol. 4495 file 50030-E-1-40 pt. 1, date redacted by ATI staff, message NATO Paris to External, "Overall Strategic Military Concept and Measures to Implement This Concept"; 25 March 1957, JPC, "Measures to Implement the Strategic Concept (MC 48/2)."

128. DGHIST, 112.3M2.009 (D226), 21 June 1963, DMO&P, "Queries and Suggestions by Members of Parliament: Appointment of Special Committee on National Defence"; DGHIST, Raymont Collection, file 1310E, COSC, 10 June 1958, 623rd meeting.

129. NAC, RG 25 vol. 4495 file 50030-E-1-40 pt. 1, 9 May 1957, message NATO Paris to External, "Overall Strategic Military Concept MC 14/2 and MC 48/2."

130. NAC, RG 25 vol. 4495 file 50030-E-1-40 pt. 1, 1 June 1957, message NATO Paris to External, "Council Meeting May 31."

Chapter 4

1. There are two superb books on Canada's nuclear energy and research efforts: Robert Bothwell's *Eldorado: Canada's National Uranium Company* (Toronto: University of Toronto Press, 1984) and *Nucleus: The History of Atomic Energy of Canada, Limited* (Toronto: University of Toronto Press, 1988). This information is drawn from both works.

2. Ibid.

3. Goodspeed, *DRB*, 45–68. There is a short, privately published biography on Dr. Solandt. However, Dr. George Lindsey informed me that he had edited it to remove any discussion of Solandt's involvement in nuclear research. This was done because Dr. Lindsey "did not want the media to portray Dr. Solandt as a 'nuclear monster' after his death." (Author's brief conversation with Dr. Lindsey, September 1995, Toronto).

4. U of T Archives, Solandt Papers, file B91-0015/011, 26 September 1985, "The Atomic Bomb." Solandt's own observations make for interesting reading and should be published as a stand-alone piece in the future.

5. U of T Archives, Solandt Papers, file B91-0015/011, n.d., "Directive to Solandt from A/ VM T. M. Wilbon."

6. U of T Archives, Solandt Papers, file B91-0015/011, n.d., "Joint Terms of Reference of the Air Staff (Weapon Requirements) and MAP (Research and Development) Representatives on the Atomic Bomb Survey Mission."

7. U of T Archives, Solandt Papers, file B91-0015/011, 10 November 1945, G-2 USSBS, "Intelligence Memorandum: Japanese Survey of Atomic Bombing of Hiroshima and Nagasaki"; November 1945, Solandt study, "Casualties Due to the Atomic Bomb at Hiroshima and Nagasaki"; March 1951, Health and Welfare Canada, "The Effects of an Atomic Bomb Explosion on Structures and Personnel"; See also DGHIST, Edmond Cloutier, *Medical Aspects of Atomic Warfare* (Ottawa: King's Printers, 1948).

8. NAC, RG 24 vol. 4197 file 266-04-3311 pt. 1, 29 March 1950, Director of Scientific Intelligence, "Vulnerability Study: Visit to Washington."

9. Ibid.

10. See John May, *The Greenpeace Book of the Nuclear Age: The Hidden History, the Human Cost* (New York: Pantheon Books, 1989), 63–73. See also Jonathan M. Weisgall, *Operation CROSSROADS: The Atomic Tests at Bikini Atoll* (Annapolis, MD: Naval Institute Press, 1994), 138–140.

11. U of T Archives, Solandt Papers, file B91-0015/011, 21 February 1987, Omond Solandt unpublished paper, "Canadian Involvement with Nuclear Weapons, 1946 to 1956."

12. J. H. W. Knox, "An RCN Engineer's Outline of RCN History: Part II," in James A. Boutillier, ed., *The RCN in Retrospect, 1910–1968* (Vancouver: University of British Columbia Press, 1982), 217–333; Letter from Keith P. Farrell to Sean Maloney, 7 December 1995.

13. German, *The Sea Is at Our Gates*, 205.

14. Unpublished article submitted by Capt. (Navy) K. P. Farrell for the Naval Technical History Project, "The St. Laurent Class: The First Canadian Designed Destroyers: An Exercise in Damage Control," April 1993; Letter from Keith P. Farrell to Sean Maloney, December 7, 1995.

15. Letter from Keith P. Farrell to Sean Maloney, 7 December 1995. See also Michael A. Henessy, "The Rise and Fall of a Canadian Maritime Policy, 1939–1965: A Study of Industry, Navalism, and the State," (PhD diss., University of New Brunswick, 1995), 230–250 for a discussion of *St. Laurent* construction politics.

16. DGHIST, file 410 B25.019 (D 021), 19 November 1953, DCGS to HQ 25 CIBG, "Atomic, Biological, and Chemical Defence: Equipment and Training."

17. DGHIST, file 410 B25.019 (D 021), 5 December 1953, HQ 25 CIBG to distribution list, "Atomic Weapons."

18. Ibid.

19. Ibid.

20. There is no mention of nuclear weapons plans or training in the official history of the Canadian Army in Korea, Wood's *Strange Battleground*. For a full examination of American nuclear weapons during Korea, see Rosemary Foot's *The Wrong War: American Policy and the Dimensions of the Korean Conflict, 1950–1953* (Ithaca, New York: Cornell University Press, 1985).

21. See RG 24 vol. 21171 file 1439-2 vol. 1 for the minutes and supporting data for the first sixteen meetings of the JSWC. For the best work so far on Canada's biological weapons program, see John Bryden, *Deadly Allies: Canada's Secret War 1937–1947* (Toronto: McClelland and Stewart Publishers, 1989).

22. See RG 24 vol. 21171 file 1439-2 vol. 1 and vol. 2 for the minutes and supporting data of the JSWC.

23. DGHIST, Raymont Study, 151–152.

24. RG 24 vol. 21171 file 1439-2 vol. 2, 14 September 1953, "Brief on No. 1 Radiation Detection Unit, RCE."

25. RG 24 vol. 21171 file 1439-2 vol. 2, 30 December 1952, "Announcement to JSWC regarding 1 RDU assistance to AECL Atomic Energy Project, Chalk River"; May, *Greenpeace Book of the Nuclear Age*, 100–104. May reproduces verbatim the Bertini report on the accident.

26. DDRS, 1979 frame 37A, JSPC to JCS, "Foreign Observers at Operation TEAPOT," 21 January 1955.

27. U of T Archives, Solandt Papers, file B91-0015/011, 21 February 1987, Omond Solandt unpublished paper, "Canadian Involvement with Nuclear Weapons, 1946 to 1956"; DGHIST, file 94/121, n.d., C. P. McNamara (DRB Canada) and W. G. Penney (Ministry of Supply UK), "The Technical Feasibility of Establishing an Atomic Weapons Proving Ground in the Churchill Area." Another six sites were surveyed, but there is no note of where they were. The DRB special weapons testing range at Suffield, Alberta, was probably one of them.

28. Robert S. Norris, Andrew S. Burroughs, and Richard W. Fieldhouse, *British, French, and Chinese Nuclear Weapons* (Boulder, Colorado: Westview Press, 1994), 20.

29. DGHIST, file 193.009 (D53), 29 September 1953, memo Solandt to Foulkes; Canadian

Op ANTLER documents acquired under ATI, 29 April 1959, JSWPC to Joint Staff, "Reports"; 21 September 1959, JSWPC to DRB, "AWRE Reports." Canada eventually received reports based on the air and ground shock instrumentation.

30. U of T Archives, Solandt Papers, file B91-0015/011, 21 February 1987, Omond Solandt unpublished paper, "Canadian Involvement with Nuclear Weapons, 1946 to 1956"; See also Denys Blakeway and Sue Lloyd-Roberts, *Fields of Thunder: Testing Britain's Bomb* (London: George, Allen and Unwin, 1985) and Lorna Arnold, *A Very Special Relationship: British Atomic Weapon Trials in Australia* (London: Her Majesty's Stationary Office, 1987). Totem 1 and 2 yielded 10 and 8 kt, respectively, and were tower-mounted tests. See also Canadian Op ANTLER documents acquired under ATI, 29 April 1959, JSWPC to Joint Staff, "Reports"; 21 September 1959, JSWPC to DRB, "AWRE Reports"; Norris, Burroughs, and Fieldhouse, *British, French, and Chinese*, 27. The British allowed two USAF B-29s to sample the clouds produced during TOTEM. In return, the RAF was allowed to deploy sampling aircraft to the American CASTLE test series.

31. DGHIST, file 193.009 (D53), 29 September 1953, memo Solandt to Foulkes, draft letter to British Chiefs of Staff.

32. DGHIST, Raymont Collection, file 1308, minutes of the 567th meeting of the Chiefs of Staff Committee, 30 July 1954.

33. Princeton University, J. V. Forrestal Papers, box 83, Correspondence 1949 "C," letter Forrestal to Claxton, 11 February 1949; Letter Forrestal to Claxton, 17 February 1949.

34. Princeton University, Allen Dulles Papers, box 95, file "Heeney, ADP," letter Heeney to Dulles, 5 October 1961; Letter Dulles to Heeney, 15 October 1961.

35. USNARA, RG 59 E 3077 250/62/30/3 box 1, file: Ottawa 1962 1/a, memo Delmar Carson to Rufus Z. Smith, 11 May 1962.

36. USN OA, Adm. George W. Anderson Jr., Oral History, 1:174–177, 219.

37. DDEL, Lauris Norstad Papers, file "F," letter Gruenther to Foulkes, 18 May 1954.

38. DDEL, Norstad Papers, file "F," letter Norstad to Foulkes, 28 March 1958.

39. DGHIST, Raymont Collection, file 497, 26 June 1958, memo Foulkes to Pearkes, "Visit of the President of the United States and Mrs. Eisenhower."

40. NAC, MG 30 E809 vol. 1, file "General Correspondance 1954–1964," 24 December 1957, letter De Wolfe to Burke; 15 January 1958, letter Burke to De Wolfe.

41 LGen A. Chester Hull, interview with the author, 29 December 1995, Trenton, Ontario.

42. NAC, RG 24 file 1439. 2 vol. 1, 18 August 1952, minutes of the 16th meeting of the Joint Special Weapons Committee.

43. U of T Archives, Solandt Papers, file B91-0015/011, 21 February 1987, Omond Solandt unpublished paper, "Canadian Involvement with Nuclear Weapons, 1946 to 1956."

44. Ibid.

45. This organization was the predecessor to the Joint Strategic Target Planning Staff established in the 1960s. See MGFA, NATO Documents Collection, 31 January 1952, JCS, "Information for General Eisenhower on Availability of Atomic Weapons"; UPS microfilm, *The JCS: Strategic Issues I*, reel 4, 0064-0065, memo by CNO to JCS, "Revision of Information for General Ridgway on Availability of Atomic Weapons," 16 May 1953; See also Maloney, *Securing Command of the Sea*, 163–165.

46. UPS microfilm, *The JCS: Strategic Issues 1*, reel IV, frame 0015-0024, JCS, "Exercise PROPHECY," 13 January 1953; frame 0029-0037, JCS, "Atomic Warfare Indoctrination Course for Allied High Commanders and Key Staff Officers," 13 March 1953; frame 0038-0047 JCS JSPC, "Information for NATO Commands Concerning Atomic Weapons," 23 March 1953. McMahon himself noted in later years that his legislation was not a good idea and constrained NATO far too much.

47. DDRS, 1976 frame 76 247C, message USLO SACLANT to JCS, 27 February 1954.

48. Ibid.

49. UPS microfilm, *The JCS: Strategic Issues 1*, reel IV, frame 0077-0085, JSPC to JCS, "Nuclear Weapons Utilization Planning in NATO," 30 March 1954.

50. NAC, RG 25 vol. 5958 file 50219-AL-40, 8 December 1954, memo to Pearson, "Agreement for the Cooperation Between the United States and NATO Regarding Atomic Information"; memo Foulkes to Under Secretary of State for External Affairs, "Proposed NATO Agreement for Exchange of Atomic Information"; 14 December 1954, message Wilgress to Pearson, "Proposed Agreement for Exchange of Atomic Information"; NAC, RG 2 vol. 2657 file 4 January–1 March 1955, Cabinet Conclusions.

51. NSA, n.d., "Agreement Between the Parties to the North Atlantic Treaty for Co-operation Regarding Atomic Information."

52. NAC, RG 25 vol. 5958 file 50219-AL-40, December 9, 1954, memo from Wilgress to Pearson, "Agreement for Co-operation Regarding Atomic Information."

53. USN OA, "Semi-Annual Report of the Secretary of the Navy, 1 Jan–10 Jun 57"; Captain David Holt, Canadian Army, interview with the author, Lahr, Germany, 12 February 1993. Note that Ridgway had organized the Special Weapons Branch at the U.S. Army School in Oberammergau as early as January 1953 to train staff officers in atomic operations, but courses were constrained by the lack of information. It came under the operational control of SACEUR in 1966. See The NATO School (SHAPE), "The NATO Military Guide, January 1990."

54. For the text of the U.K.-U.S. agreement, see John Baylis, *Anglo-American Defence Relations 1939–1984*, 2nd ed. (New York: St. Martin's Press, 1984), 85–87. See also PRO DEFE, 7 file 1517, 9 June 1958, Foreign Office to the Atomic Energy Authority, draft history "The UK-U.S.-Canadian Collaboration in the Field of Atomic Energy 1940–1957."

55. U.S. NARA, RG 59 file 877415-2503-3, FOIA request, memo Palmer to Merchant, "Initialing of Agreements with Canada and the United Kingdom for the Exchange of Atomic Information for Mutual Defence Purposes," 7 June 1955.

56. U.S. NARA, RG 59 file 877415-2503-3, FOIA request, memo Smith to Yingling, "Agreement for Cooperation with Canada Under Atomic Energy Act of 1954," 1 March 1955.

57. For an extended discussion, see Timothy J. Botti, *The Long Wait: The Forging of the Anglo-American Nuclear Alliance, 1945–1958* (New York: Greenwood Press, 1987), particularly chap. 18.

58. FOIA, Statement by Deputy Assistant Secretary of State Elbrick before the Subcommittee on Agreements for Cooperation of the Joint Committee on Atomic Energy, 11 July 1955.

59. Ibid.

60. FOIA, "Agreement Between the Government of The United States of America and the Government of Canada for Cooperation Regarding Atomic Information For Mutual Defence Purposes," n.d.

61. FOIA, memo SECDEF to the President, 10 June 1955; DGHIST, Raymont Collection, file 1329, Cabinet Defence Committee, 105th meeting, 7 June 1955. Note that the United States did test an Arctic nuclear reactor in Greenland in 1960. The PM-3A reactor was constructed in tunnels under the icecap at Camp Century, an Arctic research base. See George J. Dufek, "Nuclear Power for the Polar Regions," *National Geographic*, May 1962, 712–730.

62. FOIA, Heeney to Dulles, "Exchange of Notes," 5 August 1955.

63. Canadian Op ANTLER documents acquired under ATI, 29 April 1959, JSWPC to Joint Staff, "Reports"; 21 September 1959, JSWPC to DRB, "AWRE Reports"; Department of Energy, January 1982, "Announced United States Nuclear Tests, July 1945 through December 1981."

64. NAC, RG 24 acc 83-84/25 vol. 225 file 2001-91-012 vol. 1, 31 January 1955, Joint Staff to distribution list, "Exercise DESERT ROCK VI."

65. NAC, RG 24 acc 83-84/25 vol. 225 file 2001-91-012 vol. 1, 29 October 1954, JSWPC to COSC, "Attendance of Canadian Observers at Exercise DESERT ROCK."

66. NAC, RG 24 acc 83-84/25 vol. 225 file 2001-91-012 vol. 1, 9 May 1955, CJSMW to Foulkes, "Canadian Participation—Operation TEAPOT." In terms of r's of gamma radiation, Dyer took 2240; Rayner, 2120; Rockingham, 2270; Walsh, 2320; Carpenter, 2300.

67. NAC, RG 24 acc 83-84/25 vol. 225 file 2001-91-012 vol. 1, n.d., HQ U.S. Army G-3, "Canadian Participation in Operation TEAPOT."

68. NAC, RG 24 acc 83-84/25 vol. 225 file 2001-91-012 vol. 1, n.d., Brigadier G. Walsh, "Observations on Atomic Bomb Tests (7–16 Apr 55)"; Defence Nuclear Agency, 23 November 1981, "Fact Sheet: TEAPOT Series."

69. NAC, RG 24 acc 83-84/25 vol. 225 file 2001-91-012 vol. 1, n.d., Brigadier G. Walsh, "Observations on Atomic Bomb Tests (7–16 Apr 55)."

70. Defence Nuclear Agency, 23 November 1981, "Fact Sheet: TEAPOT Series"; LCol R. A. Klaehn, "The Story of Exercise SAPLING," and H. E. Cameron, "Some Highlights of Exercise SAPLING," *Canadian Army Journal* (July 1955): 2–17.

71. NAC, RG 24 acc 83-84/25 vol. 1888.1 vol. 4, 22 March 1955, memo Longair to Maclure, "Operation BUFFALO"; 4 March 1955, JSWPC, "Participation in UK Trials: BUFFALO"; 18 April 1955, Foulkes to CJSM London, "Canadian Participation in UK Atomic Trials."

72. Arnold gives an incorrect yield of 60 kt as does Blakeway. Note that May in *The Greenpeace Book of the Nuclear Age* gives a 98 kt yield to G-2 rather than 60, but he does not substantiate this figure. Norris, Burroughs, and Fieldhouse, *British, French, and Chinese Nuclear Weapons* (33) does substantiate this. The yield of G-2 was deliberately under-reported by the British because its yield was far in excess of what had been planned and caused greater fallout across Australia.

73. Denys Blakeway and Sue Lloyd-Roberts, *Fields of Thunder: Testing Britain's Bomb* (London: George, Allen and Unwin, 1985), 95–106; and Lorna Arnold, *A Very Special Relationship: British Atomic Weapon Trials in Australia* (London: HMSO, 1987), 132–139. See also Canadian Op ANTLER documents acquired under ATI, 29 April 1959, JSWPC to Joint Staff, "Reports"; 21 September 1959, JSWPC to DRB, "AWRE Reports."

74. Hansen, *U.S. Nuclear Weapons*, 71–74; Defence Nuclear Agency, 29 January 1983, "Fact Sheet: Operation RED WING"; U.S. Department of Energy, January 1982, "Announced United States Nuclear Tests, July 1945 through December 1981."

75. Norris, Burroughs, and Fieldhouse, *British, French, and Chinese*, 28.

76. NAC, RG 24 acc 83-84/25 vol. 1888.1 vol. 4, 20 April 1955, Longair to DRB, "Reports from AWRE." A sampling of report titles includes: "Safety Levels for Contamination from Fall-Out from Atomic Weapons"; "On a Method of Estimating Atmospheric Diffusion"; "The Rise of a Cloud Produced by a Nuclear Explosion"; A Reanalysis of Fall-Out Data from TOTEM"; "Formula for the Dependence of Medium Range Fallout on the Yield and Height of Burst of an Atomic Weapon." See NAC, RG 24 acc 83-84/25 vol. 1888.1 vol. 1, 18 April 1956, AVM Smith to JSWPC, "Operation BUFFALO: Transmittal of Documents to Mr. Hugh Cameron."

77. NAC, RG 24 acc 83-84/25 vol. 1888.1 vol. 4, 19 July 1955, Foulkes to CJSM London, "Canadian Participation in UK Atomic Trials."

78. NAC, RG 24 acc 83-84/25 vol. 1888.1 vol. 6, 15 October 1955, message CJSL to Foulkes.

79. NAC, RG 24 acc 83-84/25 vol. 1888.1 vol. 4, 19 August 1955, DRB to JSWPC, "Operation BUFFALO: RCAF Equipment for Test."

80. NAC, RG 24 acc 83-84/25 vol. 1888.1 vol. 6, 22 November 1955, handwritten note from JSWPC to Joint Staff.

81. NAC, RG 24 acc 83-84/25 vol. 1888.1 vol. 6, 3 November 1955, AVM D. M. Smith to JSWPC, "Operation BUFFALO: Weapon Yields"; 8 November 1955, Longair to DRB Chemical Lab Shirley Bay, "Operation BUFFALO."

82. NAC, RG 24 acc 83-84/25 vol. 1888.1 vol. 6, n.d., "BUFFALO Administrative Notice No. 21: Operation BUFFALO Security Classifications."

83. Blakeway and Lloyd-Roberts assume Canadians were part of the Commonwealth Indoctrination Force, but Arnold mentions only Australian and British personnel. Canadian records do not show that Canadian officers participated in the CIF during BUFFALO.

84. NAC, RG 24 acc 83-84/25 vol. 1888.1 vol. 3, February 1956, "Operations Order No. 1 for Operation BUFFALO"; 18 November 1955, "Operation BUFFALO: Preliminary Statement of RDU Tasks When Integrated in UK Teams."

85. NAC, RG 24 acc 83-84/25 vol. 1888.1 vol. 3, 18 February 1957, JSWPC to COSC, "Operational BUFFALO Canadian Participation—Final Report"; Arnold, *Very Special Relationship*, 140–170; Blakeway and Lloyd-Roberts, *Fields of Thunder*, 132.

86. NAC, RG 24 acc 83-84/25 vol. 1888.1 vol. 3, 16 April 1957, "Operation BUFFALO Final Report—1 RDU."

87. Ibid.

88. Ibid.

89. NAC, RG 24 acc 83-84/25 vol. 1888.1 vol. 3, 18 February 1957, JSWPC to COSC, "Operational BUFFALO Canadian Participation—Final Report."

90. See Joseph Levitt's *Pearson and Canada's Role in Nuclear Disarmament and Arms Control Negotiations* (Kingston: McGill-Queen's University Press, 1995) for a full view of this topic from 1945 to 1957.

91. NAC, RG 24 acc 83-84/167 vol. 4175 file 1930-106-1 pt. 1, 31 August 1956, memo DRB to DEA, "Control of Tests of Atomic Weapons."

92. NAC, RG 24 acc 83-84/167 vol. 4175 file 1930-106-1 pt. 1, 5 October 1956, memo Foulkes to Under Secretary of State for External Affairs, "Disarmament—Limitations of Atomic Tests."

93. NAC, RG 24 acc 83-84/125 vol. 225 file 2001.91/016, 20 March 1957, Director of Weapons and Development to Director of Military Training, "Participation in U.S. Atomic Tests—1957"; 14 March 1957, CJSMW to COSC, "Canadian Request for Atomic Information—Participation in U.S. Atomic Tests—1957"; 22 March 1957, JSWPC to Foulkes, "Canadian Request for Atomic Information: Canadian Participation in Operation PLUMBBOB."

94. NAC, RG 24 acc 83-84/125 vol. 225 file 2001.91/016, n.d., RAdm Horacio Rivero USN to CJSMW, "Canadian Participation in Operation PLUMBBOB."

95. Canadian Op PLUMBBOB documents acquired under ATI, 17 May 1957, "List of Officers Nominated as Being Available to Attend a Nuclear Weapons Test."

96. USNARA, RG 59 box 2878, Embassy Ottawa to Department of State, "Canadian Acceptance of Invitation to Attend Nuclear Test Shot," 16 May 1957; message Embassy Ottawa to Department of State, "Canadian Acceptance of Invitation to Attend Nuclear Test Shot," 6 August 1957.

97. Canadian Op PLUMBBOB documents acquired under ATI, October 1957, "A Report on the Activities Connected with the Formation, Operation, and Close-Out of the Canadian Administrative Group during Operation PLUMBBOB 1 May 57–1 Oct 57," prepared by Wing Commander D. T. Bain, RCAF.

98. Thomas H. Saffer and Orr Kelly, *Countdown Zero: GI Victims of U.S. Atomic Testing* (New York: Penguin Books, 1982), 83–84.
99. Canadian Op PLUMBBOB documents acquired under ATI, 8 July 1957, CAG to COSC, "Operation PLUMBBOB—BOBCAT ONE."
100. NAC, RG 24 acc 83-84/49 vol. 4175 file 1930-106-1 pt. 1, 10 July 1961, J. C. Arnell to the CAS, "The Testing of Nuclear Weapons."
101. See Saffer and Kelley, *Countdown Zero*, 60, 82; DDRS, 1979 frame 110B, memo to the President from the AEC, 7 August 1957. The pertinent portion reads: "Another shot recently added to the series is an experimental firing designed to assist in developing [deleted] tactical weapons." The word "clean" fits nicely into the deleted portion.
102. Canadian Op PLUMBBOB documents acquired under ATI, 4 September 1957, A. E. Ritchie, "Report on Attendance at Nevada Nuclear Test Scheduled for September 1, 1957."
103. Ibid.
104. Ibid.
105. Ibid.
106. Howard L. Rosenberg, *Atomic Soldiers: American Victims of Nuclear Experiments* (Boston: Beacon Press, 1980), 90–124; Defence Nuclear Agency, 15 September 1981, "Fact Sheet: PLUMBBOB Series"; Canadian Op PLUMBBOB documents acquired under ATI, October 1957, "A Report on the Activities Connected with the Formation, Operation, and Close-Out of the Canadian Administrative Group during Operation PLUMBBOB 1 May 57–1 Oct 57" prepared by Wing Commander D. T. Bain, RCAF. I attempted to conduct interviews with members of 7 Platoon in the Summer of 1996. The ones with whom I spoke were suspicious and were unwilling to give me a narrative of what they did on the exercise or other pertinent information. Inclusion of 7 Platoon in PLUMBBOB appears to have been opportunistic on the part of the army or Foulkes. There is no evidence that 7 Platoon performed "guinea pig" functions, at least with Canadian knowledge. They do not appear to have been subjected to the same sorts of psychological and physical tests that some American units were subjected to in other test events. In any event, other Canadian army units did not participate in other tests, so any form of Canadian comparative study must be ruled out. It is unclear how extensively 7 Platoon was debriefed after its experience and what was then done with that information. On the other hand, many, many DRB files remain classified.
107. Canadian Op PLUMBBOB documents acquired under ATI, 20 June 1957, "JOHN Shot—Operation PLUMBBOB, Information for RCAF Observers."
108. Rosenberg, *Atomic Soldiers*, 89–90; FOIA, SAI, "Radiation Dose Estimate, Project 53.5, Shot JOHN, Operation PLUMBBOB," 15 April 1983.
109. DGHIST, Raymont Collection, file 1309A, Chiefs of Staff Comittee Special meeting, 28 January 1957.
110. DGHIST, 79/429 vol. 7B, 4 Jul 57, "Divisional Items of Interest"; Wilfred E. Oulton, *Christmas Island Cracker* (London: Thomas Harmsworth Publishers, 1987), 292. See also Kenneth Hubbard, *Operation GRAPPLE: Testing Britain's First H-Bomb* (London: Ian Allen Inc, 1985).
111. Canadian Op ANTLER documents acquired under ATI, 4 June 1957, Foulkes to External Affairs, "Operation ANTLER"; 21 May 1957, message DRB to CANRESEARCH London; 25 March 1957, message CANRESEARCH London to DRB; 13 March 1957, message CJSL to Joint Staff, "Canadian Participation in ANTLER and Assignment"; 8 February 1957, COSC to CJSL, "Operation SAPPHIRE: Canadian Participation"; Arnold, *Very Special Relationship*, 173.
112. Arnold, *Very Special Relationship*, 174.
113. Arnold, *Very Special Relationship*, 186–190; Canadian Op ANTLER documents

acquired under ATI, 4 December 1957, DArmE to JSWC, "Operation ANTLER—Aerial Survey Report."

114. Canadian Op ANTLER documents acquired under ATI, 29 April 1959, JSWPC to Joint Staff, "Reports"; 21 September 1959, JSWPC to DRB, "AWRE Reports."

115. USNARA, RG 218 box 79 file CCS 471.6 4-25-50 section 20, message to MOD (Canada) from USREP NATO MILCOMTE, Washington, 5 April 1958; RG 218 box 79 file CCS 471.6 4-25-50 section 18, JSPC to JCS, "HARDTACK Observers," 7 January 1958.

Chapter 5

1. See Ian Lumsden, ed., *Close the 49th Parallel Etc.: The Americanization of Canada* (Toronto: University of Toronto Press, 1970); James M. Minifie, *Peacemaker or Powder Monkey: Canada's Role in a Revolutionary World* (Toronto: McClelland and Stewart, 1960); J. L. Granatstein and Norman Hillmer, *For Better or For Worse: Canada and the United States to the 1990s* (Toronto: Copp ClarkPitmen, 1991); Gerard S. Vano, *Canada: The Strategic and Military Pawn* (New York: Praeger, 1988); Reg Whitaker and Gary Marcuse, *Cold War Canada: The Making of a National Insecurity State, 1945–1957* (Toronto: University of Toronto Press, 1995). The rhetoric is less than facetious.

2. Jockel, *No Boundaries*, 93; FOIA, NORAD Historical Office, "NORAD History Highlights," undated.

3. USNARA, RG 218 JCS chairman's files, Arthur Radford file 381, memo to Radford from JSPC, "NSC Briefing on the Vulnerability of SAC," 18 October 1955; NAC, RG 24 vol. 20710 file csc. 232, 11 June 1956, memo to the CDC, "Authority to Conduct Joint Site Surveys for the Northward Extention of the Air Defence Combat Zone."

4. DDRS, 1978 frame 238 B and C, report by CoS USAF to JCS, "A Combined Canada–United States North American Air Defence Command," 5 December 1955.

5. CIIA, John Holmes Papers, file C/III/12D, letter Air Marshal C. R. Dunlap to Clive Baxter; DDRS, 1978 frame 238 B and C, report by CoS USAF to JCS, "A Combined Canada–United States North American Air Defence Command," 5 December 1955; DDRS, 1978 frame 238 B, report by the JSPC to JCS, "Integration of Operational Control of the Continental Air Defences of Canada and the United States During Peacetime," 9 January 1956; DGHIS, Carstairs Papers, 5 December 1957, "Steps in Development of Integration of Operational Control of Canadian and Continental United States Air Defence Forces in Peacetime," 5 December 1957.

6. Jockel, *No Boundaries*, 102.

7. Campney did not want to commit "on the fly" to a potentially expensive Canadian participation in the air defence system without serious and drawn out consultation.

8. DGHIST, Carstairs Papers, 12 June 1957, aide memoir from Foulkes to Pearkes, "Integration of Operational Control of Canadian and Continental United States Air Defence Forces in Peacetime."

9. DGHIST, Raymont Collection, file 1308A, COSC, 1 February 1957, 604th meeting.

10. Jockel, *No Boundaries*, 103; DGHIST, Carstairs Papers, 12 June 1957, aide memoire from Foulkes to Pearkes, "Integration of Operational Control of Canadian and Continental United States Air Defence Forces in Peacetime."

11. UVIC, Pearkes Papers, "Interview with General Charles Foulkes, March 9, 1967."

12. DGHIST, Carstairs Papers, 12 June 1957, aide memoir from Foulkes to Pearkes, "Integration of Operational Control of Canadian and Continental United States Air Defence Forces in Peacetime."

13. See Reginald Roy's biography of Pearkes, *For Most Conspicuous Bravery* (Vancouver: University of British Columbia Press, 1977), particularly chaps. 13 and 14.

14. DGHIST, Carstairs Papers, 12 June 1957, aide memoir from Foulkes to Pearkes, "Integration of Operational Control of Canadian and Continental United States Air Defence Forces in Peacetime."

15. UVIC, Pearkes Papers, "Interview with General Charles Foulkes, March 9, 1967."

16. Ibid.

17. Ibid.

18. DGHIST, Carstairs Papers, 12 June 1957, aide memoir from Foulkes to Pearkes, "Integration of Operational Control of Canadian and Continental United States Air Defence Forces in Peacetime"; 1 August 1957, "Joint Statement by the Secretary of Defence of the United States and the Minister of National Defence of Canada"; 5 December 1957, "Steps in Development of Integration of Operational Control of Canadian and Continental United States Air Defence Forces in Peacetime."

19. USNARA, RG 59 box 3218 file 742.5/7-2857, 28 July 1957, memcon, "Common Command Arrangements for Continental Air Defence."

20. DGHIST, Carstairs Papers, 3 September 1957, message Foulkes to Partridge.

21. Ibid.

22. DGHIST, Carstairs Papers, 1 October 1957, memo Foulkes to Pearkes, "Progress Resume: Integration of North American Air Defence Forces."

23. John Hilliker and Donald Barry, *Canada's Department of External Affairs*, (Kingston: McGill-Queen's University Press, 1995), 2:143–146; Jockel, *No Boundaries*, 108–109.

24. CIIA, Holmes Papers, file C/III/12D, n.d., letter Air Marshal C. R. Dunlap to Clive Baxter; 5 December 1972, letter Holmes to Roy.

25. DGHIST, Carstairs Papers, 18 October 1957, memo Smith to Pearkes.

26. UVIC, Pearkes Papers, "Interview with General George Pearkes, April 7, 1969."

27. English, *Worldly Years*, 190–191; Denis Smith, *Rogue Tory: The Life and Legend of John G. Diefenbaker* (Toronto: Macfarlane, Malcom and Ross, 1995), 206–207; Robert Bothwell et al., *Canada Since 1945*, rev. ed. (Toronto: University of Toronto Press, 1989), 186–189.

28. Bothwell et al., *Canada Since 1945*, 177.

29. Ibid.

30. DGHIST, Raymont Study.

31. UVIC, Pearkes Papers, "Interview with General Charles Foulkes, March 9, 1967."

32. DGHIST, Raymont Study.

33. UVIC, Pearkes Papers, "Interview with Air Chief Marshal F. R. Miller, June 20, 1967."

34. UVIC, Pearkes Papers, "Interview with General Charles Foulkes, March 9, 1967." It is, of course, a matter of speculation as to whether or not Foulkes ever used this to lever any policy decisions out of Diefenbaker.

35. Ibid.

36. Ibid.

37. Reg Roy's interview with Pearkes in April 1969 belies this. See "Interview with General George Pearkes, April 7, 1969" in the Pearkes Papers, UVIC.

38. DGHIST, Raymont Study; see also Roy, *For Most Conspicuous Bravery*, chaps. 14, 15, and 16.

39. DGHIST, Raymont Study; see also Roy, *For Most Conspicuous Bravery*, chaps. 14, 15, and 16; UVIC, Pearkes Papers, "Interview with General Charles Foulkes, June 5, 1967." Note that, in Reg Roy's interview with Green in December 1971, Green continually skated around these issues. See "Interview with the Honourable Howard Green, December 16, 1971."

40. UVIC, Pearkes Papers, "Interview with General George Pearkes, April 7, 1969."

41. Ibid.

42. Smith, *Rogue Tory*, 261.

43. Robertson's story is told in Jack Granatstein's *A Man of Influence: Norman A. Robertson and Canadian Statecraft 1929–68* (Toronto: Deneau Publishers, 1981).

44. USNARA, RG 59 E 3077 250/62/30/3 box 1, file: Neutralism, Anti-Americanism 1960–62 1.14, letter Livingston Merchant to Ivan White, 4 April 1961.

45. Granatstein, *Man of Influence*, 325.

46. USNARA, RG 59 E 3077 250/62/30/3 box 1, file Ottawa (General) 1961 1/A, memcon Rufus Z. Smith and Jean Fornier, 2 June 1961.

47. Granatstein, *Man of Influence*, 326.

48. DGHIST, Raymont Study, 116–117.

49. DGHIST, Raymont Collection, 30 November 1979, "The Evolution of the Structure of the Department of National Defence 1945–68."

50. Ibid.

51. Basil Robinson, *Diefenbaker's World: A Populist in Foreign Affairs* (Toronto: University of Toronto Press, 1989), 4.

52. Ibid., 4–5.

53. See NAC, RG 25 vol. 4498 file 50030-K-40 pts. 1 to 3 for the minutes and memoranda of the POEADQ from the years 1951 to 1955.

54. Ibid.

55. For example, the sheer amount of paper in the panel files balloons between 1957 and 1961, when compared to the earlier years.

56. See DGHIST, file 25/8 vols. 1 and 2 for the minutes and memoranda of the POEADQ from the years 1957 to 1961.

57. Douglas, *Creation of a National Air Force*, 624; Greenhous et al, *Crucible of War*, 63, 96.

58. DGHIST, Raymont Collection, file 497, 26 June 1958, memo Foulkes to Pearkes, "Visit of the President of the United States."

59. DDEL, Norstad Papers, box 65, file: FOULKES through FRASER, message SHAPE to Foulkes, 9 February 1957.

60. Granatstein, *Generals*, 163.

61. Graham, *Price of Command*, 4.

62. Wood, *Strange Battleground*, 10; UVIC, Pearkes Papers, "Interview with Lt-Gen S. F. Clark, July 7, 1971."

63. USASK, Diefenbaker Centre, MG 01/v1/100/D 316 conf., 5 March 1960, letter from "PhD" to Diefenbaker.

64. DGHIST, Raymont Collection, file 1309A, 19 March 1957, COSC, 608th meeting.

65. *The NATO Letter*, May 1957, 3; Marc Trachtenberg, ed., *The Development of American Strategic Thought 1945–1969: Basic Documents from the Eisenhower and Kennedy Periods Volume 1* (New York: Garland, 1988), 168–170.

66. DGHIST, Raymont Collection, file 1309A, 30 May 1957, COSC, 609th meeting.

67. Ibid.

68. NAC, RG 25 vol. 4499 file 50030-K-40 pt. 4, 12 July 1957, memo to DCosPlans and Policy, SHAPE from SHAPE Annual Review Team.

69. NAC, RG 25 vol. 4499 file 50030-K-40 pt. 4, 3 April 1957, "SHAPE Planning Guidance: Pattern of Canadian Land Forces 1960/62."

70. Ibid.

71. Ibid.

72. NAC, RG 25 vol. 4499 file 50030-K-40 pt. 4, n.d. "Comparison of SACLANT Minimum Force Requirements Against Force Figures in Canadian Reply to ARQ 1957."

73. NAC, RG 25 vol. 4500 file 50030-K-40 1957–58, 3 October 1957, letter to Leger from Foulkes, "NATO Supreme Commanders' Minimum Force Study MC 70."

74. NAC, RG 25 vol. 4499 file 50030-K-40 pt. 4, 31 October 1957, memo DL1D to USSEA, "Panel on Economic Aspects of Defence Questions: Friday November 1st." External Affairs used guilty language in its internal analysis of the affair. They were worried that Foulkes would figure out what had happened and "would try to pin it on us."

75. NAC, RG 25 vol. 4500 file 50030-K-40 FP 57-58, 10 October 1957, message NATO Paris to External, "SACEUR's Contribution to MC 70."

76. NAC, RG 25 vol. 4499 file 50030-K-40 pt. 4, 30 October 1957, memo USSEA to DL1D, "Panel on Economic Aspects of Defence—Friday November 1st."

77. Chistian Tuschhoff, *Nuclear History Program Occasional Paper 9: Causes and Consequences of Germany's Deployment of Nuclear Capable Delivery Systems 1957–1963* (College Park, MD: Center for International and Security Studies, 1994), 20–21.

78. NAC, RG 25 vol. 4500 file 50030-K-40 FP 57-58, 10 October 1957, message NATO Paris to External, "SACEUR's Contribution to MC 70."

79. NAC, RG 25 vol. 4500 file 50030-K-40 FP 57-58, 8 October 1957, message External Ottawa to NATO Paris, " SACEUR's Contribution to MC 70."

80. DGHIST, Raymont Collection, file 1332, 19 September 1957, Cabinet Defence Committee, 115th meeting.

81. Ibid.

82. Ibid.

83. Ibid.

84. NAC, RG 2 vol. 1893 file, 16 August–23 September 1957, Cabinet Conclusions.

85. DGHIST, Raymont Collection, file 1309A, 10 October 1957, COSC, 623th meeting.

86. NAC, RG 25 vol. 4495 file 50030-E-1-40 pt. 1, 8 November 1957, JPC, "SACLANT Minimum Forces Study, 1958–1962, SACEUR Minimum Forces Study, 1958–1962."

87. Ibid.

88. Ibid.

89. Ibid.

90. Ibid.

91. NAC, RG 25 vol. 4500 file 50030-K-40 FP 57-58, 24 October 1957, message External Ottawa to NATO Paris, "Restricted Meeting of the NATO Council."

92. Ibid.

93. NAC, RG 25 vol. 4499 file 50030-K-40 pt. 4, 31 October 1957, memo DL1D to USSEA, "Panel on Economic Aspects of Defence Questions: Friday November 1st."

94. DDEL, Norstad Papers, file FOULKES through FRASER, memo Mare to Norstad, 9 August 1957.

95. DGHIST, file 25/8 vol. 1, 1 November 1957, POEADQ, 47th meeting.

96. DGHIST, Raymont Collection, file 1332, 12 November 1957, Cabinet Defence Committee, 116th meeting.

97. Ibid.

98. DGHIST, Raymont Collection, file 1332, 13 November 1957, Cabinet Defence Committee, special meeting.

99. DDEL, Norstad Papers, file: DIEFENBAKER through DOVAS, 22 November 1957, letter Norstad to Diefenbaker.

100. See John G. Diefenbaker, *One Canada: Memoirs of the Right Honourable John G. Diefenbaker; Volume 2: The Years of Achievement 1956 to 1962* (Toronto: Macmillan of Canada, 1976); B. Robinson, *Diefenbaker's World.*

101. NAC, RG 25 vol. 4499 file 50030-K-40 pt. 4, n.d., draft by F. G. Hooton, "Stockpiling of Atomic Warheads in Europe: Provision of IRBM's to Europe. The Problem of Control"; NAC, RG 25 vol. 4499 file 50030-K-40 pt. 5, 18 November 1957, memo to the POEADQ, "Stockpiling of Atomic Warheads for Tactical Weapons in Europe."

102. NAC, RG 25 vol. 4499 file 50030-K-40 pt. 5, 18 November 1957, memo to the POEADQ, "Stockpiling of Atomic Warheads for Tactical Weapons in Europe."

103. Ibid.

104. DGHIST, file 25/8 vol. 1, 22 November 1957, POEADQ, 48th meeting.

105. Ibid.

106. Ibid.

107. NAC, RG 25 vol. 4499 file 50030-K-40 pt. 4, 28 November 1957, memo to USSEA to DL(1), "Meeting of the Panel on the Economic Aspects of Defence Questions"; NAC, RG 49 (DDP) vol. 708 file 247-5 vol. 4, 29 November 1957, POEADQ, 49th meeting.

108. NAC, RG 25 vol. 4499 file 50030-K-40 pt. 5, 27 November 1957, draft memo to Cabinet, "Stockpiling of Nuclear Weapons in NATO Countries."

109. DGHIST, file 25/8 vol. 1, 6 December 1957, POEADQ, 50th meeting.

110. DGHIST, Raymont Collection, file 1309A, 18 December 1957, COSC, special meeting.

111. NAC, RG 2 vol. 1893 file, 12 November–15 December 1957, 12 December 1957, Cabinet Conclusions.

112. NSA, Background Paper for NATO Heads of Government Meeting, Paris, 16–18 December 1957, "NATO Defence Policy and Strategy," 4 December 1957; PRO DEFE 6, 13 December 1957, JPS, "Minimum Essential Requirements—MC 70: Report by the Joint Planning Staff."

113. NSA, message Paris to U.S. Secretary of State, "Summary of First Closed Session of NATO Heads of Government Meeting," 17 December 1957; message Paris to U.S. Secretary of State, "Morning and Afternoon Meetings: December 18th," 18 December 1957.

114. NAC, RG 25 vol. 4499 file 50030-K-40 pt. 5, 22 January 1958, memo Foulkes to Leger, "Future Ministerial Meetings."

115. NSA, message Paris to U.S. Secretary of State, "NAC Meeting—Defence Conference," 30 January 1958.

116. NAC, RG 25 vol. 4499 file 50030-K-40 pt. 5, 25 January 1958, message NATO Paris to External, "Preparations for Defence Conference"; 29 January 1958, NATO Paris to External, "Defence Conference."

117. DGHIST, file 25/8 vol. 1, 31 January 1958, POEADQ, 51st meeting.

118. DGHIST, Raymont Collection, file 1310E, 13 February 1958, COSC, 619th meeting.

119. DGHIST, Raymont Collection, file 1310E, 13 February 1958, COSC, 619th meeting, attachment: "Canadian Preliminary Comments on MC 70."

120. DGHIST, file 25/8 vol. 1, 20 March 1958, POEADQ, 52nd meeting. See attachment, "Report by the Chairman Chiefs of Staff Committee on MC 70—Minimum Essential Force Requirements 1958–1963."

121. Ibid.

122. U.S. DOS, *FRUS 1958–1960 Volume VII Part 1: Western European Integration and Security; Canada* (Washington, DC: GPO, 1993), 315–316, message from U.S. Delegation to NATO to State, "NAC Meeting April 23 1958—item II—Minimum Essential Force Requirements (MC 70)," 23 April 1958.

123. Tuschhoff, *Causes and Consequences*, 9.

124. DGHIST, 121.013 (D1), 22 April 1963, memo ACNS to DL, "RCN Future Requirements Planning Guide for the Period 1964–74."

125. NSA, JCS JSPC, "Atomic Support of Allied Forces," 15 April 1957.

126. Ibid.

127. NSA, memo SACEUR to JCS, "Release of Tactical Target Materials," 18 June 1957.

128. Mark Cioc, *Pax Atomica: The Nuclear Defence Debate in West Germany During the Adenauer Era* (New York: Columbia University Press, 1988), 21–37.

129. NSA, memo Twining to SECDEF, "Proposed Changes to the Atomic Energy Act of 1954," 12 May 1958.

130. Ian Clark, *Nuclear Diplomacy and the Special Relationship: Britain's Deterrent and America, 1957–1962* (Oxford: Clarendon Press, 1994), 90–92. For example, the British manufactured the RED SNOW nuclear weapon based on American Mk. 28 plans.

131. DGHIST, Raymont Collection, file 1310C, 13 April 1959, COSC, special meeting.

Chapter 6

1. DGHIST, Carstairs Papers, *Hansard* extracts, 22 October and 4, 5, 6 November 1957.

2. The American State Department was following the NORAD debate closely. The American Ambassador in Canada, Livingston Merchant, noted at this point that: "Questions may presage effort to make political issue on alleged transfer [of] sovereignty without consulting parliament, liberal opposition of course agreed to NORAD before [the] last election and present tactic could backfire on them." USNARA, RG 59, box 3218, message Merchant to Dulles, 6 November 1957.

3. And Foulkes was trying to get the U.S. JCS to accept some form of NORAD-NATO relationship but was rebuffed. See note 28 below on the matter.

4. DGHIST, Carstairs Papers, *Hansard* extracts, 26 November 1957.

5. USASK, Diefenbaker Centre, MG 01/v1/108, 22 October 1957, memo Foulkes to Pearkes, "Integration of Operational Control of Canadian and Continental American Air Defence Forces in Peacetime."

6. DGHIST, Carstairs Papers, *Hansard* extracts, 5 December 1957.

7. DGHIST, Carstairs Papers, *Hansard* extracts, 4 January 1958.

8. DGHIST, Carstairs Papers, 25 November 1957, memo Foulkes to Pearkes, "Continental Defence."

9. DGHIST, Carstairs Papers, *Hansard* extracts, 4 January 1958.

10. NAC, MG 26 N2, vol. 3 file 100, n.d., untitled, detailed single-spaced five page brief on air Defence issues.

11. For those unfamiliar with Canada's parliamentary government, if a minority government does not believe that it can effectively govern or if the opposition successfully acquires a vote of no confidence in Parliament, the government must hold a general election. The objective is to gain a majority in the House of Commons so that legislation can be passed by the majority government with little interference from the opposition. In a majority government, the opposition cannot effectively block legislation unless MPs from the government vote with them on an issue, which almost never happens. Consequently, the main weapons in the hands of the opposition are sarcasm, innuendo, media leaks, grandstanding, and any means available to embarrass and harrass the government and its attempt to implement policy. Needless to say, this is a highly adversarial environment.

12. USNARA, RG 59 box 3218, message Mechant to Dulles, 15 November 1957; message Embassy Ottawa to State, "Questioning in Parliament on the North American Air Defence Command," 22 November 1957.

13. DGHIST, Carstairs Papers, *Hansard* extracts, 13, 19, 20, 30 May 1958 and 2 June 1958.

14. DGHIST, Carstairs Papers, *Hansard* extracts, 10 June 1958.

15. USNARA, RG 59, message Merchant to Dulles, 30 April 1958.

16. DGHIST, Carstairs Papers, *Hansard* extracts, 10 June 1958. American observers in Ottawa noted that this was "primarily an internal wrangle on a constitutional issue rather than a disagreement with the concept of an integrated command itself." See USNARA, RG 59 box 3218, message Embassy Ottawa to State, "Further Parliamentary Discussion of North American Air Defence Command (NORAD)," 8 January 1958.

17. DGHIST, Carstairs Papers, *Hansard* extracts, 10 June 1958.

18. DGHIST, Carstairs Papers, *Hansard* extracts, 11 June 1958.

19. Ibid.

20. Ibid.

21. DGHIST, Carstairs Papers, *Hansard* extracts, 19 July 1958.

22. Minifie eventually wrote a book entitled *Peacemaker or Powder Monkey: Canada's Role in a Revolutionary World* (Toronto: McClelland and Stewart, 1960). This work argued that there was no Soviet threat, so Canada should become neutral and interpose

itself between the superpowers in order to restrain the United States from precipitous action. In Minifie's view, Canada was a mere satellite of the United States, and in order to retain her sovereignty, Canada should divest itself of NORAD and NATO. The book was avidly read by university intellectuals, students, pundits, and young bureaucrats in the 1960s. It contributed to the creation of a mindset that viewed Canadian efforts at generating future strategic policy as futile, a mindset that dominated Canadian thought into the 1970s and 1980s.

23. USNARA, RG 59 box 3218, message Merchant to Dulles, 27 June 1958.

24. Ibid.

25. USNARA, RG 59 box 3218, message Thompson to Dulles, 13 June 1958; message Merchant to Dulles, 20 June 1958.

26. It is interesting to note that U.S. State Department message traffic from Ottawa to Washington regularly included press attitude surveys and summaries on a wide variety of issues. The NORAD affair was no exception. Until someone embarks on a systematic study of Canadian media attitudes towards defense issues in the 1950s, these surveys must suffice for now. See, for example, USNARA, RG 59 box 3218, messages Merchant to Dulles for the dates 14 November 1957; 21 May 1958; and 2 June 1958.

27. Ironically, Foulkes and COSC wanted some connection between NORAD and NATO, but the JCS did not agree and would not be convinced to do so. A phrase that Slemon and Partridge included in their original terms of reference, "cooperation with NATO commands," was deleted. The JCS motives are obscure, but were in line with their 1950–51 desire to keep continental defense matters at arms length from NATO. Canadian planners thought that security was an issue. Both Canadian and American planners did not want to submit their plans to the NAC in the way SACEUR had to for the MC 70 problem. See DGHIST, Raymont Collection, file 1310E, 24 January 1958, COSC, 617th meeting; and DGHIST, file 112.3M2.009 (D208), 11 February 1958, Joint Staff, "NORAD Integration with NATO." See also DGHIST, vol. 73/1223 file 2002, Air Officers Commanding Conference, March 1958, Foulkes discussion.

28. DGHIST, file 112.3M2.009 (D208), 8 October 1957, "North American Air Defence Command (NORAD) Proposed Mission and Terms of Reference"; USNARA, RG 59 box 3218, "Revised Terms of Reference for the Commander in Chief, North American Air Defence Command," 16 May 1958.

29. Ibid.

30. DGHIST, 20 October 1978, Slemon-Douglas-McAndrew interview.

31. USNARA, RG 59 box 3218, memo from Jandrey to Murphy, "Canadian Embassy Enquiry Regarding Article Entitled 'Air Defence Unit Has No Atom Curb' by Jack Raymond" in the 7 October edition of the *New York Times*, box 2879, message to distribution list from State, "Defence Text," 9 October 1958; message State to Distribution List, 7 October 1958.

32. USNARA, RG 59 box 3218, memo from Porter to Murphy, 13 October 1958; memcon, Canadian embassy officials and U.S. State Department representatives, 14 October 1958.

33. NAC, RG 25 vol. 4499 file 50030-K40 pt. 5, 14 November 1958, memo to Undersecretary of State for External Affairs, "Acquisition of Defensive Nuclear Weapons by Canada."

34. DGHIST, file 88/175, "Agreement Between the Government of Canada and the Government of the United States of America Concerning the Organization and Operation of the North American Air Defence Command (NORAD)."

35. FOIA, USAF, Thomas W. Ray, *ADC Historical Study No. 20: Nuclear Armament, Its Acqusition, Control and Application to Manned Interceptors 1951–1963* (Washington, DC: USAF, 1964); "ADCOM's Fighter Interceptor Squadrons," *The Interceptor* 21, no. 1 (January 1979).

36. FOIA, USAF, Ray, *ADC Historical Study No. 20*; "ADCOM's Fighter Interceptor Squad-

rons," *Interceptor*. Note that in Robert S. Norris, William M. Arkin, and William Burr, "Appendix B Deployments by Country, 1951–1977," *Bulletin of the Atomic Scientists* 55, no. 6 (1999): 66–67, and Robert S. Norris, William M. Arkin, and William Burr, "How Much Did Japan Know?" *Bulletin of the Atomic Scientists* 56, no. 1 (2000): 11–13, the U.S. Government denies that nuclear air defense weapons were deployed to Iceland or Greenland and a released document suggests that nuclear Falcon was only deployed to Canada in 1965. Yet the ADC historical study has nuclear capability inspections conducted on squadrons based in Canada, Iceland, and Greenland in 1962. In 1963, a squadron at one of the four sites in question had an accident involving an MB-1 "being readied for alert duty." In another section, the ADC study notes that the 59th FIS at Goose Bay had only access to inert training versions of the GAR-11 prior to Canadian government approval to store nuclear air-to-air weapons in Canada. Ergo, some of the information contained in the "Appendix B" data is incorrect.

37. Schaffel, *Emerging Shield*, 225–230; NORAD History Office, "NORAD Resource Statistics Book 1958–1976."

38. USNARA, RG 59 box 3219, memorandum for files, "Canadian Revisions to Draft Notes on Use of Air-to-Air Nuclear Weapons Over Canadian Territory by the United States Air Force," 8 January 1957.

39. Ibid.

40. FOIA, USAF, Ray, "BOMARC and Nuclear Armamant."

41. USNARA, RG 59 box 3218, memcons Canadian Embassy–U.S. State Department, "U.S.-Canadian Air Defence Arrangements," 15 January 1957 and 6 February 1957.

42. USNARA, RG 59 box 3218, memcon U.S. State Department, "U.S.-Canadian Air Defence Questions," 29 January 1957. There was also some concern by both parties that if the arrangement were announced in the NAC, it would cause some irritation over "preferential treartment." See memcon, State Department, "U.S.-Canadian Air Defence Arrangements," 1 February 1957.

43. USNARA, RG 59 box 3219, memo, Elbrick to Dulles, "Proposed Agreement Permitting Use of Air-to-Air Nuclear Missiles Over Canada," 17 January 1957.

44. USNARA, RG 59 box 3218, memcon State Department, "U.S.-Canadian Air Defence Arrangements," 5 February 1957.

45. DGHIST, Raymont Collection, file 629, 8 October 1958, memo for cabinet, "Acquisition and Storage of Defensive Nuclear Weapons and Warheads in Canada." Appendix A has the appropriate chronology.

46. USNARA, RG 59 box 3218, memo, Sprague to McElroy, 21 May 1957; box 3219, memo, Loper to Nugent, 5 June 1957; memo, Parsons to Elbrick, "Proposed Extention of Agreement Permitting Use of Air-to-Air Nuclear (MB-1) Rockets over Canada," 5 June 1957.

47. DGHIST, Raymont Collection, file 629, 8 October 1958, memo for cabinet, "Acquisition and Storage of Defensive Nuclear Weapons and Warheads in Canada."

48. USNARA, RG 59 box 3218, letter, Elbrick to Robertson, 29 January 1958.

49. USNARA, RG 59 box 3219, memo, Jones to Murphy, "Proposed Amendment to MB-1 Rocket Overflight Agreement with Canada," 3 January 1958.

50. USNARA, RG 59 box 3219, memo, Sprague to Murphy, 25 March 1958.

51. DGHIST, Raymont Collection, file 629, 8 October 1958, memo for cabinet, "Acquisition and Storage of Defensive Nuclear Weapons and Warheads in Canada"; USNARA, RG 59 box 3218, Robertson to Dulles, "Exchange of Notes," 12 May 1958.

52. DGHIST, Raymont Collection, file 629, 8 October 1958, memo for cabinet, "Acquisition and Storage of Defensive Nuclear Weapons and Warheads in Canada."

53. Schaffel, *Emerging Shield*, 199–200.

54. Letter, Lloyd Burnham to Maloney, 15 April 1996; D. S. Terrell, "What is SAGE?" *Roundel* June 1961, 21–23.

55. FOIA, McMullen, *Interceptor Missiles in Air Defence*, 41–64; See also FOIA, Ray, *ADC Historical Study No. 21.*

56. There also was an "Air Force–Canada Committee," probably the American name for it. This entity referred back information from the USAF's coordination staff in Ottawa, which was established to act as the American liaison for USAF-oriented projects on Canadian soil. For the scant documentation of the AF-Canada Committee, see USNARA, RG 341 box 82, minutes, 9 December 1955; 16 December 1955; 9 March 1956; 19 March 1956; 6 April 1956.

57. Of which two USAF squadrons would go to Alaska, two to northeast Canada, fifty-nine to CONUS, and twelve RCAF squadrons across Canada. See DGHIST, file 112.3M2.009 (D 208), 5 February 1957, Army LO to ADC to DMO&P, "Continental Air Defence Objectives Plan, 1956–66."

58. DGHIST, file 112.3M2.009 (D 208), 26 February 1957, memo, CGS to DMO&P, "Continental Air Defence Objectives Plan, 1956–66." The selection of Canada to host SAGE actually went back to a CUSMSG recommendation in September 1956 and the Cabinet Defence Committee took note of this and agreed that SAGE would be good for Canada. See DepCinCNORAD to USAF HQ, 13 November 1957, "Installation of SAGE in the North Bay Sector"; NAC, RG 24 acc 83/84/167 vol. 222 file 1400-14 pt. 2, 9 November 1956, memo to CDC, "Introduction of Automaticity into the Air Defence Control System in Canada."

59. DGHIST, file 112.3M2.009 (D 208), 29 November 1957, RCAF HQ to COSC, "Air Defence Combat Zone Ground Environment in Canada."

60. DGHIST, file 79/429 vol. 7A, divisional items of interest, weeks ending 8 February 1957 and 1 March 1957.

61. DGHIST, Raymont Collection, file 10, 19 August 1958, "Relative Effectiveness of Weapons Systems for the Arrow Aircraft."

62. DGHIST, Hendrick Papers, Daily Dairy, 25 March 1957; 16 April 1957; 28 August 1957; Stewart, *Shutting Down the National Dream*, 198–203; Hansen, *U.S. Nuclear Weapons*, 106–107.

63. DGHIST, file 112.3M2.009 (D 208), 7 June 1957, memo, CORE to CGS, "CF-105-Costs and Effectiveness."

64. DGHIST, Raymont Collection, file 1332, 19 September 1957, Cabinet Defence Committee, 115th meeting.

65. DGHIST, Raymont Collection, file 1309A, 24–25 October 1957, COSC, 613th meeting.

66. Ibid.

67. DGHIST, Raymont Collection, file 11, 28 October 1957, memo to the CDC, "Air Defence-CF-105 (Arrow) Aircraft Programme."

68. DGHIST, Hendrick Papers, Daily Dairy, 29 October 1957.

69. Ibid.

70. DGHIST, Raymont Collection, file 10, 28 July 1958, memo to CDC, "Air Defence-CF 105 (Arrow) Aircraft Programme."

71. DGHIST, Raymont Collection, file 1309A, 3–4 December 1957, COSC, special meeting.

72. Ibid.

73. DGHIST, Raymont Collection, file 995, 12 December 1957, message Canadian Embassy, Washington to External, "USA Proposals RE: Closer Integration of Atomic Capabilities in Defence of North America."

74. Ibid.

75. Ibid.

76. Ibid.

77. Ibid.

78. DGHIST, Raymont Collection, file 1309A, 18 December 1957, 20 December 1957, COSC, special meeting.

79. DGHIST, Raymont Collection, file 995, 3 January 1958, memo to the CDC, "United States Proposals for Closer Integration of Atomic Capabilities in the Defence of North America"; 13 January 1958, memo, Foulkes to COSC, "United States Proposals for Closer Integration of Atomic Capabilities in the Defence of North America," file 1310E, 20 January 1958, COSC, 616th meeting.

80. DGHIST, Raymont Collection, file 995, 21 January 1958, Foulkes to Sparling, "United States Proposals for Closer Integration of Atomic Capabilities in the Defence of North America."

81. DGHIST, Raymont Study, 249–250.

82. Ibid; DGHIST, Foulkes Papers, Arrow Folder 14-2, "The Story of the CF-105 AVRO Arrow, 1952–1962."

83. DGHIST, Hendrick Papers, Daily Dairy, 22 April 1958.

84. DGHIST, file 112.3M2.009 (D 260), 8 January 1958, extract, COSC, 615th meeting; extract, COSC, 616th meeting.

85. DGHIST, Hendrick Papers, Daily Dairy, 30 May 1958.

86. Ibid.

87. Ibid.

88. Ibid.

89. Ibid.

90. DGHIST, Raymont Collection, file 1310E, 3 April 1958, COSC, special meeting; 18 April 1958, COSC, 620th meeting.

91. DGHIST, file 112.012(D260), 14 May 1958, "Report by the Joint Planning Committee to the COSC on the Review of Air Defence Against the Manned Bomber Threat."

92. Ibid.

93. Ibid.

94. Ibid.

95. Ibid.

96. DGHIST, file 112.012(D260), 12 May 1958, "DRB Air Defence Study—Conclusions."

97. Ibid.

98. DGHIST, file 112.012(D260), 5 June 1958, D Arty to DMO&P, "Review of Air Defence Against the Manned Bomber." The army continued throughout 1958 to incorporate Nike Hercules into the system but to no avail. See DGHIST, file 112.1(D 184), 27 June 1958, D Arty to CGS, "Air Defence Plan."

99. DGHIST, Raymont Collection, file 1310E, 10 June 1958, COSC, 623rd meeting. It should also be noted that DRB was continually trying to extend the air combat zone along with its radars and interceptor bases further north, away from the population centers in eastern Canada. This would, in the COSC's view, add unacceptable costs to an already costly system since the locations that the DRB wanted to place these units were in completely undeveloped, wooded country. See DGHIST, file 112.3M2.009 (D 208), n.d., memo to COSC, "DRB Proposals for Northward Extension of the Air Defence System"; 5 June 1958, memo to S/ORG, "Canadian BOMARC and Interceptor Installations."

100. DGHIST, Hendrick Papers, Daily Dairy, 9 July 1958. Note that the conventional warhead in the film was a test warhead, not a mature system, and technical problems resulted in its cancellation. See FOIA, USAF, Ray, "BOMARC and Nuclear Armamant."

101. DGHIST, Raymont Study, 251.

102. Ibid.

103. DGHIST, Raymont Collection, file 1310E, 14 and 15 July 1958, COSC, special meeting; Special Meeting.

104. This had, in fact, been discussed by the panel back in January 1958. The USAF was unable to do so because of its commitment to the F-102, F-106, and F-108 series of aircraft. The USAF strongly encouraged CF-105 production and "were interested in seeking ways of helping Canada financially to introduce CF-105's into RCAF service. One way of doing this might be for the [U.S.] to purchase the CF-105's and then return them to the RCAF for Canadian use. A factor in the USAF's unwillingness to buy CF-105s for their own use was the proposed reduction in manned interceptor squadrons and the stretching out of their own contracts as the U.S. tried to answer their own policy questions." See DGHIST, 31 January 1958, POEADQ, 51st meeting.

105. NAC, RG 25 vol. 4501 file 50030-K-2-40 pt. 1, 29 July 1958, POEADQ, 54th meeting.

106. DGHIST, Raymont Collection, file 1332, 28 July 1958, Cabinet Defence Committee, 119th meeting.

107. DGHIST, Raymont Collection, file 1332, 15 August 1958, Cabinet Defence Committee, 120th meeting.

108. DGHIST, Raymont Study, 252.

109. Ibid.

110. Ibid, 255.

111. NAC, MG 32 B19 vol. 22 file 201-250/58, 22 August 1958, memo for cabinet, "Recommendations of the Cabinet Defence Committee: Air Defence Requirements."

112. NAC, RG 2, 28 August 1958, Cabinet Conclusions.

113. Ibid.

114. DGHIST, Raymont Study, 256.

115. NAC, RG 2, Cabinet Conclusions, 28 August 1958, 3 September 1958, 7 September 1958; DGHIST, Raymont Study, 250.

116. DGHIST, Raymont Collection, file 1332, Cabinet Defence Committee, 121st meeting, 21 August 1958; file 629, "Record of Cabinet Decision Meeting of September 8th, 1958: Air Defence Requirements Recommendations of the Cabinet Defence Committee."

117. USASK, Diefenbaker Papers, MG 01/v1/Arrow Conf file, 5 September 1958, memo, Bryce to the Prime Minister, re: the 105 problem.

118. Ibid.

119. Ibid.

120. NAC, RG 25 vol. 4499 file 50030-K40 pt. 5, 11 September 1958, "DND Suggestions on Cost Sharing."

121. NAC, RG 25 vol. 4499 file 50030-K40 pt. 5, POEADQ, 57th meeting 10 September 1958; 58th meeting, 12 September 1958; USNARA, RG 59 box 3218, memcon Norman Robertson and Woodbury Willoughby, "Canadian Proposal to Supply U.S. Air Force with the Canadair CL-44 Airframe," 17 September 1958; message State to Embassy, Ottawa, 6 November 1958.

122. NAC, RG 25 vol. 4499 file 50030-K40 pt. 5, 30 September 1958, POEADQ paper, "Sharing of Production Tasks in North American Defence."

123. Ibid.

124. NAC, MG 32 B9 vol. 22, Black File, 2 December 1958, memo to cabinet, "Joint RCAF-USAF Air Defence Program: Pinetree Extention, SAGE and BOMARC Cost-Sharing."

125. NAC, RG 2, 15 October 1958, Cabinet Conclusions.

126. Ibid.

127. DGHIST, vol. 73/1223 file 2002, Air Officers Commanding Conference, 17–19 March 1959, Foulkes discussion.

128. NAC, RG 2, 15 October 1958, Cabinet Conclusions.

129. Ibid.

130. Ibid.

131. Ibid.

132. DGHIST, Hendrick Papers, Daily Dairy, 27 October 1958.

133. Ibid.

134. Ibid.

135. Ibid.

136. DGHIST, Hendrick Papers, Daily Dairy, 28 October 1958.

137. DGHIST, Hendrick Papers, Daily Dairy, 14 November 1958.

138. Note that the NSC planners did not understand that the BOMARC and Arrow were complementary systems and that Canada was not replacing the CF-105 with BOMARC.

139. USNARA, RG 273, "NSC 5822: Certain Aspects of U.S. Relations with Canada," 12 December 1958.

140. Ibid.

141. NAC, RG 24 vol. 20711 file csc 2-3-2 pt. 6, 15 December 1958, "Draft Statement Regarding the Acquisition and Control of Nuclear Weapons for Possible Use in the House of Commons."

142. Ibid.

143. NAC, RG 24 vol. 20711 file csc 2-3-2 pt. 6, 15 December 1958, "Problems Connected with the Acquisition and Control of Defensive Nuclear Weapons in Canada."

144. USNARA, RG 59 box 3218, file 742.5/12-15-58, message, Dulles to Eisenhower, 15 December 1958.

145. USNARA, RG 273, "Annex to NSC 5822/1: Canadian Access to Nuclear Weapons in Peacetime," 30 December 1958.

146. Ibid.

147. Ibid.

148. Ibid.

149. Ibid.

150. Ibid.

151. NAC, RG 2, 9 December 1958, Cabinet Conclusions.

152. DGHIST, Raymont Collection, file 1310C, 4 April 1959, COSC, 629th meeting.

153. DGHIST, file 79/429 vol. 9, VCAS "Divisional Items of Interest for Week Ending 30 Jan 59."

154. DGHIST, file 79/429 vol. 9, VCAS "Divisional Items of Interest for Week Ending 13 March 59.

155. DGHIST, Raymont Collection, file 1310C, 10 February 1958, COSC, special meeting; 12 February 1958, COSC, special meeting.

156. DGHIST, Raymont Collection, file 1310C, 19 February 1958, COSC, special meeting; Raymont Study, 258–259.

157. DGHIST, Foulkes Papers, Arrow folder 14-2, "The Story of the CF-105 AVRO Arrow, 1952–1962."

158. DGHIST, file 79/333, 26 March 1959, memo, Campbell to Pearkes, "Arrow Cancellation—Disposal of Material."

159. Both Stewart and Campagna note this in their works and the motion picture portrays it in a lavish fashion.

160. DGHIST, Raymont Collection, file 631, 19 August 1958, "Report on the Development of the CF-105 Aircraft and Associated Weapons Systems 1952–1958." See the Hansard extracts attached.

161. The existing literature on the Arrow affair assigns several different reasons for the cancellation. Jon McLin's *Canada's Changing Defence Policy, 1957–1963: The Problems of a Middle Power in Alliance* (Baltimore, MD: Johns Hopkins University Press, 1967, p. 84) states that the project was cancelled due to sheer cost. Murray Peden's *Fall of an Arrow* (Toronto: Stoddart, 1987) agrees that it cost too much, but goes on to state that

this was done to maintain a balanced force structure. Grieg Stewart's *Shutting Down the National Dream: A.V. Roe and the Tragedy of the Avro Arrow* (Toronto: McGraw-Hill Ryerson, 1988) reaches no specific conclusion. E. K. Shaw's *There Never Was An Arrow* (Toronto: Steel Rail Educational Publishing, 1979, p. 124) argues that there was a loss of Canadian confidence it its dealings with the United States coupled with a cultural inferiority complex. This prevented the full realization of the aircraft's potential. Palmiro Campagna's *Storms of Controversy: The Secret Avro Arrow Files Revealed* (Toronto: Stoddart, 1992, pp. 163, 173) presents a convoluted conspiracy thesis that attributes the aircraft's demise to the American's pushing BOMARC as a replacement to the CF-105 or that the CIA deliberately undermined the program since the Arrow could shoot down the U-2 and SR-71 aircraft. James Dow's *The Arrow* (Toronto: James Lorimer, 1979, pp. 140–141) suggests that the problems and costs involved with the weapons system got out of control under both the St. Laurent and Diefenbaker governments and that this was recognized too late and there was not enough money to complete the project.

162. DGHIST, volume 73/1223 file 2002, Air Officers Commanding Conference, March 1958, Campbell discussion.

Chapter 7

1. DGHIST, Raymont Collection, file 1310E, 10 June 1958, COSC, 623rd meeting; NAC, RG 24 vol. 25, file 1200 pt. 2 v. 12, 5 November 1959, APCC, "Surface to Surface Missiles."

2. Marvin L. Worley, Jr., *New Developments in Army Weapons, Tactics, Organization, and Equipment* (Harrisburg, PA: Military Service Publishing, 1958), 8–24.

3. NAC, RG 24 vol. 25, file 1200 pt. 2 v. 12, 5 November 1959, APCC, "Surface to Surface Missiles"; DGHIST, Raymont Collection, file 139, 2 February 1960, memo, Secretary COSC to COSC, "Purchase of Honest John in Lieu of Lacrosse."

4. NAC, RG 24 vol. 25, file 1200 pt. 2 v. 12, 5 November 1959, APCC, "Surface to Surface Missiles."

5. DGHIST, file G8467-9/13, 14 March 1960, memo to the Cabinet Defence Committee, "Procurement of 762mm Rocket (Honest John) in Lieu of Lacrosse"; 25 March 1960, record of Cabinet Defence Committee Decision, "Procurement of 762mm Rocket (Honest John) in Lieu of Lacrosse"; UVIC, Pearkes Papers, 18 February 1971, "Interview with Lt-Gen S.F. Clark."

6. DGHIST, Raymont Collection, file 1310E, 20 January 1958, COSC, 616th meeting.

7. Ibid.

8. DGHIST, file 112.012 (D1), 1 January 1958, "Canada–United States Future Defence Analysis MCC 600/2."

9. Ibid.

10. NAC, RG 24 vol. 112 file 096 107.4 v. 1, 30 January 1958, memo, De Wolfe to Foulkes, "Co-Ordinated Canada–United States Defence of North America Against Submarines"; DGHIST, file 112.3M2.009 (D 260), 8 January 1958, "Extract from minutes of the 615th Meeting of the COSC."

11. NAC, RG 24 vol. 130 file 098.108, "Maritime Commander Atlantic Emergency Defence Plan—1958."

12. Ibid.

13. Ibid.

14. DGHIST, 17 July 1958, Naval Board Minutes, 573rd meeting; NAC, RG 24 vol. 8161 file 1660-78, 26 February 1958, "Report on REGSUBEX, 10–13 Sep 57."

15. W. M. Diggle, "Evolution of the Argus," *Roundel* (May 1958): 2–32; DGHIST, file R A/C C, n.d., Canadair sales pamphlet, "Argus MK II Maritime Patrol Aircraft"; DGHIST, file R A/C/ C, n.d., "Argus Statistics."

16. ATI, 25 July 1958, aide memoir for the Chief of the Air Staff, "Requirements for Nuclear Weapons."

17. Hansen, *U.S. Nuclear Weapons*, 207–208; USN OA, "CinCLANTFLEET Annual Report 1 July 1958–30 June 1959."

18. Hansen, *U.S. Nuclear Weapons*, 207–208; USN OC, "Report of the Commander-in-Chief U.S. Atlantic Fleet Upon Being Relieved, period 1 July 1959–29 February 1960."

19. ATI, February 1959, "Special Weapons Requirements for Maritime Warfare."

20. Ibid.

21. Ibid.

22. DGHIST, Raymont Collection, file 184, 17 November 1955, "A Paper on the Control and Operation of Helicopters in the Canadian Services"; 10 April 1959, memo to COSC, "Helicopters for Antisubmarine Warfare."

23. DGHIST, Raymont Collection, file 184, 9 September 1959, "Staff Characteristics for an Escort Borne ASW Helicopter."

24. Al Adcock, *H-3 Sea King in Action* (Carrollton, TX: Squadron Signal Publications, 1995), 7.

25. USNARA, RG 218 JCS 1959 vol. 5162 file CINCLANT, 1959, message, CinCLANT to JCS, 12 February 1959.

26. Ibid.

27. ATI, 1 May 1959, memo, Bean to Campbell, "Special Weapons: RCN/RCAF ASW Requirements"; 28 May 1959, memo, Bean to Campbell, "Special Weapons Requirements for Maritime Warfare."

28. USN OA, "Annual Report CinCLANTFLEET 1 July 1958–30 June 1959"; "Report of the Commander in Chief U.S. Atlantic Fleet Upon Being Relieved, Period 1 July 1959–29 February 1960."

29. ATI, 27 July 1967, agreement signed between Adm. T. H. Moorer, USN and Air Marshal F. R. Sharp, RCAF, "Canadian Forces–United States Navy Supplementary Arrangement for United States Naval Forces At A Base in Canada"; NSA, "Report of the Command in Chief of the U.S. Atlantic Fleet Upon Being Relieved Period 1 July 1962–30 April 1963."

30. PRO DEFE 6, 8 November 1957, JPS, "SACEUR's Emergency Defence Plan 1958."

31. Chuck Yaeger and Leo Janos, *Yeager*, 304–305.

32. Robert Jackson, *Strike Force: The USAF in Britain Since 1948* (London: Robson Books, 1988), chap. 5; Tom Compere, ed., *The Air Force Blue Book: The USAF Yearbook; Volume I* (New York: Military Publishing Institute, 1959), 310–311.

33. NSA, memo SHAPE to distribution list, "Public Information Policy: EX FULL PLAY," 26 April 1958.

34. NAC, RG 49 (DDP) vol. 708 file 247-5 vol. 4, 25 July 1958, POEADQ, meeting.

35. DGHIST, Raymont Collection, file 25/8 vol. 1, 23 October 1958, POEADQ, 59th meeting; 6 August 1958, 56th meeting; 3 December 1958, 60th meeting.

36. DGHIST, Raymont Collection, file 1310C, 26 January 1959, COSC, special meeting.

37. DGHIST, Raymont Collection, file 1310C, 5 February 1959, COSC, special meeting.

38. DGHIST, vol. 73/1223 file 2002, "Minutes of a Conference of Air Officers Commanding and Air Officers Held in the Air Council Room at Air Force Headquarters, Ottawa 17 to 19 March 1959."

39. Ibid.

40. Ibid.

41. Ibid.

42. NAC, RG 24 vol. 18149 file 981.101.87 vol. 1, 1 April 1959, "Operational Characteristic for a Strike/Attack Aircraft."

43. NAC, MG 32 B9 vol. 82, 30 March 1963, memo, G. P. G. Reid to Minister of National Defence.

44. NAC, RG 2, 19 June 1959, Cabinet Conclusions.

45. Ibid.

46. NAC, RG 2, 2 July 1959, Cabinet Conclusions; DGHIST, Raymont Collection, file 1310C, 30 June 1959, COSC, 639th meeting.

47. DDEL, Norstad Papers, box 49 file: Canada (2), "Excerpt from a Statement Made in the House of Commons on Thursday, 2 July 1959 by the Canadian Minister of National Defence Concerning the Re-equipping of the First Canadian Air Division."

48. Hans-Jurgan Becker, *Flugzeuge die Geschichte machen Starfighter F-104* (Stuttgart: Motorbuch Verlag, 1992), chap. 4.

49. Milberry, *Canadair Sabre*, 285–314.

50. DGHIST, Raymont Collection, file 1311, 23 September 1959, "Meeting of Minister of National Defence and Associate Minister of National Defence and Chiefs of Staff with the West German Minister of Defence, the German Ambassador to Canada, and Staffs."

51. NAC, RG 24 vol. L280 file 1038-110 F-104G, 16 December 1960, message Canadian Embassy, Bonn to External, Ottawa, "Proposed Special Mission to Europe on Cooperation on the F-104G Programme."

52. Phillip Fiddell, *F-104 Starfighter in Action* (Carrollton, TX: Squadron/Signal Publications, 1993), 4–22.

53. Fiddell, *F-104 Starfighter in Action*, 37.

54. DGHIST, Air Council minutes, 5 August 1959, "Operational Characteristics for a Strike/ Recce Aircraft."

55. DGHIST, Air Council minutes, 13 July 1960, "Operational Requirements Status Report on Armament and Recce Equipments of the CF-104."

56. Brigadier General Herb Sutherland, interview with the author, Ottawa, 15 January 1992.

57. NAC, RG 24 vol. 6280 file 1035-110-F104G, 26 October 1960, "Supporting Data for Air Council Meeting: Meeting at AIRCENT on F-104 Aircraft."

58. Ibid.

59. NAC, RG 24 vol. 6280 file 1035-110-F104G, 25 November 1960, "Minutes of the F. 104 Co-ordination Meeting Held at AIRCENT on 8 November 1960."

60. Hansen, *U.S. Nuclear Weapons*, 164.

61. NAC, RG 24 vol. 6280 file 1035-110-F104G, 28 May 1962, message, SACEUR to RCAF.

62. DGHIST, Air Council minutes, 26 October 1960, "CF-104 Programme-Bullpup Missiles."

Chapter 8

1. DGHIST, Raymont Collection, file 1332, 22 April 1959, Cabinet Defence Committee.

2. Ibid.

3. NAC, MG 26 N2, Pearson Papers, vol. 112. file: National Defence Debate Material (3), 25 May 1959, "Notes for Statement by the Prime Minister in the House of Commons of the Agreement with the United States for Co-operation on the Uses of Atomic Energy for Mutual Defence Purposes."

4. USNARA, RG 59 box 3219, message, Willoughby to Merchant, "Proposed Revision of MB-1 Overflight Agreement with Canada," 17 March 1959.

5. USNARA, RG 59 box 3219, memo to Mr. Parker, "Revision of MB-1 Overflight Agreement," 6 February 1959.

6. Hilliker and Barry, *Canada's Department of External Affairs*, 2:148–150.

7. UVIC, Pearkes Papers, "Interview with General Charles Foulkes, June 5, 1967."

8. USNARA, RG 59 E 3077 250/62/30/3 box 1, file: Basic Policy: Canada 1.15, memcon Heeney and Armstrong, 29 August 1960.

9. Ibid.

10. Ibid.
11. George Kitching, *Mud and Green Fields* (St. Catherines: Vanwell Publishing, 1993), 274.
12. Hilliker and Barry, *Canada's Department of External Affairs*, 2:148–151.
13. USNARA, RG 59 E 3077 250/62/30/3 box 1, file: NATO 1959-62 3/A, memcon W. H. Barton and Rufus Z. Smith, "NATO Ministerial Meeting in Oslo," 22 May 1961.
14. USNARA, RG 59 E 3077 250/62/30/3 box 1, file: Nationalism, Neutrality, Anti-Americanism 1960–62 1.14, memo, Tyler to McGhee, "Canadian Nationalism," 9 March 1962.
15. USNARA, RG 59 E3077 box 1, vol. 250/62/30/3 file: NATO, memo, Byrnes to Parker, "Recent Instances of Canadian Opposition to U.S. Positions in NATO," 21 May 1959.
16. DGHIST, Hendrick Papers, Daily Dairy, 19 June 1959.
17. NAC, MG 32 B9 vol. 24 file 151-200/60, 30 June 1959, diplomatic note, Herter to Heeney; 22 June 1960, memo to cabinet, "MB-1 Overflight Agreement"; DGHIST, Hendrick Papers, Daily Dairy, 24 June 1959.
18. NAC, MG 30 E144 vol.1 file: U.S.-Ambassador to Washington, 30 June 1959, memo for file, "Conversation with the Minister (Mr. Green)."
19. Ibid.
20. Ibid.
21. Harrison, *Reluctant Ally*, 121, 135; DDRS, 1978 frame 74 C & D, state department study, "France and NATO," 25 September 1965.
22. U.S. DOS, *FRUS 1958–1960 Vol. VII Part 1*, p. 759, memcon, "Secretary's Conversations in Ottawa," 11 July 1959.
23. DGHIST, Hendrick Papers, Daily Dairy, 8 July 1959.
24. B. Robinson, *Diefenbaker's World*, 108.
25. Harrison, *Reluctant Ally*, 51.
26. Note that "Fail Safe" is a different concept from the later "Airborne Alert" concept, though the movie *Fail Safe* confuses the two. The movie *Dr. Strangelove* correctly identifies the activity depicted in the movie as Airborne Alert. See also Scott D. Sagan, *The Limits of Safety* (Princeton: Princeton University Press, 1994), 163–164.
27. DGHIST, Arnell Papers, 3 June 1958, memo, Foulkes to Pearkes, "USAF Flights Carrying Nuclear Weapons Overflying Canadian Territory."
28. Ibid.
29. DGHIST, Raymont Collection, file 2006, 19 March 1959, "Address by General Charles Foulkes to Air Officers Commanding Conference."
30. There were continual Ferret operations throughout the 1940s and 1950s that sometimes resulted in shootdowns of American and British aircraft. One of the more spectacular missions involved the simultaneous night penetration of the Soviet Union by three RB-45s wearing RAF markings. These aircraft were conducting radar mapping operations for SAC and V-Force navigation. There were, of course, the U-2 missions that started in July 1956. See Ben R. Rich and Leo Janos, *Skunk Works* (New York: Little Brown., 1994), 145–147; James Bamford, *The Puzzle Palace* (New York: Penguin Books, 1983), 232–245; Paul Lashmare, "Skullduggery at Sculthorpe," *Aeroplane Monthly*, October 1994, 10–15.
31. See the BBC documentary program "TimeWatch" episode entitled "Spies in the Sky" which aired on 9 February 1994.
32. R. Cargill Hall, "The Truth About Overflights," *Military History Quarterly* 9, no. 3 (Spring 1997): 25–38.
33. DGHIST, Arnell Papers, 3 June 1958, memo, Foulkes to Pearkes, "USAF Flights Carrying Nuclear Weapons Overflying Canadian Territory."
34. ATI, NORAD has, unfortunately, divested itself of the pre-1978 Soviet penetration of North American airspace statistics.

35. NAC, MG 32 B 19, vol. 11 file 15-90, 2 September 1958, memo, CAS to MND, "RCAF Reconnaissance Mission"; 28 August 1958, memo, director of air intelligence to CAS, "APEX ROCKET—408 Squadron." RG 25 at NAC has several still-classified files relating to this and similar operations.

36. USNARA, RG 59 box 3219, n.d., "Proposed Press Release—Operation SKY HAWK."

37. USNARA, RG 59 box 3219, memo, Dale to White, "NORAD-SAC Exercise, "Operation SKY HAWK," 12 August 1959.

38. DGHIST, Hendrick Papers, Daily Dairy, 28 August 1959; USNARA, RG 59 box 3219, message, Embassy Ottawa to State, 3 September 1959.

39. USNARA, RG 59 box 3219, memo, Byrns to Rewinkel, "Proposed Press Release for Operation SKY HAWK," 4 September 1959.

40. U.S. DOS, *FRUS 1958–1960 Vol. VII Part 1*, p. 765, message, Wigglesworth to State, 29 August 1959.

41. U.S. DOS, *FRUS 1958–1960 Vol. VII Part 1*, p. 767, message, Eisenhower to Diefenbaker, 1 September 1959.

42. U.S. DOS, *FRUS 1958–1960 Vol. VII Part 1*, p. 768, message, Diefenbaker to Eisenhower, 6 September 1959.

43. DGHIST, Hendrick Papers, Daily Dairy, 2 September 1959; 16 September 1959; USNARA, RG 59 box 3219, n.d., letter, Murphy to Twining.

44. USNARA, RG 59 box 3219, letter, Merchant to Wigglesworth, 30 October 1959.

45. DGHIST, Raymont Collection, file 1310C, 7 July 1959, COSC, 641st meeting; 16 July 1959, 642nd meeting; 23 July 1959, 643rd meeting; 24 July 1959, 644th meeting.

46. NAC, RG 2, 22 September 1959, Cabinet Conclusions; DGHIST, Raymont Collection, file 996, 2 October 1959, message, External to Washington, DC, "Storage of Defensive Nuclear Weapons at Goose Bay and Harmon Air Force Base."

47. NAC, MG 32 B9, vol. 24 file 51-100/60, 2 March 1960, memo to cabinet, "Storage of Air-to-Air Defensive Nuclear Weapons at Goose Bay and Harmon Air Force Base."

48. DGHIST, Hendrick Papers, Daily Dairy, 18 November 1959.

49. USNARA, RG 59 box 3219, message, Paris to Ottawa, 24 September 1959; DGHIST, Hendrick Papers, Daily Dairy, 24 September 1959.

50. DGHIST, Hendrick Papers, Daily Dairy, 12 November 1959.

51. USNARA, RG 59 box 3219, memcon, "Suggestions for Improving Politico-Military Relations with Canada," 20 October 1959. Notably, State was unimpressed with the ad hoc nature of existing consultation measures and wanted to place more emphasis on the PJBD instead.

52. USNARA, RG 59 box 3219, message Ottawa to State, "Some Canadian Thoughts on United States—Canadian Defence Arrangements," 13 October 1959.

53. NAC, RG 24 vol. 20711 csc 2-3-2 pt. 6, 29 October 1959, "Storage of Nuclear Weapons in Canada."

54. USNARA, RG 59 box 3219, "Summary Record of the Meeting November 8–9, 1959 Camp David, Maryland."

55. USNARA, RG 59 box 3219, "Summary Record of the Meeting November 8–9, 1959 Camp David, Maryland."

56. DGHIST, Hendrick Papers, 9 November 1959, "Canada-U.S. Ministerial Meeting."

57. Ibid.

58. Ibid.; USNARA, RG 59 box 3219, "Summary Record of the Meeting November 8–9, 1959 Camp David, Maryland."

59. Ibid.

60. Ibid.

61. Ibid.

62. Ibid.

63. Ibid.

64. Ibid.

65. Ibid.

66. B. Robinson, *Diefenbaker's World*, 113–114.

67. NAC, RG 2 vol. 2752 file D-1-6-D 1960-61-62, 7 December 1959, "Draft of Proposed Agreement with the United States on the Acquisition of Nuclear Warheads for Canadian Forces."

68. Ibid.

69. Roy, *For Most Conspicuous Bravery*, 342; B. Robinson, *Diefenbaker's World*, 113–114.

70. Polmar, *Strategic Air Command*, 49–50; Jackson, *Strike Force*, 83, 89–90.

71. USNARA, RG 59 box 3219, memo to file, "SAC Canadian Overflights," 26 November 1957.

72. USNARA, RG 59 box 3219, memo to file, "Canadian Overflight," 1 March 1957.

73. USNARA, RG 59 box 3219, memo to file, "NN Canada—Operational Requests," 28 May 1957.

74. USNARA, RG 59 box 3219, letter, Irwin to Murphy, 25 October 1957; letter, Murphy to Sprague, 12 October 1957.

75. DGHIST, Raymont Collection, file 1085, 12 May 1958, memo for the CDC, "USAF Requirement for Refuelling Facilities in Canada."

76. DGHIST, Raymont Collection, file 1085, 21 March 1958, memo Miller to Campbell, "Air Defence of Refuelling Bases"; 30 April 1958, Aide Memoir on Aerial Refuelling Bases.

77. DGHIST, Raymont Collection, file 1085, 12 May 1958, memo for the CDC, "USAF Requirement for Refuelling Facilities in Canada."

78. DGHIST, Raymont Collection, file 1086, 26 May 1958, "Chief of Staff Views on USAF Refuelling Facilities in Canada."

79. Ibid.

80. DGHIST, Raymont Collection, file 1086, 14 May 1958, letter, CoS Ops USAF to CAS, "Aerial Refuelling Base Requirements in Canada."

81. DGHIST, Raymont Collection, file 1085, 7 March 1958, letter, Sparling to Twining.

82. DGHIST, Raymont Collection, file 1086, 23 August 1958, message, JCS to COSC; 20 June 1958, letter, Leger to Merchant.

83. NAC, RG 24 vol. 549 file 096103.v.3, 20 October 1958, memo, USAF CCS to CAS; 19 May 1959, message, Commander, Northern NORAD Region to distribution list, "Orbit and Dispersal Evacuation of SAC Aircraft."

84. NAC, RG 24 vol. 549 file 096103.v.3, 19 May 1959, message, Commander, Northern NORAD Region to distribution list, "Orbit and Dispersal Evacuation of SAC Aircraft."

85. NAC, RG 24 vol. 549 file 096103.v.3, 24 October 1958, memo, CPlansI to VCAS, "SAC Hostile Action Evacuation Plan."

86. Scott D. Sagan, *Limits of Safety*, 118–119; Schaffel, *Emerging Shield*, 258–260.

87. USASK, Diefenbaker Papers, reel 26, 6 June 1959, "Background Information on Voice Transmission Via the Moon for the Opening of the PARL"; 6 June 1959, "Press Release." Note that Eisenhower and Diefenbaker once conducted a radio conversation that was relayed from Washington, DC to Millstone Hill, Massachusetts, PARL, and then Ottawa. This was done to officially open PARL.

88. NAC, RG 24 acc 83-84/167, vol. 7407, file 173-1 pt. 3, 30 October 1964, "Summary of Activities for [DRB] Meeting."

89. Schaffel, *Emerging Shield*, 258–260.

90. DGHIST, Raymont Collection, file 1332, 28 April 1958, 117th CDC meeting.

91. See Kevin C. Ruffner, ed., *CORONA: America's First Satellite Program* (Washington, DC: CIA History Staff, 1995).

92. Curtis Peebles, *Guardians: Strategic Reconaissance Satellites* (Novato, CA: Presidio Press, 1987), 306.

93. NAC, RG 24 acc 83-84/167 vol. 7407 file 173-1 pt. 1, 24 June 1958, memo to COSC, "Defence Research Board Meeting."

94. NSA, US DOD, Office of the Director of Defence Research and Engineering, "Report No. 10: Military Space Projects March-April-May 1960."

95. Peebles, *Guardians*, 309–312. There were several follow-on projects, one of which was the 1970s DSP infrared detection satellite.

96. "Inuvik is the Place of Man," *Sentinel*, November–December 1970, 22–23; NAC, MG 32 B19 vol. 35 file 54-204, 27 April 1961, "Alert Wireless Station"; 14 April 1959, memo, Miller to Starnes; memo, Clark to Harkness, "U.S. Army Northern Operations—1960"; See also Larry Clark, *Doomsday Minus Four: Nuclear Brinksmanship and Beyond in the Canadian North* (Toronto: Douglas and McIntyre, 1981); Mike Frost and Michel Gratton, *Spyworld: Inside the Canadian and American Intelligence Establishments* (Toronto: Doubleday Canada Inc., 1994).

97. NAC, RG 24 vol. 549 file 096-103 v.1, 10 May 1955, HQ 64th Air Division, "Air Defence Warnings, Military Emergency and Conditions of Air Defence Preparedness."

98. Ibid; NAC, RG 24 vol. 549 file 096-103 v.3, 30 December 1957, memo, ADO-2 to DADO, "Alert Systems"; 21 July 1955, memo, AoC ADC to CAS, "Air Defence Alerting Responsibilities."

99. These were early American nuclear weapon control arrangements that were dispensed with by 1957–58.

100. ATI, "DND War Book: Fourth Draft, 18 October 1955."

101. Ibid.

102. NAC, RG 24 vol. 549 file 096-103 v.3, 30 December 1957, memo, ADO-2 to DADO, "Alert Systems"; NAC, RG 24 vol. 549 file 096-103 v.4, 5 May 1959, JPC, "Canadian Forces States of Military Vigilance;" USNARA, RG 218 JCS 1959 file 9050/3203, J-5 report, "NATO Alert System MC 67/1," 23 July 1959.

103. USNARA, RG 218 JCS 1957 file CCS 354.2 U.S., 12 April 1957, message, Chief of Ops to SECDEF and JCS, "Report of May Exercise of JCS Emergency Telephone Conference," 24 June 1957; memo, JCS to CNO, "Alert Exercise 31 May 1957," 27 May 1957; SECDEF to JCS, "Results Obtained from Ex. DODEP, 12 April 1957."

104. USNARA, RG 59 box 3218, letter, Heeney to Murphy, 18 January 1957; NAC, RG 24 vol. 112 file 096 107.4 v.1, 28 April 1958, memo to CDC, "Canada-U.S. Bilateral Arrangements with Respect to the Declaration of an Alert."

105. USNARA, RG 59 box 3218, memcon, "Proposed Coordination of U.S.-Canadian Alert Arrangements," 1 March 1957; letter, Dulles to Heeney, 1 March 1957; letter, Dulles staff to Sprague, 25 March 1957; letter, Sprague to Murphy, 9 May 1957.

106. USNARA, RG 59 box 3218, letter, Murphy to Heeney, 8 May 1957.

107. NAC, RG 24 vol. 549 file 096-103 v.2, 2 April 1957, memo, CAS to AoC ADC, "Air Defence Emergency Information to and from UK and Europe."

108. USNARA, RG 59 box 3218, message Ottawa to State, 10 July 1957.

109. NAC, RG 24 vol. 112 file 096 107.4 v.1, 28 April 1958, memo to CDC, "Canada-U.S. Bilateral Arrangements with Respect to the Declaration of an Alert."

110. Telecon with Bruce Blair, 18 July 1997.

111. Dwight D. Eisenhower, *Waging Peace: The White House Years 1956–1961* (Garden City, NY: Doubleday, 1965), 275–276; Alexander L. George and Richard Smoke, *Deterrence in American Foreign Policy: Theory and Practice* (New York: Columbia University Press, 1974), 309–310.

112. Confidential discussion with senior RCAF officer.

113. Attempts by the NORAD history office to track this down have come up with nothing.

114. USNARA, RG 59 box 3218, message, Ottawa to State, 22 July 1958.

115. Ibid.

116. Diefenbaker, *One Canada: Memoirs*, 90.

117. UVIC, Pearkes Papers, Foulkes interview, 9 March 1967.

118. Ibid.

119. USNARA, RG 59 box 3218, message, Ottawa to State, 4 September 1958; message, State to Ottawa, 10 September 1958; Diefenbaker, *One Canada: Memoirs*, 90.

120. DGHIST, Raymont Collection, file 1340, 9 December 1958, record of cabinet decision.

121. NAC, RG 24 vol. 549 file 096 103 v.3, "Extract from Chiefs of Staff Committee Meeting Held 15 Jan 59."

122. Ibid.

123. NAC, RG 24 vol. 549 file 096 103 v.3, 23 December 1958, JPC to COSC, "Canadian Forces States of Increased Military Vigilance."

124. Ibid.

125. NAC, RG 24 vol. 549 file 096 103 v.3, 24 April 1961, "Supporting Data for Air Council: Standardization of Alert Systems."

126. NAC, RG 24 vol. 549 file 096 103 v.3, n.d., "Conditions of Readiness and States of Alert."

127. DGHIST, Raymont Collection, file 34, 6 April 1959, letter, LePan to Foulkes, "Contingency Planning for Berlin." See also Sean M. Maloney, "Berlin Contingency Planning: Prelude to Flexible Response, 1958–1963," *MilitarGeschichte*, Spring 1997.

128. USNARA, RG 59 box 3219, State Department aide—Memoire, 29 April 1959.

129. USNARA, RG 59 box 3219, memcon, "CinCNORAD—Authority to Increase the State of Readiness of NORAD Forces," 15 April 1959; memo, Merchant to Murphy, "CinCNORAD's Authority to Increase Readiness of Forces Under His Operational Control," 23 April 1959; memcon, "Request for Canadian Concurrence to Increase Operational Readiness of NORAD Forces in Event Western Powers are Denied Access to Berlin," 29 April 1959.

130. USNARA, RG 59 box 3219, letter, Shuff to Murphy, 12 May 1959; memo to files, "CinCNORAD Authority to Increase States of Readiness of NORAD Forces," 13 May 1959.

131. USNARA, RG 59 box 3219, memcon, "U.S. Proposal for Canadian Concurrence to Increase Operation Readiness of NORAD Forces in Event Western Powers are Denied Access to Berlin," 26 May 1959.

132. USNARA, RG 59 box 3219, letter, Heeney to Herter, 30 September 1959.

133. Scott Sagan, "Nuclear Alerts," in Lynn-Jones et al., eds., *Nuclear Diplomacy and Crisis Management* (Cambridge, MA: MIT Press, 1990), 160–161.

134. These included CinCPAC, CinCLANT (who was also NATO SACLANT) CinCEUR, CinCCONAD (who was also CinCNORAD), CinCSAC, CinCNELM, and CinCAL[aska]. SACEUR, though an American officer, reported to the NAC.

135. NAC, RG 24 vol. 109 file 096.105.6, 19 January 1960, memo, CJSM(W) to CAS, "Emergency Action, JCS"; 3 December 1959, memo for the JCS, "Agenda for JCS Emergency Conference."

136. USN OA, Strategic Plans Division, box 315, chart, "HF Radio AJCC to Overseas Commands."

137. Jacob Neufeld, *Ballistic Missiles in the United States Air Force 1945–1960* (Washington, DC: Office of Air Force History, 1990), 233–237.

138. DGHIST, Raymont Collection, file 941, 13 June 1958, memo, CAS to COSC, "USAF ICBM Sites"; 6 March 1958, memo, CAS to COSC, "USAF ICBM Sites."

139. Sagan, *Limits of Safety*, 163; Thomas Power, *Design for Survival* (New York: Pocket Books, 1965), 142–143.

140. DDRS, frame 77 286 A and B, n.d., presidential national security notebook, "Airborne Alert Tests"; USNARA, RG 59 box 3219, letter, Rae to Courtney, 11 September 1958; memo, Farley to SECSTATE, "Strategic Air Command Exercise HEADSTART," 13 September 1958.

141. USNARA, RG 59 box 3219, letter, Rae to Courtney, 11 September 1958.

142. USNARA, RG 218, memo, CoS USAF to JCS, "SAC Exercise STEEL TRAP," 24 July 1959; RG 59 box 3219, letter, Murphy to Heeney, 24 July 1959.

143. USNARA, RG 59 box 3219, memcon, "Request for Clearance of SAC Exercise 'Airborne Alert' under the "XYZ Procedures," 13 February 1959.

144. USNARA, RG 59 box 3219, memcon, "SAC Overflights," 9 March 1959.

145. USNARA, RG 59 box 3219, letter, Farley to Murphy, "SAC Airborne Alert Exercise," 6 April 1959.

146. USNARA, RG 59 box 3219, diplomatic note, Heeney to State, 9 July 1959.

147. USNARA, RG 218, memo, CoS USAF to JCS, "SAC Exercise STEEL TRAP," 24 July 1959; Hansen, *U.S. Nuclear Weapons*, 154–157.

148. USNARA, RG 59 box 3219, letter, Willoughby to Merchant, "Proposed Revision of XYZ Procedures Governing Nuclear Overflights of Canada in Other Than Interception Missions," 17 March 1959.

149. USNARA, RG 59 box 3219, diplomatic note, Heeney to State, 12 October 1959.

150. NAC, RG 2, 29 March 1960; 2 June 1960, Cabinet Conclusions.

151. Sagan, *Limits of Safety*, 194.

152. NSA, memo, McNamara to JCS, "Strategic Air Command Airborne Alert Plan (CHROME DOME)," 16 August 1961.

153. Sagan, *Limits of Safety*, 194.

Chapter 9

1. UVIC, Pearkes Papers, Foulkes interview, 9 March 1967. Diefenbaker cut Commissioner Nicholson's pension by 20% when he retired because of a previous dispute over the use of the RCMP for riot control in Newfoundland.

2. NAC, RG 2, 12 January 1960, Cabinet Conclusions.

3. UVIC, Pearkes Papers, Foulkes interview, 9 March 1967.

4. Ibid.

5. DGHIST, Raymont Collection, file 2005, "Address by General Charles Foulkes to the Air Officers Commanding Conferences," 19 March 1959.

6. Ibid.

7. Ibid.

8. Ibid.; DGHIST, Raymont Collection, file 2005, "Address by General Charles Foulkes to the Air Officers Commanding Conferences, 19 March 1959."

9. USASK, Diefenbaker Papers, vol. 53, 6 January 1960, memo, Pearkes to Prime Minister.

10. Ibid.

11. USASK, Diefenbaker Papers, vol. 53, 11 January 1960, memo, Pearkes to Prime Minister.

12. Ibid.

13. Ibid.

14. NAC, RG 2, 12 January 1960, Cabinet Conclusions.

15. USASK, Diefenbaker Papers, vol. 53, 13 January 1960, memo, Bryce to Prime Minister.

16. NAC, RG 2, 13 January 1960, Cabinet Conclusions.

17. Ibid.

18. DGHIST, Raymont Collection, file 309, 18 January 1960, *Hansard* extract.

19. See McLin, *Canada's Changing Defence Policy*, 138.

20. DGHIST, Raymont Collection, file 309, 9 February 1960, *Hansard* extract.

21. DGHIST, Raymont Collection, file 1309B, 21 January 1960, COSC, 654th meeting.

22. That is, two engines were needed for redundancy. The CF-104 only had one.

23. DGHIST, Raymont Collection, file 1309B, 28 January 1960, COSC, 655th meeting.

24. Ibid.

25. NAC, RG 2, 4 February 1960; 8 March 1960, Cabinet Conclusions.

26. DGHIST, Raymont Collection, file 2008, "Shorthand Transcript 1960 AOsC Conference."

27. Ibid.

28. Ibid.

29. Ibid.

30. Douglas, *Creation of a National Airforce*, 476; Larry Milberry, *Sixty Years: The RCAF and CF Air Command 1924–1984* (Toronto: McGraw-Hill Ryerson, 1984), 427.

31. DGHIST, Raymont Collection, file 2008, "Shorthand Transcript 1960 AOsC Conference."

32. Ibid.

33. Ibid.

34. Ibid.

35. Ibid.

36. Ibid.

37. Ibid.

38. Knowlton Nash, *Kennedy and Diefenbaker: The Feud That Helped Topple a Government* (Toronto: McClelland and Stewart, 1990), 145–146; Paul Hellyer notes on p. 28 of his work *Damn the Torpedoes: My Fight to Unify Canada's Armed Forces* (Toronto: McClelland and Stewart, 1990) that Bill Lee was a graduate of the USAF public relations school.

39. USASK, Diefenbaker Papers, vol. 45, 28 September 1962, letter, Andras to Diefenbaker, and attached memo.

40. U.S. DOS, *FRUS 1958–1960 Vol. VII*, 790–791, memcon, "BOMARC Program," 14 April 1960.

41. U.S. DOS, *FRUS 1958–1960 Vol. VII*, 793–795, memcon, Eisenhower and Foulkes, 9 May 1960.

42. Ibid.

43. NAC, MG 32 B19 vol. 12 file 15–120, 16 May 1960, memo, Campbell to Pearkes, "U.S. Increased Readiness"; NAC, RG 2, 16–17 May 1960, Cabinet Conclusions; Michael R. Beschloss, *May Day: Eisenhower, Khurshchev, and the U-2 Affair* (New York: Harper and Row, 1986), 281.

44. NAC, RG 2, 14 May 1960, Cabinet Conclusions.

45. NAC, RG 2, 16 May 1960, Cabinet Conclusions.

46. NAC, RG 25, vol. 4501 file 50030-k-2-40 pt. 1, 31 May 1960, POEADQ, 65th meeting.

47. Ibid.

48. Ibid.

49. Ibid.

50. USNARA, RG 59 E3077 box 1, file: Amb. Wigglesworth 1960 1-A-2, memo, Wigglesworth to Willoughby, 31 March 1960.

51. U.S. DOS, *FRUS 1958–1960 Vol. VII*, 797–799, memorandum of discussion at the 446th meeting of the National Security Council.

52. Ibid.

53. U.S. DOS, *FRUS 1958–1960 Vol. VII*, 801–807, memcon, "Meeting with Prime Minister Diefenbaker," 3 June 1960.

54. Louis Henkin, ed. *Arms Control: Issues for the Public* (Englewood Cliffs, NJ: Prentice-Hall, 1961), 42–45.

55. Canada, France, Great Britain, Italy, the United States, Bulgaria, Czechoslovakia, Poland, Romania, and the USSR were the members. This was not a UN organization, though it did send material to the UN Secretary General.

56. Albert Legault and Michel Fortmann, *A Diplomacy of Hope: Canada and Disarmament, 1945–1988* (Kingston: McGill-Queen's University Press, 1992), 170.

57. See Granatstein, *Generals*, 116–144.

58. See Granatstein, *Man of Influence*, 333; Legault and Fortmann, *Diplomacy of Hope*, 178–180.

59. For more on Burns's views, see his work *Megamurder* (Toronto: Clarke, Irwin, 1966), particularly pp. 2–3, 150–151, 241.

60. DGHIST, Raymont Collection, file 1309B, 6 May 1960, COSC, 661st meeting.

61. Legault and Fortmann, *Diplomacy of Hope*, 184.

62. This was in fact based on the 1958 Rapacki Plan, a Polish attempt (read: Soviet attempt) to reduce NATO's nuclear advantage while the Soviets still held the conventional advantage.

63. Legault and Fortmann, *Diplomacy of Hope*, 162.

64. Ibid., 187.

65. Ibid.

66. Ibid., 187–188.

67. Arthur H. Dean, *Test Ban and Disarmament: The Path of Negotiation* (New York: Harper and Row, 1966), 23.

68. USNARA, RG 59 E3077 box 1 250/62/30/3 file: Ottawa 1962 1A, letter, Smith to Carlson, 21 February 1962.

69. NAC, MG 32 B9 vol. 24, file 202-250/60, 24 June 1960, memo to Cabinet, "Nuclear Weapons Policy."

70. Ibid.

71. Ibid.

72. DGHIST, Hendrick Papers, "Canada–United States Ministerial Committee on Joint Defence, 12 and 13 July 1960."

73. Ibid.

74. Ibid.

75. Ibid.

76. Ibid.

77. Ibid.

78. USNARA, RG 59 E3077 250/62/30/3 box 1 file: Basic Policy: CDN 1.15, memcon, Heeney and Armstrong, 29 August 1960.

79. NAC, RG 2, 14 July 1960, Cabinet Conclusions.

80. NAC, RG 2, 15 July 1960; 9 August 1960; 12 August 1960; 17 August 1960; 21 September 1960, Cabinet Conclusions. The Congo operation was a peripheral operation outside the NATO area but conducted in support of a NATO ally (Belgium) to prevent the Soviets and Chinese from exploiting the power vacuum left by the withdrawing Belgians.

81. McLin, *Canada's Changing Defence Policy*, 153–154.

82. NAC, MG 30 E144 file: United States Ambassador to Washington memoranda and correspondence, 23 September 1960, memcon, Herter, Heeney, and Green.

83. Ibid.

84. Ibid.

85. U.S. DOS, *FRUS 1958–1960 Vol. VII*, 609–611, memcon, Eisenhower and Norstad, 3 August 1960.

86. See Robert R. Bowie, *Nuclear History Program Occasional Paper 7: The North Atlantic Nations Tasks for the 1960's* (College Park, MD: University of Maryland Center for International Security Studies, 1991).

87. Ibid., xv.

88. Ibid., xix.

89. U.S. DOS, *FRUS 1958–1960 Vol. VII*, 611–614, memcon, Eisenhower, Bowie, and Goodpaster, 16 August 1960.

90. Ibid.

91. U.S. DOS, *FRUS 1958–1960 Vol. VII*, 628–632, memcon, Eisenhower, Bowie, Norstad, and Goodpaster, 12 September 1960.

92. USNARA, RG 218 JCS 1960 NATO file 9050/3000, memo, Secretary JCS to SECDEF, "NATO Long Range Planning," 28 October 1960.

93. Ibid.

94. DDEL, Norstad Papers, information released under mandatory review, memo, Stoessel to SECSTATE, 28 July 1961; DGHIST, file 112.1.003 (D13), 15 November 1960, memo to COSC, "Briefing on ACE Mobile Forces."

95. DGHIST, file 25/8 vol. 1, 21 October 1960, POEADQ, 69th meeting.

96. USASK, Diefenbaker Papers, vol. 45, 25 August 1960, "PJBD Journal of Discussions and Decision."

97. ATI, 26 August 1960, memo, CAS to VCAS, "Acquisition of Nuclear Weapons."

98. NAC, MG 32 (B19), 7 July 1960, "History of Events Leading Up to the Present Status for a Draft Agreement on Acquisition and Storage of Nuclear Weapons for Canadian Forces."

99. DGHIST, Raymont Collection, file 302, 1 December 1960, memo to the Minister, "Special Ammunition Storage Sites in Europe."

100. NAC, RG 24, acc 83-84/167 vol. 2063 file 5301-66, 19 November 1959, memo, DGNO, "Mk. 101 Depth Bomb Installation CS2F A/C"; 4 April 1960, memo, CJSW to CAS, "Armament-Bombs and Bombing Systems"; 3 May 1960, memo, Naval Secretary to DeHaviland, "CS2F Aircraft-Mk 101 Depth Bomb Installation."

101. NAC, RG 24, acc 83-84/167 vol. 2063 file 5301–66, 26 September 1960, memo, RCN DAE to DGNO, "Mk 101 Depth Bomb—Dummy Store."

102. NAC, RG 24 acc 83-84/167 vol. 2063 file 5301–66, 21 October 1960, memo to A/CNTS (AIR), "CS2F Aircraft—Mk. 101 Depth Bomb."

103. FOIA, McMullen, "ADC Historical Study No. 30: Interceptor Missiles in Air Defence," 98.

104. Ibid.

105. NAC, MG 32 B19 vol. 17 file 26–117 vol. 2, 4 November 1960, memo, Dwyer to Roberts, "BOMARC-Construction Status and Cost Summary as of 3 November 1960"; DGHIST, file 79/429 vol. 10, VCAS, divisional items of interest, 11 March 1960.

106. DGHIST, file 79/429 vol. 10, VCAS, divisional items of interest, 17 June 1960; 25 November 1960; NAC, RG 24 acc 83-84/167 vol. 2063 file 5301–66, 4 May 1960, memo, CJSW to CAS, "Armament-Bombs and Bombing Systems Mk 104 Mod 0 and Mk 106 Mod 0 Practice Bombs."

107. DGHIST, file 76/264, 13 July 1960, Air Council minutes.

108. Maloney, *War Without Battles*, 141.

109. NAC, RG 2, 21 September 1960, Cabinet Conclusions; DGHIST, Raymont Collection, file 629, n.d., "The Development of the Introduction of the BOMARC Ground to Air Guided Missile and the MB-1 Air to Air Guided Missile on Canadian-Manned Interceptors for the RCAF For the Defence of Canada."

110. U.S. DOS, *FRUS 1958–1960 Vol. VII*, 812–813, "Secretary's Delegation to the Fifteenth Session of The United Nations General Assembly," 27 September 1960.

111. Ibid.

112. Donald M. Fleming, *So Very Near: The Political Memoirs of the Honourable Donald M. Fleming; Volume 2: The Summit Years* (Toronto: McClelland and Stewart, 1985), 215.

113. G. W. L. Nicholson, *The Gunners of Canada: History of the Royal Regiment of Canadian Artillery*, Vol. 2, *1919–1967* (Toronto: McClelland & Stewart, 1972), 138.

114. UVIC, Pearkes Papers, "Interview with the Honourable Douglas Harkness, 22 June 1966."

115. Fleming, *So Very Near*, 238.

116. NAC, MG 32 B19 vol. 28 file 42–66 vol. 9, 20 September 1961, letter, Harkness to Dr. B. P. Gregory.

117. DGHIST, Raymont Collection, file 997, 14 October 1960, "Brief for the Chairman, Chiefs of Staff on the Status of Nuclear Agreements Pending."

118. NAC, MG 32 (B19) vol. 57, 17 November 1960, "Ministerial Brief: Characteristics of Nuclear Weapons of Interest to Canada."

119. Ibid.

120. ATI, 25 November 1960, message, External Ottawa to Washington, DC, "Acquisition of Nuclear Weapons"; Peyton V. Lyon, *Canada in World Affairs 1961–1963* (Toronto: Oxford University Press, 1968), 83.

121. Lyon, *Canada in World Affairs*, 84.

122. NAC, RG 25 vol. 4500 file 5003-k-40 pt. 6, 25 November 1960, Joint Staff, "Nuclear Weapons for NATO Forces."

123. Ibid.

124. Granatstein, *Man of Influence*, 345.

125. Ibid.

126. NAC, RG 2 vol. 2752 file D-1-1-D 1960-61-62, 5 December 1960, memo for Cabinet Defence Committee, "Nuclear Weapons for NATO and NORAD Forces."

127. Ibid.

128. Ibid.

129. Ibid.

130. Granatstein, *Man of Influence*, 356.

131. Ibid.

132. DGHIST, Raymont Collection, file 302, 6 December 1960, record of decision, Cabinet meeting, "Nuclear Weapons Policy; Irish Resolution in the United Nations and Other Aspects."

133. Ibid.

134. NAC, RG 25, vol. 4501 file 50030-k-2-40 pt. 1, 6 December 1960, POEADQ, 71st meeting.

135. Ibid.

136. Ibid.

137. Ibid.

138. DGHIST, Raymont Collection, file 302, 9 December 1960, memo, Miller to Harkness, "Control of Canadian Nuclear Weapons."

139. Ibid.

Chapter 10

1. DGHIST, Raymont Collection, file 302, 30 December 1960, letter, Harkness to Green; 13 January 1961, letter, Green to Harkness.

2. David. L. Bashow, *Starfighter* (Toronto: Fortress Publications, 1990), 9.

3. ATI, 10 January 1961, memo, DMTR to COR, "Nuclear Weapons Policy"; 20 January 1961, COR(coord), "Nuclear Weapons: CF-104 and BOMARC Programmes."

4. ATI, 28 March 1961, CAS to VCAS, "Lead Times on Nuclear Weapons"; COR to VCAS, "Progress of RCAF Actions to Acquire a Nuclear Capability."

5. Ignatieff, *Making of a Peacemonger*, 184.

6. Ibid., 187.

7. Ibid., 188–190.

8. NAC, MG 26 N2 vol. 114, nuclear weapons storage folder, 9 January 1961, "Approved by Policy Committee, National Liberal Rally, Defence Policy."

9. NAC, MG 26 N2 vol. 113, nuclear defence folder, 27 January 1960, statement by Mr. Pearson, "Control and Ownership of Tactical and Defensive Nuclear Weapons."

10. McLin, *Canada's Changing Defence Policy*, 140.

11. NAC, MG 32 B 19 vol. 27 file 42–66 vol. 4, 1 Feb 61, letter, Riddell to Harkness.

12. NAC, MG 32 B 19 vol. 27 file 42–66 vol. 4, 8 Feb 61, letter, Harkness to Goldman.

13. NAC, MG 32 B 19 vol. 27 file 42–66 vol. 4, 15 Feb 61, letter, Harkness to Endicott.

14. NAC, MG 32 B 19 vol. 27 file 42–66 vol. 4, 23 Feb 61, memo, Harkness to Diefenbaker.

15. DGHIST, Raymont Collection, file 302, 2 February 1961, memo, Hendrick to Miller, "United States/Canada Atomic Arrangements."

16. Ibid.

17. Ibid.

18. Nash, *Kennedy and Diefenbaker*, 11.

19. Ibid., 13.

20. Ibid., 63–64; Smith, *Rogue Tory*, 380.

21. USNARA, RG 59 E3077 box 1 file: Ambasador Merchant, 8 February 1961, letter, Armstrong to Merchant.

22. As quoted in Nash, *Kennedy and Diefenbaker*, 66.

23. NAC, MG 30 E144 vol. 1 file: Ambassador to the United States 1961–1962, 9 January 1961, letter, Heeney to Green.

24. DGHIST, Raymont Collection, file 302, 8 February 1961, memo, Lawson to Miller, "Nuclear Weapons for the Canadian Forces."

25. DGHIST, Raymont Collection, file 302, 9 February 1961, memo, Miller to Bryce.

26. DGHIST, Raymont Collection, file 302, 13 February 1961, memo, Miller to Robertson; 13 February 1961, memo, Robertson to Miller, "Prime Minister's Visit to Washington."

27. NAC, RG 2, 14 February 1961, Cabinet Conclusions.

28. Ibid.

29. NAC, RG 2, 17 February 1961, Cabinet Conclusions.

30. Nash, *Kennedy and Diefenbaker*, 90–91.

31. U.S. DOS, *FRUS 1961–1963 Vol. XIII*, 1140–1149, memcon, "Visit of Canadian Prime Minister Diefenbaker," 20 February 1961.

32. Ibid.

33. Ibid.

34. NAC, RG 2, 21 February 1961, Cabinet Conclusions.

35. Nash, *Kennedy and Diefenbaker*, 94–95.

36. NAC, RG 2, 25 February 1961, Cabinet Conclusions.

37. FOIA, message Commander ADC to Chief of Staff USAF, Washington, DC, 16 February 1961.

38. NAC, RG 2, 2 March 1961, Cabinet Conclusions.

39. PRO, CAB 131/25, February 1961, draft memo, UK MOD, "NATO Strategy and Nuclear Weapons."

40. Ibid.

41. Ibid.

42. Ibid.

43. USNARA, RG 218 JCS 1961 file 9050/3070 NATO, J-5 report, "NATO Strategy and Nuclear Weapons," 28 February 1961.

44. Ibid.

45. USNARA, RG 218 JCS 1961 file 9050/3070 NATO, JCS, "NATO Strategy and Nuclear Weapons," 17 March 1961.

46. Ibid.

47. "SACEUR's Views—1961: Speech to the NATO Parliamentarians, 13 November 1961," *Survival* 4, (1962): 13–14.

48. U.S. DOS, *FRUS 1961–1963 Vol. XIII*, 253–256, memcon, Norstad and Rusk, "NATO Problems," 1 February 1961; See also pp. 269–272, message, Bonn to State, 10 April 1961.

49. DGHIST, file 400.01(D1), 18 March 1961, COSC, "The Concept of the Employment of the Canadian Armed Forces in the Event of Unlimited Nuclear War."

50. Ibid.

51. Ibid.

52. Ibid.

53. Ibid.

54. Ibid.

55. Ibid.

56. Ibid.; DGHIST, file 81/674 vol. 2, 12 July 1961, "The Tasks and Problems of the Canadian Army: CGS Talk to National Defence College."

57. NAC, RG 24 acc 83-84/215 vol. 26 file 1200 pt. 2 vol. 18, APCC, "Tasks and Aims of the Army, 1961–1963."

58. DGHIST, July 1961, "The Report of the Ad Hoc Committee on Naval Objectives."

59. Ibid.

60. Ibid.

61. Ibid.

62. Ibid.

63. Ibid.

64. Douglas Harkness spoke at the conference but the transcribers deliberately did not record his speech.

65. DGHIST, file: Air Marshal Dunlap Speeches—1963, "Remarks by Air Marshal Dunlap, National Defence College Kingston, Ontario, 19 July 1963."

66. DGHIST, Raymont Collection, file 2008, "Shorthand Transcript of 1961 AOsC Conference, 21–22 March 1961."

67. Ibid.

68. Ibid.

69. Ibid.

70. Ibid.

71. Ibid.

72. Ibid.

73. Ibid.

74. Ibid.

75. Ibid.

76. Ibid.

77. Ibid.

78. Ibid.

79. Jane E. Stromseth, *The Orgins of Flexible Response* (Oxford: Oxford University Press, 1988), 28–30.

80. DGHIST, Raymont Collection, file 302, 1 March 1961, letter, Harkness to Green.

81. DGHIST, Raymont Collection, file 302, 2 March 1961, letter, Bryce to Harkness.

82. DGHIST, Raymont Collection, file 302, 30 March 1961, letter, Green to Harkness.

83. DGHIST, Raymont Collection, file 302, 26 April 1961, letter, Robertson to Miller.

84. DGHIST, Raymont Collection, file 302, 4 May 1961, letter, Harkness to Green.

85. Granatstein, *Man of Influence*, 348.

86. DGHIST, Raymont Collection, file 302, 5 May 1961, note to file, "Acquisition of Nuclear Weapons for Canadian Forces"; Smith, *Rogue Tory*, 382.

87. DGHIST, Raymont Collection, file 302, 5 May 1961, letter, Green to Harkness.

88. DGHIST, Raymont Collection, file 302, 11 May 1961, letter, Harkness to Diefenbaker.

89. ATI, 21 April 1961, memo to CAS, "Lead Times—Nuclear Weapons Systems."

90. DGHIST, 79/429 vol. 12, VCAS, "Divisional Items of Interest for Week Ending 15 June 1962."

91. ATI, 8 May 1961, memo, CAS to Minister, "Lead Times—Nuclear Weapons Systems."

92. DGHIST, Raymont Collection, file 302, 15 May 1961, memo, Miller to Harkness, "Nuclear Weapons."

93. DGHIST, Raymont Collection, file 302, attachment to 11 May 1961 letter, Harkness to Diefenbaker.

94. Ibid.

95. Ibid.

96. Ibid.

97. Ibid.

98. Ibid.

99. Ibid.

100. Ibid.

101. DGHIST, Raymont Collection, file 303, n.d., letter, Harkness to Green; NAC, MG 32 B19 vol. 30 file 44–89, 11 April 1961, memo, Miller to Harkness, "F-101B Aircraft-Weapons."

102. U.S. DOS, *FRUS 1961–1963 Vol. XIII*, 1152–1153, message, Rusk to State, 14 May 1961; USNARA, RG 59 E3077 250/68/30/3 box 1, file: NATO 1959–62 3A, "Canadian External Affairs Minister Green's Remarks at Oslo," 9 May 1961.

103. Nash, *Kennedy and Diefenbaker*, 104–105.

104. USNARA, RG 59 E3077 250/68/30/3 box 1 file: Neutralism, Nationalism, Anti-Americanism 1960–62 1.14, letter, Merchant to White, 4 April 1961.

105. Smith, *Rogue Tory*, 384.

106. Ibid.

107. Ibid., 123.

108. U.S. DOS, *FRUS 1961–1963 Vol. XIII*, 1153–1155, memcon, Diefenbaker and Kennedy, "Cuba and Latin America," 17 May 1961.

109. U.S. DOS, *FRUS 1961–1963 Vol. XIII*, 1155–1156, memcon, Diefenbaker and Kennedy, "Canada, the OAS, and IA—ECOSOC," 17 May 1961.

110. U.S. DOS, *FRUS 1961–1963 Vol. XIII*, 1157–1158, memcon, Diefenbaker and Kennedy, "NATO and Nuclear Weapons," 17 May 1961.

111. Ibid.; Nash, *Kennedy and Diefenbaker*, 117–118.

112. U.S. DOS, *FRUS 1961–1963 Vol. XIII*, 1161–1162, memcon, Diefenbaker and Kennedy, "Triangular Aircraft Agreement," 17 May 1961.

113. Ibid.

114. Smith, *Rogue Tory*, 388; Nash, *Kennedy and Diefenbaker*, 121.

115. Nash, *Kennedy and Diefenbaker*, 11.

116. NAC, RG 2, 6 June 1961, Cabinet Conclusions.

117. NAC, RG 2, 9 and 12 June 1961, Cabinet Conclusions.

118. NAC, MG 32 B19, vol. 30, file 44–89, "Remarks by the Honourable Douglas S. Harkness, PC, GM, MP Minister of National Defence at the Handing-Over Ceremony of the F-101, July 24, 1961."

119. Sean M. Maloney, "Notfallplanung fur Berlin: Vorlaufer der Flexible Response 1958–1963," *MiltarGeschichte* Heft 1.1, Quartal 1997 7 Jahrgang.

120. NAC, RG 2, 24 July 1961, Cabinet Conclusions.

121. Ibid.

122. The French struck FLN rebel sanctuary areas in Tunisia as part of their ongoing Alge-

rian campaign, which prompted a substantial outcry in the world community since Tunisia was not a belligerent.

123. NAC, RG 2, 24 July 1961, Cabinet Conclusions.

124. Ibid.

125. Ibid.

126. DGHIST, Raymont Collection, file 303, 24 July 1961, memo, Armstrong to Miller; 31 July 1961, memo, Robertson to Miller, "Negotiations with the U.S. Concerning the Provisions of Stock-piles of Nuclear Weapons for Canadian Forces."

127. U.S. DOS, *FRUS 1961–1963 Vol. XIII*, 1162–1163, message, Washington to Ottawa, 3 August 1961.

128. Maloney, *War Without Battles*, 158.

129. DGHIST, Raymont Collection, file 303, 8 August 1961, memo, Miller to Harkness, "Negotiations with the U.S. Government Concerning the Acquisition of Nuclear Weapons for Canadian Forces"; 8 August 1961, memo, Miller to Robertson, "Negotiations with the U.S. Concerning the Provision of Stockpiles of Nuclear Weapons for Canadian Forces."

130. Nash, *Kennedy and Diefenbaker*, 137.

131. DGHIST, file 114.3Q1 (D14), 10 August 1961, message, NATO Paris to External Affairs, "Germany and Berlin—Military Build Up."

132. Ibid.

133. Ibid.

134. DGHIST, file 114.3Q1 (D14), 3 August 1961, aide memoir, "Berlin Contingency Planning"; 9 August 1961, "Supporting Data to Aide Memoir Berlin Contingency Planning"; 12 August 1961, memo, DMO&P, "Dispatch of a Second Brigade Group to Germany."

135. Lyon, *Canada in World Affairs*, 92.

136. NAC, RG 2, 17 August 1961, Cabinet Conclusions.

137. Ibid.

138. Ibid.; NAC, RG 2, 21 August 1961, Cabinet Conclusions.

139. NAC, RG 2, 22 August 1961, Cabinet Conclusions.

140. NAC, RG 2, 23 August 1961, Cabinet Conclusions.

141. Ibid.

142. Louis Halle, *The Cold War as History* (New York: Harper Collins Publishers, 1991), 398.

143. U.S. Department of Energy, "Announced United States Nuclear Tests July 1945 through December 1981," January 1982.

144. Nash, *Kennedy and Diefenbaker*, 138; NAC, RG 2, 14 September 1961, Cabinet Conclusions.

145. Ibid.

146. Ibid.

147. Lyon, *Canada and World Affairs*, 95.

148. Ibid.

149. Ibid.

150. Ibid., 100.

151. U.S. DOS, *FRUS 1961–1963: Western Europe and Berlin*, microfiche supplement, frame 180, message, NATO Paris to State, 19 September 1961.

152. ATI, n.d., "Implications of the Acquisition of Nuclear Weapons by the RCAF."

153. Bashow, *Starfighter*, 11–13; DGHIST, file 79/429 vol. 11, "AMTS Divisional Items of Interest for Week Ending 18 Aug 61"; letter, Col. William Anderson to Maloney, 13 June 1995; confidential interview.

154. ATI, 25 May 1961, DAMTS to CAS, "Implications of Acquisition of Nuclear Weapons by RCAF."

155. Ibid., ATI, 1 August 1961, memo, COR to D/VCAS.

156. ATI, 31 May 1961, "Report on a Visit to SHAPE, 1 Air Division, and USAF(E) Formations. Subject Some Preparations Required to Give 1 Air Division an Atomic Strike Capability."

157. ATI, 29 May 1961, Minutes of Current Planning Committee Meeting 5/61; 29 May 1961, memo, CPers to VCAS, "Security Clearence Problems: Personnel to RCAF ZED List." The RCAF planners knew that they might be tasked to provide coverage of two ATAF targets in northern Germany and six ATAF targets in Italy.

158. NAC, RG 24 acc 83-84/49 vol. 4175 file 1930-106-1 pt. 1, 8 May 1961, memo, CAS to MND, "Lead Times: Nuclear Weapons Systems."

159. Group Captain Rayne (Joe) Schultz, interview by the author, 16 January 1996, Ottawa, Ontario.

160. NAC, RG 24 acc 83/84/167 vol. 3734 file 8100 vol. 9, 7 March 1961, memo to ACNS(A&W), "Special Weapons Training for Canadian Aircrew/Nuclear Safety for Canadian Aircrew."

161. Stuart E. Soward, *Hands to Flying Stations: A Recollective History of Canadian Naval Aviation; Volume II: 1955–1969* (Victoria, BC: Neptune Developments, 1995), 260.

162. ATI, 4 October 1961, memo, AMTS to CNTS, "Nuclear Weapons Compatibility CS2F-2."

163. ATI, 4 October 1961, memo, AMTS to CNTS, "Nuclear Weapons Compatibility CS2F-2"; 24 October 1961, memo, RCAF LO to CAS, "Special Weapons Compatibility—P2V7 Neptune."

164. ATI, 4 October 1961, "Supporting Data for Air Council Meeting: Proposed Organization to Effect the Introduction and Maintenance of Nuclear Weapons."

165. DGHIST, Raymont Collection, file 303, 18 October 1961, memo to Cabinet, "General Agreement on Atomic Weapons."

166. Granatstein, *Man of Influence*, 349.

167. DGHIST, Raymont Collection, file 303, 11 October 1961, "Joint Staff Working Paper: Nuclear Weapons for Canadian Forces."

168. Ibid.

169. Ibid.

170. Ibid.

171. Ibid.

172. DGHIST, Raymont Collection, file 303, 26 October 1961, memo, Miller to Joint Staff.

173. DGHIST, Raymont Collection, file 140, 6 July 1961, memo, Clark to Harkness, "Status Report: 762mm Rocket System (Honest John)."

174. DGHIST, Raymont Collection, file 303, 25 October 1961, memo, Walsh to Harkness, "Control and Storage of Nuclear Warheads for 1 SSM Battery."

175. NAC, RG 24 acc 83-84/215 file 1200 pt. 4.2 vol. 16, 14 December 1960, memo to VCGS, "Support Arrangements: Surface-to-Surface Missile battery, RCA"; Maloney, *War Without Battles*, 142–143. Technically, there were Special Ammunition Storage Sites where the warheads were stored and ready for use. Then there were Support Sites where third-line maintenance on the warheads was carried out in peacetime. The third type were Depot Sites where war reserve weapons and replacement components were held. See DGHIST, file 112.9M2.009 (D216), 24 July 1961, DMO&P, "Special Support of Atomic Activity in Northern Army Group."

176. NAC, RG 2, 21 and 30 November 1961, Cabinet Conclusions.

177. Milberry, *Sixty Years*, 334–335; "Canada's VooDoos: Withdrawal of Last CF-101s from Service," *Air Clues* 39, no. 2 (February 1985); *416 Squadron*, privately published squadron history (n.d.); Kevin Keaveney, *McDonnell F-101B/F* (Arlington, TX: Aerofax, 1984), 5–6; Lou Drendel and Paul Stevens, *VooDoo* (New Carrollton, TX: Squadron/Signal Publications, 1985), 55–58.

178. ATI, 24 November 1961, memo to CAS, "Nuclear Weapons—CF-101B"; 15 December 1961, memo, AMTS to CAS, "Nuclear Weapons—CF-101B."
179. Soward, *Hands to Flying Stations*, 260–261.
180. DGHIST, 79/429 vol. 12, VCAS, "Divisional Items of Interest for Week Ending 9 December 1961."
181. ATI, 11 December 1961, memo, Campbell to Miller, "Nuclear Weapons-Requirements for RCAF Air Defence Interceptor Squadrons."
182. DGHIST, Raymont Collection, file 303, 19 December 1961, letter, Harkness to Green.
183. McLin, *Canada's Changing Defence Policy*, 143.

Chapter 11

1. Smith, *Rogue Tory*, 430–432.
2. See Sean M. Maloney and Joel J. Sokolsky, "Ready, Willing, and Able: The RCN and Nuclear Weapons, 1955–1970," unpublished conference paper, September 1992; Brigadier General Herb Sutherland (CF Ret'd), interview with the author, Ottawa, 5 March 1992.
3. ATI, 22 January 1962, memo, Acting VCAS to CPlans I, "Nuclear Weapons."
4. Nash, *Kennedy and Diefenbaker*, 152.
5. B. Robinson, *Diefenbaker's World*, 239.
6. Lyon, *Canada in World Affairs*, 105–106; McLin, *Canada's Changing Defence Policy*, 142.
7. Nash, *Kennedy and Diefenbaker*, 153.
8. U.S. DOS, *FRUS 1961–1963 Vol. XIII*, 1167–1168, message, Embassy Canada to State, 27 February 1962.
9. Lyon, *Canada in World Affairs*, 107–108.
10. Ibid., 109.
11. Granatstein, *Man of Influence*, 349.
12. Lyon, *Canada in World Affairs*, 110–111; *Hansard*, House of Commons Debates, 20 March 1962.
13. Nash, *Kennedy and Diefenbaker*, 151.
14. U.S. DOS, *FRUS 1961–1963 Vol. XIII*, 1172–1177, letter, Merchant to Ball, 5 May 1962.
15. Ibid.
16. Ibid.
17. Ibid.
18. Nash, *Kennedy and Diefenbaker*, 160.
19. U.S. DOS, *FRUS 1961–1963 Vol. XIII*, 357–360, meeting, Stikker and Rusk, "NATO Nuclear Questions," 5 February 1962; 360–364, meeting, Stikker and Kennedy, "Call of Secretary General of NATO," 6 February 1962.
20. Robert S. Jordan, *Political Leadership in NATO: A Study in Multinational Diplomacy* (Boulder, CO: Westview Press, 1979), 145–146.
21. PRO, DEFE 4/143, 1 March 1962, JPS, "NATO Strategy and the Role of NATO Forces."
22. Maloney, *War Without Battles*, 200.
23. PRO, DEFE 5/125, 20 March 1962, Chiefs of Staff Committee, "Control of Nuclear Weapons."
24. Ignatieff, *Making of a Peacemonger*, 197.
25. NAC, RG 25 vol. 4486 file 50030-40 pt. 8, 14 February 1962, DEA study for George Ignatieff—Personal, "NATO Long Term Planning: The Resumption of the Debate."
26. Ibid.
27. Ibid.
28. Ibid.

29. Ibid.

30. Ibid.

31. Ibid.

32. U.S. DOS, *FRUS 1961–1963 Vol. XIII*, 372–373, letter, Taylor to Kennedy, "The New U.S. Strategy," 3 April 1962; PRO, DEFE 5/126, 17 April 1962, "Brief for Anglo-French Staff Talks"; DEFE 13/254, 23 April 1962, message, BDS Washington to MOD London.

33. PRO, DEFE 4/143, JPS, "SACEUR's Revised Emergency Defence Plan."

34. Ibid.

35. See, for example, NAC, RG 25 vol. 4496 file 50030-E-1-40 pt. 2, 30 January 1962, message, Heeney to External, "NATO Military Planning"; NAC, RG 2, 24 April 1962, Cabinet Conclusions.

36. Stromseth, *Origins of Flexible Response*, 43–47.

37. Maloney, *War Without Battles*, 199. This work mistakenly puts the Athens meeting in May 1963, not 1962.

38. U.S. DOS, *FRUS 1961–1963 Vol. XIII*, 384–387, state and Defence paper, "Suggested NATO Nuclear Program," 22 March 1962.

39. Ibid.

40. For the text of the Ann Arbor Speech, see Schuyler Foerster and Edward N. Wright, eds., *American Defence Policy*, 6th ed. (Baltimore, MD: Johns Hopkins University Press, 1990), 295–297.

41. Lyon, *Canada in World Affairs*, 91.

42. Granatstein, *Man of Influence*, 351.

43. DGHIST, file 90/302, 29 June 1962, memo, Carpenter to Miller, "Report of the Special Studies Group—Long Range Objectives for the RCAF."

44. Ibid.

45. Ibid.

46. DGHIST, file 90/302, 23 July 1962, memo, Campbell to Carpenter.

47. Fleming, *So Very Near*, 460–461.

48. DGHIST, Raymont Collection, file 303, 28 March 1962, tear sheet from "The Nation's Business."

49. NAC, MG 26 N6, defence folder: memos on defence policy 1962–65, 9 March 1962, memo to distribution list, personal and confidential, "Defence Policy."

50. Ibid.

51. Ibid.

52. NAC, MG 26 N2, vol. 49, file 806.2, 29 March 1962, letter, Curtis to Pearson.

53. NAC, MG 26 N2, vol. 49, file 806.2, 5 April 1962, letter, Pearson to Curtis.

54. Granatstein, *Man of Influence*, 350; Smith, *Rogue Tory*, 442–445.

55. DGHIST, file 79/429 vol. 12, AMTS, "Divisional Items of Interest for Week Ending 12 Jan 62."

56. DGHIST, file 79/429 vol. 12, AMTS, "Divisional Items of Interest for Week Ending 9 Feb 62."

57. DGHIST, file 79/429 vol. 12, AMTS, "Divisional Items of Interest for Week Ending 8 Jun 62 and 14 Sep 62."

58. ATI, 8 March 1962, memo, Smith to Campbell, "Aide Memoire: Timing Required for the Acquisition of Nuclear Warheads—North Bay BOMARC."

59. Ibid.

60. Ibid.

61. K. G. Roberts, "Air Defence Goes Underground," *Roundel* (September 1963): 8–13; T. G. Coughlin, "City in a Mountain," *Roundel* (June 1961): 24–26.

62. ATI, 10 April 1962, "Aide Memoire: Timing Required for the Acquisition of Nuclear

Weapons—CF-101B Program"; 19 February 1962, "Visit Report—CJS(W) and Pentagon CF-101B Program-Scheduling of Preparations to Accept Nuclear Weapons 13–15 Feb 62."

63. Ibid.

64. ATI, 12 March 1962, memo, DADSI to CAS, "Status of Actions to Provide Nuclear Capability, CF-101B/MB-1(ADC)."

65. ATI, 10 April 1962, "Aide Memoire: Timing Required for the Acquisition of Nuclear Weapons—CF-101B Program."

66. ATI, 7 May 1962, memo, Hendrick to Miller, "Release of Military Atomic Information"; 23 July 1962, memo, CAS to COSC, "CF-101B Program-Special Weapons Service-to-Service Agreement."

67. ATI, 7 May 1962, minute sheet, DNDO to DArmEng.

68. ATI, 10 April 1962. "Aide Memoire: Timing Required for the Acquisition of Nuclear Weapons—CF-101B Program."

69. ATI, 10 April 1962, "Aide Memoire: Timing Required for the Acquisition of Nuclear Weapons—CF-104."

70. ATI, 7 March 1962, memo, CPS to DArmEng, "Status of Actions to Provide a Nuclear Capability—CF-104/Mk 28 Mod 1 (Air Div)."

71. ATI, 29 June 1962, CPlansI to VCAS, "Nuclear Weapons—Draft Schedule Proposed Government-to-Government Agreement."

72. ATI, 7 August 1962, memo, CAS to COSC, "Nuclear Weapons—Proposed Government to Government Agreement."

73. ATI, 8 March 1962, memo, CNS to CAS, "Special Weapons Planning."

74. ATI, 9 April 1962, memo, CAS to CNS, "Special Weapons Planning."

75. ATI, 30 April 1962, memo, DArmEng to DMO, "Training-ASW Special Weapons/ Neptune Aramament Personnel Nominated"; 9 April 1962, D/VCAS to COps, "Nuclear Weapons—Maritime."

76. ATI, 18 April 1962, memo, ADSI 4 to DA PRog, "Special Weapons—CF-101B Programme."

77. ATI, n.d., memo, CAS to air member, CJS(W), "RCAF/USN Nuclear Programme."

78. ATI, 11 September 1962, message, CANAIRHED to RCAF Liaison Officer AFSWC Kirtland AFB.

79. ATI, 10 August 1962, memo, Cameron to Reyno, "RCAF/RCN/USN Nuclear Programs."

80. ATI, 1 August 1962, memo, D/VCAS to VCAS, "Acquisiton of Nuclear Weapons."

81. Ibid.

82. DGHIST, Raymont Collection, file 303, 10 August 1962, memo, Campbell to Harkness, "Nuclear Weapons for Air Defence."

83. Ibid.

84. ATI, 10 August 1962, memo, Campbell to Harkness, "Nuclear Weapons for Air Defence."

85. DGHIST, Raymont Collection, file 303, n.d., memo, Campbell to Miller, "Acquisition of Nuclear Weapons—BOMARC."

86. DGHIST, Raymont Collection, file 303, 6 September 1962, memo, CAS to COSC, "Nuclear Weapons for Defence."

87. Some of these reasons were elaborated on in a separate RCAF memo discussing the issue. See ATI, 6 September 1962, memo, Campbell to Miller, "Nuclear Weapons for Defence."

88. Bill Green, *First Line*, 365.

89. FOIA, USAF, Ray, *ADC Historical Study No. 20.*

90. ATI, 6 September 1962, memo, Campbell to Miller, "Nuclear Weapons for Defence"; NAC, MG 32 B19, vol. 57, 17 August 1962, memo, Harkness to Diefenbaker.

91. USNARA, RG 59 E3077 box 1 250/62/30/3 file: Ottawa memcons 1/A.8, memcon Campbell/Smith, 23 May 1962.

92. See Laurence Chang and Peter Kornbluh, eds., *The Cuban Missile Crisis 1962: A National Security Archive Documents Reader* (New York: New Press, 1992), 352–354; James G. Blight and David A. Welch, *On the Brink: Americans and Soviets Reexamine the Cuban Missile Crisis* (New York: Hill and Wang, 1989), 374–376.

93. DGHIST, 23 May 1962, naval board minutes; "FALLEX 62," *Survival* 5 (1963): 19–22.

94. Ibid.

95. Ibid.; ATI, 18 October 1955, "DND War Book"; December 1962, "DND War Book."

96. Chang and Kornbluh, *Cuban Missile Crisis*, 356–357; Peter T. Haydon, *The 1962 Cuban Missile Crisis: Canadian Involvement Reconsidered* (Toronto: Canadian Institute of Strategic Studies, 1993), 224; German, *Sea Is at Our Gates*, 263.

97. Granatstein, *Man of Influence*, 351.

98. Fleming, *So Very Near*, 578.

99. FOIA, USAF, "History of the Air Defence Command, January–June 1964 Vol. 1: Narrative."

100. Chang and Kornbluh, *Cuban Missile Crisis 1962*, 357–360; Blight and Welch, *On the Brink*, 378.

101. Steven J. Zaloga, *Target America: The Soviet Union and the Strategic Arms Race, 1945–1964* (Novato CA: Presidio Press, 1993), 208–209; Mary S. McAuliffe, *CIA Documents on the Cuban Missile Crisis 1962* (Washington, DC: CIA History Staff, 1992), 143.

102. John Lewis Gaddis, *We Now Know: Rethinking Cold War History* (Oxford: Clarendon Press, 1997), 274; Anatoli I. Gribikov and William Y. Smith, *Operation ANADYR: U.S. and Soviet Generals Recount the Cuban Missile Crisis* (Chicago: Edition q, 1994), 26.

103. Haydon, *1962 Cuban Missile Crisis*, 226; German, *Sea Is at Our Gates*, 263.

104. German, *Sea Is at Our Gates*, 263.

105. Oleg Sarin and Lev Dvoretsky, *Alien Wars: The Soviet Union's Aggressions Against the World, 1919–1989* (Novato, CA: Presidio Press, 1997), 145.

106. USN OA, Admiral Robert Lee Dennison Oral History, 283.

107. Dino A. Brugioni, *Eyeball to Eyeball: The Inside Story of the Cuban Missile Crisis* (New York: Random House, 1990), 319–320.

108. Ibid., 333.

109. B. Robinson, *Diefenbaker's World*, 285.

110. NAC, MG 32 (B19) vol. 57, 27 August 1963, Douglas Harkness, "The Nuclear Arms Question and the Political Crisis Which Arose from It in January and February 1963."

111. Chang and Kornbluh, *Cuban Missile Crisis 1962*, 365–367; Blight and Welch, *On the Brink*, 379; Sagan, *Limits of Safety*, 94–96.

112. Haydon, *1962 Cuban Missile Crisis*, 125.

113. NAC, MG 32 (B19) vol. 57, 27 August 1963, Douglas Harkness, "The Nuclear Arms Question and the Political Crisis Which Arose from It in January and February 1963."

114. Ibid.

115. Brugioni, *Eyeball to Eyeball*, 333.

116. NAC, MG 32 (B19) vol. 57, 27 August 1963, Douglas Harkness, "The Nuclear Arms Question and the Political Crisis Which Arose from It In January and February 1963."

117. Granatstein, *Man of Influence*, 352.

118. B. Robinson, *Diefenbaker's World*, 287.

119. Brugioni, *Eyeball to Eyeball*, 334.

120. Diefenbaker, *One Canada*, 82.

121. Ibid, 83.

122. Chang and Kornbluth, *Cuban Missile Crisis 1962*, 366.

123. Sagan, *Limits of Safety*, 103.

124. NAC, MG 32 (B19) vol. 57, 27 August 1963, Douglas Harkness, "The Nuclear Arms Question and the Political Crisis Which Arose from It in January and February 1963."

125. Ibid.

126. Ibid.

127. Brugioni, *Eyeball to Eyeball*, 334.

128. DGHIST, Hendrick Papers, Daily Dairy, 25 October 1962.

129. Ibid.

130. NAC, MG 32 (B19) vol. 57, 27 August 1963, Douglas Harkness, "The Nuclear Arms Question and the Political Crisis Which Arose from It in January and February 1963."

131. ATI, December 62, "Department of National Defence War Book."

132. Ibid.

133. Ibid.

134. Ibid.

135. DGHIST, file 71/493, n.d., Chief of the Air Staff, "Exercise BOOK CHECK: Sequence of Events."

136. NAC, MG 32 (B19) vol. 57, 27 August 1963, Douglas Harkness, "The Nuclear Arms Question and the Political Crisis Which Arose from It in January and February 1963."

137. DGHIST, Hendrick Papers, Daily Dairy, 25 October 1962.

138. Ibid.

139. Ibid.

140. Ibid.

141. NAC, RG 2, 23 October 1962, Cabinet Conclusions.

142. Ibid.

143. NAC, MG 32 (B19) vol. 57, 27 August 1963, Douglas Harkness, "The Nuclear Arms Question and the Political Crisis Which Arose from It in January and February 1963."

144. Ibid.

145. B. Robinson, *Diefenbaker's World*, 288.

146. Fleming, *So Very Near*, 565; Nash, *Kennedy and Diefenbaker*, 197. Ignatieff even went to Soest to visit with 4 Brigade during the crisis because he felt so lonely in Paris. See Maloney, *War Without Battles*, 173.

147. Nash, *Kennedy and Diefenbaker*, 196; Haydon, *1962 Cuban Missile Crisis*, 229.

148. Lieutenant General A. Chester Hull, CF Ret'd, telephone interview by the author, 15 June 1997.

149. Bashow, *Starfighter*, 17.

150. Maloney, *War Without Battles*, 174.

151. Ibid., 173–175; NSA, Cuban Missile Crisis microfilm, frame 1325, message, JCS to State, 25 October 1962.

152. Haydon, *1962 Cuban Missile Crisis*, 129; NAC, RG 24 vol. 549 file 096.103 v.3, 25 October 1962, message, AOC PD to CAS.

153. NAC, RG 2, 24 October 1962, Cabinet Conclusions.

154. Ibid.

155. NAC, MG 32 (B19) vol. 57, 27 August 1963, Douglas Harkness, "The Nuclear Arms Question and the Political Crisis Which Arose from It in January and February 1963."

156. Ibid.

157. NSA, Cuban Missile Crisis microfilm, frame 1211, message, Ottawa to State from Ivan White, 24 October 1962; NAC, RG 24 vol. 549 file 096.103 v.3, 24 October 1962, message, CANAIRHED to CANAIRDEF.

158. DGHIST, file 87/95, Headquarters of the Commander in Chief Atlantic Command, "CinCLANT Historical Account of the Cuban Crisis—1963," p. 121; Haydon, *1962*

Cuban Missile Crisis, 230–231; DGHIST, 24 October 1962, naval board minutes, special meeting.

159. Soward, *Hands to Flying Stations*, 280.

160. ATI, 24 October 1962, message, Gerhardt to Miller.

161. Ibid.

162. Lieutenant General A. Chester Hull, CF Ret'd, telephone interview by the author, 15 June 1997; confidential interviews.

163. Nash, *Kennedy and Diefenbaker*, 200–201; DGHIST, Hendrick Papers, Daily Dairy, 25 October 1962. See also NAC, MG 32 B 13 vol. 12 file 45, "Text of a Television Interview with the Secretary of State for External Affairs on the CBC, October 22, 1962." This transcript is misdated.

164. NAC, RG 2, 25 October 1962, Cabinet Conclusions.

165. Diefenbaker, *One Canada*, 87–88; Haydon, *1962 Cuban Missile Crisis*, 142.

166. DGHIST, file 87/95, Headquarters of the Commander in Chief Atlantic Command, "CinCLANT Historical Account of the Cuban Crisis—1963," 122; German, *Sea Is at Our Gates*, 268.

167. Chang and Kornbluth, *Cuban Missile Crisis 1962*, 376–377.

168. DGHIST, file 87/95, Headquarters of the Commander in Chief Atlantic Command, "CinCLANT Historical Account of the Cuban Crisis—1963," 122; NAC, RG 24 vol. 549 file 096.103 v.3, 25 October 1962, message, AOC PD to CAS.

169. German, *Sea Is at Our Gates*, 268–270.

170. DGHIST, file 80/381, 30 October 1962, message, CANCOMARLANT to COMASWFORLANT.

171. DGHIST, file 80/381. See message traffic from period 30 October to 15 November 1962.

172. Haydon, *1962 Cuban Missile Crisis*, 163.

173. DGHIST, file 80/381. See message traffic for 2 and 6 November 1962.

174. See NAC, RG 24 vol. 20710 file 232, 7 May 1963, Cabinet Defence Committee, 139th meeting where the participants disagree with the American argument that SACEUR, SACLANT, and CinCNORAD should retain pre-delegated defensive nuclear weapons use. The Canadian view was that use should take place in any circumstances only after consultation between the President and the Prime Minister "where practical."

175. See USN OA, oral history of Admiral George William Anderson, vol. 2, pp. 174–177, 388–389.

176. DGHIST, file 80/381, 2 November 1962, message COMASWFORLANT to CANCOMARLNAT, "ASW Surveillance Operations."

177. Confidential interviews. Yet another unconfirmed rumor is that an RCAF Argus with a nuclear depth bomb on board had an engine fire and had to divert to the Azores.

178. NAC, RG 2, 30 October 1962, Cabinet Conclusions.

179. Ibid.

180. Sagan, *Limits of Safety*, 99.

181. NAC, RG 24 vol. 549 file 096.103 v.s, 27 November 1962, message CANAIRHED to CANAIRDEF.

182. NAC, MG 32 (B19) vol. 57, 27 August 1963, Douglas Harkness, "The Nuclear Arms Question and the Political Crisis Which Arose from It in January and February 1963."

183. ATI, 13 November 1962, memo CAS to VCAS, "Time Factors—Delivery of Nuclear Warheads."

184. NAC, MG 32 (B19) vol. 57, 27 August 1963, Douglas Harkness, "The Nuclear Arms Question and the Political Crisis Which Arose from It in January and February 1963."

185. Ibid.

186. Granatstein, *Man of Influence*, 354.

187. NAC, MG 32 (B19) vol. 57, 27 August 1963, Douglas Harkness, "The Nuclear Arms Question and the Political Crisis Which Arose from It in January and February 1963."

188. Judy LaMarsh, *Memoirs of a Bird in a Gilded Cage* (Toronto: McClelland and Stewart, 1969), 15.

189. When Dunlap replaced Campbell as CAS, he appears to have altered the previous policy over the "conventionality" of the CF-104 force. He later told Harkness in February 1963 that the aircraft could in fact be equipped with conventional weapons. See NAC, MG 32 B19, vol. 17 file 26–117 vol. 3, 1 February 1963, memo, Dunlap to EAMND, "Nuclear Armament and Equipment RCAF/USAF Cost Summary."

190. LaMarsh, *Memoirs of a Bird*, 19

191. Ibid., 20.

192. Ibid., 26.

193. Peter C. Newman, *The Distemper of Our Times* (Toronto: McClelland and Stewart, 1978), 475–477.

194. Ibid.

195. DGHIST, Foulkes Papers, file: Nuclear Weapons, undated briefing, "Is there a Nuclear Commitment?"

196. DGHIST, Foulkes Papers, file: Nuclear Weapons, undated briefing, "Should Canada Acquire Nuclear Weapons?"

197. U.S. DOS, *FRUS 1961–1963 Vol. XIII*, 458, message, Rusk to State, 15 December 1962.

198. U.S. DOS, *FRUS 1961–1963 Vol. XIII*, 455, "Scope Paper Prepared for the NATO Ministerial Meeting," 6 December 1962.

199. U.S. DOS, *FRUS 1961–1963 Vol. XIII*, 461, message, State to U.S. Embassy Italy, 18 December 1962.

200. Jocelyn Maynard Ghent, "Canadian-American Relations and the Nuclear Weapons Controversy, 1958–1963," (PhD diss., University of Illinois, 1976), 212–213; Granatstein, *Man of Influence*, 354.

201. See Andre J. Pierre, *Nuclear Politics: The British Experience with an Independent Strategic Force 1939–1970* (Toronto: Oxford University Press, 1972) and especially Ian Clark's *Nuclear Diplomacy and the Special Relationship: Britain's Deterrent and America, 1957–1962* (Oxford: Clarendon Press, 1994).

202. Stromseth, *Origins of Flexible Response*, 77.

203. Ibid.

204. NAC, RG 25 vol. 4486 file 50030-40 pt. 9, 19 April 1963, "Notes on Defence Topics—Discussions between Mr. Pearson and Mr. Macmillan."

205. B. Robinson, *Diefenbaker's World*, 300–303; Smith, *Rogue Tory*, 465.

206. Lyon, *Canada in World Affairs*, 89.

Chapter 12

1. See Sean M. Maloney, "Notfallplanung fur Berlin: Vorlaufer der Flexible Response 1958–1963," *Militargeschichte* Heft 1 1 Quartal 1997 7 Jahrgang; see also Deborah Shapley, *Promise and Power: The Life and Times of Robert McNamara* (Boston: Little, Brown, 1993), 145; NAC, RG 25, vol. 4533 file: 50030 AB-40 pt. 5, 30 July 1962, message, External to Paris, "Reactions to Norstad's Resignation"; 27 July 1962, message, Paris to External, "French Reactions to Norstad's Resignation"; 26 July 1962, message, Paris to External, "Appointment of Lemnitzer as SACEUR and Brit Defence Policy."

2. NAC, MG 32B(9) vol. 82, Norstad conference file, "Transcript of General Norstad's Press Confernce, 3 January 1963."

3. LaMarsh, *Memoirs of a Bird*, 30.

4. See B. Robinson, *Diefenbaker's World*, 303–304. Smith in *Rogue Tory* sits on the fence on the Norastad press conference and suggests that it was "by accident or design" (467). See Fleming, *So Very Near*, 579.

5. Smith, *Rogue Tory*, 462.

6. NAC, MG 32 (B19) vol. 57, 27 August 1963, Douglas Harkness, "The Nuclear Arms Question and the Political Crisis Which Arose from It in January and February 1963."

7. He also had his staff generate a public record chronology for use in Defence debates in the House. See NAC, MG 26 N2 vol. 114, file: Nuclear Weapons Storage, 9 December 1962, "Chronology of Defence."

8. LaMarsh, *Memoirs of a Bird*, 28.

9. NAC, MG 26 N2, vol. 49, file 806.2, 3 January 1963, memo, JWP to Pearson.

10. NAC, MG 26 N2, vol. 49, file 806.2, January 1963, CN telecable to Pearson.

11. NAC, MG 26 N2, vol. 50, file 806.2 pt. 3, 12 January 1963, Scarborough speech transcript.

12. Ibid.

13. Ibid.

14. Ibid.

15. Ibid.

16. NAC, MG 26 N2, vol. 114 file: Nuclear Weapons, 12 January 1963, "Lester Pearson Interview Recorded on 12 January 1963 as Used on F.Y.I."

17. English, *Worldly Years*, 251.

18. NAC, MG 32 (B19) vol. 57, 27 August 1963, Douglas Harkness, "The Nuclear Arms Question and the Political Crisis Which Arose from It in January and February 1963."

19. Ibid.; Lyon, *Canada in World Affairs*, 142–144.

20. NAC, MG 32 (B19) vol. 57, 27 August 1963, Douglas Harkness, "The Nuclear Arms Question and the Political Crisis Which Arose from It in January and February 1963"; Fleming, *So Very Near*, 581–582.

21. Ibid.

22. Fleming, *So Very Near*, 583.

23. *Hansard*, House of Commons Debates, 25 January 1962.

24. NAC, MG 32 N2 vol. 110 file: National Defence—General (1), 24 January 1963, "Notes for Mr. Pearson's remarks in the House of Commons during the Foreign Policy and Defence Policy Debate, January 24 and 25, 1963."

25. Lyon, *Canada in World Affairs*, 153.

26. NAC, MG 32 (B19) vol. 57, 27 August 1963, Douglas Harkness, "The Nuclear Arms Question and the Political Crisis Which Arose from It in January and February 1963."

27. U.S. DOS, *FRUS 1961–1963 Vol. XIII*, 1193, memo, Tyler to Ball, "Proposed Press Statement on United States–Canadian Negotiations Regarding Nuclear Weapons," 29 January 1963.

28. U.S. DOS, *FRUS 1961–1963 Vol. XIII*, 1195–1196, state department press release, "United States and Canadian Negotiations Regarding Nuclear Weapons," 30 January 1963; see also Fleming, *So Very Near*, 587–588.

29. NAC, MG 32 (B19) vol. 57, 27 August 1963, Douglas Harkness, "The Nuclear Arms Question and the Political Crisis Which Arose from It in January and February 1963."

30. Fleming, *So Very Near*, 588–589; Lyon, *Canada in World Affairs*, 171.

31. Lyon, *Canada in World Affairs*, 160–163.

32. NAC, MG 32 (B19) vol. 57, 27 August 1963, Douglas Harkness, "The Nuclear Arms Question and the Political Crisis Which Arose from It in January and February 1963."

33. The best description of this event so far has been in Donald Fleming's memoir, *So Very Near*, 597–598.

34. U.S. DOS, *FRUS 1961–1963 Vol. XIII*, 1196–1198, 3 February 1963, message, Butterworth to State.
35. Charles Ritchie, *Storm Signals: More Undiplomatic Diaries, 1962–1971* (Toronto: Macmillan of Canada, 1983), 47.
36. NAC, RG 2, 8 February 1963, Cabinet Conclusions.
37. Ibid.
38. Lyon, *Canada in World Affairs*, 196–200.
39. McLin, *Canada's Changing Defence Policy*, 164–165.
40. USNARA, RG 59 3060 AII 250/63/11/03 box 1, file: Defence Affairs Canada, Nuclear Weapons, memo, Johnson to Gilpatric, 10 April 1963.
41. Lyon, *Canada in World Affairs*, 204–210.
42. Mitchell Sharp, *Which Reminds Me . . . A Memoir* (Toronto: University of Toronto Press, 1994), 106; See also Paul Martin, *A Very Public Life: So Many Worlds* (Ottawa: Deneau Publishers, 1985), 2:384.
43. Sharp, *Which Reminds Me*, 105.
44. P. Martin, *Very Public Life* 2:374.
45. Sharp, *Which Reminds Me*, 107.
46. Ibid., 109.
47. P. Martin, *Very Public Life*, 2:375.
48. Sharp, *Which Reminds Me*, 167.
49. P. Martin, *Very Public Life*, 2:376.
50. Ibid., 458.
51. Ibid., 479.
52. Walter L. Gordon, *A Political Memoir* (Toronto: McClelland and Stewart, 1977), 177.
53. Ibid., 277.
54. Ibid., 177.
55. DGHIST, Raymont Study, vol. 2, 276.
56. Ibid., 167–168.
57. Paul Hellyer, *Damn the Torpedoes: My Fight to Unify Canada's Armed Forces* (Toronto: McClelland and Stewart, 1990), 33.
58. Granatstein, *Man of Influence*, 357.
59. Hilliker and Barry, *Canada's Department of External Affairs*, 2:258–260.
60. See Gustave Morf, *Terror in Quebec: Case Studies of the FLQ* (Toronto: Clarke, Irwin, 1970) and Louis Fournier, *FLQ: Anatomy of an Underground Movement* (Toronto: NC Press, 1984), 82–83.
61. Gordon, *Political Memoir*, 157.
62. NAC, RG 24 vol. 20710 file 2-3-2, 1 May 1963, Cabinet Defence Committee, 138th meeting.
63. Ibid.
64. Ibid.
65. NAC, RG 24 vol. 20710 file 2-3-2, 7 May 1963, Cabinet Defence Committee, 139th meeting.
66. Ibid.
67. NAC, RG 2, 9 May 1963, Cabinet Conclusions.
68. Ibid.
69. Ibid.
70. Ibid.
71. Ibid.
72. Ibid.
73. Ibid.
74. Ibid.

75. Ibid.

76. U.S. DOS, *FRUS 1961–1963 Vol. XXIII*, 1201–1206, telegram, Hyannisport to State, 11 May 1963.

77. Ibid.

78. Ibid.; LBJL, VP security collection, container 12, "Briefing Book: Visit of PM Pearson, May 10–11, 1963."

79. U.S. DOS, *FRUS 1961–1963 Vol. XXIII*, 1201–1206, telegram, Hyannisport to State, 11 May 1963.

80. NAC, RG 2, 14 May 1963, Cabinet Conclusions.

81. U.S. DOS, *FRUS 1961–1963 Vol. XXIII*, 1201–1206, telegram, Hyannisport to State, 11 May 1963.

82. DGHIST, Raymont Collection, file 1086, February 1963, "Joint Statement by the Department of National Defence of Canada and the Department of National Defence, United States"; 6 March 1963, message, Washington, DC to External, "SAC: Phase Out of Refuelling Facilities"; USNARA, RG 59 vol. 3060 box 1, AII/250/63/11/03 file: Defence Affairs: Canada, memo, Newman to Johnson, "U.S. Military Activities Affecting Canada," 9 April 1963.

83. NAC, RG 25 vol. 4486 file: 50030-40 pt. 9, 24 January 1963, message, Paris to External, "The Future of NATO."

84. NAC, RG 25 vol. 4486, file: 50030-40 pt. 9, 19 April 1963, "Notes on Defence Topics—Discussions Between Mr. Pearson and Mr. Macmillan."

85. DGHIST, file 79/34, 26 November 1962, "Multilateral Seabased MRBM Force—Summary of U.S. Briefing."

86. DGHIST, Raymont Collection, file 1311A, 2 May 1963, COSC, 738th meeting; 16 May 1963, COSC, 740th meeting.

87. DGHIST, file 79/34, 3 May 1963, "Multilateral Seabased MRBM Force—The Canadian Position."

88. NAC, RG 2, 15 May 1963, Cabinet Conclusions.

89. Ibid.

90. NAC, RG 2, 16 May 1963, Cabinet Conclusions.

91. P. Martin, *Very Public Life*, 2:460.

92. NAC, RG 2, 20 May 1963, Cabinet Conclusions.

93. This was proposed back in November 1962. See USNARA, RG 200 box 82, "NATO Defence Data Program," 30 November 1962; and U.S. DOS, *FRUS 1961–1963 Vol. XXIII*, 575–578, "NATO Ministerial Meeting, Ottawa, May 22–24 1963," 17 May 1963; 579–582, "United States Delegation to the Thirty-First Ministerial Meeting of the North Atlantic Council," 23 May 1963.

94. U.S. DOS, *FRUS 1961–1963 Vol. XXIII*, 582–587, memcon, Kennedy and Stikker, "European Situation," 28 May 1963.

95. Ibid.

96. U.S. DOS, *FRUS 1961–1963 Vol. XXIII*, 587–589, message, State to certain missions, "NATO Ministerial Meeting, Ottawa," 29 May 1963.

97. David N. Schwartz, *NATO's Nuclear Dilemmas* (Washington, DC: Brookings Institution, 1983), 122.

98. DGHIST, Raymont Collection, file 1311, 12 July 1963, COSC, 744th meeting.

99. Ibid.

100. Ibid.

101. NAC, RG 2, 18 July 1963, Cabinet Conclusions.

102. Ibid.

103. NAC, RG 2, 25 July 1963, Cabinet Conclusions.

104. NAC, RG 24 vol. 20710 file 2-3-2, 2 August 1963, Cabinet Defence Committee, 140th meeting.

105. NAC, RG 2, 16 August 1963, Cabinet Conclusions; ATI, "Copy of Press Release Issues 16 Aug 63 by the Office of the Prime Minister."
106. DGHIST, file 73/276 vol. 2, 29 August 1963, memo, CAS to distribution list, "Implementation of Nuclear Weapon Programs."
107. NAC, MG 26 N3 vol. 285 file 856.21 (conf), n.d., "Statement to Be Made by the Prime Minister in the House of Commons"; 1 October 1963, memo, Robertson to Prime Minister, "Nuclear Agreement Concerning U.S. Forces at Goose Bay and Harmon Air Force Base"; NAC, RG 2, 9 May 1963, Cabinet Conclusions.
108. Newman, *Distemper of Our Times*, 38–39.
109. NAC, MG 32 B9 vol. 87, file: Report to the House, Defence, Canada, "Confidential Supplement to the Records of the Special Committee on Defence: Supplement A."
110. Ibid.
111. Ibid.
112. Ibid.
113. Ibid.
114. Ibid.
115. Ibid.
116. Ibid.
117. Ibid.
118. Ibid.
119. NAC, MG 32 B9 vol. 87, file: Report to the House, Defence, Canada, "Confidential Supplement to the Records of the Special Committee on Defence: Supplement B."
120. Ibid.
121. Ibid.
122. NAC, MG 32 B9 vol. 87, file: Report to the House, Defence, Canada, n.d., "Draft Report: Special Committee on Defence." This section is a concise summation of the committee's conclusions and not a verbatim summation.
123. Ibid.
124. FOIA, History and Research Division, HQ Strategic Air Command, "History of the Joint Strategic Target Planning Staff: Background and Preparation of SIOP-62"; see Anthoney Gray's novel, *The Penetrators* (New York: G.P. Putnam, 1965) for a fictional depiction of JSTPS activities. It is clear that Gray either worked in SAC HQ/JSTPS or knew people who did. The novel is a plea against placing too much emphasis on ICBMs over manned bombers.
125. U.S. DOS, *FRUS 1961–1963 Vol. VIII*, 138–152, raft memo, McNamara to Kennedy, "Recommended Long Range Nuclear Delivery Forces 1963–1967," 23 September 1961.
126. David Alan Rosenberg, "U.S. Nuclear War Planning, 1945–1960," in *Strategic Nuclear Targeting*, ed. Desmond Ball and Jeffrey Richelson (Ithaca New York: Cornell University Press, 1986), 35–56.
127. Desmond Ball, "The Development of the SIOP, 1960–1983," in *Strategic Nuclear Targeting*, ed. Ball and Richelson, 57–83; David Alan Rosenberg, ed., "Nuclear War Planning," in *The Laws of War: Constraints on Warfare in the Western World*, ed. Michael Howard, George J. Andreopoulos, and Mark R. Shulman (New Haven, CT: Yale University Press, 1996), 160–190.
128. U.S. DOS, *FRUS 1961–1963 Vol. VIII*, 126–129, memo, Taylor to Kennedy, "Strategic Air Planning and Berlin," 19 September 1961.
129. FOIA, History and Research Division, HQ Strategic Air Command, January 1964, "History of the Joint Strategic Target Planning Staff: Preparation of SIOP-63"; U.S. DOS, *FRUS 1961–1963 Vol. VIII*, 82, memcon, Kaysen and Rowan, 25 May 1961.
130. Rosenberg, "Nuclear War Planning," Michael Howard, George J. Andreopoulos, and Mark R. Shulman, eds. *The Laws of War: Constraints on Warfare in the Western World*

(New Haven, CT: Yale University Press, 1994), 178–179; U.S. DOS, *FRUS 1961–1963 Vol. VIII*, 125, editorial note No. 41.

131. Rosenberg, "Nuclear War Planning," 178–179.

132. Power, *Design for Survival*, 178–179.

133. U.S. DOS, *FRUS 1961–1963 Vol. VIII*, 138–152, draft memo, McNamara to Kennedy, "Recommended Long Range Nuclear Delivery Forces 1963–1967," 23 September 1961.

134. U.S. DOS, *FRUS 1961–1963 Vol. VIII*, 543–560, "Summary record of the 520th Meeting of the National Security Council: Soviet Military Capabilities," 5 December 1963.

135. USNARA, Office of the Secretary of Defence History section, oral history interview, Gen. Lyman L. Lemnitzer, 19 January 1984.

136. Hellyer, *Damn the Torpedoes*, 117–118; letter, Paul Hellyer to Maloney, 16 August 1995.

137. Col. Fred Lockwood, USAF Ret'd, interview by the author, 28 December 1993, Henderson Village, NY; Adm. Yogi Kaufman, USN Ret'd, telephone interview by the author, 10 August 1995.

138. USNARA, RG 218 JCS 1961 box 149 file 9051/112 ACE, JCS, "Establishment of SACEUR Liaison Officer to JSTPS," 13 April 1961.

139. DDEL, Norstad Papers, Mobile Force folder, message, JCS to USCINCEUR; USCINCEUR to JCS, 12 January 1962.

140. FOIA, History and Research Division, HQ Strategic Air Command, "History of the Joint Strategic Target Planning Staff: Preparation of SIOP-64 Vol. 1—Narrative."

141. FOIA, History and Research Division, HQ Strategic Air Command, "History of the Joint Strategic Target Planning Staff: Revisions 1-8 to SIOP-64."

142. Ibid.

143. Lockwood interview.

144. Lockwood interview; Kaufman interview.

145. FOIA, History and Research Division, HQ Strategic Air Command, "History of the Joint Strategic Target Planning Staff: Revisions 1–8 to SIOP-64."

146. Lockwood interview; Kaufman interview; Colonel John David, telephone interview by the author, 22 February 1993; Schultz interview.

Chapter 13

1. NAC, MG 32 B9 vol. 87, House of Commons, "Confidential Supplement to the Records of the Special Committee on Defence, November 1963."

2. DDEL, Norstad Papers, file: NAC Meeting (3), 26 January 1961, "SACEUR's Briefing of NATO Council at SHAPE."

3. NAC, MG 26 N6 file: Defence Correspondance, 11 July 1963, letter, George Drew to Pearson.

4. Donald T. Steury, ed., *Intentions and Capabilities: Estimates on Soviet Strategic Forces, 1950–1983* (Washington, DC: CIA History Staff, 1996), 204–205.

5. Ray Bonds, ed., *The Soviet War Machine* (New York: Chartwell Books, 1976), see map p. 73. This map was adapted from a U.S. Air Force study.

6. *From Snark to Peacekeeper: A Pictoral History of Strategic Air Command Missiles* (Offut, NE: Office of the Historian HQ Strategic Air Command, 1990), 51–61.

7. Robert Berman and Bill Gunston, *Rockets and Missiles of World War III* (New York: Exeter Books, 1983), 27; Hansen, *U.S. Nuclear Weapons*, 107; Kenneth P. Werrell, *The Evolution of the Cruise Missile* (Maxwell AFB, AK: Air University Press, 1985), 108–112.

8. Sokolsky, *Seapower in the Nuclear Age*, 60–61; Thomas Cochrane, William Arkin, and Robert S. Norris, *Nuclear Weapons Databook: U.S. Nuclear Forces and Capabilities*, vol. 1 (New York: Ballinger, 1984), 11; Berman and Gunston, *Rockets and Missiles*, 33.

9. USN OA, "Report of the Commander in Chief U.S. Atlantic Fleet Upon Being Relieved, Period 1 July 1964 to 30 April 1965"; Mats Berdal, *Forging a Maritime Alliance: Norway and the Evolution of American Maritime Strategy, 1845–1960* (Oslo: Iinstitutt for Forsvarsstudier, 1993), 116–124; W. Bauss, ed., *Radio Navigation Systems for Aviation and Maritime Use: A Comparative Study* (New York: Pergamon Press, 1963), 119–126.

10. Humphrey Wynn, *RAF Nuclear Deterrent Forces* (London: HMSO, 1994), 363–370, 493–497.

11. DDEL, Norstad Papers, Mobile Force folder, message, JCS to USCINCEUR; USCINCEUR to JCS, 12 January 1962.

12. Norris, Burroughs, and Fieldhouse, *British, French, and Chinese*, 49; Wynn, *RAF Nuclear Deterrent Forces*, 552–553.

13. John Fricker, "Lockheed F-104 Starfighter," *Wings of Fame: The Journal of Classic Combat Aircraft* 2 (1996): 93, 98.

14. Simon Duke, *United States Military Forces and Installations in Europe* (Oxford: Oxford University Press, 1989), 178, 288–189; William M. Arkin and Richard Fieldhouse, *Nuclear Battlefields: Global Links to the Arms Race* (Cambridge, MA: Ballinger, 1985), 219, 233.

15. Fricker, "Lockheed F-104 Starfighter," 93–94.

16. Jean-Jacques Petit, "Le F-100 dans l'Armee' de l'Air," *Le Fana de l'Aviation*, no. 282 (May 1993): 50–57; Chris Ashworth, *RAF Bomber Command 1936–1968* (Somerset, UK: PSL Publishing, 1995), 161; Robert Jackson, *Canberra: The Operational Record* (Washington, DC: Smithsonian Institution Press, 1989), 39–44; letter and attachment, Brevt Colonel M. Paulissen to Maloney, 10 February 1995, "History of the Belgian Army," in Fricker, "Lockheed F-104 Starfighter," 93, 98; P. A. van de Werve, "The Royal Netherlands Air Force," *Royal Air Forces Quarterly* 1, no. 2 (Summer 1962): 99–105; Fricker, "Lockheed F-104 Starfighter"; Bob Archer, "USAFE 1970–1979: A Decade of Airpower," *Wings of Fame: The Journal of Classic Combat Aircraft* 4 (1996): 138–157; Becker, *Starfighter F-104*, 115–126; Robert Robinson, *USAF Europe 1948–1965* (New Carrollton, TX: Squadron/Signal Publications, 1982); NSA, Presidential Briefing Book—1966: "Army's PERSHING Surface-to-surface Ballistic Missile is Being Optimized for the Quick Reaction Alert Role"; Robert Robinson and David Menard, *F-100 Super Sabre* (New Carrollton, TX: Squadron-Signal Publications, 1992).

17. Fricker, "Lockheed F-104 Starfighter."

18. FOIA, USNARA, RG 200 box 21 tab 7, "Analysis of SACEUR Emergency Defence Plans and Related Postures," 18 May 1964.

19. Archer, "USAFE 1970–1979: A Decade of Airpower"; Cecil Brownlow, "F-105D's Limited War Capability Boosted," *Aviation Week and Space Technology*, 25 February 1963, 105–111; Harvey, *Strike Command*, 178–186; See also Bill Yenne, *Aircraft of the U.S. Air Force and Its NATO Allies* (New York: Gallery Books, 1987).

20. FOIA, USNARA, RG 200 box 21 tab 7, "Analysis of SACEUR Emergency Defence Plans and Related Postures," 18 May 1964.

21. Ivo H. Daalder, *The Nature and Practice of Flexible Response: NATO Strategy and Theater Nuclear Forces Since 1967* (New York: Columbia University Press, 1991), 108–109.

22. DGHIST, Raymont Collection, file 1391, 13 October 1966, Defence Council—minutes, 200th meeting.

23. NSA, Cuban Missile Crisis microfilm collection, frame 1325/2, message, JCS to SECSTATE, 25 October 1962.

24. ATI, 29 May 1961, minutes of Current Planning Committee meeting, May 1961.

25. NSA, memo for SECDEF, "Tactical Fighters for NATO Europe," 8 September 1961;

Ray Bonds, ed., *Soviet War Machine*, see map p. 73. This map was adapted from a U.S. Air Force study.

26. Colonel John David, interview.

27. DGHIST, file: Air Marshal Dunlap Speeches—1963, 16 January 1963, "Address to General Officers Commanding Conference."

28. Bashow, *Starfighter*, 28–30; letter, LCol William Anderson to Maloney, 13 September 1996.

29. Maloney, *War Without Battles*, 242.

30. Bashow, *Starfighter*, 54–58.

31. Correspondance LGen Reg Lane (CF Ret'd) with Sean Maloney, 1 December 1995.

32. Bashow, *Starfighter*, 30; NAC, RG 24 acc 86-87/65 box 16 vol. 1, 17 April 1964, message, USAFE to CANAIRDIV Metz; NAC, RG 24 acc 86-87/165 box 16 vol. 2, 11 May 1967, "Summaries of Briefings Presented to Joint RCAF/USAF Operational Review Board—CF-104/Mk. 57 NWS."

33. NAC, RG 24 acc 86-87/65 box 18 vol. 3, file 3313-22, n.d., "Draft Safety Rules for the Non-U.S. NATO CF-104/ MK 28 RE and MK 28 EX Weapons Systems"; 3 December 1963, memo to DADSI, "CF-104 Plan of System Operation"; Hansen, *U.S. Nuclear Weapons*, 151–154. A 1993 conversation by the author in Ottawa with a retired brigadier general, who was a former RCAF group captain, on the yields of the weapons in question resulted in glib astonished disbelief when confronted with the megaton-yield range of the weapons. He claimed that the Americans would never allow NATO, let alone Canada, access to such weapons, and that all weapons were in the kt-yield range. At least two secondary sources, Bashow's *Starfighter* (p. 61) and Becker's *Starfighter F-104* (p. 114), cite the average yield of the weapons as approximately 1 MT.

34. Hansen, *U.S. Nuclear Weapons*, 158–161; NAC, RG 24 acc 86-87/165 box 18 vol. 3 file 3313–22, 1 February 1966, CDS to COMMATCOM, "Nuclear Weapons Safety— CF-104 Limitations on Operations"; 14 February 1969, message CANFORCHED to CANAIRDIV; 20 Feb 69, message CANFORCHED to CANAIRDIV; 3 February 1969, memo to DNW, "1 Air Division Stockpile No. 2 Weapon."

35. Hansen, *U.S. Nuclear Weapons*, 164–166; NAC, RG 24 acc 86-87/165 box 18 vol. 2 file 3313–22, 28 February 1966, message, USAFE to CANAIRDIV, "Mk-57 Weapon"; NAC, RG 24 acc 86-87/165 box 18 vol. 3 file 3313–22, 15 June 1966, "CFHQ Nuclear Weapon Instruction NWI 306 (Second Issue)."

36. NAC, RG 24 acc 86-87/165 box 18 vol. 1, 25 May 1964, memo, DNW to DARMENG, "CF-104 Nuclear Weapons Safety Operational Duals—Project ABALONE"; 19 May 1964, message, RCAF LO Kirtland AFB to CANAIRHED, "Project ABALONE"; 20 April 1964, memo, DARMENG to Lockheed, "CF-104D Aircraft-Project ABALONE: Electrical Compatibility Trials"; 10 April 1964, memo, CAS to RCAF LO Kirtland AFB, "CF-104D Armament Installations T&DI Project ABALONE"; NAC, RG 24 acc 86-87/165 box 18 vol. 2, 11 May 1967, "CFHQ/VCDS/DNW Report on the Operational Review of the CF-104/CF-104D/Mk. 57 Nuclear Weapons Systems."

37. Hansen, *U.S. Nuclear Weapons*, 166–168; David Anderson, telephone interview by the author, 10 April 1996; NAC, RG 24 acc 86-87/165 box 18 vol. 4, 31 May 1968, memo to distribution list, "CF-104/CF-104D Mk. II Checklists."

38. NAC, RG 24 acc 86-87/165 box 18 vol. 4, 15 February 1967, message CANAIRDIV to CANFORCEHED; 26 January 1967, message CANFORCHED to CANAIRDIV; 15 December 1966, memo, DConP to distribution list, "RCAF/USAFE CF-104 Technical Agreement Amendment #5."

39. Letter, LCol William Anderson to Maloney, 13 June 1995.

40. Ibid.

41. Correspondance, LGen Reg Lane to Maloney, 1 December 1995.

42. Letter LCol William Anderson to Maloney, 31 June 1995; Schultz interview; confidential interviews.

43. LCol William Anderson, telephone interviews by the author, 28 November 1996; 23 July 1997.

44. Correspondance, LGen Reg Lane to Maloney, 1 December 1995.

45. Ibid.; Irving Breslauer, "Fourth Allied Tactical Air Force," *Sentinel*, January 1967, 18–20.

46. USNARA, RG 218 JCS 1961 box 147 file 9050/4900 NATO, 5 October 1962, JCS report by the J-1, "Emergency Personnel Requirements Program for Allied Command Europe"; BGen Herb Sutherland, telephone interview by the author, 25 February 1994; see also "The Control of Nuclear Weapons," *Survival* 6 (1964): 278–279.

47. BGen Herb Sutherland, telephone interview, 25 February 1994; USNARA, RG 218 JCS 1961 box 147 file 4050/6000 NATO, 22 March 1963, JCS decision, "Requirement for U.S. Teletype (Off-Line Crypto)."

48. NAC, RG 24 acc 86-87/165 box 16 vol. 2, 11 May 1967, "Summaries of Briefings Presented to Joint RCAF/USAF Operational Review Board—CF-104/Mk. 57 NWS."

49. NAC, RG 24 acc 86-87/165 box 18 vol. 1, 3 December 1963, DADSI, "CF-104 Plan of System Operation."

50. FOIA, USNARA, RG 200 box 21 tab 7, "Analysis of SACEUR Emergency Defence Plans and Related Postures," 18 May 1964.

51. NAC, RG 24 acc 86-87/165 box 16 vol. 2, 11 May 1967, "Summaries of Briefings Presented to Joint RCAF/USAF Operational Review Board—CF-104/Mk. 57 NWS."

52. NAC, RG 24 acc 86-87/165 box 18 vol. 1, 3 December 1963, DADSI, "CF-104 Plan of System Operation."

53. Ibid.

54. Sutherland interview.

55. NAC, RG 24 acc 86-87/165 box 18 vol. 1, 3 December 1963, DADSI, "CF-104 Plan of System Operation."

56. LCol William Anderson, telephone interview by the author, 28 November 1996.

57. Ibid.

58. FOIA, USNARA, RG 200 box 21 tab 7, "Analysis of SACEUR Emergency Defence Plans and Related Postures," 18 May 1964.

59. See Paul Stares, *Command Performance: The Neglected Dimension of European Security* (Washington, DC: Brookings Institution, 1991), 130, 224.

60. Hellyer, *Damn the Torpedoes*, 75.

61. Letter, Paul Hellyer to Maloney, 16 August 1995.

62. He noted in a speech that newspaper reports of 1 MT weapons were "gross exagerrations." See DGHIST, file: Air Marshal Dunlap Speeches—1963, 19 July 1963, "Remarks by Air Marshal Dunlap, National Defence College."

63. NAC, MG 26 N6 file: Defence Correspondence, 11 July 1963, letter, Geroge Drew to Pearson.

64. Jackson, *Canberra*, 39–44; Fricker, "Starfighter"; Archer, "USAFE 1970–1979."

65. NAC, RG 24 acc 83-84/167 vol. 6281, file 1038-1110 F-104G.3 v.2, "Notes on the Recce Meeting Held at GMOD on 6–7 Feb 1962."

66. Confidential interview.

67. Ibid.

68. Hellyer, *Damn the Torpedoes*, 117–118; letter, Hellyer to Maloney, 16 August 1995; NAC, RG 24 acc 86-87/165 box 18 vol. 2, 11 February 1965, memo, DNW to NW2, "CF-104 Nuclear-Conventional Weapons Interface."

69. LCol William Anderson, telephone interview by author, 28 November 1996; NAC, RG

24 acc 86-87/165 box 18 vol. 2, 4 March 1965, memo, DARMEng to DNW, "CF-104 Aircraft Armament Installations Conventional Weapons Systems—Nuclear Safety Implications"; 11 February 1965, memo, DNW to NW2, "CF-104 Nuclear-Conventional Weapons Interface."

70. See Tony Geraghty's excellent *Beyond the Front Line: The Untold Exploits of Britain's Most Daring Cold War Spy Mission* (London: Harper Collins Publishers, 1996) for a discussion of BRIXMIS operations and the treaties which permitted this activity. See also Maloney, *War Without Battles*, 42, 390–391.

71. William Dickson, David Anderson, William Anderson, Joe Schultz, and Tom Henry/ Jack Orr interviews and correspondence.

72. House of Commons, SCOND, 28 and 29 June 1966; DGHIST, file 73/430, "RCAF Programme of Activities 1961–66"; FOIA, NORAD Historical Office, 31 December 1982, "NORAD Resource Statistics Book."

73. NAC, RG 24 acc 86-82/165 box 17 file 3313-20 vol. 2, 21 October 1969, DNW-2, "Nuclear Weapons Field Activities: CIM-10B/BUIC III Operational Review History."

74. FOIA, NORAD Historical Office, 31 December 1982, "NORAD Resource Statistics Book."

75. Ibid.; Drendel and Stevens, *VooDoo*, 26, 48; Keaveney, *McDonnell F-101B/F*, 1–6; SCOND, 28 and 29 June 1966.

76. Hansen, *U.S. Nuclear Weapons*, 177–179.

77. DGHIST, Hendrick Papers, Daily Dairy, 4 October 1963.

78. ATI, 16 October 1963, memo, DCE to COR, "Programme of Acquisition of Nuclear Weapons."

79. DGHIST, Hendrick Papers, Daily Dairy, 18 February 1964.

80. NAC, RG 24 vol. 8 file 3315–22 vol. 2, 27 October 1966, memo, CDS to Comd ADC, "Changes to Supplementary Arrangements for CIM-10B and CF101/AIR-2A Weapons Systems"; 24 September 1963, memo, DAFT to DOE, "Trip Report—Lowry Technical Training Centre USAF."

81. A. M. Lee, *Chatham: An Airfield History* (Fredericton, NB: Unipress, 1989), 45–46.

82. Letter, D. A. Nicks to Maloney, 16 February 1994.

83. Ibid.

84. Ibid.; ATI, 11 September 1963, memo to CAE, "Organization and Establishment for Safety and Inspection of Special Weapon in the RCAF."

85. FOIA, NORAD Historical Office, 31 December 1982, "NORAD Resource Statistics Book."

86. NAC, RG 24 acc 86-82/165 box 17 file 3313–20 vol. 2, n.d., "BOMARC Operational Review: Briefing by ADCHQ"; ATI, 7–8 November 1963, DADSI to DOE, "Visit Report to HQ USAF."

87. NAC, RG 24 vol. 8 file 3315–22 vol. 2, 3 January 1964, message, CinCNORAD to Air Marshal Dunlap.

88. ATI, 8 January 1964, memo, Campbell to Miller; memo, Martin to Pearson.

89. NAC, RG 24 vol. 8 file 3315–22 vol. 2, 1 January 1964, message, Austin to Hendricks.

90. Ibid.

91. ATI, 6 December 1963, memo, Hellyer to Martin.

92. FOIA, USAF, Ray, "BOMARC and Nuclear Armamant."

93. DGHIST, file 79/34, 9 July 1963, memo, ACN (A&W) to CNS, "Effectiveness of Naval (RCN) Response to the Threat Now and in the Foreseeable Future—1970s."

94. Ibid.

95. DGHIST, file 79/34, 22 November 1963, memo to distribution list, "Visit Report of J. S. Vigder, DOR(N)."

96. Ibid.

97. Ibid.

98. DGHIST, file 124.019(D1), "The Future Fleet: A Presentation to the Naval Staff—November 1963."

99. Ibid.

100. DGHIST, file 79/34, 6 May 1963, memo, ACNS (A&W) to CNS, "Nuclear Warheads for the Canadian Forces."

101. DGHIST, NPPCC files, 3 March 1964, "Supplement to the Minutes of the 293rd Meeting of the Naval policy Coordinating Committee: Nuclear Weapons for Anti-Submarine Warfare."

102. See NAC, RG 24 vol. 573 file 098.1058, 25 May 1962, memo, VCAS to CAS, "Employment and Control of RCN Fixed Wing Aircraft." Note that these documents were marked "RCAF Eyes Only."

103. DGHIST, NPPCC files, 3 March 1964, "Supplement to the Minutes of the 293rd Meeting of the Naval policy Coordinating Committee: Nuclear Weapons for Anti-Submarine Warfare."

104. Ibid.; Maloney and Sokolsky, "Ready, Willing, and Able."

105. DGHIST, Naval Board files, 13 March 1964, Naval Board, 724th meeting.

106. DGHIST, Raymont Collection, file 1311, 30 April 1964, COSC, 764th meeting.

107. Ibid.

108. Ibid.

109. "Composition of the Fleet," *Crowsnest*, March–April 1965, 36.

110. DGHIST, file 124.019(D1), 6 January 1964, "Study on Size and Shape of the Royal Canadian Navy 1964–1974."

111. Ibid.

112. Ibid.

113. Ibid.

114. Ibid.

115. Michael A. Hennessy, "The Rise and Fall of a Canadian Maritime Policy, 1939–1965: A Study of Industry, Navalism and the State" (PhD diss., University of New Brunswick, 1995), 385–418.

116. DGHIST, Raymont Collection, file 384, 31 January 1967, "Maritime Systems Study."

117. Ibid.

118. Ibid.

119. Ibid.

120. USNARA, RG 200 box 23 file 16/32, memo to the President, "Anti-Submarine Warfare Forces FY 1965–1969," 18 October 1963; memo for the President, "Recommended FY 1966–FY 1970 Anti-Submarine Warfare Forces," 20 October 1964.

121. Hansen, *U.S. Nuclear Weapons*, 207–209; Friedman, *World Naval Weapons Systems*, 415–416; Polmar, *Ships and Aircraft of the U.S. Fleet (14th Ed)*, 58–63, 481–482.

122. Ibid., Hansen, *U.S. Nuclear Weapons*, 84, 86, 208; Cochrane, Arkin, and Norris, *Nuclear Weapons Databook*, 267–268.

123. *Jane's Fighting Ships 1971–72*, 41–49.

124. Confidential interview.

125. Maloney, *War Without Battles*, 201. Note that the details of NATO nuclear Defence planning in Central Region are included in this book, including maps.

126. Ibid., 205.

127. Ibid.

128. Ibid., 289.

129. Ibid., 209.

130. NAC, RG 24 acc 83-84/215 file 1200 pt. 4.2 vol. 16, 14 December 1960, 4 CIBG to VCGS, "Support Arrangements: Surface-to-Surface Missile Battery, RCA"; confidential interview.

131. Dan G. Loomis, "Not Much Glory: An Account of the Canadian Forces Adaptation to the FLQ Crisis and Other Low Intensity Conflicts," (1984) draft manuscript stored at the Fort Frontenac Library, Kingston, Ontario, p. 287.

132. Crow interview; Hansen, *U.S. Nuclear Weapons*, 193; DGHIST, file 83/601, 1967, "Drill for Assembly of Honest John Rocket 762mm MGR 1B (M50)."

133. Hansen, *U.S. Nuclear Weapons*, 174.

134. Maloney, *War Without Battles*, 137.

135. Barney Oldfield, "The Lance: Shoot and Scoot," *NATO's Fifteen Nations*, April–May 1975, 78–82; NSA, memorandum for the President, "Progam of Cooperation to Replace Honest John with Lance in Non-U.S. NATO Forces," 9 June 1966; Cochran, Arkin, and Norris, *Nuclear Weapons Databook*, 284–285.

136. Hansen, *U.S. Nuclear Weapons*, 173–176.

137. LCol R. C. Stowell, telephone interview by the author, 27 July 1997.

Chapter 14

1. See Patrick M. Morgan, *Deterrence: A Conceptual Approach* (Beverly Hills, CA: Sage Publications, 1977) and Herman Kahn, *On Escalation* (Baltimore, MD: Pelican Books, 1965).

2. That is, provide a new direction for disarmament policy established under Pearson in the 1950s. See Joseph Levitt, *Pearson and Canada's Role in Nuclear Disarmament and Arms Control Negotiations 1945–1957* (Kingston: McGill-Queen's University Press, 1993).

3. Janne E. Nolan discusses the divergence between American civilian and uniformed nuclear policy makers in *Guardians of the Arsenal: The Politics of National Strategy* (New York: Basic Books, 1989).

SELECTED BIBLIOGRAPHY

Personal and Association Papers

National Archives of Canada, Ottawa:
Jeffry V. Brock Papers
E. L. M. Burns Papers
Brooke Claxton Papers
Gordon Churchill Papers
Harry George DeWolf Papers
John G. Diefenbaker Papers
Howard Green Papers
Douglas Harkness Papers
A. D. P. Heeney Papers
Andrew McNaughton Papers
Lester B. Pearson Papers

Director General, History, Ottawa:
Carstairs Arnell Papers
Charles Foulkes Papers
Max Hendrick Papers
Charles Raymont Collection

University of Toronto Archives, Toronto:
O. M. Solandt Papers
C. P. Stacey Papers

Trinity College Archives, Toronto:
George Ignatieff Papers

Canadian Institute of International Affairs, Toronto:
John Holmes Papers

University of Victoria Archives, Victoria:
George Pearkes Papers

Dwight D. Eisenhower Library, Abilene, KS:
John Foster Dulles Papers
Alfred Gruenther Papers
Lauris Norstad Papers

U.S. National Archives and Record Administration, Washington, DC:
Lyman L. Lemnitzer Papers
Robert S. McNamara Papers

U.S. Navy Operational Archives, Washington, DC:
Arleigh Burke Papers
Forrest Sherman Papers

Library of Congress, Manuscript Division, Washington, DC:
Lynde McCormick Papers

Yale University, New Haven, CT:
Dean Acheson Papers

Archives Record Groups

Director General, History, Ottawa:
Memoranda of the Cabinet Defence Committee
Memoranda of the Chiefs of Staff Committee
Memoranda of the Joint Planning Committee
Raymont Collection

Dwight D. Eisenhower Library, Abilene, KS:
White House Office: Office of the Special Assistant for National Security Affairs, 1952–61
White House Office: National Security Council Staff Papers, 1948–61

John F. Kennedy Library, Boston:
National Security Files
Department of Defence
Department of State

Lyndon B. Johnson Library, Austin, TX:
National Security File

National Archives of Canada, Ottawa:
RG 2: Cabinet Memoranda and Conclusions
RG 24: Department of National Defence
RG 25: External Affairs
RG 49: Department of Defence Production

Public Record Office, Kew (London):
ADM 204 Admiralty Research Laboratory Files
ADM 205 First Sea Lord's Records
ADM 223 Monthly Intelligence Reports
DEFE 4 Chiefs of Staff Committee Minutes, 1947–1957
DEFE 6 Chiefs of Staff Committee Joint Planning Staff Documents, 1947–1959
DEFE 7 NATO-General
DEFE 11 Chiefs of Staff Committee Registered Files, 1946–1964
DEFE 13 Private Office Papers, 1950–1965

U.S. National Archives and Record Administration, Washington, DC:
RG 59: State Department
RG 218: Joint Chiefs of Staff

U.S. Navy Operational Archive, Washington, DC:
Strategic Plans Division 1945–1955
CinCLANTFLT Annual Reports, 1946–1970
CinCPACFLT Annual Reports, 1946–70
Annual Reports to the Secretary of the Navy 1952–1965

Interviews and Correspondence

General J. V. Allard, Canadian Army
Colonel William J. Anderson, RCAF
Lieutenant General M. R. Dare, Canadian Army
Air Marshal C. Dunlap, RCAF
Keith P. Farrell
Major General J. C. Gardner, Canadian Army
General Sir John Hackett, British Army
Colonel Tom Henry, Canadian Forces
Lieutenant General A. Chester Hull, RCAF
VAdm Yogi Kaufman, USN
Major General George Kitching, Canadian Army
Lieutenant General Reg Lane, RCAF
Colonel Fred Lockwood, USAF
Group Captain Robert Schultz, RCAF
Brigadier General Herb Sutherland, RCAF
Major General A. J. Tedlie, Canadian Army

Oral Histories

U.S. Navy Operational Archive, Washington, DC:
Adm. George Anderson, USN
Adm. Robert B. Carney, USN
Adm. Charles K. Duncan, USN
Adm. William M. Fechteler, USN

Office of the Secretary of Defence, Historical Section:
General L. L. Lemnitzer

Published Document Collections

U.S. Joint Chiefs of Staff:
Records of the Joint Chiefs of Staff Part II: 1946–1953; Europe and NATO. Lanham, MD:
    University Publications of America, 1980. (microfilm)
Records of the Joint Chiefs of Staff Part II: 1946–1953; Strategic Issues 1. Lanham, MD:
    University Publications of America, 1980. (microfilm)
Records of the Joint Chiefs of Staff Part II: 1946–1953; Strategic Issues 2. Lanham, MD:
    University Publications of America, 1980. (microfilm)
Records of the Joint Chiefs of Staff Part II: 1946–1953; The United States. Lanham, MD:
    University Publications of America, 1980. (microfilm)

Records of the Joint Chiefs of Staff Part II: 1946–1953; The U.S. and the Soviet Union. Lanham, MD: University Publications of America, 1979. (microfilm)

U.S. Department of State:
Foreign Relations of the United States 1950 Volume I: National Security Affairs; Foreign Economic Policy. Washington, DC: GPO, 1977.
Foreign Relations of the United States 1950 Volume III: Western Europe. Washington, DC: GPO, 1977.
Foreign Relations of the United States 1951 Volume I: National Security Affairs; Foreign Economic Policy. Washington, DC: GPO, 1979.
Foreign Relations of the United States 1951 Volume II: The United Nations; The Western Hemisphere. Washington, DC: GPO, 1979.
Foreign Relations of the United States 1951 Volume III: European Security and the German Question Part 1. Washington, DC: GPO, 1981.
Foreign Relations of the United States 1952–1954 Volume II: National Security Affairs Parts 1 and 2. Washington, DC: GPO, 1986.
Foreign Relations of the United States 1952–1954 Volume VI: Western Europe and Canada. Washington, DC: GPO, 1986.
Foreign Relations of the United States 1958–1960 Volume VII: Western European Integration and Security; Canada Parts 1 and 2. Washington, DC: GPO, 1993.
Foreign Relations of the United States 1961–63 Volume XIII: Western Europe and Canada. Washington, DC: GPO, 1994.

Published Official Documents

Department of National Defence, Canada:
Canada's Defence Programme 1955–56. Ottawa: Queen's Printer, 1956.
Canada's Defence Programme 1956–57. Ottawa: Queen's Printer, 1957.
Defence 1959. Ottawa: Queen's Printer, 1959.
Defence in the 1970's. Ottawa: Queen's Printer, 1971.
Pearkes, G. R. *Statements on Defence Policy and Its Implementation.* Ottawa: Queen's Printer, 1960.
Report of the Department of National Defence for the Fiscal Year Ending 31 March 1950. Ottawa: Queen's Printer, 1950.
Report of the Department of National Defence for the Fiscal Year Ending 31 March 1951. Ottawa: Queen's Printer, 1951.
Report of the Department of National Defence for the Fiscal Year Ending 31 March 1952. Ottawa: Queen's Printer, 1952.
Report of the Department of National Defence for the Fiscal Year Ending 31 March 1953. Ottawa: Queen's Printer, 1953.
Report of the Department of National Defence for the Fiscal Year Ending 31 March 1954. Ottawa: Queen's Printer, 1954.
Report of the Department of National Defence for the Fiscal Year Ending 31 March 1955. Ottawa: Queen's Printer, 1955.

North Atlantic Treaty Organization:
NATO Basic Documents.: 4th ed. Brussels: NATO Information Service, 1989.
The NATO Handbook 1952. Bosch, Netherlands: NATO Information Service, 1952.
The NATO Handbook 1953. Bosch, Netherlands: NATO Information Service, 1953.
The North Atlantic Treaty Organization 1956. Bosch, Netherlands: NATO Information Service, 1956.

The North Atlantic Treaty Organization 1959. Bosch, Netherlands: NATO Information Service, 1959.

The North Atlantic Treaty Organization 1962. Bosch, Netherlands: NATO Information Service, 1962.

SACLANT Information Pamphlet. Norfolk, VA, [n.d.]

Published Official Histories

Canada:

Douglas, W. A. B. *The Creation of a National Air Force: The Official History of the Royal Canadian Air Force Volume II*. Toronto: University of Toronto Press, 1986.

Goodspeed, D. J. *DRB: A History of the Defence Research Board of Canada*. Ottawa: Queen's Printer, 1958.

Greenhous, Brereton, Stephen J. Harris, William C. Johnston, and William G. P. Rawling. *The Crucible of War 1939–1945: The Official History of the Royal Canadian Air Force Volume III*. Toronto: University of Toronto Press, 1994.

Hilliker, John. *Canada's Department of External Affairs Volume 1: The Early Years, 1909–1946*. Montreal and Kingston: McGill-Queen's University Press, 1990.

Hilliker, John, and Donald Barry. *Canada's Department of External Affairs Volume 2: Coming of Age, 1946–1968*. Montreal and Kingston: McGill-Queen's University Press, 1995.

Wood, Herbert Fairlie. *Strange Battleground: The Official History of the Canadian Army in Korea*. Ottawa: Crown Publishers, 1966.

United Kingdom:

Wynn, Humphrey. *RAF Nuclear Deterrent Forces*. London: HMSO, 1994.

United States:

Knaack, Marcel Size. *Post-World War II Fighters*. Washington, DC: Office of Air Force History, 1986.

McAuliffe, Mary S. *CIA Documents on the Cuban Missile Crisis 1962*. Washington, DC: CIA History Staff, 1992.

Neufeld, Jacob. *Ballistic Missiles in the United States Air Force 1945–1960*. Washington, DC: Office of Air Force History, 1990.

Poole, Walter S. *The History of the Joint Chiefs of Staff Vol. IV 1950–1952*. Washington, DC: Historical Division Joint Secretariat Joint Chiefs of Staff, December 1979.

Ruffner, Kevin C., ed. *CORONA: America's First Satellite Program*. Washington, DC: CIA History Staff, 1995.

Schaffel, Kenneth. *The Emerging Shield: The Air Force and the Evolution of Continental Air Defence 1945–1960*. Washington, DC: Office of Air Force History, 1991.

Steury, Donald T., ed. *Intentions and Capabilities: Estimates on Soviet Strategic Forces, 1950–1983*. Washington, DC: CIA History Staff, 1996.

Watson, Robert. *The History of the Joint Chiefs of Staff Vol. V The Joint Chiefs of Staff and National Policy, 1953–1954*. Washington, DC: Historical Division, Joint Chiefs of Staff, 1986.

Unpublished Theses and Dissertations

Clark, Robert H. "Canadian Weapons Acquisition: The Case of the BOMARC Missile." MA thesis, Royal Military College of Canada, 1983.

Eyre, K.C. "Custos Borealis: The Military in the Canadian North." PhD diss., King's College, 1987.

Ghent, Jocelyn Maynard. "Canadian-American Relations and the Nuclear Weapons Controversy, 1958–1963." PhD diss., University of Illinois, 1976. University Microfilms International Order Number 76-24,087.

Hennessy, Michael A. "The Rise and Fall of a Canadian Maritime Policy, 1939–1965: A Study of Industry, Navalism and the State." PhD diss., University of New Brunswick, 1995.

Rennie, Carl G. "The Mobilization of Manpower for the Canadian Army During the Korean War, 1950–1951." MA thesis, Royal Military College of Canada, 1982.

Autobiographies and Biographies

Allard, Jean Victor, and Serge Bernier. *Memoirs*. Vancouver: UBC Press, 1988.

Bothwell, Robert, and William Kilbourn. *C.D. Howe: A Biography*. Toronto: McClelland and Stewart, 1979.

Brock, Jeffry V. *With Many Voices: Memoirs of a Sailor*. Vols. 1 and 2. Toronto: McClelland and Stewart, 1983.

Burcuson, David Jay. *True Patriot: The Life of Brooke Claxton 1998–1960*. Toronto: University of Toronto Press, 1993.

English, John. *Shadow of Heaven: The Life of Lester Person, Volume One: 1897–1948*. London: Vintage UK, 1989.

————. *The Worldly Years: The Life of Lester B. Pearson, 1949–1972*. Toronto: Random House of Canada, 1993.

Gordon, Walter. *A Political Memoir*. Toronto: McClelland and Stewart, 1977.

Graham, Dominick. *The Price of Command: A Biography of General Guy Simonds*. Toronto: Stoddart Publishing, 1993.

Granatstein, J. L. *A Man of Influence: Norman A. Robertson and Canadian Statecraft, 1929–1968*. Ottawa: Deneau Publishers, 1981.

Hellyer, Paul. *Damn the Torpedoes: My Fight to Unify Canada's Armed Forces*. Toronto: McClelland and Stewart, 1990.

Ignatieff, George. *The Making of a Peacemonger: The Memoirs of George Ignatieff*. Toronto: University of Toronto Press, 1985.

LaMarsh, Judy. *Memoirs of a Bird in a Gilded Cage*. Toronto: McClelland and Stewart, 1969.

Martin, Paul. *A Very Public Life: So Many Worlds*. 2 vols. Ottawa: Deneau Publishers, 1984.

Morton, Desmond. "He Did What Had to Be Done," *Toronto Star Saturday Magazine*, June 1990, 16.

Newman, Peter C. *Renegade in Power: The Diefenbaker Years*. Toronto: McClelland and Stewart, 1963.

Pearson, Lester B. *Mike: The Memoirs of the Rt. Hon. Lester B. Pearson*. 3 vols. Toronto: University of Toronto Press, 1972.

Pickersgill, J. W. *My Years with Louis St Laurent: A Political Memoir*. Toronto: University of Toronto Press, 1975.

Pope, Maurice A. *Soldiers and Politicians*. Toronto: University of Toronto Press, 1962.

Reid, Escott. *Radical Mandarin: The Memoirs of Escott Reid*. Toronto: University of Toronto Press, 1989.

Ritchie, Charles. *Storm Signals: More Undiplomatic Diaries, 1962–1971*. Toronto: Macmillan, 1983.

Robinson, Basil. *Diefenbaker's World: A Populist in Foreign Affairs*. Toronto: University of Toronto Press, 1989.

Shapely, Deborah. *Promise and Power: The Life and Times of Robert McNamara*. Boston: Little, Brown, 1993.

Sharp, Mitchell. *Which Reminds Me . . . A Memoir*. Toronto: University of Toronto Press, 1994.

Smith, Denis. *Rogue Tory: The Life and Legend of John G. Diefenbaker*. Toronto: Macfarlane, Walter and Ross, 1995.

Stursberg, Peter. *Lester Pearson and the American Dilemma*. Toronto: Doubleday Canada, 1980.

Thomson, Dale C. *Louis St. Laurent: Canadian*. Toronto: Macmillan Canada, 1967.

Trudeau, Pierre. *Memoirs*. Toronto: McClelland and Stewart, 1993.

Worthington, Larry. *Worthy: A Biography of Major General F.F. Worthington*. Toronto: Macmillan Canada, 1961.

Published Secondary Sources

Adcock, Al. *Sea King in Action*. Carrollton, TX: Squadron/Signal Publications, 1995.

Allison, Graham T., Albert Carnesale, and Joseph S. Nye, Jr. *Hawks, Doves, and Owls: An Agenda for Avoiding Nuclear War*. New York: W.W. Norton, 1985.

Andrew, Arthur. *The Rise and Fall of a Middle Power: Canadian Diplomacy from King to Mulroney*. Toronto: Lorimer, 1993.

Anglin, Gerald. "The Russian Subs on Our Coastline," *Maclean's* 1 (April 1951): 14–16.

Arkin, William M., and Richard Fieldhouse. *Nuclear Battlefields: Global Links to the Arms Race*. Cambridge, MA: Ballinger, 1985.

Axworthy, Thomas S., and Pierre Elliott Trudeau, eds. *Towards a Just Society: The Trudeau Years*. Toronto: Viking Books, 1990.

Bacevich, A. J. *The Pentomic Era: The U.S. Army Between Korea and Vietnam*. Washington, DC: National Defence University Press, 1988.

Ball, Desmond, and Jeffrey Richelson, eds. *Strategic Nuclear Targeting*. Ithaca: Cornell University Press, 1986.

Bashow, David L. *Starfighter*. Stoney Creek, Ontario: Fortress Publications, 1990.

Becker, Hans-Jurgan. *Flugzeuge die Geschichte machen Starfighter F-104*. Stuttgart: Motorbuch Verlag, 1992.

Beschloss, Michael R. *May Day: Eisenhower, Khrushchev and the U-2 Affair*. New York: Harper and Row, 1986.

Blair, Bruce. *Strategic Command and Control: Redefining the Nuclear Threat*. Washington DC: Brookings Institution, 1985.

———. *The Logic of Accidental Nuclear War*. Washington, DC: Brookings Institution, 1993.

Bland, Douglas. *Chiefs of Defence: Government and the Unified Command of the Canadian Armed Forces*. Toronto: Canadian Institute of Strategic Studies, 1995.

———. *The Administration of Defence Policy in Canada, 1947 to 1985*. Kingston, Ontario: Ronald P. Frye, 1987.

———. *The Military Committee of the North Atlantic Alliance: A Study in Structure and Strategy*. New York: Praeger, 1991.

Blight, James G., and David A. Welch. *On the Brink: Americans and Soviets Reexamine the Cuban Missile Crisis*. New York: Hill and Wang, 1989.

Bothwell, Robert. *Canada and the United States: The Politics of Partnership*. Toronto: University of Toronto Press, 1992.

———. *Eldorado: Canada's National Uranium Company*. Toronto: University of Toronto Press, 1984.

———. *Nucleus: The History of Atomic Energy of Canada Limited*. Toronto: Toronto University Press, 1995.

Botti, Timothy J. *The Long Wait: The Forging of the Anglo-American Nuclear Alliance, 1945–1958*. New York: Greenwood, 1987.

Boutillier, James, ed. *The RCN in Retrospect, 1910–1968*. Vancouver: UBC Press, 1982.

Bracken, Paul. *The Command and Control of Nuclear Forces*. New Haven, CT: Yale University Press, 1983.

Breslauer, Irving. "Fouth Allied Tactical Air Force." *Sentinel*, January 1967, 18–20.

Brewin, Andrew. *Stand on Guard: The Search for a Canadian Defence Policy*. Toronto: McClelland and Stewart, 1965.

Brownlow, Cecil. "F-105D's Limited War Capability Boosted.," *Aviation Week and Space Technology*, February 25, 1963, 105–111.

Bruce-Briggs, B. *The Shield of Faith: A Chronicle of Strategic Defense from Zeppelins to Star Wars*. New York: Simon and Schuster, 1988.

Brugioni, Dino A. *Eyeball to Eyeball: The Inside Story of the Cuban Missile Crisis*. New York: Random House, 1990.

Burns, E. L. M. *Megamurder*. Toronto: Clarke-Irwin, 1966.

Buteux, Paul. *The Politics of Nuclear Consultation in NATO 1965–1980*. New York: Cambridge University Press, 1983.

Campagna, Palmiro. *Storms of Controversy: The Secret Avro Arrow Files Revealed*. Toronto: Stoddart, 1992.

Canadian Institute of International Affairs. *Canada in World Affairs 1961–1963*. Toronto: Oxford University Press, 1968.

Carter, Ashton, ed. *Managing Nuclear Operations*. Washington, DC: Brookings Institution, 1987.

Chang, Lawrence, and Peter Kornbluh. *The Cuban Missile Crisis 1962*. New York: New Press, 1992.

Charles, Daniel. *Nuclear Planning in NATO: Pitfalls of First Use*. Cambridge: Ballinger, 1987.

Cioc, Mark. *Pax Atomica: The Nuclear Defence Debate in West Germany During the Adenauer Era*. New York: Columbia University Press, 1988.

Clark, Ian. *Nuclear Diplomacy and the Special Relationship: Britain's Deterrent and America, 1957–1962*. Oxford: Clarendon Press, 1994.

Clarkson, Stephen., ed. *An Independent Foreign Policy for Canada?* Toronto: McClelland and Stewart, 1968.

Clements, W. I. "The Evolution and Status of Maritime Command." *Roundel* (October 1961): 2–9.

Cochrane, Thomas, William Arkin, and Robert S. Norris. *Nuclear Weapons Databook: U.S. Nuclear Forces and Capabilities*. Vol. 1. New York: Ballinger, 1984.

Cook, Don. *Forging the Alliance: NATO 1945–1950*. New York: Arbor House/William Morrow, 1989.

Coughlin, T. G. "City in a Mountain." *Roundel* (June 1961): 24–26.

Crane, Brian. *An Introduction to Canadian Defence Policy*. Toronto: Canadian Institute of Strategic Studies, 1964.

Cuthberson, Brian. *Canadian Military Independence in the Age of the Superpowers*. Toronto: Fitzhenry and Whiteside, 1977.

Daalder, Ivo H. *The Nature and Practice of Flexible Response: NATO Strategy and Theater Nuclear Forces Since 1967*. New York: Columbia University Press, 1991.

Diggle, W. M. "Evolution of the Argus." *Roundel* (May 1958): 2–32.

Dow, James. *The Arrow*. Toronto: James Lorimer, 1979.

Duke, Simon. *United States Military Forces and Installations in Europe*. Oxford: Oxford University Press, 1989.

Eayrs, James. *In Defence of Canada: Growing Up Allied*. Toronto: University of Toronto Press, 1980.

―――. *In Defence of Canada: Indo-China: Roots of Complicity*. Toronto: University of Toronto Press, 1983.

―――. *In Defence of Canada: Peacemaking and Deterrence*. Toronto: University of Toronto Press, 1972.

―――. *Northern Approaches: Canada and the Search for Peace*. Toronto: Macmillan, 1961.

Farrell, K. P. "The Progress of DDH 280." *Sentinel* (March 1969): 10–13.

Feaver, Peter Douglas. *Guarding the Guardians: Civilian Control of Nuclear Weapons in the United States*. Ithaca: Cornell University Press, 1992.

Fiddell, Phillip. *F-104 Starfighter in Action*. Carrollton, TX: Squadron/Signal Publications, 1993.

Foerster, Schuyler, and Edward N. Wright. *American Defence Policy*. 6th ed. Baltimore: Johns Hopkins University Press, 1990.

Foot, Rosemary. *The Wrong War: American Policy and the Dimensions of the Korean Conflict, 1950–1953*. Ithaca: Cornell University Press, 1985.

Fricker, John. "Lockheed F-104 Starfighter." *Wings of Fame: The Journal of Classic Combat Aircraft* 2 (1996): 90–100.

Friedman, Norman. *The Naval Institute Guide to World Naval System*. Annapolis, MD: Naval Institute Press, 1989.

―――. *The Postwar Naval Revolution*. Annapolis, MD: Naval Institute Press, 1989.

Gaddis, John Lewis. *The United States and the End of the Cold War: Implications, Reconsiderations, Provocations*. New York: Oxford University Press, 1992.

―――. *We Now Know: Rethinking Cold War History*. Oxford: Clarendon Press, 1997.

George, Alexander L., and Richard Smoke. *Deterrence in American Foreign Policy: Theory and Practice*. New York: Columbia University Press, 1974.

German, Tony. *The Sea Is at Our Gates: The History of the Canadian Navy*. Toronto: Maclelland and Stewart, 1991.

Granatstein, J. L. *Canadian Foreign Policy: Historical Readings*. Toronto: Copp-Clark, 1986.

―――. *The Generals: The Canadian Army's Senior Commanders in the Second World War*. Toronto: Stoddart, 1993.

Granatstein, J. L., and Norman Hillmer. *For Better or For Worse: Canada and the United States to the 1990s*. Toronto: Copp Clark Pitman, 1991.

Granatstein, J. L., and Robert Bothwell. *Pirouette: Pierre Trudeau and Canadian Foreign Policy*. Toronto: University of Toronto Press, 1990.

Green, Bill. *The First Line: Air Defence in the Northeast 1952 to 1960*. Fairview, PA: Wonderhorse Publications, 1994.

Gribikov, Anatoli I., and William Y. Smith. *Operation ANADYR: U.S. and Soviet Generals Recount the Cuban Missile Crisis*. Chicago: Edition q, 1994.

Griffiths, R. W. "King Neptune." *Sentinel* (July-August 1968): 6–8.

Gwynn, Richard. *The Northern Magus*. Toronto: McClelland and Stewart, 1980.

Haftendorn, Helga. *NATO and the Nuclear Revolution: A Crisis of Credibility, 1966–1967*. Oxford: Clarendon Press, 1997.

Halle, Louis. *The Cold War as History*. Rev. ed. New York: Harper Perennial, 1991.

Hansen, Chuck. *U.S. Nuclear Weapons: The Secret History*. New York: Orion, 1988.

Harrison, Michael M. *The Reluctant Ally: France and Atlantic Security*. Baltimore: Johns Hopkins University Press, 1981.

Haydon, Peter T. *The 1962 Cuban Missile Crisis: Canadian Involvement Reconsidered*. Toronto: Canadian Institute of Strategic Studies, 1993.

Head, Ivan, and Pierre Trudeau. *The Canadian Way: Shaping Canada's Foreign Policy, 1968–1984*. McClelland and Stewart, 1995.

Holmes, John W. *The Better Part of Valour: Essays on Canadian Diplomacy.* Toronto: McClelland and Stewart, 1970.

———. *The Shaping of Peace: Canada and the Search for World Order.* 2 vols. Toronto: University of Toronto Press, 1979.

Howard, Michael, George J. Andreopoulos, and Mark R. Shulman, eds. *The Laws of War: Constraints on Warfare in the Western World.* New Haven, CT: Yale University Press, 1996.

Jackson, Robert. *Canberra: The Operational Record.* Washington, DC: Smithsonian Institution, 1989.

———. *Strike Force: The USAF in Britain Since 1948.* London: Robson Books, 1986.

Jockel, Joseph T. *No Boundaries Upstairs: Canada, The United States and the Origins of North American Air Defence, 1945–1958.* Vancouver: UBC Press, 1987.

Jordan, Robert S., ed. *Generals in International Politics: NATO's Supreme Allied Commander Europe.* Lexington: University Press of Kentucky, 1987.

———. *Political Leadership in NATO: A Study in Multinational Diplomacy.* Boulder, CO: Westview Press, 1979.

Kealy, J. D. F., and E. C. Russell. *A History of Canadian Naval Aviation.* Ottawa: Queen's Printers, 1965.

Keating, Tom. *Canada and World Order: The Multilateralist Tradition in Canadian Foreign Policy.* Toronto: McClelland and Stewart, 1993.

Keaveney, Kevin. *McDonnell F-101B/F.* Arlington, TX: Aerofax, 1984.

Kinzey, Bert. *F-89 Scorpion.* Waukesha, WI: Detail and Scale, 1992.

Kissinger, Henry. *Nuclear Weapons and Foreign Policy.* Washington, DC: Council on Foreign Relations, 1957.

Kramer, Mark. "The Lessons of the Cuban Missile Crisis for Warsaw Pact Nuclear Operations." *Cold War International History Project Bulletin* no. 5 (Spring 1995): 112–113.

Kronenberg, Vernon J. *All Together Now: The Organization of the Department of National Defence in Canada 1964–1972.* Toronto: Canadian Institute of International Affairs, 1973.

Lee, A. M. *Chatham: An Airfield History.* Fredericton, NB: Unipress Ltd., 1989.

Legault, Albert, and Michel Fortmann. *A Diplomacy of Hope: Canada and Disarmament, 1945–1988.* Kingston: McGill-Queen's, 1992.

Levant, Victor. *Quiet Complicity: Canadian Involvement in the Vietnam War.* Toronto: Between the Lines Press, 1986.

Levitt, Joseph. *Pearson and Canada's Role in Nuclear Disarmament and Arms Control Negotiations 1945–1957.* Kingston: McGill-Queen's, 1995.

Lumsden, Ian, ed. *Close the 49th Parallel Etc.: The Americanization of Canada.* Toronto: University of Toronto Press, 1970.

Lyon, Peyton V. *Canada and World Affairs 1961–1963.* Toronto: Oxford University Press, 1968.

Maier, Klaus, and Norbert Wiggershaus, eds. *Das Nordatlantishe Bundnis 1949–1956.* Munich: R. Oldenbour Verlag, 1993.

Maloney, Sean M. "Dr. Strangelove Visits Canada: Projects RUSTIC, EASE, and BRIDGE 1959–1966." *Canadian Military History* (Spring 1997), 42–58.

———. "Notfallplannung fur Berlin: Vorlaufer der Flexible Response 1958–1963." *Militargeschichte* Heft 1.1, Quartal 1997 7 Jahrgang.

———. *Securing Command of the Sea: NATO Naval Planning, 1948–1954.* Annapolis, MD: Naval Institute Press, 1995.

———. *War Without Battles: Canada's NATO Brigade in Germany, 1951–1993.* Toronto: McGraw-Hill Ryerson, 1997.

Martin, Laurence. *NATO and the Defence of the West*. New York: Holt, Rhinehart and Winston, 1985.

May, John. *The Greenpeace Book of the Nuclear Age: The Hidden History, the Human Cost*. New York: Pantheon Books, 1989.

McLin, John B. *Canada's Changing Defence Policy 1957–1963*. Baltimore, MD: Johns Hopkins, 1967.

Merchant, Livingston T., ed.. *Neighbors Taken for Granted: Canada and the United States*. New York: Frederick Praeger Press, 1966.

Middlemiss, D. W., and J. J. Sokolsky. *Canadian Defence Decisions and Determinants*. Toronto: Harcourt Brace and Jovanovich, 1989.

Midgley, John J. *Deadly Illusions: Army Policy for the Nuclear Battlefield*. London: Westview Press, 1986.

Milberry, Larry. *Sixty Years: The RCAF and CF Air Command 1924–1984*. Toronto: McGraw-Hill Ryerson, 1984.

———. *The Avro CF-100*. Toronto: CANAV Books, 1986.

———. *The Canadair Sabre*. Toronto: CANAV Books, 1986.

Mills, Carl. *Banshees in the Royal Canadian Navy*. Toronto: Banshee Publication, 1991.

Minifie, James M. *Peacemaker or Powder Monkey: Canada's Role in a Revolutionary World*. Toronto: McClelland and Stewart, 1960.

Morgan, Patrick M. *Deterrence: A Conceptual Approach*. Beverely Hills, CA: Sage Publications, 1977.

Nash, Knowlton. *Kennedy and Diefenbaker: The Feud That Helped Topple a Government*. Toronto: McClelland and Stewart, 1990.

Nicks, Don. *Lahr Schwarzwald: Canadian Forces Base Lahr 1967–1992*. Ottawa, 1993.

Nolan, Janne E. *Guardians of the Arsenal: The Politics of Nuclear Strategy*. New York: Basic Books, 1989.

Norris, Robert S., Andrew S. Burroughs, and Richard W. Fieldhouse. *British, French and Chinese Nuclear Weapons*. Boulder, CO: Westview Press, 1994.

Organ, Richard, Ron Page, Don Watson, and Les Wilkenson. *Avro Arrow: The Story of the Avro Arrow from Its Evolution to Its Extinction*. Rev. ed. Erin, Ontario: Boston Mills Press, 1992.

Pearson, Geoffrey. *Seize the Day: Lester B. Pearson and Crisis Diplomacy*. Ottawa: Carleton University Press, 1993.

Peden, Murray. *Fall of an Arrow*. Toronto: Stoddart, 1987.

Polmar, Norman, ed. *Strategic Air Command: People, Aircraft and Missiles*. Baltimore: Nautical and Aviation Publishing, 1979.

Rankin-Lowe, Jeff. "Royal Canadian Air Force 1950–1959 Part II." In *Wings of Fame: The Journal of Classic Combat Aircraft*. Vol. 3. London: Aerospace Publishing Ltd., 1996.

Reid, Escott. *Time of Fear and Hope: The Making of the North Atlantic Treaty, 1947–1949*. Toronto: McClelland and Stewart, 1977.

Richelson, Jeffrey T., and Desmond Ball. *The Ties That Bind: Intelligence Cooperation Between the UKUSA Countries*. Boston: Allen Unwin, 1985.

Roberts, K. G. "Air Defence Goes Underground." *Roundel* (September 1963): 8–13.

Robinson, Robert. *USAF in Europe 1948–1965*. Carrollton, TX: Squadron/Signal Publications, 1982.

Rosenberg, David Alan. "The Origins of Overkill: Nuclear Weapons and American Strategy 1945–1960." *International Security* no. 4 (Spring 1993): 12–70.

Ross, Douglas A. *In the Interests of Peace: Canada and Vietnam, 1954–73*. Toronto: University of Toronto Press, 1984.

Sagan, Scott D. *The Limits of Safety: Organizations, Accidents, and Nuclear Weapons*.

Princeton, NJ: Princeton University Press, 1993.

Sarin, Oleg, and Lev Dvoretsky. *Alien Wars: The Soviet Union's Aggressions Against the World 1919–1989*. Novato, CA: Presidio Press, 1997.

Schwartz, David N. *NATO's Nuclear Dilemmas*. Washington, DC: Brookings Institution, 1983.

Shaw, E. K. *There Never Was an Avro Arrow*. Toronto: Steel Rail Educational Publishing, 1979.

Sokolsky, Joel J., and Joseph T. Jockel, eds. *Fifty Years of Canada-United States Defence Cooperation: The Road from Ogdensburg*. Lewiston, NY: Edwin Mellen Press, 1992.

Soward, Stuart. *Hands to Flying Stations: A Recollective History of Canadian Naval Aviation; Volume II: 1955–1969*. Victoria, British Columbia: Neptune Developments, 1995.

Stacey, C. P. *Canada and the Age of Conflict Volume 2: 1921–1948 The Mackenzie King Era*. Toronto: University of Toronto Press, 1984.

Stewart, Grieg. *Shutting Down the National Dream: A.V. Roe and the Tragedy of the AVRO Arrow*. Toronto: McGraw-Hill Ryerson, 1988.

Stewart, Larry, ed. *Canadian Defence Policy: Selected Documents 1964–1981*. Kingston, Ontario: Queen's University, 1981.

Stromseth, Jane E. *The Origins of Flexible Response*. Oxford: Oxford University Press, 1988.

Sullivan, Jim. *S2F Tracker in Action*. Carrollton, TX: Squadron-Signal Publications, 1990.

van de Werve, P. A. "The Royal Netherlands Air Force." *Royal Air Forces Quarterly* 1, no. 2 (Summer 1962): 99–105.

Warnock, John W. *Partner to Behemoth: The Military Policy of a Satellite Canada*. Toronto: New Press, 1970.

Weisgall, Jonathan M. *Operation Crossroads: The Atomic Tests at Bikini Atoll*. Annapolis, MD: Naval Institute Press, 1995.

Worley, Marvin L. *New Developments in Army Weapons, Tactics, Organization, and Equipment*. Harrisburg, PA: Military Service Publishing, 1958.

Yeager, Chuck, and Leo Janos. *Yeager: An Autobiography*. New York: Bantam Books, 1985.

Zaloga, Steven J. *Target America: The Soviet Union and the Strategic Arms Race 1945–1964*. Novato, CA: Presidio Press, 1993.

INDEX

ABOUT THE AUTHOR

Dr. Sean M. Maloney is from Kingston, Ontario, and served in Germany as the historian for 4 Canadian Mechanized Brigade, the Canadian Army's contribution to the North Atlantic Treaty Organization during the Cold War. The author of several works dealing with the modern Canadian Army and peacekeeping history, including the controversial *Canada and UN Peacekeeping: Cold War by Other Means, 1945–1970* (2002), *Chances for Peace: The Canadians and UNPROFOR 1992–1995* (2002), and the forthcoming *Operation KINETIC: The Canadians in Kosovo, 1999–2000*, Maloney has extensive field-research experience throughout the Balkans, the Middle East, and Afghanistan. He currently teaches in the Royal Military College War Studies Programme and is a senior research fellow at the Queen's Centre for International Relations.